SOFT COMPUTING AND ITS APPLICATIONS

Volume I: A Unified Engineering Concept

SOFT COMPUTING AND ITS APPLICATIONS

Volume I: A Unified Engineering Concept

Kumar S. Ray, PhD

Apple Academic Press

TORONTO   NEW JERSEY

Apple Academic Press Inc. | Apple Academic Press Inc.
3333 Mistwell Crescent | 9 Spinnaker Way
Oakville, ON L6L 0A2 | Waretown, NJ 08758
Canada | USA

©2015 by Apple Academic Press, Inc.

First issued in paperback 2021

Exclusive worldwide distribution by CRC Press, a member of Taylor & Francis Group
No claim to original U.S. Government works

ISBN 13: 978-1-77463-086-0 (pbk)
ISBN 13: 978-1-926895-38-3 (hbk)

Library of Congress Control Number: 2014938389

Library and Archives Canada Cataloguing in Publication

Ray, Kumar S., author
Soft computing and its applications/Kumar S. Ray, PhD.

Includes bibliographical references and index.
Contents: Volume I. A unified engineering concept -- Volume II.
Fuzzy reasoning and fuzzy control.
ISBN 978-1-77188-047-3 (set).--ISBN 978-1-926895-38-3 (v. 1 :
bound).--ISBN 978-1-77188-046-6 (v. 2 : bound)
1. Soft computing. 2. Fuzzy logic. I. Title. II. Title: Unified engineering concept.. III. Title:
Fuzzy reasoning and fuzzy control

QA76.9.S63R37 2014	006.3	C2014-902599-8

Apple Academic Press also publishes its books in a variety of electronic formats. Some content that appears In print may not be available in electronic format. For information about Apple Academic Press products, visit our website at **www.appleacademicpress.com** and the CRC Press website at **www.crcpress.com**

ABOUT THE AUTHOR

Kumar S. Ray, PhD

Kumar S. Ray, PhD, is a professor in the Electronics and Communication Science Unit at the Indian Statistical Institute, Kolkata, India. He is an alumnus of the University of Bradford, UK. He was a visiting faculty member under a fellowship program at the University of Texas, Austin, USA. Professor Ray was a member of the task force committee of the Government of India, Department of Electronics (DoE/MIT), for the application of AI in power plants. He is the founder and member of the Indian Society for Fuzzy Mathematics and Information Processing (ISFUMIP) and a member of the Indian Unit for Pattern Recognition and Artificial Intelligence (IUPRAI). In 1991, he was the recipient of the K. S. Krishnan memorial award for the best system-oriented paper in computer vision. He has written a number of research articles published in international journals and has presented at several professional meetings. He also serves as a reviewer of several international journals.

His current research interests include artificial intelligence, computer vision, commonsense reasoning, soft computing, non-monotonic deductive database systems, and DNA computing.

He is the co-author of two edited volumes on approximate reasoning and fuzzy logic and fuzzy computing, and he is the co-author of *Case Studies in Intelligent Computing-Achievements and Trends*. He has is also the author of *Polygonal Approximation and Scale-Space Analysis of Closed Digital Curves*, published Apple Academic Press, Inc.

CONTENTS

LIST OF ABBREVIATIONS

AI	Artificial intelligence
ANFIS	Adaptive network-based fuzzy inference system
BMI	Body mass index
CI	Computational intelligence
EC	Evolutionary computing
EP	Extension principle
FAM	Fuzzy associative memory
FIS	Fuzzy inference system
FLS	Fuzzy logic system
FTT	Fuzzy type theory
GMDH	Group method of data handling
GTU	Generalized theory of uncertainty
HMIQ	High machine intelligence quotient
LOWA	Linguistic ordered weighted averaging
MF	Membership functions
MFL	Mathematical fuzzy logic
MP	Modus ponens
MSE	Mean square error
NN	Neural networks
OWA	Ordered weighted averaging
PNL	Precisiated natural language
PT	Probability theory
RFV	Random fuzzy variable
RMS	Root mean square
SAM	Standard additive model
SC	Soft computing
WEG	World of Euclidean Geometry

Dedicated to

Dhira Ray (wife)
Aratrika Ray (daughter)

PREFACE

The term 'soft computing' means the final result of computation based on imperfect information is tolerant to imprecision, uncertainty and partial truth. The final result of computation, which is usually represented by a fuzzy set, can be flexibly interpreted (depending upon the process of defuzzification) as per the need of the problem at hand. The basic feature 'tolerance' is the hallmark of the method of soft computing by which it is different from the existing approach to computing (the so-called hard computing), which is essentially based on the data/information of perfect measurement and whose semantic is either true or false. The topic soft computing has a very soft boundary and is based on several methods of intelligent computation. The basic ingredients of the topic soft computing are fuzzy set, fuzzy logic, rough set, neuro-fuzzy, fuzzy-genetic and many such hybrid approaches. But a very careful inspection of this methodology of soft computing reveals that fuzzy set and fuzzy logic are in the vanguard of technical development of soft computing. Hence the present volume on soft computing, with an aim to introduce the notion of the same, starts with the topic fuzzy set and fuzzy logic and its various approaches in the fields of fuzzy reasoning (approximate reasoning). It is to be noted that a remarkable feature of fuzzy logic is its capability to mimic the human cognitive process of thinking and reasoning, which are essentially the expressions of human perceptions. Thus fuzzy logic becomes an essential tool for commonsense reasoning and computations with perceptions. In addition to fuzzy set, the concept of rough set is also useful to represent the vagueness in the information (data) available to us. Hence the fuzzy rough or rough fuzzy approach to soft computation becomes an important ingredient of soft computing. However in the present volume we restrict ourselves to in-depth study on fuzzy set, fuzzy logic and introduction to rough set. These areas of soft computing technology essentially build up the plinth of the notion of soft computing. Standing on this plinth we promise to move forward through fuzzy reasoning and fuzzy control, which are discussed in a separate volume of this two-volume publication. Thus the basic aim is to study and analyze imprecision, uncertainty and vagueness of our real world is to reveal the mystery of our Nature.

At this juncture we want to convey a message to the readers that the real world is a mixed environment; it is neither completely fuzzy nor completely non fuzzy (crisp). It is a combination of both and change from fuzzy to non fuzzy and vice versa are very gradual, not at all abrupt. Therefore to describe our universe in a more complete fashion we do not want to make the domain of soft computing a competitor of its counterpart, which is hard computing, as stated above. Rather one should be the complement of other and we strive to have a peaceful co-existence of both methods to describe our real world.

This book on soft computing is highly useful for academics and researchers of different institutions and industries for the applications of soft computing as tools in diverse domains of engineering. This book can also be used as a textbook by undergraduate and post-graduate students of different engineering branches such as Electrical Engineering, Control Engineering, Electronics and Communication Engineering, and Computer Sciences and Information Sciences. Research scholars and professional researchers of different institutions and organizations of different areas such as Control and Robotics, Knowledge Engineering (Database + Artificial Intelligence), Artificial Intelligence, Common Sense Reasoning, Image Processing, Computer Vision (Pattern Classification and Object Recognition) and Web Engineering can utilize the concept of soft computing as an important tool of engineering. This book has a combined flavor of theory and practice and it presents several experimental results on synthetic data and real life data. Thus the book provides a unified platform for applied scientists and engineers.

— Kumar S. Ray, PhD

CHAPTER 1

NOTION OF SOFT COMPUTING

1.1 INTRODUCTION

The term "soft computing" was coined by L.A. Zadeh in early nineties. Fuzzy set and fuzzy logic, which were born in mid-sixties, are in the vanguard of technical development of "soft computing" whose aim and objective are to capture the world of vagueness, imprecision, and uncertainty where the mystery of nature lies. The word 'soft' means that the process of computation (using domain specific heuristic/meta heuristics and implicit model of environment) is qualitatively imprecise which lacks rigor but which is robust, tractable, and low cost. The final result of such computation is also qualitatively imprecise and has sufficient semantic flexibility to mimic the cognitive process of human ability for approximate reasoning (decision making and problem solving) and thinking, which are by nature tolerant to vagueness, imprecision, uncertainty, and partial truth. Soft computing (SC) is essentially a paradigm of fusion methodology: fusion between fuzzy set and neural network, fuzzy set and genetic algorithm, fuzzy set and rough set, neuro fuzzy genetic, quantum fuzzy, fuzzy DNA, and so on.

In traditional 'hard' computing, the prime objectives are precision, certainty, and rigor. By contrast, the point of departure in soft computing is the thesis that precision and certainty carry a cost and that computation, reasoning, and decision making should exploit (wherever possible) the tolerance for imprecision and uncertainty. For instance, let us consider the problem of parking a car. Most people are able to park a car quite easily because the final position of the car and its orientation are not specified precisely. If they were, the difficulty of parking would grow geometrically with the increase in precision and eventually would become unmanageable for humans. What is important to observe is that the problem of parking is easy for humans when it is formulated imprecisely and difficult to solve by traditional methods because such methods do not exploit the tolerance for imprecision.

The exploitation of the tolerance for imprecision and uncertainty underlies the remarkable human ability to understand distorted speech, decipher sloppy handwriting, comprehend nuances of natural language, summarize text, recognize and classify images, drive a vehicle in dense traffic and, more generally, make rational decisions in an environment of uncertainty and imprecision. In effect, in raising the banner of 'exploit the tolerance for imprecision and uncertainty', soft computing uses the human mind as a role model and, at the same time, aims at a formalization of the cognitive processes humans employ so effectively in the performance of daily tasks.

The paradigm of *Soft Computing* is comparatively new and is evolving rapidly. Soft computing causes a paradigm shift (breakthrough) in the field of engineering and science since, it can solve problems that cannot be solved by traditional analytic methods. In addition, soft computing yields rich knowledge representation (symbol and pattern), flexible knowledge acquisition (by machine learning from data and by interviewing experts), and flexible knowledge processing (inference by interfacing between symbolic and pattern knowledge), which enable intelligent system to be constructed at low cost and which can be considered as a measure for 'high machine intelligence quotient (HMIQ)'.

On the other hand, the paradigm of *Computational Intelligence* (CI) has gained popularity in recent years. According to some researchers there is a close similarity between the two paradigms, namely SC and CI. At the same time, some researchers find a clear difference between them. So, the coincidences and discrepancies in between SC and CI should be considered when we try to establish the basic notion of SC.

At this juncture we try to explore several answers that have been suggested in the past, each of which uses a different approach and emphasizes different aspects.

These include the following features of SC:
- Fusion methodologies,
- Essential properties of constituents of SC,
- As complement of hard computing,
- Tolerant to imprecision and uncertainty,
- Heuristics and Meta Heuristics (MH) in SC,
- Quantum vagueness and fuzzy set in SC, and
- Fuzzifying information content of DNA strands for SC.

As stated earlier, it is interesting to consider other terms closely related to SC as is the case of CI, and analyze the level of intersection or even the coincidence between these two concepts [179].

SOFT COMPUTING AS FUSION METHODOLOGIES

As already mentioned, the idea of SC as the fusion of several preexisting techniques goes beyond putting different techniques in a single toolbox. The fusion is basically a symbiosis in nature. According to many researchers, the symbiotic feature is one of the most significant features of SC. In this sense one of the main characteristics of SC is that of hybridization. Hybrid (fusion) approaches could be considered as one of the main contributions of SC, with neuro-fuzzy systems being the first and probably the most popular hybrid approach.

Neuro-fuzzy systems incorporate elements from Fuzzy Logic (FL) and Neural Networks (NN).

This idea of hybridization originates from two observations:

- Fuzzy Systems are neither capable of learning, adaptation, or parallel computation, whereas these characteristics are clearly attributed to NNs.
- NNs lack flexibility, human interaction, interpretability, or knowledge representation, which lies at the core of FL.

Similar arguments are used latter to generate other hybrid approaches like Genetic Fuzzy Systems, where the main aim is to join the robust search capabilities of evolutionary computing (EC), and the already mentioned properties of FL.

From this point of view, SC, that started as the partnership of fuzzy logic, neurocomputing, and probabilistic reasoning, has evolved to integrate many symbiotic approaches among those techniques. This idea of hybridization, being central in SC, is reflected by different authors.

As an example, the following quotation gives a clear view of the role of hybridization

"SC's main characteristic is its intrinsic capability to create hybrid systems that are based on a (loose or tight) integration of constituent technologies. This integration provides complementary reasoning and searching methods that allow us to combine domain knowledge and empirical data to develop flexible computing tools and solve complex problems."

Figure 1 gives a pictorial view of this concept. Many hybrid approaches appear at bottom of the four boxes representing the main constituents of SC (the arrows show the origin of the hybridized components).

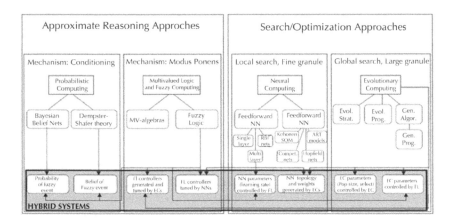

FIGURE 1 Soft computing as a fusion methodology to Bonissone *et al.* [33]

Some examples are the "FL controllers tuned by NNs", where the originating components are fuzzy logic and multilayer perceptron, or the "NN topology and weights generated by ECs" obtained as a result of merging multilayer perceptrons and evolutionary computing.

This central role of hybridization is also represented by Figure 2, through the idea of different *hybrid approaches* appearing as the intersecting areas of the main components of SC.

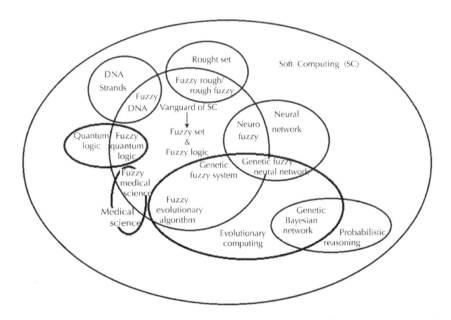

FIGURE 2   Soft computing (SC) viewed as a fusion methodology.

In summary, The SC has been defined as the mixture of several preexisting techniques, but pointing out the importance of the interaction in between those techniques, formalized in terms of different hybrid approaches.

Zadeh established the definition of soft computing in the following terms:

Basically, soft computing is not a homogeneous body of concepts and techniques. Rather, it is a partnership of distinct methods that in one way or another conform to its guiding principle.

At this juncture, the dominant aim of soft computing is to exploit the tolerance for imprecision and uncertainty to achieve tractability, robustness, and low solutions cost. The principal constituents of soft computing are fuzzy logic, neurocomputing, and probabilistic reasoning, with the latter subsuming genetic algorithms, belief networks, chaotic systems, and parts of learning theory. In the partnership of fuzzy logic, neurocomputing, and probabilistic reasoning, fuzzy logic is mainly concerned with imprecision and approximate reasoning, neurocomputing with learning and curve-fitting, and probabilistic reasoning with uncertainty and belief propagation.

It is therefore clear that rather than a precise definition for soft computing, it is instead defined by extension, by means of different concepts and techniques which attempt to overcome the difficulties which arise in real problems which occur in a world which is vague, imprecise, uncertain and, difficult to categorize.

Before we proceed any further to explore the basic notion of SC, we try to clarify the three keywords, the three pillars of the SC doctrine namely vagueness, imprecision, and uncertainty through the following simple illustrative example;

Let us consider the following assertions about a man:

- The man is about eighty to eighty five years old (pure imprecision).
- The man is very old (imprecision and vagueness).
- The man is probably from German (uncertainty).

In the first case, there is lack of knowledge due to lack of measure of the specific numerical value of age. In the second case, there is lack of precise definition of the term 'old' and the modifier 'very' only indicates a rough qualitative degree of the term 'old' and the third case expresses, uncertainty about a well-defined proposition, perhaps based on statistics.

With these basic impressions in mind about the three keywords, we try to establish the fundamental slogan of SC, that is 'tolerance (tolerance for vagueness, imprecision, uncertainty, and partial truth) is the hallmark of soft computing paradigm,.

SOFT COMPUTING DEFINED BY ESSENTIAL PROPERTIES OF ITS CONSTITUENTS

As previously stated, the definition merely based on the enumeration of constituent though not being exhaustive. Therefore, it is necessary to consider the properties of those constituents in order to determine what, if any, are the common (essential) properties of SC. One of the existing definition of SC is as follows:

> "Every computing process that purposely includes imprecision into the calculation on one or more levels and allows this imprecision either to change (decrease) the granularity of the problem, or to "soften" the goal of optimization at some stage, is defined as to belonging to the field of soft computing."

This is a quite general definition including all those techniques and approaches that have been previously described as the constituents of soft computing. Thus, SC purposely includes imprecision into the calculation changing (relaxing) the level of description of the problem or the level of achievement of the goal. But it is important to note that the imprecision is not a desired target, but a mean or even a need to achieve a higher order objective that could be summarized as "solvability" of the problem. If we go by this approach, it is possible to say that soft computing encompasses two main conceptual components, namely approximate reasoning and function approximation and optimization. This view is already presented in Figure 1, where the corresponding techniques are located in two main boxes referring to those two conceptual components.

Approximate reasoning is considered when relaxing the level of description of the problem (decrease the granularity) while function approximation and optimization is considered by relaxing the level of achievement of the goal (soften the goal of optimization).

Thus, we can say that SC techniques are those reasoning and optimization techniques that assume and integrate imprecision when solving a problem either as a consequence of the presence of that imprecision in the available information or as a mean to overcome complexity and achieve feasibility/solvability. From that point, and considering again that soft computing is an evolving concept, its evolution can be easily interpreted in terms of the integration of new topics/techniques that are in accordance with these properties and the corresponding conceptual components. In fact, *granular computing* is one new and important technique to be integrated in SC. Granular computing clearly matches with the idea of relaxing the level of description of the problem or the model in order to achieve suitable solutions to complex problems. As a matter of fact, granular computing encompasses concepts from (among others) rough sets and fuzzy sets theories, both of them considered as constituents of SC [179].

SOFT COMPUTING AS A COMPLEMENT OF HARD COMPUTING

The paradigm soft computing differs from the paradigm hard computing (conventional approaches), which is less flexible and computationally more rigorous.[1] The main reason for moving from hard to soft computing is the observation that the computational effort required by conventional approaches which makes in many cases the problem almost infeasible, is a cost paid to gain a precision that in many applications is not really needed or, at least, can be relaxed without a significant effect on the solution. In other words, we can assume that this imprecision is a small price to be paid for obtaining more economical, less complex, and more feasible solutions (consider the car parking example as stated earlier).

To talk in terms of optimization is very academic, but there are several practical situations where sub-optimal solutions (or even feasible solutions) are enough. Hence, at the time of designing optimal solution of a given problem, we have to consider the difference between obtaining a solution that satisfies our needs or getting lost when searching for the optimal solution. It is again the concept of softening the goal of optimization as stated in previous section.

Alternative view of SC as opposed to hard computing is as follows:

The distinguishing feature of soft computing is straightforward. Hard computing uses an explicit model of the process under consideration while soft computing does not do this. Instead, as an indispensable preliminary step, it infers an implicit model from the problem specification and the available data. Thus, we can say that building the explicit model is a first step in the process of finding the optimal solution, while, in absence of such an explicit model, the use of an implicit model usually drives us to a (sub-optimal) solution satisfying our needs. Considering again the "view of SC" as blending approximate reasoning and function approximation/optimization, this idea concentrates on the second part, the one usually assigned to neural networks and evolutionary computation, that could obviously integrate other optimization techniques as new components of soft computing.

---

[1]It is to be noted that in many engineering and scientific design studies based on traditional analytic approach, a term 'factor of safety' is used to make the final designed parameters over designed to take care of natural uncertainties (namely earthquake, flood, and so on). Thus, the traditional approach to hard computing is also very much aware of the notion of tolerance to uncertainty. Also, it is a fact that in real life there are many situations where precision and rigor are very much necessary even at the cost of money.

In the same way that evolutionary computation gained some presence in the field, meriting for a soloist role in the ensemble (and not a secondary role as occurred in some initial definitions), other new bio-inspired search and optimization techniques have appeared on stage more recently to play similar roles as EC. And even heuristic techniques (see detail discussion in the following section) that emerged inspired by the principle that satisfaction is better than optimization could be considered as part of soft computing.

In any case, some limits are needed since function approximation and optimization is a large area not completely contained in SC, for example numerical optimization techniques are clearly out of the scope of SC.

A different approach to the same idea of Soft Computing as opposite to Hard Computing is stated by Bonissone in terms of approximate versus precise models, instead of implicit versus explicit models:

In ideal problem formulations, the systems to be modeled or controlled are described by complete and precise information.

As we attempt to solve real-world problems, however, we realize that they are typically ill-defined systems, difficult to model and with large-scale solution spaces. In these cases, precise models are impractical, too expensive, or nonexistent. The relevant available information is usually in the form of empirical prior knowledge and input-output data representing instances of the systems behavior.

Figure 3 has been adapted from this concept by including the idea of explicit and implicit models to integrate both conceptions. The Figure clearly states the role of SC as the machinery to cope with problems that are out of the scope of the more traditional hard computing techniques. In fact the figure describes SC as the way of approaching problems when a precise model is either unavailable or unaffordable due to its complexity.

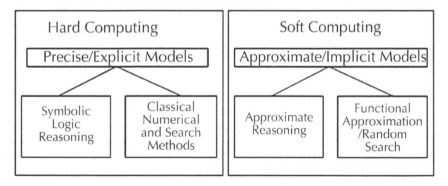

FIGURE 3   Hard and Soft Computing [149].

SOFT COMPUTING TOLERANT TO UNCERTAINTY AND IMPRECISION

The SC techniques are meant to operate in an environment that is subject to uncertainty and imprecision.

According to Zadeh, the guiding principle of soft computing is:

"Exploit the tolerance for imprecision, uncertainty, partial truth, and approximation to achieve tractability, robustness, low solution cost, and better rapport with reality."

Imprecision results from our limited capability to resolve detail and encompasses the notions of partial, vague, noisy, and incomplete information about the real world. In summary, the SC is designed to cope with all those "uncomfortable characteristics" that real world uses to add to the problems under consideration. In other words, it becomes not only difficult or even impossible, but also inappropriate to apply hard computing techniques when dealing with situations in which the required information is not available, the behavior of the considered system is not completely known or the measures of the underlying variables are noisy.

The idea stated above is the most important when we talk about SC as a tool to cope with uncertainty and imprecision. But we can go one step further and analyze those situations where imprecision is not a drawback of the information we are managing but an intrinsic characteristic of that information. In that sense it is quite important to distinguish between measurements and perceptions, and to discriminate those situations where we work on the basis of imprecise measurements from those others where we compute with perceptions. Computing with perceptions is clearly an approach to approximate reasoning (again one of the constituents of soft computing).

In that sense, soft computing as a tool to cope with uncertainty and imprecision should clearly include computing with words and perceptions as one of its basic components. In fact, quite similar sentences to that previously quoted are used by Zadeh to describe the potential use of *computing with words* as well as *its computational theory of perceptions*. Computing with words is inspired by the remarkable human capability to perform a wide variety of physical and mental tasks without any measurements and any computations. As a methodology, computing with words provides a foundation for a computational theory of perceptions.

A basic difference between perceptions and measurements is that, in general, measurements are crisp whereas perceptions are fuzzy. One of the fundamental aims of science has been and continues to be that of progressing from perceptions to measurements. One of the potential achievements of soft computing is to return to perceptions in order to take profit of its qualities as a carrier for intrinsically imprecise information.

HEURISTICS AND META HEURISTICS IN SC

Among the SC components, instead of EA (which can represent only one part of the search and optimization methods used), heuristic algorithms and even MHs should be considered [31].

There is usually controversy about the difference between metaheuristics (MHs) and heuristics, and, while it is not our intention here to enter into this debate, we are interested in offering a brief reflection on both concepts.

A large number of heuristic procedures have been developed to solve specific optimization problems with a great success, and the best of these have been extracted and used in other problems or in more extensive contexts. This has contributed to the scientific development of this field of research and to the extension of the application of its results.

The term MHs is derived from the combination of the word heuristics with the prefix meta (meaning beyond or of a higher level), and, although there is no formal definition for the term MHs, the following two proposals give a clear representation of the general notion of the term:

- Osman and Laporte [31]: "An iterative generation process which guides a subordinate heuristic by combining intelligently different concepts for exploring and exploiting the search space".
- Voss et al. [31]: "An iterative master process that guides and modifies the operations of subordinate heuristics to efficiently produce high quality solutions".

It is clear that MHs are more broad-brushed than heuristics. The limitation in the above definitions consists in assuming that MHs are a master process to generate, search, guide, or control subordinate heuristics. In the broader framework of SC, the subordinate processes do not need to be heuristics, but are in fact SC components (which might include global search methods, such as EA). We prefer to use the etymological sense of Meta, as "of a higher level", a connotation that is widely used in logic, reasoning and AI, therefore, we propose a formal distinction between meta-level and object level. At the object level we have problem-solver models based on any technique (may be based on SC components). At the meta-level we have the designers, controllers, or guides of the object-level models.

Within this definition of MHs, we also like to distinguish between offline and online MHs. Offline MHs deal with the design of the object-level model—once the design is complete, a run-time object-level model is generated and used to solve the problem without any further modification. Online MHs deal with the monitoring, guidance, and control of the run-time model.

We consider three main groups of MHs. From these, we then describe the new MHs which have emerged, briefly dwelling on the less developed or less popular ones because they are more recent [31].

EVOLUTIONARY MHS

These MHs are by far the most popular and define mechanisms for developing an evolution in the search space of the sets of solutions in order to come close to the ideal solution with elements, which will survive in successive generations of populations. In the context of soft computing, the hybridizations which take these MHs as a reference are fundamental (See Figure 4)

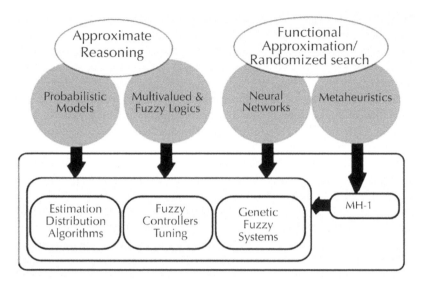

FIGURE 4   Representation of evolutionary MHs.

Although this is a very important and a very wide area (covering everything from the fuzzy genetic systems to the adjustment of the fuzzy controllers with EA, to the evolution of Bayesian belief networks, to EDA, bio-inspired systems, and so on), it is beyond the scope of this book. Another important reference is the concept of meta-GA, in which MH1 was used both at the meta-level and at the object level [31].

RELAXATION MHS

A real problem may be relaxed when it is simplified by eliminating, weakening, or modifying one of its characteristic elements. Relaxation MHs are strategies for relaxing the problem in heuristic design, and which are able to find solutions for problems which would otherwise have been very difficult to solve without the use of this methodology. Examples of these are rounding up or down or adjustments in nature, as occurring when an imprecisely and linguistically expressed quantity is associated with an exact numerical value.

From this point of view, a real alternative is to flexibilize exact algorithms, introducing fuzzy stopping criteria, which eventually leads to rule-based relaxation MHs, admitting the vagueness of coefficients, justifying algorithms for resolving problems with fuzzy parameters and relaxing the verification of restrictions, allowing certain violations in their fulfillment (See Figure 5).

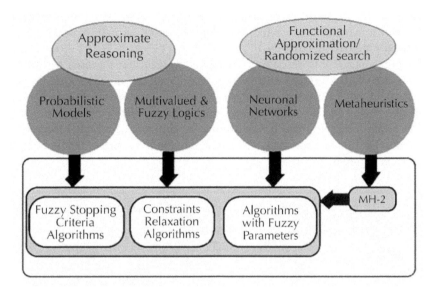

FIGURE 5   Representation of relaxations MHs.

In order to illustrate some of these MHs more specifically, we consider algorithms with fuzzy stop criteria [31]. We know that the stop criteria fix the end conditions of an algorithm's iterative procedure, establishing these criteria from the problem's theoretical features, from the type of solution being sought and from the type of algorithm used.

If a given algorithm provides the succession (x_n) of feasible solutions, some of the most frequent stop criteria are:

- Step 1. Stop the process after N iterations,
- Step 2. Stop the process when the relative or absolute distance between two elements in the succession from a certain iteration is less than or equal to a prefixed value, and
- Step 3. Stop the process when a prefixed measure $g(x_n)$ satisfies a certain condition such as being less than or equal to a constant.

In short, it can be said that an algorithm determines a reference set and stops when the set specified in the stop criteria has been obtained. The flexibilization of exact algorithms with the introduction of fuzzy stop criteria therefore assumes that the reference set is considered to be a fuzzy set, and the stop criteria are fixed according to the membership degree of the elements.

SEARCH MHS

Generally speaking, these are probably the most important MHs, and their basic operation consists in establishing strategies for exploring the solution space of the problem and iterating the starting-point solutions. Although at first sight they might appear to be similar to the evolutionary search methods, they are not since the evolutionary search methods base their operation on the evolution of a population of individuals in the search space. These MHs are usually described by means of various metaphors, which classify them as bio-inspired, sociological, based on nature, and so on, this makes them extremely popular.

However, outside this descriptive framework, given that a search can be made by means of a single search procedure (or by more than one in which case the search methods could either cooperate with each other or not) the search MH (without this classification being exclusive for this section) can be considered as individual or multiple, allowing in this last case the possibility for different agents to cooperate with each other. The different options which can emerge in the context of soft computing are shown in Figure 6.

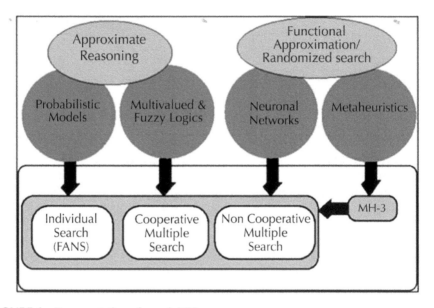

FIGURE 6   Representation of search MHs.

Among the best known individual MHs are hill climbing, greedy like, multi-start, variable neighborhood, simulated annealing, taboo, and so on which have their own fuzzy extensions.

Independent of their specific method of action, all these MHs explore the search space according to evaluations of the objective function of the specific problem which is being solved, and this explicitly supposes performing numerical valuations with the help of an objective function in a precisely defined space. Only too often, however, the objective function represents some vaguely established property, and the search space (or the neighborhoods being searched) has no clearly defined boundaries, and this makes it logical to focus the application of these MHs with theoretical elements from the sphere of fuzzy logic and fuzzy sets. It is precisely in this context that FANS-type algorithms emerge. FANS is a neighborhood search method where the solutions are evaluated not only in terms of the objective functions but also through the use of fuzzy properties and concepts which enable qualitative valuations on the solutions. It is also a method which may be adapted to the context since its behavior varies according to the state of the search through the use of various administrators. FANS is based on four main components that is operator (O), fuzzy valuation (FV), operator scheduler (OS), and neighborhood scheduler (NS), and a diagram of the algorithm is shown below to display the interaction between these four components [31]:

```
Proceedure FANS
Begin
    While   ( not - finalization )   Do
        /* the ne1ghbourhood scheduler 1s called   */
        NS - > Run (o,μ (), S_our, S_new, ok) ;
        If  (S_new 18 good enought in terms of μ()) Then
            S_our = Snew ;
            adaptFuzzyVal (μ(), S_our) ;
        Else
            /*  No good enough solution was found   */
            /* wtith the current operator   */
            /*  We change it with the operator scheduler */
            OS - > RUN(O) ;
        endlf
        If (trappedCondition ( ) )   Then
            doRestart () ;
        endlf
    endDo
End.
```

If, however, the search procedure is performed using various MHs, there is always the possibility of cooperation between these, and therefore the generalization of everything described so far to the context of parallelism, something which is obviously beyond the scope of this chapter but which is interesting to reflect on since, with the proliferation of parallel computing, more powerful work stations and faster communication networks, parallel implementations of MHs have emerged as something natural and provide an interesting alternative for increasing the speed of the search for solutions. Various strategies have correspondingly been proposed and applied and these have proved to be very efficient for resolving large-scale problems and for finding better solutions than those of their sequential counterparts due to the division of the search space, or because they have improved the intensification and diversification of the search. As a result, parallelism (and therefore multiple MHs) not only constitutes a way of reducing the execution times of individual MHs, but also of improving their effectiveness and robustness.

In the soft computing framework, the basic idea which has been developed so far has consisted in supposing that there is a set of resolving agents which are basically algorithms for solving combinatorial optimization problems, and to execute them co-operatively by means of a coordinating agent to solve the problem in question, taking the generality based on the minimum knowledge of a problem as a fundamental prem-ise. Each solving agent acts autonomously and only communicates with a coordinating agent to send it the solutions as it finds them and to receive guidelines about how to proceed. The coordinating agent receives the solutions found by each solving agent for the problem, and following a fuzzy rule base to model its behavior, it creates the guidelines which it then sends to them, thereby taking total control of the strategy.

QUANTUM VAGUENESS AND FUZZY SET IN SC

Due to the scientific revolution brought about by the discovery of quantum mechan-ics in the first third of the 20th century, a basic change happened in the relationship between the exact scientific theory of physics and the phenomena observed in basic experiments. Objects of quantum mechanics do not behave like objects of classical theories in physics; they are not particles and they are not waves, they are differ-ent. This change led to a new mathematical conceptual fundament in physics. Werner Heisenberg, Niels Bohr, and others introduced new objects and theoretical terms to the new quantum mechanics theory that differ significantly from those in classical phys-ics. Their properties are completely new and not comparable with those of observables in classical theories such as Newton's mechanics or Maxwell's electrodynamics.

THE CONCEPT OF STATE IN QUANTUM MECHANICS

The state of a quantum mechanical system is much more difficult to determine than that of classical systems as we cannot measure sharp values for both variables (posi-tion and momentum) simultaneously. This is the meaning of Heisenberg's uncertainty principle. We can experiment with quantum mechanical objects in order to measure a position value, and we can also experiment with these objects in order to measure their momentum value. However, we cannot conduct both experiments simultaneously and thus are not able to get both values for the same point in time respectively. However, we can predict these values as outcomes of experiments at this point in time. Since predictions are targeted on future events, we cannot valuate them with logical values "true" or "false", but with probabilities.

In quantum mechanics, we have to use a modified concept of the state: the state of a quantum mechanical system consists of the probability distributions of all the ob-ject's properties that are formally possible in this physical theory. Max Born proposed an interpretation of this non-classical peculiarity of quantum mechanics – the quantum mechanical wave function is a "probability-amplitude". The absolute square of its value equals the probability of it having a certain position or a certain momentum if we measure the position or momentum respectively. The higher the probability of the po-sition value, the lesser that of the momentum value and vice versa. In 1932, John von Neumann published the *Mathematical Foundations of Quantum Mechanics*, in which he defined the quantum mechanical wave function as a one-dimensional subspace of an abstract Hilbert space, which is defined as the state function of a quantum mechani-cal system or object. Its absolute square equals the probability density function of it having a certain position or a certain momentum in the position or momentum representation of the wave function respectively. Unfortunately there is no joint probability distribution for events in which both variables have a certain value simultaneously, as there is no classical probability space that comprises these events. Such pairs would describe classical states. Thus, the quantum mechanical object's state function embodies the probabilities of all properties of the object, but it delivers no joint probability distribution for all these properties. We need a radically different kind of uncertainty theory which is not describable in terms of probability distributions.

It is therefore necessary to have a new view on fuzzy set theory, quantum mechanics, probability theory, and perhaps even more theories dealing with uncertainty, to embed them in one network of "uncertainty theories" and to explain their differences and their commonalities as inter-theoretical relationships. This view demands a new direction of research analyzing and reconstructing scientific theories – in the first instance, quantum mechanics and fuzzy set theory. Perhaps we can add the theories of Dempster-Shafer, certainty factors, belief functions, and so on. This approach will have a great significance to understanding many concepts of uncertainty in science and technology and their relation to reality. Moreover, we can expect to get an overview of intended applications of these network elements and their cross connections.

Lotfi Zadeh published a paper "Toward a Generalized Theory of Uncertainty (GTU)". He started with the following words: "It is a deep-seated tradition in science to view uncertainty as a province of probability theory. The Generalized Theory of Uncertainty (GTU), which is mentioned in this context, breaks with this tradition and views uncertainty in a broader perspective". In Zadeh's favored GTU probabilistic and "statistical information is just one – albeit an important one of many forms of information". It is desirable to proceed to embed fuzzy set theory and consequently fuzzy set technology into the whole system of classical and non-classical science and technology.

FUZZY QUANTUM LOGIC

Since for any element a of a logic L and for any state p the number $p(a)$ belongs to the unit interval, states can be treated as fuzzy subsets of a universe L, and conversely, propositions can be treated as fuzzy subsets of a universe S. This second possibility allows us to utilize the fuzzy set theory with the aid of the following theorem of Maczynski [178].

Theorem 1.1. If L is a logic with an ordering set of probability measures S, then each $a \in L$ includes a function $a: L \rightarrow [0, 1]$, where $\underline{a}(p) = p(a)$ for all $p \in S$. The set of all functions $\underline{L} = \{\underline{a} : a \in L\}$ satisfies the following condition:

According to this theorem, we see that any logic L with an ordering set of states' S is isomorphic to a family $\mathbb{L}$ of fuzzy subsets of S equipped with the standard fuzzy set inclusion and complementation, and such that membership functions of elements of $\mathbb{L}$ satisfy the orthogonality postulate.

By simply translating Maczynski's [178] results into the language of fuzzy sets, we can check that the fuzzy orthogonality postulate is satisfied in $\mathbb{F}$ if and only if in $\mathbb{F}$ the following conditions are satisfied:

- 1.1. $\mathbb{F}$ contains the empty set $\emptyset$.

- 1.2. $\mathbb{F}$ is closed under the standard fuzzy set complementation.

- 1.3. If $A_1, A_2,....$ are pair-wise weakly disjoint, then $\sum_i \mu_{A_i} \leq 1$ and $\cup_i A_i \in \mathbb{F}$.

Definition 1.1. By a fuzzy quantum logic, we mean any family of fuzzy sets in which the fuzzy orthogonality postulate or, equivalently, conditions (1.1)–(1.3) are satisfied..

The most standard example of fuzzy quantum logic can be obtained via the Maczynski theorem from the traditional quantum logic of projectors on a Hilbert space H. Let P(H) be such a logic and let S(H) denote the set of all density matrices on H. The family $\mathbb{L}(S(H))$ of all fuzzy subsets of S(H), the membership functions of which are defined by:

$$\mu_P(\rho) = Tr(\rho P) \text{ for all } \rho \in S(H) \tag{1.1}$$

where $P \in \mathbb{L}(S(H))$ denotes the fuzzy subset of *S(H)* generates by the projector $P \in P(H)$, is a fuzzy quantum logic isomorphic to *P(H)*. Probability measures on *$\mathbb{L}(S(H))$* generated by density matrices are of the form:

$$m_\rho: \mathbb{L}(S(H)) \to [0,1], \ m_\rho(P) = Tr(\rho P) \tag{1.2}$$

FUZZY QUANTUM SPACES

The notion of a fuzzy quantum space was introduced by Dvurecenskij and Chovanec [73] as a fuzzy generalization of a quantum space of Suppes [269]. This notion also shows remarkable similarities to the notion of a fuzzy quantum logic.

Definition 1.2. A fuzzy quantum space is a family $\mathbb{M}$ of fuzzy subsets of a universe *U* such that:

s.1. $\mathbb{M}$ contains the empty set $\emptyset$.

s.2. $\mathbb{M}$ is closed under the standard fuzzy set complementation.

s.3. If $\mu_A(x) = 1/2$ for all $x \in U$, then $A \notin \mathbb{M}$.

s.4. If $A_1, A_2,....$ are pair-wise weakly disjoint, then $\cup_i A_i \in \mathbb{M}$.

When we compare Definition 1.2 with Definition 1.1 of fuzzy quantum logic we see that the conditions (s.1) and (1.1), as well as conditions (s.2) and (1.2), are identical. However, the union in the condition (s.4) is the standard (Zadeh) fuzzy set union whose membership function is defined as the point-wise supremum of membership functions of sets A_i:

$$\mu \cup_i A_i(x) = \sup_i(\mu_{A_i}(x)) \tag{1.3}$$

While in the analogous condition (1.3) of the definition of fuzzy quantum logic, Giles' bold union is utilized. Moreover, according to the condition (1.3) of Definition 1.1 the algebraic sum of membership functions of pair-wise weakly disjoint sets should not exceed 1. This is a very restrictive condition and mainly due to this condition, fuzzy quantum logics have the sophisticated structure of an orthocomplemented orthomodular set.

Let us note that in the definition of a fuzzy quantum space M of Dvurecenskij and Chovanec there is nothing which could prevent M from containing a noncrisp, weakly empty set, weak universe, or sets of the form cA, which explains why in the condition (s.3) of Definition 1.2 nonexistence of a fuzzy set with membership function constantly equal to 1/2 had to be assumed separately. This condition was adopted by Dvurecenskij and Chovanec because of mathematical convenience.

Thus, fuzzy quantum state and fuzzy quantum logic are important constituents of SC paradigm [234].

FUZZIFYING INFORMATION CONTENT OF DNA STRANDS FOR SC

Fuzzifying information content of DNA strands by Ray *et. al.* [238] [237] is a recent development of SC tools. It adds a new dimension to the existing similarity-based fuzzy reasoning method by bringing it down to nanoscale computing. Here the logical aspect of fuzzy reasoning is replaced by DNA chemistry. To achieve this goal, we first fuzzify the synthetic DNA sequence which is called fuzzy DNA and which handles the vague concept of human reasoning. We adopt the basic notion of DNA computing based on standard DNA operations. In the present model, we consider double stranded DNA sequences with a specific aim of measuring similarity between two DNA sequences. The present wet lab procedure can exploit massive parallelism of DNA computing. The end result of the wet lab algorithm produces multi-valued status which can be linguistically interpreted to match the perception of human expert.

In this work, we attempt to realize the basic approach to the similarity-based fuzzy reasoning by synthetic fuzzy DNA. We replace the logical aspect of fuzzy reasoning by DNA chemistry. In our DNA computing model, we choose double stranded DNA molecules for a specific aim of measuring similarity between two DNA sequences. The similarity measure between two DNA sequences is essential for realizing similarity-based fuzzy reasoning in the wet lab algorithm. In the present approach, whenever we talk about DNA sequences, we essentially mean double stranded fuzzy DNA sequences. For fuzzification of synthetic double stranded DNA sequence, we have used another sequence representing the membership value of the double stranded DNA sequence.

FUZZIFICATION OF DNA SEQUENCE

For fuzzification of DNA sequences which are used for wet lab DNA computing, we consider DNA sequences of variable lengths which indicate a specific membership value (See Table 1). Without any lack of generality, depending upon the need and attitude of the designer, we can have different membership values with different DNA sequences. These variable lengths of DNA sequences are attached with each five-base long DNA sequence to indicate its membership value. As we always deal with double stranded DNA sequences, each five-base DNA sequence is coupled with its complementary pair. Similarly each variable length DNA sequence representing the membership value of five-base DNA sequence is also coupled with its complementary pair.

FUZZY DNA

We introduce the concept of fuzzy DNA as follows. Let, our universe of discourse is discrete. Let an arbitrary five-base DNA sequence be a basic element of discrete universe (refer Table 2 to Table 4). Thus, several elements of discrete universe are represented by several five-base DNA sequences which are arbitrarily chosen. For instance, the universe height (Ht) (See Table 2) is discretized (quantized) as shown by the left most column of Table 2 and each discrete element of the quantized universe of Ht is represented by five-base DNA sequence, that is, the discrete element $4'3 \leq Ht < 4'6"$ ≡ TAATTTAATT, and so on. Each segment of discrete universe is linguistically termed as very short, very tall, and so on. (see the right most column of Table 2 to Table 4). Later, this individual linguistic term will be treated as primary fuzzy set over the respective discrete universe of height (Ht), weight (wt), and body mass index (BMI) (See Table 2 to Table 4). Thus, a five-base DNA sequence (coupled with its complementary pair), taken from any Table 2 to Table 4, attached with an appropriate DNA sequence of variable length (coupled with its complementary pair) taken from Table 1, together form a fuzzy DNA. For example:

$$\begin{pmatrix} CTAAGATCCATGCCG \\ GATTCTAGGTACGGC \end{pmatrix}$$

It is a fuzzy DNA. For wet lab computation, a string of fuzzy DNA sequence consists of several fuzzy DNAs represents a primary fuzzy set over a given discrete universe. Note that, whenever we talk about DNA sequences we always considered double stranded DNA sequences. Such double stranded DNA sequence is necessary to perform a specific task of similarity measurement between two primary fuzzy sets in our wet lab computation which is discussed in [237]. A primary fuzzy set, say, 'under weight' define over discrete universe of Body Mass Index (BMI) is represented as shown in Figure 1.

TABLE 1   Representation of the DNA sequences with their membership value

Membership value	DNA sequence (5' to 3')
0.1	A
0.2	AT
0.3	ATC
0.4	ATCC
0.5	ATCCA
0.6	ATCCAT
0.7	ATCCATG
0.8	ATCCATGC
0.9	ATCCATGCC
1.0	ATCCATGCCG

TABLE 2   Quantization of height (A domain)

Quantized Universe	DNA Oligonucleotide Sequence (5' to 3')	Linguistic Value
4' ≤ Ht < 4'3"	CTGGA	Very Short (I)
4'3 ≤ Ht < 4'6"	TAATT	Very Short (II)
4'6" ≤ Ht < 4'9"	GATCC	Short (I)
4'9 ≤ Ht < 5'	ATTTT	Short (II)
5' ≤ Ht < 5'3"	TCAGC	Medium Height (I)
5'3" ≤ Ht < 5'6"	CGAAT	Medium Height (II)
5'6" ≤ Ht < 5'9"	AATGT	Tall (I)
5'9" ≤ Ht < 6'	CCGGA	Tall (II)
6' ≤ Ht < 6'3"	ATCGT	Very Tall (I)
6'3" ≤ Ht ≤ 6'6"	TTAGA	Very Tall (II)

TABLE 3   Quantization of weight (B domain)

Quantized Universe	DNA Oligonucleotide Sequence (5' to 3')	Linguistic Value
80 lb ≤ Wt < 90 lb	ATTCA	Very Light (I)
90 lb ≤ Wt < 100 lb	GCCAA	Very Light (II)
100 lb ≤ Wt < 110 lb	TTCGT	Light (I)
110 lb ≤ Wt < 120 lb	CAAAC	Light (II)
120 lb ≤ Wt < 130 lb	CGGAA	Medium Weight (I)
130 lb ≤ Wt < 140 lb	ATCCG	Medium Weight (II)
140 lb ≤ Wt < 150 lb	GGAAT	Heavy (I)
150 lb ≤ Wt < 160 lb	GTAGC	Heavy (II)
160 lb ≤ Wt < 170 lb	ATCCC	Very Heavy (I)
170 lb ≤ Wt ≤ 180 lb	TAGGA	Very Heavy (II)

TABLE 4   Quantization of body mass index (C domain)

Quantized Universe	DNA Oligonucleotide Sequence (5' to 3')	Linguistic Value
BMI < 18.5	CTAAG	Under Weight
18.5 ≤ BMI < 25	AGGAA	Normal Weight
25 ≤ BMI < 30	TAGCT	Over Weight
30 ≤ BMI < 35	GCGCG	Obesity (Class I)
35 ≤ BMI < 40	GTAAC	Obesity (Class II)
40 ≤ BMI	AAATA	Morbid Obesity

µ = 1.0   µ = 0.8   µ = 0.6   µ = 0.5   µ = 0.3

5'CTAAGATCCATGCCGAGGAAATCCATGCTAGCTATCCATGCGCGATCCAGTAACATCAAA

3'GATTCTAGGTACGGC TCCTT TAGGTACGATCGATAGGTACGCGCTAGGTCATTGTAG TTT

TAAT3'
ATTA5'

Similarly, we can represent other primary fuzzy sets in terms of double strand-ed fuzzy DNA sequences. Whenever a primary fuzzy set is represented by a double stranded fuzzy DNA sequence, as shown in Figure 1, the membership value of each fuzzy DNA, that is,

$$\left(\begin{matrix} \text{CTAAGATCCATGCCG} \\ \text{GATTCTAGGTACGGC} \end{matrix} \right)$$

$$\left(\begin{matrix} \text{AGGAAATCCATGC} \\ \text{TCCTTTAGGTACG} \end{matrix} \right)$$

Given in descending order.

For the details of the abstract of fuzzy DNA computing, the syntax of fuzzy DNA computing and the semantic of fuzzy DNA computing interested readers are referred to [237].

SOFT COMPUTING VERSUS COMPUTATIONAL INTELLIGENCE

Once considered many different ways to define SC, another interesting question is its relation with other terms as "Computational Intelligence" (CI). Is there any differ-ence between Soft Computing and Computational Intelligence? Are simply different terms for the same topic? Is it (CI) a competitor of Artificial Intelligence (AI)? Is the meaning of the word "intelligence" in CI paradigm significantly different from that of AI paradigm? In AI, domain specific information (heuristic) essentially establishes the notion of intelligence. How the term "intelligence" is unifiedly defined and for different constituents of the paradigm of CI? In author's opinion (author of the book) any machine implementable algorithm which passes Turing test is computationally intelligent and there by belongs to the category of CI. Thus we may further claim any machine implementable algorithm from the domain of traditional hard comput-ing which passes Turing test is also computationally intelligent. According to Zadeh [65], Computational Intelligence is defined as the combination of soft computing and numerical processing.

To have a better understanding about the paradigm CI, let us consider some exist-ing definitions of Computational Intelligence (CI).

We follow a similar sequence that we have already considered for SC, that is, definition by essential properties, as a family of techniques or as complementary to something else. It would be much more difficult to find a parallel structure to that of Soft Computing as a tool to cope with uncertainty and imprecision, and maybe that is the apparent difference between the two terms.

Following the same order previously considered we start with a definition based on the component technologies and their essential properties, and in that sense we can directly consider the one applied by the Computational Intelligence Society of IEEE, a society using the slogan 'Mimicking nature for problem solving'. A slogan that is clearly reflected in the following statement (from http://ieee-cis.org/about_cis/scope/):

> "The Field of Interest of the Society shall be the theory, design, application and development of biologically and linguistically motivated computational paradigms."

From this statement, we can deduce that CI could be defined as the area of research that studies biologically and linguistically motivated computational paradigms, having apparently nothing to do with the corresponding definition of SC. But only the first part of the statement was included in the previous quotation, let us now analyze the second part:

'Emphasizing neural networks, connectionist systems, genetic algorithms, evolutionary programming, fuzzy systems, and hybrid intelligent systems in which these paradigms are contained.'

And what we find now is quite similar to the definition of SC as a family of techniques we have considered previously. And what is even more interesting is the explicit reference to hybridization, another distinctive characteristic of SC. It is also possible to recover other citations using the same approach of definition by components, as in the following one by Pedrycz.

> "Computational intelligence is a recently emerging area of fundamental and applied research exploiting a number of advanced information processing technologies. The main components of CI encompass neural networks, fuzzy set technology, and evolutionary computation."

Consequently, if we approach CI from the point of view of components, the result is quite close; maybe we miss in the case of CI the field of Probabilistic Reasoning, a topic that has an important role in SC. This absence is also supported by the first definition, since (at least in a first view) Probabilistic Reasoning is neither biologically nor linguistically motivated.

Continuing the parallel description of SC and CI, we find now the idea of "complementary or opposite to something else". In that sense, while SC is defined as based on approximate or implicit models being somehow a complement to Hard Computing, the following quotation taken from Duch, locates Computational Intelligence in a quite similar position:

> "Computational Intelligence is a branch of science studying problems for which there are no effective computational algorithms."

This statement could be read as expressing the idea of CI being the branch of science considering those problems for which there is not an exact model, plus those cases where the model exist but its consideration is not computationally effective, that is when we need to reduce the granularity or soften the goal. Both ideas are stated previously as descriptions of SC as the opposite to hard computing or based on its essential properties.

So, apparently there may be some attempts to draw a notional difference between the paradigm of soft computing and the paradigm of computational intelligence, essentially there is no such conceptual difference between the two paradigms of computing. Also note that in the paradigm of traditional hard computing the term 'factor of safety' as stated earlier, faces the challenge of all real life uncertainty. Hence, according to the author of the book, instead of doing any quarrel and competitions among different paradigms (tha is SC, CI, and hard computing), it is much better to have a peaceful co-existence of all the existing paradigms of computing with an aim to face the challenge of the nature which continuously offers vagueness, imprecision, and uncertainty in our real life problems. Depending upon the need of the problem and the particular situation at hand we should choose a particular paradigm of computation (or combination of paradigms) to get the problem solved.

1.2   SCOPE FOR FUTURE WORK

The new wave of theoretical contributions and practical applications that followed the seminal works by Zadeh has had a remarkable inspirational effect on numerous disciplines. Activities in soft computing have increased since the field started. They do not only focus on theoretical descriptions, but also provide a collection of real-world problems and techniques that are used to solve them.

Industry has benefited from adopting these techniques to address a variety of problems that can be seen also by the diverse range of products developed. Lately, it has been noticed that publications tend to combine the different sub-fields which seems to indicate that there are much more applications to come.

The SC is an evolving collection of methodologies, which aims to exploit tolerance for imprecision, uncertainty, and partial truth to achieve robustness, tractability, and low cost. The SC provides an attractive opportunity to represent the ambiguity in human thinking with real life uncertainty. Fuzzy logic (FL), neural networks (NN), and evolutionary computation (EC) are the core methodologies of soft computing. However, FL, NN, and EC should not be viewed as competing with each other, but synergistic and complementary instead. The SC has been theoretically developed for the past decade, since L. A. Zadeh proposed the concept in the early 1990s. The SC is causing a paradigm shift (breakthrough) in engineering and science fields since it can solve problems that have not been able to be solved by traditional analytic methods [tractability (TR)]. In addition, SC yields rich knowledge representation (symbol and pattern), flexible knowledge acquisition (by machine learning from data and by interviewing experts), and flexible knowledge processing (inference by interfacing between symbolic and pattern knowledge), which enable intelligent systems to be constructed at low cost HMIQ. This chapter briefly reviews applications of SC in several industrial fields to show the various innovations by TR, HMIQ, and low cost in industries that have been made possible by the use of SC. Our aim is to remove the gap between theory and practice and attempts to learn how to apply soft computing practically to industrial systems from examples/analogy reviewing many application papers.

INDUSTRIAL INNOVATION USING SOFT COMPUTING

The SC was proposed for construction of new generation artificial intelligence (HMIQ, human-like information processing) and for solving nonlinear and mathematically un-modeled systems (tractability) (TR) [297]. In addition, SC can be implemented at low cost (LC). The SC is the fusion or combination of fuzzy, neuro, and evolutional computing [273]. Later, chaos computing and immune networks were added to explain so-called complex systems, cognitive distributed artificial intelligence, and reactive distributed artificial intelligence [209]. It has been proven that nonlinear mapping obtained by neural networks can be approximated to any desired accuracy by the use of fuzzy systems. As neural networks have flexible learning capabilities, it is possible to develop nonlinear models using only input/output (I/O) data. However, it is often cumbersome to fine-tune the modeling accuracy of neural networks, because it may be difficult to explain logically the cause and result in the excitation-response relationships. On the other hand, fuzzy systems provide clear advantages in knowledge representation and acquisition. For example, knowledge is easily introduced in parallel to an adaptive fuzzy neural network by constructing a hierarchical diagnosis structure and modifying rules by available structured knowledge or modifying and adjusting fuzzy inference for pattern recognition with lack of input data by some complementary knowledge [243]. Fuzzy systems, however, have been missing adaptation capabilities for a long time. Jang and Sun have shown that under the condition of minor restrictions, functional behaviors of radial basis function networks, and fuzzy inference systems are the same [142]. On the other hand, local models in blended multiple model structures for nonlinear systems (fast fuzzy neural networks) have been recently investigated [142].

For example, [142] presents type-I fuzzy systems implemented using Gaussian radial basis function neural networks as local models in blended model structures for nonlinear systems. This fuzzy neural network is actually an extended radial basis function network that is obtained by replacing the output layer weights with a linear function of the network inputs. Each neuron represents a local linear model with its corresponding validity function (membership function). Furthermore, the radial basis function network is normalized like fuzzy membership functions. The side effects of normalizing should be considered, as all validity functions for a specific input combination sum up to one. The Gaussian validity functions determine the regions of the input space where each neuron is active. The input space becomes larger when dynamic systems are represented by these networks. A fast fuzzy neural network with general parameter learning is developed. It is especially suitable for real-time fault diagnosis since what we have to do is to only observe changes in a general parameter. It was implemented with a digital signal processor (DSP) and integrated RISC machine [142]. Recurrent fuzzy neural networks are recommended as a means to reduce the size of the input space. They are able to yield adaptive self-tuning, self-organizing, and automated design functions for nonlinear systems and systems for which suitable mathematical models are not obtained. They are also used for cognitive (fuzzy decision tree, and so on) and reactive (multiagent system coordination, and so on) decision making. The DSPs and advanced computer systems are at present utilized to implement soft computing. Neuro computing and evolutionary computations usually need a lot of computational time, which is the disadvantage of the implementation of soft computing. Recently developed fuzzy neural networks enable solutions to be obtained for problems that have not been able to be solved by traditional analytical methods (hard computing), since function approximation is used rather than parameter optimization (TR). Tractability enables industrial systems to become increasingly innovative.

Evolutionary computation has been developed and modified for applications of optimization for large-scale and complex systems. Data mining, for which soft computing is an effective and a promising approach, has been attracting the attention of researchers in industry [137]. Data mining is expected to be applied to large-scale process plants and electric power systems for decision support and optimization (TR).

Soft computing has recently been playing an important role in advanced knowledge processing. An advanced learning method using a combination of perception and motion has been introduced. Emergent, self-organizing, reflective, and interactive (among human beings, environment, and artificial intelligence) knowledge processing is considered by using soft computing and by borrowing ideas from bio-information processing. Soft computing provides rich knowledge representation (symbol and pattern), flexible knowledge acquisition (by learning from data and by interviews with experts), and knowledge processing (inference by interface between symbolic and pattern knowledge). Therefore, it is straightforward to construct low-cost intelligent systems. The various kinds of artificial intelligence (cognitive and reactive AI) make industrial systems intelligent. Such an intelligent system has adaptive, autonomous, decision support, optimization, and emergent functions (HMIQ). This HMIQ enables innovations in industry. Soft computing has been used considerably in human-related fields such as, manufacturing automation and robotics and transportation.

The applications of SC range from the purely theoretical ones, those which develop new lines in abstract mathematics or logic, passing across the areas of multimedia, preference modeling, information retrieval, hybrid intelligent systems, image processing, and so on to practical applications domains such as robotics and manufacturing, actuarial science, nuclear, or medical engineering.

- *Pure and applied Mathematics*: Theoretical foundations of soft computing techniques stem from purely mathematical concepts. The basic mathematical formalisms of fuzzy logic and soft computing have triggered a renewed interest in some old theories, such as that of residuated lattices or the theory of t-norms and copulas, and have initiated a complete redesign of well-established areas such as the theory of differential equations (with the addition of fuzziness), topology (including similarity spaces, tolerance spaces, approximation spaces), development, and algebraic study of new logical systems for dealing with vagueness, imprecision and uncertainty, and so on.
- *Extended Tools for Fuzzy and similarity-based Reasoning*: Existing tools for knowledge representation and reasoning, such as Prolog-based implementations, are being extended to the framework of fuzzy logic or, even, lattice-valued logics. In this sense, we can cite the works [143]. Some other approaches also include the adaptation of enhancements and specific optimization methods, such as the tabulation (or tabling) methods for logic programming.

- **Case-based Reasoning**: This model of reasoning incorporates problem solving, understanding and learning, and integrates all of them with memory processes. It involves adapting old solutions to meet new demands, using old cases to explain new situations or to justify new solutions, and reasoning from precedents to interpret a new situation. Recent research is demonstrating the role of soft computing tools, both individually and in combination, for performing different tasks of case based reasoning with real life applications [182].
- **Multimedia Processing**: Due to their strong learning and cognitive ability, SC techniques have found applications in multimedia processing and nowadays, there is a wide range of research areas of SC in multimedia processing including video sequence, color quantization, image retrieval, meeting video, document image analysis, image segmentation, and biometric application. The increased possibilities to capture and analyze images have contributed to create the new scientific field of image processing that has numerous commercial, scientific, industrial, and military applications [176].
- **Preference Modeling and, Decision Making**: Although standard approaches to decision-making problems assumed by default that all the information is expressed in the same preference representation format; in real practice this is hardly possible. As a result, new fuzzy approaches to integrating different preference representation formats in decision-making are of great importance. Moreover, missing information poses additional difficulties that have to be addressed when dealing with real decision-making problems, which leads to topics that are naturally included within the boundaries of fuzzy logic and soft computing. In this respect, theoretical studies on areas such as extensions of fuzzy sets (type-2 fuzzy sets, L-fuzzy sets, interval-valued fuzzy sets, and fuzzy rough sets) or aggregation operators (fuzzy measures, linguistic aggregators, and inter-valued aggregators) are especially useful. Some specific application domains of preferences modeling are the following: data-base theory, classification and data mining, information retrieval, non-monotonic reasoning, recommendation systems, and so on [144].
- **Knowledge Engineering Applications**: With the advent of artificial intelligence, the emphasis on knowledge engineering moved from social and philosophical concepts to the problem of knowledge representation in computers. The inherent synergy of the different methods of soft computing allows to incorporate human knowledge effectively, deal with imprecision and uncertainty, and learn to adapt to unknown or changing environments for better performance. One can see applications to several areas related to management of knowledge, such as knowledge representation, knowledge acquisition, knowledge-based inference, modeling and developing knowledge-based systems, knowledge integration, and knowledge discovery.
- **Ontologies and the Semantic Web**: When analyzing information on the web, one has to note the difference between information produced primarily for human consumption and that produced mainly for machines; on the other hand, one has to keep track of information uncertainty. The increasing interest in ontology-based, standard representations of belief-based, possibilistic and probabilistic information, as well as other types of uncertainty, is bringing soft computing tech-

niques for uncertainty representation and processing to the forefront of semantic web research. In the last few years, a number of seminal workshops and seminars have spread the interest for these issues within both the Semantic Web and the fuzzy logic or soft computing communities. Fuzzy logic has been used to bridge the gap among intuitive knowledge and machine-readable knowledge systems. Much research is also being done on techniques for extracting incomplete, partial or uncertain knowledge, as well as on handling uncertainty when representing extracted information using ontologies for example, to achieve semantic interoperability among heterogeneous systems. Semantic Web demands the management of large amounts of fuzzy data and the extraction of fuzzy information. Therefore, automatic tools for reasoning about fuzzy dependencies are necessary; in this line we can cite [50].

- **Business and Economics**: Soft computing methods can be used in an uncertain economic decision environment to deal with the vagueness of human thought and the difficulties in estimating inputs. There is a plethora of applications of soft computing in business and economics, which range from marketing (analysis of customer's purchasing attitudes, fraud detection, and service quality), to finance (stock market predicting schemes, portfolio selection, risk management, and loan assessment systems), electronic business (e-commerce decisions, personalization, and risk analysis in e-commerce), and son on.

- **Medical Engineering**: Successful diagnoses and surgical outcomes depend on the experience and skill of examiners and surgeons, but dependence on the subjective abilities of these healthcare professionals carries with it the risk of failure. Teaching these feelings to beginners is a very difficult task, because the skill of diagnose the feelings is based on subjective evaluation. Thus, the medical industry requires new engineering technologies, such as soft computing techniques, to assess information objectively. While recent developments in medical engineering have been achieved by state-of-the-art of intelligent computing techniques, including computer-aided diagnosis, computer-aided radiography, computer-assisted surgery, developments in soft computing, including information processing, signal/image processing, and data mining seems to be specially promising in this field.

- **Information Retrieval**: Information retrieval aims at defining systems able to provide a fast and effective content-based access to a large amount of stored information. Currently, soft computing techniques are being used to model subjectivity and partiality in order to provide an adaptative environment of information retrieval, one which learns the user's concept of relevance. The modeling is performed by the knowledge representation components of SC such as fuzzy logic, probabilistic reasoning, and rough sets. This way, the application of soft computing techniques can be of help to obtain greater flexibility in IR systems.

- **Fuzzy Control Applications**: The first application of fuzzy logic to control systems was the design of a fuzzy algorithm for regulating a steam engine by given Mamdani and Assilian [180]. After this starting point, the research and applications of fuzzy control progressed rapidly. Hard computing methodologies are not useful for the construction of the robot control systems of acceptable cost; it is the use of soft computing techniques what allows to overcome the problem of complexity of control systems and, in addition, provides them with abilities of tolerance for imprecise data, high efficiency, and performance.

- ***Robotics***: This field has a number of subareas which can profit from soft computing techniques. For instance, the drive control of a robot is often performed by a neuro-fuzzy system that generates action commands to the motors; the input of this system comes from the surrounding information, in terms of data obtained by the vision subsystem and the goal identifying device. Then, fuzzy inference mechanisms are usually provided by neural networks. Moreover, the systems are taught how to behave by means of adjusting its knowledge base by a neural network learning technique.

Based upon the facts and figures as stated above the author of the volume has an opinion that the salient features of soft computing paradigm are as follows:

- The SC is tolerant for imprecision and uncertainty.
- Also soft computing is marked as a representation of HMIQ.

However, according to the author of the volume the real world is a mixed environment and in this environment everything is neither fuzzy nor nonfuzzy; it is a combination of both and sometimes the changeover from fuzzy to nonfuzzy and vice versa is very gradual. Hence, there is no reason to assume that soft computing paradigm is the only approach to tackle the challenge of the real life problem. Depending upon the need and situation at hand we may consider the paradigm of hard computing also. There may be an attempt to fuse the paradigm of soft computing and the paradigm of hard computing and both of the paradigms can be considered as effective tools for the solution of our real life problems.

KEYWORDS

- **Computational intelligence**
- **Fuzzy logic**
- **Metaheuristics**
- **Neural networks**
- **Quantum mechanics**

CHAPTER 2

FUZZY SETS, FUZZY OPERATORS, AND FUZZY RELATIONS

2.1 INTRODUCTION

With the advent of fuzzy set and fuzzy logic, in mid 1960s, a new paradigm of computing, which is tolerant for imprecision, uncertainty and partial truth was introduced. In 1965, Zadeh introduced fuzzy set for generating implicit model of complex real life situation. But the basic notion of fuzzy logic was developed much earlier.

Aristotle posited the "Laws of Thought" to develop a concise theory of logic and mathematics.

One of these, the "Law of the Excluded Middle," states that every proposition must either be True (**T**) or False (F). Parminedes proposed the first version of this law around 400 B.C and faced strong criticisms. For example, Heraclitus proposed that things could be simultaneously True and not True. Infact Plato first laid the foundation for fuzzy logic, indicating that there was a third region (beyond **T** and **F**) where these opposites "tumbled about."

In the eighteenth century, David Hume (1711–1776) and Immanuel Kant (1724–1804) were inquiring about such concepts. They concluded that reasoning is acquired by gaining experiences throughout our lives.

Hume believed in the logic of commonsense, and Kant thought that only mathematicians could provide clear and precise definitions; both believed that there were conflicting principles that had no solution. In conclusion, both detected conflicting principles within the so-called classical logic.

In the early twentieth century, the British philosopher and mathematician Bertrand Russel reported the idea that classical logic inevitably leads to contradictions. A study on the "vagaries of language", concluded that the vagueness is precisely one degree.

The theory of "vague sets" was proceeded from the work of German philosopher Max Black (1973), who was aware of Quantum Vagueness and who realized the problem of modeling "vagueness". He differed from Russell in that he proposed that traditional logic could be used by representing vagueness at an appropriate level of detail and suggested that Russell's definition of vagueness confuses vagueness with generality. He discussed vagueness of terms or symbols by using borderline cases, where it is unclear whether the term can be used to describe the case. When discussing scientific measurement he pointed out 'the indeterminacy, which is the characteristic of vagueness is present in all scientific measurement'. An idea put forward by Black is the idea of a consistency profile or curve to enable some analysis of the ambiguity of a word or symbol. To the fuzzy logic community these curves bear a strong resemblance to the membership functions of (type-1)-fuzzy sets.

A systematic alternative to the bi-valued logic of Aristotle was proposed by Lukasiewicz around 1920. He described a three-valued logic. The third value proposed by Lukasiewicz can best be translated as the term "possible". He assigned it a numeric value between **T** and **F**. Eventually, he proposed an entire notation and axiomatic system from which he hoped to derive modern mathematics. Later, Lukasiewicz developed four-valued logics and five-valued logics.Subsequently he declared that in principle there was nothing to prevent the derivation of an infinite-valued logic. Łukasiweicz felt that three-and infinite-valued logics were the most intriguing, but he ultimately settled on a four-valued logic because it seemed to be the most easily adaptable to Aristotelian logic.Knuth also proposed a three-valued logic similar to Lukasiewicz's, from which he speculated that mathematics would become even more elegant than in traditional bi-valued logic.

The notion of an infinite-valued logic was introduced in Zadeh's seminal work "Fuzzy Sets" where he described the mathematics of fuzzy set theory, and by extension fuzzy logic. This theory proposed making the membership functions linguistic truth values (that is true, false, very true, more or less false, and so on) operate over the range of real numbers [0,1]. New operations for the calculus of logic were proposed, and showed to be in principle at least a generalization of classic logic.

Fuzzy logic provides an inference methodology that approximates human reasoning capabilities to be applied to knowledge-based systems. The theory of fuzzy logic provides a mathematical strength to capture the uncertainties associated with human cognitive processes, such as thinking and reasoning.

The conventional approaches to knowledge representation lack the means for representing the meaning of fuzzy concepts. As a consequence, the approaches based on first order logic and classical probability theory do not provide an appropriate conceptual framework for dealing with the representation of commonsense knowledge, since such knowledge is by its nature both lexically imprecise and noncategorical.

The development of fuzzy logic was motivated in large measure by the need for a conceptual framework, which can address the issue of uncertainty and lexical imprecision.

Some of the salient features of fuzzy logic are as follows:

- Approximate reasoning based on fuzzy logic is generalization of exact reasoning based on two valued logic. For instance, generalized modus ponens(an inference mechanism for fuzzy logic based approximate reasoning) is generalization of modus ponens(an inference mechanism for two valued based exact reasoning).
- In fuzzy logic, everything is expressed in terms of degree of possibility (not probability).
- In fuzzy logic, knowledge is represented by fuzzy constraint on a collection of linguistic variables.

- In fuzzy logic, inference is imprecise and is treated as a process of propagation of fuzzy constraints.
- Any logic can be converted to fuzzy logic.
- The most important aspects of fuzzy logic based systems, which we should consider to achieve better performance under specific applications are;
- Fuzzy systems are suitable for generating implicit model of complex uncertain environment, which cannot be described, in a cost effective manner, by classical mathematical model.
- Fuzzy logic is a precise logic for inference under incomplete or uncertain environment.

Most important fact is that, fuzzy sets and fuzzy logic can jointly quantify human perception, through the representation of membership function of a fuzzy set, in a simplified computational form for machine implementation of human cognitive process.

Traditionally, fuzzy logic has been viewed as a theory for dealing with uncertainty about complex systems. A modern complementary perspective is however, to view fuzzy logic as an approximation theory. This perspective on fuzzy logic brings to the surface the underpinning of the theory the cost- precision trade-off. Indeed, providing a cost-effective solution to wide range of real world problems is the primary reason that fuzzy logic has found so many successful applications in industry to date.

In fuzzy logic, which is also sometimes called diffuse logic, there are not just two alternatives but a whole continuum of truth values for logical propositions. A propositions 'A' can have the truth value 0.4 and its complement 'A^c' the truth value 0.5. According to the type of negation operator that is used, the two truth values must not be necessarily add up to 1.

Fuzzy logic has a weak connection to probability theory. Probabilistic methods that deal with imprecise knowledge are formulated in the Bayesian framework, but fuzzy logic does not need to be justified using a probabilistic approach. The common route is to generalize the findings of multivalued logic in such a way as to preserve part of the algebraic structure.

Fuzzy logic can be used as an interpretation model for the properties of neural networks, as well as for giving a more precise description of their performance. We can show that fuzzy operators can be conceived as generalized output functions of computing units. Fuzzy logic can also be used to specify networks directly without applying a learning algorithm. An expert in a certain field can sometimes produce a simple set of control rules for a dynamical system with less effort than the work involved in training neural network. A classical example proposed by Zadeh to the neural network community is developing a system to park a car. It is straightforward to formulate a set of fuzzy rules for this task, but it is not immediately obvious how to build a network to do the same for how to train it. Fuzzy logic is now being used in many products of industrial and consumer electronics for which a good control system is sufficient and where the question of optimal control does not necessarily arise.

In 1974, S. Assilian and E.H. Mamdani in United Kingdom developed the first fuzzy controller, which was for controlling a steam generator. In 1976, Blue Circle Cement and SIRA in Denmark developed a cement kiln controller – which is the first industrial application of fuzzy logic. The system went to operation in 1982.

In the 1980's, several important industrial applications of fuzzy logic was launched successfully in Japan. After eight years of persistent research, development and deployment efforts, Yasunobu and his colleagues at Hitachi put a fuzzy logic-based automatic train control system into operation in Sendai city's subways system in 1987. Another early successful industrial application of fuzzy logic is a water-treatment system developed by Fuji Electric. These and other applications motivated many Japanese engineers to investigate a wide range of novel fuzzy logic applications. This leads to the fuzzy boom.

The fuzzy boom in Japan was a result of close collaboration and technology transfer between universities and industries. Two large-scale national research projects were established by two Japanese government agencies in 1987, the better know of the two is the Laboratory for international Fuzzy Engineering Research (LIFE). In late January 1990, Matsushita Electric Industrial Co. named their newly developed fuzzy controlled automatic washing machine "Asai-go (beloved wife) Day Fuzzy" and launched a major commercial campaign for the "fuzzy" product. This campaign turns out to be a successfully marketing effort not only for the product, but also for the fuzzy logic technology. A foreign word pronounced "fuzzy" was thus introduced to Japan with a new meaning 'intelligence'. Many other home electronics companies followed Panasonic's approach introduced fuzzy vacuum cleaners, fuzzy rice cookers, fuzzy refrigerators, fuzzy camcorders (for stabilizing an image under hand jittering), camera for smart auto-focus, and others. This resulted in fuzzy vogue in Japan. As a result, the consumers in Japan recognized the Japanese word "fuzzy", which won the gold prize for the new word in 1990. This fuzzy boom in Japan triggered a broad and serious interest in this technology in Korea, Europe, and to a lesser extent, in the United States, where fuzzy logic was invented.

Fuzzy logic has also found its applications in the financial area. The first financial trading system using fuzzy logic was Yamaichi Fuzzy Fund. It handles 65 industries and a majority of the stocks listed on Nikkei Dow and consists of approximately 800 fuzzy rules. Rules are determined monthly by a group of experts and modified by senior business analysts as necessary. The system was tested for two years, and its performance in terms of the return and growth exceeds the Nikkei Average by over 20%. While in testing, the system recommended "sell" 18 days before the Black Monday in 1987. The system went to commercial operation in 1988.

The first special-purpose VLSI chip for performing fuzzy logic inferences was developed by M. Togai and H. wanted in 1986. These special-purpose VLSI chips can enhance the performance of fuzzy rule-based systems for real-time applications. Several companies were formed (for example, Togai Infralogic, APTRONIX, INFORM) to commercialize hardware and software tools for developing fuzzy systems. Vendors of conventional control design software also started introducing toolbox for designing fuzzy systems. The Fuzzy Logic Toolbox for MATLAB, for instance, was introduced as an add-on component MATLAB IN 1994.

Followed by the Japanese, the Chinese, the Russians, the Germans, the French, the Italians, the Spanish, the Dutch, the Indians, the Poles, and at last the rest of the world started cultivating and nourishing the thoughts and concepts of fuzzy sets and fuzzy logic, the brain child of Zadeh, and thus generated a global slogan "Fuzzy Logic everywhere".

Fuzzy logic is not fuzzy. Fuzzy logic is essentially precise logic of imprecision and approximate reasoning. Fuzzy logic may be viewed as an attempt to mimic the cognitive process of human thinking and commonsense reasoning.

One very salient feature of fuzzy logic, which is most of the time unrecognized, is its high power of precisiation. Fuzzy logic is much more than a logical system. It has many facets, viz, logical, fuzzy set theoretic, epistemic, and relational. Fuzzy logic has a non-standard perspective and its distinguishing features are graduation, granulation, precisiation, and the concept of a generalized constraint.

Zadeh not only introduced the concept of fuzzy sets, but also a methodology for the representation of commonsense knowledge using fuzzy sets, and a way of making inferences with such knowledge once represented. He established the grounds for a coherent logic of commonsense reasoning, to such an extent that Approximate Reasoning and Fuzzy Logic are almost interchangeable terms. Thus the concept of fuzzy set and the concept of fuzzy logic are closely associated with each other.

Boole made great advances by mathematizing an important part of exact reasoning, translating its pieces of discourse into mathematical equations solved with an especial calculus. Pólya made great advances in the modeling of Plausible Reasoning by means of Probability theory. And Zadeh made great advances by functionally modeling an important part of inexact reasoning that at the end is a typical kind of reasoning with which we argue every day on everything. Atleast, if Boole modeled the exact syllogism, Zadeh began the modeling of the approximate syllogism. The father of fuzzy set and fuzzy logic, Zadeh, can be viewed as a philosopher of the era, which is continuously facing the challenges of imprecision, uncertainty, and vagueness of the real world in which the mystery of nature lies.

2.2 FUZZY SET

In representing human understanding of various kinds of real world activities, Zadeh formally introduced the concept of a fuzzy set. A fuzzy set is the theoretical primitive of fuzzy mathematics just as a classical set is the theoretical primitive of classical mathematics. In fuzzy set theory, classical sets are called crisp sets, in order to distinguish them from fuzzy sets [97].

A (classical) set is characterized by objects, which are called members of the set. Like (classical) set, a fuzzy set is also characterized by its members. But unlike (classical) set, members of the universal set X may or may not belong to the fuzzy subset to some degree.

Definition 2.1 A fuzzy set A in a given universe X is characterized by a membership function $\mu_A(x)$ which associates with each point in X, real number in the interval [0,1] with the value $\mu_A(x)$ at x representing the grade of membership of x in A.

In order to have a better understanding of a fuzzy set, let us elaborate some basic concepts, associated with the Definition 2.1 of fuzzy set. By a fuzzy set, we mean:

- A set of elements, for example, m (man) ∈M (men);
- A label, for example, X (height of men), for an attribute of elements m∈M;
- An adjective/adverb, for example, A (tall man) associated with height of men;
- A referential set, for example, R (the interval [0,250] cms.) associated with height of men and,
- A purely subjective assignment function

$$\mu : X \rightarrow [0,1]$$

known as membership function, to denote a concept of grade/degree with which an elements x∈ X may belong to the fuzzy set A. Throughout this chapter, a fuzzy set A in X represented by the collection of pairs (x, μ_A (x)) as:

$$A = [(x, \mu_A (x)) \mid u \in X, \mu_A (x) > 0]. \tag{2.1}$$

When X is finite, may use

$$A = \Sigma_{x \in X} \, \mu_A (x) / x. \tag{2.2}$$

Example 2.1 In Figure 1 the membership function of the fuzzy set of real numbers "close to 1", is represented as

$$\mu(x) = \exp (-\beta (x - 1)^2) \tag{2.3}$$

where β is a positive real number.

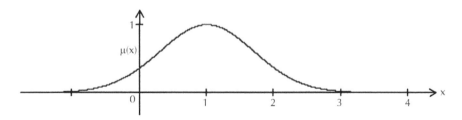

FIGURE 1   A membership function for "x is close to 1".

If X = {x_1, ……,x_n} is a finite set and A is a fuzzy set in X then we use the notation;

$$A = \mu_1/x_1 + \text{………} + \mu_n/x_n$$

where the term μ_i/x_i, i = 1,…..,n signifies that μ_i is the grade of membership of x_i in A and the plus sign represents the union.

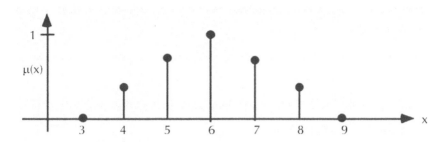

FIGURE 2 A discrete membership function for "x is close to 1".

Example 2.2 Suppose we want to define the set of natural numbers "close to 6".This can be expressed by (see Figure 2)

$$A = 0.0/3 + 0.3/4 + 0.6/5 + 1.0/6 + 0.6/7 + 0.3/8 + 0.0/9.$$

Example 2.3 Consider a universal set X which is defined on the age domain (See Table 1);

$$X = \{3, 15, 25, 35, 45, 55, 65, 75, 85\}.$$

TABLE 1 Example of fuzzy set

age(element)	infant	young	adult	senior
3	1	0	0	0
15	0.1	0.2	0.1	0
25	0	1	0.9	0
35	0	0.8	1	0
45	0	0.4	0.9	0.1
55	0	0.1	0.5	0.2
65	0	0	0.3	0.6
75	0	0	0.1	1
85	0	0	0	1

The fuzzy sets "infant", "young", "adult" and "senior" are defined over the discrete universe as shown in Table 1.

Let us illustrate the concept of membership function by considering the problem of buying a cheap car. Cheap can be represented as a fuzzy set on universe of prices, and depends on person's financial capacity. From the Figure 3 the term cheap is roughly interpreted as follows:

- Below 2000$ cars are considered as cheap, and process make no real difference to buyer's eyes.
- Below 2000$ and 3500$, a variation in the price induces a weak preference in favor of the cheapest car.
- Between 35000$ and 5000$, a small variation in the price induces a clear preference in favor of the cheapest car.
- Beyond 5000$ the costs are too high (out of consideration).

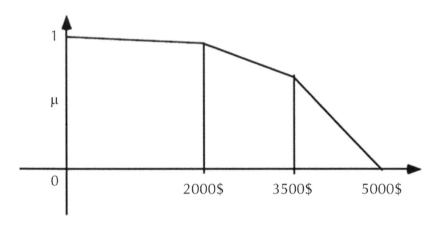

FIGURE 3   Membership function of "cheap".

TYPICAL MEMBERSHIP FUNCTIONS

In theory, membership functions usually can take any form. But in practice commonly used membership functions are triangular, Gaussian (bell-shaped), S-function, and γ -functions. In the following we outline such functions.

THE γ-FUNCTION

This function has 2 parameters α and β. It is formally defined by

$$\left. \begin{array}{ll} \gamma(x;\,\alpha,\beta) = 0, x \leq \alpha, & \\ \qquad\qquad = (x - \alpha)/(\beta - \alpha) & \alpha < x \leq \beta, \\ \qquad\qquad = 1 & x > \beta \end{array} \right\}. \quad (2.4)$$

The Figure 4 describes the graphical representation of the γ-function. The membership function of the fuzzy set 'old' is represented by the γ-function.

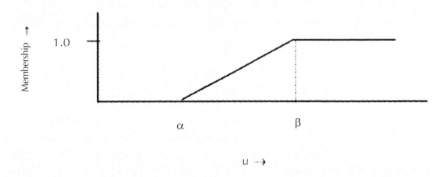

FIGURE 4 Representation of γ-function.

THE S-FUNCTION

This function is a smooth version of the γ-function mentioned above. It is formally defined as follows:

$$
\left.
\begin{aligned}
S(x;\,\alpha,\beta,\gamma\,) &= 0, x \leq \alpha, \\
&= 2[(x-\alpha)/(\gamma-\alpha)]^2, && \alpha < x \leq \beta, \\
&= 1 - 2[\tfrac{x-\gamma}{((\gamma-\alpha)]}]^2 && \beta < x \leq \gamma \\
&= 1, && x > \gamma.
\end{aligned}
\right\} \quad (2.5)
$$

Typical form of the S-function is presented in Figure 5 below. The membership function of the fuzzy set 'old' is represented by the s-function.

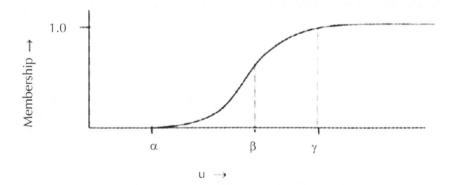

FIGURE 5 Representation of S-function.

THE L-FUNCTION

This function is the converse of the γ-function. It can be methematically expressed as:

$$
\begin{aligned}
L(x;\ \alpha,\beta) &= 1, x \leq \alpha, \\
&= (\alpha - x)/(\beta - \alpha) & \alpha < x \leq \beta, \\
&= 0 & x > \beta
\end{aligned} \Bigg\} \quad (2.6)
$$

One typical form of the L-function is presented in Figure 6. L-functions are generally used to represent the fuzzy linguistic statement *positive small*. Suppose u is a fuzzy variable, which should essentially have a positive value. Now, as u increases its membership should decrease. As a second example, suppose we are interested to describe the average intensity of the pixels (points) in an image by a fuzzy linguistic: *not very dark*. So, until the average intensity exceeds $\alpha(= 50, say)$, its membership of being not very dark is 1 and falls off if the average intensity exceeds α.

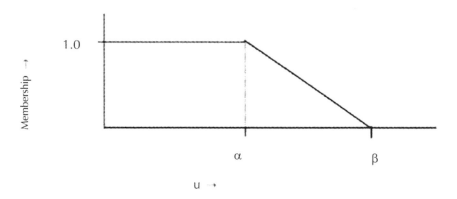

FIGURE 6   Representation of L-function.

THE TRIANGULAR MEMBERSHIP FUNCTION

The triangular membership function can be formally defined as follows:

$$
\begin{aligned}
\wedge (x;\ \alpha,\beta,\gamma) &= 0, x \leq \alpha, \\
&= (x - \alpha)/(\beta - \alpha) & \alpha < x \leq \beta, \\
&= \frac{\alpha - x}{\beta - \alpha} & \beta < x \leq \gamma, \\
&= 0, x > \gamma
\end{aligned} \Bigg\} .(2.7)
$$

One typical plot of the triangular membership function is given in Figure 7.

The YOUNG membership function, can be represented by the triangular membership function. We can set age $\alpha = 20$, $\beta = 25$, and $\gamma = 30$ as the typical parameter for the YOUNG membership function in order to represent it by a triangular membership function.

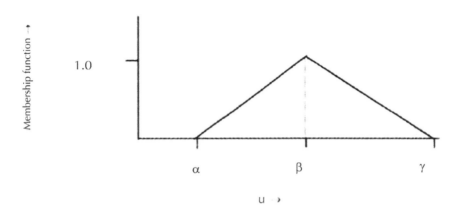

FIGURE 7   Representation of Triangular membership function.

THE $\prod$ - FUNCTION

The $\prod$ - function can be formally described as follows:

$$
\begin{aligned}
\prod(x;\ \alpha,\beta,\gamma,\delta) &= 0, x \le \alpha, \\
&= (x - \alpha)/(\beta - \alpha) \qquad \alpha < x \le \beta, \\
&= 1 \qquad\qquad\qquad \beta < x \le \gamma, \\
&= \frac{\gamma - x}{\delta - \gamma}, \gamma < x \le \delta \\
&= 0, \qquad\qquad x > \delta.
\end{aligned}
\right\} .(2.8)
$$

One typical plot of the $\prod$ - function is given in Figure 8. The $\prod$ - function is used to represent the fuzzy linguistic statement *neither so high nor so low.* For example suppose we want to express that today is *neither so hot nor so cold.* This can be represented by a fuzzy membership curve plotted against temperature. It may be noted that for temperature below a threshold th_1 and above a threshold th_2, the membership of the said curve should be close to one and it should have fall offs below th_1 and above th_2. Thus a $\prod$ - function is an ideal choice for the representation of the fuzzy linguistic *neither so hot nor so cold.*

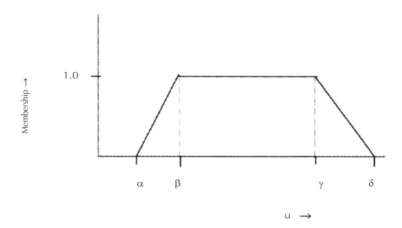

FIGURE 8   Representation of Π-function.

THE GAUSSIAN MEMBERSHIP FUNCTION

A Gaussian membership function is represented as:

$$G(x; m, \sigma) = \exp[-\{(x - m)/\sqrt{2}\sigma\}^2] \tag{2.9}$$

where the parameters m and σ control the center and width of the membership function. A plot of the Gaussian membership function is shown in Figure 9.

The Gaussian membership function has a wide application in the literature on fuzzy sets and systems. The YOUNG membership function illustrated earlier, for instance, can also be described by a Gaussian membership function with mean m = 22 years, say. Smaller the value of variance of the curve, higher is its sharpness around the mean.

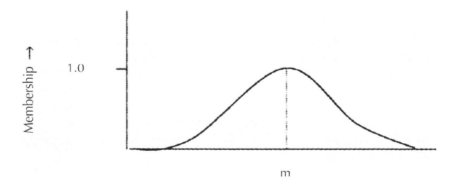

FIGURE 9   Representation of Gaussian Membership function.

We state some definitions of fuzzy sets.

Definition 2.2 *The support of a fuzzy set A is the set of all points x in X such that* $\mu_A(x) > 0$. *Formally,*

$$\text{Support(A)} = \{x \mid \mu_A(x) > 0\} \tag{2.10}$$

Definition 2.3 *The core of a fuzzy set A is the set of points x in X such that* $\mu_A(x) = 1$. *Formally,*

$$\text{Core(A)} = \{x \mid \mu_A(x) = 1\}. \tag{2.11}$$

Definition 2.4 A fuzzy set with non-empty core is called normal. In other words, A is normal if $\exists x$, $\mu_A(x) = 1$.

Definition 2.5 *A crossover point denotes a point x in X where* $\mu_A(x) = 0.5$. *Mathematically,*

$$\text{Crossover (A)} = \{x \mid \mu_A(x) = 0.5\}. \tag{2.12}$$

Definition 2.6 The height of a fuzzy set A, denoted by h(A) is the largest membership value obtained by any element in the set.

$$h(A) = \mathop{\sup}_{x \in X} \mu_A(x) \tag{2.13}$$

Definition 2.7 An α –level set of a fuzzy set A of X is a non-fuzzy set denoted by $[A]^\alpha$ and is defined by

$$[A]^\alpha = \begin{cases} (x \in X \mid \mu(x) \geq \alpha) & if\, \alpha > 0 \\ cl(suppA) & if\, \alpha = 0 \end{cases} \tag{2.14}$$

where cl (supp A) denotes the closure of the support of A.

Example 2.4 Let X = {3, 4, 5, 6, 7, 8, 9}, and

$$A = \{0.0/3 + 0.3/4 + 0.6/5 + 1.0/6 + 0.6/7 + 0.3/8 + 0.0/9\}.$$

In this case

$$[A]^\alpha = \begin{cases} (4, 5, 6, 7, 8) & if\ 0 \leq \alpha \leq 0.3 \\ (5, 6, 7) & if\ 0.3 < \alpha \leq 0.6 \\ (6) & if\ 0.6 < \alpha \leq 1. \end{cases} \tag{2.15}$$

Example 2.5 For the fuzzy set

$$A = \{0.1/x_1 \ , \ 0.5/x_2 \ , \ 0.7/x_3 \ , \ 0.9/x_4 \ , \ 1.0/x_5 \ , \ 0.5/x_6 \}$$

Support (A)=$\{x_1, x_2, x_3, x_4, x_5, x_6\}$ since for all the elements x_1, x_2, x_3 , x_4, x_5, x_6 of set A the membership values are greater than 0.

Core (A) = $\{x_5\}$ since $\mu_A(x_5) = 1$.

Crossover point (A) = $\{x_2, x_6\}$ since both at $x = x_2$ and x_6 the membership value is 0.5.

$A_\alpha|_{\alpha=0.7} = \{x_1, x_2, x_3, x_4, x_5\}$ because for all these elements the membership values are greater than or equal to 0.7.

Definition 2.8 A fuzzy set A of X is called convex if

$$\mu_A(\lambda x_1 + (1 - \lambda x_2)) \geq \min(\mu_A(x_1), \mu_A(x_2)), \ x_1, x_2 \in X \text{ and } \lambda[0, 1]. \quad (2.16)$$

Alternatively, a fuzzy set is convex, if$[A]^\alpha$is a convex subset of $X \forall \alpha \in [0, 1]$.

In many situations people are only able to characterize numeric information imprecisely. For example, people use terms such as, about 5000, near zero, or essentially bigger than 5000. These are examples of fuzzy numbers. Using the theory of fuzzy subsets we can represent these fuzzy numbers as fuzzy subsets of the set of real numbers while Boolean operations such as union and intersection can be carried out on any fuzzy sets. The fuzzy numbers can be used to perform arithmetic operations such as, addition, subtraction, multiplication and division [97].

Definition 2.9 A fuzzy number A is a fuzzy set of the real line with a normal, (fuzzy) convex and continuous membership function of bounded support. The family of fuzzy numbers will be denoted by F.

The Figure 10 shows the pictorial representation of a fuzzy number.

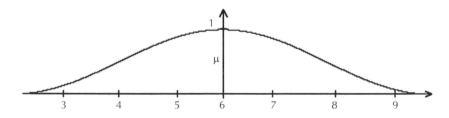

FIGURE 10   Representation of a Fuzzy number.

Definition 2.10 A quasi fizzy number A is a fuzzy set of the real line with a normal fuzzy convex and continuous membership function satisfying the limit conditions

$$\lim_{x \to \infty} A(x) = 0, \lim_{x \to -\infty} A(x) = 0. \tag{2.17}$$

Let A be a fuzzy number. Then $[A]^{\gamma}$ is a closed convex (compact) subset of R for all $\gamma \in [0, 1]$. Let us introduce the notations

$$a_1(\gamma) = \min [A]^{\gamma}, a_2(\gamma) = \max [A]^{\gamma}.$$

In other words, $a_1(\gamma)$ denotes the left-hand side and $a_2(\gamma)$ denotes the right-hand side of the γ – cut. It is easy to see that

$$\alpha \leq \beta \text{ then } [A]^{\alpha} \supset [A]^{\beta}. \tag{2.18}$$

Furthermore, the left-hand side function

$$a_1: [0, 1] \to R$$

is monoton increasing and lower semicontinuous, and the right-hand side function

$$a_2 : [0, 1] \to R$$

is monoton decreasing and upper semicontinuous. We use the notation

$$[A]^{\gamma} = [a_1(\gamma), a_2(\gamma)].$$

The support of A as shown in Figure 11 is the open interval $(a_1(0), a_2(0))$.

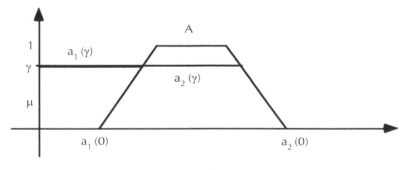

FIGURE 11   The support of A is $(a_1(0), a_2(0))$.

If A is not a fuzzy number then there exists an $\gamma \in [0, 1]$ such that $[A]^\gamma$ is not a convex subset of R (See Figure 12).

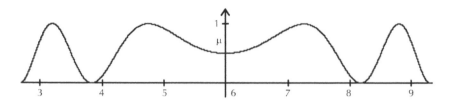

FIGURE 12   Representation of Not fuzzy number.

Definition 2.11 A fuzzy set A is called triangular fuzzy number A = (a, α, β) with peak (or center) at a, left width $\alpha > 0$ and right width $\beta > 0$ if its membership function has the following form

$$\mu(x) = \begin{cases} 1 - \frac{a-x}{\alpha} \, if \, a - \alpha \leq x \leq a \\ 1 - \frac{x-a}{\beta} \, if \, a \leq x \leq a + \beta \\ 0 \qquad\qquad otherwise. \end{cases} \qquad (2.19)$$

It can easily be verified that

$$[A]^\gamma = [a - (1 - \gamma)\alpha, a + (1 - \gamma)\beta], \forall \gamma \in [0, 1]. \qquad (2.20)$$

The support of A is $(a - \alpha, b + \beta)$.

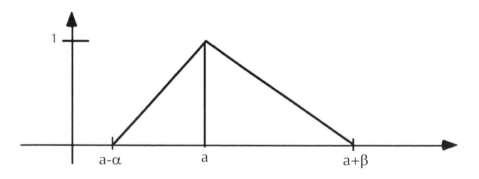

FIGURE 13   Triangular fuzzy number.

A triangular fuzzy number with center at a may be seen as a fuzzy quantity "x is approximately equal to a" (See Figure 13).

In the following we state different types of triangular fuzzy numbers;

- *Positive triangular fuzzy number:* A positive triangular fuzzy number A is denoted as $A = (a_1, a_2, a_3)$ where a_i's > 0 for all i= 1, 2, 3.

- *Negative triangular fuzzy number:* A negative triangular fuzzy number A is denoted as $A = (a_1, a_2, a_3)$ where a_i's < 0 for all i= 1, 2, 3.*Note:* A negative Triangular fuzzy number can be written as the negative multiplication of a positive Triangular fuzzy number. *for example:* When A = (-3, -2, -1) is a negative triangular fuzzy number this can be written as A=-(1, 2, 3).

- *Equal Triangular fuzzy number:* Let $A = (a_1, a_2, a_3)$ and B (b_1, b_2, b_3) be two triangular fuzzy numbers. If A is identically equal to B only if $a_1 = b_1$, $a_2 = b_2$ and $a_3 = b_3$.

The Figure 14 shows a α-cut of a triangular fuzzy number.

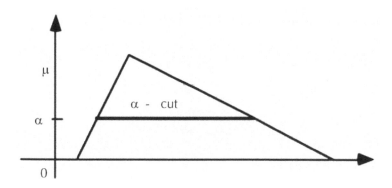

FIGURE 14   A α- cut of a triangular fuzzy number.

Definition 2.12 A fuzzy set A is called trapezoidal fuzzy number A = (a, b, α, β) with tolerance interval [a, b], left width α and right width β if its membership function has the following form

$$\mu(x) = \begin{cases} 1 - \frac{a-x}{\alpha} & if\ a \leq x \leq a + \beta \\ 1 & if\ a \leq x \leq b \\ 1 - \frac{x-b}{\beta} & if\ a \leq x \leq b + \beta \\ 0 & otherwise. \end{cases} \tag{2.21}$$

It can easily be shown that

$$[A]^\gamma = [a - (1 - \gamma)\alpha, b + (1 - \gamma)\beta], \forall \gamma \in [0, 1]. \tag{2.22}$$

The support of A is $(a - \alpha, b + \beta)$.

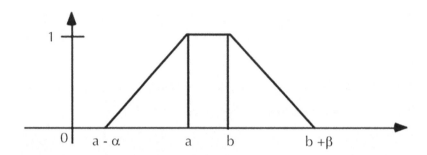

FIGURE 15   Trapezoidal fuzzy number.

A trapezoidal fuzzy number may be seen as a fuzzy quantity "x is approximately in the interval [a, b]"(see Figure 15).

Definition 2.13 Any fuzzy number A ∈ Fcan be described as:

$$\mu(x) = \begin{cases} L\left(\frac{a-x}{\alpha}\right) & \text{if } x \in [a-\alpha, a] \\ 1 & \text{if } x \in [a, b] \\ R\left(\frac{x-b}{\beta}\right) & \text{if } x \in [b, b+\beta] \\ 0 & \text{otherwise;} \end{cases} \tag{2.23}$$

where [a, b] is the peak or core of A

$$L: [0,1] \rightarrow [0,1], R: [0,1] \rightarrow [0,1]$$

are continuous and non-increasing shape functions with $L(0) = R(0) = 1$ and $R(1) = L(1) = 0$. We call this fuzzy interval of LR-type and refer to it by

$$A = (a, b, \alpha, \beta)_{LR}. \tag{2.24}$$

The support of A is $(a - \alpha, b + \beta)$.

Let $A = (a,b, \alpha, \beta)_{LR}$ be a fuzzy number of type LR. If $a = b$ then we use the notation

$$A = (a, \alpha, \beta)_{LR} \tag{2.25}$$

and say that A is a quasi-triangular fuzzy number. Furthermore if L(x) = R(x) = 1 − x then instead of A = (a,b, α, β)$_{LR}$ we simply write

$$A = (a,b, \alpha, \beta) \,.(2.26)$$

2.2.1 THE MAGNITUDE OF FUZZY SET

The magnitude of a fuzzy set A is represented by the cardinality of the fuzzy set. We can measure the cardinality of a fuzzy set A as follows;

- We can sum up the membership degrees of fuzzy set A. It is called "**scalar cardinality**".

$$|A| = \sum_{x \in X} i_A(x).$$

According to this method, the cardinality of fuzzy set "senior" (in Example 2.3) is,

$$|senior| = 0.1 + 0.2 + 0.6 + 1 + 1 = 2.9$$

.

- We can take the ratio between the cardinality of the fuzzy set A with that of universal set X.

$$\|A\| = \frac{|A|}{|X|}.$$

This is called "relative cardinality". In the case of "senior",

$$|senior| = 2.9, |X| = 9$$

Therefore, $\|senior\| = 2.9 / 9 = 0.32$

we can express the cardinality as fuzzy set.

Definition 2.14 Let's consider α-*cut* set (crisp set) A_α, of A. The number of elements is $|A_\alpha|$. The possibility for number of elements in A to be $|A_\alpha|$ is α. The membership degree of fuzzy cardinality $|A|$ is defined as:

$$\mu_{|A|}(|A_\alpha|) = \alpha, \alpha \in \Lambda_A \ (2.27)$$

Where A_α is a α-*cut* set and Λ_A is a level set.

Example 2.6 If we cut fuzzy set "senior" (with respect to Example 2.3) at $\alpha = 0.1$ there are 5 elements in the α-*cut* set.

$senior_{0.1} = \{45,55,65,75,85\}, |senior_{0.1}| = 5.$ *In the same manner, there are 4 element sat* $\alpha = 0.2$

there are 3 elements at $\alpha = 0.6$ there are 2 elements at $\alpha = 1$. Therefore the fuzzy cardinality of "senior" is :

$$|senior| = \{(5,0.1),(4,0.2),(3,0.6),(2,1)\}$$

SUBSET OF FUZZY SET

Let there be two fuzzy sets A and B. If the degrees of membership values of the two sets are same, we call "A and B are equivalent". That is,

$$A = B$$

$$\text{if } i_A(x) = i_B(x), \quad \forall x \in X$$

If $\mu_A(x) \neq \mu_B(x)$ for any element, then $A \neq B$. If the following relation is satisfied in the fuzzy set A and B, A is a *subset* of B (Figure 16), that is,

$$i_A(x) \leq i_B(x), \quad \forall x \in X \ .$$

This relation is expressed as $A \subseteq B$. We call that A is a subset of B. If the following relation holds, A is a *proper subset* of B; that is,

$$i_A(x) < i_B(x), \quad \forall x \in X \ .$$

This relation can be written as

$$A \subset B \text{ if } A \subseteq B \text{ and } A \neq B \ .$$

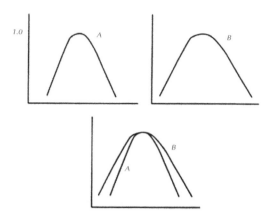

FIGURE 16   Subset $A \subset B$

Definition 2.15 Let A and B be fuzzy subsets of a classical set X. We say that A is a subset of B if $\mu_A(x) \leq \mu_B(x)$, $\forall x \in X$.

The Figure 17 represents A as subset of B.

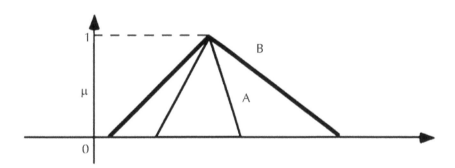

FIGURE 17   A is a subset of B.

Definition 2.16 Given two fuzzy sets A and B on a finite universe X, the degree to which one set belongs to another can be stated as:

$$S(A, B) = \frac{|A \cap B|}{|A|}$$

$$\frac{1}{|A|} \left(|A| - \sum_{x \in X} \max\{0, A(x) - B(x)\} \right)$$

$$= \frac{1}{|A|} \left(|B| - \sum_{x \in X} \max\{0, B(x) - A(x)\} \right)$$

$$= \frac{1}{|A|} \left(\sum_{x \in X} \min\{A(x), B(x)\} \right) \tag{2.28}$$

The above expression can be depicted by the Figure 18.

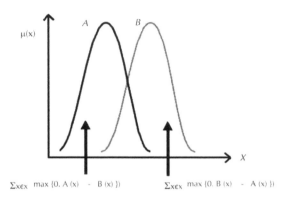

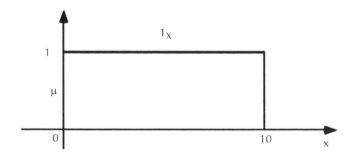

FIGURE 18   Representation of subsethood.

Definition 2.17 Let A and B are fuzzy subsets of a classical set X. A and B are said to be equal, denoted A = B, if A ⊂ B and B ⊂ A. We note that A = B if and only if $\mu_A(x) = \mu_B(x)$ for x ∈ X.

Definition 2.18 The empty fuzzy subset of X is defined as the fuzzy subset ∅ of X such that ∅ (x) = 0 for each x ∈ X.

Note that, ∅ ⊂ A holds for any fuzzy subset A of X.

Definition 2.19 The largest fuzzy set in X, called universal fuzzy set in X, denoted by 1_X, is defined by $1_X(x) = 1$, ∀x∈ X.

It is easy to see that A ⊂ 1_v holds for any fuzzy subset A of X.

The Figure 19 shows the graph of the universal fuzzy subset in X = [0, 10].

FIGURE 19   The graph of the universal fuzzy subset in X = [0, 10].

Definition 2.20 Let A be a fuzzy number. If supp(A) = $\{x_0\}$ then A is called a fuzzy point and we use the notation A = $\bar{x}_0$.

The Figure 20 shows a fuzzy point.

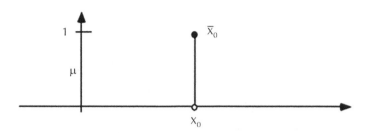

FIGURE 20   Fuzzy point.

Let A = $\bar{x}_0$ be a fuzzy point. It is easy to see that $[A]^y = [x_0, x_0] = \{x_0\}$, A$y \in$ [0, 1].

CLASSIFICATION FUZZY SETS

Different types of fuzzy sets are stated below:

- Ordinary fuzzy set $\mu_A : X \rightarrow [0,1]$ which is abbreviated as $A : X \rightarrow [0,1]$, that is, each element of X is assigned a particular real number (that is, precise membership grade). It is called type-1 fuzzy set.

- *L − fuzzy set* is abbreviated as, $A : X \rightarrow L$, where L is a partial order set.

- *Interval − valued fuzzy set is abbreviated as, $A : X \rightarrow \varepsilon([0,1])$,* where $\varepsilon([0,1])$ is the family of all closed interval in [0, 1]. The Figure 21 shows an example of interval-valued fuzzy set.

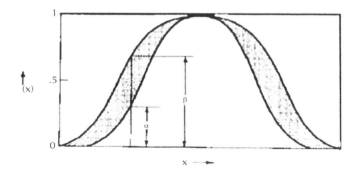

FIGURE 21   An example of an interval-valued fuzzy set (μA (a) = $\{\alpha, \beta\}$.

- Fuzzy sets of type-K is interval-valued fuzzy set which possess fuzzy intervals Type -2: $A: X \rightarrow \Xi([0,1])$, where $\Xi([0,1])$: fuzzy power set of $[0,1]$, the set s defined on $[0,1]$. Figure 22 represents Type-2 fuzzy set where the value of membership function is given by a fuzzy set.

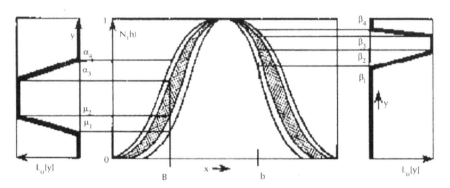

FIGURE 22   Illustration of the concept of a fuzzy set of type 2.

Example 2.7 Consider set A = "adult" (see Example 2.3). The membership function of this set maps entire range of 'age' to 'infant', 'young', 'adult' and 'senior'. The values of membership for 'infant', 'young' etc. are fuzzy sets (see Figure 23). Thus the set 'adult' is a type-2 fuzzy set. The sets 'infant', 'young', and so on are type-1 fuzzy sets. In the same way, if the values of membership function of 'infant', 'young', and so on are type-2, the set 'adult' is type-3.

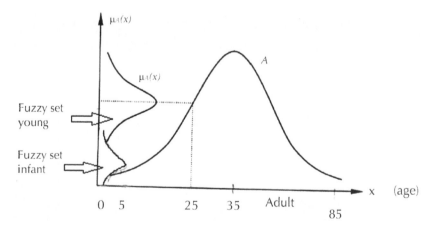

FIGURE 23   Fuzzy set (Type 2)

- Level-K fuzzy sets indicates that elements in a universal set are themselves fuzzy sets. The 'level-1 fuzzy set' is a fuzzy set whose elements are not fuzzy sets (that is ordinary elements).

  Level-2: $A: \Xi(X) \rightarrow [0, 1]$. Figure 24 shows a level-2 fuzzy set.

Example 2.8 Fuzzy set "x is close to r" where x: a fuzzy variable and r: a particular number, for example, 5.

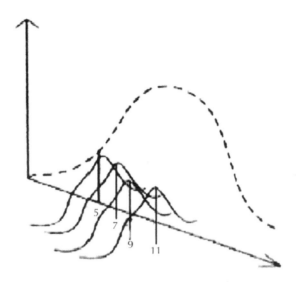

FIGURE 24   Example of level-2 fuzzy set.

Level 3: The Figure 25 depicts level-3 fuzzy set.

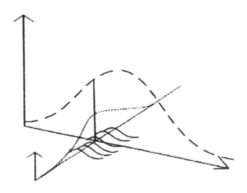

FIGURE 25   Example of level 3 fuzzy set.

- Combinations of interval-valued, L, Type-K, level-K fuzzy sets.

2.2.2   OPERATION OF FUZZY NUMBER

Operation of fuzzy number can be generalized from that of crisp interval. Let's have a look at the operation of interval [172].

OPERATION ON INTERVAL

$$\forall a_1, a_3, b_1, b_3 \in \Re$$

$$A = [a_1, a_3], B = [a_1, b_3]$$

Assuming A and B as numbers expressed as interval, main operations of interval are:

1.   Addition

$$[a_1, a_3](+)[b_1, b_3] = [a_1 + b_1, a_3 + b_3]. \qquad (2.29)$$

2.   Substraction

$$[a_1, a_3](-)[b_1, b_3] = [a_1 - b_3, a_3 - b_1]. \qquad (2.30)$$

3.   Multiplication

$$[a_1, a_3](\bullet)[b_1, b_3] = [a_1 \bullet b_1 \wedge a_1 \bullet b_3 \wedge a_3 \bullet b_1 \wedge a_3 \bullet b_3, a_1 \bullet b_1 \vee a_1 \bullet b_3 \vee a_3 \bullet b_1 \vee a_3 \bullet b_3]$$
$$(2.31)$$

4.   Division

$$[a_1, a_3](/)[b_1, b_3] = [a_1 / b_1 \wedge a_1 / b_3 \wedge a_3 / b_1 \wedge a_3 / b_3, a_1 / b_1 \vee a_1 / b_3 \vee a_3 / b_1 \vee a_3 / b_3]$$
$$(2.32)$$

excluding the case $b_1 = 0$ *or* $b_3 = 0$.

5.   Inverse interval

$$[a_1 a_3]^{-1} = [1/a_1 \wedge 1/a_3, \ 1/a_1 \vee 1/a_3] \qquad (2.33)$$

excluding the case $a_1 = 0$ or $a_3 = 0$

When previous sets A and B is defined in the positive real number $\Re+$, the operations of multiplication, division, and inverse interval are written as,

(3*) Multiplication

$$[a_1,a_3](\bullet)[b_1,b_3]=[a_1 \bullet b_1, a_3 \bullet b_3] \qquad (2.34)$$

(4*) Division

$$[a_1,a_3](/)[b_1,b_3]=[a_1/b_3, a_3/b_1] \qquad (2.35)$$

(5*) Inverse Interval

$$[a_1,a_3]^{-1} = [1/a_3, 1/a_1] \qquad (2.36)$$

(6) Minimum

$$[a_1,a_3](\wedge)[b_1,b_3]=[a_1 \wedge b_1, a_3 \wedge b_3] \qquad (2.37)$$

(7) Maximum

$$[a_1,a_3](\vee)[b_1,b_3]=[a_1 \vee b_1, a_3 \vee b_3] \qquad (2.38)$$

Example 2.9 Consider two intervals A and B,

$$A=[3,\ 5],\ B=[-2,7].$$

We get the following results:

$$A+B=[3-2,5+7]=[1,12],$$

$$A(-)B=[3-7,5-(-2)]=[-4,7],$$

$$A(\bullet)B =[3\bullet(-2)\wedge3\bullet7\wedge5\bullet(-2)\wedge5\bullet7,\ \ 3\bullet(-2)\vee...]$$

$$=[-10,35],$$

$$A(/)B =[3/(-2)\wedge3/7\wedge5/(-2)\wedge5/7,\ \ 3/(-2)\vee...]$$

$$= [-2.5, \quad 5/7] \text{ and } B^{-1} = [-2,7]^{-1} = \left[\frac{1}{(-2)} \wedge \frac{1}{7}, \frac{1}{(-2)} \vee \frac{1}{7}\right] = \left[-\frac{1}{2}, \frac{1}{7}\right].$$

OPERATION OF α – CUT INTERVAL

We consider that α – cut interval of fuzzy number $A = [a_1, a_3]$ as crisp set:

$$A_\alpha = \left[a_1^{(\alpha)}, a_3^{(\alpha)}\right], \forall \alpha \in [0,1], a_1, a_3, a_1^{(\alpha)}, a_3^{(\alpha)} \in R$$

So that A_α is a crisp interval. As a result, the operations of interval stated above can be applied to the α - cut interval A_α,

If α – cut interval B_α of fuzzy number B is given as:

$$B = [b_1, b_3], \; b_1, b_3 \in R,$$

Then

$$B_\alpha = \left[b_1^{(\alpha)}, b_3^{(\alpha)}\right], \forall \alpha \in [0,1], \; b_1^{(\alpha)}, b_3^{(\alpha)} \in R,$$

Operations between A_α and B_α are described as follows:

$$\left[a_1^{(\alpha)}, a_3^{(\alpha)}\right](+)\left[b_1^{(\alpha)}, b_3^{(\alpha)}\right] = \left[a_1^{(\alpha)} + b_1^{(\alpha)}, a_3^{(\alpha)} + b_3^{(\alpha)}\right] \quad (2.39)$$

$$\left[a_1^{(\alpha)}, a_3^{(\alpha)}\right](-)\left[b_1^{(\alpha)}, b_3^{(\alpha)}\right] = [a_1^{(\alpha)} - b_3^{(\alpha)}, a_3^{(\alpha)} - b_1^{(\alpha)}]. \quad (2.40)$$

These operations can be also applicable to multiplication and division in the same manner.

Previous operations of interval are also applicable to fuzzy number. Since outcome of fuzzy number (fuzzy set) is in the shape of fuzzy set, the results are expressed in membership function.

$$\forall x, y, z \in \Re$$

Addition: $A(+)B$

$$\mu_{A(+)B}(Z) = \hat{e}_{z=x+y} (\mu_A(x) \wedge \mu_B(y))$$

$$(2.41)$$

Subtraction: $A(-)B$

$$\mu_{A(-)B}(Z) = \bigvee_{z=x-y} (\mu_A(x) \wedge \mu_B(y)) \tag{2.42}$$

Multiplication: $A(\bullet)B$

$$\mu_{A(\bullet)B}(Z) = \hat{e}_{z=x\bullet y} (\mu_A(x) \wedge \mu_B(y)) \tag{2.43}$$

Division: $A(/)B$

$$\mu_{A(/)B}(Z) = \hat{e}_{z=x/y} (\mu_A(x) \wedge \mu_B(y)) \tag{2.44}$$

Minimum: $A(\wedge)B$

$$\mu_{A(\wedge)B}(Z) = \hat{e}_{z=x\wedge y} (\mu_A(x) \wedge \mu_B(y)) \tag{2.45}$$

Maximum: $A(\vee)B$

$$\mu_{A(\vee)B}(Z) = \hat{e}_{z=x\vee y} (\mu_A(x) \wedge \mu_B(y)) \tag{2.46}$$

We can multiply a scalar value to the interval. For instance, multiplying $a \in R$,

$$a[b_1, b_3] = [a \bullet b_1 \wedge a \bullet b_3, a \bullet b_1 \vee a \bullet b_3] \tag{2.47}$$

Example 2.10 Let us consider a scalar multiplication to interval. Let the scalar value be negative;

$$-4.14[-3.55, 0.21] = [[(-4.15)] \bullet (-3.55) \wedge (-4.15) \bullet 0.21, (-4.15) \bullet (-3.55) \vee (-4.15) \bullet 0.21]$$

$$= [14.73 \wedge -0.87, 14.73 \vee -0.87]$$

$$= [-0.87, 14.73].$$

We can also multiply scalar value to α - cut interval of fuzzy number.

$$\forall \alpha \in [0,1], \ b_1^{(\alpha)}, b_3^{(\alpha)} \in R$$

$$a\left[b_1^{(\alpha)}, b_3^{(\alpha)}\right] = \left[a \bullet b_1^{(\alpha)} \wedge a \bullet b_3^{(\alpha)}, a \bullet b_1^{(\alpha)} \vee a \bullet b_3^{(\alpha)}\right] \qquad (2.48)$$

Example 2.11 Let us consider two fuzzy sets A and B. These fuzzy sets are defined on discrete numbers; that is,

$$A = \{(2, 1), (3, 0.5)\}, B = \{(3, 1), (4, 0.5)\}.$$

For all $x \in A, y \in B, z \in A(+)B$, fuzzy set A(+)B is represented as follows:

1. for $z < 5$,

    $$\mu_{A(+)B}(Z) = 0.$$

2. $z = 5$

    results from $x + y = 2 + 3$

    $$\mu_A(2) \wedge \mu_B(3) = 1 \wedge 1 = 1$$

    $$\mu_{A(+)B}(5) = \underset{5=2+3}{\vee}(1) = 1.$$

3. $z = 6$

    results from $x + y = 3 + 3$ or $x + y = 2 + 4$

    $$\mu_A(3) \wedge \mu_B(3) = 0.5 \wedge 1 = 0.5$$

    $$\mu_A(2) \wedge \mu_B(4) = 1 \wedge 0.5 = 0.5$$

    $$\mu_{A(+)B}(6) = \underset{\substack{6+3+3\\6-2+4}}{\vee}(0.5, 05) = 0.5.$$

4. $z = 7$

    results from $x + y = 3 + 4$

    $$\mu_A(3) \wedge \mu_B(4) = 0.5 \wedge 0.5$$

    $$\mu_{A(+)B}(7) = \underset{7=3+4}{\vee}(0.5) = 0.5.$$

5. for $z > 7$

    $$\mu_{A(+)B}(Z) = 0.$$

Therefore, $A(+)B$ can be written as ,

$$A(+)B = \{(5,1), (6,0.5), (7,0.5)\} \cdot$$

Example 2.12 Let's consider $A(-)B$ between previously defined fuzzy sets A and B. For $x \in A$, $y \in B$, $z \in A(-)B$, fuzzy set $A(-)B$ is represented as follows:

1. For $z < -2$,

    $$\mu_{A(-)B}(Z) = 0 \cdot$$

2. $z = -2$

    results from $x - y = 2 - 4$

    $$\mu_A(2) \wedge \mu_B(4) = 1 \wedge 0.5 = 0.5$$

    $$\mu_{A(-)B}(-2) = 0.5 \cdot$$

3. $z = -1$

    results from *x-y=2-3 or x-y=3-4*

    $$\mu_A(2) \wedge \mu_B(3) = 1 \wedge 1 = 1$$

    $$\mu_A(3) \wedge \mu_B(4) = 0.5 \wedge 0.5 = 0.5$$

    $$\mu_{A(-)B}(-1) = \underset{\substack{-1=2-3 \\ -1=3-4}}{\vee}(1,0.5) = 1 \cdot$$

4. $z = 0$

    results from $x - y = 3 - 3$

    $$\mu_A(3) \wedge \mu_B(3) = 0.5 \wedge 1 = 0.5$$

    $$\mu_{A(-)B}(0) = 0.5 \cdot$$

5. For $z \geq 1$

    $$\mu_{A(-)B}(z) = 0$$

Therefore, $A(-)B$ can be written as,

$$A(-)B = \{(-2,0.5),(-1,1),(0,0.5)\}.$$

Example 2.13 Let's consider the operation Max $A(\vee)B$ between A and B.

For $x \in A, y \in B, z \in A(\vee)B$, fuzzy set $A(\vee)B$ is represented as,

1. $z \le 2$

    $\mu_{A(\vee)B}(z) = 0$.

2. $z = 3$

    results from $x \vee y = 2 \vee 3$ and $x \vee y = 3 \vee 3$

    $\mu_A(2) \wedge \mu_B(3) = 1 \wedge 1 = 1$

    $\mu_A(3) \wedge \mu_B(3) = 0.5 \wedge 1 = 0.5$

    $\mu_{A(\vee)B}(3) = \underset{\substack{3=2\vee 3 \\ 3=3\vee 3}}{\vee}(1, 0.5) = 1$.

3. $z = 4$

    results from $x \vee y = 2 \vee 4$ and $x \vee y = 3 \vee 4$

    $\mu_A(2) \wedge \mu_B(4) = 1 \wedge 0.5 = 0.5$

    $\mu_A(3) \wedge \mu_B(4) = 0.5 \wedge 0.5 = 0.5$

    $\mu_{A(\vee)B}(4) = \underset{\substack{4=2\vee 4 \\ 4=3\vee 4}}{\vee}(0.5, 0.5) = 0.5$.

4. $z > 5$

    $\mu_{A(\vee)B}(z) = 0$.

    so $A(\vee)B$ is defined to be

    $A(\vee)B = \{(3, 1), (4 \ \ 0.5)\}$.

We see the results of operations are fuzzy sets. We realize that the extension principle (see section 2.17.5) is applied to the operation of fuzzy number.

2.2.3 TRIANGULAR FUZZY NUMBER

Among the various shapes of fuzzy number, triangular fuzzy number (TFN) is the most popular one [172]. In Definition 2.11 we have already stated TFN. According to Definition 2.11, a fuzzy number represented with three points is interpreted, in terms of membership function as follows (see Figure 26)

$$\mu_{(A)}(x) = \begin{cases} 0, & x < a_1 \\ \dfrac{x - a_1}{a_2 - a_1} & a_1 \le x \le a_2 \\ \dfrac{a_3 - x}{a_3 - a_2} & a_2 \le x \le a_3 \\ 0, & x > a_1 \end{cases} \tag{2.49}$$

If you get crisp interval by α-cut operation, interval A_a shall be obtained as follows:

$\forall \alpha \in [0,1]$ from

$$\frac{a_1^{(\alpha)} - a_1}{a_2 - a_1} = \alpha, \quad \frac{a_3 - a_3^{(\acute{a})}}{a_3 - a_2} = \alpha$$

we get, $\quad a_1^{(\alpha)} = (a_2 - a_1)\alpha + a_1$

$$a_3^{(\alpha)} = -(a_3 - a_2)\alpha + a_3$$

Thus, $\quad A_\alpha = [a_1^{(\alpha)}, a_3^{(\alpha)}]$

$$= [(a_2 - a_1)\alpha + a_1, -(a_3 - a_2)\alpha + a_3] \tag{2.50}$$

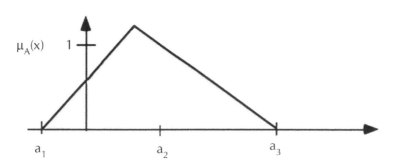

FIGURE 26 Triangular fuzzy number $A = (a_1, a_2, a_3)$.

Example 2.14 For the triangular fuzzy number $A = (-5, -1, 1)$ as shown in Figure 27, the membership function is:

$$\mu_{(A)}(x) = \begin{cases} 0, & x < 5 \\[2mm] \dfrac{x+5}{4}, & -5 \le x \le 1 \\[4mm] \dfrac{1-x}{2}, & -1 \le x \le 1 \\[4mm] 0 & x > 1 \end{cases} \qquad (2.51)$$

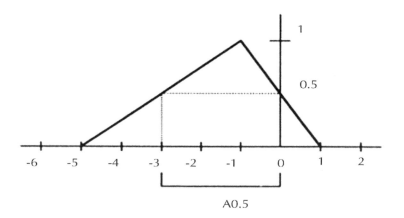

FIGURE 27 $\alpha = 0.5$ cut of triangular fuzzy number $A = (-5, -1, 1)$.

$\alpha -$ cut interval from the fuzzy number is

$$\frac{x+5}{4} = \alpha \Rightarrow \quad x = 4\alpha - 5$$

$$\frac{1-x}{2} = \alpha \Rightarrow \quad x = -2\alpha + 1$$

$$A_{\acute{a}} = \left[a_1^{(\acute{a})}, a_3^{(\acute{a})} \right] = \left[4\acute{a} - 5, -2\acute{a} + 1 \right]$$

if $\alpha = 0.5$, substituting 0.5 for α, we get $A_{0.5}$

$$A_{0.5} = \left[a_1^{(0.5)}, a_3^{(0.5)} \right] = [-3, 0].$$

ARITHMETIC OPERATIONS OF TRIANGULAR FUZZY MEMBER NUMBER

Operations of Triangular Fuzzy Number using function principle can be stated as follows:

Let A= (a_1, a_2, a_3) and B (b_1, b_2, b_3) then,

- *Addition*: A + B = $(a_1 + b_1, a_2 + b_2, a_3 + b_3)$.

- *Subtraction*: A - B = $(a_1 - b_3, a_2 - b_2, a_3 - b_1)$.

- *Multiplication*: A × B = (min $(a_1 b_1, a_1 b_3, a_3 b_1, a_3 b_3), a_2 b_2$, max ($a_1 b_1, a_1 b_3, a_3 b_1, a_3 b_3$)).

- *Division*: A/ B = (min $(a_1 / b_1, a_1 / b_3, a_3 / b_1, a_3 / b_3), a_2 / b_2$, max $(a_1 / b_1, a_1 / b_3, a_3 / b_1, a_3 / b_3)$).

Example 2.15 Let A = (2, 4, 6) and B = (1, 2, 3) be two fuzzy numbers. Then:

- A + B= (3, 6, 9)

- A - B = (-1, 2, 5)

- A × B = (2, 8, 18)

- $\frac{A}{B} = \left(\frac{2}{3}, \frac{4}{2}, \frac{6}{1} \right) = (0.66, 2, 6)$

- A - A(-4, 0, 4)

- $\frac{A}{A} = \left(\frac{2}{6}, \frac{4}{4}, \frac{6}{2} \right) = (0.33, 1, 3)$

REMARK 2.1

Note that $A - A \neq 0$, $\dfrac{A}{A} \neq 1$, where 0 and 1 are singletons whose fuzzy representations are $(0, 0, 0)$ and $(1, 1, 1)$. It follows that the C solution of the fuzzy linear equation $A + B = C$ is not as we would expect, $B = C - A$.

For example, $A + B = (2, 4, 6) + (1, 2, 3) = (3, 6, 9) = C$.

But $(1, 2, 3) = (3, 6, 9) - (2, 4, 6) = (-3, 2, 6) \neq B$.

The same annoyance appears when solving the fuzzy equation $A \times B = C$ whose solution is not given by $B = \dfrac{C}{A}$.

For example, $A \times B = (2, 8, 18) = C$.

But $B = \dfrac{(2,8,18)}{(2,4,6)} = \left(\dfrac{2}{6}, \dfrac{8}{4}, \dfrac{18}{2}\right) = (0.33, 2, 9) \neq B$.

Thus, it is not possible to solve the inverse problems exactly using the standard fuzzy arithmetic operators.

Example 2.16 α – level intervals from α – cut operation in the above two triangular fuzzy numbers A and B are

$$A_\alpha = \left[a_1^{(\alpha)}, a_3^{(\alpha)}\right] = \left[(a_2 - a_1)\alpha + a_1, -(a_3 - a_2)\alpha + a_3\right]$$

$$= \left[5\alpha - 3, -2\alpha + 4\right].$$

$$B_\alpha = \left[b_1^{(\alpha)}, b_3^{(\alpha)}\right] = \left[(b_2 - b_1)\alpha + b_1, -(b_3 - b_2)\alpha + b_3\right]$$

$$= \left[\alpha - 1, -6\alpha + 6\right].$$

Obtaining the addition of two α – cut intervals A_α and B_α,

$$A_\alpha(+)B_\alpha = [6\alpha - 4, -8\alpha + 10],$$

for $\alpha = 0$ and $\alpha = 1$, we get

$$A_0(+)B_0 = [-4, 10]$$

$$A_1(+)B_1 = [2, 2] = 2.$$

Therefore, the obtained three points from this procedure coincide with the three points of triangular fuzzy number $(-4, 2\ 10)$ obtained from the result $A(+)B$ given in the previous example.

Similarly, obtaining $A_\alpha(-)B_\alpha$,

$$A_\alpha(-)B_\alpha = [1\ \alpha - 9, -3\alpha + 5]$$

for $\alpha = 0$ and $\alpha = 1$, we get,

$$A_0(-)B_0 = [-9,\ 5]$$

$$A_1(-)B_1 = [2, 2] = 2.$$

These three points also coincide with the three points of A(-)B = (-9, 2, 5) of the previous example.

Thus, we can perform operations between fuzzy number using α-cut interval.

2.2.4 OPERATION OF GENERAL FUZZY NUMBERS

So far we have considered simplified procedure of addition and subtraction using three points of triangular fuzzy number. But, fuzzy numbers may have general form. Hence, we have to deal the operations with their membership functions [172].

Example 2.17 We consider two triangular fuzzy numbers,

$$A = (-3, 2, 4), B = (-1, 0.6)$$

and their membership functions,

$$\mu_{(A)}(x) = \begin{cases} 0, & x < 3 \\ \dfrac{x+3}{2+3} & -3 \leq x \leq 2 \\ \dfrac{4-x}{4-2} & 2 \leq x \leq 4 \\ 0, & x > 4 \end{cases}$$

and

$$\mu_{(B)}(y) = \begin{cases} 0, & y < -1 \\ \dfrac{y+1}{0+1} & -1 \le y \le 0 \\ \dfrac{6-y}{6-0} & 0 \le y \le 6 \\ 0, & y > 6 \end{cases}.$$

We perform the addition operation using their membership functions.

For the two fuzzy number $x \in A$ and $y \in B$, $z \in A(+)B$ is obtained by their membership functions.

Let us consider, $z = 8$. Addition to make $z = 8$ is possible for following cases:

$$2 + 6, 3 + 5, 3.5 + 4.5, \ldots$$

Therefore,

$$\mu_{A(+)B} = \bigvee_{8=x+y} \left[\mu_A(2) \wedge \mu_B(6), \mu_A(3) \wedge \mu_B(5), \mu_A(3.5) \wedge \mu_B(4.5), \ldots \right]$$

$$= \vee \left[1 \wedge 0 \quad 0.5 \wedge 1/6, \quad 0.25 \wedge 0.25, \ldots \right]$$

$$= \vee \left[0, 1/6, 0.25, \ldots \right]$$

If we continue these operations for all $z \in A(+)B$, we get the following membership functions. These are identical to the three point expression for triangular fuzzy number $A = (-4, 2, 10)$

$$\mu_{A(+)B}(z) = \begin{cases} 0 & z < -4 \\ \dfrac{z+4}{6} & -4 \le z \le 2 \\ \dfrac{10-z}{8} & 2 \le z \le 10 \\ 0 & z > 10 \end{cases}$$

There in no simple method using there point expression for multiplication or division operation. So it is necessary to use membership functions.

Example 2.18 We consider two triangular fuzzy numbers A and B

$$A = (1, \ 2,4), \ B = (2, \ 4, \ 6)$$

and their membership functions;

$$\mu_{(A)}(x) = \begin{cases} 0, & x < 1 \\ x-1 & 1 \le x < 2 \\ -\dfrac{1}{2}x + 2, & 2 \le x < 4 \\ 0, & x \ge 4 \end{cases}$$

and

$$\mu_{(B)}(y) = \begin{cases} 0, & y < 2 \\ \dfrac{1}{2}y - 1 & 2 \le y < 4 \\ -\dfrac{1}{2}y + 3, & 4 \le y < 6 \\ 0, & y \ge 6 \end{cases}$$

We calculate the multiplication $A\ (\bullet)B$ of A and B, as follows:
For $z = x \bullet y = 8$, either $z = 2 \bullet 4$ or $4 \bullet 2$.

Therefore, $\mu_{A(\bullet)B} = \underset{x \bullet y = 8}{\vee} \left[\mu_A(2) \wedge \mu_B(4) \wedge \mu_B(2), ... \right]$

$$= \vee[1 \wedge 1, 0 \wedge 0, ...]$$

$$= \ 1.$$

For $Z = x \bullet y = 12$, $3 \bullet 4$, $4 \bullet 3$, $2.5 \bullet 4.8$, ...are possible
Therefore,

$$\mu_{A(\bullet)B} = \underset{x \bullet y = 12}{\vee} \left[\mu_A(3) \wedge \mu_B(4), \mu_A(4) \wedge \mu_B(3), \mu_A(2.5) \wedge \mu_B(4.8), ... \right]$$

$$= \vee [0.5 \wedge 1, 0 \wedge 0.5, 0.75 \wedge 0.6, ...]$$

$$= \vee [0.5, \ 0 \quad 0.6, ...]$$

$$= \ 0.6 \ .$$

According to this procedure, if we consider membership function for all $z \in A \ (\bullet)B$, we get fuzzy number as in Figure 28. Since this shape is in curve, it is not a triangular fuzzy number. But we can express it as a triangular fuzzy number by approximating $A \ (\bullet)B$ as,

$$A(\bullet)B \cong (2, 8, 24) ,$$

where we have two end points have 2 and 24 and one peak point at 8.

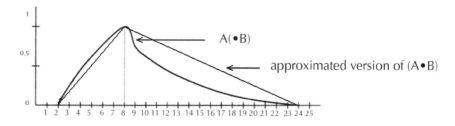

FIGURE 28   Multiplication $A \ (\bullet)B$ of triangular fuzzy number.

APPROXIMATION OF TRIANGULAR FUZZY NUMBER

We can approximate values of multiplication and division as triangular fuzzy numbers. We demonstrate this result through the following examples;

Example 2.19. Let us consider α - cuts of two fuzzy numbers,

$$A = (1, 2, 4), \ B = (2, 4, 6) .$$

$$A_\alpha = [(2 - 1)\alpha + 1, \quad -(4 - 2)\alpha + 4]$$

$$= [\alpha + 1, -2\alpha + 4] .$$

$$B_\alpha = [(4 - 2)\alpha + 2, -(6 - 4)\alpha + 6]$$

$$= [2\alpha + 2, -2\alpha + 6].$$

For all $\alpha \in [0,1]$, multiply A_α with B_α which are two crisp intervals. Now in $\alpha \in [0, 1]$, we see that elements of each interval are positive numbers. So multiplication operation of the two intervals is as follows;

$$A_\alpha (\bullet) B_\alpha = [\alpha + 1, -2\alpha + 4]$$

$$(\bullet)[2\alpha + 2, -2\alpha + 6]$$

$$= [(\alpha + 1)(2\alpha + 2), (-2\alpha + 4)(-2\alpha + 6)]$$

$$= [2\alpha^2 + 4\alpha + 2, 4\alpha^2 - 20\alpha + 24].$$

For, $\alpha = 0$,

$$A_0 (\bullet) B_0 = [2, 24],$$

and for $\alpha = 1$,

$$A_1 (\bullet) B_1 = [2 + 4 + 2, 4 - 20 + 24] = [8,8] = 8.$$

Therefore, we obtain a triangular fuzzy number which is an approximation of $A (\bullet) B$ as shown in Figure 28.

$$A(\bullet)B \cong [2, 8, 24].$$

Example 2.20 Let's express approximated value of $A (/)B$ in a triangular fuzzy number. Divide interval A_α by B_α. We reconsider the sets A and B in the previous example. For $\alpha \in [0, 1]$, since element in each interval has positive number, we get $A_\alpha (/)B_\alpha$ as follows.

$$A_\alpha (/)B_\alpha = [(\alpha + 1)/(-2\alpha + 6), (-2\alpha + 6)/(2\alpha + 2)].$$

For $\alpha = 0$,

$$A_0(/)B_0 \ = [1/6, \quad 4/2]$$

$$= [0.17, 2],$$

and for $\alpha = 1$,

$$A_1(/)B_1 \ = [(1+1)/(-2+6), \quad (-2+4)/(2+2)]$$

$$= [2/4, 2/4]$$

$$= 0.5.$$

Therefore, the approximated value of $A(/)B$ is,

$$A(/)B \ = (0.17, \ 0.5, \ 2).$$

2.2.5   OTHER TYPES OF FUZZY NUMBER

In Definition 2.12 we have also stated about trapezoidal fuzzy number. This shape is originated from the fact that there are several points whose membership degree is maximum $(\alpha = 1)$. In terms of membership function we can represent (See Figure 29) a trapezoidal fuzzy number A as

$$A = (a_1, a_2, a_3, a_4),$$

where the membership function of this fuzzy number is:

$$\mu_{(A)}(x) = \begin{cases} 0, & x < a_1 \\[2mm] \dfrac{x - a_1}{a_2 - a_1}, & a_1 \le x \le a_2 \\[2mm] 1 & a_2 \le x \le a_3 \\[2mm] \dfrac{a_4 - x}{a_4}, & a_3 \le x \le a_4 \\[2mm] 0, & x \ge a_4 \end{cases} \qquad (2.53)$$

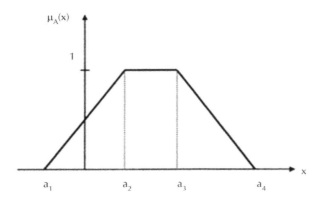

FIGURE 29 Trapezoidal fuzzy number $A = (a_1, a_2, a_3, a_4)$.

$\alpha - cut$ interval for this shape is written below.

$$\forall \alpha \in [0, 1]$$

$$A_{\acute{a}} = \left[(a_2 - a_1)\,\acute{a} + a_1, \quad -(a_4 - a_3)\,\acute{a} + a_4 \right]$$

when $a_2 = a_3$, the trapezoidal fuzzy number coincides with triangular one.

OPERATIONS OF TRAPEZOIDAL FUZZY NUMBER

We consider the operations of trapezoidal fuzzy number [172].

- Addition and subtraction between trapezoidal fuzzy numbers become trapezoidal fuzzy number.
- Multiplication, division, and inverse need not be trapezoidal fuzzy number.
- Max and Min of fuzzy number is not always in the form of trapezoidal fuzzy number.

As in triangular fuzzy number, addition and subtraction are simply defined as follows:

- Addition

$$A(+)B = (a_1, a_2, a_3, a_4)(+)(b_1, b_2, b_3, b_4) \tag{2.54}$$

$$= (a_1 + b_1, a_2 + b_2, a_3 + b_3, a_4 + b_4).$$

- Subtraction

$$A(-)B = (a_1 - b_4, a_2 - b_3, a_3 - b_2, a_4 - b_1) \tag{2.55}$$

Multiplication and division operations are done using membership function. In many cases the results of operation from multiplication and division are approximated trapezoidal shape.

Example 2.21 Multiply two trapezoidal fuzzy numbers as given below.

$$A = (1, 5, 6, 9)$$

$$B = (2, 3, 5, 8)$$

For exact value of the calculation, the membership functions are used and the result is shown in (Figure 30). For the approximation operation, we use α - cut interval

$$A_\alpha = [4\alpha + 1, \ -3\alpha + 9]$$

$$B_\alpha = [\alpha + 2, \ -3\alpha + 8]$$

Since, for all $\alpha \in [0, 1]$, each element for each interval is positive, multiplication between α – cut intervals becomes,

$$A_\alpha(\bullet)B_\alpha = [(4\alpha + 1)(\alpha + 2), \ (-3\alpha + 9)(-3\alpha + 8)]$$

$$= [4\alpha^2 + 9\alpha + 2, \ 9\alpha^2 - 51\alpha + 72]$$

For, $\alpha = 0$,

$$A_0(\bullet)B_0 = [2, 72],$$

and for $\alpha = 1$,

$$A_1(\bullet)B_1 = [4 + 9 + 2, \ 9 - 51 + 72]$$

$$= [15, 30].$$

Therefore, using four points in $\alpha = 0$ and $\alpha = 1$, we obtain the approximated value as trapezoidal fuzzy number shown in Figure 30.

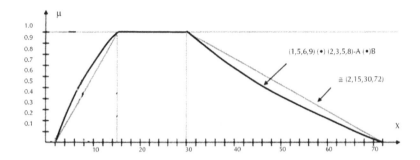

FIGURE 30 Multiplication of trapezoidal fuzzy number $A(\cdot)B$.

Generalizing trapezoidal fuzzy number, we get flat fuzzy number. Flat fuzzy number is for fuzzy number A satisfying following

$$\exists m_1, m_2 \in R, \; m_1 < m_2$$

$$\mu_A(x) = 1, \qquad m_1 \le x \le m_2 .$$

In this case, not like trapezoidal form, membership function in $x < m_1$ and $x < m_2$ need not be a line as shown in Figure 31.

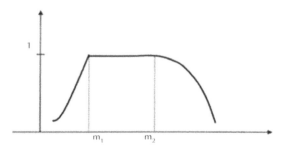

FIGURE 31 Flat fuzzy number.

BELL SHAPE FUZZY NUMBER

Bell shape fuzzy number as shown in Figure 32 is defined as follows (Figure 32);

$$\mu_f(x) = \exp\left\{\frac{-(x - m_f)^2}{2\delta_f^2}\right\} \tag{2.56}$$

where μ_f is the mean of the function and δ_f is the standard deviation.

α-cut method is a standard method for performing different arithmetic operations like addition, multiplication, division, subtraction. We show that alpha-cut method can be used for finding n^{th} root of fuzzy number.

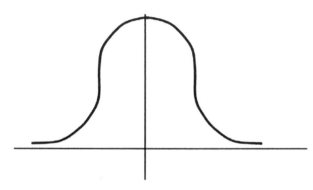

FIGURE 32   bell shape fuzzy number.

2.2.6   ARITHMETIC OPERATION OF FUZZY NUMBERS USING α-CUT METHOD [68]

In this section we consider arithmetic operation on fuzzy numbers using α-cut method.

ADDITION OF FUZZY NUMBERS

Let X = [a, b, c] and Y = [p, q, r] be two fuzzy numbers whose membership functions are

$$\mu_X(x) = \begin{cases} \dfrac{x - a}{b - a}, & a \le x \le b \\ \dfrac{c - x}{c - b}, & b \le x \le c \end{cases}$$

and

$$\mu_Y(x) = \begin{cases} \dfrac{x - p}{q - p}, & p \le x \le q \\ \dfrac{r - x}{r - q}, & q \le x \le r. \end{cases}$$

Then $\alpha_X = [(b\text{-}a)\,\alpha + a, c - (c\text{-}b)\alpha]$ and $\alpha_Y = [(q\text{-}p)\,\alpha + p, r - (r\text{-}q)\alpha]$ are the α-cuts of fuzzy numbers X and Y respectively. To calculate addition of fuzzy numbers X and Y we first add the α-cuts of X and Y using arithmetic.

$$\alpha_X + \alpha_Y = [(b\text{-}a)\,\alpha + a, c - (c\text{-}b)\,\alpha] + [(q\text{-}p)\,\alpha + p, r - (r\text{-}q)\alpha] = [a + p + (b - a + q - p)\,\alpha,\, c + r - (c - b + r - q)\,\alpha] \qquad (2.57)$$

To find the membership function $\mu_{X+Y}(x)$ we equate to x both the first and second component in (2.57) which gives:

$$x = a + p + (b - a + q - p)\alpha \text{ and}$$
$$x = c + r - (c + r - b - q)\alpha.$$

Now, expressing α in terms of x and setting $\alpha = 0$ and $\alpha = 1$ in (2.57) we get α together with the domain of x,

$$\alpha = \frac{x - (a+p)}{(b+q) - (a+p)}, \ (a + p) \leq x \leq (b + q)$$

and

$$\alpha = \frac{(c+r) - x}{(c+r) - (b+q)}, \ (b + q) \leq x \leq (c + r)$$

which yield

$$\mu_{X+Y}(x) = \begin{cases} \dfrac{x - (a + p)}{(b + q) - (a + p)}, & (a + p) \leq x \leq (b + q) \\[2mm] \dfrac{(c + r) - x}{(c + r) - (b + q)}, & (b + q) \leq x \leq (c + r). \end{cases}$$

SUBTRACTION OF FUZZY NUMBERS

Let X= [a, b, c] and Y= [p, q, r] be two fuzzy numbers. Then:

$$\alpha_X = [(b - a)\alpha + a, c - (c - b)\alpha] \text{ and}$$

$$\alpha_Y = [(q - p)\alpha + p, r - (r - q)\alpha]$$

are the α-cuts of fuzzy numbers X and Y respectively. To calculate subtraction of fuzzy numbers X and Y we first subtract the α-cuts of X and Y using interval arithmetic.

$$\alpha_X - \alpha_Y =$$
$$[(b-a)\alpha + a, c - (c-b)\alpha] - [(q-p)\alpha + p, r - (r-q)\alpha]$$

$$= [((b-a)\alpha + a - (r - (r-q)\alpha), c - (c-b)\alpha - ((q-p)\alpha + p)]$$

$$= [(a-r) + (b-a+r-q)\,\alpha, (c-p) - (c-b+q-p)\,\alpha]. \qquad (2.58)$$

To find the membership function $\alpha_{X-Y}(x)$ we equate to x both the first and second component in (2.58) which gives

$$x = (a-r) + (b-a+r-q)\,\alpha, \text{ and } x = (c-p) - (c-b+q-p)\,\alpha.$$

Now, expressing α in terms of x and setting $\alpha = 0$ and $\alpha = 1$ in (2.58) we get α together with the domain of x,

$$\alpha = \frac{x - (a-r)}{(b-q) - (a-r)}, (a-r) \leq x \leq (b-q)$$

and

$$\alpha = \frac{(c-p) - x}{(c-p) - (b-q)}, (b-q) \leq x \leq (c-p)$$

which yield

$$\mu_{X-Y}(x) = \begin{cases} \dfrac{x - (a-r)}{(b-q) - (a-r)}, & (a-r) \leq x \leq (b-q) \\ \dfrac{(c-p) - x}{(c-p) - (b-q)}, & (b-q) \leq x \leq (c-p). \end{cases}$$

MULTIPLICATION OF FUZZY NUMBERS

Let X= [a, b, c] and Y= [p, q, r] be two positive fuzzy numbers. Then $\alpha_X = [(b-a)\alpha + a, c - (c-b)\alpha]$ and $\alpha_Y = [(q-p)\alpha + p, r - (r-q)\alpha]$

are the α-cuts of fuzzy numbers X and Y respectively. To calculate multiplication of fuzzy numbers X and Y we first multiply the α-cuts of X and Y using interval arithmetic.

$$\alpha_X * \alpha_Y =$$

$$[(b-a)\alpha + a, c - (c-b)\alpha] * [(q-p)\alpha + p, r - (r-q)\alpha]$$

$$= [((b-a)\alpha + a) * ((q-p)\alpha + p), (c - (c-b)$$
$$\alpha) * (r - (r-q)\alpha)] \tag{2.59}$$

To find the membership function $\mu_{XY}(x)$ we equate to x both the first and second component in (2.59) which gives

$$x = (b-a)(q\text{-}p)\alpha^2 + ((b\text{-}a)p + (q\text{-}p)a)\alpha + ap.$$

and

$$x = (c\text{-}b)(r\text{-}q)\alpha^2 - ((r\text{-}q)c + (c\text{-}b)r)\alpha + cr$$

Now, expressing α in terms of x and setting $\alpha = 0$ and $\alpha = 1$ in (2.59) we get α together with the domain of x,

$$\alpha = \frac{-((b-a)p + q - p)a) + \sqrt{((b-a)p + q - p)a)^2 - 4(b-a)(q-p)(ap-x)}}{2(b-a)(q-p)}, ap$$
$$\le x \le bq$$

and

$$\alpha = \frac{((r-q)c + (c-b)r) - \sqrt{((r-q)c + (c-b)r)^2 - 4(c-b)(r-q)(cr-x)}}{2(c-b)(r-q)}, bq \le x$$
$$\le cr$$

which yield

$$\mu_{XY}(X) = \begin{cases} \dfrac{-((b-a)p + q - p)a) + \sqrt{((b-a)p + q - p)a)^2 - 4(b-a)(q-p)(ap-x)}}{2(b-a)(q-p)}, ap \le x \le bq \\[4mm] \dfrac{((r-q)c + (c-b)r) - \sqrt{((r-q)c + (c-b)r)^2 - 4(c-b)(r-q)(cr-x)}}{2(c-b)(r-q)}, bq \le x \le cr. \end{cases}$$

DIVISION OF FUZZY NUMBERS

Let X= [a, b, c] and Y= [p, q, r] be two positive fuzzy numbers. Then $\alpha_X = [(b-a)\alpha + a, c - (c-b)\alpha]$ and $\alpha_Y = [(q-p)\alpha + p, r - (r-q)\alpha]$ are the α -cuts of fuzzy numbers X and Y respectively. To calculate division of fuzzy numbers X and Y we first divide the α-cuts of X and Y using interval arithmetic.

$$\frac{\alpha_X}{\alpha_Y} = \frac{[(b-a)\alpha+a,c-(c-b)\alpha]}{[(q-p)\alpha+p,r-(r-q)\alpha]} = \left[\frac{(b-a)\alpha+a}{r-(r-q)\alpha}, \frac{c-(c-b)\alpha}{(q-p)\alpha+p}\right]. \tag{2.60}$$

To find the membership function $\mu_{X/Y}(x)$ we equate to x both the first and second component in (2.60) which give

$$x = \frac{[(b-a)\alpha+a}{r-(r-q)\alpha} \text{ and } x = \frac{c-(c-b)\alpha}{(q-p)\alpha+p}.$$

Now, expressing α in terms of x and setting $\alpha= 0$ and $\alpha = 1$ in (2.60) we get α together with the domain of x,

$$\alpha = \frac{xr-a}{(b-a)+(q-r)x}, \frac{a}{r} \leq x \leq b/q$$

and

$$\alpha = \frac{c-px}{(c-b)+(q-p)x}, b/q \leq x \leq c/p$$

which yield

$$\mu_{\frac{X}{Y}}(x) = \begin{cases} \frac{xr-a}{(b-a)+(q-r)x}, & \frac{a}{r} \leq x \leq \frac{b}{q} \\ \frac{c-px}{(c-b)+(q-p)x}, & b/q \leq x \leq c/p. \end{cases}$$

INVERSE OF FUZZY NUMBER

Let X=[a, b, c] be a positive fuzzy number. Then $\alpha_X = [(b-a)\alpha + a, c - (c-b)\alpha]$ is the α-cut of fuzzy numbers X. To calculate inverse of fuzzy number X we first take the α-cut of X using interval arithmetic.

$$\frac{1}{\alpha_X} = \frac{1}{[(b-a)\alpha+a,c-(c-b)\alpha]} = \left[\frac{1}{c-(c-b)\alpha}, \frac{1}{(b-a)\alpha+a}\right]. \tag{2.61}$$

To find the membership function $\mu_{1/x}(x)$ we equate to x both the first and second component in (2.61), which gives

$$X = \frac{1}{c-(c-b)\alpha} \text{ and } X = \frac{1}{(b-a)\alpha+a}.$$

Now, expressing α in terms of x and setting $\alpha = 0$ and $\alpha = 1$ in (2.61) we get α together with the domain of x,

$$\alpha = \frac{cx-1}{x(c-b)}, \frac{1}{c} \le x \le \frac{1}{b} \text{ and}$$

$$\alpha = \frac{1-ax}{x(b-a)}, \frac{1}{b} \le x \le \frac{1}{a} \text{ which give,}$$

$$\mu_{\frac{1}{x}}(x) = \begin{cases} \frac{cx-1}{x(c-b)}, & \frac{1}{c} \le x \le \frac{1}{b} \\ \frac{1-ax}{x(b-a)}, & \frac{1}{b} \le x \le \frac{1}{a} \end{cases}$$

EXPONENTIAL OF A FUZZY NUMBER

Let $X = [a, b, c] > 0$ be a fuzzy number. Then $\alpha_x = [(b-a)\alpha + a, c - (c-b)\alpha]$ is the α-cut of fuzzy numbers x. To calculate exponential of fuzzy number x we first take the exponential of the α-cut of X using interval arithmetic.

$$\exp(\alpha_x) = \exp([b-a]\alpha + a, c - (c-b)\alpha]) =$$
$$[\exp((b-a)\alpha + a), \exp(c-(c-b)\alpha] \quad (2.62)$$

To find the membership function $\mu_{\exp(x)}(x)$ we equate to x both the first and second component in (2.62) which gives

$$x = \exp((b-a)\alpha + a) \text{ and}$$

$$x = \exp(c-(c-b)\alpha).$$

Now, expressing α in terms of x and setting $\alpha = 0$ and $\alpha = 1$ in (2.62) we get α together with the domain of x,

$$\alpha = \frac{\ln(x) - a}{b - a}, \exp(a) \le x \le \exp(x) \text{ and}$$

$$\alpha = \frac{c - \ln(x)}{c - b}, \exp(b) \le x \le \exp(c)$$

which yield,

$$\mu_{exp(X)}(x) = \begin{cases} \frac{\ln(x)-a}{b-a}, & \exp(a) \le x \le \exp(x) \\ \frac{c-\ln(x)}{c-b}, & \exp(b) \le x \le \exp(c). \end{cases}$$

LOGARITHM OF A FUZZY NUMBER

Let X= [a, b, c] be a fuzzy number. Then $\alpha_X = [(b-a)\alpha + a, c - (c-b)\alpha]$ is the α-cut of fuzzy numbers X. To calculate logarithm of the fuzzy number X we first take the logarithm of the α-cut of X using interval arithmetic.

$$\ln(\alpha_X) = \ln([b\text{-}a]\,\alpha + a, c - (c\text{-}b)\,\alpha]) =$$

$$[\ln((b\text{-}a)\alpha + a), \ln(c\text{-}(c\text{-}b))]. \tag{2.63}$$

To find the membership function $\mu_{\ln(X)}(x)$ we equate to x both the first and second component in (2.63) which gives

$$x = \ln((b\text{-}a)\,\alpha + a) \text{ and}$$

$$x = \ln(c\text{-}(c\text{-}b)).$$

Now, expressing α in terms of x and setting $\alpha = 0$ and $\alpha = 1$ in (2.63) we get α together with the domain of x,

$$\alpha = \frac{\exp(x)-a}{b-a}, \ln(a) \le x \le \ln(b) \text{ and}$$

$$\alpha = \frac{c-\exp(x)}{c-b}, \ln(b) \le x \le \ln(c)$$

which yield

$$\mu_{\ln(X)}(x) = \begin{cases} \frac{\exp(x)-a}{b-a}, & \ln(a) \le x \le \ln(b) \\ \frac{c-\exp(x)}{c-b}, & \ln(b) \le x \le \ln(c). \end{cases}$$

SQUARE ROOT OF FUZZY NUMBER BY α-CUT METHOD

Let X = [a,b,c] > 0 be a fuzzy number. Then $\alpha_X = [(b-a)\alpha + a, c - (c-b)\alpha]$ is the α-cut of the fuzzy numbers X. To calculate square root of the fuzzy number X we first take the square root of α-cut of X using interval arithmetic.

$$\sqrt{a_x} = \sqrt{[(b-a)\alpha + a, c - (c-b)\alpha]} =$$

$$[\sqrt{(b-a)\alpha + a}, \sqrt{c - (c-b)\alpha}\,] \qquad (2.64)$$

To find the membership function $\mu_{\sqrt{x}}(x)$ we equate to x both the first and second component in (2.64), which gives

$$x = \sqrt{(b-a)\alpha + a} \text{ and}$$

$$x = \sqrt{c - (c-b)\alpha}.$$

Now, expressing α in terms of x and setting $\alpha = 0$ and $\alpha = 1$ in (2.64) we get α together with the domain of x,

$$\alpha = \frac{x^2 - a}{b - a}, \ \sqrt{a} \le x \le \sqrt{b} \text{ and}$$

$$\alpha = \frac{c - x^2}{c - b}, \ \sqrt{b} \le x \le \sqrt{c}$$

which yield

$$\mu_{\sqrt{x}}(x) = \begin{cases} \frac{x^2 - a}{b - a}, & \sqrt{a} \le x \le \sqrt{b} \\ \frac{c - x^2}{c - b}, & \sqrt{b} \le x \le \sqrt{c}. \end{cases}$$

N^{TH} ROOT OF A FUZZY NUMBER

Let X = [a,b,c]> 0 be a fuzzy number. Then $\alpha_X = [(b-a)\alpha + a, c - (c-b)\alpha]$ is the α-cut of the fuzzy numbers X. To calculate square n^{th} root of the fuzzy number X we first take the nth root of the α-cut of X using interval arithmetic.

$$(\alpha_X)^{1/n} = ([(b-a)\alpha + a, c - (c-b)\alpha])^{1/n} =$$

$$[(b(-a)\alpha)^{1/n}, \left(c - (c-b)\alpha\right)^{\frac{1}{n}}] \qquad (2.65)$$

To find the membership function $\mu_{n\sqrt{x}}(x)$ we equate to x both the first and second component in (2.65) which gives

$$x = (b(-a)\alpha)^{1/n} \text{ and } x = (c - (c-b)\alpha)^{1/n}.$$

Now expressing α in terms of x and setting $\alpha = 0$ $and \alpha = 1$ in (2.65) we get α together with the domain of x,

$$\alpha = \frac{x^n - a}{b - a}, \ \sqrt[n]{a} \le x \le \sqrt[n]{b} \text{ and}$$

$$\alpha = \frac{c-x^n}{c-b}, \sqrt[n]{b} \leq x \leq \sqrt[n]{c}$$

which yield

$$\mu_{\sqrt[n]{A}}(x) = \begin{cases} \frac{x^n-a}{b-a}, & \sqrt[n]{a} \leq x \leq \sqrt[n]{b} \\ \frac{c-x^n}{c-b}, & \sqrt[n]{b} \leq x \leq \sqrt[n]{c} \end{cases}.$$

2.3   METRICS FOR FUZZY NUMBERS

Let A and B be fuzzy numbers with $[A]^\alpha = [a_1(\alpha), \ a_2(\alpha)]$ and $[B]^\alpha = [b_1(\alpha), \ b_2(\alpha)]$. We metricize the set of fuzzy numbers by the metrics

2.3.1   HAUSDORFF DISTANCE

$$D(A,B) = \overset{sup}{\alpha \in [0,1]} \max \{|a_1(\alpha) - b_1(\alpha)|, \ |a_2(\alpha) - b_2(\alpha)|\}. \quad (2.66)$$

that is D (A,B) is the maximal distance between α level sets of A and B. Figure 33 shows the Hausdorff distance between symmetric triangular fuzzy numbers A and B.

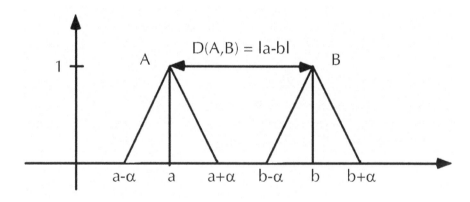

FIGURE 33   Hausdorff distance between symmetric triangular fuzzy numbers A and B.

C_∞ DISTANCE

$$C_\infty(A,B) = \|A-B\|_\infty = \sup\{|A(u)-B(u)| \mid u \in \mathbb{R}\}. \quad (2.67)$$

That is C_∞ (A,B) is the maximal distance between the membership grades of A and B. C(A,B) = 1 if the supports of A and B are disjunctive see Figure 34.

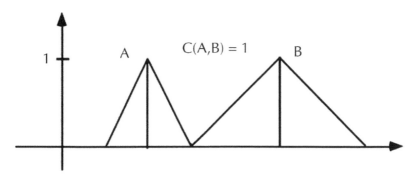

FIGURE 34 C(A,B) = 1 whenever the supports of A and B are disjunctive.

HAMMING DISTANCE

Suppose A and B fuzzy sets in X. Then their Hamming distance, denoted by H (A,B), is defined by

$$H(A,B) = \int_X |A(x) - B(x)|\, dx. \tag{2.68}$$

DISCRETE HAMMING DISTANCE

Suppose A and B discrete fuzzy sets

$$A = \mu_1 / x_1 + \ldots + \mu_n / x_n, \ B = v_1/x_1 + \ldots + v_n/x_n.$$

Then their Humming distance is defined by

$$H(A,B) = \sum_{j=1}^{n} |\mu_j - v_j|. \tag{2.69}$$

Remark 2.2 D (A,B) is a better measure of similarity than C_∞ (A,B), because C_∞ (A,B) $\leq$ 1 holds even though the supports of A and B are very far from each other.

Definition 2.21 Let f be a fuzzy function from F to F. Then f is said to be continuous in metric D if $\forall \epsilon > 0$ there exists $\delta > 0$ such that if

$$D(A,B) \leq \delta$$

then

$$D(f(A), f(B)) \leq \epsilon.$$

In a similar way we can define the continuity of fuzzy functions in metric C_∞.

Definition 2.22 Let f be a fuzzy function from $F(R)$ to $F(R)$. Then f is said to be continuous in metric C_∞ $\forall \varepsilon > 0$ there exists $\delta > 0$ such that if

$$C_\infty (A,B) \leq \delta$$

then

$$C_\infty (f(A), f(B)) \leq \varepsilon.$$

Remark 2.3 In the definition of continuity in metric C_∞ the domain and the range of f can be the family of all fuzzy subsets of the real line, while in the case of continuity in metric D the domain and the range of f is the set of fuzzy numbers.

2.4   DIFFERENCE IN FUZZY SET

The difference in crisp set is defined as follows

$$A - B = A \cap \sim B$$

In fuzzy set, there are two means of obtaining the difference

SIMPLE DIFFERENCE

Example 2.22 Using standard complement and intersection (min) operations, the difference operation, A - B becomes,

$$A = \{(x_1, 0.3), (x_2, 0.7), (x_3, 1), (x_4, 0)\}$$

$$B = \{(x_1, 0.5), (x_2, 0.4), (x_3, 1), (x_4, 0.1)\}$$

$$\sim B = \{(x_1, 0.5), (x_2, 0.6), (x_3, 0), (x_4, 0.9)\}$$

$$A - B = A \cap \sim B = \{(x_1, 0.3), (x_2, 0.6), (x_3, 0), (x_4, 0)\}.$$

BOUNDED DIFFERENCE

Definition 2.23 For operator θ, we define the membership function as:

$$\mu_{A\theta B}(X) = Max[0, \mu_A(x) - \mu_B(x)] \tag{2.70}$$

By the definition, bounded difference of preceding two fuzzy sets is as follows;

$$A \ \theta \ B = \{(x_1, 0), (x_2, 0.3), (x_3, 0), (x_4, 0)\}$$

2.5   DISTANCE IN FUZZY SET

The concept 'distance' is designated to describe the difference. But it has different mathematical measure from the 'difference' introduced in the previous section. Measure for distance are defined in the following.

HAMMING DISTANCE

It is represented as:

$$d(A, B) = \sum_{i=1, x_i \in X}^{n} |\mu_A(x_i) - \mu_B(x_i)|. \tag{2.71}$$

Example 2.23 Following A and B for instance,

$$A = \{(x_1, 0.4), (x_2, 0.8), (x_3, 1), (x_4, 0)\}$$

$$B = \{(x_1, 0.4), (x_2, 0.3), (x_3, 0), (x_4, 0)\}$$

Hamming distance; *d (A, B)*:

$$d(A, B) = |0| + |0.5| + |1| + |0| = 1.5$$

Hamming distance has the following properties:

$$d(A, B) \geq 0$$

$$d(A, B) = d(B, A) \qquad\qquad \text{commutativity}$$

$$d(A, C) \leq d(A, B) + d(B, C) \qquad\qquad \text{transitivity}$$

$$d(A, A) = 0.$$

Assuming n elements in universal set X; that is, $|X| = n$, the relative Hamming distance is,

$$\delta(A, B) = \frac{1}{n} d(A, B)$$

EUCLIDIAN DISTANCE

It is represented as:

$$e(A, B) = \sqrt{\sum_{i=1}^{n} (\mu_A(x) - \mu_B(x))^2} \tag{2.72}$$

Example 2.24 Euclidean distance between sets A and B used for the previous Hamming distance is

$$e(A, B) = \sqrt{0^2 + 0.5^2 + 1^2 + 0^2} = \sqrt{1.25} = 1.12$$

and relative Euclidean distance is

$$\varepsilon(A, B) = \frac{e(A, B)}{\sqrt{n}}$$

MINKOWSKI DISTANCE

It is represented as,

$$d_w(A, B) = \left(\sum_{x \in X} |\mu_A(x) - \mu_B(x)|^w \right)^{1/w}, \qquad w \in [1, \infty] \tag{2.73}$$

For w = 1, Minkowski distance reduces to Hamming distance and for w = 2 Minkowski distance reduces to Euclidean distance.

2.6   CARTESIAN PRODUCT OF FUZZY SET

Definition 2.24 Second power of fuzzy set A is defined as follows:

$$\mu_{A^2}(x) = [\mu_A(x)]^2, \qquad \forall x \in X$$

Similarly m^{th} power the fuzzy set A^m may be computed as,

$$\mu_{A^m}(x) = [\mu_A(x)]^m, \quad \forall x \in X \tag{2.74}$$

Definition 2.25 Cartesian product applied to multiple fuzzy set can be defined as follows.

Denoting $\mu_{A_1}(x), \mu_{A_2}(x), ..., \mu_{A_n}(x)$ as membership functions of $A_1, A_2, ..., A_n$ for $\forall x_1 \in A_1, x_2 \in A_2, ..., x_n \in A_n$.

Then, the possibility for n-tuple $(x_1, x_2, ..., x_n)$ to be involved in fuzzy set $A_1 \times A_2 \times ... \times A_n$ is:

$$\mu_{A_1 \times A_2 \times ... \times A_n}(x_1, x_2, ..., x_n) = Min[\mu_{A_1}(x_1), ..., \mu_{A_n}(x_n)] \tag{2.75}$$

Example 2.25 The objective in climate control is to find the optimum conditions in terms of both temperature T and humidity H. Suppose that the discrete sets of temperature and humidity are given by $T = \{T_1, T_2, T_3, T_4\}$ and $H = \{H_1, H_2, H_3\}$ respectively:

Let the derived temperature by discrete fuzzy set be:

$$A = \{^{0.12}/_{T_1}, ^{0.65}/_{T_2}, ^{1}/_{T_3}, ^{0.25}/_{T_4}\};$$

and the derived level of humidity be:

$$B = \{^{0.5}/_{H_1}, ^{0.9}/_{H_2}, ^{0.1}/_{H_3}\}.$$

Therefore, the Cartesian product A × B is:

$$A \times B = \{^{0.12}/_{T_1 H_1}, ^{0.12}/_{T_1 H_2}, ^{0.1}/_{T_1 H_3}, ^{0.5}/_{T_2 H_1},$$

$$^{0.65}/_{T_2 H_2}, ^{0.1}/_{T_2 H_3}, ^{0.5}/_{T_3 H_1}, ^{0.9}/_{T_3 H_2},$$

$$^{0.1}/_{T_3 H_3}, ^{0.25}/_{T_4 H_1}, ^{0.25}/_{T_4 H_2}, ^{0.1}/_{T_4 H_3}\}.$$

The optimum conditions are $T = T_3$ and $H = H_2$.

2.7   OPERATORS ON FUZZY SET

Definition 2.26 Let A be a fuzzy set on X, and $\mu_A(x)$ the degree to which x is a member of A. Let $c(S)$ denote the *fuzzy complement* of A of type c, defined by the function $c:[0,1] \rightarrow [0,1]$, which assigns a value $c(\mu_A(x))$ to all x in X, $c(\mu_A(x))$ may be interpreted both as the degree to which x is a member of c(A), and as the degree to which x is not a member of A. The fuzzy complement function, c, must satisfy at least the following two axiomatic requirements:

- axiom 1 (boundary conditions): $c(0)=1$, and $c(1) = 0$;

- axiom 2 (monotonicity): $\forall x, y \in [0,1]$, if $x \leq y$, then $c(x) \geq c(y)$.

In addition, it is desirable in many practical cases that c also satisfies the following requirements:

- axiom 3 (continuity): c is a continuous function;

- axiom 4 (involutivity): c is *involutive*, namely, $\forall x, y \in [0,1]$, $c(c(x))= x$.

Several different complement functions, c, which satisfy the axiomatic requirements of Definition 2.26, have appeared in the literature.

Some examples are as follows.s

1.   The standard complement:

$$c\left(\mu_S(x)\right) = 1 - \mu_S(x) \qquad\qquad \mu_S(x) \in [0,1] \qquad\qquad (2.76)$$

This form of complement, which satisfies all four axiomatic requirements, has been used in the majority of fuzzy applications.

2.   Step-threshold complement

$$c\left(\mu_A(x)\right) = \begin{cases} 1 & \text{for}\,\mu_A(x) \leq t \\ 0 & \text{for}\,\mu_A(x) > t \end{cases}$$

where

$$, \mu_A(x) \in [0,1], t \in [0,1]. \qquad\qquad (2.77)$$

This form of complement satisfies only the axiomatic skeleton (Axioms 1 and 2).

3.   Sugeno class complement:

$$c_\lambda \mu_A(x)) = \frac{1-\mu_A(x)}{1+\lambda \mu_A(x)}, \mu_A(x) \in [0,1], \lambda \in (-1, \infty) \qquad (2.78)$$

which satisfies all four axiomatic requirements.

Lemma 2.1 In case of fuzzy set the law of excluded middle is not valid.

Example 2.26 Let $\mu_A(x) = 1/2$, $\forall x \in R$, then it is easy to see that

$$\sim\mu_A(x)\vee\mu_A(x) = \max\{\sim\mu_A(x),\mu_A(x)\} = \max\{1 - 1/2, 1/2\} = 1/2 \neq 1.$$

Lemma 2.2 In case of fuzzy set the law of noncontradiction is not valid.

Example 2.27 Let $\mu_A(x) = 1/2$, $\forall x \in R$, then it is easy to see that

$$\sim\mu_A(x)\wedge\mu_A(x) = \min\{\sim\mu_A(x),\mu_A(x)\} = \min\{1 - 1/2, 1/2\} = 1/2 \neq 0.$$

Definition 2.27 The fuzzy union of two fuzzy set A and B on X, denoted $A \cup B$, is specified by a function u:

$$u: [0, 1] \times [0, 1] \rightarrow [0, 1]. \tag{2.79}$$

The fuzzy union function u must satisfy at least the following axiomatic requirements, for any $a, b, d \in \{x | x \in C, |x| \leq 1\}$:

- axiom 1 (boundary conditions): $u(a, 0) = a$;

- axiom 2 (monotonocity): $b \leq d$ implies $u(a, b) \leq u(a, d)$;

- axiom 3 (commutativity): $u(a, b) = u(b, a)$;

- axiom 4 (associativity): $u(a, u(b, d)) = u(u(a, b), d)$.

In some cases, it may be desirable that u also satisfies the following requirements:

- axiom 5 (continuity): u is a continuous function;

- axiom 6 (superidempotency): $u(a, a) > a$;

- axiom 7 (strict monotonicity): $a \leq c$ and $b \leq d$ implies $u(a, b) \leq u(c, d)$.

Below are some examples of commonly used fuzzy union functions, expressed in the form of membership functions:

$$\text{Maximum (Standard Union): } \mu_{A \cup B} = \max[\mu_A, \mu_B] \tag{2.80}$$

$$\text{Algebraic Sum: } \mu_{A \cup B} = \mu_A + \mu_B - \mu_A \cdot \mu_B \tag{2.81}$$

$$\text{Bounded Sum: } \mu_{A \cup B} = \min[1, \mu_A + \mu_B]. \tag{2.82}$$

The properties of fuzzy union functions must satisfy, as specified by Definition 2.27, are equivalent to properties of functions known in the literature s *t-conorms*. For this reason, fuzzy union functions are also known as *t*-conorms.

In general, the intersection of two fuzzy sets A and B on X is denoted by $A \cap B$. The properties which fuzzy intersection functions must satisfy are the same as properties of functions known in the literature as *t-norms*.

Commonly used fuzzy intersection function, expressed in the form of membership functions, are

$$\text{Minimum (Standard Intersection): } \mu_{A \cap B} = \min [\mu_A, \mu_B] \qquad (2.83)$$

$$\text{Algebraic Product: } \mu_{A \cap B} = \mu_A \cdot \mu_B \qquad (2.84)$$

$$\text{Bounded Difference: } \mu_{A \cap B} = \max [0, \mu_A + \mu_B - 1]. \qquad (2.85)$$

Example 2.28 Let us consider the fuzzy sets A and B,

$$A = \{^0/_1, ^{0.2}/_2, ^{0.8}/_3, ^1/_4, ^1/_5\} \text{ and}$$

$$B = \{^{0.1}/_1, ^{0.4}/_2, ^{0.5}/_3, ^{0.7}/_4, ^{0.3}/_5\}.$$

Therefore,

$A \cap B$ (using min operator) = $\{^0/_1, ^{0.2}/_2, ^{0.5}/_3, ^{0.7}/_4, ^{0.3}/_5\}$,

$A \cap B$ (using product operator) = $\{^0/_1, ^{0.08}/_2, ^{0.4}/_3, ^{0.7}/_4, ^{0.3}/_5\}$,

$A \cup B$ (using max operator) = $\{^0/_1, ^{0.4}/_2, ^{0.8}/_3, ^1/_4, ^1/_5\}$,

$\sim A$ (Complement of A) = $\{^1/_1, ^{0.8}/_2, ^{0.2}/_3, ^0/_4, ^0/_5\}$,

$\sim B$ (Complement of B) = $\{^{0.9}/_1, ^{0.6}/_2, ^{0.5}/_3, ^{0.3}/_4, ^{0.7}/_5\}$ and

$\sim(A \cap B) = \sim A \cup \sim B = \{^1/_1, ^{0.8}/_2, ^{0.5}/_3, ^{0.3}/_4, ^{0.7}/_5\}$.

(De Morgan's law using max and min operator)

Table 2. provides the basic characteristics of standard fuzzy set operators.

TABLE 2   Characteristics of standard fuzzy set operators

Involution	$\sim\sim A = A$
Commutativity	$A \cup B = B \cup A$ $A \cap B = B \cap A$
Associativity	$(A \cup B) \cup C = A \cup (B \cup C)$
Distributivity	$(A \cap B) \cap C = A \cap (B \cap C)$ $A \cap (B \cup C) = (A \cap B) \cup (A \cap C)$ $A \cup (B \cap C) = (A \cup B) \cap (A \cup C)$
Idempotency	$A \cup A = A$ $A \cap A = A$
Absorption	$A \cup (A \cap B) = A$ $A \cap (A \cup B) = A$
Absorption by X and $\oslash$	$A \cup X = X$ $A \cap \oslash = \oslash$
Identity	$A \cup \oslash = A$ $A \cap X = A$
De Morgan's law	$\sim(A \cap B) = \sim A \cup \sim B$ $\sim(A \cup B) = \sim A \cap \sim B$
Equivalence formula	$(\sim A \cup \sim B) \cap (A \cup \sim B) = (\sim A \cap \sim B) \cup (A \cap B)$
Symmetrical difference formula	$(\sim A \cap B) \cup (A \cap \sim B) = (\sim A \cup \sim B) \cap (A \cup B)$

2.8   OTHER OPERATIONS IN FUZZY SET

DISJUNCTIVE SUM

Disjunctive sum is "exclusive OR" operation. It is represented as,

$$A \oplus B = (A \cap \sim B) \cup (\sim A \cap B)$$

By means of fuzzy union (max) and fuzzy intersection (min), the disjunctive sum in fuzzy set is represented by the following example.

EXAMPLE 2.29

$$A = \{(x_1, 0.3), (x_2, 0.7), (x_3, 1), (x_4, 0)\}$$

$$B = \{(x_1, 0.5), (x_2, 0.4), (x_3, 1), (x_4, 0.1)\}$$

$$\sim A = \{(x_1, 0.7), (x_2, 0.3), (x_3, 0), (x_4, 1)\}$$

$$\sim B = \{(x_1, 0.5), (x_2, 0.6), (x_3, 0), (x_4, 0.9)\}$$

$$A \cap \sim B = \{(x_1, 0.3), (x_2, 0.6), (x_3, 0), (x_4, 0)\}$$

$$\sim A \cap B = \{(x_1, 0.5), (x_2, 0.3), (x_3, 0), (x_4, 0.1)\}.$$

And as a consequence,

$$A \oplus B = (A \cap \sim B) \cup (\sim A \cap B) =$$

$$\{(x_1, 0.5), (x_2, 0.6), (x_3, 0), (x_4, 0.1)\}.$$

The key idea of "exclusive OR" is elimination of common area from the union of A and B. With this idea, we can define an operator Δ for the exclusive OR disjoint sum as follows.

$$\mu_{A\Delta B}(x) = |\mu_A(x) - \mu_B(x)|.$$

Example 2.30 If we reconsider the previous example, we get,

$$A = \{(x_1, 0.3), (x_2, 0.7), (x_3, 1), (x_4, 0)\}$$
$$B = \{(x_1, 0.5), (x_2, 0.4), (x_3, 1), (x_4, 0.1)\}$$
$$A \Delta B = \{(x_1, 0.2), (x_2, 0.3), (x_3, 0), (x_4, 0.1)\}$$

2.9 GEOMETRIC INTERPRETATION OF FUZZY SETS

Kosko introduced a very useful graphical representation of fuzzy sets. Figure 35 shows an example in which the universal set consists only of the two elements x_1 and x_2. Each point in the interior of the unit square represents a subset of X. The convention is that the coordinates of the representation correspond to the membership values of the elements in the fuzzy set. The point (1, 1), for example, represents the universal set X, with membership function $\mu_A(x_1) = 1$ and $\mu_A(x_2) = 1$. The point (1, 0) represents the set $\{x_1\}$ and the point (0, 1) the set $\{x_2\}$. The crisp subsets of X are located at the vertices of the unit square. The geometric visualization can be extended to an *n*-dimensional hypercube.

Kosko calls the inner region of a unit hypercube in an *n*-dimensional space the *fuzzy region*. We find here all combinations of membership values that a fuzzy set could assume. The point M in Figure 35 corresponds to the fuzzy set D = $\{0.5/x_1 + 0.3/x_2\}$. The center of the square represents the most diffuse of all possible fuzzy sets of X, that is the set O = $\{0.5/x_1 + 0.5/x_2\}$.

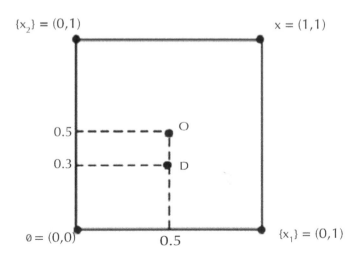

FIGURE 35 Geometric representation of fuzzy sets.

Example 2.31 Nonfuzzy or crisp subsets of X are given by mappigs $\mu : X \rightarrow [0,1]$, and are located at the 2^n corners of the n-dimensional unit hypercube I^n. We have represented the fuzzy hypercube I^2 in Figure 36, and I^3 in Figure 37. The n-dimensional hypercube I^n is graphically not representable for $n \geq 4$.

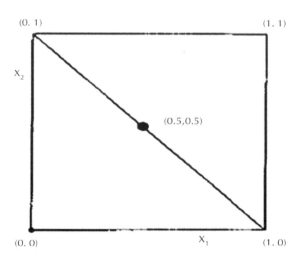

FIGURE 36 Two dimensional hypercube with I^2 with the 4 nonfuzzy subsets (0,0),(0,1),(1,1) and the fuzzy set(0.5,0.5).

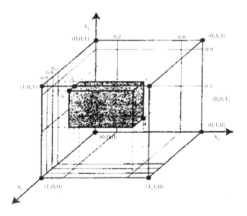

FIGURE 37 Three dimensional hypercube I^3 with its $2^3=8$ nonfuzzy sets. The points $\lambda=(0.9,0.2,0.9)$, $\mu=(0.7,0.8,0.5)$, and $\xi=(0.8,0.2,0.9)$ represents fuzzy sets.

According to the geometric representation the degree of fuzziness of a fuzzy set is measured by its *entropy*. In the geometric visualization, this corresponds inversely to the distance between the representation of the set and the center of the unit square.

The set O in Figure 38 has the maximum possible entropy. The vertices represent the crisp sets and have the lowest entropy that is zero. The fuzzy concept of entropy is mathematically different from the entropy concept in physics or information theory. Sometimes the term entropy is called as index of fuzziness which is also called crispness, certitude, ambiguity, and so on.

Thus, we adopt a preliminary definition of the entropy of a fuzzy set D as the quotient of the distance d_1 (according to some metric) of the corner which is nearest to the representation of D to the distance d_2 from the corner which is farthest away. Figure 38 shows the two relevant segments.

The entropy E(D) of D is therefore:

$$E(D) = \frac{d_1}{d_2}.$$

According to this definition the entropy is bounded by 0 and 1. The maximum entropy is reached at the center of the square.

The union or intersection of sets can be also visualized using this representation. The membership function for the union of two sets A and B can be defined as:

$$\mu_{A \cup B}(x) = \max(\mu_A(x), \mu_B(x)) \ \forall x \in X \tag{2.86}$$

and corresponds to the maximum of the corresponding coordinates in the geometric visualization. The membership function for the intersection of two sets A and B is given by

$$\mu_{A \cap B}(x) = \min(\mu_A(x), \mu_B(x)) \ \forall x \in X. \tag{2.87}$$

Together with the points representing the sets A and B, Figure 39 shows the points which represent their union and intersection.

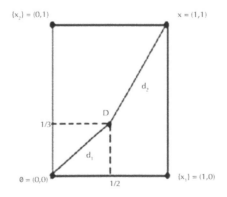

FIGURE 38 Distance of the set D to the universal and to the void set.

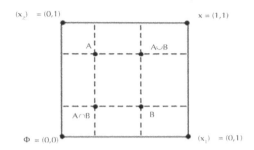

FIGURE 39   Intersection and union of two fuzzy sets.

The union or intersection of two fuzzy sets is in general a fuzzy, not a crisp set. The complement A^c of a fuzzy set A can be defined with the help of the membership function μ_{A^c} given by

$$\mu_{A^c}(x) = 1 - \mu_A(x) \; \forall x \in X. \tag{2.88}$$

Figure 39 shows that the representation of A must be transformed into another point at the same distance from the center of the unit square. The line joining the representation of A and A^c goes through the center of the square. Figure 40 also shows how to obtain the representations for $A \cup A^c$ and $A \cap A^c$ using the union and intersection operators as stated earlier. For fuzzy sets, it holds in general that

$$A \cup A^c \neq X \text{ and } A \cap A^c \neq \emptyset$$

which is not true in classical set theory. This means that the principle of excluded middle and absence of contradiction do not necessarily hold in fuzzy logic.

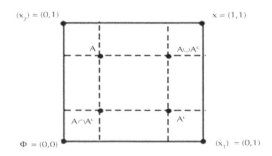

FIGURE 40   Compliment A^c of a fuzzy set.

Kosko [170] establishes a direct relationship between the entropy of fuzzy sets and the geometric representation of the union and intersection operations. To compute the entropy of a set, we need to determine the distance between the origin and the coordinates of the set. This distance is called the *cardinality* of the fuzzy set.

Definition 2.28 *Let A be a subset of universal set X. The cardinality |A| of A is the sum of the membership values of all elements of X with respect to A, that is:*

$$|A| = \Sigma_{x \in X} \mu_A(x)$$

This definition of cardinality corresponds to the distance of the representation of A from the origin using a *Manhattan metric*.

The Figure 41 shows how to define the entropy of a set A using the cardinality of the sets $A \cup A^c$ and $A \cap A^c$. The entropy concept introduced previously in an informal manner can then be formalized with our next definition.

Definition 2.29 *The real value*

$$E(A) = \frac{|A \cap A^c|}{|A \cup A^c|}$$

is called the entropy of the fuzzy set A.

The entropy of a crisp set is always zero, since for a crisp set $A \cap A^c = \emptyset$. In fuzzy set theory E(A) is a value in the interval [0.1], since $A \cap A^c$ can be non-void.

Some authors take the geometric definition of entropy as given and derive Definition 2.29 as a theorem, which is called the *fuzzy entropy theorem* [170]. Here we take the definition as given, since the geometric interpretation of fuzzy union and intersection depends on the exact definition of the fuzzy operators.

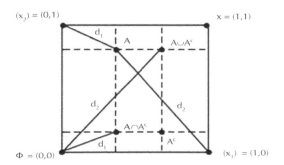

FIGURE 41   Geometric representation of the entropy of a fuzzy set.

2.10   T-OPERATORS

The triangular norm (T-norm) and the triangular conorm (T-conorm) are frequently used in fuzzy set theory in defining intersection and union of fuzzy sets. Zadeh's conventional T-operators 'min' and 'max' have been extensively used in many design of fuzzy systems. Let us define T-operators in the following.

Definition 2.30 Let T: $[0,1] \times [0,1] \rightarrow [0,1]$. T is a T-norm, if and only if, for all x,y,z$\in$ [0,1]:

1.   T(x,y) = T(y,x),

2.   T(x,y) $\leq$ T(x,z), if y $\leq$ z,

3.   T(x, T(y,z)) = T(T(x,y),z).

4.   T(x,1) = x.

The basic T-norm are shown in Table 3.

TABLE 3   Basic T-norms

Minimum (Gödel)	min (a,b) = min {a,b}
Lukasiewicz	T_L (a, b) = max {a + b − 1, 0}
Product	T_P (a, b) = ab
Weak	T_W (a,b) = $\begin{cases} min\{a, b\} \; if \; max\{a, b\} = 1 \\ 0 \qquad\qquad\quad otherwise \end{cases}$
Hamacher	H_γ (a, b) = $\frac{ab}{\gamma+(1-\gamma)(a+b-ab)}$, $\gamma \geq 0$
Dubois and Prade	D_α (a, b) = $\frac{ab}{max\{a,b,\alpha\}}$, $\alpha \in (0,1)$
Yager	Y_P (a,b)=1−min{1, $\sqrt[p]{[(1-a)^p + (1-b)^p]}$}, p > 0
Frank	F_λ (a, b) = $\begin{cases} min\{a, b\} & if \; \lambda = 0 \\ T_p(a,b) & if \; \lambda = 1 \\ T_L(a, b) & if \; \lambda = \infty \\ 1 - log_\lambda\left[\left[1 + \frac{(\lambda^a - 1)(\lambda^b - 1)}{\lambda-1}\right]\right] & otherwise \end{cases}$

A T-norm is Archimedean, if and only if,
1. $T(x,y)$ is continuous,
2. $T(x,x) < x$, for all $x \in (0,1)$.
   Archimedean T-norm is strict, if and only if,
3. $T(x', y') < T(x,y)$, if $x' < x, y' < y$, for all $x', y', x,y \in (0,1)$.

Definition 2.31 Let $T^*: [0,1] \times [0,1] \to [0,1]$. T^* is a T-conorm, if and only if, for all $x,y,z \in (0,1)$;
1. $T^* (x,y) = T^*(y,x)$,
2. $T^* (x,y) \leq T^* (x,z)$, if $y \leq z$,
3. $T^* (x, T^*(y,z)) = T^* (T^* (x,y),z)$,
4. $T^* (x,0) = x$.

Some basic T-conorms are given in Table 4.

TABLE 4   Basic T-conorms

Maximum (Gödel)	$T^*\max (a, b) = \max \{ a, b\}$
Lukasiewicz	$T^*(a, b) = \min \{ a + b, 1 \}$
Probabilistic	$T^*(a, b) = a + b - ab$
Strong	$T^*STRONG (a, b) = \begin{cases} \max\{a,b\} & if \ \min\{a,b\} = 0 \\ 1 & otherwise \end{cases}$
Hamacher	$T^*HOR_\gamma (a, b) = \dfrac{a+b-(2-\gamma)ab}{1-(1-\gamma)ab}, \gamma \geq 0$
Yager	$T^*YOR_p (a, b) = \min \{ 1, \sqrt[p]{a^p + b^p} \}, p > 0.$

A T-conorm is Archimedean, if and only if,
1. $T^* (x,y)$ is continuous,
2. $T^* (x,x) > x$, for all $x \in (0,1)$.
   An Archimedean T-conorm is strict, if and only if,
3. $T^* (x',y') < T^* (x,y)$, if $x' < x, y' < y$, for all $x', y', x,y \in (0,1)$.

Example 2.32 Let
$T(x, y) = \max \{x + y - 1, 0\}$
be the Łukasiewicz t-norm. Then we have

$$(A \cap B) (x) = \max \{A(x) + B(x) - 1, 0 \},$$

for all $x \in X$.

Let A and B be fuzzy subsets of

$$X = \{x_1, x_2, x_3, x_4, x_5, x_6, x_7\}$$

and be defined by

$$A = \{0.0/x_1 + 0.3/x_2 + 0.6/x_3 + 1.0/x_4 + 0.6/x_5 + 0.3/x_6 + 0.0/x_7\}$$

$$B = \{0.1/x_1 + 0.3/x_2 + 0.9/x_3 + 1.0/x_4 + 1.0/x_5 + 0.3/x_6 + 0.2/x_7\}.$$

Then A $\cap$ B has the following form,

$$A \cap B = \{0.0/x_1 + 0.0/x_2 + 0.5/x_3 + 1.0/x_4 + 0.6/x_5 + 0.0/x_6 + 0.2/x_7\}.$$

Example 2.33 Let

$T^*(x, y) = \min \{x + y, 1\}$

be the Łukasiewicz t-conorm. Then we have

$$(A \cup B)(x) = \min \{A(x) + B(x), 1\},$$

for all $x \in X$.

Let A and B be fuzzy subsets of

$$X = \{x_1, x_2, x_3, x_4, x_5, x_6, x_7\}$$

and be defined by

$$A = \{0.0/x_1 + 0.3/x_2 + 0.6/x_3 + 1.0/x_4 + 0.6/x_5 + 0.3/x_6 + 0.0/x_7\}$$

$$B = \{0.1/x_1 + 0.3/x_2 + 0.9/x_3 + 1.0/x_4 + 1.0/x_5 + 0.3/x_6 + 0.2/x_7\}.$$

Then A $\cup$ B has the following form

$$A \cup B = \{0.1/x_1 + 0.6/x_2 + 1.0/x_3 + 1.0/x_4 + 1.0/x_5 + 0.6/x_6 + 0.2/x_7\}.$$

We list some important properties of T and T* in the following:

1. $T(x,y) = T(y,x)$, $T^*(x,y) = T^*(y,x)$ (commutativity),
2. $T(x,T(y,z)) = T(T(x,y),z)$, $T^*(x, T^*(y,z)) = T^*(T^*(x,y),z)$ (associativity),
3. $T(x, T^*(y,z)) = T^*(T(x,y), T(x,z))$, $T^*(x,T(y,z)) = T(T^*(x,y), T^*(x,z))$ (distributivity),
4. $T(T^*(x,y),x) = x$, $T^*(T(x,y),x) = x$ (absorption),
5. $T(x,x) = x$, $T^*(x,x) = x$ (idempotency).

2.11   AGGREGATION OPERATORS [293]

Aggregation and fusion of information are basic concerns for all kinds of knowledge based systems. The basic purpose of aggregation is to use simultaneously different pieces of information (provided by several expert/sources) in order to come to a meaningful conclusion or a decision. Several research groups are directly interested in finding solution to this problem. Among them the multi-criteria community, the sensor fusion community, the decision-making community, the data mining community, and so on, are very much interested to apply such techniques. Each of this group uses or proposes some methodologies in order to perform an intelligent aggregation, as for instance the use of rules, the use of neuronal networks, the use of fusion specific techniques, the use of probability theory, evidence theory, possibility theory and fuzzy set theory, and so on. But all this approaches are based on some numerical aggregation operator [293].

2.11.1   MONOTONIC IDENTITY COMMUTATIVE AGGREGATION (MICA) OPERATORS

Let us look at the process for combining the individual ratings $(A_1(x), ..., A_n(x))$ of an alternative x. We consider a basic assumption that the operation is *pointwise* and *likewise*. By pointwise we mean that for every alternative x, A(x) just depends upon $A_j(x)$, j=1,...,n. By likewise we mean that the process used to combine the A_j is the same for all the x.

Let us denote the pointwise process to combine the individual ratings as

$$A(x) = \text{Agg}[A_1(x), ..., A_n(x)].$$

In the above Agg is called the aggregation operator and the $A_j(x)$ are the arguments.

More generally, we can consider this as an operator

$$a = \text{Agg}(a_1, ..., a_n)$$

where the a_i and a are values from the membership grade space, normally the unit interval.

Let us look at the minimal requirements associated with Agg. We first note that the combination of the individual ratings should be independent of the choice of indexing of the criteria. This implies that a required property that we must associate with the Agg operator is that of commutativity. The indexing of the arguments does not matter. We note that the commutativity property represents the arguments of the Agg operator, as an unordered collection of possible duplicate values; such an object is a bag. For an individual rating, A_j, the membership grade $A_j(x)$ indicates the degree or strength to which this rate suggests that x is the appropriate (best compromise) solution. In particular if for a pair of elements x_1 and x_2 it is the case that

$$A_j (x_1) \geq A_j (x_2), \qquad\qquad (2.89)$$

then we say that the j-th rating is preferring x_1 as the output over x_2.

From this we can reasonably conclude that if all criteria prefer x_1 over x_2 as output then the overall ratings should prefer x, over x₂.

This observation imposes a monotonicity condition on the **Agg** operation.

In particular if $A_j (x_1) \geq A_j (x_2)$, for all j, then

$$A (x_1) \geq A (x_2). (2.90)$$

Hence, another condition is added to the aggregation operator. Assume that there exists some criterion whose value does not matter. The implication of this is that the criterion provides no information regarding what should be the overall rating.It should not affect the final A. The first observation we can make is that whatever rating this criterion provides should not make any distinction between the potential overall ratings.

Hence, we see that the aggregation operator needs an *identy element*.

In summary, Agg satisfies three conditions:
- Commutativity,
- Monotonicity,
- A fixed identity.

These conditions are based on the three requirements: that the indexing of the criteria be unimportant, a positive association between individual criterion rating and total rating, and irrelevant criteria play no role in the decision process. These operators are called Monotonic Identity Commutative Aggregation (MICA) operators.MICA-operators are the most general class for aggregation in fuzzy modeling. They include t-norms, t-conorms, compensatory, and averaging operators.

Assume X is a set of elements. A bag drawn from X is any collection of elements, which is contained in X. A bag is different from a subset in that it allows multiple copies of the same element. A bag is similar to a set in that the ordering of the elements in the bag does not matter. If A is a bag consisting of a,b,c,d we denote this as

$$A = <a,b,c,d>.$$

Assume A and B are two bags. We denote the sum of the bags

$$C = A \oplus B$$

where C is the bag consisting of the members of both A and B.

Example 2.34 Let A = <a,b,c,d> and

$$B = <b,\ c,\ c>$$

then

$$A \oplus B <a,b,c,d,b,c,c>.$$

Let Bag (X) be the set of all bags of the set X.

Definition 2.32 A function F: Bag (X) $\rightarrow$ X is called a bag mapping from Bag (X) into the set X. Bag mappingis commutative in the sense that the ordering of the elements does not matter.

Definition 2.33 Let A = $<a_1, ..., a_n>$ andB = $<b, ..., b_n>$ be two bags of the same cardinality n. If the elements in A and B can be indexed in such way that $a_i \geq b_i$ for all i then we denote this by A $\geq$ B.

Definition 2.34 A bag mapping

M: Bag ([0,1]) $\rightarrow$ [0,1] is called MICA operator if it satisfies the following two properties

(i) If A $\geq$ B then M(A) $\geq$ M(B)
(ii) For every bag A there exists an element, u $\in$ [0,1], called the identity of A such that if

$$C = A \oplus <u>$$

then M(C) = M(A).

Thus the MICA operator is endowed with two properties in addition to the inherent commutativity of the bag operator, *monotonicity and identity.*

- The requirement of monotonicity appears natural for an aggregation operator in that it provides some connection between the arguments and the aggregated value.
- The property of identity allows us to have the facility for aggregating data, which does not affect the overall result. This becomes useful for enabling us to include importance among other characteristics.

There exists a class of operators called t-norms that provide way of quantitatively implementing the type of "anding" aggregation implied by the "all" requirement. A closely related class of operators, called t-conorms, provide a way of implementing of type "oring" operator. In this section we briefly discuss these operators and point out some properties relevant to our discussion.

Definition 2.35 An n-ary aggregation operator (n $\geq$ 2) is a mapping Agg: [0, 1]^n $\rightarrow$ [0, 1].

If there are n fuzzy sets A_1, ..., A_n on X to be aggregated, then we have A = Agg(A_1, ..., A_n) and for all x $\in$X,

$$Agg(A_1, ..., A_n) (x) = Agg(A_1(x), ..., A_n(x)). \qquad (2.91)$$

We consider intersection-like and union-like operators called t-norms and t-conorms, respectively.

2.11.2   T-NORMS AND T-CONORMS

Definition 2.36 An aggregation operatorT: $[0, 1]^2 \rightarrow [0, 1]$ is called a t-norm if the following are satisfied for all a, b, c $\in$ [0, 1]:
1. $T(a, 1) = a$ (boundary condition),
2. $b \leq c$ implies $T(a, b) \leq T(a, c)$ (monotonicity),
3. $T(a, b) = T(b, a)$ (commutativity),
4. $T(a, T(b, c)) = T(T(a, b), c)$ (associativity).

Example 2.35 Let a, b $\in$ [0, 1]. The following are t-norms:
1. min-operator $T(a, b) = \min\{a, b\}$,
2. algebraic product $T(a, b) = ab$,
3. bounded difference $T(a, b) = \max\{0, a+b-1\}$.

There are lots of other t-norms. If $A, B \in F(U)$ then for any t-norm T we haveT($A, B) \leq A \wedge B$.

Definition 2.37 An aggregation operator $T^*: [0, 1]^2 \rightarrow [0,1]$ is called a t-conorm if the following conditions are satisfied for all a,b,c $\in$ [0,1]:
1. $T^*(a,0)$ a (boundary condition),
2. $b \leq c$ implies $T^*(a,b) \leq T^*(a,c)$ (monotonicity),
3. $T^*(a,b) = T^*(b,a)$ (commutativity),
4. $T^*(a,T^*(b,c)) = T^*(T^*(a,b),c)$ (associativity).

Example 2.36 Let a, b $\in$ [0,1]. The following are t-conorms:
1. max-operator $T^*(a,b) = \max\{a,b\}$,
2. algebraic sum $T^*(a,b) = a+b - ab$,
3. bounded sum $T^*(a,b) = \min\{1, a+b\}$.

There are lots of other t-conorms. If $A, B \in F(U)$ then for any t-conormT* we have $A \vee B \leq T^*(A, B)$.

2.11.3   COMPENSATORY OPERATORS

Several authors noticed that t-norms and t-conorms lack of compensation behavior and that this particular property seems crucial in the aggregation process. They discover that in a decision making context humans do not follow exactly the behavior of a t-norm (nor of a t-conorm) when aggregating.

In order to get closer to the human aggregation process, they proposed an operator on the unit interval based on t-norms and t-conorms:

$$Z_\gamma(x_1, ..., x_n) = \left(\prod_{i=1}^{n} x_i\right)^{1-\gamma} . \left(1 - \prod_{i=1}^{n}(1 - x_i)\right)^\gamma. \qquad (2.92)$$

Here the parameter γ indicates the degree of compensation. This operator is a particular case of the exponential compensatory operators:

$$E_\gamma^{T,S}(x_1, ..., x_n) = (T(x_1, ..., x_n))^{1-\gamma} . (T(x_1, ..., x_n))^\gamma. \qquad (2.93)$$

where T is a t-norm and S is t-conorm.

It is important to notice that the exponential compensatory operators are not associative for γ different from 0 or 1.

Another class of non-associative t-norm and t-conorm-based compensatory operator is the convex-linear compensatory operator:

$$L_\gamma^{T,S}(x_1, ..., x_n) = (1-\gamma).T(x_1, ..., x_n) + \gamma.T^*(x_1, ..., x_n). \qquad (2.94)$$

Setting the value of the parameter γ is a delicate issue. Zimmerman and Zysno calculated the best γ to match the human behavior. Yager and Rybalov proposed a method based on fuzzy modeling techniques to compute the parameter γ:

$$\gamma = \frac{T(x_1, ..., x_n)}{T(x_1, ..., x_n) + T(1-x_1, ..., 1-x_n)} \qquad (2.95)$$

where $T(x_1, ..., x_n)$ is called the highness and $T(1- x_1, ..., 1 - x_n)$ the lowness.

Another approach to the construction of compensatory operators based on t-norms and t-conorms. They based their construction on the additive generators of continuous Archimedean t-norms and t-conorms. Their associative compensatory operator is defined by:

$$C(x, y) = f^{-1}(f(x) + f(y)) \qquad (2.96)$$

Where the function f is defined by:

$$F(x) = \begin{cases} -g\left(\frac{x}{e}\right) if x \leq e \\ h\left(\frac{x-e}{1-e}\right) if x \geq e \end{cases} \qquad (2.97)$$

where g is an additive generator of a t-norm, h is an additive generator of a t-conorm and e is a neutral element.

Fuzzy set theory provides a host of attractive aggregation connectives for integrating membership values representing uncertain information. These connectives can be categorized into three classes union, intersection and compensation connectives.

Union produces a high output whenever any one of the input values representing degrees of satisfaction of different features or criteria is high.Intersection connectives produce a high output only when all of the inputs have high values. Compensative connectives have the property that a higher degree of satisfaction of one of the criteria can compensate for a lower degree of satisfaction of another criterion to a certain extent.

In the sense, union connectives provide full compensation and intersection connectives provide no compensation. In a decision process the idea of trade-offs corresponds to viewing the global evaluation of an action as lying between the worst and the best local ratings. This occurs in the presence of conflicting goals, when a compensation between the corresponding compabilities is allowed. Averaging operators realize trade-offs between objectives, by allowing a positive compensation between ratings.

2.11.4 AVERAGING OPERATORS

Sometimes it is useful to find an "average" fuzzy set from a collection of fuzzy sets.

Let us consider column vectors a,b$\in[0,1]^n$ such that a = $[a_1 \ldots a_n]^T$ and b = $[b_1 \ldots b_n]^T$ and also denote $\bar{a}$ = $[a,a \ldots a]^T$ for all a $\in[0,1]$. Note that $\bar{a} \in[0,1]^n$. Now we stipulate the following definition.

Definition 2.38 An aggregation operator m: $[0,1]^n \rightarrow [0,1]$ is a mean operator if

1. $m(\bar{a})$ = a for all a $\in[0,1]$ (idempotency),

2. $m(a) = m(a_\pi)$, where π is any permutation on {1, ..., n} and $a_\pi = [a_{\pi(1)} \ldots a_{\pi(n)}]^T$ (symmetry on all its aguments),

3. $m(0) = 0, m(1) = 1$ (boundary conditions),

4. for any pair a,b $[0,1]^n$, if $a_i \leq b_i$ for all i $\in$ {1, ..., n} then $m(a) \leq m(b)$ (monotonic in all its arguments),

5. m is continuous.

Example 2.37 Let us definite generalized p-mean m: $[0,1]^n \rightarrow [0,1]$ such that for all a $\in [0,1]^n$,

$$m_p(a) = \left(\frac{\sum_{i=n}^n (a_i)^p}{n} \right)^{\frac{1}{p}}.$$

If p = 1 then m_1 gives the arithmetic mean. If p = -1, then m_{-1} gives the harmonic mean. For p $\rightarrow 0$ the mapping $m_p \rightarrow G$, where G is the geometric mean. For p $\rightarrow -\infty$ the mapping $m_p \rightarrow$ min, and for p $\rightarrow \infty$ the mapping $m_p \rightarrow$ max. For the geometric and haromoic means we demand that $a_i \neq 0$, for all i $\in$ {1, ..., n}.

Averaging operators represent a wide class of aggregation operators. We prove that whatever is the particular definition of an averaging operator, m, the global evaluation of an action will lie between the worst and the best local ratings:

Lemma 2.3 If m is an averaging operator then

$$\min \{x, y\} \leq m (x, y) \leq \max \{x, y\}, \forall x, y \in [0, 1]$$

Proof. From idempotency and monotonicity of m it follows that
$$\min \{x, y\} = m (\min \{x, y\}, \min \{x, y\}) \leq m (x, y)$$
and $m (x, y) \leq m (\max \{x, y\}, \max \{x, y\}) = \max \{x, y\}$.

Averaging operators have the following interesting properties:

Property 2.1 A strictly increasing averaging operator cannot be associative.

Property 2.2 The only associative averaging operators are defined by

$$m (x, y, \alpha) = \begin{cases} y \ if x \leq y \leq \alpha \\ \alpha \ if x \leq \alpha \leq y \\ x \ if \alpha \leq x \leq y \end{cases}$$

where $, \alpha \in [0, 1]$.

An important family of averaging operators is formed by quasi-arithmetic means

$$m (a_1, ..., a_n) = f^{-1} \left(\frac{1}{n} \sum_{i=1}^{n} f (a_i) \right).$$

This family has been characterized by Kolmogorov as being the class of all decomposable continuous averaging operators. For example, the quasi-arithmetic mean of a_1 and a_2 is defined by

$$m (a_1, a_2) = f^{-1} \left(\frac{f(a_1) + f(a_2)}{2} \right).$$

The Table 5 shows the most often used mean operators.

TABLE 5   Mean operators

Name	m (x, y)
harmonic mean	$2xy/ (x + y)$
geometric mean	$\sqrt{xy}$
arithmetic mean	$(x + y)/ 2$
dual of geometric mean	$1 - \sqrt{(1 - x)(1 - y)}$
dual of harmonic mean	$(x + y - 2xy) / (2 - x - y)$
median	$med (x, y, \alpha) = \begin{cases} y \ if x \leq y \leq \alpha \\ \alpha \ if x \leq \alpha \leq y \ \alpha \in (0, 1) \\ x \ if \alpha \leq x \leq y \end{cases},$
generalized p- mean	$((x^p + y^p)/2)^{1/p} \quad p \geq 1$

The process of information aggregation appears in many applications related to the development of intelligent systems. We have seen aggregation in neural networks, fuzzy logic controllers, vision systems, expert systems and multi-criteria decision aids. In 1988 Yager introduced a new aggregation technique based on the ordered weighted averaging (OWA) operators [97, 294].

2.11.5 OWA-OPERATORS

Definition 2.39 An OWA operator of dimension n is a mapping F: $R^n \rightarrow R$, that has an associated weighting vector W = $(w_1, w_2, \ldots, w_n)^T$ such as $w_i \in [0, 1]$, $1 \leq i \leq n$, and

$$w_1 + \ldots + w_n = 1.$$

Furthermore

$$F(a_1, \ldots, a_n) = w_1 b_1 + \ldots + w_n b_n = \sum_{j=1}^{n} w_j b_j$$

where b_j is the j-th largest element of the bag $\langle a_1, \ldots, a_n \rangle$.

Example 2.38 Assume W = $(0.4, 0.3, 0.2, 0.1)^T$ then
F (0.7,1, 0.2, 0.6) = $0.4 \times 1 + 0.3 \times 0.7 + 0.2 \times 0.6 + 0.1 \times 0.2 = 0.75$.

A fundamental aspect of this operator is the re-ordering step, in particular an aggregate a_i is not associated with a particular weight w_i but rather a weight is associated with a particular ordered position of aggregate. When we view the OWA weights as a column vector we shall find it convenient to refer to the weights with the low indices as weights at the top and those with the higher indices with weights at the bottom. It is noted that different OWA operators are distinguished by their weighting function. In 1988 Yager pointed out three important special cases of OWA aggregations:

1. F* In this case W = W* = $(1, 0 \ldots, 0)^T$ and

$$F^* (a_1, \ldots, a_n) = \max \{a_1, \ldots, a_n\},$$

2. F_* : In this case W = W_* = $(0, 0 \ldots, 1)^T$ and

$$F_* (a_1, \ldots, a_n) = \min \{a_1, \ldots, a_n\},$$

3. F_A In this case W = W_A = $(1/n, \ldots, 1/n)^T$ and

$$F_A(a_1, ..., a_n) = \frac{a_1 + ... + a_n}{n}.$$

The ordered weighted averaging operators as stated in Definition 2.39 can be further explained by the following examples.

Example 2.39 Let a = [5 6 4]^T and π is a permutation on {1, ..., n} such that elements of a are changed in decreasing order. Therefore, a_π = [6 5 4]^T, and w = [0.2 0.7 0.1]^T. Then, F(a) = 0.2 × 6 + 0.7 × 5 + 0.1 × 4 = 5.1.

Example 2.40 Let X = {1, 2, 3, 4} with fuzzy sets

$$A_1 \triangleq [0.0 \ 0.5 \ 0.1 \ 1.0]^T \text{ and } A_2 \triangleq [0.1 \ 0.4 \ 1.0 \ 0.0]^T$$

Hence,

$$A_{\pi,1} \triangleq [1.0 \ 0.5 \ 0.1 \ 0.0]T \text{ and } A_{\pi,2} \triangleq [1.0 \ 0.4 \ 0.1 \ 0.0].$$

Moreover, let the associating vector for the OWA operator F be w =[0.1 0.9]^T. Then, for F(A_1, A_2) we have

F(A_1, A_2) (1) = 0.1. 1.0 + 1.0. 0.9 = 1.0

F(A_1, A_2) (2) = 0.1. 0.5 + 0.9. 0.4 = 0.41

F(A_1, A_2) (3) = 0.1. 0.1 + 0.9. 0.1 = 0.1

F(A_1, A_2) (4) = 0.1. 0.0 + 0.9. 0.0 = 0.0.

Note that F(A_1, A_2) (x) = F(A_1 (x), A_2 (x)) for all x∈X.

The OWA operator F_A is called window-type operator. A window type OWA operator (see Figure 42) takes the average of the m arguments around the center. For this class of operators we have,

$$w_i = \begin{cases} 0 & if \ i < \kappa \\ \frac{1}{m} & if \ k \leq i < \kappa + m \\ 0 & if \ i \geq \kappa + m. \end{cases}$$

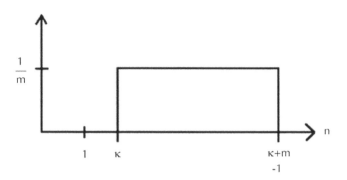

FIGURE 42   Window type OWA operator.

A number of important properties can be associated with OWA operators. We shall now discuss some of these. For any OWA operator F holds

$$F_*(a_1, ..., a_n) \leq F(a_1, ..., a_n) \leq F^*(a_1, ..., a_n).$$

Thus the upper an lower star OWA operator are its boundaries. From the above it becomes clear that for any F

$$\text{Min } \{(a_1, ..., a_n) \leq F(a_1, ..., a_n) \leq \text{max } \{a_1, ..., a_n\}.$$

The OWA operator can be seen to be *commutative*. Let $(a_1, ..., a_n)$ be a bag of aggregates and let $\{d_1, ..., d_n\}$ be any *permutation* of the a_i. Then for any OWA operator

$$F(a_1, ..., a_n) = F(d_1, ..., d_n).$$

A third charactreristic associated with these operators is *monotonicity*. Assume a_i and c_i are a collection of aggregates, $i=1, ..., n$ such that for each i, $a_i \geq c_i$. Then

$$F(a_1, ..., a_n) \geq F(c_1, c_2 ..., c_n)$$

where F is some fixed weight OWA operator.

Another characteristic associated with these operators is *idempotency*. If $a_i = a$ for all *i* then for any OWA operator

$$F(a_1, ..., a_n) = \text{a}.$$

Consider the two characterizing measures associated with the weighting vector w of an OWA operator.

1.   The measure of orness of the aggregation, is defined as:

$$\text{orness } (w) = \frac{1}{n-1} \sum_{i=1}^{n} (n - i) w_i \qquad (2.98)$$

$$= \frac{1}{n-1} \times [(n - 1)w_1 + \cdots + w_{n-1}]$$

$$= w_1 + \frac{n-2}{n-1} \times w_2 + \cdots + \frac{1}{n-1} \times w_{n-1} .$$

It characterizes the degree to which the aggregation is like an or operation. orness (w) $\in$ [0,1] holds for any weighting vector.

It is possible to have an andness-measure by defining

$$\text{andness } (w) = 1 - \text{orness } (w). \qquad (2.99)$$

Generally, an OWA operator with much of nonzero weights w near the top is an *orlike* operator, that is, orness (w) $\geq$ 0.5 and when much of the weights are nonzero near the bottom, the OWA operator is an and like operator, that is andness (w) $\geq$ 0.5.

Lemma 2.4 Consider the vectors $w^* = [1 \ 0 \ \ldots \ 0]^T$, $w_o = [0 \ 0 \ \ldots \ 0 \ 1]^T$, and $w_A = [1/n \ 1/n \ \ldots \ 1/n]^T$. Then it can easily be shown that

1.   orness $(w^*) = 1$,
2.   orness $(w_o) = 0$,
3.   orness $(w_A) = 0.5$.

Proof:

$$\text{orness}(W^*) = \frac{1}{n-1} \left((n - 1)w_1 + \cdots + w_{n-1} \right)$$

$$= \frac{1}{n-1} \left((n - 1) + \cdots + 0 \right) = 1.$$

$$\text{orness}(W_*) = \frac{1}{n-1} \left((n - 1)w_1 + \cdots + w_{n-1} \right)$$

$$= \frac{1}{n-1} \left(0 + \cdots + 0 \right) = 0.$$

$$\text{orness}(W_{mean}) = \frac{1}{n-1} \left[\frac{n-1}{n} + \cdots + \frac{1}{n} \right] = \frac{n(n-1)}{2n(n-1)} = 0.5.$$

Example 2.41 Let $W = (0.8, 0.2, 0.0)^T$. *Then*

$$orness(W) = \frac{1}{2} (2 \times 0.8 + 0.2) = 0.8 + \frac{1}{2} \times 0.2 = 0.9$$

and

$$andness(W) = 1 - orness \ (W) = 1 - 0.9 = 0.1.$$

This means that that OWA operator, defined by

$$F(a_1, a_2, a_3) = 0.8b_1 + 0.2b_2 + 0.0b_3 = 0.8b_1 + 0.2b_2$$

where b_j is the j-th largest element of the bag

$$<a_1, a_2, a_3>,$$

is an orlike aggregation.

Example. 2.42

Suppose we have n applicants for a Ph.D. program. Each application is evaluated by experts, who provides ratings on each of the criteria from the set

1. 3 (high)
2. 2 (medium)
3. 1(low) .

Compensative connectives have the property that a higher degree of satisfaction of one of the criteria can compensate for a lower degree of satisfaction of another criterion.

Oring criterion means full compensation and *Anding* criterion means no compensation.

We illustrate the effect of compensation rate on the overall rating:

Let us have the following ratings (3, 2, 1). If $w = (w_1, w_2, w_3)$ is an OWA weight then

$orness(w_1, w_2, w_3) = w_1 + \frac{1}{2}w_2.$

Min operator: the overall rating is

min {3, 2, 1} = 1.

in this case there is no compensation, because

orness (0, 0, 1) = 0.

Max operator: the overall rating is

max {3, 2, 1} = 3.

In this case there is full compensation, because

orness (1, 0 0) = 1.

Mean operator: the overall rating is $\frac{1}{3}$ (3+2+1) = 2 and in this case the measure of compensation is 0.5, because

orness (1/3, 1/3, 1/3) = 1/3 + 1/2 × 1/3 = 1/2.

An andlike operator: the overall rating is

0.2 × 3 + 0.1 × 2 + 0.7 × 1 = 1.5.

In this case the measure of compensation is 0.25, because

orness (0.2, 0.1, 0.7) = 0.2 + 1/2 × 0.1 = 0.25.

An orlike operator: the overall rating is

0.6 × 3 + 0.3 × 2 + 0.1 × 1 = 2.5 .

In this case the measure of compensation is 0.75, because

orness (0.6, 0.3, 0.1) = 0.6 + 1/2 × 0.3 = 0.75.

The following theorem shows that as we move weight up the vector we increase the orness, while moving weight down causes to decrease orness (w).

Theorem 2.1 Assume w and w' are two n-dimendional OWA operators, such that

$$w = (w_1, w_2, \dots, w_n)^T,$$

and

$$w' (w_1, \dots, w_j + \varepsilon, \dots, w_k - \varepsilon, \dots, w_n)^T$$

where $\varepsilon > 0, j < k$. Then orness (w') > orness (w).
Proof. From the definition of the measure of orness we get

$$\text{orness (w')} = \frac{1}{n-1} \sum_{i=1}^{n} (n - i) w'_i$$

$$= \frac{1}{n-1} \sum_{i=1}^{n} (n - i) w_i + (n\text{-}j) \varepsilon - (n\text{-}k) \varepsilon.$$

Hence,
orness (w') = orness (w) + $\frac{1}{n-1} \varepsilon$ (k-j).
Since k > j we get
orness (w') > orness (w).

1.   The measure of dispersion (or entropy) of the aggregation, is defined as

$$\text{disp (w)} = - \sum_{i=1}^{n} w_i \ln w_i \tag{2.100}$$

and it measures the degree to which w takes into account all information in the aggregation.

We can see when using the OWA operator as an averaging operator disp(w) measures the degree to which we use all the aggregates equally.

If F is an OWA aggregation with weights w_i the dual of F, denoted $\hat{F}$, is an OWA aggregation of the same dimension where the weights $\hat{w}_i$ are $\hat{w}_i = w_{n-i+1}$.

We can easily see that if F and $\hat{F}$ are duals then
disp($\hat{F}$) = disp(F) and orness ($\hat{F}$) = 1 – orness (F) = andness (F).
Hence, if F is orlike its dual is andlike.
Example 2.43 Let w = (0.3 0.2 0.1 0.4)^T then
$\hat{w} = (0.4\ 0.1\ 0.2\ 0.3)^T$
and

orness (F) = $\frac{1}{3}$ (3 × 0.3 + 2 × 0.2 + 0.1) $\approx$ 0.466
orness ($\hat{F}$) = $\frac{1}{3}$ (3 × 0.4 + 2 × 0.1 + 0.2) $\approx$ 0.533.

2.11.6 QUANTIFIER GUIDED AGGREGATION

An important application of the OWA operators is in the area of quantifier guided aggregation. Assume

$$\{A_1, ..., A_n\}$$

is a collection of criteria. Let x be an object such that for any criterion A_i, A_i (x) $\in$ [0,1] indicates the degree to which this criterion is satisfied by x. If we want to find out the degree to which x satisfies "all the criteria" denoting this by D(x), we get the following degree (this is due to Bellman and Zadeh)

$$D(x) = \min \{A_1 (x), ..., A_n (x)\},$$

where x to satisfies A_1 and A_2 and ... A_n.

If we want to find out the degree to which x satisfies "at least one of the criteria", denoted by E(x), we get

$$E(x) = \max \{A_1(x), ..., A_n (x)\},$$

where x satisfies either A_1 or A_2 or ... A_n.

Instead of considering a solution which satisfies one of these extreme condition, "all" or "at least one", we may consider that x satisfies most or at least half of the criteria. Based on the concept of Zadeh's linguistic quantifiers we can achieve quantifier guided aggregations [96].

Definition 2.40 A quantifier Q is called regular monotonically non-decreasing if,

$$Q(0)=0, Q(1)=1, \text{ and } r_1 > r_2 \implies Q(r_1) \geq Q(r_2),$$

and regular monotonically non-increasing if,

$$Q(0)=1, Q(1)=0, \text{ and } r_1 < r_2 \implies Q(r_1) \geq Q(r_2),$$

The Figure 43 shows the basic pattern of monotone linguistic quantifier.

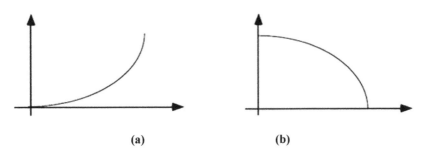

(a)   **(b)**

FIGURE 43   (a, b). Monotone linguistic quantifiers.

Definition 2.41 A quantifier Q is called regular unimodal if,

$$Q(r) = \begin{cases} 0 & if\ r = 0 \\ monotitonically\ increasing & if\ 0 \leq r \leq a \\ 1 & if\ a \leq r \leq b, 0 < a < b < 1 \\ monotonically\ decreasing & if\ ;b \leq r \leq r \leq 1 \\ 0 & if\ r = 1. \end{cases}$$

The Figure 44 shows the basic pattern of unimodal linguistic quantifier.

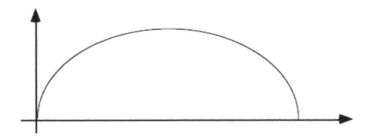

FIGURE 44   Unimodal linguistic quantifier.

With $a_i = A_i(x)$, the overall valuation of x is $F_Q(a_1, ..., a_n)$ where F_Q is an OWA operator. The weights associated with this quantified guided aggregation are obtained as follows (see Figure 45):

$$w_i = Q(\tfrac{i}{n}) - Q(\tfrac{i-1}{n}),\ i = 1, ..., n. (2.101)$$

The Figure 45 shows the operation involved in determining the OWA weights directly from the quantifier guiding the aggregation.

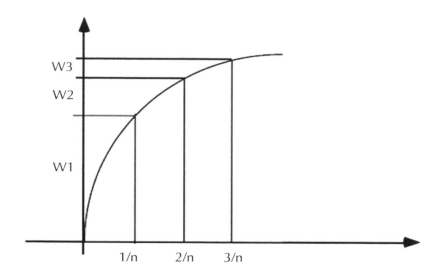

FIGURE 45   Determining weights from a quantifier.

Theorem 2.2 If we construct the weights w_i via the method stated above we get,

$$\sum_{i=1}^{n} w_i = 1$$

and $w_i \in [0,1]$ for any mapping

$$Q: [0,1] \rightarrow [0,1],$$

satisfying the conditions of a regular non-decreasing quantifier.
Proof:
From the non-decreasing property we get the inequality

$$Q(\tfrac{i}{n}) \geq Q(\tfrac{i-1}{n}).$$

Hence, $w_i \geq 0$. Since $Q(r) \leq 1$ then $w_i \leq 1$. Further, we see that

$$\sum_{i=1}^{n} w_i = \sum_{i=1}^{n} [\ Q(\tfrac{i}{n}) - Q(\tfrac{i-1}{n})] = Q(\tfrac{n}{n}) - Q(\tfrac{0}{n}) = 1 - 0 = 1.$$

Any function satisfying the conditions of a regular non-decreasing quantifier is an acceptable OWA weight generating function.

Let us look at the weights generated by some basic types of quantifiers. The quantifier, for all Q_*, is defined such that

$$Q_* (r) = \begin{cases} 0 \text{ for } r < 1, \\ 1 \text{ for } r = 1. \end{cases}$$

Using the method for generating weights,

$$w_i = Q_* \ Q(\tfrac{i}{n}) - Q_*(\tfrac{i-1}{n})$$

we have

$$w_i = \begin{cases} 0 \text{ for } i < n, \\ 1 \text{ for } i = n. \end{cases}$$

In this case,

$$w_i = \begin{cases} 0 & \text{for } i < 1 \\ 1 & \text{for } i = 1. \end{cases}$$

This is exactly what we denoted as W_*.
The Figure 46 shows the quantifier all.

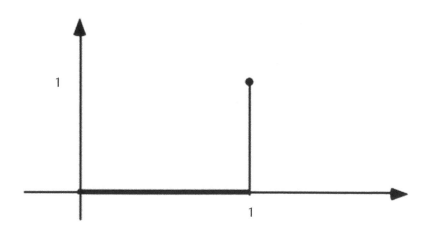

FIGURE 46   The quantifier all.

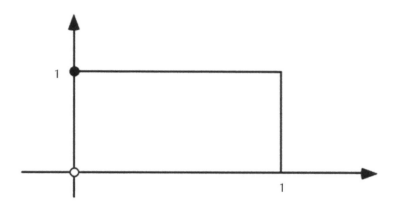

FIGURE 47   The quantifier there exists.

For the quantifier there exists (see Figure 47) we have

$$Q^*(r) = \begin{cases} 0 \text{ for } r = 0, \\ 1 \text{ for } r > 0. \end{cases}$$

In this case we get
$w_1 = 1$, $w_i = 0$, for $i \neq 1$.
This is exactly what we denoted as W*.
Next we consider the quantifier defined by
$Q(r) = r$.
This is an identity or linear type quantifier. In this case we have

$$w_i = Q(\tfrac{i}{n}) - Q(\tfrac{i-1}{n}) = \frac{i}{n} - \frac{i-1}{n} = \frac{1}{n}.$$

This provides the pure averaging OWA aggregation operator.
The Figure 48 shows the identity quantifier i.
According to Yager, we can calculate

$$F_Q(a_1, a_2, \ldots, a_n)$$

for Q being a regular non-decreasing quantifier as follows:
Step 1. Calculate

$$Q(\tfrac{i}{n}) - Q(\tfrac{i-1}{n}).$$

Step 2. Calculate

$$F_Q(a_1, a_2, \ldots, a_n) = \sum_{i=1}^{n} w_i b_i,$$

where b_i is the i-th biggest element in the queue $(a_1, a_2, ..., a_n)$.

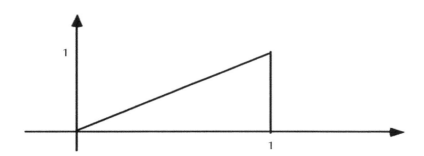

FIGURE 48 The identity quantifier.

Example 2.44 The weights of the window-type OWA operator can be derived from the quantifier

$$Q(r) = \begin{cases} 0 & \text{if} & r \le \frac{k-1}{n}, \\ 1 - \frac{(k-1+m)-nr}{m} & \text{if} & \frac{k-1}{n} \le r \le \frac{k-1+m}{n}, \\ 1 & \text{if} & \frac{k-1+m}{n} \le r \le 1. \end{cases}$$

The standard degree of orness associated with a Regular Increasing Monotone (RIM) linguistic Quantifier Q (See Figure 49).

$$\text{Orness (Q)} = \int_0^1 Q(r)dr$$

is equal to the area under the quantifier. This definition for the measure of orness of quantifier provides a simple useful method for obtaining this measure

Consider the family of RIM quantifiers

$$Q_\alpha(r) = r^\alpha, \alpha \ge 0. \tag{2.102}$$

It is clear that

$$\text{Orness (Q)} = \int_0^1 Q(r)dr = \frac{1}{a+2} =$$

and $orness\,(Q_\alpha)\,<\,0.5$ for $\alpha\,>\,1,$ $orness\,(Q_\alpha)=0.5$ for $\alpha=1$ and $orness\,(Q_\alpha)\,>0.5$ for $\alpha<1.$

For example, if $\alpha=2$ then we get

$$orness\,(Q_\alpha)=\int_0^1 r^2 dr=\frac{1}{2+1}=1/3 \,.$$

A number of interesting properties can be associated with this measure of orness. If Q_1 and Q_2 are two quantifiers such that

$$Q_1(r)\geq Q_2(r)$$

for all r then

$$orness\,(Q_1)\geq orness\,(Q_2).$$

In addition since any regular quantifier is normal we see that

$$orness\,(Q)=0 \iff Q=Q_*$$

where q_* is the quantifier for all.

If we consider again the quantifier

$$Q\,(r)=r^\alpha,\,\alpha\geq 0,$$

then there are three special cases of these family are worth noting
- For $\alpha=1$ we get $Q(r)=r$. This called the *unitor* quantifier.
- For $\alpha\to\infty$ we get Q_*, the universal quantifier.
- For $\alpha\to\infty$ we get Q*, the existential quantifier.

A proportional type quantifier, such as most, can be represented as a fuzzy set Q of the segment [0,1], where Q is the linguistic quantifier.

In this representation, the fuzzy set Q is defined such that for each $r\in[0,1]$, the membership grade Q(r), indicates the degree to which the proportion r satisfies the concept, linguistic quantifier, which Q is representing.

Assume $X=\{x_1,\,...,\,x_n\}$ is some collection of objects and A is some concept expressed as a fuzzy set of X.

A quantified proposition is a statement of the form:
Q X's are A.
Examples of these kinds of statements

MOST STUDENTS ARE YOUNG.

The truth value of these quantified propositions can be evaluated using the OWA aggregation operator.

Once having obtained the weights from quantifier Q, we can obtain the truth τ, of the proposition

Q X's are A

as

$$\tau = \sum_{i=1}^{n} w_i\, b_i$$

where b_i is the i-th largest element from the bag

$$< A(x_1), A(x_2) \ldots, A(x_n)>.$$

Example 2.45 Let us have five students with ages

$$\{21, 22, 24, 22, 38\},$$

and suppose that the degrees of youngness of students obtained from a fuzzy set for young students

$$A(u) \begin{cases} 1 & \text{if } u \leq 22 \\ 1 - \dfrac{u - 22}{8} & \text{if } 22 \leq u \leq 30 \\ 0 & \text{otherwise}. \end{cases}$$

That is $A(21) = 1$, $A(22) = 1$, $A(24) = 0.75$, $A(22) = 1$ and $A(38) = 0$.

If we order the bag

$<1, 1, 0.75, 1, 0>$

in monotone decreasing order then we get:

$(1, 1, 1, 0.75, 0)$.

Let us define the quantifier most by the following membership function

$$Q(r) = \begin{cases} 1 & \text{if } r \geq 0.8 \\ 1 - \dfrac{0.8 - r}{0.6} & \text{if } 0.2 \leq r \leq 0.8 \\ 0 & \text{otherwise}. \end{cases}$$

So, the OWA weights are

$w_1 = Q(0.2) - Q(0) = 0,$

$w_2 = Q(0.4) - Q(0.2) = 1/3,$

$w_3 = Q(0.6) - Q(0.4) = 1/3,$

$w_4 = Q(0.8) - Q(0.6) = 1/3,$

$w_5 = Q(1) - Q(0.8) = 0.$

Then the degree of truth (which can be considered as the units score of the bag, if the elements of the bag are criteria satisfactions) is:

$$\tau = 0 \times 1 + \frac{1}{3} \times 1 + \frac{1}{3} \times 1 + \frac{1}{3} \times 0.75 + 0 \times 0 = \frac{11}{12} \simeq 0.9.$$

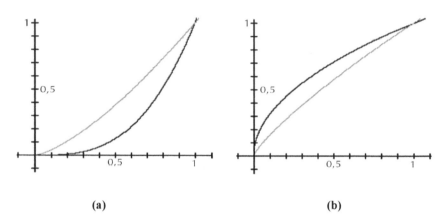

(a)   (b)

FIGURE 49   Risk averse and risk pro RIM linguistic quantifiers.

2.11.7   MINIMAL VARIABILITY OWA OPERATOR WEIGHTS

One important issue in the theory of Ordered Weighted Averaging (OWA) operators is the determination of the associated weights. One of the first approaches, suggested by O'Hagan, determines a special class of OWA operators having maximal entropy of the OWA weights for a given level of orness. Algorithmically it is based on the solution of a constrained optimization problem. Another consideration that may be of interest to a decision maker involves the variability associated with a weighting vector. In particular, a decision maker may desire low variability associated with a weighting vector. In particular, a decision maker may desire low variability associated with a chosen weighting vector. In this section, using the Kuhn-Tucker second-order sufficiency conditions for optimality, we analytically derive the minimal variability weighting vector for any level of orness [98].

Definition 2.42 An OWA operator of dimension n is a mapping F: $R^n \rightarrow R$ that has an associated weighting vector W = $(w_1, ..., w_n)^T$ of having the properties $w_1 + ... + w_n = 1, 0 \leq w_i \leq 1, I = 1, ..., n$, and such that

$$F(a_1, ..., a_n) = \sum_{i=1}^{n} w_i b_i,$$

where b_j is the jth largest element of the collection of the aggregated objects $\{a_1, ..., a_n\}$.

A fundamental aspect of this operator is the re-ordering step, in particular an aggregate a_i is not associated with a particular weight w_i but rather a weight is associated with a particular ordered position of aggregate. When we view the OWA weights as a column vector we find it convenient to refer to the weights with the low indices as weights at the top and those with the higher indices with weights at the bottom. It is noted that different OWA operators are distinguished by their weighting function.

Yager introduced a measure of orness associated with the weighting vector W of an OWA operator, defined as

$$\text{orness}(W) = \sum_{i=1}^{n} \frac{n-i}{n-1} \cdot w_i \, .$$

and it characterizes the degree to which the aggregation is like an or operation. it is clear that orness(W) $\in$ [0, 1] holds for any weighting vector.

It is clear that the actual type of aggregation performed by an OWA operator depends upon the form of the weighting vector. A number of approaches have been suggested for obtaining the associated weights, that is, quantifier guided aggregation, exponential smoothing and learning.

Another approach, suggested by O'Hagan, determines a special class of OWA operators having maximal entropy of the OWA weights for a given level or orness. This approach is based on the solution of the following mathematical programming problem:

maximize disp(W) = $- \sum_{i=1}^{n} w_i \ln w_i$

$$\text{subject to orness}(W) = \sum_{i=1}^{n} \frac{n-i}{n-1} \cdot w_i \, . = \alpha, 0 \leq \alpha \leq 1 \qquad (2.103)$$

$w_1 + ... + w_n = 1, 0 \leq w_i, i = 1, ..., n.$

We want to determine the minimal variability weighting vector under given level of orness. We measure the variance of a given weighting vector as

$$D^2(W) = \sum_{i=1}^{n} \frac{1}{n} \cdot \left(w_i - E(W) \right)^2 = \frac{1}{n} \sum_{i=1}^{n} w_i^2 - \left(\frac{1}{n} \sum_{i=1}^{n} w_i \right)^2 = \frac{1}{n} \sum_{i=1}^{n} w_i^2 - \frac{1}{n^2} \, ,$$

where E(W) = $(w_1 + ... + w_n)/n$ stands for the arithmetic mean of weights.

To obtain minimal variability OWA weights under given level of orness we need to solve the following constrained mathematical programming problem

$$\text{minimize } D^2(W) = \frac{1}{n} \sum_{i=1}^{n} w_i^2 - \frac{1}{n^2}$$

$$\text{subject to orness}(w) = \sum_{i=1}^{n} \frac{n-i}{n-1} \cdot w_i \, . = \alpha, 0 \leq \alpha \leq 1 \qquad (2.104)$$

$$w_1 + ... + w_n = 1, 0 \leq w_i, i = 1, ..., n.$$

Using the Kuhn–Tucker second-order sufficiency conditions for optimality, we can solve problem (2.104) analytically and derive the exact minimal variability OWA weights for any level of orness.

The optimal weighting vector

$$W^* = (0, \ldots, 0, w_p^* , \ldots, w_q^* , 0, \ldots, 0)^T$$

is feasible if and only if $w_p^*, w_q^* \in [0, 1]$.

We find

$$w_p^*, w_q^* \in [0, 1] \Longleftrightarrow \alpha \in \left[1 - \frac{1}{3} \cdot \frac{2q+p-2}{n-1}, 1 - \frac{1}{3} \cdot \frac{q+2p-4}{n-1} \right].$$

The following (disjunctive) partition of the unit interval (0, 1) is crucial in finding an optimal solution to problem (2.104):

$$(0, 1) = \bigcup_{r=2}^{n-1} J_{r,n} \cup J_{1,n} \cup \bigcup_{s=2}^{n-1} J_{1,s} \tag{2.105}$$

where

$$J_{r,n} = \left(1 - \frac{1}{3} \cdot \frac{2n+r-2}{n-1}, 1 - \frac{1}{3} \cdot \frac{2n+r-3}{n-1} \right], r = 2, \ldots, n-1,$$

$$J_{1,n} = \left(1 - \frac{1}{3} \cdot \frac{2n-1}{n-1}, 1 - \frac{1}{3} \cdot \frac{n-2}{n-1} \right),$$

$$J_{1,s} = \left[1 - \frac{1}{3} \cdot \frac{s-1}{n-1}, 1 - \frac{1}{3} \cdot \frac{s-2}{n-1} \right), s = 2, \ldots, n-1.$$

Consider the problem (2.104) and suppose that $\alpha \in J_{r,s}$ for some r and s from partition (2.105). Such r and s always exist for any $\alpha \in (0, 1)$, furthermore, $r = 1$ or $s = n$ should hold.

Then

$$W^* = (0, \ldots, 0, w_r^* , \ldots, w_s^* , 0, \ldots, 0)^T \tag{2.106}$$

where

$$w_j^* = 0, \text{ if } j \notin I_{\{r,s\}},$$

$$w_r^* = \frac{2 (2s+r-2) - 6(n-1)(1-\alpha)}{(s-r+1) (s-r+2)},$$

$$w_s^* = \frac{6(n-1)(1-\alpha)-2\,(s+2r-4)}{(s-r+1)\,(s-r+2)}, \tag{2.107}$$

$$w_j^* = \frac{s-j}{s-r}\cdot w_r + \frac{j-r}{s-r}\cdot w_s, \text{ if } j \in I_{\{r+1,s-1\}}.$$

and $I_{\{r+1,s-1\}} = \{r+1, \ldots, s-1\}$. We note that if $r = 1$ and $s = n$ then we have

$$\alpha \in J_{1,n} = \left(1 - \frac{1}{3}\cdot\frac{2n-1}{n-1}, \ 1 - \frac{1}{3}\cdot\frac{n-2}{n-1}\right),$$

and

$$W^* = \left(w_1^* , \ldots, w_n^*\right)^T,$$

where

$$w_1^* = \frac{2\,(2n-1)-6(n-1)(1-\alpha)}{n(n+1)},$$

$$w_n^* = \frac{6(n-1)(1-\alpha)-2\,(n-2)}{n(n+1)},$$

$$w_j^* = \frac{n-j}{n-1}\cdot w_1 + \frac{j-1}{n-1}\cdot w_n, \text{ if } j \in \{2, \ldots, n-1\}.$$

Futhermore, from the construction of W^* it is clear

$$\sum_{i=1}^{n} w_i^* = \sum_{i=r}^{s} w_i^* = 1, w_i^* \geq 0, \qquad i = 1,2, \ldots, n,$$

and orness $(W^*) = \alpha$, that is, W^* is feasible for problem (2.104).

Note that, W^* satisfies the Kuhn-Tucker second-order sufficiency conditions for optimality.

Example 2.46 We want to determine the minimal variability five-dimensional weighting vector under orness levels $\alpha = 0, 0.1, \ldots, 0.9$ and 1.0. First, we construct the corresponding partition as

$$(0,1) = \bigcup_{r=2}^{4} J_{r,5} \cup J_{1,5} \cup \bigcup_{s=2}^{4} J_{1,s}.$$

where

$$J_{r,s} = \left(\frac{1}{3} \cdot \frac{5-r-1}{5-1}, \frac{1}{3} \cdot \frac{5-r}{5-1}\right] = \left(\frac{4-r}{12}, \frac{5-r}{12}\right],$$

for r = 2, 3, 4 and

$$J_{1,5}\left(\frac{1}{3} \cdot \frac{5-2}{5-1}, \frac{1}{3} \cdot \frac{10-1}{5-1}\right) = \left(\frac{3}{12}, \frac{9}{12}\right),$$

and

$$J_{1,s} = \left[1 - \frac{1}{3} \cdot \frac{s-1}{5-1}, 1 - \frac{1}{3} \cdot \frac{s-2}{5-1}\right] = \left[\frac{13-s}{12}, \frac{14-s}{12}\right],$$

for s = 2,3,4, and, therefore we get,

$$(0,1) = \left[0, \frac{1}{12}\right] \cup \left(\frac{1}{12}, \frac{2}{12}\right] \cup \left(\frac{2}{12}, \frac{3}{12}\right] \cup \left(\frac{3}{12}, \frac{9}{12}\right) \cup \left[\frac{9}{12}, \frac{10}{12}\right) \cup \left[\frac{10}{12}, \frac{11}{12}\right) \cup \left[\frac{11}{12}, \frac{12}{12}\right).$$

Without loss of generality we can assume that $\alpha < 0.5$, because if a weighting vector W is optimal for problem (2.104) under some given degree of orness, $\alpha < 0.5$, then its reverse, denoted by W^R, and defined as

$$w_i^R = w_{n-i+1}$$

is also optimal for problem (2.104) under degree of orness (1-α). As shown by Yager, we find that

$$D^2(W^R) = D^2(W) \text{ and orness } (W^R) = 1 - \text{orness (W)}.$$

Therefore, for any $\alpha < 0.5$, we can also solve problem (2.104) by solving it for level of orness (1- α) and then taking the reverse of that solution.

Then we obtain the optimal weights from (2.107) as follows

- if $\alpha = 0$ then $W^*(\alpha) = W^*(0) = (0,0,\ldots,0.1)^T$ and, therefore,

$$W^*(1) = (W^*(0))^R = (1,0,\ldots,0,0)^T.$$

- if $\alpha = 0.1$ then

$$\alpha \in J_{3,5} = \left(\frac{1}{12}, \frac{2}{12}\right],$$

and the associated minimal variability weights are

$$w_1^* (0.1) = 0,$$

$$w_2^* (0.1) = 0,$$

$$w_3^* (0.1) = \frac{2(10+3-2)-6(5-1)(1-0.1)}{(5-3+1)(5-3+2)} = \frac{0.4}{12} = 0.0333,$$

$$w_5^* (0.1) = \frac{2}{5-3+1} \cdot w_3^* (0.1) = 0.6334,$$

$$w_4^* (0.1) = \frac{1}{2} \cdot w_3^* (0.1) + \frac{1}{2} \cdot w_5^* (0.1) = 0.3333.$$

So,

$$W^* (\alpha) = W^*(0,1) = (0,0,0.033, 0.333, 0.633)^T,$$

and, consequently,

$$W^*(0.9) = (W^*(0.1))^R = (0.633, 0.333, 0.033, 0,0)^T.$$

with variance $D^2 (W^*(0.1)) = 0.0625.$
- if $\alpha = 0.2$ then

$$\alpha \in J_{2.5} = \left(\frac{2}{12}, \frac{3}{12} \right]$$

and in a similar manner we find that the associated minimal variability weighting vector is

$$W^* (0.2) = (0.0, 0.04, 0.18, 0.32, 0.46)^T,$$

and therefore,

$$W^*(0.8) = (0.46, 0.32, 0.18, 0.04, 0.0)^T,$$

with variance $D^2 (W^*(0.2)) = 0.0296.$
- if $\alpha = 0.3$ then

$$\alpha \in J_{1,5} = \left(\frac{3}{12}, \frac{9}{12}\right]$$

and in a similar manner we find that the associated minimal variability weighting vector is

$$W^* (0.3) = (0.04, 0.12, 0.20, 0.28, 0.36)^T,$$

and therefore,

$$W^*(0.7) = (0.36, 0.28, 0.20, 0.12, 0.04)^T,$$

with variance $D^2 (W^*(0.3)) = 0.0128$.

- if $\alpha = 0.4$ then

$$\alpha \in J_{1,5} = \left(\frac{3}{12}, \frac{9}{12}\right]$$

and in a similar manner we find that the associated minimal variability weighting vector is:

$$W^* (0.4) = (0.12, 0.16, 0.20, 0.24, 0.28)^T,$$

and therefore,

$$W^*(0.6) = (0.28, 0.24, 0.20, 0.16, 0.12)^T,$$

with variance $D^2 (W^*(0.4)) = 0.0032$.

if $\alpha = 0.5$ then

$$W^*(0.5) = (0.2, 0.2, 0.2, 0.2, 0.2)^T,$$

with variance $D^2 (W^*(0.5)) = 0$.

We extend the power of decision making with OWA operators by considerations of minimizing variability into the process of selecting the optimal alternative. The particular significance of this work is the development of a methodology to calculate the minimal variability weights in an analytic way.

2.12   PROBABILITY VERSUS POSSIBILITY

Since Zadeh proposed the fuzzy concept in 1965, there have been many discussions about the relationship between the fuzzy theory and probability theory. Both theories express uncertainty, have their values in the range of [0, 1], and have similarities in many aspects. In this section, we review the definition of the two theories and compare them [172].

2.12.1   *PROBABILITY THEORY*

Probability theory deals with the probability for an element to occur in universal set. We call the element as **event** and the set of possible events as sample space. In the sample space, the elements, that is, events are **mutually exclusive**.

Example 2.47 When we play a six-side-dice, the sample space is $S = \{1, 2, 3, 4, 5, 6\}$. Among these six events, only one event can occur. The probability for any of these six events is $1/6$.

An event might contain multiple elements. Consider two events A and B as follows.

$$A = \{1,3,5\}, \qquad B = \{1,\ 2,\ 3\}$$

The union and the intersection of these two events are,

$$A \cup B = \{1,2,3,5\}, \qquad A \cap B = \{1,\ 3\}$$

and the complement of the event A is

$$\overline{A} = \{2,4,6\}.$$

To express the probability of events to occur in the sample space, we can define the *probability distribution* as follows.

The probability distribution P is a numerically valued function that assigns a number $P(A)$ to event A so that the following aximoms hold. In the axioms, S denotes the sample space.

$$0 \le P(A) \le 1,$$

$$P(S) = 1,$$

For the mutually exclusive events $A_1, A_2, \dots$ (that is, for any $i \ne j$,

$$A_i \cap A_j = \Phi)$$

$$P\left(\bigcup_{i=1}^{\infty} A_i\right) = \sum_{i=1}^{\infty} P(A_i).$$

$P(A)$ is the probability of an event A and the sample space S is the domain of probability distribution function. In the Example 2.47 of a six-side-dice, the probability P is,

$$P(i) = \frac{1}{6}, \quad i = 1, 2, \ldots 6,$$

We state the following properties of probability distribution.

$$P(A \cup B) = P(A) + P(B) - P(A \cap B).$$

$$P(A \cup B) = P(A) + P(B), \text{ if } A \cap B = \emptyset.$$

$$P(A) + P(\sim A) = 1.$$

Now assume that there are two sample spaces S and S', and an event A can occur in S and B in S'. When these events can occur in the mutually independent manner, the *joint probability P(AB)* for both A and B to occur is

$$P(AB) = P(A).P(B).$$

The *Conditional probability* $P(A \mid B)$ for A provided that the event B has occurred is

$$P(A \mid B) = \frac{P(AB)}{P(B)}$$

2.12.2 POSSIBILITY DISTRIBUTION

Fuzzy set A is defined on an universal set X and each element in the universal set has its membership degree in [0, 1] for the set A.

$$\mu_A(x) > 0 \text{ for } x \in A = 0 \text{ otherwise.}$$

The membership function μ_A can be defined as a possibility distribution function for the set A on the universal set X. The possibility of element x is denoted as $\mu_A(x)$ and these possibilities define the fuzzy set A.

We know the probability distribution P is defined on a sample space S and the sum of these probabilities should be equal to 1. Meanwhile, the possibility distribution is defined on an universal set X but there is no limit for the sum.

Example 2.48 Suppose the following proposition:
   "Dona has x sisters."

$$P(A) = \sum_{x \in a} \mu_A(x) P(x).$$

Both the probability distribution and possibility distribution can be used to define the variable x in N (Table 6). If we use the probability distribution P, the probability of having x sister(s) is defined by $P(x)$. By the possibility distribution μ, we define the possibility with x sisters as $\mu_A(x)$. The set N is considered as a sample space in the probability distribution and as a universal set in the possibility distribution.

TABLE 6   Possibility and Probability

x	1	2	3	4	5	6	7	8	9	10
$P(x)$	0.4	0.3	0.2	0.1	0	0	0	0	0	0
$\mu(x)$	0.9	1.0	1.0	0.7	0.5	0.2	0.1	0	0	0

We see that the sum of the probabilities is equel to 1 but that of the possibilities is greater than 1. In (Table 6), we can see that higher possibility does not always means higher probability. But lower possibility leads to lower probability. So we can say that the possibility is the upper bound of the probability.

2.12.3   COMPARISON BETWEEN PROBABILITY AND POSSIBILITY

Probability and possibility have something in common they both describe uncertainty. The possibility can be regarded as the upper bound of probability value. That is, the possibility $\mu(A)$ and probability $P(A)$ of an event A have the following relation.

$$\mu(A) \geq P(A).$$

If the events $A_1, A_2, ..., A_n$ are mutually exclusive, the probability of union of the these events is equivalent to the sum of the probabilities of each event, and that of intersection is equivalent to the multiplication.

$$P\left(\bigcup_i A_1\right) = \sum_i P(A_i)$$

$$P\left(\bigcap_i A_1\right) = P(A_1). \ P(A_2) \cdot .... \cdot P(A_n)$$

The possibility for union of those events has the maximum value and that for intersection has the minimum. (Table 7) compares the characteristics of possibility with those of probability.

$$\mu\left(\bigcup_i A_i\right) = Max_i \, \mu(A_i)$$

$$\mu(\bigcap_i Ai) = Min_i \, \mu(A_i)$$

TABLE 7   Comparison between Possibility and Probability [172]

	Possibility	Probability
Domain	Universal set X	Sample space S
Range	[0.1]	[0.1]
Constraints	none	$\sum_i P(A_i) = 1$
Union	$\mu\left(\bigcup_i A_i\right) = Max_i \, \mu(A_i)$	$P\left(\bigcup_i A_i\right) = \sum_i P(A_i)$
Intersection	$\mu\left(\bigcap_i A_i\right) = Min_i \, \mu(A_i)$	$P\left(\bigcap_i A_i\right) = P(A_1) \cdot P(A_2) \cdot ... \cdot P(A_n)$

2.13   FUZZY EVENT

When dealing with the ordinary probability theory, an event has its precise boundary. For instance, if an even is $A = \{1,3,5\}$, its boundary is sharp and thus it can be represented as a crisp set. When we deal an event whose boundary is not sharp, it can be considered as a fuzzy set, that is, a fuzzy event. For example,

$$B = \text{"small integer"} = \{(1,0.9),(2,0.5),(3,0.3)\}..$$

How would we deal with the probability of such fuzzy events? We can identify the probability in two manners. One is dealing with the probability as a crisp value (crisp probability) and the other as a fuzzy set (fuzzy probability) [172].

2.13.1 CRISP PROBABILITY OF FUZZY EVENT

Let a *Crisp event* A be defined in the space R^n. All events in the space R^n are mutually exclusive and probability of each event is ,

$$P(AB) = P(A) \cdot P(B)$$

and for discrete event in the space R^n,

$$P(A) = \sum_{x \in a} P(x)$$

.

Let $\mu_A(x)$ be the *membership function* of the event(set) A and the *expectation* of $\mu_A(x)$ be $E_P(\mu_A)$. Then the following relationship is satisfied.

$$P(A) = \int_A \mu_A dP = E_P(\mu_A)$$

For discrete elements,

$$P(A) = \sum \mu_A(x) P(x).$$

Let event A be a *fuzzy event* or a fuzzy set considered in the space R^n.

$$A = \{(x, \mu_A(x)) | x \in R^n\}.$$

The probability for this fuzzy set is defined as follows:

$$P(A) = \int_A \mu_A dP = E_P(\mu_A)$$

and alternatively.

$$P(A) = \sum_{x \in A} \mu_A(x)P(x).$$

Example 2.49 Assume that the sample space S= $\{a,b,c,d\}$ is given as in (Figure 50) Each element is mutually exclusive, and each probability is given as,

$$P(a) = 0.2, P(b) = 0.5, P(c) = 0.2, P(d) = 0.1.$$

We consider a crisp event $A = \{a,b,c\}$ in the sample space S with its characteristic function given as (Figure 51),

$$\mu_A(a) = \mu_A(b) = \mu_A(c) = 1, \quad \mu_A(d) = 0$$

The probability of the crisp event A can be calculated from the following procedure.

$$P(A) = 1 \times 0.2 + 1 \times 0.5 + 1 \times 0.2 = 0.9.$$

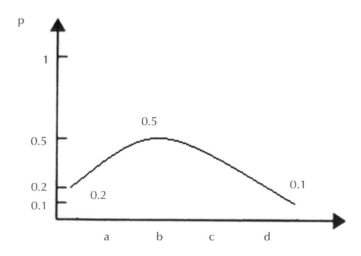

FIGURE 50   Sample space S and Probability.

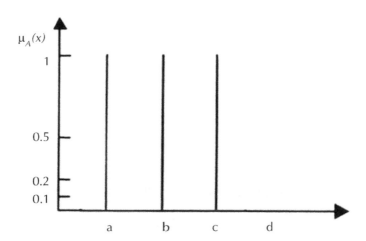

FIGURE 51   Crisp event A.

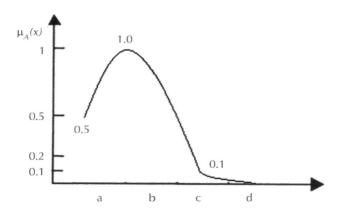

FIGURE 52   Fuzzy event A.

We consider the event A as a fuzzy event (Figure 52). That is,

$$A = \{(a,0.5),(b,1),(c,0.1)\}.$$

The crisp probability for the fuzzy event A is,

$$P(A) = 0.5 \times 0.2 + 1 \times 0.5 + 0.1 \times 0.2 = 0.62.$$

2.13.2 FUZZY PROBABILITY OF FUZZY EVENT

Consider the following fuzzy event in the sample space S.

$$A = \{(x, \mu_A(x)) | x \in S\}$$

The α – cut set of the event(set) A is given as the following crisp set.

$$A_\alpha = \{x | \mu_A(x) \geq \alpha\}$$

The probability of the α – cut event is as follows:

$$P(A_\alpha) = \sum_{x \in A_\alpha} P(x)$$

Here, A_α is the union of mutually exclusive events. The probability of A_α is the sum of the probability of each event in the α-cut set A_α. For the probability of the α-cut event, we can say that, "the possibility of the probability of set A_α to be $P(A_\alpha)$ is α". Considering this interpretation, there are multiple cases for the fuzzy probability $P(A)$ according to the value α.

Fuzzy event A, its α – cut event A_α and the probability (A_α) and probability $P(A_\alpha)$ are provided from the above procedure.

The fuzzy probability $P(A)$ is defined as follows:

$$P(A) = \{(P(A_\alpha), \alpha) | \alpha \in [0,1]\}.$$

Of course, the value of α is an element in the level set of fuzzy set A.

Example 2.50 Assume the probability of each element in the sample space $S = \{a, b, c, d\}$ as shown in (Figure 53)

$$P(a) = 0.2, P(b) = 0.3, P(c) = 0.4, P(d) = 0.1$$

A fuzzy event A is given in (Figure 54)

$$A = \{(a,1), (b,0.8), (c,0.5), (d,0.3)\}.$$

Considering the α – cut event A_α, we get crisp events.

$$A_{0.3} = \{a,b,c,d\}$$

$$A_{0.5} = \{a,b,c\}$$

$$A_{0.8} = \{a,b\}.$$

Since these are crisp events, we can easily calculate the probabilities of each $\alpha -$ cut event.

$$P(A_{0.3}) = 0.2 + 0.3 + 0.4 + 0.1 = 1$$

$$P(A_{0.5}) = 0.2 + 0.3 + 0.4 + 0.9$$

$$P(A_{0.8}) = 0.2 + 0.3 + 0.5$$

$$P(A_{1}) = 0.2.$$

Now, the possibility for this fuzzy event A to be $P(A_{\alpha})$ is α, and the probability of the fuzzy event A is given as follows (Figure 55):

$$P(A) = \{(1,0.3),(0.9,0.5),(0.5,0.8),(0.2,1)\}.$$

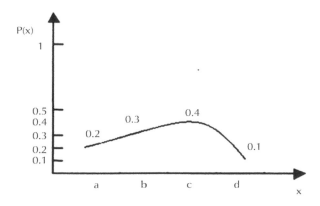

FIGURE 53   Sample space $S = \{a, b, c, d\}$.

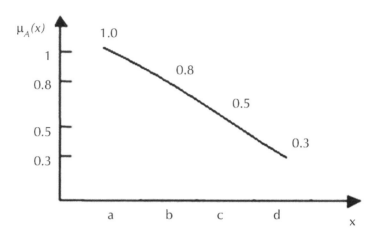

FIGURE 54   Fuzzy event *A*.

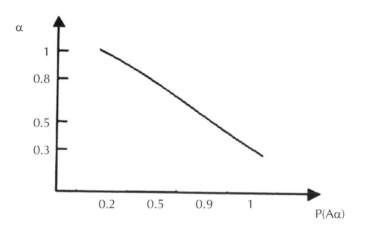

FIGURE 55   Fuzzy probability

2.14   UNCERTAINTY

Suppose students *a, b, c* and, *d* take the entrance examination for college *A*. The possibility for each student to enter the college is 0.2, 0.5, 0.9, and 1 respectively. At this point, the possibilities can be identified as a fuzzy set. That is, let the college be a fuzzy set *A* and *a, b, c,* and *d* be the elements of *A*. The possibilities to be contained in *A* can be expressed as the values of membership function (Figure 56).

$$\mu_A(a) = 0.2, \quad \mu_A(b) = 0.5, \quad \mu_A(c) = 0.9, \quad \mu_A(d) = 1.$$

When discussing the possibilities to be in A, which of these elements a, b, c, and d has the largest uncertainty?

First, the element d has the concrete possibility, we say it has the least uncertainty. The element a, on the other hand, has almost no possibility to pass the examination. This student does not expect too much for his success and we might say he has relatively less uncertainty. However, the student b might have the most uncertainty since he has the possibility 0.5.

When the possibility is near to 0.5. the uncertainty gets the highest. As the possibility approaches 0 or 1, the uncertainty decreases.

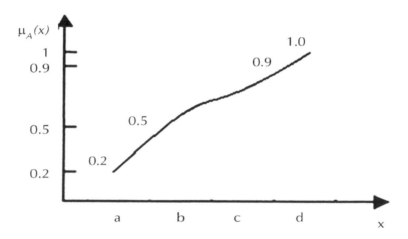

FIGURE 56 Fuzzy set A.

2.14.1 FUZZINESS OF FUZZY SET

Suppose students a, b, c, and d apply to B college and consider B as a fuzzy set. The possibilities for those students to succeed in the entrance examination are shown in the following membership functions (Figure 57).

$$\mu_B(a) = 0.4, \quad \mu_B(b) = 0.7, \quad \mu_B(c) = 0.6, \mu_B(d) = 0.5.$$

Comparing the fuzzy sets A and B, which one is more uncertain? Comparisons element by element, the elements of B are more uncertain (the values of membership functions are closer to 0.5). So, the fuzzy set B has more uncertain states comparing with A. So as to speak, B is relatively more fuzzy.

If we consider another fuzzy set C, each element of which having its membership degree 0.5, the fuzzy set C has the largest degree of fuzziness (uncertainty)

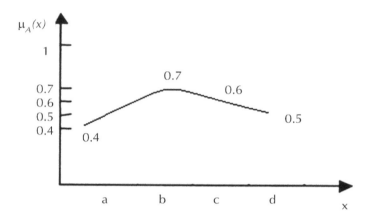

FIGURE 57   Fuzzy set B.

2.15   MEASURE OF FUZZINESS

Fuzziness is termed for the case when representation of uncertainty level is needed. The function for this fuzziness is called *measure of fuzziness*. The function f denoting the measure of fuzziness is

$$f : P(X) \rightarrow R.$$

In the function, $P(X)$ is the power set gathering all subsets of the universal set X, and R is the real number domain. The function f grants the real value $f(A)$ to the subset A of X, and the value indicates the fuzziness of set A, there are conditions for the measures to observe.

- $f(A) = 0$ if A is a crisp set.
The fuzziness should have the value 0 when the set is crisp.
- If the uncertainty of A is less than that B, the measures value $f(A)$ should be less than $f(B)$. We denote it by $A<B$ and say that A is sharper than B. The following relation is satisfied.

$$f(A) \le f(B)$$

The relation implies the monotonicity property [172].

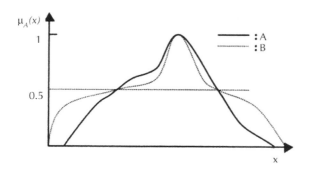

FIGURE 58 When A is sharper than B, $f(A) \leq f(B)$.

Example 2.51 Consider the two fuzzy sets A and B as presented in (Figure 58). The fact that A is sharper than B is defined as follows, that is, if $A < B$ holds;

$$\text{If } \mu(x) \leq \tfrac{1}{2}, \quad \mu_A(x) \leq \mu_B(x) \text{ and}$$

$$\text{If } \mu(x) \geq \tfrac{1}{2}, \quad \mu_A(x) \geq_B (x).$$

Thus, the relation $f(A) \leq f(B)$ is satisfied.

- If the fuzziness is the maximum, the measure $f(A)$ has the maximum value.

Example 2.52 For the deep understanding of the above condition, we consider the case that the uncertainty is the maximum. If the membership degree of each element x in fuzzy set A is 0.5, the uncertainty has the maximum. That is, for all elements $x \in A$, i, $_A(x) = 0.5$, and then the fuzziness measure $f(A)$ is also the maximum (Figure 59).

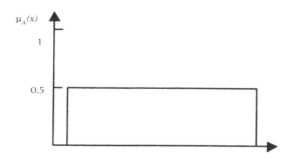

FIGURE 59 Maximum uncertainty $f(A)$.

2.15.1 MEASURE USING ENTROPY

In this section, a fuzziness measure based on Shannon's entropy is explained. Shannon's entropy is widely used in measuring the amount of uncertainty or information, and is considered as the fundamental theory in the information theory [172].

Definition 2.43 (Shannon's entropy)

$$H(P(x)) = -\sum_{x \in X} P(x) \log_2 P(x), \qquad \forall x \in X,$$

and $P(x)$ denotes the probability distribution in the universal set X for all $x \in X$.

Example 2.53 To know more about the entropy, consider the following examples with two probability distributions P and P'.

FOR PROBABILITY DISTRIBUTION P

For the universal set $X = \{a, b, c\}$, the probability distribution P is given as,

$$P(a) = 1/3, \quad P(b) = 1/3, \quad P(c) = 1/3,$$

$$P(a) + P(b) + P(c) = 1.$$

The probabilities of all elements in X are equal to each other, and the sum of probabilities is 1. The uncertainty of one element's occurrence is measured by Shannon's entropy.

$$H(P) = \left[\frac{1}{3} \log_2 \frac{1}{3} + \frac{1}{3} \log_2 \frac{1}{3} + \frac{1}{3} \log_2 \frac{1}{3} \right]$$

$$= -\log_2 \frac{1}{3} = \log_2 3 = 1.6.$$

FOR PROBABILITY DISTRIBUTION P'

Assume there is a probability distribution P' for X as follows.

$$P(a) = 1/2, \quad P'(b) = 1/2, \quad P'(c) = 0$$

The uncertainty is,

$$H(P') = \left[\frac{1}{2}\log_2\frac{1}{2} + \frac{1}{2}\log_2\frac{1}{2} + 0\right]$$

$$= -\log_2\frac{1}{2} = \log_2 2 = 1.$$

The uncertainty for P is greater than that of P'.

In the above example, when the probability distribution is P', the possibility for the element c to occur is 0. So we do not need to consider c. But in the probability distribution P, we need to consider the three elements, a, b, c. So the uncertainty $H(P)$ is greater than $H(P')$. When there are only two events and the probability of each event is 0.5, the amount of information is the maximum at 1 as in the case P'

Since the Shannon's entropy is based on the probability distribution, the total probabilities of all elements is 1.

$$\sum_X P(x) = 1.$$

But for fuzzy sets, this restriction is unnecessary. If a fuzzy set A is defined in the universal set X by a membership function $\mu_A(x)$, the following restriction is not required.

$$\sum_X \mu_A(x) = 1 \text{ (not necessary).}$$

Now referring to what we have seen, define a measure of fuzziness $f(A)$ of a fuzzy set A[1].

Definition 2.44

$$f(A) = -\sum_{x \in X}[\mu_A(x)\log_2\mu_A(x) + (1 - \mu(x))\log_2(1 - \mu_A(x))]$$

This is the sum of the uncertainties of a fuzzy set A defined by the membership function $\mu_A(x)$ and its complement ~A defined by $\left[1 - \mu_A(x)\right]$.

The normalized measure of fuzziness $\hat{f}(A) = \dfrac{f(A)}{|X|}$.

---

[1]Note that the degree of fuzziness as stated by Kosko (see section 2.9) is different from the measure of fuzziness as stated in Definition 2.44.

In the above, $|X|$ denotes the cardinality of the universal set X and the normalized measure observes the following relation.

$$0 \le \hat{f}(A) \le 1$$

This measure satisfies the first two conditions of measure of fuzziness (see section 2.15).

Example 2.54 Suppose that there are two fuzzy sets A and A' in $X = \{a,b,c\}$.
- Assume that a fuzzy set A is given as

$$A = \{(a,0.5),(b,0.2),(c,1)\}.$$

The fuzziness of the fuzzy set A is,

$$f(A) = -(0.5\log 0.5 + 0.5\log + 0.5 + 0.2\log 0.2 + 0.8\log 0.8 + 1\log 1 + 0)$$

$$= -\left(\log_2 \frac{1}{2} + \frac{1}{5}\log_2 \frac{1}{5} + \frac{4}{5}\log_2 \frac{4}{5} \right)$$

$$= \log_2 2 + \frac{1}{5}\log_2 5 + \frac{4}{5}\log_2 \frac{5}{4}$$

$$= \log_2 5 - 0.6 = 1.7.$$

and the normalized measure yields,

$$\hat{f}(A) = \frac{f(A)}{|X|} = \frac{1.7}{3} = 0.57.$$

- The fuzzy set A' is given as follows.

$$A' = \{(a,0.5),(b,0.5),(c,0.5)\}$$

The fuzziness for the fuzzy set A' is,

$$f(A') = -(0.5\log_2 0.5 + 0.5\log_2 0.5 + 0.5\log_2 0.5)$$

$$+ 0.5\log_2 0.5 + 0.5\log_2 0.5 + 0.5\log_2 0.5)$$

$$= -(3\log_2 0.5) = 3\log_2 2 = 3,$$

and the normalized measure is,

$$\hat{f}(A) = \frac{f(A')}{|X|} = \frac{3}{3} = 1$$

The membership degrees of all elements in A' are 0.5. So the uncertainty of the fuzzy set A' is larger. Consequently, the fuzziness of A' is greater than that of A

$$f(A) < f(A').$$

We state that the uncertainty is the largest when the membership degrees are all 0.5. and the normalized fuzziness of such fuzzy set is 1.

2.15.2   MEASURE USING METRIC DISTANCE

Another measure of fuzziness is the one that is based on the concept of metric distance. We talked about Hamming distance and Euclidean distance in sec 2.5. A crisp set C that corresponds to a fuzzy set A is introduced for the distance measure (Figure 60).

$$\mu_C(x) = 0 \qquad if\ \mu_A(x) \le \frac{1}{2} \qquad and$$

$$\mu_C(x) = 1 \qquad if\ \mu_A(x) > \frac{1}{2}.$$

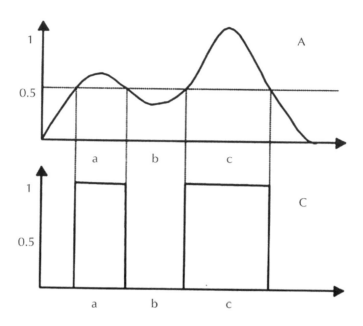

FIGURE 60   Fuzzy set *A* and its corresponding crisp set *C*.

If the set *C* is defined as such, the measure of fuzziness is the distance between the fuzzy set *A* and the crisp set *C*. For the measure of distance, we can use Hamming distance or Euclidean distance (see section 2.5).

According to Hamming distance the measure of fuzziness $f(A)$ is,

$$f(A) = \sum_{x \in X} |\mu_A(x) - \mu_C(x)| \text{ and}$$

according to Euclidean distance the measure of fuzziness *f(A)* is,

$$f(A) = \left(\sum_{x \in x} [\mu_A(x) - \mu_C(x)]^2 \right)^{\frac{1}{2}}.$$

If the values of membership function are closer to 0.5, the measure of fuzziness is larger.

Example 2.55 Consider the sets *A* and *A'* of Example 2.54. According to Hamming distances $f(A)$ and $f(A')$ are calculated as;

$$f(A) = |0.5 - 0| + |0.2 - 0| + |1 - 1|$$

$$= 0.5 + 0.2 + 0 = 0.7, \text{ and}$$

$$f(A') = |0.5 - 0| + |0.5 - 0| + |0.5 - 0|$$

$$= 0.5 + 0.5 + 0.5 = 1.5.$$

The relation $f(A) < f(A')$ holds. The Hamming measure of fuzziness can be normalized as,

$$\hat{f}(A) = \frac{f(A)}{0.5|X|} = \frac{0.7}{0.5 \times 3} = 0.47.$$

Therefore,

$$0 \leq \hat{f}(A) \leq 1.$$

2.16 TYPE-2 FUZZY SETS

Type-2 fuzzy set was introduced as an extension of a type-1 fuzzy set by Zadeh. Mizumoto and Tanaka studied the set theoretic operations and properties of membership grades of such sets and examined their operations of algebraic product and algebraic sum. Karnik and Mendel extended the algorithms for performing union, intersection and complement for type-2 fuzzy sets. Type-2 fuzzy sets and related tools have now been widely used in many fields.

Type-2 fuzzy set is shown in Figure 61. Type 2 fuzzy sets are designed by making membership function in three dimensions where each element in type 2 fuzzy sets has membership value in range [0, 1]. The third dimension is an extension and adds degrees of freedom to get more information in representing fuzzy sets. Type 2 fuzzy sets are very useful when there is a difficulty in determining appropriate membership function for a fuzzy set and problem related with ambiguity.

The Figure 61 shows the main difference between both types in the membership function in which type 2 fuzzy set forms boundary values that are defined as the lower and upper membership functions. Both functions define the upper and lower membership values of each value of horizontal axis.

Type 2 fuzzy sets have fuzzy membership value. Membership value in type 2 fuzzy sets can be any value in range [0, 1]. This membership is called primary membership.

Related with each primary membership, there is a secondary membership (also has a value in range [0,1]).Figure 62 shows the visualization of type 2 fuzzy sets.

Horizontal axis x in Figure 62 shows main variable as member of fuzzy set, axis of u shows primary membership value, and the vertical axis shows secondary membership for each primary membership.

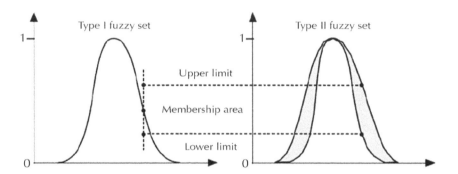

FIGURE 61   Construction of type 2 fuzzy set from type 1 fuzzy set.

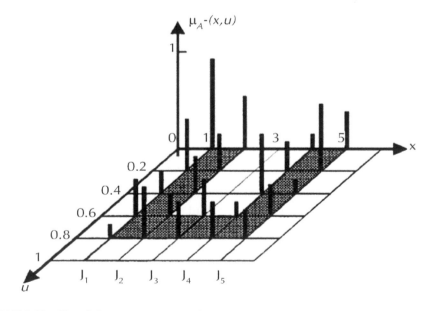

FIGURE 62   Type 2 fuzzy sets representation.

In this section, we define type-2 fuzzy sets and some important associated concepts. We provide simple mathematically expression to represent type-2 fuzzy sets [183].

Definition 2.45 A *type-2 fuzzy set,* denoted $\tilde{A}$, is characterized by a *type-2 membership function* $\mu_{\tilde{A}}(x, u)$, where $x \in X$ and $u \in J_x \subseteq [0, 1]$, that is,

$$\tilde{A} = \{((x, u), \mu_{\tilde{A}}(x, u)) | \forall x \in X, \forall u \in J_x \subseteq [0, 1]\} \qquad (2.108)$$

in which $0 \leq \mu_{\tilde{A}}(x, u) \leq 1$. $\tilde{A}$ can also be expressed as

$$\tilde{A} = \int_{x \in X} \int_{u \in J_x} \mu_{\tilde{A}}(x, u)/(x, u) J_x \subseteq [0, 1] \qquad (2.109)$$

where $\int \int$ denotes union over all admissible x and u. For discrete universes of discourse $\int$ is replaced by Σ.

In Definition 2.45, the first restriction that $\forall u \in J_x \subseteq [0, 1]$ is consistent with the type-1 constraint that $0 \leq \mu_A(x) \leq 1$, that is, when uncertainties disappear a type-2 membership function reduces to a type-1 membership function, in which case the variable u equals $\mu_A(x)$ and $0 \leq \mu_A(x) \leq 1$. The second restriction that $0 \leq \mu_{\tilde{A}}(x, u) \leq 1$ is consistent with the fact that the amplitudes of a membership function lie between or be equal to 0 and 1.

Example 2.56 Figure 62 depicts $\mu_{\tilde{A}}(x, u)$ for discrete X = {1, 2, 3, 4, 5} and U={0, 0.2, 0.4, 0.6, 0.8}.

Definition 2.46 At each value of x, say $x = x'$, the 2-D plane whose axes are u and $\mu_{\tilde{A}}(x', u)$ is called a *vertical slice* of $\mu_{\tilde{A}}(x, u)$. *A secondary membership function* is a vertical slice of $\mu_{\tilde{A}}(x, u)$. It is $\mu_{\tilde{A}}(x = x', u)$ for $x \in X$ and $\forall u \in J_{x'} \subseteq [0, 1]$, that is,

$$\mu_{\tilde{A}}(x = x', u) \equiv \mu_{\tilde{A}}(x') = \int_{u \in J_{x'}} fx'(u)/u \, J_{x'} \subseteq [0, 1] \; (2.110)$$

in which $0 \leq f_{x'}(u) \leq 1$.

Remark 2.4 As $\forall x' \in X$, we drop the prime notation on $\mu_{\tilde{A}}(x')$, and refer to $\mu_{\tilde{A}}(x')$ as a secondary membership function; it is a type-1 fuzzy set, which we also refer to as a *secondary set*.

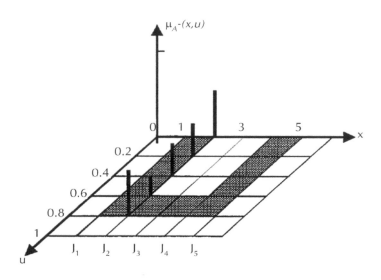

FIGURE 63   example of a vertical slice for the type 2 membership function.

Example 2.57 The type-2 membership function that is depicted in Figure 62 has five vertical slices associated with it. The one at x=2 is depicted in Figure 63. The secondary membership function at x=2 is $\mu_{\tilde{A}}(2) = 0.5/0 + 0.35/0.2 + 0.35/0.4 + 0.2/0.6 + 0.5/0.8$.

We can reinterpret a type-2 fuzzy set as the union of all secondary sets. Thus, using (2.110), *we can re-express $\tilde{A}$ in a vertical-slice manner*, as

$$\tilde{A} = \{(x, \mu_{\tilde{A}}(x)) \mid \forall x \in X\} \tag{2.111}$$

or, as

$$\tilde{A} = \int_{x \in X} \mu_{\tilde{A}}(x)/x = \int_{x \in X} \left[\int_{u \in J_x} f_x(u)/u \right]/x \qquad J_x \subseteq [0,1]. \tag{2.112}$$

Definition 2.47 The *domain* of a secondary membership function is called the *primary membership* of x.

Remark 2.5 In (2.112), J_x is the primary membership of x, where $J_x \subseteq [0, 1]$ for $\forall x \in X$.

Definition 2.48 The *amplitude* of a secondary membership function is called the *secondary grade*.

Remark 2.6 In (2.112), $f_x(u)$ is a *secondary grade*. In (2.108), $\mu_{\tilde{A}}(x', u')(u' \in X, u' \in J_{x'})$ is a secondary grade.

Remark 2.7 If X and J_x are both discrete then the right-most part of (2.112) is expressed as

$$\tilde{A} = \Sigma_{x \in X} \ [\Sigma_{u \in J_x} f_x(u)/u]/x$$

$$= \Sigma_{i=1}^{N} \ [\Sigma_{u \in J_i} f_{x_i}(u)/u]/x_i$$

$$= [\Sigma_{k=1}^{M_1} f_{x_1}(u_{1k})/u_{i_k}]/x_1 + \ ... + [\Sigma_{k=1}^{M_N} f_{x_N}(u_{NK})/u_{N_K}]/x_N. \ (2.113)$$

In this equation, + also denotes union.

Remark 2.8 Note that x has been discretized into N values and at each of these values u has been discretized into M_i values. The discretization along each u_{ik} does not have to be same, which is why we have shown a different upper sum for each of the bracketed terms. If, however, the discretization along each u_{ik} is the same, then $M_1 = M_2 ... = M_n \equiv M.$

Example 2.58 In Figure 62, the union of the five secondary membership functions at x = 1,2,3,4,5 is $\mu_{\tilde{A}}(x, u)$. Observe that the primary membership are

$$J_1 = J_2 = J_4 = J_5 = \{0, 0.2, 0.4, 0.6, 0.8\} \text{ and } J_3 = \{0.6, 0.8\}$$

and, we have only included values in J_3 for which $\mu_{\tilde{A}}(x, u) \neq 0.$

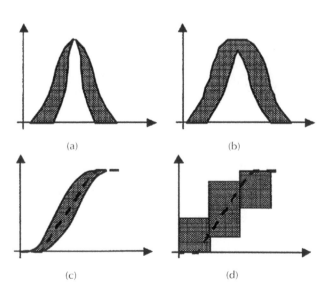

(a)

(b)

(c)

(d)

FIGURE 64 FOUs. (a) GaussianMFwith uncertain standard deviation. (b) Gaussian. MF with uncertain mean. (c) Sigmoidal MF with inflection uncertainties.(d) Granulated sigmoidal MF with granulation uncertainties

Definition 2.49 Uncertainty in the primary memberships of a type-2 fuzzy set, $\tilde{A}$, consists of a bounded region that we call the *footprint of uncertainty* (FOU). It is the union of all primary memberships, that is,

$$\text{FOU}(\tilde{A}) = U_{x \in X} \, J_x. \tag{2.114}$$

The shaded region in Figure 64 is the FOU.

Remark 2.9 The term *footprint of uncertainty* is very useful, because it not only focuses our attention on the uncertainties inherent in a specific type-2 membership function, whose shape is a direct consequence of the nature of these uncertainties.

Remark 2.10 It is also provides a very convenient verbal description of the entire domain of support for all the secondary grades of a type-2 membership function.

Remark 2.11 It also lets us depict a type-2 fuzzy set graphically in two-dimensions instead of three dimensions, and thus simplifies the first difficulty about type-2 fuzzy sets because of its three-dimensional nature, which makes them very difficult to draw.

Remark 2.12 The shaded FOUs imply that there is a distribution that sits on top of its – the new third dimension of type-2 fuzzy sets. The shapes of the said distribution depends on the specific choices made for the secondary grades.

Remark 2.13 When all the grades are equal to one, the resulting type-2 fuzzy sets are called *interval type-2 fuzzy sets*. Such sets are the most widely used type-2 fuzzy sets to date.

Definition 2.50 For discrete universes of discourse X and U, an *embedded type-2 set* $\tilde{A}_e$ has N elements, where $\tilde{A}_e$ contains exactly one element from $J_{x_1}, J_{x_2}, \ldots, J_{x_N}$, namely $u_1, u_2, \ldots, u_N$, each with its associated secondary grade, namely $f_{x_1}(u_1), f_{x_2}(u_2), \ldots, f_{x_N}(u_N)$, that is,

$$\tilde{A}_e = \sum_{i=1}^{N} [f_{x_i}(u_i)/u_i]/x_i \qquad u_i \in J_x \subseteq U = [0, 1]. \tag{2.115}$$

Remark 2.14 Set $\tilde{A}_e$ is embedded in $\tilde{A}$, and, there are a total of $\prod_{i=1}^{N} M_i \, \tilde{A}_e$.

Definition 2.51 For discrete universes of discourse X and U, an *embedded type-1 set* A_e has N elements, one each from $J_{x_1}, J_{x_2}, \ldots, J_{x_N}$, namely $u_1, u_2, \ldots, u_N$, that is,

$$A_e = \sum_{i=1}^{N} u_i/x_i \; u_i \in J_{x_i} \subseteq U = [0, 1]. \tag{2.116}$$

Remark 2.15 Set A_e is the union of all the primary memberships of set $\tilde{A}_e$ in (2.115), and, there are a total of $\prod_{i=1}^{N} M_i A_e$.

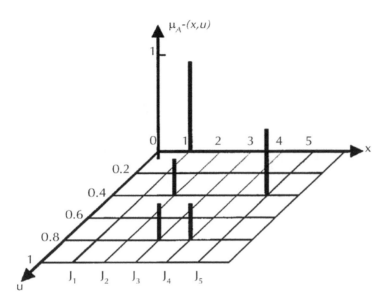

FIGURE 65 Example of an embedded type-2 set associated with the type-2 membership function

Example 2.59 Figure 65 depicts one of the possible 1250 embedded type-2 sets for the type-2 membership function that is depicted in Figure 62. Observe that the embedded type-1 set that is associated with this embedded type-2 set is $A_e = 0/1 + 0.4/2 + 0.8/3 + 0.8/4 + 0.4/5$.

Definition 2.52 *A type-1 fuzzy set is expressed as a type-2 fuzzy set*, provided the type-2 representation is $(1/\mu_F(x))/x$ or $1/\mu_F(x) \forall_x \in X$, for short.

Remark 2.16 The notation $1/\mu_F(x)$ means that the secondary membership function has only one value in its domain, namely the primary membership $\mu_F(x)$, at which the secondary grade equals 1.

2.16.1 CANONICAL REPRESENTATION FOR TYPE-2 FUZZY SETS

So far we have emphasized the vertical-slice representation (decomposition) of type-2 fuzzy set as given in (2.112). In this section, we provide canonical representation for a type-2 fuzzy set in terms of *wavy slices*. This representation makes very heavy use of embedded type-2 fuzzy sets as stated in Definition 2.50.

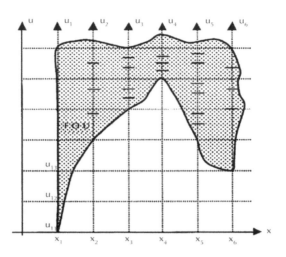

FIGURE 66   Example of a FOU on discretized x- and u-axes. Here N = 6.

Now we stipulate the following results:

Theorem 2.3 [183] Consider the general FOU that is depicted in Figure 66. We call each point along the u_i line a *node*. Each node among the u_i-axis is contained in exactly

$$n_l = \prod_{j=1, j \neq 1}^{N} M_j \qquad (2.117)$$

embedded (type-2 or type-1) sets, where $l = 1, 2, \dots, N$.

Next, we present a new decomposition for a type-2 fuzzy set that we refer to as a *Representation Theorem*.

Theorem 2.4 [183] Let $\tilde{A}_e^j$ denote the jth type-2 embedded set for type-2 fuzzy set $\tilde{A}$, that is,

$$\tilde{A}_e^j \equiv \{(u_i^j, f_{x_i}(u_i^j)), i = 1, \dots, N\} \qquad (2.118)$$

where

$$u_i^j \in \{u_{i_k}, k = 1, \dots, M_i\}. \qquad (2.119)$$

Then $\tilde{A}$ can be represented as the union of its type-2 embedded sets, that is,

$$\tilde{A} = \sum_{j=1}^{n} \tilde{A}_e^j \qquad (2.120)$$

where

$$n \equiv \prod_{i=1}^{N} M_i. \qquad (2.121)$$

Remark 2.17 In order to implement (2.120), we need a constructive method for specifying each $\tilde{A}_e^j$. Note that j is the solution to the following combinatorial assignment problem. Determine all possible combinations $(a_1, a_2, ..., a_N)$ such that $(u_{1a_1}, u_{2a_2}, ..., u_{Na_N}) \rightarrow j$, where $a_1 \in \{1, 2, ..., M_1\}$ $a_2 \in \{1, 2, ..., M_2\} ..., a_N \in \{1, 2, ..., M_N\}$, and $j = 1, 2, ..., \prod_{i=1}^{N} M_i$.

Remark 2.18 Theorem 2.4 expresses $\tilde{A}$ as a union of simpler type-2 fuzzy sets, the $\tilde{A}_e^j$. They are simpler because their secondary membership functions are singletons. Whereas (2.112) is a vertical slice representation of $\tilde{A}$ and (2.120) is a *wavy slice* representation of $\tilde{A}$.

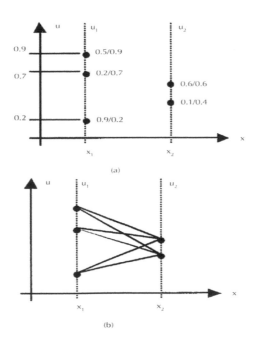

FIGURE 67 (a) Vertical-slice representation for $\tilde{A}$. (b) Six embedded type-2 fuzzy sets, each connected by a line from x_1 to x_2.

Example 2.60 Consider the following type-2 fuzzy set:

$$\tilde{A} = (0.5/0.9)/x_1 + (0.2/0.7)/x_1 + (0.9/0.2/x_1 + (0.6/0.6)/x_2 + (0.1/0.4)/x_2. \tag{2.122}$$

The vertical-slice representation of $\tilde{A}$ is depicted in Figure 67. Observe that $M_1^A = 3$, $M_2^A = 2$, and $n_A = M_1^A M_2^A = 6$. Hence, there are six embedded type-2 sets, namely

$$\tilde{A}_e^1 = (0.5/0.9)/x_1 + (0.6/0.6)/x_2 \tag{2.123a}$$

$$\tilde{A}_e^2 = (0.5/0.9)/x_1 + (0.1/0.4)/x_2 \tag{2.123b}$$

$$\tilde{A}_e^3 = (0.2/0.7)/x_1 + (0.6/0.6)/x_2 \tag{2.123c}$$

$$\tilde{A}_e^4 = (0.2/0.7)/x_1 + (0.1/0.4)/x_2 \tag{2.123d}$$

$$\tilde{A}_e^5 = (0.9/0.2)/x_1 + (0.6/0.6)/x_2 \tag{2.123e}$$

$$\tilde{A}_e^6 = (0.9/0.2)/x_1 + (0.1/0.4)/x_2 \tag{2.123f}$$

It is very easy to see that $\tilde{A} = \sum_{j=1}^{6} \tilde{A}_e^j$.

We apply the Representation Theorem 2.4 to the derivation of formulas for union, intersection and complement of type-2 fuzzy sets, without using the Extension Principle.

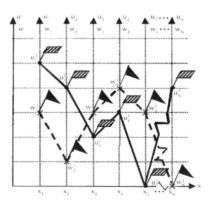

FIGURE 68   Two representative embedded type-2 fuzzy sets. The filled circles and rectangular flags denote the primary memberships and secondary grades for $\tilde{A}$, whereas the crosses and triangular flags denote the primary memberships and secondary grades for $\tilde{B}$. The solid and dashed curves are associated with the embedded type-1 fuzzy sets, A and B, respectively.

UNION OF TYPE-2 FUZZY SETS

Consider two type-2 fuzzy sets $\tilde{A}$ and $\tilde{B}$, where

$$\tilde{A} = \sum_{x \in X} \mu_{\tilde{A}}(x)/(x) = \sum_{x \in X} \left[\sum_{u \in J_x^u} f_x(u)/u \right]/x \qquad J_x^u \subseteq [0,1] \tag{2.124}$$

and

$$\tilde{B} = \sum_{x \in X} \mu_{\tilde{B}}(x)/(x) = \sum_{x \in X} \left[\sum_{w \in J_x^w} g_x(w)/w \right]/x \, J_x^w \subseteq [0,1] \tag{2.125}$$

From Representation Theorem 2.4, it follows that

$$\tilde{A} \cup \tilde{B} = \sum_{j=1}^{n_A} \tilde{A}_e^j \cup \sum_{i=1}^{n_B} \tilde{B}_e^j = \sum_{j=1}^{n_A} \sum_{i=1}^{n_B} \tilde{A}_e^j \cup \tilde{B}_e^j \tag{2.126}$$

This demonstrates that to evaluate $\tilde{A} \cup \tilde{B}$ we need to evaluate the union of type-2 embedded sets, that is, we need to evaluate $\tilde{A}_e^j \cup \tilde{B}_e^j (\forall i, j)$.

Two representative embedded type-2 fuzzy sets are depicted in Figure 68. Each embedded type-2 set has only one node on its u_l or w_k-axes. The rectangular and triangular flags denote the secondary grades at each node, and are merely meant as a pneumonic for those grades.

Recall that a type-1 fuzzy set can be interpreted as a type-2 fuzzy set all of whose secondary grades equal unity (that is, all flags equal 1). In fact, a type-1 fuzzy set is an instance of a type-2 fuzzy set. It is a crisp version of a type-2 fuzzy set. Given that this is the case, it seems sensible to consider using the type-1 definitions for union, intersection, and complement as a starting point and generalizing them to a *fuzzy* type-1 fuzzy set – a type-2 fuzzy set. Next, we show that by taking this approach we do not need to use, the Extension Principle.

Recall, from Definition 2.51, that $\tilde{A}_e^j$ and $\tilde{B}_e^i$ are the embedded type-1 fuzzy sets that are associated with $\tilde{A}_e^j$ and $\tilde{B}_e^i$, respectively. In the type-1 case

$$A_e^j \cup B_e^i = u_1^j \vee w_1^i / x_1 + u_2^j \vee w_2^i / x_2 + \ldots + u_N^j \vee w_N^i / x_N \tag{2.127}$$

which (see Definition 2.52) can be expressed as a type-2 set, as follows:

$$A_e^j \cup B_e^i = [1/ u_1^j \vee w_1^i]/ x_1 + [1/ u_2^j \vee w_2^i]/x_2 + \ldots + [1/u_N^j \vee w_N^i]/x_N \tag{2.128}$$

Observe that in this representation, the "flag" (that is, secondary grade) at each $u_l^j \vee w_l^i$ point is unity.

In the type-2 case, where the flags start out being different at each u_l^j and w_l^i points, we need to keep track of them as we perform $A_e^j \cup B_e^i$. Call the flag (see Figure 68, for example, for l=2) at u_l^j which occurs when $x = x_l, f_{xl}\left(u_l^j\right),$ and the flag at w_l^i , which also occurs when $x = x_l, g_{xl}\left(w_l^j\right)$. Let h be some operation (defined below) on the two flags that produces a new flag that uniquely identifies $u_l^j \vee w_l^i$. Call this new flag $F_{xl}\left(u_l^j, w_l^j\right)$, that is,

$$F_{xl}\left(u_l^j, w_l^j\right) = h\left[f_{xl}\left(u_l^j\right), g_{xl}\left(w_l^j\right)\right]. \qquad (2.129)$$

In analogy to (2.128), we now *define* $\tilde{A}_e^j \cup \tilde{B}_e^i$ as follows:

$$\tilde{A}_e^j \cup \tilde{B}_e^i \equiv \left[F_{x_1}\left(u_1^j, w_1^j\right)/u_1^j \vee w_1^i\right]/x_1 + \ldots + \left[F_{x_N}\left(u_N^j, w_N^j\right)/u_N^j \vee w_N^i\right]/x_N.$$
$$\qquad (2.130)$$

This is a very plausible way to define the union of embedded type-2 fuzzy sets, since it reduces to type-1 definition of union when all flags equal unity. It also establishes the constraint that h(1, 1) = 1, which forces the type-2 result in (2.130) to reduce to the type-1 result in (2.128) when all uncertainties disappear.

Next, we demonstrate that an appropriate choice for h is a t-norm. We begin by requiring h to have the following four properties:

Property 1 $h(a, b) = h(b, a)$;

Property 2 $0 \le h \le (a, b) \le 1$;

Property 3 $h(1, 1) = 1$;

Property 4 $h(a, 0) = h(0, b) = 0.$

Property 1 is intuitive, because it should not matter in which order we handle the flags a and b, Property 2 is also intuitive, because h (a,b) is another flag, which means that it is a secondary grade for a secondary membership function, and all secondary grades must be bounded according to Definition 2.45. We have already justified Property 3. Property 4 involves flags that each have zero values. Such flags (which are perfectly permissible) allow secondary membership functions to have zero (that is, vacuous) secondary grades at specific values of primary memberships. Property 4 requires that a vacuous flag in one fuzzy set must remain vacuous in any fuzzy set derived from it, which again seems plausible. It is now obvious, from the properties of a t-norm that.

Lemma 2.5 Under the four properties just stated, h is a t-norm.

Remark 2.19 We could require a different Property 4, for example, h (a, 0) = a and h (0, b) = p, in which case h is a t-conorm. We find such a requirement for h is much less plausible than Property 4, hence we recommend h as a t-norm.

Remark 2.20 The Extension Principle can claim that (2.130) is exactly what is achieved by applying the existing formula for the union of two type-2 fuzzy sets to to $\tilde{A}_e^j$ and $\tilde{B}_e^i$, and it is correct (when h is a t-norm). However, we obtain (2.130) without applying Extension Principle.

Now we stipulate the following result,

Theorem 2.5 [183] The union of two type-2 fuzzy sets $\tilde{A}$ and $\tilde{B}$ is given as

$$\tilde{A} \cup \tilde{B} = \sum_{j=1}^{n_A}\sum_{i=1}^{n_B} \{[\ f_{x_1}(u_1^j,\ w_1^i)/\ u_1^j \vee w_1^i]/\ x_1 + \ldots + [F_{x_N}(u_N^j,\ w_N^j)/ \ u_N^j \vee w_N^i]/\ x_N$$

(2.131)

where

$$F_{x_1}\left(u_1^j,\ w_i^i\right) = h\left[F_{x_i}(u_i^j)\ g_{x_i}(w_i^j)\right] = f_{x_i}(u_i^j) * g_{x_i}(w_i^j)]$$ (2.132)

and $*$ is a t-norm (for example, minimum, product, and so on). Equation (2.131) can also be expressed as

$$\tilde{A} \cup \tilde{B} = \sum_{j=1}^{M_1\ (u_1)}\sum_{i=1}^{M_1\ (w_1)} [\ F_{x_1}\left(u_1^j,\ w_1^i\right)/\ u_1^j \vee w_1^i]/\ x_1 + \ldots + \sum_{j=1}^{M_N\ (u_N)}\sum_{i=1}^{M_N\ (w_N)} [F_{x_N}\left(u_N^j,\ w_N^j\right)/\ u_N^j \vee w_N^i]/\ x_N$$

(2.133)

Remark 2.21 Equation (2.131) is the *wavy-slice* expression for $\tilde{A} \cup \tilde{B}$, but it is not recommended for computing purposes because it involves an enormous number of terms. Equation (2.133), on the other hand, which a *vertical-slice* expression for $\tilde{A} \cup \tilde{B}$, and is very practical for computing purposes.

Remark 2.22 The union of $\tilde{A}$ and $\tilde{B}$ is the discrete version of the first expression in (2.112), that is,

$$\tilde{A} \cup \tilde{B} \Leftrightarrow \mu_{\tilde{A}\cup\tilde{B}}(x,v) = \sum_{x\in X}\mu_{\tilde{A}\cup\tilde{B}}(x)/x$$

(2.134)

Remark 2.23. From the Extension Principle, we obtain the following expression for $\mu_{\tilde{A}\cup\tilde{B}}(x)$.

$$\mu_{\tilde{A}\cup\tilde{B}}(x) = \sum_{u\in J_x^u}\sum_{w\in J_x^w} f_x(u) * g_x(w)/(u \vee w)\ x \in X.$$ (2.135)

Remark 2.24 An alternative approach to express (2.135), in terms of the secondary membership function of $\tilde{A}$ and $\tilde{B}$, that is $\mu_{\tilde{A}}(x)$ and $\mu_{\tilde{B}}(x)$, is

$$\mu_{\tilde{A}\cup\tilde{B}}(x) = \sum_{u\in J_x^u} \sum_{w\in J_x^w} f_x(u) * g_x(w)/(u \vee w) \tag{2.136}$$

$$\equiv \mu_{\tilde{A}}(x) \sqcup \mu_{\tilde{B}}(x) \qquad x \in X$$

where $\sqcup$ denotes the so-called *join* operation. The use of the notation $\mu_{\tilde{A}}(x) \sqcup \mu_{\tilde{B}}(x)$ to indicate the join between the secondary membership functions $\mu_{\tilde{A}}(x)$ and $\mu_{\tilde{B}}(x)$ is, of course, a shorthand notation for the operations in the middle of (2.136).

Remark 2.25 Equation (2.133) is exactly the same as the combination of (2.134) and (2.135), because each term of (2.133) is the same as (2.135).

Remark 2.26 The result of (2.135) is derived from the Extension Principle, and we have obtained the same result without it.

Remark 2.27 If the fourth property for h is changed, then our results in (2.133) remains unchanged, but (2.135) is no longer valid because it is in terms of a t-norm (since the Extension Principle is in terms of a t-norm).

Remark 2.28 Each of the N terms in (2.133) is a join operation, so that we can describe the union of $\tilde{A}$ and $\tilde{B}$ as the union of N joins. The term "join" is very useful because we can linguistically describe $\tilde{A} \cup \tilde{B}$.

INTERSECTION OF TYPE-2 FUZZY SETS

As the derivation of the intersection of two type-2 fuzzy sets $\tilde{A}$ and $\tilde{B}$ is similar to the derivation of the union of those two sets, we simply state the formulas and summarize the results in Theorem 2.6.

$$\tilde{A} \cap \tilde{B} = \sum_{j=1}^{n_A} \tilde{A}_e^j \cap \sum_{i=1}^{n_B} \tilde{B}_e^i = \sum_{j=1}^{n_A} \sum_{i=1}^{n_B} \tilde{A}_e^j \cap \tilde{B}_e^i \tag{2.137}$$

$$A_e^j \cap B_e^i = u_1^j \wedge w_1^i / x_1 + u_2^j \wedge w_2^i / x_2 + \ldots + u_N^j \wedge w_N^i / x_N \tag{2.138}$$

$$A_e^j \cap B_e^i = [1/u_1^j \wedge w_1^i]/x_1 + [1/u_2^j \wedge w_2^i]/x_2 + \ldots + [1/u_N^j \wedge w_N^i]/x_N \tag{2.139}$$

$$\tilde{A}_s^j \cap \tilde{B}_s^i \equiv [\, F_{x_1} (u_1^j,\, w_1^i)/u_1^j \wedge w_1^i]\, /\, x_1 + \ldots + [F_{x_N}(\, u_N^j \wedge w_N^i)\, /$$
$$u_N^j \wedge w_N^i]\, / x_N \tag{2.140}$$

Theorem 2.6 [183] The *intersection* of two type-2 fuzzy sets $\tilde{A}$ and $\tilde{B}$ is given as

$$\tilde{A} \cap \tilde{B} = \sum_{j=1}^{n_A} \sum_{i=1}^{n_B} \{[\, F_{x_1} (u_1^j,\, w_1^i)/u_1^j \wedge w_1^i]/x_1 + \ldots + [F_{x_N} (\, u_N^j \wedge w_N^i)$$
$$u_N^j \wedge w_N^i]\, / x_N \tag{2.141}$$

where $F_{x_i} (u_i^j, w_i^i)$ is given in (2.132). Equation (2.141) can also be expressed as

$$\tilde{A} \cap \tilde{B} = \sum_{j=1}^{M_1\,(u_1)} \sum_{i=1}^{M_1\,(w_1)} [F_{x_1}(u_1^j,\, w_1^i)/\, u_1^j \wedge w_1^i)]/\, x_1 + \ldots +$$
$$\sum_{j=1}^{M_N\,(u_N)} \sum_{i=1}^{M_N\,(w_N)} [\, F_{x_N}(u_N^j,\, w_N^i)/\, u_N^j \wedge w_N^i]/\, x_N \tag{2.142}$$

Remark 2.29 The intersection of $\tilde{A}$ and $\tilde{B}$ is the discrete version of the first expression in (2.112), that is,

$$\tilde{A} \cap \tilde{B} \Leftrightarrow \mu_{\tilde{A} \cap \tilde{B}}(x,\, v) = \sum_{x \in X} \mu_{\tilde{A} \cap \tilde{B}}(x)/x \tag{2.143}$$

Remark 2.30 From the Extension Principle, we obtain the following expression for $\mu_{\tilde{A} \cap \tilde{B}}(x)$.
$$\mu_{\tilde{A} \cap \tilde{B}}(x) = \sum_{u \in J_x^u} \sum_{w \in J_x^w} f_x (u) * g_x (w)/(u \wedge w), \qquad x \in X. \tag{2.144}$$

Remark 2.31 An alternative approach to express (2.144), in terms of the secondary membership functions of $\tilde{A}$ and $\tilde{B}$, that is $\mu_{\tilde{A}} (x)$ and $\mu_{\tilde{B}} (x)$, is

$$\mu_{\tilde{A} \cap \tilde{B}}(x) = \sum_{u \in J_x^u} \sum_{w \in J_x^w} f_x (u) * g_x (w)\, /\, u \wedge w \equiv \mu_{\tilde{A}}(x) \sqcap \mu_{\tilde{B}}(x) \qquad x \in X \tag{2.145}$$

where $\sqcap$ denotes the so-called *meet* operation. The use of the notion $\mu_{\tilde{A}}(x) \sqcap \mu_{\tilde{B}} (x)$ to indicate the meet between the secondary membership functions $\mu_{\tilde{A}} (x)$ and $\mu_{\tilde{B}} (x)$ is, of course, a shorthand notation for the operations in the middle of (2.145).

Remark 2.32 Equation (2.142) is exactly the same as the combination of (2.143) and (2.144), because each term of (2.142) is the same as (2.144).

Remark 2.33. The result of (2.144) is derived from the Extension Principle, and we have obtain the same result without it.

Statement of Remark 2.27 also applies here.

Remark 2.33 Each of the N terms in (2.142) is a meet operation, so that we can describe the intersection of $\tilde{A}$ and $\tilde{B}$ as the union of N meets. The term "meet" is very useful because we can linguistically describe $\tilde{A} \cap \tilde{B}$.

COMPLEMENT OF TYPE-2 FUZZY SETS

The final application of the Representation Theorem 2.4 is to compute the complement of $\tilde{A}$.

Theorem 2.7 The complement of type-2 fuzzy set $\tilde{A}$ is given as

$$\sim\tilde{A} = \sum_{j=1}^{n_A}(\sum_{i=1}^{N}[f_{x_i}(u_i^j)/(1-u_i^j)]/x_i) \tag{2.146}$$

where n_A is given by (2.121). Equation (2.146) can also be expressed as

$$\sim\tilde{A} = \sum_{i=1}^{N}(\sum_{j=1}^{M_i}[f_{x_i}(u_i^j)/(1-u_i^j)]/x_i) \tag{2.147}$$

Remark 2.34 As the complement of $\tilde{A}$ is another type-2 fuzzy set, it follows from the discrete version of the first expression in (2.112), that is,

$$\sim\tilde{A} \Leftrightarrow \mu_{\sim\tilde{A}}(x,v) = \sum_{x \in X} \mu_{\sim\tilde{A}}(x)/x \tag{2.148}$$

Remark 2.35 From the Extension Principle, we obtain the following expression for $\mu_{\sim\tilde{A}}$;

$$\mu_{\sim\tilde{A}}(x) = \sum_{u \in J_x^u} f_x(u)/(1-u) \equiv \sim \mu_{\tilde{A}}(x) \qquad x \in X \tag{2.149}$$

in which $\sim$ denotes the so-called *negation* operation. The use of the notation $\sim\mu_{\tilde{A}}(x)$ to indicate the negation of the secondary membership function $\mu_{\tilde{A}}(x)$ is yet another shorthand notation, but this time for the operations in the middle of (2.149).

Remark 2.36 Equation (2.147) is exactly the same as the combination of (2.148) and (2.149), because each term of (2.147) is the same as (2.149).

Remark 2.37 The result of (2.149) is derived from the Extension Principle, and we have obtained the same result without it.

Remark 2.38 Each of the N terms in (2.147) is a negation operation, so that we can describe the complement of $\tilde{A}$ as the union of N negations. The term "negation" is very useful because we can linguistically describe $\tilde{A}$.

2.16.2 INTERVAL TYPE-2 FUZZY SETS

Interval type-2 fuzzy sets are the most widely used type-2 fuzzy sets because they are simple to use and because, at present, it is very difficult to justify the use of any other kind (for example, there is no best choice for a type-1 fuzzy set, so to compound this nonuniqueness by leaving the choice of the secondary membership functions arbitrary is hardly justifiable). When the type-2 fuzzy sets are interval type-2 fuzzy sets, all secondary grades (flags) equal 1 [for example, in (2.124) and (2.125), $\forall f_{x_i}\left(u_i^j\right) = 1$

and $\forall g_{x_i}\left(w_i^i\right) = 1$]. In this case we can treat embedded type-2 fuzzy sets as embedded tyuple-1 fuzzy sets [for example, (2.130) is the same as (2.128)] so that no new concepts are needed to derive the union, intersection, and complement of such sets. After each derivation, we merely append interval secondary grades to all the results in order to obtain the final formulas for the union, intersection, and complement of interval type-2 fuzzy sets [289].

Example 2.61 The Figure 69(a). shows type-1 fuzzy set. We consider the discrete domain, and the type 1 fuzzy set is represented as $\{0/2, 0.5/3, 1/4, 1/5, 0.6$ $7/6, 0.33/7, 0/8\}$.

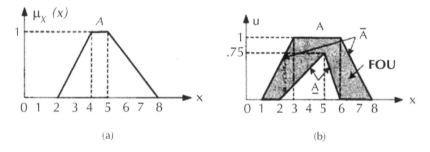

(a)   (b)

FIGURE 69   Examples of a T1 FS (a) and an IT2 FS (b).

The *membership function* (MF), type 1 fuzzy set can either be chosen based on the user's opinion (hence, the MFs from two individuals could be quite different depending upon their experiences, perspectives, cultures, and so on) or, it can be designed using optimization procedures.

There are limitations in the ability of type 1 fuzzy set to model and minimize the effect of uncertainties because a type 1 fuzzy set is certain in the sense that its membership grades are crisp values. Recently, type-2 FSs, characterized by MFs that are themselves fuzzy, have been attracting interests. Interval type-2 fuzzy set, a special case of type 2 fuzzy set, is widely used for its reduced computational cost.

The Figure 69(b). shows an interval type-2 fuzzy set $\tilde{A}$. Observe that unlike a type 1 fuzzy set whose membership for each element is a number, the membership of an interval type-2 fuzzy set is an interval. For instance, the membership of number 3 is [0.25, 1]. and the membership of number 5 is [0.75,1], Observe also that an IT2 FS is bounded from the above and below by two T1 FSs, $\bar{A}$ and $\underline{A}$, which are called upper MF (UMF) and lower MF (LMF), respectively. The area between $\bar{A}$ and $\underline{A}$ is the footprint of uncertainty (FOU).

Type-2 fuzzy sets are particularly useful when it is difficult to determine the exact MF, or in modeling the diverse opinions from different individuals. The MFs can be constructed from surveys or using optimization algorithms.

Various classes of Type-2 membership functions (MFs) are inspected, but a Interval Type-2 fuzzy sets, has been widely investigated and applied in various contexts such as decision making, time-series forecasting, control of mobile robots, and so on. Interval Type-2 fuzzy sets are the most widely used Type-2 fuzzy sets because they are simple to use and because it is very difficult to justify the use of any kind of Type-2 fuzzy sets. In this case, the MF $\mu_A(a)$ is an Interval Type-2 fuzzy set so that it can be represented by its lower and upper bounds (that is by two Type-1 MFs). This situation is depicted in Figure 70 and compared with other typologies of non Interval Type-2 MFs (denoted as General Type-2 MFs) [182].

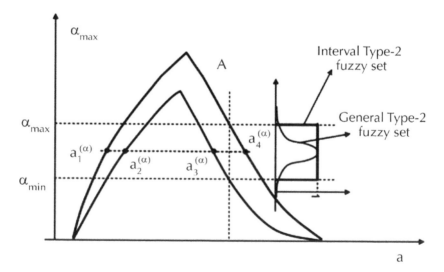

FIGURE 70   Example of an interval Type-2 MF.

In order to identify how to operate on this class of more complex fuzzy sets, the concept of interval of confidence of Type-2 is introduced. Let us recall now some basic notions. Assume that the lower and upper bounds of an interval of confidence, instead of being ordinary numbers, are fuzzy numbers, that themselves have intervals of confidence. We denote this kind of Type-2 interval of confidence as

$$A = [[a_1, a_2], [a_3, a_4]] ,$$

such that $a_1 \leq a_2 \leq a_3 \leq a_4$. When $a_1 = a_2$ and $a_3 = a_4$ the interval of confidence of Type-2 becomes an interval of Type-1 and if $a_1 = a_2 = a_3 = a_4$ the interval becomes of Type-0 (that is, a number). Consider now a sequence of intervals of confidence of Type-2 that depends on α, that is:

$$\forall \alpha \in [0, 1], \forall a_1^{(\alpha)}, a_2^{(\alpha)}, a_3^{(\alpha)}, a_4^{(\alpha)}$$

$$A_\alpha = [[a_1^{(\alpha)}, a_2^{(\alpha)}], [a_3^{(\alpha)}, a_4^{(\alpha)}]],$$

such that $a_1^{(\alpha)} \leq a_2^{(\alpha)} \leq a_3^{(\alpha)} \leq a_4^{(\alpha)}$.

To perform algebraic operations on Type-2 fuzzy sets let us consider now that a fuzzy number of Type-2 can be constructed in two ways.

1.   Given a Type-1 fuzzy number A and a convex fuzzy subset B we build a Type-2 fuzzy number as shown in Figure 71 (a). Note that we can identify a gamma of Type-1 MFs belonging to the range $[B,A]$, as for example the dotted MF.

2.   The second kind of construction considers a Type-1 fuzzy number A and its translation of a certain Δa thus obtaining Figure 71 (b).

The latter interpretation is commonly used. It can be seen as a blurring of a Type-1 MF around a central value, thus producing the corresponding Type-2 MF. Otherwise, the former representation is the one where the fuzzy subset B is naturally the inner MF (that is, a lower bound) and the fuzzy set A corresponds to the outer MF (that is, an upper bound). Thus we can construct the Type-2 MF in the context of uncertainty representation.

We can also consider the relation among Type-2 MF and random fuzzy variable (RFV). Let us consider a Type-2 fuzzy number by its α-cuts

$$[[a_1^{(\alpha)}, a_2^{(\alpha)}], [a_3^{(\alpha)}, a_4^{(\alpha)}]].$$

Now, let us assign to each segment $[a_1^{(\alpha)}, a_2^{(\alpha)}]$ and $[a_3^{(\alpha)}, a_4^{(\alpha)}]$ a probability density function (pdf) $f_L(\alpha, x)$ and $f_R(\alpha, x)$ respectively. Therefore, in the interval of confidence, the lower and the upper bounds become random variables. Figure 72 shows this concept, with F_L and F_R the probability distribution functions associated.

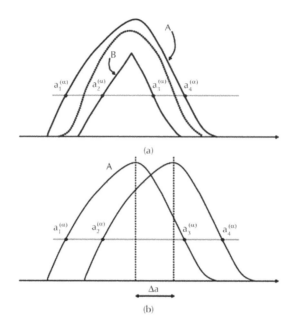

FIGURE 71   Two ways of building a Type-2 fuzzy number (a) and (b).

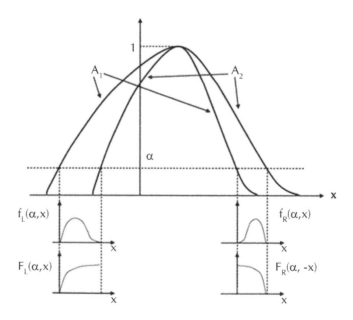

FIGURE 72   Random fuzzy variables embedded in Type-2 MFs.

The envelope of a RFV is a Type-2 fuzzy number, and the operations on the RFV are necessarily performed by sum-product convolution (since the confidence interval is represented by two pdfs). The operations on Type-2 fuzzy numbers can be performed by max-min convolution that corresponds to the use of the so called Extension Principle (EP) by Zadeh. They also show that the application of EP can be turned into working directly on $\alpha-$cuts, under the assumption of independent variables. Anyway, the use of RFV, is necessary when systematic errors or their corrections are partially unknown, so that standard approaches produce a wrong evaluation of uncertainty. In this case a particular class of rectangular Type-1 MF is embedded into the RFV, in order to model systematic errors or their incomplete correction.

INTERVAL TYPE-2 FUZZY LOGIC SYSTEM (IT2 FLS)

The Figure 73 shows the schematic diagram of an IT2 FLS. It is similar to its T1 counterpart, the major difference being that at least one of the FSs in the rule base is an IT2 FS. Hence, the outputs of the inference engine are IT2 FSs, and a type-reducer is needed to convert them into a T1 FS before defuzzification can be carried out [289].

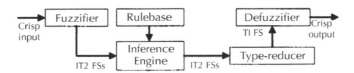

FIGURE 73 An Interval type 2 fuzy logic system.

In practice the computations in an IT2 FLS can be significantly simplified. Consider the rulebase of an IT2 FLS consisting of N rules assuming the following form:

$$R^n : IF\ x_1\ is\ \tilde{X}_1^n\ and...\ x_I\ is\ \tilde{X}_I^n,\ THEN\ y\ is\ Y^n\ n=1,2...N$$

where $\tilde{X}_i^n$ ($i = 1,...,I$) are IT2 FSs, and $Y^n = [\underline{y}^n, \overline{y}^n]$ is an interval, which can be understood as the centroid of a consequent IT2 FS^2, or the simplest TSK model, for its simplicity. In many applications we use $\underline{y}^n = \overline{y}^n$, that is, each rule consequent is a crisp number.

Assume the input vector is $x' = (x'_1,\ x'_2 .....x'_I)$. Typical computations in an IT2 FLS involve the following steps: [147]

1. Compute the membership of x'_i on each

$$X_{i,}^n[\mu \underline{X}_i^n(x_i^n), \mu \overline{X}_i^n((x_i'))], = 1,2,.........I, n = 1,2,......N$$

2. Compute the firing interval of the nth rule, $F^n(x')$:

$$F^n(x') = [\mu_{\underline{X}_1^n}(x_1') \times ... \times \mu_{\underline{X}_I^n}(x_I'), \mu_{\overline{X}_1^n}(x_1') \times ... \times \mu_{\overline{X}_I^n}(x_I')] \equiv \left[\underline{f^n}, \overline{f^n}\right], n = 1, ..., N$$

(2.150)

Note that the minimum, instead of the product, can be used in (2.150).

3. Perform type-reduction to combine $F^n(x')$ and the corresponding rule consequents. There are many such methods. The most commonly used one is the
center-of-sets type reducer:

$$Y_{cos}(x') = \bigcup_{\substack{f^n \in F^n(x') \\ y^n \in Y^n}} \frac{\sum_{n=1}^{N} f^n y^n}{\sum_{n=1}^{N} f^n} = [y_l, y_r]$$

(2.151)

It has been shown that:

$$y_l = \min_{k \in [1, N-1]} \frac{\sum_{n=1}^{k} \overline{f^n} y^n + \sum_{n=k+1}^{N} \underline{f^n} y^n}{\sum_{n=1}^{k} \overline{f^n} + \sum_{n=k+1}^{N} \underline{f^n}} \equiv \frac{\sum_{n=1}^{L} \overline{f^n} y^n + \sum_{n=L+1}^{N} \underline{f^n} y^n}{\sum_{n=1}^{L} \overline{f^n} + \sum_{n=L+1}^{N} \underline{f^n}}$$

(2.152)

$$y_r = \max_{k \in [1, N-1]} \frac{\sum_{n=1}^{k} \underline{f^n} \overline{y^n} + \sum_{n=k+1}^{N} \overline{f^n} \overline{y^n}}{\sum_{n=1}^{k} \underline{f^n} + \sum_{n=k+1}^{N} \overline{f^n}} \equiv \frac{\sum_{n=1}^{R} \underline{f^n} \overline{y^n} + \sum_{n=R+1}^{N} \overline{f^n} \overline{y^n}}{\sum_{n=1}^{R} \underline{f^n} + \sum_{n=R+1}^{N} \overline{f^n}}$$

(2.153)

where the *switch points* L and R are determined by

$$\underline{y}^L \leq y_l \leq \underline{y}^{L+1}$$

(2.154)

$$\underline{y}^R \leq y_r \leq \underline{y}^{R+1}$$

(2.155)

and $\{\underline{y}^n\}$ and $\{\overline{y}^n\}$ have been sorted in ascending order, respectively.

4. Compute the defuzzified output as, $y = \frac{y_l + y_r}{2}$, where (2.156)

y_l and y_r can be computed using the Karnik-Mendel (KM) algorithms [147] as
follows:

KM ALGORITHM FOR COMPUTING y_l.

Step 1. Sort $\underline{y}_n$ $(n = 1,2, ...,N)$ in increasing order and call the sorted $\underline{y}^n$ by the same name, but now $\underline{y}^1 \leq \underline{y}^2 \leq ... \leq \underline{y}^N$. Match the weights $F^n(x')$ with their respective $\underline{y}^n$ and renumber them so that their index corresponds to the renumbered $\underline{y}^n$.

Step 2. Intialize f^n by setting

$$f^n = \frac{\underline{f}^n + \overline{f}^n}{2} \quad n=1,2, ..., N \tag{2.157}$$

and then compute

$$y = \frac{\sum_{n=1}^N \underline{y}^n f^n}{\sum_{n=1}^N f^n} \tag{2.158}$$

Step 3. Find switch point k $(1 \leq k \leq N - 1)$ such that

$$\underline{y}^k \leq y \leq \underline{y}^{k+1} \tag{2.159}$$

Step 4. Set

$$f^n = \begin{cases} \overline{f}^n & n \leq k \\ \underline{f}^n & n > k \end{cases} \tag{2.160}$$

and compute

$$y' = \frac{\sum_{n=1}^N \underline{y}^n f^n}{\sum_{n=1}^N f^n} \tag{2.161}$$

Step 5. Check if $y'= y$. If yes, stop and set $y_l = y$ and $L = k$. If no, go to Step 6.

Step 6. Set $y = y'$ and go to Step 3.

KM ALGORITHM FOR COMPUTING y_r:

Step 1. Sort $\overline{y}^n$ $(n = 1,2, ...,N)$ in increasing order and call the sorted $\overline{y}^n$ by the same name, but now $\overline{y}^1 \leq \overline{y}^2 \leq \cdots \leq \overline{y}^N$. Match the weights $F^n(x')$ with their respective $\overline{y}^n$ and renumber them so that their index corresponds to the renumbered $\overline{y}^n$.

Step 2. Initialize f^n by setting

$$f^n = \frac{\underline{f}^n + \overline{f}^n}{2} \quad n=1,2, ..., N \tag{2.162}$$

and then compute

$$y = \frac{\sum_{n=1}^{N} \overline{y}^n f^n}{\sum_{n=1}^{N} f^n} \tag{2.163}$$

Step 3. Find switch point k $(1 \leq k \leq N - 1)$ such that

$$\overset{-k}{y} \leq y \leq \overset{-k+1}{y} \tag{2.164}$$

Step 4. Set

$$f^n = \begin{cases} \underline{f}^n & n \leq k \\ \overline{f}^n & n > k \end{cases} \tag{2.165}$$

and compute

$$y' = \frac{\sum_{n=1}^{N} \overline{y}^n f^n}{\sum_{n=1}^{N} f^n} \tag{2.166}$$

Step 5. Check if $y' = y$. If yes, stop and set $y_r = y$ and $R - k$. If no, go to Step 6.

Step 6. Set $y = y'$ and go to Step 3.

The main idea of the **KM** algorithm is to find the switch points for y_l and y_r. Take y_l for example. y_l is the minimum of $Y_{cos}(x')$. Since $\underline{y}^n$ increases from the left to the right along the horizontal axis of Figure 74, we choose a large weight (upper membership grade) for $\underline{y}^n$ on the left and a small weight (lower membership grade) for $\underline{y}^n$ on the right. The KM algorithm finds the switch point L. For $n \leq L$, the upper membership grades are used to calculate y_l; for $n > L$, the lower membership grades are used. This ensures y_l be the minimum.

y_l and y_r can also be computed more efficiently by many other algorithms.

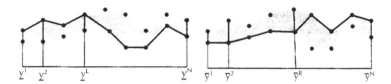

(left) Computing y_l; switch from the upper; (right) Computing y_r; switch from the lower firing

(left) level to the lower firing level; (right) level to the upper firing level.

FIGURE 74   Illustration of the switch points in computing y_l and yr.

There are many other ways to perform type-reduction and defuzzification. However, the KM method is the most widely used approach. So far IT2 FLSs have been used in almost all application areas of T1 FLSs, and better performances are reported from many experiments. The reason may be that IT2 FLSs can achieve input-output mappings which cannot be obtained from T1 FLSs. However, there is no theoretical results on when and how IT2 FLSs can outperform T1 FLSs [289].

Example 2.62 In this section, the mathematical operations in an IT2 FLS are illustrated using an example. Consider an 1T2 FLS that has two inputs (x_1 and x_2) and one output (y). Each input domain consists of two IT2 FSs, shown as the shaded areas in Figure 75

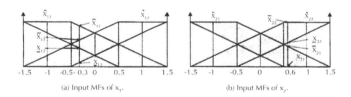

(a) Input MFs of x_1.   (b) Input MFs of x_2.

FIGURE 75   Membership Functions of the Interval Type 2 Fuzzy Logic System.

The rule base has the following four rules:

$$R^1: IF x_1 \text{ is } \tilde{X}_{11} \text{ and } x_2 \text{ is } \tilde{X}_{21}, THEN \ y \text{ is } Y^1$$

$$R^2: IF x_1 \text{ is } \tilde{X}_{11} \text{ and } x_2 \text{ is } \tilde{X}_{22}, THEN \ y \text{ is } Y^2$$

$$R^3: IF x_1 \text{ is } \tilde{X}_{12} \text{ and } x_2 \text{ is } \tilde{X}_{21}, THEN \ y \text{ is } Y^3$$

$$R^4: IF x_1 \text{ is } \tilde{X}_{12} \text{ and } x_2 \text{ is } \tilde{X}_{22}, THEN \ y \text{ is } Y^4$$

The complete rule base and the corresponding consequents are given in Table 8.

TABLE 8 Rulebase and consequence of the IT2 FLS

x_1 \ x_2	$\tilde{X}_{21}$	$\tilde{X}_{22}$
$\tilde{X}_{11}$	$Y^1 = [\underline{y}^1, \overline{y}^1] = [-1, -0.9]$	$Y^2 = [\underline{y}^2, \overline{y}^2] = [-0.6, -0.4]$
$\tilde{X}_{12}$	$Y^3 = [\underline{y}^3, \overline{y}^3] = [0.4, 0.6]$	$Y^4 = [\underline{y}^4, \overline{y}^4] = [0.9, 1]$

Consider an input vector x' = (x_1', x_2') = (-0.3, 0.6). The firing intervals of the four IT2 FSs are:

$$\left[\mu\underline{X}_{11}(x_1'), \mu\overline{X}_{11}(x_1')\right] = [0.4, 0.9] \qquad (2.167)$$

$$\left[\mu\underline{X}_{12}(x_1'), \mu\overline{X}_{12}(x_1')\right] = [0.1, 0.6] \qquad (2.168)$$

$$\left[\mu\underline{X}_{21}(x_2'), \mu\overline{X}_{21}(x_2')\right] = [0, 0.45] \qquad (2.169)$$

$$\left[\mu\underline{X}_{22}(x_2'), \mu\overline{X}_{22}(x_2')\right] = [0.55, 1] \qquad (2.170)$$

The firing intervals of the four rules are given in Table 9. [289]

TABLE 9 Firing intervals of rules

Rule No.	Firing Interval	Consequent

R^1: $\left[\underline{f}^1, \overline{f}^1\right] = [\mu\underline{X}_{11}(x_1) \cdot \mu\underline{X}_{21}(x_2'), \mu\overline{X}_{11}(x_1') \cdot \mu\overline{X}_{21}(x_2')] \rightarrow [\underline{y}^1, \overline{y}^1] = [-1, -0.9]$

$$= [0.4 \times 0, 0.9 \times 0.45] = [0, 0.405]$$

R^2: $\left[\underline{f}^2, \overline{f}^2\right] = [\mu\underline{X}_{11}(x_1') \cdot \mu\underline{X}_{22}(x_2'), \mu\overline{X}_{11}(x_1') \cdot \mu\overline{X}_{22}(x_2')] \rightarrow [\underline{y}^2, \overline{y}^2] = [-0.6, -0.4]$
$$= [0.4 \times 0.55, 0.9 \times 1] = [0.22, 0.9]$$

R^3: $\left[\underline{f}^3, \overline{f}^3\right] = [\mu\underline{X}_{12}(x_1') \cdot \mu\underline{X}_{21}(x_2'), \mu\overline{X}_{12}(x_1') \cdot \mu\overline{X}_{21}(x_2')] \rightarrow [\underline{y}^3, \overline{y}^3] = [0.4, 0.6]$
$$= [0.1 \times 0, 0.6, \times 0.45] = [0, 0.27]$$

R^4: $\left[\underline{f}^4, \overline{f}^4\right] = [\mu\underline{X}_{12}(x_1') \cdot \mu\underline{X}_{22}(x_2'), \mu\overline{X}_{12}(x_1') \cdot \mu\overline{X}_{22}(x_2')] \rightarrow [\underline{y}^4, \overline{y}^4] = [-0.9, 1]$
$$= [0.1 \times 0.55, 0.6, \times 1] = [0.055, 0.6]$$

From the KM algorithms, we find that $L = 1$ and $R = 3$. So,

$$y_l = \frac{\overline{f}^1 \underline{y}^1 + \underline{f}^2 \underline{y}^2 + \underline{f}^3 \underline{y}^3 + \underline{f}^4 \underline{y}^4}{\overline{f}^1 + \underline{f}^2 + \underline{f}^3 + \underline{f}^4}$$

$$= \frac{0.405 \; x \; (-1) + 0.22 \; x \; (-0.6) + 0 \; x \; 0.4 + 0.055 x 0.9}{0.405 + 0.22 + 0 + 0.055}$$

$$= -0.7169$$

$$y_r = \frac{\underline{f}^1 \overline{y}^1 + \underline{f}^2 \overline{y}^2 + \underline{f}^3 \overline{y}^3 + \overline{f}^4 \overline{y}^4}{\underline{f}^1 + \underline{f}^2 + \underline{f}^3 + \overline{f}^4}$$

$$= \frac{0 \; x \; (-0.9) + 0.22 \; x \; (-0.4) + 0 \; x \; 0.6 + 0.6 \; x \; 1}{0 + 0.22 + 0 + 0.6}$$

$$= 0.6244$$

Finally, the crisp output of the IT2 FLS, y, is:

$$y = \frac{y_l + y_r}{2} = \frac{-0.7169 + 0.6244}{2} = -0.0463.$$

2.16.3 SOME REMARKS ON FUZZY SETS OF TYPE-2

The fundamental object for a "fuzzy set theory" is an algebra of truth values. For ordinary fuzzy sets, or fuzzy sets of type-1, that algebra, which we denote by **I**, is the unit interval with the usual max, min, and negation, and constants 0 and 1 [286].

A fuzzy subset of a set S (usually referred to as a **fuzzy set**) is a mapping $f\colon S \to [0,1]$, and operations on these mappings come pointwise from operations on $[0,1]$, yielding the algebra of fuzzy subsets of S. To understand the algebraic properties of the algebra of fuzzy subsets of S, one must understand those of **I**. This is a special case of a general phenomenon.

There are many ways to generalize the notion of fuzzy subset of type-1. For example, instead of taking mappings $f\colon S \to [0,1]$ we can take other relations in $S \times [0,1]$. But in the spirit of fuzzy sets, we want a mapping that associates with an element $s \in S$ something that is a measure of a degree of "belonging." So the natural thing to do is to generalize the algebra **I** of truth values. What does this mean? A reasonable meaning is to use an algebra **A** of truth values that contains **I** as a subalgebra, or more precisely that contains a subalgebra isomorphic to **I**. Then, mappings of a set into **A** that go into that subalgebra would be ordinary fuzzy sets. But **I** should be contained in **A** in a special way. There should be a "natural" copy of it in **A**.

A common generalization of the algebra **I** is an algebra $I^{[2]}$ consisting of pairs (a, b) with $0 \le a \le b \le 1$, and appropriate coordinate operations. Mappings $f: S \to I^{[2]}$ are interval-valued fuzzy sets, which have come to play a big role in applications. The applications of type-2 fuzzy sets tend to be applications of interval-valued ones.

Type-2 fuzzy sets are mappings into the set of fuzzy subsets of the unit interval. The usual operations put on $Map([0,1], [0,1])$ to make it into an appropriate algebra are certain convolutions of the operations of **I**, and are the ones proposed by Zadeh, resulting in an algebra **M** of truth values. Again, mappings $f: S \to M$ are fuzzy sets of type-2. Not only are **I** and $I^{[2]}$ subalgebras of **M**, but they are characteristic subalgebras. This means that automorphisms of **M** induce automorphisms of these subalgebras. Intuitively, **M** has no flther subalgebra isomorphic to **I** sitting in **M** in the same way, and similarly for $I^{[2]}$ [286].

Type-1 Fuzzy Sets

The fundamental object for a "fuzzy set theory" is a algebra of truth values. For ordinary fuzzy sets, or fuzzy sets of type-1, that algebra is

$$\mathbf{I} = ([0, 1], \vee, \wedge, ', 0, 1) \tag{2.171}$$

with operations

$$x \ y = max \ \{x, y\} \tag{2.172}$$

$$x \wedge y = min \ \{x, y\}$$

$$x' = 1 - x$$

and the nullary operations 0 and 1. The following equations hold in the algebra **I**.

1. $x \wedge x = x; x \vee x = x$ (idempotent)
2. $x \wedge y = y \wedge x; x \vee y = y \vee x$ (commutative)
3. $x \wedge (y \wedge z) = (x \wedge y) \wedge z; x \vee (y \vee z) = (x \vee y) \vee z$ (associative)
4. $x \wedge (y \vee y) = x; x \vee (x \wedge y) = x$ (absorption laws)
5. $x \wedge (y \ z) = (x \ y) \vee (x \ z); x \vee (y \wedge z) = (x \vee y) \wedge (x \vee z)$ (distributive laws)
6. $0 \vee x = x; 1 \wedge x = x$ (identities)
7. $x'' = x$ (involution)
8. $(x \wedge y)' = x' \vee y'; (x \vee y)' = x' \wedge y'$ (De Morgan's laws)
9. $x \wedge x' \le y \vee y'$ (Kleene inequality)

This is summarized by saying that $([0,1], \wedge, \vee, ', 0, 1)$ is a bounded distributive lattice with an involution ' that satisfies De Morgan's laws and the Kleene inequality, that is, **I** is a **Kleene algebra**. An algebra satisfying the first eight equations is a **De Morgan algebra**. It is also true that any equation holding in $([0,1], \vee, \wedge, ', 0, 1)$ is a consequence of the equations above.

For a set S, a **fuzzy subset** of S is a mapping of S into this algebra of fuzzy truth values. The corresponding operations on the set $[0, 1]^s$ of all fuzzy subsets of S are given pointwise by the formulas

$$(A \wedge B)(s) = A(s) \wedge B(s) \qquad\qquad (2.173)$$

$$(A \vee B)(s) = A(s) \vee B(s)$$

$$A'(s) = (A(s))'$$

and the two nullary operations are given by $1(s) = 1$ and $0(s) = 0$ for all $s \in S$. Thus F $(S) = ([0, 1]^s, \vee, \wedge, ', 0, 1)$ is also a Kleene algebra. It satisfies exactly the same equations as does I. In fact, $[0, 1]^S$ may be viewed as the Cartesian product $[0, 1]^S = \Pi_{s \in S}$ $[0, 1]$ of copies of $[0,1]$, one copy for each element of S. Then the operations become coordinatewise. For example, for two elements $\{x_s\}_{s \in S}$ and $\{y_s\}_{sS}$ in $\Pi_{s \in S} [0,1]$, $\{x\}_{sS}$ $\vee \{y_s\}_{s \in S} = \{x_s \vee y_s\}_{s \in S}$. These are just two ways of viewing the same thing, and this is clearly a general phenomenon.

The converse also holds: if an equation holds in $([0, 1]^s, \vee, \wedge, ', 0, 1)$, then it holds in $\Pi_{s \in S}[0, 1]$ with the coordinate operations. So to determine what equations hold in F (S) it suffices to determine those that hold in I. More is true. There is a three-element Kleene algebra, in fact the three element chain, denoted 3, with the obvious operations, that satisfies exactly the same equations as does I. This is expressed by saying that 3 and I generate the same variety. A **variety** of algebras is a class of algebras that is closed under taking subalgebras, homomorphic images, and products. The variety generated by an algebra is the smallest variety containing that algebra. A pertinent point is that two algebras generate the same variety if and only if they satisfy exactly the same equations.

Quite frequently, in applications an additional operation is put on I, that of a t-norm. A **t-norm** on $[0, 1]$ is a binary operation Δ on $[0, 1]$ satisfying, for all $x, y, z \in [0, 1]$,

1. $1 \Delta x = x$ (1 is an identity element)
2. $x \Delta y = y \Delta x$ (commutativity)
3. $(x \Delta y) \Delta z = x \Delta (y \Delta z)$ (associativity)
4. $x \Delta (y \ z) = (x \ y) \vee (x \Delta z)$ (monotonicity)

In both applications and theory of fuzzy sets, t-norms play a big role. The basic examples from which others are built are the following:

- $x \Delta y = x \wedge y$ (minimum)
- $x \Delta y = xy$ (product)
- $0 \vee (x + y - 1)$ (Lukasiewicz t-norm).

In interval-valued and in type-2 fuzzy sets, t-norms will no doubt come to play an increasingly important role.

INTERVAL-VALUED FUZZY SETS

For interval-valued fuzzy sets, the algebra of truth values is:

$$\mathbf{I}^{[2]} = ([0, 1]^{[2]}, \vee, \wedge, ', (0, 0), (1, 1)) \tag{2.174}$$

with

$$[0, 1]^{[2]} = \{(a, b) : a, b \in [0, 1], a \le b\} \tag{2.175}$$

$$(a, b) \vee (c, d) = (a \vee c, b \vee d)$$

$$(a, b) \wedge (c, d) = (a \wedge c, b \wedge d)$$

$$(a, b)' = (b', a')$$

and the nullary operations $(0, 0)$ and $(1, 1)$. This algebra is a bounded distributive lattice with an involution ' that satisfies De Morgan's laws. It is not a Kleene algebra. For a set S, an **interval-valued fuzzy subset** of S is a mapping into this algebra of truth values, with operations on the set of such mappings given point-wise, and as in the type-1 case, yielding again an algebra $I(S)$ of the same type satisfying exactly the same equations. Here, there is a four-element De Morgan algebra that generates the same variety as does $\mathbf{I}^{[2]}$.

Type-2 Fuzzy Sets

The algebra of truth values for fuzzy sets of type-2 is much more complicated than those for type-1 and interval-valued ones. The basic set is that of all mappings of $[0, 1]$ into $[0, 1]$, and the operations are certain convolutions of operations on $[0, 1]$,

Definition 2.53 On $[0,1]^{[0,\,1]}$, let

$$(f \cup g)(x) \underset{y \vee z = x}{\vee} (f(y) \wedge g(z))$$

$$(f \cap g)(x) = \underset{y \wedge z = x}{\vee} (f(y) \wedge g(z)) \tag{2.176}$$

$$f^*(x) = \underset{y' = x}{\vee} f(y) = f(x')$$

$$\bar{1}(x) = \begin{cases} 1 \ if \ x = 1 \\ 0 \ if \ x \ne 1 \end{cases}$$

$$\bar{0}(x) = \begin{cases} 1 \ if \ x = 0 \\ 0 \ if \ x \neq 0 \end{cases}$$

The algebra of truth values for type-2 fuzzy sets is

$$M = \left([0,1]^{[01]}, \sqcup, \sqcap, *, \bar{0}, \bar{1}\right) \tag{2.177}$$

A fuzzy subset of type-2 of a set S is a mapping $f: S \rightarrow [0,1]^{[01]}$, and operations on the set $F_2(S)$ of all such fuzzy subsets are given pointwise from the operations in M. Thus we have the algebra $F_2(S) = \left(Map(S, [0,1]^{[0,1]}), \sqcup, \sqcap, *, \bar{0}, \bar{1}\right)$ of fuzzy subsets of type-2 of the set S. Again, the same equations hold in $F_2(S)$ as in M. At this point, it is not clear how type-2 generalizes type-1 and interval-valued fuzzy sets. At least, the algebras of truth values of type-1 and of interval-valued fuzzy sets should be subalgebras of M.

Determining the properties of the algebra M is a bit tedious, but is helped by introducing the auxiliary operations in the following definition.

Definition 2.54 For $f \in M$, let f^L and f^R be the elements of M defined by

$$f^L(x) = \vee_{y \leq x} f(y) \tag{2.178}$$

$$f^R(x) = \vee_{y \geq x} f(y) .$$

Note that f^L is monotone increasing, f^R is monotone decreasing, and they are the pointwise smallest such that lie above f. The point of this definition is that the operations $\sqcup$ and $\sqcap$ in **M** can be expressed in terms of the pointwise max and min of functions, as follows.

Theorem 2.8 *The following hold for all* $f, g \in$ **M**.

$$f \sqcup g = (f \wedge g^L) \vee (f^L \wedge g) = (f \vee g) \wedge (f^L \wedge g^L)$$

$$f \sqcap g = (f \wedge g^R) \vee (f^R \wedge g) = (f \vee g) \wedge (f^R \wedge g^R) \tag{2.179}$$

Using these auxiliary operations, it is fairly routine to verify the following properties of the algebra **M**.

Corollary 2.1 *Let* $f, g, h \in$ **M**. *The basic properties of* M *follow.*

1. $f \sqcup f = f; f \sqcap f = f$ *(indempotent)*

2. $f \sqcup g = g \sqcup f; f \sqcap g = g \sqcap f$ (commutative)

3. $\bar{1} \sqcap f = f; \bar{0} \sqcup f = f$ (identity for each operation)

4. $f \sqcup (g \sqcup h) = (f \sqcup g) \sqcup h; f \sqcap (g \sqcap h) = (f \sqcap g) \sqcap h$ (associative)

5. $f \sqcup (f \sqcap g) = f \sqcap (f \sqcup g)$

6. $f^{**} = f$

7. $(f \sqcup g)^* = f^* \sqcap g^*; (f \sqcap g)^* = f^* \sqcup g^*$ (De Morgan laws)

Notice that this list does not include the absorption laws or distributive laws. In particular, the algebra **M** is not a lattice.

2.17   RELATION

A classical relation can be considered as a set of tuples, where a tuple is an ordered pair. A binary tuple is denoted by(u,v), a ternary tuple is denoted by (u, v, w), and an *n*-ary tuple is denoted by $(x_1, x_2, \dots, x_n)$.

Example 2.63 Let X be the domain of boy {John, Charles, James}, and Y be the domain of girl {Diana, Rita, Eva}.The relation "brother-sister" on X × Y is,can be expressed as,

{(Charles, Diana), (John, Eva),(James, Rita) }.

Definition 2.55 Let $X_1, \dots, X_n$ be classical sets. The subsets of the Cartesian product $X_1 \times \dots \times X_n$ are called an n-ary relations. If $X_1 = \dots = X_n$ and $R \subset X^n$ then R is called an n-ary relation in X.

Let R be binary relation in R. Then the characteristic function R is defined as

$$\chi_R(x_1, x_2) = \begin{cases} 1 \ if (x_1, x_2) \in R \\ 0 \ otherwise \, . \end{cases}$$

Let R be a binary relation in a classical set X. Then

Definition 2.56 R is reflexive if $\forall x \in X: (x,x) \in R$.

Definition 2.57 R is anti-reflexive if $\forall x \in X: (x,x) \notin R$.

Definition 2.58 R is summetric if from $(x_1, x_2) \in R \rightarrow (x_1, x_2) \in R, \forall x_1, x_2 \in X$.

Definition 2.59 R is anti-symmetric if $(x_1, x_2) \in R$ and $(x_1, x_2) \in R$ then $x_1 = x_2, \forall x_1, x_2 \in X$.

Definition 2.60 R is transitive if $(x_1, x_2) \in R$ and $(x_2, x_3) \in R$ then $(x_1, x_3) \in R, \forall x_1, x_2, x_3 \in X$.

Some important properties of binary relations are:

Property 2.3 R is an equivalence relation if, R is reflexive, symmetric and transitive.

Property 2.4 R is a partial order relation if it is reflexive, anti-symmetric and transitive.

Property 2.5 R is a total order relation if it is partial ordr and $\forall x_1$, $x_2 \in R, (x_1, x_2) \in R$ or $(x_1, x_2) \in R$ hold.

2.17.1 FUZZY RELATION

Definition 2.61 Let X and Y be nonempty sets. A fuzzy relation R is a fuzzy subset of X × Y.

In other words, $R \in F(X \times Y)$.
If X = Y then we say that R is a binary fuzzy relation in X.

Let R be a binary fuzzy relation. Then $R(x_1, x_2)$ is interpreted as the degree of membership of the ordered pari (x_1, x_2) in R.

Example 2.64 A binary fuzzy relation on
X = {1, 2, 3},
Say "approximately equal" can be represented as,

$$R(1, 1) = R(2, 2) = R(3, 3) = 1$$

$$R(1, 2) = R(2, 1) = R(2, 3) = R(3, 2) = 0.7$$

$$R(1, 3) = R(3, 1) = 0.2$$

The membership function of R is given by

$$R(x_1, x_2) = \begin{cases} 1 & \text{if } u = v \\ 0.7 & \text{if } |u - v| = 1 \\ 0.2 & \text{if } |u - v| = 2 \end{cases}$$

In matrix notation it can be represented as

$$\begin{array}{c c c c} & 1 & 2 & 3 \\ \begin{matrix} 1 \\ 2 \\ 3 \end{matrix} & \begin{pmatrix} 1 & 0.8 & 0.2 \\ 0.7 & 1 & 0.7 \\ 0.2 & 0.7 & 1 \end{pmatrix} \end{array}.$$

Remark 2.15 The relation is one of the key concepts in mathematics. The same is true for the fuzzy relation in fuzzy mathematics.

Example 2.65 Let X={horse, donkey} and Y={mule, cow}. The fuzzy relation R-labelled "similarity" may be, for example, as follows;

"similarity" = 0.8/(horse, mule) + 0.4/(horse, cow) + 0.9 /(donkey, mule) + 0.2/(donkey, cow).

The particular grades of membership give the degree to which the respective animals are similar, for example, a horse and a mule are similar to the degree 0.8, that is quite considerably, while a donkey and a cow are similar to the degree 0.2 only, that is not very much. Thus, as opposed to the nonfuzzy case in which any two elements may only be or not be in a relation, we now have the strength of the relation: from being fully in relation (1), through all the intermediate values (between 1 and 0), to not being fully in relation (0).

Let us notice that the above fuzzy relation "similarity", as well as any fuzzy relation in a finite Cartesian product, may be represented in the following matrix form:

mule cow

$$\text{"similarity"} = \begin{array}{c} \text{horse} \\ \text{donkey} \end{array} \begin{bmatrix} 0.8 & 0.4 \\ 0.9 & 0.2 \end{bmatrix}$$

The matrix form is very convenient for dealing with fuzzy relations.

Definition 2.62 A fuzzy relation R is called
i.   reflexive if and only if for all x ∈ X: R(x, x) = 1,
ii.   symmetric if and only if for all x,y∈ X: R(x, x) = R(y, x),
iii.   t-transitive if and only if for all x,y,z∈ X: T(R(x, y), R(y, z)) ≤ R(z, x).

A reflexive, symmetric and t-transitive fuzzy relation is called t-equivalence relation. Detail classification of fuzzy relation is discussed in section 2.17.4.

GENERATING FUZZY RELATION

As fuzzy relations are fuzzy sets on X × Y all aggregation operators are applicable.

Example 2.66 Let X = {A, B, C} be a set of three persons labeled 1, 2 and 3, respectively, and Y = {D, E} be a set of two different cars labeled by 1 and 2 respectively. We define two fuzzy relations R and Q on X × Y meaning "x likes y" and "x wants to buy y", as follows:

$$R = \begin{bmatrix} 0.3 & 0.9 \\ 1.0 & 0.0 \\ 0.1 & 0.6 \end{bmatrix} \quad Q = \begin{bmatrix} 0.5 & 0.8 \\ 1.0 & 0.2 \\ 0.0 & 1.0 \end{bmatrix}$$

We define an OWA operator u with associated weighting vector w = $[0.2 \ 0.8]^T$. Therefore,

$$X(R, Q) = \begin{bmatrix} 0.34 & 0.82 \\ 1.00 & 0.04 \\ 0.02 & 0.68 \end{bmatrix}$$

The entries in (R, Q) are created as follows:

Entry $(1,1)$: $a = (0.3\ 0.5) \Rightarrow a_\pi = (0.5\ 0.3)$.
Hence, $u(a) = 0.2 \times 0.5 + 0.8 \times 0.3 = 0.34$.

Entry $(2, 1)$: $a = (1.0\ 1.0) \Rightarrow a_\pi = a$.
Hence, $u(a) = 0.2 \times 1 + 0.8 \times 1 = 1.00$.

Entry $(2, 2)$: $a = (0.0\ 0.2) \Rightarrow a_\pi = (0.2\ 0.0)$.
Hence, $u(a) = 0.2 \times 0.2 + 0.8 \times 0 = 0.04$.

Entry $(3, 1)$: $a = (0.1\ 0.0) \Rightarrow a_\pi = a$.
Hence, $u(a) = 0.2 \times 0.1 + 0.8 \times 0 = 0.02$.

Entry $(3, 2)$: $a = (0.6\ 1.0) \Rightarrow a_\pi = (1.0\ 0.6)$.
Hence, $u(a) = 0.2 \times 1 + 0.8 \times 0.6 = 0.68$.

We can now define a fuzzy relation R on $X \times Y$ by means of fuzzy sets $A \in F(U)$ and $B \in F(V)$, as follows:

Entry $(1, 2)$: $a = (0.9\ 0.8) \Rightarrow a_\pi = (0.9\ 0.8)$.
Hence, $u(a) = 0.2 \times 0.9 + 0.8 \times 0.8 = 0.82$.

Definition 2.63 Let $A \in F(X)$, $B \in F(Y)$ and Agg: $[0,1]^2 \to [0,1]$ be any aggregation operator. A fuzzy relation R on $X \times Y$ is an Agg-relation if for all $(x,y) \in X \times Y$, $R(x,y) = \text{Agg}(A(x), B(y))$.

- If Agg is the min-operator then we may write $R = A x\, B$. In this case R is also called as Cartesian product of A and B.
- A many-valued implication operator i: $[0,1]^2 \to [0,1]$ gives the membership values for all pairs $(x,y) \to [0,1] \in X \times Y$ in the fuzzy relation $R \subseteq X \times Y$ meaning "if x is in A then y is in B". Notice that $A(x)$ and $B(y)$ may be considered as truth values for the propositions "x is in A" and "y is in B" respectively.
- If Agg is a many-valued implication operator i, $A \in F(X)$ and $B \in F(Y)$ then we assign for all $(x,y) \in X \times Y$,

$$R(x,y) = i(A(x), B(y)) = A(x) \to B(y).$$

Of course, we write $R = A \to B$.
There is a large class of aggregation operators which may be unused to determine $A \to B$.

Example 2.67 Let $a,b, \in [0, 1]$. The following operators are (just a few examples) widely used in applications:

- Lukasiwitcz implication $a \rightarrow b = \min\{1, 1 - a + b\}$.
- Gödel implication $a \rightarrow b = \begin{cases} 1, & if\ a \le b, \\ b, & otherwise. \end{cases}$
- Mamdani implication $a \rightarrow b = \min\{a, b\}$.
- Larsen implication $a \rightarrow b = ab$.
- Kleene-Dienes implication $a \rightarrow b = \max\{1 - a, b\}$.

Example 2.68 Let $X = \{1,2,3,4\}$ and $A \in F(X)$ such that $A \triangleq [0.0\ 0.5\ 0.1\ 1.0$. Let $Y = \{1,2,3\}$ and $B \in F(Y)$ such that $B \triangleq [0.1\ 0.4\ 1.0]^2$. Using Mamdani implication we have

$$R = A \rightarrow B = \begin{bmatrix} 0.0 & 0.0 & 0.0 \\ 0.1 & 0.4 & 0.5 \\ 0.1 & 0.1 & 0.1 \\ 0.1 & 0.4 & 1.0 \end{bmatrix}.$$

2.17.2 OPERATIONS ON FUZZY RELATIONS

Fuzzy relations are very important because they can describe interactions between variables. Let R and S be two binary fuzzy relations on $X \times Y$.

Definition 2.64 The intersection of R and S is defined by:

$$(R \wedge S)(x, y) = \min\{R(x, y), S(x, y)\}.$$

Definition 2.65 The union of R and S is defined by:

$$(R \vee S)(x, y) = \max\{R(x, y), S(x, y)\}.$$

Example 2.69 Let $X = \{9, 10, 11\}$ and $Y = \{1, 2, 3, 4\}$. Let us define two binary relations

$$R = \text{"x is much larger than y"}$$

$$\begin{array}{cccc} & & & x_1 \\ y_1 & y_2 & y_3 & y_4 = x_2 \\ & & & x_3 \end{array} \left(\begin{array}{cccc} 0.9 & 0.1 & 0.1 & 0.7 \\ 0 & 0.9 & 0 & 0 \\ 0.9 & 1 & 0.7 & 0.9 \end{array} \right) \text{ and }$$

$$S = \text{"x is much close to y"}$$

$$y_1 \quad y_2 \quad y_3 \quad y_4 = \begin{matrix} x_1 \\ x_2 \\ x_3 \end{matrix} \begin{pmatrix} 0.5 & 0 & 0.9 & 0.6 \\ 0.9 & 0.5 & 0.6 & 0.7 \\ 0.3 & 0 & 0.8 & 0.6 \end{pmatrix}.$$

The intersection of R and S means that "x is much large than y" **and** "x is much close to y"

$$y_1 \quad y_2 \quad y_3 \quad y_4$$

$$(R \wedge S)(x,y) = \begin{matrix} x_1 \\ x_2 \\ x_3 \end{matrix} \begin{pmatrix} 0.5 & 0 & 0.1 & 0.6 \\ 0 & 0.5 & 0 & 0 \\ 0.3 & 0 & 0.7 & 0.6 \end{pmatrix}.$$

The union of R and S means that "x is much larger than y" **or** "x is much close to y".

$$y_1 \quad y_2 \quad y_3 \quad y_4$$

$$(R \vee S)(x,y) = \begin{matrix} x_1 \\ x_2 \\ x_3 \end{matrix} \begin{pmatrix} 0.9 & 0 & 0.9 & 0.7 \\ 0.9 & 0.9 & 0.6 & 0.7 \\ 0.9 & 1 & 0.8 & 0.9 \end{pmatrix}.$$

Consider a classical relation R.

$$R(x, y) = \begin{cases} 1 & \text{if } (x,y) \in [a, b] \times [0,c] \\ 0 & otherwise \end{cases}.$$

It is clear that the projection (or **Shadow**) of R on the X-axis is the closed interval [a,b] and its projection on the Y-axis is [0,c] (see Figure 76).
If R is a classical relation in X × Y then

$$\Pi_X = \{x \in X | \exists y \in Y : (x, y) \in R\}$$

$$\Pi_Y = \{y \in Y | \exists x \in X : (x, y) \in R\}$$

where Π_X denotes projection on X and Π_Y denotes projection on Y.

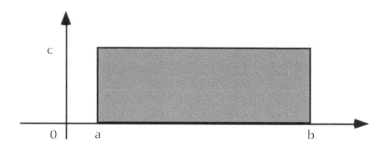

FIGURE 76   Projection of R on the x axis is [a,b] and on the y axis is [0,c].

Definition 2.66 Let R be a fuzzy binary fuzzy relation on X × Y. The projection of R on X is defined as

$$\Pi_X (x) = \sup \{R (x,y)|\, y \in Y\}$$

and the projection of R on Y is defined as

$$\Pi_Y (y) = \sup \{R (x,y)|\, x \in X\}.$$

Example 2.70 Consider the relation
R = "x is considerable larger than y"

$$\begin{array}{cccc} y_1 & y_2 & y_3 & y_4 \end{array} = \begin{array}{c} x_1 \\ x_2 \\ x_3 \end{array}\begin{pmatrix} 0.8 & 0.1 & 0.1 & 0.7 \\ 0 & 0.8 & 0 & 0 \\ 0.9 & 1 & 0.7 & 0.8 \end{pmatrix}$$

Then the projection on X means that

- x_1 is assigned the highest membership degree from the tuples $(x_1, y_1), (x_1, y_2), (x_1, y_3), (x_1, y_4)$, that is $\Pi_X (x_1)= 1$, which is the maximum of the first now.
- x_2 is assigned the highest membership degree from the tuples $(x_2, y_1), (x_2, y_2), (x_2, y_3), (x_2, y_4)$, that is $\Pi_X (x_2)= 0.8$, which is the maximum of the second row.
- x_3 is assigned the highest membership degree from the tuples $(x_3, y_1), (x_3, y_2), (x_3, y_3), (x_3, y_4)$, that is $\Pi_X (x_3) = 1$, which is the maximum of the third row.

The Figure 77 shows the shadows of a fuzzy relation.

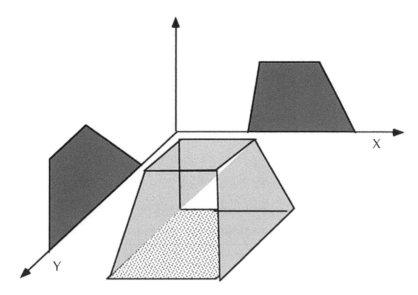

FIGURE 77   Shadows of a fuzzy relation.

Example 2.71 Let $\tilde{R}$ be a fuzzy relation defined by the following relational matrix. The first, second and total projections are then shown at the appropriate places below.

		y_1	y_2	y_3	y_4	y_5	y_6	1st projection $[\mu_R^{(1)}(x)]$
R:	x_1	.1	.2	.4	.8	1	.8	1
	x_2	.2	.4	.8	1	.8	.6	1
	x_3	.4	.8	1	.8	.4	.2	1

The relation resulting from applying an operation of projection to another relation is also called a "shadow". Let us now consider a more general space: $X = X_1 \times \ldots \times X_n. R_q$ be a projection on $X_{i_1} \times \ldots \times X_{i_k}$, where $(i_1, \ldots, i_k)$ is a subsequence of $(1, \ldots, n)$. It is obvious that distinct fuzzy relations in the same universe can have the same projection. There must, however, be a uniquely defined largest relation $R_{qL}(X_1 \times \ldots \times X_n)$ with $\mu_{R_q}(x_{i_1} \times \ldots \times x_{i_k})$ for each projection. This largest relation is called the *cylindrical extension of the projection relation.*

Definition 2.67 $R_{qL} \subseteq X$ is the largest relation in X the projection of which is $R_q. R_{qL}$ is then called the cylindrical extension of R_q and R_q the base of R_{qL} .

Example 2.72 The cylindrical extension of $R^{(2)}$ (example 2.71) is

$R_2:$

	y_1	y_2	y_3	y_4	y_5	y_6
x_1	.4	.8	1	1	1	.8
x_2	.4	.8	1	1	1	.8
x_3	.4	.8	1	1	1	.8

Definition 2.68 Let R be a fuzzy relation on $X = X_1 \times ... \times X_n$ and R_1 and R_2 be two fuzzy projections on $X_1 \times ... \times X_r$ respectively, with $s \leq r + 1$ and R_{1L}, R_{2L} their respective cylindrical extensions.

The join of R_1 and R_2 is then defined as $R_{1L} \cap R_{2L}$ and their meet as $R_{1L} \cup R_{2L}$

For all $x \in X$ and $y \in Y$.

The Figure 78 pictorially represents the intuitive concept of cylindrical extension. Figure 79(a,b) pictorially represents the intuitive concept of reconstruction of relation R from its two projections on x and y axis.

Remark 2.16 I) It is not always possible to recover the original relation from the cylindric extension of one of its projections. Information is lost when a fuzzy relation is replaced by any of its projections.

II) Sometimes it can be reconstructed from the intersection of a set of its projections. This intersection is called "the cylindric closure".

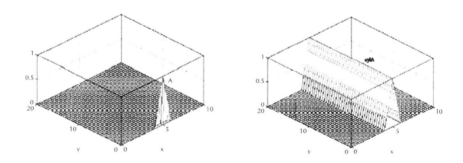

FIGURE 78   Cylindrical extension of fuzzy set of x on y.

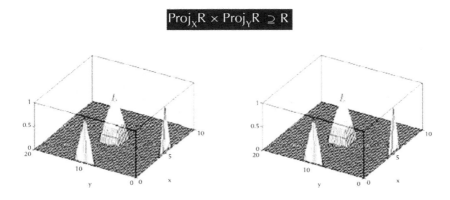

FIGURE 79   a) Projection of R on x and y, b)Reconstruction of R from its projection on x and y axis.

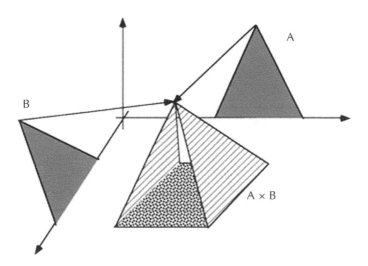

FIGURE 80   Cartesian product of fuzzy relations.

Definition 2.69 The Cartesian product of $A \in F\ (X)$ and $B \in F\ (Y)$ is defined as

$$(A \times B)(x,y) = \min\ \{\ A(x),\ B(y)\}.$$

It is clear that the Cartesian product of two fuzzy sets is a fuzzy relation in $X \times Y$(see Figure 80).

If A and B are normal then $\prod_Y (A \times B) = B$ and $\prod_X (A \times B) = A$. For instance,

$$\prod_X (x) = \sup\{(A \times B)(x,y)|y\}$$

$$= \sup \{ A(x) \wedge B(y) | y$$

$$= \min \{A(x), \sup \{B(y)\} | y\}$$

$$= \min \{A(x), 1\} = A(x).$$

Definition 2.70 The sup-min composition of a fuzzy set $C \in F(X)$ and a fuzzy relation $R \in F(X \times Y)$ is defined as

$$(C \circ R)(y) = \frac{sup}{x \in X} \min \{C(x), R(x,y)\}$$

for all $y \in Y$.

The composition of a fuzzy set C and a fuzzy relation R can be considered as the shadow of the relation R on the fuzzy set C (see figure 81).

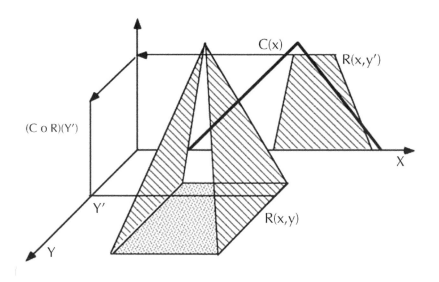

FIGURE 81   Shadow of a relation R on the fuzzy set C.

Example 2.73 Let A and B be fuzzy numbers and let

$$R = A \times B$$

a fuzzy relation.

Observe the following property of composition

- $AoR = Ao\ (A \times B) = A,$
- $BoR = Bo\ (A \times B) = B.$

Example 2.74 Let C be a fuzzy set in the universe of discourse {1,2,3} and let R be a binary fuzzy relation in {1,2,3}. Assume that

$$C = 0.2/1 + \tfrac{1}{2} + 0.2/3$$

and

$$R = \begin{matrix} & 1 & 2 & 3 \\ 1 & \\ 2 & \\ 3 & \end{matrix}\begin{pmatrix} 1 & 0.8 & 0.3 \\ 0.8 & 1 & 0.8 \\ 0.3 & 0.8 & 1 \end{pmatrix}.$$

Using the definition of sup-min composition we get

$$C o R = (0.2/1 + 1/2 + 0.2/3)\ o\ \begin{matrix} & 1 & 2 & 3 \\ 1 & \\ 2 & \\ 3 & \end{matrix}\begin{pmatrix} 1 & 0.8 & 0.3 \\ 0.8 & 1 & 0.8 \\ 0.3 & 0.8 & 1 \end{pmatrix} = 0.8/1 + 1/2 + 0.8/3.$$

Example 2.75 Let C be a fuzzy set in the universe of discourse [0,1] and let R be a binary fuzzy relation in [0,1]. Assume that $C(x) = x$ and

$$R(x,y) = 1 - |x\text{-}y|.$$

Using the definition of sup-min composition we get

$$(C o R)(y) = \underset{x \in [0,1]}{\sup}\ \min\ \{x, 1 - |x - y|\} = \frac{1+y}{2}$$

for all $y \in [0,1]$.

Definition 2.71 Let $R \in F(X \times Y)$ and $S \in F(Y \times Z)$. The sup-min composition of R and S, denoted by R o S is defined as

$$(R o S)(x, z) = \underset{v \in Y}{\sup}\ \min\ \{R\ (x,y), S\ (y,z)\}.$$

It is clear that R o S is a binary fuzzy relation in $X \times Z$.

Example 2.76 Consider two fuzzy relations
R = "x is considerable larger than y"

$$\begin{array}{c} \\ \\ = \end{array} \begin{array}{c} \\ x_1 \\ x_2 \\ x_3 \end{array} \begin{array}{cccc} y_1 & y_2 & y_3 & y_4 \\ \left(\begin{array}{cccc} 0.8 & 0.1 & 0.1 & 0.7 \\ 0 & 0.8 & 0 & 0 \\ 0.9 & 1 & 0.7 & 0.8 \end{array} \right) \end{array}$$

$$S = \text{"y is very close to z"} = \begin{array}{c} y_1 \\ y_2 \\ y_3 \\ y_4 \end{array} \begin{array}{ccc} z_1 & z_2 & z_3 \\ \left(\begin{array}{ccc} 0.4 & 0.9 & 0.3 \\ 0 & 0.4 & 0 \\ 0.9 & 0.5 & 0.8 \\ 0.6 & 0.7 & 0.5 \end{array} \right) \end{array}$$

Then their composition is;

$$R \, o \, S = \begin{array}{c} x_1 \\ x_2 \\ x_3 \end{array} \begin{array}{ccc} z_1 & z_2 & z_3 \\ \left(\begin{array}{ccc} 0.6 & 0.8 & 0.5 \\ 0 & 0.4 & 0 \\ 0.7 & 0.9 & 0.7 \end{array} \right) \end{array}$$

Formally,

$$\begin{array}{c} x_1 \\ x_2 \\ x_3 \end{array} \begin{array}{cccc} y_1 & y_2 & y_3 & y_4 \\ \left(\begin{array}{cccc} 0.8 & 0.1 & 0.1 & 0.7 \\ 0 & 0.8 & 0 & 0 \\ 0.9 & 1 & 0.7 & 0.8 \end{array} \right) \end{array} o \begin{array}{c} y_1 \\ y_2 \\ y_3 \\ y_4 \end{array} \begin{array}{ccc} z_1 & z_2 & z_3 \\ \left(\begin{array}{ccc} 0.4 & 0.9 & 0.3 \\ 0 & 0.4 & 0 \\ 0.9 & 0.5 & 0.8 \\ 0.6 & 0.7 & 0.5 \end{array} \right) \end{array} = \begin{array}{c} x_1 \\ x_2 \\ x_3 \end{array} \begin{array}{ccc} z_1 & z_2 & z_3 \\ \left(\begin{array}{ccc} 0.6 & 0.8 & 0.5 \\ 0 & 0.4 & 0 \\ 0.7 & 0.9 & 0.7 \end{array} \right) \end{array}$$

that is, the composition of R and S is nothing else, but the classical product of the matrices R and S with the difference that instead of addition we use maximum and instead of multiplication we use minimum operator.

PROPERTIES OF MIN-MAX-COMPOSITION

ASSOCIATIVITY.

Definition 2.72 The max-min-composition is associative, if,

$$(R_3 {}^O R_2) {}^O R_1 = R_3 {}^O (R_2 \, o \, R_1)_.$$

Hence $R_1 {}^O R_1 \, o \, R_1 = R_1^3$; the 3rd power of a fuzzy relation is defined.

REFLEXITIVITY

Definition 2.73 Let R be a fuzzy relation in $X \times X$.

i. R is called reflexive if

$$\mu_R(x,x) = 1 \; \forall \; x\varepsilon X.$$

ii. R is called ε-reflexive if

$$\mu_R(x,x) \geq \varepsilon \qquad\qquad \forall \; x\varepsilon X.$$

iii. R is called weakly reflexive if

$$\left.\begin{array}{l}\mu_R(x,y) \leq \mu_R(x,x)\\ \mu_R(y,x) \leq \mu_R(x,x)\end{array}\right\} \forall \; x,y \; \varepsilon X.$$

Example 2.77 Let $X = \{x_1, x_2, \; x_3, \; x_4\}$ and $Y = \{y_1, y_2, \; y_3, \; y_4\}$
The following relation "y is close to x" is reflexive

$$R = \begin{array}{c|cccc} & y_1 & y_2 & y_3 & y_4 \\ \hline x_1 & 1 & 0 & .2 & .3 \\ x_2 & 0 & 1 & .1 & 1 \\ x_3 & .2 & .7 & 1 & .4 \\ x_4 & 0 & 1 & .4 & 1 \end{array}$$

If R_1 and R_2 are reflexive fuzzy relations then the max-min-composition $R_1 \; o \; R_2$ is also reflexive.

SYMMETRY

Definition 2.74 A fuzzy relation R is called symmetric if $R(x,y) = R(y,x)$.

Definition 2.75 A relation is called antisymmetric if for

$$\begin{array}{ll}x \neq y & \text{either} \quad \mu_R(x,y) \neq \mu_R(y,x)\\ \text{or} & \mu_R(x,y) = \mu_R(y,x) = 0\end{array}\right\} \forall \; x,y \; \varepsilon X$$

Definition 2.76 A relation is called perfectly antisymmetric if for $x \neq y$ whenever

$$\mu_R(x,y) > 0 \text{ then } \mu_R(y,x) = 0, \quad \forall \ x,y \ \varepsilon X$$

Example 2.78

	x_1	x_2	x_3	x_4
x_1	.4	0	.1	.8
x_2	.8	1	0	0
x_3	0	.6	.7	0
x_4	0	.2	0	0

R_1:

	x_1	x_2	x_3	x_4
x_1	.4	0	.7	0
x_2	0	1	.9	.6
x_3	.8	.4	.7	.4
x_4	0	.1	0	0

R_2:

	x_1	x_2	x_3	x_4
x_1	.4	.8	.1	.8
x_2	.8	1	0	.2
x_3	.1	.6	.7	.1
x_4	0	.2	0	0

R_3:

R_1 is a perfectly antisymmetric relation while R_2 is an antisymmetric, but not perfectly antisymmetric, relation. R_3 is a nonsymmetric relation, that is, there exist $x, y \varepsilon X$ with $\mu_R(x, y) \neq \mu_R(y, x)$, which is not antisymmetric and therefore also not perfectly antisymmetric.

We can define other concepts, such as an α-antisymmetry $(\mu_R(x, y) - \mu_R(y, x) \geq \alpha \; \forall \; x, y \varepsilon X)$. These concepts would probably be more in line with the basic ideas of fuzzy set theory. Since we shall not need this type of definition for our further considerations, we will abstain from any further definition in this direction.

Example 2.79 Let X and Y be defined as in example 2.78. The following relation is then a symmetric relation:

		y_1	y_2	y_3	y_4
	x_1	0	.1	0	.1
$R(x,y) =$	x_2	.1	1	.2	.3
	x_3	0	.2	.8	.8
	x_4	.1	.3	.8	1

Remark 2.17 For max-min-compositions the following properties hold:

If R_1 is reflexive and R_2 is an arbitrary fuzzy relation then $R_1 \; o \; R_2 \supseteq R_2$ and $R_2 \; o \; R_1 \supseteq R_2$.

If R is reflexive then $R \subseteq R \; o \; R$.
If R_1 and R_2 are reflexive relations, so is $R_1 \; o \; R_2$.
If R_1 and R_2 are symmetric then $R_1 \; o \; R_2$ is symmetric if $R_1 \; o \; R_2 = R_2 \; o \; R_1$.
If R is symmetric so is each power of R.

TRANSIVITY

Definition 2.77 A fuzzy relation R is called (max-min) transitive if $R \; o \; R \subseteq R$.

Example 2.80 Let the fuzzy relation R be defined as:

$$R = \begin{array}{c|cccc} & x_1 & x_2 & x_3 & x_4 \\ \hline x_1 & .2 & 1 & .4 & .4 \\ x_2 & 0 & .6 & .3 & 0 \\ x_3 & 0 & 1 & .8 & 0 \\ x_4 & .1 & 1 & 1 & .1 \end{array}$$

Then $R \circ R$ is

$$\begin{array}{c|cccc} & x_1 & x_2 & x_3 & x_4 \\ \hline x_1 & .1 & .6 & .4 & .2 \\ x_2 & 0 & .6 & .3 & 0 \\ x_3 & 0 & .6 & .3 & 0 \\ x_4 & .1 & 1 & 3 & .1 \end{array}$$

Now we can easily see that $\mu_{\mu_{RoR}}(x,y) \leq \mu_R(x,y)$ holds for all $x, y \, \varepsilon \, X$.

Remark 2.18 Combinations of the above properties give some interesting results for max-min-compositions:

If R is symmetric and transitive, then $\mu_R(x, y) \leq \mu_R(x, x)$ for all $x, y \, \varepsilon \, X$.

If R is reflexive and transitive, then $R_1 \circ R_2 = R$.

If R_1 and R_2 are transitive and $R_1 \circ R_2 = R_2 \circ R_1$, then R_1 is transitive.

The properties motioned in remarks 2.17 and 2.18 hold for the *max-min-composition*. For the *max-prod-composition* property (iii) of remark 2.18 is also true but not properties (i) and (iii) of remark 2.17 and property (i) of remark 2.18. For the *max-av-composition* properties (i) and (iii) of remark 2.17 hold as well as properties (i) and (iii) of remark 2.18. Property (v) of remark 2.17 is true for any cumulative operator.

2.17.3 SOME FURTHER DEFINITIONS AND OPERATIONS OF FUZZY RELATIONS

Definition 2.78 The domain of a binary fuzzy relation R(X, Y) as the fuzzy set:

$$\text{Dom } R(X) = \max_{y \in Y} R(x, y)$$

Example 2.81

$$X = \{0,1\},\, Y = \{0,1,2\}$$

$$R = \begin{matrix} & 0 & 1 \\ 0 & 0.3 & 0.7 \\ 1 & 1 & 0.4 \\ 2 & 0.6 & 0 \end{matrix} \rightarrow \text{Dom } R(X) = 1/0 + .7/1.$$

Definition 2.79 The range of a binary fuzzy relation is defined as the fuzzy set:

$$\text{Ran } R(y) = \max_{x \in X} R(x, y).$$

Example 2.82

$$X = \{0,1\},\, Y = \{0,1,2\}$$

$$R = \begin{matrix} & 0 & 1 \\ 0 & 0.3 & 0.7 \\ 1 & 1 & 0.4 \\ 2 & 0.6 & 0 \end{matrix} \rightarrow \text{Ran } R(X) = .7/0 + 1/1 + .6/2.$$

Definition 2.80 The Height of $R(X, Y)$ is a number defined by

$$h(r) = \max_{y \in Y} R(x, y),$$

where $h(r)$ is the largest membership grade in the relation

Example 2.83

$$X = \{0,1\},\, Y = \{0,1,2\}$$

$$R = \begin{matrix} & 0 & 1 \\ 0 & 0.3 & 0.7 \\ 1 & 1 & 0.4 \\ 2 & 0.6 & 0 \end{matrix} \rightarrow h(R) = 1.$$

Definition 2.81 The inverse of given fuzzy relation R is Defined as follows R^{-1} $(Y,X) = R(X,Y)$.

Example 2.84

$$X = \{0,1\},\, Y = \{0,1,2\}$$

$$
\begin{array}{cc}
 & 0 \quad 1 \\
R = \begin{array}{c} 0 \\ 1 \\ 2 \end{array} \begin{pmatrix} 0.3 & 0.7 \\ 1 & 0.4 \\ 0.6 & 0 \end{pmatrix}
\end{array}
\rightarrow R^{-1} =
\begin{array}{c} 0 \\ 1 \end{array}
\begin{pmatrix} 0.3 & 1 & 0.6 \\ 0.7 & 0.4 & 0 \end{pmatrix} .
$$

Similarly to the one-dimensional case, intersection and union operations on fuzzy relations can be defined via t-norms and t-conorms, respectively.

Definition 2.82 Let T be a t-norm and let R and G be binary fuzzy relations in X x Y. Their T-intersection is defined by

$$(R \cap G)(x, y) = T(R(x, y), G(x, y)), \in X \text{ x } Y.$$

Definition 2.81 Let S be a t-norm and let R and G be binary fuzzy relations in X x Y. Their T-union is defined by

$$(R \cup G)(x, y) = S(R(x, y), G(x, y)), \in X \text{ x } Y.$$

Definition 2.84 Let $R \in F$ (X x Y) and $G \in F$ (Y x Z). The sup-min composition of R and G, denoted by R o G is defined as

$$(R \text{ o } G)(x, z)) \sup_{y \in Y} \min \{R(x, y), G(y, z)\}.$$

It is clear R o G is a binary fuzzy relation in X x Z.

Example 2.85 Consider two fuzzy relations R $\Leftrightarrow$ "x is considerably smaller than y" G $\Leftrightarrow$ "is very close to z".

R	y_1	y_2	y_3	y_4
x_1	0.5	0.1	0.1	0.7
x_2	0	0.8	0	0
x_3	0.9	1	0.7	0.8

G	z_1	z_2	z_3
y_1	0.4	0.9	0.3
y_2	0	0.4	0
y_3	0.9	0.5	0.8
y_4	0.6	0.7	0.5

Then their sup-min composition is

R o G	z_1	z_2	z_3
x_1	0.6	0.7	0.5
x_2	0	0.4	0
x_3	0.7	0.9	0.7

Formally,

$$\begin{pmatrix} 0.5 & 0.1 & 0.1 & 0.7 \\ 0 & 0.8 & 0 & 0 \\ 0.9 & 1 & 0.7 & 0.8 \end{pmatrix} o \begin{pmatrix} 0.4 & 0.9 & 0.3 \\ 0 & 0.4 & 0 \\ 0.9 & 0.5 & 0.8 \\ 0.6 & 0.7 & 0.5 \end{pmatrix} = \begin{pmatrix} 0.6 & 0.7 & 0.5 \\ 0 & 0.4 & 0 \\ 0.7 & 0.9 & 0.7 \end{pmatrix}$$

that is, the composition of R and G is nothing else, but the classical product of the matrices R and G with the difference that instead of addition we use maximum and instead of multiplication we use minimum operation. For example,

$(R \ o \ G)(x_1, z_1) = \max \{0.5 \wedge 0.4; 0.1 \wedge 0; 1 \wedge 0.9; 0.7 \wedge 0.6\} = 0.6$

$(R \ o \ G)(x_1, z_2) = \max \{0.5 \wedge 0.9; 0.1 \wedge 0.4; 0.1 \wedge 0.5; 0.7 \wedge 0.7\} = 0.7$

$(R \ o \ G)(x_1, z_3) = \max \{0.5 \wedge 0.3; 0.1 \wedge 0; 0.1 \wedge 0.8; 0.7 \wedge 0.5\} = 0.5.$

Definition 2.85 Let T be a t-norm and let $R \in F$ (X x Y) and $G \in F$ (Y x Z). The sup-T composition of R and G, denoted by R o G is defined as

$$(R \ o \ G)(x, z)) \sup_{y \in Y} T\{R(x, y), G(y, z)\}.$$

Following Zadeh, we can define the sup-min composition of a fuzzy set and fuzzy relation as follows:

Definition 2.86 Let $C \in F$ (X) and $R \in F$ (X x Y). The membership function of the composition of f fuzzy set C and a fuzzy relation R is defined by

$$\forall y \in Y, (C \ o \ R)(y) = \sup_{x \in X} \min \{C(x), R(x,y)\}.$$

The composition of a fuzzy set C and a fuzzy relation R can be considered as a shadow of the relation R on the fuzzy set C.

In the above definition we can use any t-norm for modeling the compositional operation.

Definition 2.87 Let T be a t-norm, $C \in F(X)$ and $R \in F(X \times Y)$. A membership function of the composition of a fuzzy set C and a fuzzy relation R is defined by

$$\forall y \in Y, (C \ o \ R)(y) = \sup_{x \in X} T(C(x), R(x,y)).$$

For example, if $T_p(x, y) = xy$ is the product t-norm then the sup-T composition of a fuzzy set C and a fuzzy relation R is defined by

$$\forall y \in Y, (C \ o \ R)(y) = \sup_{x \in X} T_p(C(x), R(x,y)) = \sup_{x \in X}(C(x), R(x,y)$$

And if T_L $(x,y)) = \max \{0,x+y-1\}$ is the Lukasiewicz t-norm then we get

$\forall y \in Y, (C \text{ o } R) (y) = \sup_{x \in X} T_L (C(x), R(x,y)) = \sup_{x \in X} \max \{0, (C(x) + R(x,y)-1\}.$

Example 2.86 Let A and B be fuzzy numbers and let $R = A \times B$ be a fuzzy relation. Observe the following property of composition

$$A \text{ o } R = A \text{ o } (A \times B) = B, B \text{ o } R = B \text{ o } (A \times B) = A.$$

This fact can be interpreted as: if A and B have relation $A \times B$ and then the composition of A and A×B is exactly B, and then the composition of B and $A \times B$ is exactly A.

Example 2.87 Let C be a fuzzy set in the universe of discourse $\{1,2,3\}$ and let R be a binary fuzzy relation in $\{1,2,3\}$. Assume that

$$C = 0.2/1 + 1/2 + 0.2/3$$

and

R	1	2	3
1	1	0.8	0.3
2	0.8	1	0.8

Using Definition 2.86 we get

$$C \text{ o } R = (0.2, 1, 0.2) \text{ o } \begin{pmatrix} 1 & 0.8 & 0.3 \\ 0.8 & 1 & 0.8 \\ 0.3 & 0.8 & 1 \end{pmatrix} = (0.8, 1, 0.8)$$

Thus the result is the fuzzy set $\{0.8/1 + \frac{1}{2} + 0. 8/3\}$.

Example 2.88 Let C be a fuzzy set in the universe of discourse $[0,1]$ and let R be a binary fuzzy relation in $[0,1]$. Assume that $C(x) = x$ and $R(x,y) = 1 - |x-y|$. Using the Definition 2.86 of sup-min composition, we get

$$\forall y \in [0,1], (C \text{ o } R) (y) = \sup_{x \in [0,1]} \min\{x, 1- |x - y|\} = \frac{1+y}{2}.$$

Example 2.89 Let C be a fuzzy set in the universe of discourse $\{1,2,3\}$ and let R be a binary fuzzy relation in $\{1,2,3\}$. Assume that $C = 1/1 + 0. 2/2 + 1/3$
and

R	1	2	3
1	0.4	0.8	0.3
2	0.8	0.4	0.8
3	0.3	0.8	0

Then the sup- T_p composition of C and R is calculated by

$$C \text{ o } R = (1, 0.2, 1) \text{ o } \begin{pmatrix} 0.4 & 0.8 & 0.3 \\ 0.8 & 0.4 & 0.8 \\ 0.3 & 0.8 & 0 \end{pmatrix} = (0.4, 0.8, 0.3)$$

Thus the result is the fuzzy set $\{0.4/1 + 0.8/2 + 0.3/3\}$.

2.17.4 CLASSIFICATION OF FUZZY RELATION

We generalize the concepts of equivalence, compatibility, pre-order, and order relations of crisp relations to those of fuzzy relations. We assume relation R is defined on A×A [172].

FUZZY EQUIVALENCE RELATION

Definition 2.88 If a fuzzy relation $R \subseteq A \times A$ satisfies the following conditions, we call it a "fuzzy equivalence relation" or "similarity relation."
Reflexive relation

$$\forall x \in A \Rightarrow \mu_R(x, x) = 1$$

Symmetric relation

$$\forall x \in A \times A, \mu_R(x, x) = \mu \Rightarrow \mu_R(y, x) = \mu$$

Transitive relation

$$\forall (x, y), (y, z), (x, z) \in A \times A$$

$$\mu_R(x, z) \geq Max_y [Min [\mu_R(x, y), \mu_R(y, z)]]$$

Example 2.90 Let's consider a fuzzy relation expressed in the following matrix. Since this relation is reflexive, symmetric and transitive, we see that it is a fuzzy equivalence relation (Figure 82).

	A	b	c	d
a	1.0	0.8	0.7	1.0
b	0.8	1.0	0.7	0.8
c	0.7	0.7	0.1	0.7
d	1.0	0.7	0.7	1.0

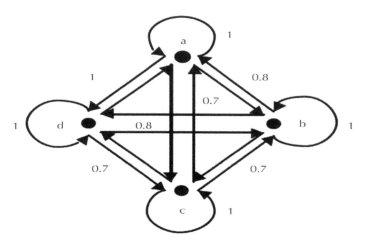

FIGURE 82   Graph of fuzzy equivalence relation.

Using this similarity relation, we can perform the following three applications.

PARTITION OF SETS

As we can partition a crisp set A into subsets A_1, A_2 ..... by the equivalence relation, fuzzy set A can also be partitioned.

Example 2.91 Let us consider a fuzzy relation R expressed in the following matrix. Figure 83 shows a partition of A by the given relation R. At this point, fuzzy equivalence relation holds in class A_1 and A_2 but not between A_1 and A_2.

	a	b	c	d	e
a	1.0	0.5	1.0	0.0	0.0
b	0.5	1.0	0.5	0.0	0.0
c	1.0	0.5	1.0	0.0	0.0
d	0.0	0.0	0.0	1.0	0.5
e	0.0	0.0	0.0	0.5	1.0

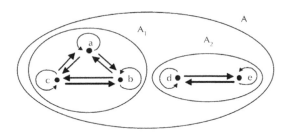

FIGURE 83   Partition by fuzzy equivalence relation.

PARTITION BY α-CUT

If α-cut is done on a fuzzy relation, we get crisp relations. If we perform α-cut on fuzzy equivalence relation, we get crisp equivalence relations. Thus the set A can be partitioned. If a partition is done on set A into subsets A_1, A_2, A_3 ..... , the similarity among elements in A_i is no less than α.

Definition 2.89 The α-cut equivalence relation R_α is defined by

$$\mu_R(x, y) = 1 \text{ if } \mu_R(x, y) \geq \alpha, \forall\ x, y\ \in\ A_i = 0 \text{ otherwise .}$$

If we apply α -cut according α_1 in level set $\{\alpha_1, \alpha_2, ...\}$ the partition we obtain is denoted by $\pi(R_{\alpha_1})$ or $\pi(A/R_{\alpha_1})$. Similarly, we get $\pi(R_{\alpha_2})$ by the procedure of α_2 -cut.

Remark 2.19 If $\alpha_1 \geq \alpha_2, R_{\alpha_1} \subseteq R_{\alpha_2}$ then $\pi(R_{\alpha_1})$ is more refined than $\pi(R_{\alpha_2})$.

Example 2.92 Let us consider a fuzzy relation R expressed in the following matrix. Partition tree of Figure 84 shows the multiple partitions by α. If we apply $\alpha = 0.5$, similarity classes are obtained as {a, b}, {d}, (c, e, f} whose elements have degrees no less than 0.5.

$$\pi(A/R_{\alpha_1}) = \{\{a, b\}, \{d\}, (c, e, f\}\}.$$

	a	b	c	d	e	f
a	1.0	0.8	0.0	0.4	0.0	0.0
b	0.8	1.0	0.0	0.4	0.0	0.0
c	0.0	0.0	1.0	0.0	1.0	0.5
d	0.4	0.4	0.0	1.0	0.0	0.0
e	0.0	0.0	1.0	0.0	1.0	0.5
f	0.0	0.0	0.5	0.0	0.5	1.0

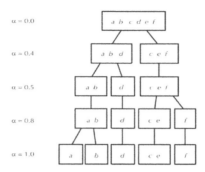

FIGURE 84   partition tree.

Set similar to element x

If similarity relation R is defined on set A, elements related to arbitrary member $x \in A$ can make up "set similar to x". Certainly this set is fuzzy one.

Example 2.93 Let us consider the member d in the fuzzy similarity relation, which is stated in previous example. Elements making similarity relation with d are a,b, and d itself. These members are expressed according to the degree of similarity with d. Thus, we get a similarity class of d.

$$\{(a, 0.4), (b, 0.4), (d, 1)\}.$$

Similarly, considering the elements similar to element e, the similarity class yields.

$$\{(c, 1), (e, 1), (f, 0.5)\}.$$

FUZZY COMPATIBILITY RELATION

Definition 2.90 If fuzzy relation R in set A satisfies the following conditions, we call it "fuzzy compatibility relation" or "resemblance relation".

Reflexive relation

$$x \in A \Rightarrow \mu_R(x, x) = 1$$

Symmetric relation

$$\forall\, x \in A \times A$$

$$\mu_R(x, y) = \mu \Rightarrow \mu_R(y, x) = \mu.$$

If fuzzy compatibility relation is given on set A, we can obtain a partition of several subsets. Subsets from this partition are called the "fuzzy compatibility classes".

If we apply α-cut to the fuzzy compatibility relation, we get α-cut crisp compatibility relation R_α.

Definition 2.91 A compatibility class A_i is defined by,

$$\mu_{R_\alpha}(x,y) = 1 \text{ if } \mu_R(x,y) \geq \alpha, \quad \forall\, x, y \in A_i$$

$$= 0 \text{ otherwise.}$$

The collection of all compatibility classes from a α-cut is called complete α-cover. Note the differences of the cover and partition.

Example 2.94 Let us consider a fuzzy relation R expressed in the following matrix. Figure 85 represents covers made by α-cut. By $\alpha = 0.7$ cut, we get compatibility class {a, b}, {c, d, e}, {d, e, f}. These compatibility classes cover the set A. The elements d and e are far from partition since they appear in dual subsets. The sequence of such compatibility classes constructs a compatibility covering tree as shown in Figure 86.

	a	b	c	d	e	f
a	1.0	0.8	0.0	0.0	0.0	0.0
b	0.8	1.0	0.0	0.0	0.0	0.0
c	0.0	0.0	1.0	1.0	0.8	0.0
d	0.0	0.0	1.0	1.0	0.8	0.7
e	0.0	0.0	0.8	0.8	1.0	0.7
f	0.0	0.0	0.0	0.7	0.7	1.0

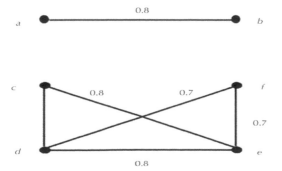

FIGURE 85   Representation of covers made by alpha cut

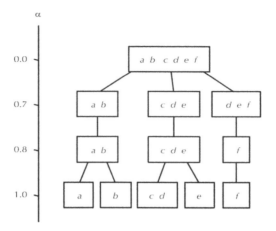

FIGURE 86   Compatibility covering tree.

FUZZY PRE-ORDER RELATION

Definition 2.92 Given fuzzy relation R in set A, if the followings are well kept for all $x, y, z, \in A$, this relation is called pre-order relation.

Reflexive relation

$$\forall\, x \in A \Rightarrow \mu_R(x, x) = 1$$

Transitve relation

$$\forall\, (x, y), (y, z) \in A \times A$$

$$\mu_R(x, z) Max_y[\, Min\, (\mu_R(x, y)\mu_R]$$

If certain relation is transitive but not reflexive, this relation is called "semi-pre-order" or "nonreflexive fuzzy pre-order".

Example 2.95 We consider a semi-pre-order relation.

	a	b	c
a	0.2	1.0	0.4
b	0.0	0.6	0.3
c	0.0	1.0	0.3

If the membership function follows the relation $\mu_R(x, x) = 0$ for all x, we use the term "anti reflexive fuzzy pre-order".

Example 2.96 The following matrix shows an anti-reflexive fuzzy pre-order relation.

	a	b	c
a	0.0	1.0	0.4
b	0.0	0.0	0.3
c	0.0	1.0	0.0

FUZZY ORDER RELATION

Definition 2.93 If relation R satisfies the followings for all $x, y, z, \in A$, it is called fuzzy order relation.

Reflexive relation

$$\forall x \in A \Rightarrow \mu_R(x, x) = 1$$

Antisymmetric relation

$$\forall (x, y), \in A \times A$$

$$\mu_R(x, y) \neq \mu_R(y, x) \text{ or } \mu_R(x, y) = \mu_R(y, x) = 0.$$

Transitive relation

$$\forall (x, y), (y, z), (x, z) \in A \times A$$

$$\mu_R(x, z) \geq Max_y \left[Min \left[\mu_R(x, y), \mu_R(y, z) \right) \right].$$

Example 2.97 For example, the relation shown in Figure 87 is a fuzzy order relation.

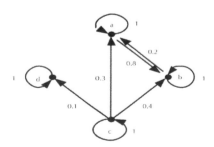

FIGURE 87   Fuzzy order relation.

Definition 2.94 We can get a corresponding crisp relation R_1 from given fuzzy order relation R by arranging the value of membership function as follows.

if $\mu_R(x, y) \geq \mu_R(y, x)$ then $\mu_{R_1}(x, y) = 1$

$\mu_{R_1}(y, x,) = 0$

if $\mu_R(x, y) = \mu_R(y, x)$ then $\mu_{R_1}(x, y) = \mu_{R_1}(y, x,) = 0.$

Example 2.98 The following matrix represents a crisp relation obtained from fuzzy order relation introduced in the previous example (Figure 88).

	a	b	c	d
a	1	1	0	0
b	0	1	0	0
c	1	1	1	1
d	0	0	0	1

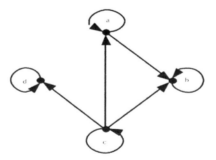

FIGURE 88   Crisp order relation obtained from fuzzy order relation.

If the corresponding order relation of a fuzzy order relation is total order or linear order, this fuzzy relation is named as "fuzzy total order".

When the second condition of the fuzzy order relation is transformed to "perfect antisymmetric", the fuzzy order relation becomes a perfect fuzzy order.

Perfect antisymmetric

$$\forall\ (x, y), \in A \times A,\ x \neq y$$

$$\mu_R(x,y) > 0 \Rightarrow \mu_R(y,x) = 0$$

When the first condition (reflexivity) does not exist, the fuzzy order relation is called "fuzzy strict order".

Definition 2.95 In the fuzzy order relation, if $R(x,y) > 0$ holds, then x dominates y and is denoted $x \geq y$. With this concept, two fuzzy sets are associated.

The one is dominating class $R_{\geq[x]}$ which dominates x and which is defined as,

$$\mu R_{\geq[x]}(y) = \mu_R(y,x)$$

The other is dominated class $\mu R_{\leq[x]}$ with elements dominated by x which is defined as,

$$\mu R_{\leq[x]}(y) = \mu_R(y,x).$$

Example 2.99 Let's consider the following matrix represented by Figure 89.

	a	b	c	d
a	1.0	0.0	0.5	0.0
b	0.7	1.0	0.7	0.0
c	0.0	0.0	1.0	0.0
d	1.0	0.9	1.0	1.0

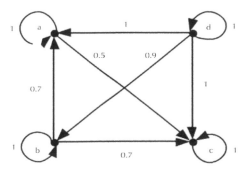

FIGURE 89 Example for dominating relation.

Dominating classes of element a and b are,

$$R_{\geq[a]} = \{(a, 1.0), (b, 0.7), (d, 1.0)\}$$

$$R_{\geq[b]} = \{(b, 1.0), (d, 0.9)\}.$$

Dominated class by a is:

$$R_{\geq[a]} = \{(a, 1.0), (c, 0.5)\}.$$

If such fuzzy order relation is given, fuzzy upper bound of subset $A' = \{x, y\}$ can be obtained by fuzzy intersection or Min operation of the dominating class.

$$\bigcap_{x \in A'} R_{\geq[x]}.$$

Example 2.100 If $A' = (a, b\}$ with respect to the above example, the fuzzy upper bound is:

$$R_{\geq[a]} \cap R_{\geq[b]} = \{a, 1.0), (b, 0.7), (d, 1.0)\} \cap \{(b, 1.0), (d, 0.9)\} = \{(b, 0.7), (d, 0.9)\}.$$

2.17.5 EXTENSION PRINCIPLE

A very important notion in fuzzy set theory is the extension principle. It provides a method for combining non-fuzzy and fuzzy concepts of different kinds including the operation of a mathematical function on fuzzy sets. Let $A_1, A_2, ..., A_n$ be fuzzy sets, defined on $U_1, U_2, ..., U_n$ respectively, and let f be a non-fuzzy function f: $U_1 \times U_2 \times ... \times U_n \to V$.

Let F be extension of f on V.

Definition 2.96 The extension of f, operating on $A_1, A_2, ..., A_n$ results in the following membership function for F

$$\mu_F(v) = \{u_1, ..., u_n | f(u_{1...}u_n)v\}\{\min(\mu A_1(u_1), ..., \mu A_n(u_n))\} \quad (2.180)$$

when $f^{-1}(v)$ exists. Otherwise, $\mu_F(v) = 0$.

Example 4.101 Let $A = \{(-1, .5), (0, .8), (1,1), (2,4)\}$ and $f(x) = x^2$.
By applying the extension principle we obtain

$$B = f(A)\{(0..8),(1,1),(4,.4)\}$$

The following Figure 90 illustrates the relationship:

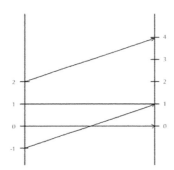

FIGURE 90 Representation of extension principle.

So far we discussed mapping from a one dimensional space X to another one dimensional space Y. In general the mapping can be defined from an n dimensional product space $X_1, X_2, \ldots, X_n$ denote fuzzy universes. The mapping function in the present context is denoted by $f(x_1, x_2, \ldots, x_n)$, where $x_1 \in X_1, x_2 \in X_2, \ldots,$ and $x_n \in X_n$. If $A_1, A_2, \ldots, A_n$ are n fuzzy sets in $X_1, X_2, \ldots$ and X_n respectively, then extension principle asserts that the fuzzy set B induced by the mapping from $A_1, A_2, \ldots, A_n$ is given by

$$B = \{\mu_B(y)/y, \text{where } y = f(x_1, x_2, \ldots, x_n)\} \text{ with}$$

$$\mu_B(y) = \max_{(x_1, x_2, \ldots, x_n) \in f^{-1}(y)} [\min \{\mu_{A\,1}(x_1), \mu_{A\,2}(x_2), \ldots, \mu_{A\,1}(x_n)\},$$

if $f^{-1}(y) \neq$ null set, $=0$, otherwise. (2.181)

Example 2.102 In this example we illustrate the extension principle for a function f of 2 variables x_1 and x_2. Let $f(x_1, x_2) = x_1 + x_2$, and

$$A_1 = \{0.2/-1, \ 0.4/0, 0.6/1\} \text{ and } A_2 = \{0.8/-1, 0.6/0, 0.7/1\}.$$

Here, $X_1 = \{-1, 0, 1\}$ and $X_2 = \{-1, 0, 1\}$.
Thus $X_1 \times X_2 = ((-1, -1), (-1, 0), (-1, 1), (0,-1), (0,0), (0, 1), (1, -1), (1, 0), (1, 1))$
Consequently, $f(-1, 0)=f(0, -1)=0+(-1)=-1,$

$$f(1, -1)=f(-1, 1)=-1 +1=0.$$

$$f(1, 0)=f(0, 1)=0, f(1, 1)=2.$$

So, $\mu_B(y)$ at y = f(-1, 0)

$$\mu_B(y) \text{ at } y = f(0,-1)$$

$$= \max[\min(0.2, 0.6), \min(0.4, 0.8)\} = 0.4.$$

Similarly, $\mu_B(y)$ at y = f(1,-1)

$$= \mu_B(y) \text{ at } y=f(-1, 1)$$

$$= \max \{\min(0.6, 0.8), \min(0.2, 0.7)\} = 0.6 \text{ and}$$

$$\mu_B(y) \text{ at } y=f(1, 0)$$

$$= \mu_B(y) \text{ at } y=f(0, 1)$$

$$= \max \{\min(0.6, 0.6), \min(0.4, 0.7)\} = 0.6, \text{ and}$$

$$\mu_B(y) \text{ at } y=f(-1, -1)$$

$$= \min(0.2, 0.8) = 0.2$$

$$\mu_B(y) \text{ at } y=f(0, 0)$$

$$= \min(0.4, 0.6) = 0.4,$$

and $\mu_B(y)$ at y=f(1, 1)

$$= \min(0.6, 0.7) = 0.6.$$

Consequently, B={0.4/ f(-1, 0), 0.6/ f(-1, 1), 0.6/ f(1, 0), 0.2/ f(-1, -1), 0.4/ f(0,0), 0.6/ f(1,1)}

$$= \{0.4/-1, 0.6/0, 0.6/1, 0.2/-2, 0.4/0, 0.6/2\}.$$

2.17.6 SPECIFICITY MEASURE OF FUZZY SETS

In this section, we discuss specificity measure of a fuzzy set, which is used in measuring the preciseness of a fuzzy information. A fuzzy set with maximum specificity value corresponds to a precise assessment of the values. In trying to capture the form of a specificity index, a number of properties are required. According to Dubois and Prade, a specificity measure Sp(A) should satisfy the following properties.

Let, a linguistic variable defined on a universe of discourse X and A,B be normalized fuzzy subsets of X.

P1. For all $A \subseteq X$, $Sp(A) \in [0,1]$.

P2. $Sp(A) = 1$, if and only if A is a singleton of X.

P3. $A \subseteq B \rightarrow Sp(A) \geq Sp(B)$.

Yager has introduced one such measure of specificity which satisfies the above properties. When X is finite, Yager has proposed the following expression for definiting the specifity.

Definition 2.97 Let us assume that A be a fuzzy set defined over the universal set X. The specificity associated withA is denoted as Sp(A) and is defined as

$$Sp(A) = \int_0^{\alpha_{max}} \frac{1}{CardA_\alpha} \, d\alpha. \tag{2.182}$$

Here, $A_\alpha = \{ x \in X \mid \mu_A \ (x) \geq \alpha \}$ and Card A denotes the cardinality of the fuzzy set A, that is, Card $A = \sum_{\alpha \in (0,1]} \alpha.A_n$.

Example 2.103 Let $X = (x_1, x_2, x_3, x_4)$, and $A = \{1.0/x_1 + 0.75/x_2 + 0.5/x_3 + 0.25/x_4\}$. In this case we find that $\alpha_{max} = 1.0$. The level sets are

$A_\alpha = \{x_1, x_2, x_3, x_4\}$ for $\alpha \geq 0.25$

$A_\alpha = \{x_1, x_2, x_3\}$ for $0.25 < \alpha \geq 0.50$

$A_\alpha = \{x_1, x_2\}$ for $0.50 < \alpha \geq 0.75$

$A_\alpha = \{x_1\}$ for $0.75 < \alpha \geq 1.00$

and from these we may get the cardinalities as

$$Card \ A_\alpha = \begin{cases} 4 \ for \alpha \geq 0.25 \\ 3 \ for \ 0.25 < \alpha \leq 0.50 \\ 2 \ for \ 0.50 < \alpha \leq 0.75 \\ 1 \ for \ 0.75 < \alpha \leq 1.00. \end{cases}$$

Therefore, we find from Definition 2.97 that $Sp(A) = 0.52$.

Let us now list some important properties associated with the above Definition 2.97.

Theorem 2.9 For all A, SP(A) assumes its maximum value 1, when $A = \{1/x\}$ for some particular $x \in X$.

Theorem 2.10 For all A, $Sp(A) \in [0,1]$ and it assumes its minimum value 0, when $A = \phi$.

Theorem 2.11 If for all A, $\mu_A(x) = k$ for all $x \in X$ then $Sp(A) = \frac{k}{n}$ where n is the cardinality of the ordinary set X.

KEYWORDS

- **Fuzzy Set**
- **Laws of thought**
- **Fuzzy number**
- **Hausdorff distance**

CHAPTER 3

FUZZY LOGIC

3.1 INTRODUCTION

Investigation on fuzzy logic began immediate after Zadeh's seminal paper on fuzzy sets. According to Zadeh [298], fuzzy logic is essentially precise logic of imprecision and approximate reasoning. Fuzzy logic is much more than a logical system. It'sIts distinguishing features are graduation, granulation, precisiation, and the concept of a generalized constraint. From the outset, it is established that fuzzy logic is similar to the nonclassical many-valued logics, which were investigated by Łukasiewicz and the Polish School of logic in the 1920s, as well as Post in the United States. An early exploration to establish a relation between fuzzy logic and many-valued logic may be found in [99]. A unified treatment of both fuzzy and many-valued logics, based on Kleene algebras, is presented in [317]. Fuzzy propositional logic is first studied in [212]. Further studies in this direction include [202] and [122]. The primary issues addressed in fuzzy logic research are the possible operations of a fuzzy logic and their algebraic properties viz. normal forms for fuzzy logic expressions; and an extensive debate on the nature of the fuzzy complement.

In 1967, Goguen proposed [107, 108] the concept of an L-fuzzy set which is a generalization of fuzzy logic to general posets. According to this work, fuzzy membership values are elements of a complete lattice-ordered semigroup, that is, a complete lattice with an additional binary operation "*" that has the lattice infimum (inf) and supremum (sup) as its zero and identity, respectively, and which is distributive over the disjunction operation. The interval [0, 1] is one particular example of a complete lattice-ordered semigroup, which happens to be an infinite chain. Examples of other posets that are not chains are also given. The work of Bellman and Giertz [19] is cited as the first study of the axiomatization of the fuzzy intersection, union, and complement operations. According to them the min and max operations for fuzzy intersection and union respectively satisfy their axioms. No unique form for the fuzzy complement is determined. The min and max operations are examples of t-norms and t-conorms, respectively. The accepted axioms of fuzzy intersection and union are identical to axioms for t-norms and t-conorms. This leads to a vast number of possible "fuzzy logics". A survey of over thirty such logical systems is available in [285]. One of the well-known results in fuzzy logic is that DeMorgan triples which satisfy the laws of contradiction and excluded middle cannot be distributive lattices. It is shown in [275] that lattices satisfying excluded middle and contradiction can possess the weaker property of modularity.

Investigations of the algebraic properties of fuzzy logics usually concentrate on the general case of a lattice rather than the special case of the interval [0, 1]. Lattices composed of a countably infinite number of infinite chains are studied in [74]. The studies in [144,], [51], and [41] concentrate on the complete lattice-ordered semigroups described by Goguen. Noncommutative lattices are studied in [103]. In 2000, Brzozowski [34] described a different algebraic structure called a DeMorgan bisemilattice. In this structure, the inf and sup operators each from a semilattice, share a common upper and lower bound, and are related by DeMorgan's laws through some involutive complement operation. This structure is used instead of complete lattice-ordered semigroups in [274] and [153]. A specific fuzzy logic, generated by combining Łukasiewicz and Product logic, is studied in [189] and shown to be isomorphic to algebraic structures called f-semifields.

The normal (canonical) form of a logic expression is a key concept in classical logic which is used for in the minimization of switching functions. Equivalent problems are much harder in many-valued and fuzzy logic. Canonical forms are studied for first-order fuzzy logics in [202], and a completeness theorem proven. Turksen [283] has studied fuzzy normal forms based on fuzzy truth tables. According to the study, a fuzzy disjunctive normal form is a crisp subset of the fuzzy conjunctive normal form, when the standard fuzzy union, intersection, and complement are used. In [284], Turksen proposes that fuzzy connectives map type-1 fuzzy sets onto a type-2 fuzzy set. In many-valued logic, Reed-Muller expressions are often used as a canonical form. Reed-Muller expressions are sum-of-product expressions, in which the product operation is a conjunction, and the sum is an exclusive-or. The minimization of these expressions is, in general, known to be NP-hard [168], [235], [316].

The fuzzy complements found in the literature are not true lattice complements. By definition, the complement of an element a in a bounded lattice with infimum 0 and supremem 1 is the unique element $\sim a$ such that $a \wedge \sim a = 0$ and $a \vee \sim a = 1$. These are identically the laws of contradiction and excluded middle. Axiomatizations of the fuzzy complement do not define the fuzzy complement in terms of the fuzzy union and intersection but rather treat it as a unary, continuous, involutive, and order-reversing function c, with boubdary conditions $c(0) = 1$ and $c(1) = 0$. Complement operations satisfying these axioms have been criticized on both philosophical [242], [268] and mathematical [39] grounds. Complement operators in intuitionistic fuzzy sets are studied in [7]. An intuitionistic fuzzy complement is defined as a function c from $L=\{(x,y) \in [0,1] \times [0,1] | x+y \leq 1\}$ to L such that $c(1, 0) = (0, 1)$, $c(0, 1) = (1, 0)$, and $\forall (a,b),(x,y) \in L$, $a \leq x$ and $y \leq b \Rightarrow c(x,y) \leq c(a,b)$. Additional studies of fuzzy complements are reported in [30,], [239], and [177].

Some criticisms of fuzzy logic, from both philosophical-logic and mathematical-logic grounds, have appeared in [3,] and [75]. A lengthy response to this criticism may be found in [173].

The complex fuzzy set theory is proposed in [236]. The operations of union and intersection therein give rise to a lattice,; which has different properties than the infinite chain [0, 1]. The lattice developed in [236] is the traditional partial ordering defined for the complex plane (based solely on the modulus of a vector in the plane), limited to the unit disc. Though there is a unique infimum for this partial ordering (0 + 0j), there is no unique supremum in the unit disc. Hence, this lattice is lower-bounded but not upper bounded. As the existence of an upper bound is required for both structures, this means that the complex fuzzy set theory presented in [236] forms neither a complete lattice-ordered semigroup, nor a DeMorgan bisemilattice.

Fuzzy set theory language and ideas are used to express basic quantum logic notions. The possibility of replacing probabilistic interpretation of quantum mechanics by interpretation based on infinite-valued logics and fuzzy set theory is outlined by Feynmann. Fuzzy logic using the Lukasicwicz operators is proposed in [174] to generate fuzzy quantum logic.

Though reversibility of computation is analyzed in detail on other frameworks, no result on the possibility of computing with fuzzy connectives without altering the global information content of the involved signals (and thus preserving thermodynamic reversibility) seem to exist in present state of art. Yet the problem has some relevance as fuzzy computation is inherently much richer than the Boolean one. In the framework of classical statistical mechanics, reversible gates can be deviseddevised, in which we can decompose any quantum computable function. Similarly an attempt has been made by Feynmann [88] to develop a reversible elementary gate which can be devised to obtain all the functions that can be expressed by means of fuzzy norm-based conjunction, disjunction, and negation.

3.2 PRELIMINARIES OF LOGIC

Classical logic is the simplest logic in which there are only two truth values for a statement or proposition, that is, there are only two possible values that we can assign to certain statement that is True (1, yes) and False (0, No). A proposition can be either true or false,; but not both at the same time. For instance, "sun rises in the east" is a true statement and has truth value 1. Normally we use 1's and 0's in two valued classical logic and true, false in propositional logic.

PROPOSITION LOGIC

Definition 3.1 A declarative statement which is either "true (1)" or "false (0)" as its truth value is called "proposition".

Example 3.1 The following sentences are propositions.

Smith hits 30 home runs in one season.	(true)
$2 + 4 = 7$	(false)
For every x, if $= \sin x$, then $f'(x) = \cos x$.	(true)
It rains now.	(true)

Example 3.2 The followings are not propositions.
1. Why are you interested in the fuzzy theory?

2. He hits 5 home runs in one season.

$$x+5 = 0$$
$$x+y = z$$

In the second example, we do not know who is "He" and thus cannot determine whether the sentence is true (1) or false (0). If "He" is replaced by "Tom", we have;

Tom hits 5 home runs in one season.

Now we can evaluate the truth value of the above sentence.

In the same way:,

$$x+5 = 0$$

is not a proposition. If the value x is replaced by -5, then the sentence:

$$-5+5 = 0$$

has its value "true".

A variable is used as a symbol representing an element in a universal set.

Definition 3.2 A proposition has its value (true or false). If we represent a proposition as a variable, the variable can have the value true or false. This type of variable is called as a "proposition variable" or "logic variable".

We can combine prepositional variables by using "connectives". The basic connectives are negation, conjunction, disjunction, and implication.

Negation

Let's assume that prepositional variable P represents the following sentence.

p : 2 is rational.

In this case, the true value of P is true.

p = true

but its negation is false and represents as follows:.

~p = false

The truth table representing the values of negation is given in (Table 1).

TABLE 1   Truth table of negation

p	~p
1	0
0	1

CONJUNCTION

If p and q are prepositional variables, their conjunction is represented as $p \wedge q$ and is interpreted as "p AND q". The truth value of the above conjunction is determined according to the truth values of p end and q (Table 2).

Example 3.3 Suppose we have two propositions p and q. We can see their conjunction is 0.

p : 2 + 2 = 4   True (1)
q : 3 + 2 = 7   False (0)
r = p ∧ q = False (0)

Therefore,

TABLE 2 Truth table of conjunction

p	q	p ∧ q
1	1	1
1	0	0
0	1	0
0	0	0

DISJUNCTION

The disjunction of two propositions p and q are represented as follows:

p ∨ q

The disjunction is interpreted as "p OR q". But it has two different meanings: "exclusive OR" and "inclusive OR". The exclusive OR is used in which two events could not happen simultaneously.

Are you awake or asleep?

The inclusive OR is used when two events can occur simultaneously.

Are you wearing a shirt or sweater?

In general, if we say the disjunction, we mean the "inclusive OR" (Table 3).

TABLE 3 Truth table of disjunction

p	q	p ∨ q
1	1	1
1	0	1
0	1	1
0	0	0

Implication

The proposition "if p, then q" is represented as follows:,

p → q

TABLE 4 Truth table of implication

p	q	p → q
1	1	1
1	0	0
0	1	1
0	0	1

Example 3.4 Consider the following propositions. We study the truth value of each proposition in varying the value of propositional variables p and q.

     p $\rightarrow$ q where a : 2 + 2 = 4, b : 3 + 3 = 6

     p $\rightarrow$ q where a : 2 + 2 = 4, b : 3 + 3 = 7

     p $\rightarrow$ q where a : 2 + 2 = 5, b : 3 + 3 = 6

     p $\rightarrow$ q where a : 2 + 2 = 5, b : 3 + 3 = 7

We can see that the above propositions are true except for the second.

The truth values of implication are summarized in Table 4. In the table, we see that the value of implication can be represented by **~p ∨ q**.

CONNECTIVES IN CLASSICAL LOGIC

We use following symbols to connect two propositions in different ways:.

     ~ is used for Negation (NOT).

     ∧ is used for Conjunction (AND).

     ∨ is used for Disjunction (OR).

     $\rightarrow$ is used for an Implication sign.

     $\leftrightarrow$ is used for Equivalence.

Based on these connectives we generate compound propositions.

Example 3.5 Let us consider two propositions

     p = "We are sitting in a bar".

     q = "We are taking beer".

Now according to above operations and truth table we have:

     ~p= "We are not sitting in a bar".

     ~q= "We are not taking beer".

     p ∨ q = "We are sitting in a bar or we are taking beer".

whichWhich means that the compound statement is true when one of the p and q is true or both p and q are true.

     p ∧ q = "We are sitting in a bar and we are taking beer"

whichWhich means that the compound statement is true when both pboth p and q are true.

     p $\rightarrow$ q = "If we are sitting in a bar then we are taking beer",

which means that the compound statement is wrong when true statement implies the wrong one.This means that the compound statement is wrong when true statement implies the wrong one. We can also say that p is a sufficient condition for p or q is a necessary condition for p.

There should be a relation between premise and conclusion in the implication, e.g.for example, Ifif I fall into the lake then I will get wet.

We also use implication in theorems.,

For example, if ABC is the right triangle with right angle at B then $AC^2 = AB^2 + BC^2$.

BASIC OPERATIONS ON TRUTH VALUES

Operations on propositional logic can be described in terms of truth tables.

Truth tables of the logical formulas are based upon the following basic operations:.

$$\sim p = 1 - p$$
$$p \lor q = \max(p,q)$$
$$p \land q = \min(p,q)$$
$$p \to q = \min\{1, 1-p+q\}$$

where p and q are two propositions and their truthfulness is used as inputs in the following truth table (Table 5).

TABLE 5 Truth table

p	q	~ p	p ∨ q	p ∧ q	p→q
0	0	1	0	0	1
0	1	1	1	0	1
1	0	0	1	0	0
1	1	0	1	1	1

Any logic formula defines a logic function, and it has its truth value. Properties of logic formulas are summarized in (Table 6).

TABLE 6 Properties of logical formulas.

(1)	Involution	$\sim\sim p = p$
(2)	Commutativity	p ∨ q=q ∧ p p ∧ q=q ∨ p
(3)	Associativity	(p ∧ q)∧ r=p ∧ (q ∧ r) (p ∨ q)∨ r=p ∨ (q ∨ r)
(4)	Distributivity	p ∨ (q ∧ r)=(p ∨ q)∧ (p ∨ r) p ∧ (q ∨ r)=(p ∧ q)∨ (p ∧ r)
(5)	Idempotency	p ∧ p=p p ∨ p=p
(6)	Absorption	p ∨ (p ∧ q)=p p ∧ (p ∨ q)=p
(7)	Absorption by 0 and 1	p ∧ 0=0 p ∨ 1=1
(8)	Identity	p ∧ 1=p p ∨ 0=p
(9)	De Morgan's law	~(p ∧ q)= ~p ∨~q ~(p ∨ q) = ~p ∧~q

TABLE 6   *(continued)*

(10)	Absorption of complement	$p \vee (\sim p \wedge q) = p \vee q$
		$p \wedge (\sim p \vee q) = p \wedge q$
(11)	Law of contradiction	$p \wedge \sim p = 0$
(12)	Law of excluded middle	$p \vee \sim p = 1$

PREDICATE LOGIC

A "predicate" is a group of words like:

"is a man"

"is green"

"is less than"

"belongs to".

They can be applied to one or more names of individuals (objects) to yield meaningful sentences,; for example:;

"Socrates is a man"

"Two is less than four"

"That hat belongs to me"

"He is John".

The names of the individuals are called individual constants.

Definition 3.3 " Predicate logic" is a logic which represents a proposition with the predicate and individual (object).

Example 3.6 The following propositions are "predicate propositions" and consist of predicates and objects.

"Socrates is a man"

Predicate: ""is a man"

Object : "Socrates".

"Two is less than four"

Predicate: "is less than"

Object : "Two", "four".

Sometimes, the objects can be represented by "variable", and then, in that case, the "predicate proposition" can be evaluated if an element in the universal set is instantiated to the variable.

Example 3.7 Let's consider the following examples:.

x is a man.

y is green.

z is less than w.

p belongs to q.

If an individual is mapped to a variable, the sentence can have its meaning and then we can evaluate the value of proposition. There are examples of individual constants for the above propositions with variables.

Thomas is a man.

His shirt is green.

Two is less than four.

This pen belongs to me.

In the first sentence, Thomas is an element in the universal set "man". The element Thomas is instantiated to the variable x, and then we know the value of the proposition is true. In the second sentence, his shirt is an object (element) corresponded to the variable y, and we can evaluate the truth value of the proposition.

In the formal language, we denote predicates by letters. For example, the sentence "x satisfies P" can be written by P(x).

Example 3.8 For example, the above expressions can be represented in the following way:.

      is_a_man(x),   is_a_man(Thomas)

      is_green(y),   is_green(his shirt)

      is_less_than(z,w), is_less_than(two, four)

      belongs_to(p,q),   belongs_ to (this pen, me)

The number of individual constants to which a given predicate is called number of places of the predicate. For instance, "is a man" is an one- place predicate, and "is less than" is a two-place predicate.

A one-place predicate determines a set of things: namely those things for which it is true. Similarly, a two-place predicate determines a set of pairs of things; that is, a two-place "relation". In general, an n-place predicate determines an n-place relation. We may think of the predicate as denoting the relation.

Example 3.9. For example, the predicate "is man" determines the set of men, and the predicated "is south of" determines the set of pairs (x, y) of cities such that x is south of y. For instance, the relation holds when x = Sydney and y = Tokyo, but not when x = New York and y = Seoul. Different predicates may determine the same relation. For example, "x is south of y" and "y is north of x".

QUANTIFIER

The phrase "for all" is called the "universal quantifier" and is denoted symbolically by $\forall$. The phrase "there exists", "there is a", or "for some" is called the "existential quantifier" and is denoted symbolically by by $\exists$.

The universal quantifier is kind of an iterated conjunction. Suppose there are only finitely-many individuals. That is, the variable x takes only the values values $a_1, a_2, ... a_n$. Then the sentence $\forall x P(x)$ has the same meaning as the conjunction conjunction $P(a_1) \wedge P(a_2) \wedge ... \wedge P(a_n)$.

The existential quantifier is kind of an iterated disjunction. If there are only finitely-many individuals $a_1, a_2, ... a_n$, then the sentence $\exists x p(x)$ has the same meaning as the disjunction $P(a_1) \vee P(a_2) \vee ... \vee P(a_n)$.

Of course, if the number of individuals is infinite, such an interpretation of the quantifier is not possible, since infinitely long sentences are not allowed.

According to De Morgan's laws, $P(a_1) \vee P(a_2) \vee ... \vee P(a_n)$ is equivalent to $\sim [\sim P(a_1) \wedge \sim P(a_2) \wedge ... \wedge \sim P(a_n)]$, where the symbol $\sim$ represents the negative operator. This suggests the possibility of defining the existential quantifier from the universal quantifier. We shall do this,; $\exists x p(x)$ will be an abbreviation for $\sim \forall x \sim P(x)$ Of course, we could also define the universal quantifier from the existential quantifier, $\forall x P(x)$ has the same meaning as $\sim \exists x \sim P(x)$.

3.3 ŁUKASIEWICZ LOGIC

In western philosophy, it is only early this century that tri-valued logic is worked out. One of the contributors to this is Bertrand Russell who while writing Principia Mathematica, he came upon the Cretans paradox at the very heart of modern mathematics.

The paradox is as follows:

'The liar from Crete said that all Cretans are liars and asked if he lied.'

Now if he did not lie then he did. If he did lie then he did not. He seems to lie and not lie at the same time. The answer is not trivial. Logic then has to contend with true, false, and indeterminance. It is in the 1920's that Jan Łukasiewicz subdivides the indeterminate into multiple sections, thus multi-valued logic. He defines indeterminacy to have a continuous spectrum of values (or grayness) between truth and false or 1 and 0. Fractions would then represent degrees of a particular proposition. In 1937 Max Black publishes a paper on vagueness. This work is largely un-noticed.

Classical logic works well for mathematical proofs, but it does not describe how we reason about most nonmathematical matters.

Example 3.10
"I will eat pizza tomorrow" (or)
"I will not eat pizza tomorrow."

Classical logic says one of those is already true. So my free will is just an illusion. To have an intermediate statement of our mind, we need a logic that can say "may be".

Łukasiewicz logic is a non-classical, and multi-valued logic, in which we assign a certain value as a truthfulness of a given statement on an interval [0, 1].

In 1920, Łukasiewicz proposed the theory of three valued logic which is generalized later on to n-valued (n=2, 3, …) logic.

3-VALUED ŁUKASIEWICZ LOGIC

In 3-valued Łukasiewicz logic we have an intermediate state between "true" and "false" which can be interpreted as "may be true" or "may be false" with numeric value of ½.

Example 3.11
I will be in America in next month   True (1)

| And I will not be in America in next month | False (0) |
| I may be in America in next month | May be (1/2) |

OPERATIONS ON 3-VALUED ŁUKASIEWICZ TRUTH EXPRESSIONS

p is any statement about which we have to make conclusions whether it is true (T), false (F), or indeterminate (I). And v (p) is a truth value of statement p which could be 1, 0, or 1/2.

According to Łukasiewicz's concept, we introduce the following operations for two primitive statements p and q and obtain their results in the following truth table (Table 7).

$$v (\sim p) = 1 - v(p)$$
$$v(p \vee q) = \max (v (p), v(q)) = v (p \cup q) = v(p) \vee v(q)$$
$$v (p \wedge q) = \min(v (p), v (q)) = v (p \cap q) = v (p) \wedge v (q)$$
$$v (p \rightarrow q) = 1 \wedge [1 - v (p) + v (q)] = \min [1, 1 - v (p) + v (q)]$$
$$v (p \leftrightarrow q) = \min [v (p \rightarrow q), v (q \rightarrow p)] = v (p \rightarrow q) \wedge v (q \rightarrow p).$$

TABLE 7   3-valued Łukasiewicz Logic

| p | q/p ~ p | p ∧ q | p ∨ q | p → q | p ↔ q |
		1 ½ 0	1 ½ 0	1 ½ 0	1 ½ 0
1	1 0	1 ½ 0	1 1 1	1 ½ 0	1 ½ 0
½	½ 1/2	½ ½ 0	1 ½ ½	1 1 ½	½ 1 ½
0	0 1	0 0 0	1 ½ 0	1 1 1	0 ½ 1

In Table 7, p and q are truth values of two different statements and q/p is the value of q on condition that p. This table is constructed by combining each value of p with all three values of q. This can be illustrated by the following example.

Example 3.12 Let usLet us consider two values of p and q

$$p = \tfrac{1}{2} \text{ and } q = 1.$$

so we consider the second row in this case.

$$\sim p = 1 - \tfrac{1}{2} = \tfrac{1}{2}$$

which is shown on the last position in second column.

$$p \wedge q = \min (1/2, 1) = (1/2)$$

which is shown on the first position in third column.

$$p \lor q = \max (1/2, 1) = 1$$

which is shown on the first position in fourth column.

$$p \rightarrow q = \min (1, 1 - 1/2 + 1) = \min (1, 3/2) = 1$$

which is shown on the first position in fifth column.

$$p \leftrightarrow q = \min (p \rightarrow q, q \rightarrow p)$$

where $q \rightarrow p = \min (1, 1 - 1 + \frac{1}{2}) = \min (1, \frac{1}{2}) = \frac{1}{2}$.
So,

$$P \leftrightarrow q = \min (1, \frac{1}{2}) = \frac{1}{2}$$

which is shown on the first position in last column.

Similarly, we can verify the results for any other combination of values of p and q.
Working rules for 3-valued Łukasiewicz Logic:
The three truth values (T, I, F or 1, ½, 0) are in order of decreasing truthfulness.
The negation of a statement of given truth values is its opposite in truthfulness
The truth value of conjunction is the falsest and of a disjunction the truest of the truth values of its components.
The truth value of $p \rightarrow q$ is the same as that of $\sim p \lor q$ except the truth value corresponding to $I \rightarrow I$.
The truth value of $p \leftrightarrow q$ is same as that of $(p \rightarrow q) \land (q \rightarrow p)$.

MODEL OPERATORS

Łukasiewicz implemented the idea of Aristotelian logic that proposition regarding future contingent matters have a truth status that does not corresponds to either of the orthodox truth values of truth and falsity. In carrying out this idea, we introduce corresponding complications into the truth rules for propositional connectives. Łukasiewicz solution to this problem consists of truth tables for any proposition or statement.

With a view to the future contingency interpretation of the third value (I), Łukasiewicz introduced modal operators of possibility and necessity (symbolically ◊ and □) into his 3 valued logic. These are represented in the truth table below (Table 8):.

TABLE 8   Modeling of 3-valued Łukasiewicz Logic

v(p)	◊ p	□ p
1	1	1
1/2	1	0
0	0	0

Thus symbolically ◊ p is true if p is either true or intermediate but is false if p is definitely false.

Example 3.13 Let us consider the future prediction about rain, i.e.that is Tomorrowtomorrow will be rain.

If this is true (v(p) = 1), then there is possibility of rain tomorrow (◊ p = 1) and also it is necessary (□ p = 1) to be true. Otherwise the values v(p) and □ p will contradict.

If it is partially true that tomorrow will be rain (v(p) = 1/2), then there is still possibility of rain (◊ p = 1), but is not necessary (□ p = 0) to be true that tomorrow will be rain.

If it is false that tomorrow will be rain (v(p) = 0), then there is no possibility of rain (◊ p = 0) and also not necessary (□ p = 0) to be true that tomorrow will be rain.

3.3.1 MODALITIES IN CLASSICAL LOGIC

Truth functional treatment of modalities is not possible in two valued logic. The closest, we can comecan come to specifying modalities in classical logic is given in Table 9.

TABLE 9   Closest specification of modalities is classical logic

v(p)	◊ p	□ p
1	1	1
0	0	0

Therefore, v(p) ≡ ◊ p and v(p)≡ □ p.

So □ p ≡ ◊ p will all be logical truths so that model distinctions collapse in 3 valued logic. However we have the desirable implications p → ◊ p, and □ p → v(p), and □ p → ◊ p without being saddled with their undesirable converses so that model distinctions are preserved.

3.3.2 COMPARISON BETWEEN 3-VALUED ŁUKASIEWICZ LOGIC AND CLASSICAL LOGIC

Three valued truth table agrees with the two valued ones only when T's (1's) and F's (0's) are involved as we can see in truth table (Table 10) of 3-valued Łukasiewicz logic,. i.e. that is,

TABLE 10   Three valued interpretation with respect to two valued logic

p	q/p	¬ p	p ∧ q			p ∨ q			p → q			p ↔ q		
			1	½	0	1	½	0	1	½	0	1	½	0
1	1	0	1	½	0	1	1	1	1	½	0	1	½	0
½	½	1/2	½	½	0	1	½	½	1	1	½	½	1	½
0	0	1	0	0	0	1	½	0	1	1	1	0	½	1

Łukasiewicz uses this 3-valued logic as a base to generalize it into n-valued Łukasiewicz Logic.

MANY-VALUED GENERALIZATION OF THE 3-VALUED ŁUKASIEWICZ LOGIC

It is a logic, in which we assign a certain value to a truthfulness of given statement on an interval [0, 1] as in classical logic we assign '0' for false statement and '1' for true statement. But sometimes, we come across many kinds of true and false statements like true, very true, very very true, ratherand rather false in our everyday life.

Truth-values are real numbers between 0 and 1 for the proposition (say p) and isare denoted by:

$$v(p) \in [0,1]$$

As Łukasiewicz generalizes 3-valued logic to many-valued logic, so the operations on truth expressions in this case are the same as in 3-valued logic case.

DIVISION OF UNIT INTERVAL

Let us divide the interval from 0 to 1 by inserting evenly spaced division points for a total of a pointsof points ($n \geq 2$).

TABLE 11   Many valued interpretation of Łukasiewicz logic

n	Division	Division Points (Truth Values)
2	1/1, 0/1	(1, 0)
3	2/2, ½, 0/2	(1, 1/2, 0)
4	3/3, 2/3, 1/3, 0/3	(1, 2/3, 1/3, 0)
⋮	⋮	⋮
⋮	⋮	⋮
⋮	⋮	⋮
n	1=(n-1)/(n-1), (n-2)/(n-1), ..., 2/n-1, 1/n-1, 0/n-1=0	

Given the propositional connectives based on the arithmetical operations and taking the members of this series as truth-values, we obtain the series Ln of Łukasiewicz many-valued logic. It is readily seen that:

L_2 is identical with two valued classical logic.

L_3 is identical with 3-valued system of Łukasiewicz.

So the above system of the series is many valued generalizations both of the classical two valued system (L_2) and of the Łukasiewicz (L_3).

Moreover we can take the further possibility of obtaining two infinite valued systems as follows:

For the system L_{s0} we consider 0 and 1 together with all the rational numbers (i.e. all fractions n/m) between 0 and 1 as truth values.

For the system L_{s1} we consider all the real numbers from the interval 0 to 1 as truth values. Thus, we can construct truth table L_n for any value of n.

4-valued Łukasiewicz Logic

Let us consider n = 4, then for L_4 the truth table is as follows (Table 12)

TABLE 12   4 valued Łukasiewicz logic

p	q/p	~p	p∧q				p∨q				p→q				p↔q			
			1	2/3	1/3	0	1	2/3	1/3	0	1	2/3	1/3	0	1	2/3	1/3	0
1	1	0	1	2/3	1/3	0	1	1	1	1	1	2/3	1/3	0	1	2/3	1/3	0
2/3	2/3	1/3	2/3	2/3	1/3	0	1	2/3	2/3	2/3	1	1	2/3	1/3	2/3	1	2/3	1/3
1/3	1/3	2/3	1/3	1/3	1/3	0	1	2/3	1/3	1/3	1	1	1	2/3	1/3	2/3	1	2/3
0	0	1	0	0	0	0	1	2/3	1/3	0	1	1	1	1	0	1/3	2/3	1

where p and q are truth values of two different statements and q/p is the value of q on the condition that p. This table is constructed by combining each value of p with all four values of q. This can be illustrated by the following example:.

Example 3.14 Let us take two values of p and q

$$P = 2/3 \text{ and } q = 1/3$$

So we see the second row in this case.

$$\sim p = 1\text{-}2/3 = 1/3$$

$$\sim q = 1\text{-}1/3 = 2/3$$

$$p \wedge q = \min (2/3,\ 1/3) = 1/3$$

which we can see on the third position in third column.

$$p \vee q = \max (2/3,\ 1/3) = 2/3$$

which we can see on the second position in fourth column.

$$p \rightarrow q = \min (1,\ 1\text{-}2/3 + 1/3) = 2/3$$

which we can see on the second position in fifth column.

$$p \leftrightarrow q = \min (p \rightarrow q,\ q \rightarrow p)$$

where

$$q \rightarrow p = \min (1,\ 1\text{-}1/3 + 2/3) = 1$$

So,

$$p \leftrightarrow q = \min (2/3, 1) = 2/3$$

which we can see this value on the third position in last column.

We can verify the results for the other combinations of the values of p and q in a similar way.

Similarly we can construct any other truth table for different values of n in L_n.

Example 3.15 Let us consider p = "appreciated customers" in a local bank, which is depended upon the amount of money on their accounts.

Following the data of customer financial situations, we evaluate the truth value of "appreciated position" in the bank by using classical and Łukasiewicz logic (Table 13).

TABLE 13   Comparative status between two valued and multivalued logic

Account No.	Deposit in millions	V(p) in classical two- valued logic	V(p) in Łukasiewicz Multi-valued logic
001-78	100	1	1
167-36	93	1	0.98
475-84	79	1	0.80
368-02	71	1	0.78
745-45	54	1	0.65
745-34	41	0	0.39
730-17	33	0	0.24
904-47	27	0	0.15
397-01	18	0	0.09
376-33	7	0	0.01

The following graph of Figure. 1 shows the difference between truth values belonging to different logical systems.

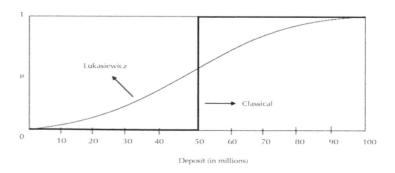

FIGURE 1   Truth value representation of classical logic and Łukasiewicz logic.

Example 3.16 Let p and q be the statements given as:

P = "Temperature in a city is high"

Q = "It is raining"

Classical logic fails here because it provides only two values for each of the above statements,; either Temperature is high [True(1)] or temperature is not high [False (0)] and either it is raining [True (1)] or it is not raining [False (0)]. Now consider the case, temperature is high and it is raining,; but we do no't know how much the level of temperature is high and how much intense the rain is? That isi.e., what is the truthfulness of the above statements p and q. That i's why, we use Łukasiewicz logic to precise the given information by assigning the value according to the truthfulness. Suppose that the statement 'p' is true in the following sense:.

$$v(p) = 1$$

that is temperature is very high.

$$v(p) = 0.9$$

that is temperature is high.

$$v(p) = 0.7$$

that is temperature is rather high.

$$v(p) = 0.5$$

that is temperature is moderately high.

Similarly, we can assign values to the statement q according to the reality.

Now take any two values of both statements.

"Temperature is rather high" with $v(q) = 0.7$

"It is raining heavily" with $v(p) = 0.9$

$v(\sim p)$= "Temperature is not rather high" = $1-v(p) = 1-0.7 = 0.3$

$v(\sim q)$= "it is not raining heavily" = $1-v(q) = 1-0.9 = 0.1$

$v(p \vee q)$= "Temperature is rather high or it is raining heavily"

$v(p \vee q)$= max $[v(p), v(q)]$ = max $[0.7, 0.9] = 0.9$

$v(p \wedge q)$= "Temperature is rather high and it is raining heavily"

$v(p \wedge q)$= min $[v(p), v(q)]$ = min$[0.7-0.9] = 0.7$

$v(p \rightarrow q)$= "if Temperature is rather high then it is raining heavily"

$v(p \rightarrow q)$= min $[1, 1-v(p) + v(q)]$ = min$[1, 1-0.7+0.9]$ = min$[1, 1.2]$=1.

3.4   FUZZY LOGIC

Fuzzy logic is a logic in which the truth values are fuzzy subsets of the unit interval with linguistic labels such as:;

True, false, not true, very true, quite true, not very true and not very false , and so on etc.

The main difference between Łukasiewicz logic and fuzzy logic is that, in Łukasiewicz logic truth value for certain statement or proposition is a single value in [0, 1], but in fuzzy logic, the truth value is a fuzzy set of the unit interval.

DISTINGUISHED FEATURES OF FUZZY LOGIC

- Fuzzy truth values are expressed in linguistic terms.
- Truth tables are imprecise in nature.
- Rules of inference are approximate rather than exact.

From these aspects fuzzy logic differs significantly from standard logical systems ranging from the classical Aristotelia logic to inductive logics and many valued logics. Fuzzy logic is fuzzy extension of a non-fuzzy multivalued logic which constitutes a base logic for fuzzy logic. In fuzzy logic we actually assign the membership degree to a statement according to the degree of truthfulness in the interval [0, 1].

It is convenient to use standard Łukasiewicz logic (which we have briefly explained with examples in the previous section) as a base logic for fuzzy logic.

3.4.1 FUZZY EXPRESSION

In the fuzzy expression (formula), a fuzzy proposition can have its truth value in the interval [0,1]. The fuzzy expression function is a mapping function from [0,1] to [0,1].

$$f : [0,1] \rightarrow [0,1]$$

If we generalize the domain in n-dimension, the function becomes as follows :

$$f : [0,1]^n \rightarrow [0,1]$$

Therefore we can interpret the fuzzy expression as an n-ary relation from n fuzzy sets to [0,1]. In the fuzzy logic, the operations such as negation ($\sim$), conjunction ($\wedge$), and disjunction ($\vee$) are used as in the classical logic.

Definition 3.4 The fuzzy logic is a logic represented by the fuzzy expression (formula) which satisfies the followings:.
- Truth values, 0 and 1, and variable   are fuzzy expressions.
- If f is a fuzzy expression, $\sim$f is also a fuzzy expression.

- If f and g are fuzzy expressions, $f \wedge g$ and $f \vee g$ are also fuzzy expressions.

3.4.2 OPERATORS IN FUZZY EXPRESSION

There are some operators in the fuzzy expression such as $\sim$ (negation), $\wedge$ (conjunction), $\vee$ (disjunction), and $\rightarrow$ (implication). However the meaning of operators may be different according to the literature. If we follow Łukasiewicz's definition, the operators are defined as follows for p, q $\in$ [0, 1].
- Negation $\sim p = 1 - p$
- Conjunction $p \wedge q = Min(p, q)$
- Disjunction $p \vee q = Min(1, 1 + q - p)$
- Implication $p \rightarrow q = Min(1, 1 + q - p)$

The properties of fuzzy operators are summarized in (Table 14).

TABLE 14   The properties of fuzzy logic operators

(1)	Involution	$\sim\sim p = p$
(2)	Commutativity	$p \wedge q = q \wedge p$
		$p \vee q = q \vee p$
(3)	Associativity	$(p \wedge q) \wedge r = p \wedge (q \wedge r)$
		$(p \vee q) \vee r = p \vee (q \vee r)$
(4)	Distributivity	$p \vee (q \wedge r) = (p \vee q) \wedge (p \vee r)$
		$p \wedge (q \vee r) = (p \wedge q) \vee (p \wedge r)$
(5)	Idempotency	$p \wedge p = p$
		$p \vee p = p$
(6)	Absorption	$p \vee (p \wedge q) = p$
		$p \wedge (p \vee q) = p$
(7)	Absorption by 0 and 1	$p \wedge 0 = 0$
		$p \vee 1 = 1$
(8)	Identity	$p \wedge 1 = p$
		$p \vee 0 = p$
(9)	De Morgan's law	$\sim(p \wedge q) = \sim p \vee \sim q$
		$\sim(p \vee q) = \sim p \wedge \sim q$

But we note that the law of contradiction and law of excluded middle are not applicable in the fuzzy logic.

Classical logic is referred to as bivalent logic where a statement (proposition) is either true or false. This is known as Aristotle's legacy. According to him p and ~p is null, an empty set. This is considered to be philosophically correct for over 2000 years. It is interesting to note that around two countries earlier, Buddha holds a completely different view. Instead of having a clear cut perspective of a black and white world, he visualizes a world filled with contradictions. Buddha says that a rose,, can be a certain degree completely red, but also at the same time it is to a certain degree not red,; i.e.that is the rose can be red and not red at the same time. This is a clear contradiction with Aristotle view. Kosko prefers Buddha principle of "A ∧ non A" to the Aristotle principle "A ∨ non A". According to Kosko, the world can be understood only if we forget the principle of non contradiction, because always the objects of the world have in the same time opposite determinations. On the other hand, Zadeh does not think that fuzzy logic is so in contrast with classical logic. Zadeh and Bellman writes, *"Although fuzzy logic represents a significant departure from the conventional approaches to the formalization of human reasoning, it constitutes – so far at least – an extension rather than a total abandonment of the currently hold views on meaning, truth, and inference"*.

3.4.3   *THE TRUTH VALUE SET OF FUZZY LOGIC*

The truth value set 'T' of fuzzy logic is assumed to be generated by a context-free grammar with a semantic rule providing a means of computing the meaning of each linguistic truth value 'τ' in 'T' as a fuzzy subset of [0, 1].

It is a countable set of the form:;

T={true,false,not true,very true,not very true,more or less true,fairly true, ...not very false,...,etc}.

Each element of this set represents a fuzzy subset of the truth value set of Łukasiewicz logic i.e.that is [0, 1]. Thus the meaning of a linguistic truth value 'τ' in 'T' is assumed to be a fuzzy subset of [0, 1], more specifically let [4]

$\mu_\tau : [0, 1] \rightarrow [0, 1]$ denote the membership function of 'τ'.

The meaning of 'τ' as a fuzzy subset of [0, 1] is expressed by:

$$\tau = \int_1^0 \mu_\tau(v)/v$$

where the integral sign denotes the union of fuzzy singletons $\mu_\tau(v)/v$, signifying that the membership of the numerical truth value 'v' with the linguistic truth value τ is $\mu_\tau(v)$ or the grade of membership of v in the fuzzy set labeled τ is $\mu_\tau(v)$.

If the support of τ is a finite subset $\{v_1, v_2, ..., v_n\}$ of [0,1], τ may be expressed as:

$$\tau = \mu_1/v_1 + v_n\ \mu_2/v_2 + ... + \mu_n/v_n, \text{ for example}$$

True = {0.4/0.6 + 0.6/0.7 + 0.8/0.8 + 0.9/0.9 + 1/1}.

Example 3.17. Suppose that the meaning of true is defined by:

$$\tau_{true}(v) = \begin{cases} 0 & \text{for } \alpha \leq v \leq \alpha \\ ((v-\alpha)/(1-\alpha))^2 & \text{for } \alpha \leq v \leq \alpha + 1/2 \\ 1 - ((v-1)(1-\alpha))^2 & \text{for } \alpha + 1/2 \leq v \leq 1 \end{cases}$$

where α is a value in [0,1].

Therefore we may write:

true = $\int_\alpha^{(\alpha+1)/2}((v-\alpha)/(1-\alpha))^2/v + \int_{(\alpha+1)/2}^1[1 - ((v-\alpha)/(1-\alpha))^2]/v$.

If v_1 = 0,1, v_2 = 0.2, ..., v_11=1 then 'true' might be written as:,
    true = {0.3/0.7 + 0.5/0.8 + 0.8/0.9 + 1/1}.

COMPARISON OF LINGUISTIC FUZZY TRUTH VALUES AND NUMERICAL ŁUKASIEWICZ TRUTH VALUES

- The Łukasiewicz truth-value set is a continuous, whereas that of fuzzy logic is a countable set. More importantly, in most applications to approximate reasoning, a small finite subset of the truth-values of fuzzy logic would in general, be sufficient because each fuzzy truth-value represents a fuzzy subset rather than a single element of [0,1]. Thus, we gain by trading the large number of simple Łukasiewicz truth-values for the small number of less simple truth-values of fuzzy logic.

- The method of approximate reasoning essentially deals with propositions which are fuzzy rather than precise, e.gFor example., "weather is very hot", "he is looking very beautiful", "soup is not very tasty", and so on. etc.

Clearly, the fuzzy truth-values of fuzzy logic are more commensurate with the fuzziness of such propositions than the numerical Łukasiewicz truth-values.

3.4.4 OPERATIONS ON FUZZY TRUTH VALUES

So far we have discussed the structure of the truth value set of fuzzy logic. Now we consider the manipulation of linguistic fuzzy truth values in interval [0, 1].

To extend the definition of negation, conjunction, and implication in Łukasiewicz logic to those of fuzzy logic it is convenient to employ an extension principle for fuzzy sets which can be stated as follows: .

EXTENSION PRINCIPLE FOR FUZZY SETS (SEE SECTION 2.17.5 OF CHAPTER 2)

For one variable:
Let us define a function 'f' mapping from X to Y
$f: X \rightarrow Y$
where

$$X = \{x_i\}, \qquad x_{(i)} \in X, , \qquad i = 1, 2, \ldots, n$$
$$Y = \{y_i\}, \qquad y_{(i)} \in Y, \qquad j = 1, 2, \ldots, m.$$

Let $A \subset X$ be a fuzzy set given by:
$$A = \{x_i, \mu_A(x_i)\}$$
where $\mu_A(x_i)$ are the membership degrees for x_i, $i = 1, 2, \ldots, n$.

Therefore we can construct
$$f(A) = \{f(x_i), \mu_{f(A)}(f(x_i))\} = B$$
where
$$\mu_{f(A)}(f(x_i)) = \max_{f(xi)} \mu_A(x_i)$$

or we can also write f(A) as:

$$f(A) = \sum_{xi} \in X \max_{f(xi)} \mu(x_i) / f(x_i) \tag{3.1}$$

Example 3.18   Let X={-2,-1,0,1,2,3} and A is fuzzy set in X given by:
$A = \{0.1/ -2 + 0.2/ - 1 + 0.3/0 + 0.5/1 + 0.8/2 + 1/3\}$ and function f is given by:
$y = 2x^2 + 1$.
Therefore, according to Equation (3.1) we get:
$\quad f(A) = 0.1/9 + 0.2/3 + 0.3/1 + 0.5/3 + 0.8/9 + 1/19$
$\quad f(A) = 0.3/1 + \max(0.2, 0.5)/3 + \max(0.1, 0.8)/9 + 1/19$
$\quad f(A) = 0.3/1 + 0.5/3 + 0.8/9 + 1/19.$

For two variables:
Let

$$X=\{x_i\}, \qquad x_i \in X, \qquad i=1,2,...,n$$
$$Y=\{y_j\}, \qquad y_j \in Y, \qquad j=1,2,...,m$$
$$Z=\{z_k\}, \qquad z_k \in Z, \qquad k=1,2,...,p$$

be the universal sets.

Let a two dimensional function

$$Z=g(X,Y) \text{ or } z_k=g(x_i,y_j).$$

We consider two fuzzy sets

$$A \subset X, A=\{x_i; \mu_A(x_i)\} \text{ and}$$
$$B \subset Y, B=\{y_j; \mu_B(y_j)\}.$$

Therefore,

$$g(A,B) \subset Z,$$

where

$g(A,B)$ in Z is a representation of function g and

$$g(A,B) = \Sigma_{(x_i,y_j) \in X \times Y} max_{g(x_i,y_j)} \min (\mu_A(x_i), \mu_B(y_j))/g(x_i,y_i) \qquad (3.2)$$

Example 3.19   Let X and Y be the two universal crisp sets given by:
X = {2, 4, 5}, and   Y = {5, 6, 7} and A, B are two fuzzy sets A $\subset$ X and B $\subset$ Y respectively defined by:
A = 'big number in X' = 0.3/2 + 0.7/4 + 1/5 B = 'big number in Y' = 0.6/5 + 0.9/6 + 1/7. For Z $\subset$ X $\times$Y
Let g(x, y) = y-x.
Therefore, according to equation (3.2), we get:,

g(A, B) = min (0.6, 0.3)/3 + min(0.6, 0.7)/1 + min(0.6,1)/0 + min(0.9, 0.3)/4
+ min (0.9, 0.7)/2 + (min 0.9,1)/1 + min (1, 0.3)/5 + min(1, 0.7)/3 + min(1, 1)/2
g(A, B) = 0.3/3 + 0.6/1 + 0.6/0 + 0.3/4 + 0.7/2 + 0.9/1 + 0.3/5 + 0.7/3 + ½
g(A, B) = 0.6/0 + max(0.6, 0.9)/1 + max(0.7, 1)/2 + max (0.3, 0.7)/3
g(A, B) = 0.6/0 + 0.9/1 + ½ + 0.7/3 + 0.3/4 + 0.3/5.

3.4.5   OPERATIONS ON FUZZY TRUTH VALUES BASED ON EXTENSION PRINCIPLE

The concept of extension principle as stated above is utilized to define negation, conjunction, disjunction, and implication in fuzzy logic. We consider linguistic fuzzy subsets τ,

that is τ: [0, 1] $\rightarrow$[0, 1] of truth expressions set.

T = {true, false, very true, very false, rather true, maybe true, bit true, etc and so on}

In which both members of set τ and their degrees are ranging from 0 to 1.

Let p and q be propositions (statements) which have logical values described by the fuzzy sets $\tau(p)$ and $\tau(q)$ where:

$$\tau(p) = \Sigma \mu_{\tau(p)}(x)/x, \ x \in [0,1]$$
$$\tau(q) = \Sigma \mu_{\tau(p)}(y)/y, \ y \in [0,1].$$

To illustrate the concept we consider some of fuzzy truth values setsset τ as follows:

Example 3.20.
   "true" = 0.7/.8 + 0.9/0.9 + 1/1
   "very true' = 0.9/0.8 + 1/0.9 + 1/1
   "fairly True" = 1/0.8 + 0.9/0.9 + 0.8/1
   "more or less true" = 0.7/0.4 + 1/0.5 + 0.7/0.6
   "less True" = 1/0.3 + 0.8/0.4 + 0.7/0.5
   "false" = 1/0 + 0.7/0.1 + 0.5/0.2
   "very False" = 1/0 + 1/0.1 + 0.9/0.2
   "not False" = 0.6/0.6 + 0.7/0.7 + 0.8/0.8 + 0.9/0.9 + 1/1.

Definition 3.5 Negation for a certain fuzzy truth value τ(p) for statement 'p' is denoted by ~τ(p) and is given by the membership function,

$$\mu_{\sim\tau(p)}(v) = 1 - \mu_{\tau(p)}(v), v \in [0,1]. \tag{3.3}$$

There is another type of negation in which we negate the statement 'p' rather than the truth value set ~τ(p).

Definition 3.6 The truth value on negate statement ~p is given by the membership function

$$\mu_{\tau(\sim p)}(v) = 1 - \mu_{\tau(p)}(1-v), v \in [0,1]. \tag{3.4}$$

Example 3.21 Let
   p = "Dona is looking beautiful".
Suppose that this statement is more or less true.
   τ(p) = "more or less true" = 0.7/0.4 + 1/0.5 + 0.7/0.6
So by equation (3.3) we get:,
   ~ τ(p) = "not more or less true"
   ~ τ(p) = 1-0.7/0.4 + 1-1/0.5 + 1-0.7/0.6
   ~ τ(p) = 0.3/0.4 + 0/0.5 + 0.3/0.6.
For the second type of negation, we make the follwingfollowing calculation:.
Consider the same proposition as stated above and according to Equation (3.4) we get:;
   ~p = "Dona is not looking beautiful"
With membership values:
   τ(~p) = 0.7/1 - 0.4 + 1/1-0.5 + 0.7/1-0.6
   τ(~p) = 0.7/0.6 + 1/0.5 + 0.7/0.4.

Definition 3.7 Conjunction between two truth fuzzy expression τ(p) and τ(q) for two propositions p and q is given by:

$$\tau(p \wedge q) = \sum_{(x,y)\in[0,1]\times[0,1]} \max_{\min(x,y)} \min\left(\mu_{\tau(p)}(x), \mu_{\tau(q)}(y)\right) / \min(x,y) \tag{3.5}$$

with
$$\tau(p) = \{x, \mu_{\tau(p)}(x)\}, \qquad x \in [0,1]$$
$$\tau(q) = \{y, \mu_{\tau(p)}(y)\}, \qquad y \in [0,1].$$

Example 3.22 Let us consider two fuzzy propositions:,

p = "John does exercise"   and

q = "John is a healthy man"

with fuzzy truth values given by:

$\tau(p)$ = "less true" = 1/0.3 + 0.9/0.4 + 0.8/0.5 and

$\tau(q)$ = "more or less true" = 0.8/0.4+1/0.5+0.7/0.6 .

According to Equation (3.5) we get:,

$\tau(p \wedge q)$ = min(1, 0.7)/min (0.3, 0.4) + min (1, 1) / min (0.3, 0.5) + min (1, 0.7) / min (0.3, 0.6) + min (0.9, 0.7)/ min (0.4, 0.4) + min (0.9, 1)/ min (0.4, 0.5) + min (0.9, 0.7) / min (0.4, 0.6) + min (0.8, 0.7)/ min (0.5, 0.4) + min (0.8, 1)/ min (0.5, 0.5) + min (0.8, 0.7) / min (0.5, 0.6).

Therefore,

$\tau(p \wedge q)$ = 0.7/0.3 + 1/ 0.3 + 0.7/0.3 + 0.7/0.4 + 0.9/0.4 + 0.7/0.4 + 0.7/0.5 + 0.8/0.5 +0.7/0.5

$\tau(p \wedge q)$ = max(0.7, 1, 0.7)/0.3 + max(0.7, 0.9, 0.7,0.7)/0.4 + max (0.8, 0.7)/0.5

$\tau(p \wedge q)$ = 1/0.3 + 0.9/0.4 + 0.8/0.5 .

So ("less true") AND ("more or less true") = "less true".

Definition 3.8 Disjunction between two truth fuzzy expressions $\tau(p)$ and $\tau(q)$ for two propositions p and q is given by:

$$\tau(p \vee q) = \sum\nolimits_{(x,y) \in [0,1] \times [0,1]} \max\nolimits_{\max(x,y)} \min\left(\mu_{\tau(p)}(x), \mu_{\tau(q)}(y)\right) / \max(x,y) \qquad (3.6)$$

Where,

$$\mu_{\tau(p \vee q)} = \max\nolimits_{\max(x,y)} \min(\mu_{\tau(p)}(x), \mu_{\tau(q)}(y)) .$$

Example 3.23 Apply the equation (3.6) to above example where:,

$\tau(p)$= "less true" = 1/0.3 + 0.9/0.4 + 0.8/0.5

$\tau(q)$= "more or less true" = 0.7/0.4 + 1/0.5 + 0.7/0.6.

Thus we get:;

$\tau(p \vee q)$=min(1, 0.7)/max (0.3, 0.4) + min (1, 1) / max (0.3, 0.5) + min (1, 0.7) / max (0.3, 0.6) + min (0.9, 0.7)/ max (0.4, 0.4) + min (0.9, 1)/ max (0.4, 0.5) + min (0.9, 0.7) / max (0.4, 0.6) + min (0.8, 0.7)/ max (0.5, 0.4) + min (0.8, 1)/ max (0.5, 0.5) + min (0.8, 0.7) / max (0.5, 0.6).

Therefore,

$\tau(p \vee q)$ =0.7/0.4+1/0.5+0.7/0.6+0.7/0.4+0.9/0.5+0.7/0.6+0.7/0.5+0.8/0.5+0.7/0.6

$\tau(p \vee q)$ = max(0.7, 0.7)/0.4 + max(1, 0.9, 0.7, 0.8)/0.5 + max (0.7, 0.7, 0.7)/0.6

$\tau(p \vee q)$ = 0.7/0.4 + 1/0.5 + 0.7/0.6 = $\tau(q)$.

So ("less true") OR ("more or less true") = "more or less true" .

Definition 3.9 Implication of two fuzzy truth expressions $\tau(p)$ and $\tau(q)$ for propositions p and q is given by:

$$\tau(p \rightarrow q) = \sum_{(x,y)\in[0,1]\times[0,1]} \max_{\min(1,1-x+y)} \min\left(\mu_{\tau(p)}(x), \mu_{\tau(p)}(y)\right) / \min(1,1-x+y) \quad (3.7)$$

with

$$\mu_{\tau(p\rightarrow q)}(v) = \max_{\min(1,1-x+y)} \min\left(\mu_{\tau(q)}(x), \mu_{\tau(q)}(y)\right)$$

Example 3.24 Let us apply the implication operation of equation (3.7) to the data of the above example. Thus we get:

$\tau(p \rightarrow q)$ = min(1, 0.7)/min (1, 1.1) + min (1, 1) / min (1, 1.2) + min (1, 0.7) / min (1, 1.3) + min (0.9, 0.7)/ min (1, 1) + min (0.9, 1)/ min (1, 1.1) + min (0.9, 0.7) / min (1, 1.2) + min (0.8, 0.7)/ min (1, 0.9) + min (0.8, 1)/ min (1, 1) + min (0.8, 0.7) / min (1, 1.1)

Therefore:,

$\tau(p \rightarrow q)$ = 0.7/1 + 1/1 + 0.7/1 +0.7/1 + 0.9/1 + 0.7/1 + 0.7/0.9 + 0.8/1 + 0.7/1
$\tau(p \rightarrow q)$ = max(0.7, 1, 0.7, 0.7, 0.9, 0.7, 0.8, 0.7)/1 + 0.7/0.9
$\tau(p \rightarrow q)$ = 0.7/0.9 + 1/1.

Equivalence relation is actually minimum of two implication, i.e.,that is:

$$\tau(p \leftrightarrow q) = \tau(p \rightarrow q) \wedge (q \rightarrow p).$$

Definition 3.10 Equivalence between two fuzzy truth expression, $\tau(p)$ and $\tau(q)$ for proposition p and q is given by,

$$\sum_{(x,y)\in[0,1]\times[0,1]} \max_{\min(x,y)} \min\left(\mu_{\tau(p\rightarrow q)}(x), \mu_{\tau(q\rightarrow p)}(y)\right) / \min(x,y) \quad (3.8)$$

Example 3.25 According to the definition 3.9 for implication of two fuzzy truth expression we get,

$$\tau(q \rightarrow p) = \sum_{(x,y)\in[0,1]\times[0,1]} \max_{\min(1,1-y+x)} \min\left(\mu_{\tau(p)}(x), \mu_{\tau(q)}(y)\right) / \min(1,1-y+x)$$

Therefore,

$\tau(q \rightarrow p)$ = 0.8/0.9 + 1/0.8 + 0.7/0.7 +0.7/1+ 0.9/0.9 +0.7/0.8+0.7/1 +0.8/1+0.7/0.9
$\tau(q \rightarrow p)$ = 0.7/ 0.7+1/ 0.8+ 0.9/0.9 +0.8/1.

and we have

$\tau(p \rightarrow q)$ = 0.7/0.9 + 1/1 .

According to equation (3.8) we get:,

$\tau(p \leftrightarrow q)$ = min(0.7, 0.7)/min (0.9, 0.7) + min (0.7, 1) / min (0.9, 0.8) + min (0.7, 0.9)/ min (0.9,0.9) + min (0.7, 0.8)/ min (0.9, 1) + min (1, 0.7) / min (1, 0.7) + min (1, 1)/ min (1, 0.8) + min (1, 0.9)/ min (1, 0.9) + min (1, 0.8) / min (1, 1)

$\tau(p \leftrightarrow q)$= 0.7/0.7 + 0.7/0.8 + 0.7/0.9 + 0.7/1 + 0.7/0.7 + 1/0.8 + 0.9/0.9 + 0.8/1
$\tau(p \leftrightarrow q)$= 0.7/0.7 + max(0.7, 1)/0.8 + max (0.7, 0.9)/0.9 + max(0.7/0.8)/1
$\tau(p \leftrightarrow q)$= 0.7/0.7 + 1/ 0.8 + 0.9/0.9 + 0.8/1.

3.4.6   BALDWIN APPROACH TO FUZZY TRUTH   VALUES

As it is difficult to define fuzzy subsets for different linguistic truth values and perform all the operations stated in the previous section, Baldwin formalizes all these fuzzy truth values and describedescribed them in a convenient way.

Let us consider

$$\tau(p)= \text{"true"}$$

With the membership function

$$\mu_{true}(v)=v.$$

Then according to Baldwin:;

$$\mu_{false}(v) = 1 - v \tag{a}$$

$$\mu_{very\ true}(v) = (\mu_{true}(v))^2 = v^2 \tag{b}$$

$$\mu_{very\ false}(v) = (\mu_{false}(v))^2 = (1-v)^2 \tag{c}$$

$$\mu_{fairly\ true}(v) = (\sqrt{\mu_{true}(v)}) = \sqrt{v} \tag{d}$$

$$\mu_{fairly\ false}(v) = \left(\sqrt{\mu_{false}(v)}\right) = \sqrt{1-v} \tag{e}$$

$$\mu_{absolutelytrue}(v) = \begin{cases} 1 & v = 1 \\ 0 & v\epsilon[0,1) \end{cases} \tag{f}$$

$$\mu_{absolutelyfalse}(v) = \begin{cases} 1 & v = 0 \\ 0 & v\epsilon(0,1] \end{cases} \tag{g}$$

$$\mu_{undefined}(v) = 1 \quad v\epsilon[0,1] \tag{h}$$

$$(3.9)$$

Example 3.26 According to Baldwin a fuzzy truth value set "true" used as a base set is given by the line y = x,; i.e.that is:

"True" = 0.0/0 = 0.1/0.1 + 0.2/0.2 + 0.3/0.3 + 0.4/0.4 + 0.5/0.5 + 0.6/0.6 + 0.7/0.7 + 0.8/0.8 + 0.9/0.9 + 1/1 .

Therefore, according to equation 3.9(a-h) we get:,

"false" = (1 - 0.0)/0 + (1 - 0.1)/0.1 + (1 - 0.2)/0.2 + (1 - 0.3)/0.3 + (1 - 0.4)/0.4 + (1 - 0.5)/0.5 + (1 - 0.6)/0.6 + (1 - 0.7)/0.7 + (1 - 0.8)/0.8 + (1 - 0.9)/0.9 + (1 - 1)/1

"false" = 1.0/0 + 0.9/0.1 + 0.8/0.2 + 0.7/0.3 + 0.6/0.4 + 0.5/0.5 + 0.4/0.6 + 0.3/0.7 + 0.2/0.8 + 0.1/0.9 + 0/1

"very true" =0.0²/0 + 0.1²/0.1 + 0.2²/0.2 + 0.3²/0.3 + 0.4²/0.4 + 0.5²/0.5 + 0.6²/0.6 + 0.7²/0.7 + 0.8²/0.8 + 0.9²/0.9 + 1²/1

"very true" = 0.0/0 + 0.0/0.1 + 0.04/0.2 + 0.09/0.3 + 0.16/0.4 + 0.25/0.5 + 0.36/0.6 + 0.49/0.7 + 0.64/0.8 + 0.81/0.9 + 1/1

"very false" = 1.0²/0 + 0.9²/0.1 + 0.8²/0.2 + 0.7²/0.3 + 0.6²/0.4 + 0.5²/0.5 + 0.4²/0.6 + 0.3²/0.7 + 0.2²/0.8 + 0.1²/0.9 + 0²/1

"very false" = 1.0/0 + 0.81/0.1 + 0.64/0.2 + 0.49/0.3 + 0.36/0.4 + 0.25/0.5 + 0.16/0.6 + 0.09/0.7 + 0.04/0.8 + 0.01/0.9 + 0/1

"rather true" = √(0.0) /0.0 + √(0.1) /0.1 + √(0.2) /0.2 + √(0.3) /0.3 + √(0.4) /0.4 + √(0.5)/0.5 + √(0.6) /0.6 + √(0.7)/0.7 + √(0.8)/0.8 + √(0.9)/0.9 + √(1)/1

"rather true" = 0/0 + 0.32/0.1 + 0.45/0.2 + 0.55/0.3 + 0.63/0.4 + 0.71/0.5 + 0.78/0.6 + 0.84/0.7 + 0.89/0.8 + 0.95/0.9 + 1/1

"rather false" = √(1)/0 + √(0.9)/0.1 + √(0.8)/0.2 + √(0.7)/0.3 + √(0.6)/0.4 + √(0.5)/0.5 + √(0.4)/0.6 + √(0.3)/0.7 + √(0.2)/0.8 + √(0.1)/0.9 + √(0)/1

"rather false" = 1/0 + 0.95/0.1 + 0.89/0.2 + 0.84/0.3 + 0.78/0.4 + 0.71/0.5 + 0.63/0.6 + 0.55/0.7 + 0.45/0.8 + 0.32/0.9 + 0/1

Absolute true has the value 1 for 1 and absolute false has the value 1 for 0. They are not fuzzy sets.

NEGATIONS IN BALDWIN APPROACH

Negations of fuzzy truth values set according to Baldwin approach are given by:

TABLE 15 Negation in Baldwins approach

$\tau(p)$	Negation~ $\tau(p)$	$\mu_{\sim\tau(p)}$
true	false	$1 - \mu_{true}(v) = 1 - v$
very true	fairly false	$1 - \mu_{verytrue}(v)$ $= 1 - (\mu_{true}(v))^2$ $= 1 - v^2$
fairly true	very false	$1 - \mu_{fairlytrue}(v)$ $= 1 - \sqrt{\mu_{true}(v)}$ $= 1 - \sqrt{v}$

3.4.7 LINGUISTIC VARIABLE

When we consider a variable, in general, it takes numbers as its value. If the variable takes linguistic terms, it is called "linguistic variable".

Definition 3.11 The linguistic variable is defined by the following quintuple:
Linguistic variable = (x, T(x), U, G, M)
x : Name of variable

T(x): Set of linguistic terms which can be a value of the variable
U: Set of universe of discourse which defines the characteristics of the variable.
G: Syntactic grammar which produces terms in
M: Semantic rules which map terms in to fuzzy sets in U

Example 3.27 Let's consider a linguistic variable "X" whose name is "Age".
X = (Age, T(Age), U,G,M)
Age : name of the variable X
T (Age) : {young, very young, very very young, ...}
U: [0, 100] universe of discourse

G (Age) : $T^{i+1} = \{young\} \cup \{very\ T^i\}$

M (young) = $\left\{ \left(u, \mu_{young}(u)\right) \middle| u \in [0,100] \right\}$

$$\mu_{young}(u) = \begin{cases} 1 & if\ u \in [0,25] \\ \left(1 + \dfrac{u-25}{5}\right)^{-2} & if\ u \in [25,100] \end{cases}$$

In the above example, the term "young" is used as a basis in the T(Age), and thus this kind of term is called a "primary term". When we add modifiers to the primary terms, we can define new terms (fuzzy terms). In many cases, when the modifier "very" is added, the membership is obtained by square operation. For example, the membership function of the term "very young" is obtained from that of "young".

$$\mu_{very\ young}\left(u\right) = \left(\mu_{young}\left(u\right)\right)^2$$

The fuzzy linguistic terms often consist of two parts:
- Fuzzy predicate (primary term) : expensive, old, rare, dangerous, good, etcand so on.
- Fuzzy modifier: very, likely, almost impossible, extremely unlikely, etcand so on.

The modifier is used to change the meaning of predicate and it can be grouped into the following two classes:
- Fuzzy truth qualifier: quite true, very true, more or less true, mostly false, etc. and so on.
- Fuzzy quantifier: many, few, almost, all, usually, etc. and so on.

In the following sections, we introduce the fuzzy predicate, fuzzy modifier, and fuzzy truth quantifier.

FUZZY PREDICATE

As we know now, a predicate proposition in the classical logic has the following form:.
    "x   is a man".
    " y is P".

x and y are variables, and "man" and "P" are crisp sets. The sets of individuals satisfying the predicates are written by "man(x)" and "P(y)".

Definition 3.12 A fuzzy predicate is a predicate whose definition contains ambiguity.

Example 3.28 For example,
    "z is expensive".
    "w is young.".

The terms "expensive" and "young" are fuzzy terms. Therefore the sets "expensive(z)" and "young(w)" are fuzzy sets.

When a fuzzy predicate "x is P" is given, we can interpret it in two ways:.
    P(x) is a fuzzy set. The membership degree of x in the set P is defined by the membership function $\mu_{P(x)}$.

$\mu_{P(x)}$ is the satisfactory degree of x for the property P. Therefore, the truth value of the fuzzy predicate is defined by the membership function, $\mu_{P(x)}$.

FUZZY MODIFIER

As we know, a new term can be obtained when we add the modifier "very" to a primary term. In this section, we see how semantic of the new term and membership function can be defined.

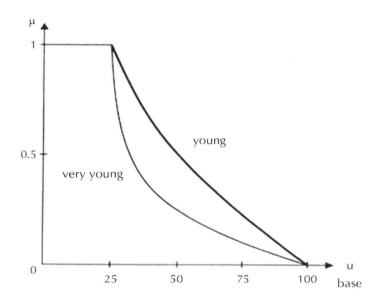

FIGURE 2   Linguistic variable "Age"

Example 3.29 Let's consider a linguistic variable "Age" in (Figure. 2) Linguistic terms "young" and "very young" are defined in the universal set U.

$U=\{u \mid u \in [0,100]\}$.

The variable Age takes a value in the set T(Age) where

T(Age) = {young, very young, very very young, ...}.

In the Figure. 2, the term "young" is represented by a membership function μ_{young} (u). When we represent the term "very young", we can use the square of μ_{young} (u) as follows:.

The graph of membership function of "very young" is given in the Figure. 2.

3.4.8   FUZZY TRUTH QUALIFIER

Baldwin defines fuzzy truth qualifier in the universal set $V = \{v \mid v \in [0,1]\}$ by Equation (3.9).

If we take baldwin's membership function μ_{true} (v), the fuzzy truth values are represented by the membership functions shown in Figure. 3.

Example 3.30 Let's consider a predicate using the primary term " young" and fuzzy truth value "very false"

P = 'Thomas is young is very false.'

Suppose the term "young" is defined by the function μ_{young} .

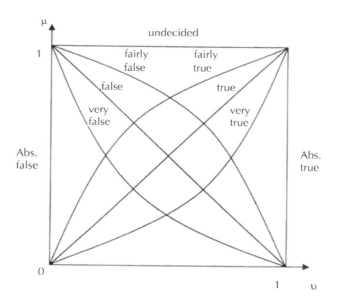

FIGURE 3   Baldwin's truth graph

$$\mu_{young}(u) = \begin{cases} 1 & u \in [0,25] \\ \left(1 + \dfrac{u-25}{5}\right)^{-2} & u \in [25,100] \end{cases}$$

The term "very false" can be defined by the following:

$$\mu_{very\ false} = \left(1 - \mu_{true}(u)\right)^2 = \left(1 - \mu_{young}(u)\right)^2$$

$$= \begin{cases} 1 & u \in [0,25] \\ \left[1 - \left(1 + \dfrac{u-25}{5}\right)^{-2}\right]^2 & u \in [25,100] \end{cases}$$

Therefore, if Thomas has age less than 25, the truth value of the predicate P is 0. If he is in [25, 100], the truth value is calculated from $\mu_{very\ false}$.

Example 3.31 Let's consider a predicate P in the following:
    P = " 20 is young.".
Assume the term "young" and " very young" are defined as shown in (Figure. 4).
    We see the membership degree of 20 in "young" is 0.9. Therefore, the truth value of the predicate P is 0.9. Now we can modify the predicate P by using fuzzy truth qualifiers as follows:

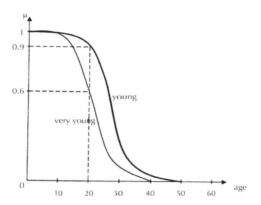

FIGURE 4 Fuzzy sets "young" and "very young."

"20 is young is true."
"20 is young is fairly true."
"20 is young is very true."
"20 is young is false."

The truth values are changed according to the qualifiers as shown in (Figure. 5).

We know already is 0.9. That is, the truth value of P is 0.9. For the predicate predicate , we use the membership function "true" in the figure and obtain the truth value 0.9. For , the membership function "fairly true" is used and 0.95 is obtained.

In the same way, we can calculate for and and summarize the truth values in the following:.

For : 0.9
For : 0.95
For : 0.81
For : 0.1.

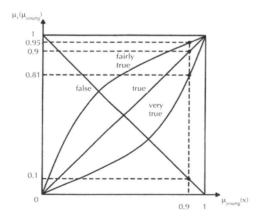

FIGURE 5 The truth values of fuzzy proposition

3.7   LINGUISTIC APPROXIMATION

Instead of handling directly the linguistic truth-value fuzzy sets we use, for represen-
tational compactness, linguistic approximations.

We represent a fuzzy statement P with fuzzy truth value τ as:,

$$p=\{(x,\mu_p(x)0\},\qquad x \in X$$

with truth value

$$\tau=\{(v,\mu_\tau(v))\},\qquad v \in V.$$

Here we have

$$(u = p) = \tau$$

After linguistic approximation

$$(u = q) = \text{it is } \tau \text{ that p.}$$

Example 3.32 Let us consider the universe X of speed with standard units, that is,
miles/hour

$$X = \{10, 20, 30, 40, 50, 60\}.$$

Let us consider the proposition p as:

p = "leopard runs fast"

$$p = 0.4/10 + 0.6/20 + 0.7/30 + 0.8/40 + 0.9/50 + 1/60$$

with truth-value set

$$\tau(p) = \text{"quite true"}$$

$$\tau(p) = 0.7/0.6 + 0.8/0.7 + 1/0.8 + 0.9/0.9 + 0.8/1 .$$

We can combine p and $\tau(p)$ in the following sentence:,

Q = "It is quite true that leopard runs fast"

given by:

$$Q = \{(x,\mu_Q(x))\}$$

where

$$\mu_Q(x)= \mu_\tau(\mu_Q(x)) .$$

So we get:

$$Q = 0/10 + 0.7/20 + 0.8/30 + 1/40 + 0.9/50 + 0.8/60.$$

3.4.9   *MODUS   PONENS   LAW   WITH   FUZZY   TRUTH-VALUES*

Modus ponens law is formulated as an IF … THEN rule and is applied to classical two
valued logic.

This law is given by:

Premise 1: $p \rightarrow q$

Premise 2: p .

Consequence: q   .

Alternatively, we can write:

$$(p \wedge (p \rightarrow q)) \rightarrow q, \quad \text{which is a tautology}$$

that is

$$\tau((p \wedge (p \rightarrow q)) \rightarrow q) = \text{"true"}$$

TABLE 16   provides the truth table of the above expressions.

$\tau(p)$	$\tau(q)$	$\tau(p \to q)$	$\tau(p \wedge (p \to q))$	$\tau((p \wedge (p \to q)) \to q)$
1	1	1	1	1
1	0	0	0	1
0	1	1	0	1
0	0	1	0	1

Our aim is to derive the fuzzy linguistic truth values for the law of Modus Ponens. We illustrate this concept with the help of the following example:.

Example 3.33 Let 'true' and 'false' be given by:

"true" = 0.7/0.8 + 0.9/0.9 + 1/1

"false" = 1/0 + 0.7/0.1 + 0.5/0.2.

We consider the fuzzy truth-values for two propositions p and q as:,

$\tau(p)$="true"

$\tau(q)$="true".

According to Equation (3.7) we get;

$$\tau(q \to p) = \sum\nolimits_{(x,y)\in[0,1]\times[0,1]} max_{\min(1,1-x+y)} \min\left(\mu_{\tau(p)}(x), \mu_{\tau(p)}(y)\right) / \min(1, 1-x+y)$$

$\tau(q \to p) = \min(0.7,\ 0.7)/\min(1,\ 1) + \min(0.7,\ 0.9)/\min(1,\ 1.1\ ) + \min(0.7,\ 1)/\min(1, 1.2\ ) + \min(0.9, 0.7)/\min(1, 0.9) + \min(0.9, 0.9)/\min(1, 1) + \min(0.9, 1)/\min(1, 1.1\ ) + \min(1, 0.7)/\min(1, 0.8\ ) + \min(1, 0.9)/\min(1, 0.9\ ) + \min(1, 1)/\min(1, 1)$

$\tau(q \to p) = 0.7/0.8 + 0.9/0.9 + 1/1.$

Now, according to Equation (3.5) we get:

$$\tau\left(p \wedge (p \to q)\right) = \sum\nolimits_{(x,y)\in[0,1]\times[0,1]} max_{\min(x,y)} \min\left(\mu_{\tau(p)}(x), \mu_{\tau(p \to q)}(y)\right) / \min(x,y)$$

- $\tau(p \wedge (p \to q)) = \min(0.7,\ 0.7\ )/\min(0.8, 0.8\ ) + \min(0.7, 0.9)/\min(0.8, 0.9) + \min(0.7, 1)/\min(0.8, 1\ ) + \min(0.9, 0.7)\ /\min(0.9, 0.8) + \min(0.9, 0.9)/\min(0.9, 0.9) + \min(0.9, 1)/\min(0.9, 1) + \min(1, 0.7)/\min(1, 0.8) + \min(1, 0.9)/\min(1, 0.9) + \min(1, 1)/\min(1, 1)$
- $\tau(p \wedge (p \to q)) = 0.7/0.8 + 0.7/0.8 + 0.7/0.8 + 0.7/0.8 + 0.9/0.9 + 0.9/0.9 + 0.7/0.8 + 0.9/0.9 + 1/1$
- $\tau(p \wedge (p \to q)) = 0.7/0.8 + 0.9/0.9 + 1/1$
- $\tau(p \wedge (p \to q)) =$ "true" $= \tau(p)$

Therefore, we can write,

$\tau(p \wedge (p \to q) \to q) = \tau(p \to q)$.

Thus:

$\tau(p \wedge (p \to q) \to q) = 0.7/0.8 + 0.9/0.9 + 1/1$,

$\tau(p \wedge (p \to q) \to q) =$ "true" .

Similarly, we can derive for both false truth-values

that is:

τ(p) = "false"

τ(q) = "false".

According to equation (3.7), we get;

$$\tau(p \to q) = \sum\nolimits_{(x,y)\in[0,1]\times[0,1]} max_{\min(1,1-x+y)} \min\left(\mu_{\tau(p)}(x), \mu_{\tau(q)}(y)\right)/\min(1,1-x+y).$$

τ(p→q)= min(1, 1)/min(1, 1) + min(1, 0.7)/min(1, 0.9) + min(1, 0.5)/min(1, 0.8) + min(0.7, 1)/min(1, 0.9) + min(0.7, 0.7)/min(1, 1) + min(0.7, 0.5)/min(1, 1.1) + min(0.5, 1)/min(1, 0.8) + min(0.5, 0.7)/min(1, 0.9) + min(0.5, 0.5)/min(1, 1)

τ(p→q)=1/1 + 0.7/0.9 + 0.5/0.8 + 0.7/0.9 + 0.7/1 + 0.5/1 + 0.5/0.8 + 0.5/0.9 + 0.5/1

τ(p→q) = max(0.5, 0.5)/0.8 + max(0.7, 0.7, 0.5)/ 0.9 + max(1, 0.7, 0.5, 0.5)/1

τ(p→q) = 0.5/0.8 + 0.7/0.9 + 1/1

τ(p→q) = True .

Now, according to Equation (3.5) we get;

$$\tau(p \wedge (p \to q)) = \sum\nolimits_{(x,y)\in[0,1]\times[0,1]} max_{\min(x,y)} \min\left(\mu_{\tau(p)}(x), \mu_{\tau(p \to q)}(y)\right)/\min(x,y)$$

- τ(p ∧ (p→q)) = min(1, 0.5)/min(0, 0.8) + min(1, 0.7)/min(0, 0.9) + min(1, 1)/min(0, 1) + min(0.7, 0.5)/min(0.1, 0.8) + min(0.7, 0.7)/min(0.1, 0.9) + min(0.7, 1)/min(0.1, 1) + min(0.5, 0.5)/min(0.2, 0.8) + min(0.5, 0.7)/min(0.2, 0.9) + min(0.5, 1)/min(0.2, 1)
- τ(p ∧ (p→q))= 0.5/0 + 0.7/0 + 1/0 + 0.5/0.1 + 0.7/0.1 + 0.7/1 + 0.5/0.2 + 0.5/0.2 + 0.5/0.2,
- τ(p ∧ (p→q))= max(0.5, 0.7, 1)/0 + max(0.5, 0.7, 0.7)/0.1 + max(0.5, 0.5, 0.5)/0.2
- τ(p ∧ (p→q))= 1/0 + 0.7/0.1 + 0.5/0.2,
- τ(p ∧ (p→q))= false = τ(p) .

Therefore we can write:,

τ(p ∧ (p→q)→q)= τ(p→q).

Thus,

τ(p ∧ (p→q)→q)= 0.5/0.8 + 0.7/0.9 + 1/1

τ(p ∧ (p→q)→q)= True.

Now we consider the following situation:,

τ(p)=True

τ(q)= False.

Therefore, according to Equation (3.7) we get:,

$$\tau(p \to q) = \sum\nolimits_{(x,y)\in[0,1]\times[0,1]} max_{\min(1,1-x+y)} \min\left(\mu_{\tau(p)}(x), \mu_{\tau(q)}(y)\right)/\min(1,1-x+y)$$

τ(p→q) = min(0.7, 1)/min(1, 0.2) + min(0.7,0.7)/min(1, 0.3) + min(0.7, 0.5)/min(1, 0.4) + min(0.9, 1)/min(1, 0.1) + min(0.9, 0.7)/min(1, 0.2) + min(0.9, 0.5)/min(1, 0.3) + min(1, 1)/min(1, 0) + min(1, 0.7)/min(1, 0.1) + min(1, 0.5)/min(1, 0.2),

τ(p→q) = 0.7/0.2 + 0.7/0.3 + 0.5/0.4 + 0.9/0.1 + 0.7/0.2 + 0.5/0.3 + 1/0 + 0.7/0.1 + 0.5/0.2,

τ(p→q) =1/0 + max(0.7, 0.9)/0.1 + max(0.7, 0.7)/0.2 + 0.5/0.3 + 0.5/0.4,

τ(p→q) =1/0 + 0.9/0.1 + 0.7/0.2 + 0.5/0.3 + 0.5/0.4,

τ(p→q) ="false".

Now, according to Equation (3.5) we get,

$$\tau(p \wedge (p \to q)) = \sum_{(x,y)\in[0,1]\times[0,1]} max_{\min(x,y)} \min\left(\mu_{\tau(p)}(x), \mu_{\tau(p \to q)}(y)\right)/\min(x+y).$$

$\tau(p \wedge (p \to q))$= min(0.7, 1)/min(0.8, 0) + min(0.7, 0.9)/min(0.8, 0.1) + min(0.7, 0.7)/min(0.8, 0.2) + min(0.7, 0.5)/min(0.8, 0.3) + min(0.7, 0.5)/min(0.8, 0.4) + min(0.9, 1)/min(0.9, 0) + min(0.9, 0.9)/min(0.9, 0.1) + min(0.9, 0.7)/min(0.9, 0.2) + min(0.9, 0.5)/min(0.9, 0.3) + min(0.9, 0.5)/min(0.9, 0.4) + min(1, 1)/min(1, 0) + min(1, 0.9)/min(1, 0.1) + min(1, 0.7)/min(1, 0.2) + min(1, 0.5)/min(1, 0.3) + min(1, 0.5)/min(1, 0.4),

$\tau(p \wedge (p \to q))$= 0.7/0 + 0.7/ 0.1 + 0.7/0.2 + 0.5/0.3 + 0.5/0.4 + 0.9/0 + 0.9 /0.1 + 0.7/0.2 + 0.5/0.3 + 0.5/0.4 + 1/0 + 0.9/0.1 + 0.7/0.2 + 0.5/0.3 + 0.5/0.4,

$\tau(p \wedge (p \to q))$= max (0.7, 0.9,1)/0 + max (0.7, 0.9, 0.9)/0.1 + max (0.7, 0.7, 0.7)/0.2 + max (0.5, 0.5, 0.5)/0.3 + max (0.5, 0.5, 0.5)/0.4

$\tau(p \wedge (p \to q))$= 1/0 + 0.9/0.1 +0.7/0.2 + 0.5/0.3 + 0.5/0.4,

$\tau(p \wedge (p \to q))$= "false".

Finally we get,

$$\tau\left((p\wedge(p \to q)) \to q\right) = \sum_{(x,y)\in[0,1]\times[0,1]} max_{\min(1,1-x+y)} \min\left(\mu_{\tau(p\wedge(p \to q))}(x), \mu_{\tau(q)}(y)\right)/\min(1,1-x+y)$$

$\tau((p\wedge(p \to q)) \to q)$= min(1.1)/min(1,1) + min(1,0.7)/min(1,1.1) + min(1,0.5)/min (1,1.2) + min(0.9,1)/min(1,0.9) + min (0.9, 0.7)/min(1,1) + min (0.9, 0.5)/min(1,1.1) + min (0.7,1)/min (1, 0.8) + min (0.7, 0.7)/min (1, 0.9) + min (0.7, 0.5)/min(1,1) + min (0.5,1)/min (1, 0.7) + min (0.5, 0.7)/min (1, 0.8) + min (0.5, 0.5)/min(1,0.9) + min (0.5,1)/ min (1, 0.6) + min (0.5, 0.7)/ min (1, 0.7) + min (0.5, 0.5)/min(1,0.8)

$\tau((p\wedge(p \to q)) \to q)$=   1/1 + 0.7/1 + 0.5/1 + 0.9/0.9 + 0.7/1 + 0.5/1 + 0.7/0.8 + 0.7/0.9 + + 0.5/1 + 0.5/0.7 + 0.5/0.8 + 0.5/0.9 + 0.5/0.6 + 0.5/0.7 + 0.5/0.8,

$\tau((p \wedge (p \to q)) \to q)$= max (1,0.7, 0.5, 0.7, 0.5, 0.5)/1 + max (0.9, 0.7, 0.5)/0.9 + max (0.7, 0.5, 0.5)/0.8 + max(0.5, 0.5)/0.7, 0.5/0.6

$\tau((p \wedge (p \to q)) \to q)$= 1/1 + 0.9/0.9 + 0.7/0.8 + 0.5/0.7, 0.5/0.6

$\tau((p \wedge (p \to q)) \to q)$= "true".

Similarly, we can verify for $\tau(p)$ = "false" and $\tau(q)$ = "true".

So, we conclude the following final result (Table 17) for fuzzy linguistic truth-values.

TABLE 17 Fuzzy Linguistic Truth values for Modus Ponens

$\tau(p)$	$\tau(q)$	$\tau(p \to q)$	$\tau(p \wedge (p \wedge q))$	$\tau((p \wedge (p \to q)) \to q)$
true	true	true	True	True
true	false	false	false	True
false	true	true	false	True
false	false	true	False	True

Hence we can state that $\tau((p \wedge (p \to q)) \to q)$ is tautology for fuzzy truth values also. Let us illustrate the law for different fuzzy truth values.

Example 3.34
$\quad$ $\tau(p)$ = "Less True" = $1/0.3 + 0.8/0.4 + 0.7/0.5$
$\quad$ $\tau(q)$ = "Very False" = $1/0 + 1/0.1 + 0.9/0.2$.
As we know, according to Equation (3.7),

$$\tau(p \to q) = \sum_{(x,y) \in [0,1] \times [0,1]} max_{\min(1,1-x+y)} \min\left(\mu_{\tau(p)}(x), \mu_{\tau(q)}(y)\right) / \min(1,1-x+y),$$

So,

- $\tau(p \to q)$= min(1,1)/min(1,0.7) + min(1,1)/min(1,0.8) + min (1, 0.9)/min (1, 0.9) + min (0.8,1)/min(1,0.6) + min(0.8,1)/min(1,0.7) + min (0.8, 0.9)/min (1, 0.8) + min (0.7,1)/min(1,0.5) + min(0.7,1)/min(1,0.6) + min (0.7, 0.9)/min (1, 0.7),
- $\tau(p \to q)$= 1/0.7 + 1/0.8 + 0.9/0.9 + 0.8/0.6 + 0.8/0.7 + 0.8/0.8 + 0.7/0.5 + 0.7/0.6 + 0.7/0.7
- $\tau(p \to q)$= max(0.8, 0.7)/0.6 + max (1, 0.8, 0.7)/0.7 + max (1, 0.8)/0.8 + 0.9/0.9

$$\tau(p \to q) = 0.8/0.6 + 1/0.7 + 1/0.8 + 0.9/0.9. \qquad (3.10)$$

Now, according to equation (3.5), we get,
$$\tau(p \wedge (p \to q)) = \sum_{(x,y) \in [0,1] \times [0,1]} max_{\min(x,y)} \min\left(\mu_{\tau(p)}(x), \mu_{\tau(p \to q)}(y)\right) / \min(x,y),$$

Therefore,

- $\tau(p \wedge (p \to q))$= min(1,0.8)/min(0.3, 0.6) + min(1,1)/min(0.3, 0.7) + min (1,1)/ min(0.3, 0.8) + min (1, 0.9)/min(0.3, 0.9) + min(0.8, 0.8)/min(0.4, 0.6) + min(0.8,1)/min(0.4, 0.7) + min(0.8, 1)/min(0.4, 0.8) +min(0.8, 0.9)/min(0.4, 0.9)+ min(0.7, 0.8)/min(0.5, 0.6) + min(0.7, 1)/min(0.5, 0.7) + min(0.7, 1)/ min(0.5, 0.8) + min(0.7, 0.9)/min(0.5, 0.9),
- $\tau(p \wedge (p \to q))$= 0.8/0.3 + 1/0.3 + 1/0.3 + 0.9/0.3 + 0.8/0.4 + 0.8/0.4 + 0.8/0.4 + 0.8/0.4 + 0.7/0.5 + 0.7/0.5 + 0.7/0.5 + 0.7/0.5,
- $\tau(p \wedge (p \to q))$= max (0.8, 1, 1, 0.9)/0.3 + max (0.8, 0.8, 0.8, 0.8)/0.4 + max (0.7, 0.7, 0.7, 0.7)/0.5,
- $\tau(p \wedge (p \to q))$= 1/ 0.3 + 0.8/0.4 + 0.7/0.5 = $\tau(p)$,
- $\tau(p \wedge (p \to q))$= $\tau(p)$.

Finally we get,

- $\tau((p \wedge (p \to q)) \to q)$= $\tau(p \to q)$
- $\tau((p \wedge (p \to q)) \to q)$= 0.8/0.6 + 1/0.7 + 1/0.8 + 0.9/0.9 (by Equation (3.10))
- $\tau((p \wedge (p \to q)) \to q)$= "fairly true".

So Modus ponens law for fuzzy truth value expressions lead to the increasing truthfulness.

But verification of the linguistic truth status of any fuzzy deduction system using truth table method is computationally very cumbersome. Hence, for any fuzzy deduction (approximate reasoning) based on fuzzy statement we look for an alternative approach in the following section.

3.4.10 APPROXIMATE REASONING BASED ON FUZZY LOGIC

"The term Approximate reasoning" refers to methods and methodologies that enable reasoning with imprecise inputs to obtain meaningful outputs.

Inference in approximate reasoning is in sharp contrast to inference in classical logic. Inference in approximate reasoning is computation with fuzzy sets that represent the meaning of a certain set of fuzzy propositions. One of the best known application areas of fuzzy logic is approximate reasoning. Approximate reasoning with fuzzy sets encompasses a wide variety of inference schemes and havehas been readily applied in many fields like decision making, expert systems, and fuzzy control. Since fuzzy logic handle approximate information in a very systematic way, it is perfect for controlling nonlinear systems and also for modeling complex systems where an inexact model exists where vagueness is common. A typical fuzzy system consists of a fuzzy rule base, membership functions, and an inference.

Let us try to formalize the rule: IF x is a banana and x is yellow THEN x is ripe. According to predicate logic for this formalization of the above rule, we need 3 predicates Banana(x),. Yellow(x), and Ripe(x), where each of these predicates has only 2 possible truth values: true or false. Using a IF-THEN (implication) operator, the above the rule can be written as :

Banana(x), Yellow(x) →Ripe(x)

where the comma in the left side of the implication sign $(\rightarrow)$ denotes logical conjunction (AND) of the antecedent predicates.

In order to allow instantiation of the antecedent predicates with primary fuzzy sets, we consider 6 fuzzy sets: YELLOW, VERY –YELLOW, MORE-OR-LESS-YELLOW, RIPE, VERY-RIPE, and MORE-OR-LESS-RIPE.

Fuzzy extensions of the above rule can be represented as:,

Rule 1: If a banana is YELLOW

THEN it is RIPE.

Rule 2: IF a banana is VERY-YELLOW

THEN it is VERY-RIPE.

Rule 3: IF a banana is MORE-OR-LESS-YELLOW

THEN it is MORE-OR-LESS-RIPE.

According to the logic of fuzzy sets, we can allow firing of these 3 rules concurrently in presence of a data element concerning color of a banana.

Formally, let x be a linguistic variable in a universe X, and A_1, A_2, and A_3 are three primary fuzzy sets under the universe X. Also assume that y be another linguistic variable in a universe Y and B_1, B_2, and B_3 are 3 primary fuzzy sets under Y. Then the implication rules between variable x and y may be described as:,

Rule 1: IF x is A_1 THEN y is B_1.

Rule 2: IF x is A_2 THEN y is B_2

Rule 3: IF x is A_3 THEN y is B_3

Suppose the fact (data) available is, x is A', where A' is semantically close to A_1, A_2, and A_3 respectively. In the subsequent discussion, we demonstrate the evaluation procedure of y is B' from the known membership distribution of x is A_1, y is B_1. x is A_2, y is B_2, x is A_3, y is B_3, and x is A'. For detail discussions see chapter 1 of volume 2 of this book.

FUZZY IMPLICATION RELATIONS

A fuzzy implication relation for a given rule : IF x is A_1 THEN y is B_1 is formally denoted by:

$$R_i(x,y) = \{\mu_{Ri}(x,y) / (x,y)\} \tag{3.11}$$

where the membership function $\mu_{Ri}(x,y)$ is constructed intuitively by many alternative ways. Some typical implication relations are presented below:.

- **Dienes–Rescher Implication:** This implication relation is a direct conse-quence of the implication function in classical propositional logic. In the logic of propositions the implication $p \rightarrow q$ (to be read as if p then q) can be proved to be equivalent to ~p ∨ q, where ~ and ∨ denote logical negation and OR op-eration respectively. Consequently, the result p $\rightarrow$ q $\equiv$ ~p ∨ q follows, where denotes an equivalence operator. Dienes –Rescher Implication relation extends the classical propositional implication formula by replacing negation by one's complement and logical OR by max operator. Thus, membership function for the implication rule : IF x is A_1 THEN y is B_1 is given by:

$$\mu_{Ri}(x,y) = Max[1 - \mu_{Ai}(x), \mu_{Bi}(y)] \tag{3.12}$$

- **Mamdani Implication:** Mamdani proposed the following two implication functions:

$$\mu_{Ri}(x,y) = Min[\mu_{Ai}(x), \mu_{Bi}(y)] \tag{3.13}$$

and

$$\mu_{Ri}(x,y) = \mu_{Ai}(x), \mu_{Bi}(y) \tag{3.14}$$

Mamdani implication functions are most widely used implications in fuzzy sys-tems and fuzzy control engineering. This implication relation is constructed based on the assumption that fuzzy IF-THEN rules are local. For example, consider the implication rule : IF height is TALL THEN speed is HIGH. By Mamdani's implication function, we do not want to mean: IF height is SHORT THEN speed is SLOW. The second rule is rather an example of a non-local rule. The knowledge engineer prefers local rules then Mamdani's implication relation should be used.

Example 3.35 In this example we illustrate the construction of fuzzy relation R using Mamdani's "Min" operator.

Let us consider the two universes volume and mass in standard units, that is m³ and kg. respectively and represent the following two crisp sets;

    X = volume = {10, 15, 20, 25} and
    Y = mass = {40, 60, 80, 100}.

Let us consider the following fuzzy conditional statement;

    IF x is small THEN y is heavy.

The above IF-THEN statement is converted into fuzzy relation R as follows:

    x is small = {1/10, 0.9/15, 0.5/20, 0.1/25} and
    y is heavy = {0.3/40, 0.6/60, 0.8/80, 1/100}.

Therefore, according to Equation (3.14) we get the fuzzy relation R as follows;

$$\underset{(4\times4)}{R} = \begin{pmatrix} 1/100 \\ 0.9/15 \\ 0.5/20 \\ 0.1/25 \end{pmatrix}_{4\times1} \min(0.3/40 \quad 0.6/60 \quad 0.8/80 \quad 1/100)_{1\times4}$$

$$= \begin{array}{c} \\ 10 \\ 15 \\ 20 \\ 25 \end{array} \begin{array}{cccc} 40 & 60 & 80 & 100 \\ \left[\begin{array}{cccc} \min(1,0.3) & \min(1,0.6) & \min(1,0,8) & \min(1,1) \\ \min(0.9,0.3) & \min(0.9,0.6) & \min(0.9,0.8) & \min(0.9,1) \\ \min(0.5,0.3) & \min(0.5,0.6) & \min(0.5,0.8) & \min(0.5,1) \\ \min(0.1,0.3) & \min(0.1,0.6) & \min(0.1,0.8) & \min(0.1,1) \end{array}\right] \end{array}$$

$$= \begin{array}{c} \\ 10 \\ 15 \\ 20 \\ 25 \end{array} \begin{array}{cccc} 40 & 60 & 80 & 100 \\ \left[\begin{array}{cccc} 0.3 & 0.6 & 0.8 & 1.0 \\ 0.3 & 0.6 & 0.8 & 0.9 \\ 0.3 & 0.5 & 0.5 & 0.5 \\ 0.3 & 0.1 & 0.1 & 0.1 \end{array}\right] \end{array}$$

Thus we translate a fuzzy IF-THEN rule to a fuzzy relation R.

- **Łukasiewicz Implication:** The propositional implication function can easily be extended in fuzzy logic by replacing negation by one's complement and logical OR by sum (+) operator. Thus, for the given fuzzy implication rule : IF x is THEN y is , the membership function of the rule may be stated as:

Since, the result may exceed 1 we express:

$$\mu_{Ri}(x, y) = Min\left[1, 1 - \mu_{Ai}(x) + \mu_{Bi}(y)\right] \tag{3.15}$$

which is known as the Łukasiewicz implication function .

Example 3.36 Based on the data of Example 3.35, we compute the fuzzy relation R according to Equation (3.15).

$$\underset{(4 \times 4)}{R} =$$

$$
\begin{array}{cccc}
 & 40 & 60 & 80 & 100 \\
\begin{array}{c}10\\15\\20\\25\end{array}
\left[
\begin{array}{cccc}
\min(1,1-1+0.3)=0.3 & \min(1,1-1+0.6)=0.6 & \min(1,1-1+0.8)=0.8 & \min(1,1-1+1)=1.0 \\
\min(1,1-0.9+0.3)=0.4 & \min(1,1-0.9+0.6)=0.7 & \min(1,1-0.9+0.8)=0.9 & \min(1,1-1+1)=1.0 \\
\min(1,1-0.5+0.3)=0.8 & \min(1,1-0.5+0.6)=1.0 & \min(1,1-0.5+0.8)=1.0 & \min(1,1-1+1)=1.0 \\
\min(1,1-0.1+0.3)=1.0 & \min(1,1-0.1+0.6)=1.0 & \min(1,1-0.1+0.8)=1.0 & \min(1,1-0.1+1)=1.0
\end{array}
\right]
\end{array}
$$

$$
=\begin{array}{c}10\\15\\20\\25\end{array}
\left[
\begin{array}{cccc}
0.3 & 0.6 & 0.8 & 1.0 \\
0.4 & 0.7 & 0.9 & 1.0 \\
0.8 & 1.0 & 1.0 & 1.0 \\
1.0 & 1.0 & 1.0 & 1.0
\end{array}
\right]
= \underset{(4\times4)}{R}.
$$

- **Zadeh Implication:** Zadeh's implication function is another form of extension of the classical propositional implication function. In the logic of proposition, the propositional implication $p \to q$ can alternatively be stated as "either p and q are true or p is false'false". Thus, $p \to q$ is equivalent to $(p \wedge q) \vee (\neg p)$ Representing logical AND by min, logical OR by max, and negation by one's complement we can state the membership function of the fuzzy implication rule: IF x is A_1 THEN y is B_1 by:

$$
\mu_{Ri}(x,y) = Max\left[Min\left(\mu_{Ai}(x), \mu_{Bi}(y)\right), \quad 1 - \mu_{Ai}(x) \right] \tag{3.16}
$$

This is known as Zadeh implication relation.

- **Gödel Implication:** The Godel implication is a popular implication formula in traditional logic. A fuzzy extension of the formula for the rule : IF x is A_1 THEN y is B_1 can be stated by representing the membership function of the

$$
\begin{aligned}
\mu_{Ri}(x,y) &= 1 \; if \; \mu_{Ai}(x) \le \mu_{Bi}(y) \\
&= \mu_{Bi}(y), otherwise
\end{aligned} \tag{3.17}
$$

There are many other implication functions commonly used in the logic of fuzzy sets.

The logic of fuzzy sets, also called fuzzy logic, is an extension of the classical propositional logic from two perspectives. First, instead of binary valuation space (truth/falsehood) of the propositional logic, fuzzy logic provides a multi-valued truth-space in [0, 1]. Second, propositional logic generates inferences based on the complete matching of the antecedent clauses with the available data, whereas fuzzy logic is capable of generating inferences even when a partial matching of the antecedent clauses against available data elements. In this section, we present three typical propositional inference rules and describe their possible extensions in fuzzy logic.

TYPICAL PROPOSITIONAL INFERENCE RULES

Let p, .q,. and r be 3 propositions.

The following 3 propositional inference rules are commonly used for logical inferencing:.

- *Modus Ponens:* Given a proposition p and a propositional implication rule , we can derive the inference q. Symbolically:.

$$p \wedge (p \rightarrow q) \rightarrow q \qquad (3.18)$$

This above inference rule is well known as modus ponens.

- *Modus Tollens:* Given a proposition ~q, and the implication rule , we can derive the inference ~p.

Symbolically:,

$$\sim q \wedge (p \rightarrow q) \rightarrow \sim p \qquad (3.19)$$

The above inference rule is known as modus tollens.

- *Hypothetical Syllogism:* Given two implication rules and , then we can easily derive an implication .

Symbolically:,

$$(p \rightarrow q) \wedge (q \rightarrow r) \rightarrow (p \rightarrow r) \qquad (3.20)$$

The above inference rule is popularly known as hypothetical syllogism or chain rule.

FUZZY EXTENSION OF THE INFERENCE RULES

The logic of fuzzy set provides a general framework for the extension of the above three propositional inference rules. Fuzzy extension of modus ponens, modus tollens, and hypothetical syllogisms are called generalized modus ponens, generalized modus tollens, and generalized hypothetical syllogism respectively.

- *Generalized Modus Ponens (GMP):* Consider a fuzzy rule : IF x is A then y is B, and a fuzzy fact: x is A'. The GMP inference rule infers y is B'. Here A' and B' are fuzzy sets such that A' is close to A, and B' is close to B. The inference rule also states that the closer the A' to A, the closer the B' to B.

    Symbolically, the GMP can be stated as follows:

    Given : IF x is A THEN y is B

    Given : x is A'

    Inferred: y is B'
- *Generalized Modus Tollens (GMT):* Given a fuzzy rule : IF x is A THEN y is B, and a fuzzy fact y is B', the GMT infers x is A', where the more is the difference between B' and B, the more is the difference between A' and A.

    Symbolically, the GMT is stated as follows :

    Given : IF x is THEN y is B

$$\text{Given: y is } \mathbf{B'}$$

Inferred: x is $\mathbf{A'}$

- ***Generalized Hypothetical Syllogism (GHS):*** Given two fuzzy rules : IF x is A THEN y is B, and IF y is B′ THEN z is C' , where A, B, and C are three fuzzy sets, and $\mathbf{B'}$ is close to B. Then the GHS infers the fuzzy fact z is C' , where C' is close to C. The closer the $\mathbf{B'}$ to B, the closer the C′ to C.

  Symbolically, we can state this rule as follows:

  Given : IF x is A THEN y is B

  Given : IF y is THEN z is C

  Inferred: z is C'

In the above definition of the inference rules, we just mentioned that is close to A, is close to B and the like. But we did not mention what we exactly mean by "close to". In fact "close to" can take any of the following forms: VERY, VERY-VERY, MORE-OR-LESS, NOT, ABOUT-TO, AROUND, and other fuzzy hedges that means a fuzzy set is approximately similar to A (see chapter 1 of vol. 2 of this book).

THE COMPOSITIONAL RULE OF INFERENCE

In this section, we present the methodology for the evaluation of fuzzy inferences for GMP, GMT , and GHS. This, however, calls for formalization of a fuzzy rule called the compositional rule of inference. The compositional rule of inference is usually applied to two fuzzy membership distributiondistributions, one of which usually have-has a smaller number of linguistic variables. The rule extends the latter membership distribution cylindrically, so as to increase its number of linguistic variables to the former distribution. The intersection of the former and the resulting distribution is then projected to desired axes. The whole process is referred to as the compositional rule of inference (see section 1.2 of chapter 1 of vol. 2 of this book).

How exactly the compositional rule of inference is applied to determine the fuzzy inferences in GMP, GMT, and GHS are presented below:

COMPUTING FUZZY INFERENCE IN GMP

Given the rule: IF x is A THEN y is B, and the observed membership distribution x is $\mathbf{A'}$,we by GMP infer: y is $\mathbf{B'}$. For evaluation of membership distribution of y is $\mathbf{B'}$, $\mu_{B'}(y)$, we need to know the membership distribution of x is $\mathbf{A'}$, $\mu_{A'}(x)$, and the membership of the fuzzy relation for the given IF – THEN rule, $\mu_R(x, y)$. This is accomplished by applying the compositional rule of inference over $\mu_A'(x)$ and $\mu_R(x, y)$.

Here x and y are linguistic variables on universes X and Y respectively. Now, in order to apply the compositional rule, we extend $\mu_A'(x)$ cylindrically and the extended distribution is, supposed $\mu_{A\,CYL}'(x, y)$. Let the intersection of $\mu_R(x, y)$ be denoted by $\mu_{A\,\mathrm{CYL}\cap R}'(x, y)$. Then $\mu_{B'}'(y)$ is computed by projecting $\mu_{A'\,CYL\cap R}(x, y)$ on Y,

Symbolically, the whole process includes the following 3 steps:

$$\mu_A'{}_{CYL}(x,y) = \mu_A'(x) \tag{3.21}$$

$$\mu_A'{}_{CYL \cap R}(x,y) = \mu_A'{}_{CYL}(x,y) \cap \mu_R(x,y) = t\left[\mu_A'{}_{CYL}(x,y), \mu_R(x,y)\right] \tag{3.22}$$

$$\mu_B'(y) = \max_{x \in X} t\left[\mu_A'{}_{CYL}(x,y), \mu_R(x,y)\right] \tag{3.23}$$

$$= \max_{x \in X} t\left[\mu_A'(x), \mu_R(x,y)\right] \tag{3.24}$$

If we take min for t-norm then the above result can directly be obtained for discrete fuzzy system by employing the max-min composition operator as presented below:

$$\mu_B'(y) = \mu_A'(x) \circ \mu_R(x,y) \tag{3.25}$$

where $\mu_A'(x)$ and $\mu_R(x,y)$ are now vector and matrices of compatible dimensions.

Example 3.37 We illustrate the computation of membership of the inferences generated using GMP. Let

$$\mu'_A(x) = [0.8 \ 0.9 \ 0.2]$$

$$\text{and } \mu_R(x,y) = \begin{bmatrix} 0.8 & 0.6 & 0.5 \\ 0.6 & 0.5 & 0.9 \\ 0.7 & 0.6 & 0.5 \end{bmatrix}.$$

The membership distribution of the derived inference is given by:

$$\mu_B'(y) = \mu_A'(x) \circ \mu_R(x,y).$$

$$= \underset{[0.8 \ \ 0.9 \ \ 0.2]}{\overset{(1 \times 3)}{}} \circ \underset{\begin{bmatrix} 0.8 & 0.6 & 0.5 \\ 0.6 & 0.5 & 0.9 \\ 0.7 & 0.6 & 0.5 \end{bmatrix}}{\overset{(3 \times 3)}{}}$$

$\quad$ = max{min(0.8, 0.8), min(0.9, 0.6), min(0.2, 0.7)}, max{ min(0.8, 0.6), min(0.9, 0.5), min(0.2, 0.6)}, max{ min(0.8, 0.5), min(0.9, 0.9), min(0.2, 0.5)}

$\quad$ = [(max(.8,.6,.2) max(.6,.5,.2) max(.5,.9,.2))]

$\quad$ = [(.8 .6 .9)].

The same result can also be obtained by applying the three basic steps of the compositional rule of inference.

Here:

$$\mu_A'{}_{\,CYL}(x, y) = \begin{bmatrix} 0.8 & 0.8 & 0.8 \\ 0.9 & 0.9 & 0.9 \\ 0.2 & 0.2 & 0.2 \end{bmatrix}$$

(see section 2.17.2 of chapter 2)

and

$$\mu_A'{}_{\,CYL \cap R}(x, y) = t\left[\mu_A'{}_{\,CYL}(x, y), \mu_R(x, y) \right]$$

$$= \begin{bmatrix} 0.8 & 0.8 & 0.8 \\ 0.9 & 0.9 & 0.9 \\ 0.2 & 0.2 & 0.2 \end{bmatrix} t \begin{bmatrix} 0.8 & 0.6 & 0.5 \\ 0.6 & 0.5 & 0.9 \\ 0.7 & 0.6 & 0.5 \end{bmatrix}$$

$$= \begin{bmatrix} 0.8 & 0.6 & 0.5 \\ 0.6 & 0.5 & 0.9 \\ 0.2 & 0.2 & 0.2 \end{bmatrix}.$$

Projecting (see section 2.17.2 of chapter 2) the resulting distribution on Y-axis, we

find $\mu_B'(y) = [0.8 \ \ 0.6 \ \ 0.9]$ which is same as obtained directly by using the max-min composition operator as shown above.

COMPUTING FUZZY INFERENCES USING GMT

Given a fuzzy rule : IF x is A THEN y is B, and a fact y is B', we by GMT infer x is A'. We present the principle of determining the membership distribution of x is A', $\mu_A'(x)$, from the membership distribution of y is B', $\mu_B'(y)$, and the membership $\mu_R(x, y)$ of the fuzzy relation between the antecedent and consequent part of the given rule. The computation involves cylindrical extension of $\mu_B'(y)$ to $\mu_B'{}_{\,CYL}(x, y)$, then intersection of $\mu_B'{}_{\,CYL}(x, y)$ with $\mu_R(x, y)$ and finally projection of the resulting relation on X-axis.

Thus, following the same steps as in the case of GMP, we get,

$$\mu_A'(x) = \max_{y \in Y} \left[t\{\mu_B'(y), \mu_R(x, y)\} \right] \tag{3.26}$$

when $\mu_B'(y)$ and $\mu_R(x, y)$ are discrete relations represented by a row vector and a matrix respectively, we can represent the above result by the following max-min composition operation :

$$\mu_A'(x) = \mu_B'(y) \circ [\mu_R(x, y)]^T \tag{3.27}$$

where T denotes the transposition operator over the given relation.

Example 3.38 This example illustrates the computation of GMT using max-min composition operator.

We take the same $\mu_R(x, y)$ as in Example 3.37, and the $\mu_B'(y)$ we obtained as the result in the example, and plan to determine $\mu_A'(x)$ by the compositional rule of inference.

Thus:,

$$\mu_A'(x) = \mu_B'(y) \circ [\mu_R(x, y)]^T$$

$$= [0.8 \ 0.6 \ 0.9] \circ \begin{bmatrix} 0.8 & 0.6 & 0.5 \\ 0.6 & 0.5 & 0.9 \\ 0.7 & 0.6 & 0.5 \end{bmatrix}^T$$

$$= [0.8 \ 0.9 \ 0.7]$$

It may be noted that $\mu_A'(x)$ thus obtained is not same as that presumed in Example 3.37.

COMPUTING FUZZY INFERENCES USING GHS

Given two fuzzy rules: IF x is A THEN y is B, and IF y is B THEN z is C, we by GHS infer IF x is A THEN z is C. Suppose, the membership $\mu_R(x, y)$ of the relation $R(x, y)$ and the membership $\mu_R(y, z)$ of the relation $R(y, z)$ are supplied, and we want to determine the membership $\mu_R(x, z)$ of the relation $R(x, z)$. We can solve the problem first by extending $\mu_R(x, y)$ to $\mu_{R \ \text{CYL}}(x, y, z)$, then by taking intersection of $\mu_{R \ \text{CYL}}(x, y, z)$ with $\mu_R(y, z)$ and finally projecting the resulting distribution onto X and Z axes.

The whole process can be described by the following expression:

$$\mu_R(x,y) = \max_{y \in Y} t\left[\mu_R(x,y), \mu_R(y,z)\right] \qquad (3.28)$$

We can represent the above expression in a closed form by using max-min composition operation:

$$\mu_R(x,z) = \mu_R(x,y) \circ \mu_R(y,z) \qquad (3.29)$$

Example 3.39 Consider the following two fuzzy rules (R):

R_1: IFage is YOUNG THEN digestion-rate is HIGH.

R_2: IF digestion-rate is HIGH THEN speed is HIGH.

Now, by GHS we infer-IF age is YOUNG THEN speed is HIGH. Let μ_R (age, digestion-rate) and μ_R (digestion-rate, speed) be the membership distribution for the relation between the antecedent and the consequent part of the first rule and the second rule respectively. We want to determine the membership μ_R (age, speed) of the relation between the antecedent and the consequent part of the derived rule.

Let

$$\mu_R\left(age, digestion-rate\right) = \begin{array}{c} \\ age \\ \downarrow \end{array} \overset{digestion-rate \rightarrow}{\begin{pmatrix} 0.2 & 0.3 & 0.6 \\ 0.4 & 0.6 & 0.5 \\ 0.3 & 0.6 & 0.9 \end{pmatrix}}$$

and

$$\mu_R\left(digestion-rate, speed\right) = \begin{array}{c} \\ digestion-rate \\ \downarrow \end{array} \overset{speed \rightarrow}{\begin{pmatrix} 0.8 & 0.7 & 0.5 \\ 0.7 & 0.7 & 0.4 \\ 0.7 & 0.4 & 0.5 \end{pmatrix}}.$$

Then we can evaluate:

$$\mu_R\left(age, speed\right) = \mu_R\left(age, digestion-rate\right) \circ \mu_R\left(digestion-rate, speed\right)$$

$$= \begin{array}{c} \\ age \\ \downarrow \end{array} \overset{speed \rightarrow}{\begin{pmatrix} 0.6 & 0.4 & 0.5 \\ 0.6 & 0.6 & 0.5 \\ 0.7 & 0.6 & 0.5 \end{pmatrix}}.$$

APPROXIMATE REASONING WITH MULTIPLE ANTECEDENT CLAUSES

Now we provide a general scheme for approximate reasoning with multiple antecedent clauses in the rule (also see chapter 1 of vol. 2 of this book). (also see chapter 1 of volume 2 of this book)

Consider the following fuzzy IF-THEN rule with two antecedent clauses :

IF x is A and y is B THEN z is C

where x, y, and z are three linguistic variables in the universes X, Y, and Z respectively, and A, B and C are three fuzzy sets under the respective universes.

Let $\mu_A(x), \mu_B(y)$ and $\mu_C(z)$ be the membership distribution of linguistic variables x, y, and z to belong to A, B, and C respectively.

Suppose, the observed distribution of x is A', $\mu_A'(x)$, and y is B', $\mu_B'(y)$, are supplied, and we want to determine the membership distribution of z is $C', \mu_C'(z)$.

Assuming Łukasiewicz implication function, the membership distribution of the given antecedent – consequent relationship can be described as:

$$\mu_R(x, y; z)$$

$$= \text{Min} \left[1, 1-t \left[(\mu_A(x), \mu_B(y)) + \mu_C(z) \right] \right.$$

$$= \text{Min} \left[1, 1 - \min(\mu_A(x), \mu_B(y)) + \mu_C(z) \right] \text{ (Taking min as the t-norm)}.$$

If $R(x, y : z)$ is a discrete relation, we can represent $\mu_R(x, y; z)$ as a relational matrix. Suppose, $x \in X = \{x_1, x_2, x_3\}$, $y \in Y = \{y_1, y_2\}$, and $z \in Z = \{z_1, z_2, z_3\}$, then $\mu_R(x, y; z)$ can be described as a (6×3) matrix with row indices x1y1, x1y2, x2y1, x2y2, x3y1, x3y2, and column indices z_1 and z_2. We can now determine $\mu_C'(z)$ by the following composition rule:

$$\mu_C'(z) = t\left(\mu_A'(x), \mu_B'(y) \right) \circ \mu_R(x, y; z) \tag{3.30}$$

Note that
$t\left(\mu_A'(x), \mu_B'(y) \right)$ has 6 components corresponding to $xy \in \{x_1 y_1 x_1 y_2, x_2 y_1, x_2 y_2, x_3 y_1, x_3 y_2\}$ and other than Łukasiewicz implication function it can assume any typical function, such as Mamdani implication, Zadeh implication, and so on.

Example 3.40 This example illustrates the numerical computations involved in Equation (3.30). Consider the fuzzy production rule with two antecedents:

IF height is TALL and weight is MODERATE THEN speed is HIGH.

Suppose $\mu_{TALL}(\text{height}) = \{0.5/5', 0.8/6', 1.0/7'\}$.

$\mu_{MODERATE}(\text{weight}) = \{0.7/45Kg, 0.9/50Kg\}$ and

$\mu_{HIGH}(\text{speed}) = \{0.6/6m/s, 0.8/8m/s, 0.5/9m/s\}$ are given.

Suppose $\mu_{TALL}'(\text{height}) = \{0.6/5', 0.7/6', 0.9/7'\}$, and

$$\mu_{MODERATE}{}'(weight) = \{0.8 / 45Kg, 0.7 / 50Kg\}$$

are also given and we want to determine $\mu_{HIGH}{}'(speed)$. It is of course assumed that the fuzzy sets $TALL' \approx$ TALL, $MODERRATE' \approx$ MODERATE, and $HIGH' \approx HIGH$; $\approx$ means close.

For solving the above problem, we first construct the fuzzy relation R(height, weight, and speed), the membership function μ_R (height, weight, and speed) of which is computed in two phases.

First phase: Computation of the membership function of antecedent clauses of the rule

$$AM = t(\mu_{TALL}(height), \mu_{MODERATE}(weight))$$

$$= \min(\mu_{TALL}(height), \mu_{MODERATE}(weight))$$

$$= \{(0.5 \wedge 0.7) / (5', 45Kg), (0.5 \wedge 0.9 / 5', 50Kg), (0.8 \wedge 0.7) / (6', 45Kg),$$

$$(0.8 \wedge 0.9) / (6', 50Kg), (1.0 \wedge 0.7) / (7', 45Kg), (1.0 \wedge 0.9) / (7', 50Kg)\}$$

$$= \{(0.5) / (5'45Kg), (0.5) / (5', 50Kg), (0.7) / (6', 45Kg), ,$$

$$(0.8) / (6', 50Kg), (0.7) / (7', 45Kg), (0.9) / (7', 50Kg)\}.$$

Second phase: Computation of the membership functions of fuzzy relation between antecedent clauses and consequent clause.

Result of the computation is presented below in matrix μ_R (height, weight, and speed). For convenience of the readers, we illustrate computation of one matrix element only corresponding to the row index $5'$, 45 Kg, and column index 6 m/s.

Here $\mu_R\left(5', 45 Kg, \dfrac{6m}{s}\right) = Min\left[1, (1 - 0.5 + 0.6)\right] = 1.0.$

Remaining elements of μ_R have been computed similarly.

$$
\mu_R(\text{height, weight; speed}) = \begin{array}{c} 5',45Kg \\ 5',50Kg \\ 6',45Kg \\ 6',50Kg \\ 7',45Kg \\ 7',50Kg \end{array} \begin{pmatrix} \overset{6\,\text{m/s}\quad 8\,\text{m/s}\quad 9\,\text{m/s}}{} \\ 1.0 \quad 1.0 \quad 1.0 \\ 1.0 \quad 1.0 \quad 1.0 \\ 0.9 \quad 1.0 \quad 0.8 \\ 0.8 \quad 1.0 \quad 0.7 \\ 0.9 \quad 1.0 \quad 0.8 \\ 0.7 \quad 0.9 \quad 0.6 \end{pmatrix}.
$$

The last part of the problem is to determine the membership distribution of the fuzzy inference: speed is HIGH'. This can be done by composing the t-norm $t(\mu_{TALL}{}'(height)$, $\mu_{MODERATE}{}'(weight))$ with μ_R (height, weight, speed).
Symbolically.

$$
\mu_{\text{HIGH}}{}'(\text{Speed})
$$

$$
= t\!\left(\mu_{TALL}{}'(\text{height}), \mu_{MODERATE}{}'(\text{weight})\right) \circ \mu_R (\text{height, weight, speed})
$$

Taking min as the t-norm, we can easily compute the above max-min composition to determine $\mu_{\text{HIGH}}{}'(\text{speed})$.

Approximate Reasoning with Multiple Rules

In this section, we present a general scheme for approximate reasoning by GMP with multiple rules each having one antecedent clause (also see chapter 1 of volume 2 of this book). Let x and y be two linguistic variables in the universes X and Y respectively. Also let A1, A2, …, An be fuzzy sets under the universe X and B1, B2, …Bn be fuzzy sets under the universe Y.

We consider the following fuzzy rules (R):

R1: IF x is A1 THEN y is B1.

R2: IF x is A_2 THEN y is B2.

R3: IF x is A_3 THEN y is B3.

Rn: IF x is An THEN y is Bn.

Let $R_i(x, y)$ be the fuzzy relation between the antecedent and the consequent part of production rule R_i.

We can then easily compute the membership distribution of R_i by:

$$
\mu_{Ri}(x, y) = f_i(\mu_{Ai}, \mu_{Bi}) \tag{3.31}
$$

where f_i is an implication function. For example, if f_i is of Mamdani type then we can write $f_i\left(\mu_{Ai},\mu_{Bi}\right)$ as min $\left(\mu_{Ai},\mu_{Bi}\right)$.

Suppose the observed distribution is x is A', where,

$A' \approx A1, A' \approx A2, A' \approx A3,...,$ and $A' \approx An$. Then we can determine the membership distribution of y is B_i' using the i-th rule only by:

$$\mu_{Bi}{}'(y) = \max\left\{\underset{x\in X}{\min}\left(\mu_{Ai}{}'(x),\mu_{Ri}(x,y)\right)\right\} \tag{3.32}$$

Thus for n rules we determine $\mu_{Bi}'(y)$ for i = 1 to n. Now for computation of $\mu_B'(y)$, we use the maximum of $\mu_{Bi}'(y)$ for i = 1 to n.

Symbolically:

$$\mu_B'(y) = \overset{n}{\underset{i=1}{\max}}\left[\mu_B'(y)\right]$$

$$= max_{i=1}^{n}\; _{x\in X}\; [max\{\min(\mu_{Ai}'(x),\mu_{Ri}(x,y))\}] \tag{3.33}$$

For discrete membership distribution we can evaluate $\mu_B'(y)$ by taking the maximum of the max-min composition operation of $\mu_{Ai}'(x)$ and $\mu_{Ri}(x,y)$.

Thus:

$$\mu_B'(y) = \overset{n}{\underset{i=1}{\max}}\left[\mu_{Ai}'(x) \circ \mu_{Ri}(x,y)\right] \tag{3.34}$$

Example 3.41 This example illustrates the computation of $\mu_B'(y)$ using the following two rules:

R1: IF height is TALL THEN speed is HIGH

R2: IF height is MEDIUM THEN speed is MODERATE.

Suppose the membership distribution of $\mu_{TALL}\left(\text{height}\right)$, $\mu_{HIGH}\left(\text{speed}\right)$, $\mu_{MEDIUM}\left(\text{height}\right)$ and $\mu_{MODERATE}\left(\text{speed}\right)$ are given from which we can construct the fuzzy relational matrices R_1 and R_2 for rule 1 and rule 2 respectively.

For brevity, we instead of computing the matrices, directly provide the matrices as follows:

$$R_1 = height \downarrow \begin{pmatrix} 0.4 & 0.5 & 0.6 \\ 0.5 & 0.7 & 0.8 \\ 0.6 & 0.7 & 0.9 \end{pmatrix} \overset{speed \rightarrow}{} and \ R_2 = height \downarrow \begin{pmatrix} 0.6 & 0.9 & 0.7 \\ 0.5 & 0.8 & 0.6 \\ 0.8 & 0.7 & 0.5 \end{pmatrix} \overset{speed \rightarrow}{}.$$

Let the membership distribution of 'height is ABOVE-AVERAGE' is given, and we want to determine the membership distribution of 'speed is ABOVE-NORMAL'. Suppose:

$$\mu_{ABOVE-NORMAL}(height) = \{0.5/5', 0.9/6', 0.8/7'\}$$

and the entries the relational matrices R_1 and R_2 correspond to the height $5', 6'$, and $7'$ respectively in order.

Then we can determine $\mu_{ABOVE-NORMAL}(speed)$ by the following formula:

$$\mu_{ABOVE-NORMAL}(speed)$$

$$= max \left[\mu_{ABOVE-AVERAGE}(height) \circ R_1, \mu_{ABOVE-AVERAGE}(height) \circ R_2 \right]$$

$$= \mu_{ABOVE-AVERAGE}(height) \circ max \left[R_1, R_2 \right]$$

$$= [0.5\ 0.9\ 0.8] \circ \begin{pmatrix} 0.6 & 0.9 & 0.7 \\ 0.5 & 0.8 & 0.8 \\ 0.8 & 0.7 & 0.9 \end{pmatrix}$$

$$= [0.8\ 0.8\ 0.8].$$

In the above computation, max $[R_1, R_2]$ was evaluated by taking the position-wise maximum of the matrices R_1 and R_2 like matrix addition, with the replacement of addition operation by max operation.

If the speed referenced in R_1 and R_2 are 5m/s, 7m/s, and 9m/s respectively in order then the membership distribution of $\mu_{ABOVE-NORMAL}(speed)$ should be described as follows:

$$\mu_{ABOVE-NORMAL}(speed) = \{0.8/5m/s, 0.8/7m/s, 0.8/9m/s\}.$$

Approximate Reasoning with Multiple Rules Each with Multiple Antecedent Clauses
To start with let us consider n rules each with two antecedent clauses only as presented follows:

   R1: IF x is A1 and y is B1 THEN z is C1.
   R2: IF x is A2 and y is B2 THEN z is C2.
   R3: IF x is A3 and y is B3 THEN z is C3.
   ....
   ....
   Rn: IF x is An and y is Bn THEN z is Cn.

Now, for the i-th rule membership distribution of the fuzzy implication relation is given by:

$$\mu_{Ri}(x, y; z) = f_i\left(t\left(\mu_{Ai}, \mu_{Bi}\right), \mu_{Ci}\right) \qquad (3.35)$$

where f_i is an implication function. If the t-norm, for example, is interpreted as the min operator, and the f_i as the Mamdani type min operator, then $\mu_{Ri} = \min\left(\min\left(\mu_{Ai}, \mu_{Bi}\right), \mu_{Ci}\right)$.

Given an observed distribution of x is A' and y is B', we can easily evaluate the membership distribution of z is C_i by the i-th rule as follows:

$$\mu_{Ci}' = t\left(\mu_A', \mu_B'\right) \circ \mu_{Ri}(x, y; z). \qquad (3.36)$$

Consequently, taking the contribution of all n rules together, we can determine the membership distribution of z is C' by taking the max of μ_C' for i = 1 to n. Symbolically:

$$\mu_C' = \max_{i=1}^{n}\left[\mu_{Ci}'\right]$$

$$= \max_{i=1}^{n}\left[t\left(\mu_A', \mu_B'\right) \circ \mu_{Ri}(x, y, z)\right] \text{ [by (3.36)]}$$

$$= \max_{i=1}^{n}\left[t\left(\mu_A', \mu_B'\right) \circ f_i\left(t\left(\mu_{Ai}, \mu_{Bi}\right), \mu_{Ci}\right)\right] \text{ (by 3.35)]} \qquad (3.37)$$

For further details on this generalized approach to approximate reasoning using fuzzy logic see chapter 1 of volume 2 of this book.

FUZZY ABDUCTIVE REASONING

The reasoning methodology introduced in the previous sections was based on GMP. There are, however, situations when we need to determine the membership distribution of the antecedent clause of a rule for an observed distribution of its consequence. This is called GMT or abductive reasoning. The adverb fuzzy has been included in the heading to distinguish it from the crisp deduction. The most important application of abductive reasoning is in diagnostic problems. In diagnostic applications, the defective item in a system need to be identified from the measurement data. Since abnormality in measurements is mainly caused by the abnormal behavior of the defective components, determination of the defective item is feasible by reasoning with GMT.

In this section we discuss the principle of abductive reasoning by two chain rules listed below:

R1: IF x is A THEN y is B.
R2: IF y is B THEN z is C.

Suppose, the observed membership distribution of z is C' is available, and we want to determine the membership distribution of x is A'. To do so, we have to apply GMT twice, once to determine the membership of y is B' and next to determine the membership of x is A'.

The entire scheme is stepwise given below:

Determine the membership distribution $\mu_{R1}(x, y)$ and $\mu_{R2}(y, z)$ by the following formula:

$$\mu_{R1}(x, y) = f\left(\mu_A(x), \mu_B(y)\right) \tag{3.38}$$

$$\mu_{R2}(y, z) = f\left(\mu_B(y), \mu_C(z)\right) \tag{3.39}$$

where f is any typical implication function.

Compute μ_B' first and then μ_A' by executing the following two steps in order:

$$\mu_B'(y) = \mu_C'(z) \circ \left[\mu_{R2}(y, z)\right]^T \tag{3.40}$$

$$\mu_A'(x) = \mu_B'(y) \circ \left[\mu_{R1}(x, y)\right]^T \tag{3.41}$$

where T denotes the transposition operation over the specified relations.

If number of chain rules increase, we can easily evaluate the membership distribution of the cause from the membership distribution of its direct or chained effect by extending the above principle.

Example 3.42 Given below a fragment of the diagnostic knowledge base of an audio player system:

R1: IF transformer secondary output is CLOSE-TO 20 V
THEN rectifier output is CLOSE-TO 12 V.
R2: IF the transformer primary input is CLOSE-TO 230 V
THEN transformer secondary output is CLOSE-TO 20 V.

We have an observation that the rectifier output is CLOSE-TO 10 V. Also suppose that the following membership distributions are available, we need to determine the membership distribution of the transformer primary input to be CLOSE-TO approximately 230V. Let the relational matrices for rule R1 and rule R2 be R1 and R2 respectively.

Then suppose:

$$\mu_{R1}\left(trans.-output, recti.-output\right) = \begin{array}{c} Transformer\ output \\ \downarrow \end{array} \begin{array}{c} Rectifier\ output \rightarrow \\ \begin{array}{ccc} 10 & 12 & 14 \end{array} \\ \begin{array}{c} 18 \\ 20 \\ 22 \end{array} \begin{pmatrix} 0.9 & 0.7 & 0.8 \\ 0.6 & 1.0 & 0.9 \\ 0.7 & 0.8 & 1.0 \end{pmatrix} \end{array}$$

$$\mu_{R2}\left(trans.-input, recti.-input\right) = \begin{array}{c} Transformer\ input \\ \downarrow \end{array} \begin{array}{c} Rectifier\ input \rightarrow \\ \begin{array}{ccc} 10 & 12 & 14 \end{array} \\ \begin{array}{c} 210 \\ 230 \\ 250 \end{array} \begin{pmatrix} 0.8 & 0.7 & 0.8 \\ 0.6 & 1.0 & 0.9 \\ 0.7 & 0.9 & 1.0 \end{pmatrix} \end{array}$$

and $$\mu_{CLOSE-TO}\left(rectifier-output\right) = \left\{ {}^{0.9}\!/_{10V}, {}^{06}\!/_{12V}, {}^{02}\!/_{14V} \right\}.$$

Note that to represent that rectifier output is CLOSED-TO 10V, we assigned a high membership value to 10V and relatively smaller membership values to 12V and 14V. By step 2 of the abductive reasoning principle, we find:

$$\mu_{CLOSE-TO}\left(transformer-output\right)$$

$$= \mu_{CLOSE-TO}\left(rectifier-output\right) \circ \left[\mu_{R1}\left(trans.-output, recti.-output\right)\right]^{T}$$

$$=\{0.9/18V.\ 0.6/20V,\ 0.7/22V\}.$$

$$\text{and } \mu_{CLOSE-TO}\left(transformer - input\right)$$

$$=\mu_{\text{CLOSE-TO}}\left(transformer - output\right) \circ [\mu_{\text{R}2}\left(trans. - input, \; trans. - output\right)]^{\text{T}}$$

$$= \left\{0.8 / 210\text{V}, \; 0.7 / 230\text{V}, \; 0.7 / 250\text{V}\right\}.$$

3.5   FUZZY LOGIC AS VIEWED BY ZADEH

Fuzzy logic is an extension of multivated logic. Its applications and objectives are quite different and novel to handle imprecision, uncertainty, and vagueness of real world problems. Fuzzy logic deals with approximate rather than precise modes of reasoning. The chains of reasoning in fuzzy logic are short in length, and rigor is not necessarily needed like classical logical systems. In fuzzy logic everything, including truth, is a matter of degree. Fuzzy logic has the greater expressive power to contain as special cases the classical two-valued and multivalued logical systems, probability theory, and probabilistic logic.

The fuzzy logic defers from traditional logical systems by the following features:

- In two-valued logical systems, a proposition p is either true or false. In multivalued logical systems, a proposition may be true or false or have an intermediate truth value, which may be an element of a finite or infinite truth value set T. In fuzzy logic, the truth values are fuzzy subsets of T. For example, if T is unit interval, then a truth value in fuzzy logic, for example, "very true," may be interpreted as a fuzzy subset of the unit interval. Thus, a fuzzy truth value is an imprecise characterization of a numerical truth value. (see section 3.4.3).
- The predicates in two-valued logic are constrained to be crisp in the sense that the denotation of a predicate must be a non-fuzzy subset of the universe of discourse. In fuzzy logic, the predicates may be either crisp ("mortal", "even", and "father of") or fuzzy ("ill", "tired", "large", "tall", "much heavier", and "friend of").
- Two-valued as well as multivalued logics allow only two quantifiers: "all" and "some." Whereas, in fuzzy logic, in addition, we have fuzzy quantifiers exemplified by "most," "many," "several," "few," "much of," "many," "several," "few," "much of," "frequently," "occasionally," "about ten," and so on. Such quantifiers are reduced to fuzzy numbers that imprecisely characterizes the cardinality of one or more fuzzy or nonfuzzy sets. A fuzzy quantifier may be viewed as a second-order fuzzy predicate. Based on this view, fuzzy quantifiers may represent the meaning of propositions containing fuzzy probabilities and thereby manipulate probabilities within fuzzy logic.
- Fuzzy logic provides a method for representing the meaning of both non-fuzzy and fuzzy predicate-modifiers exemplified by "not", "very", "more or less", "extremely", "slightly", "much", "a little", and so on. Thus, fuzzy logic handles *linguistic variables,* whose values are words or sentences in a natural or

synthetic language. For example, "Age" is a linguistic variable when its values are assumed to be "young," "old," "very young," "not very old," and so forth.

- In two-valued logical systems, a proposition p may be qualified, by associating with p a truth value, either "true" or "false"; a modal operator such as "possible" or "necessary"; and an intentional operator such as "know" or "believe."

Fuzzy logic has three principal modes of qualification:

- *Truth-qualification,* for example, (Mary is young) is not quite true, in which the qualified proposition is (Mary is young) and the qualifying truth value is "is not quite true";
- *Probability-qualfiication,* for example, (Mary is young) is unlikely, in which the qualifying fuzzy probability is "unlikely"; and
- *Possibility-qualification,* for example, (Mary is young) is almost impossible, in which the qualifying fuzzy possibility is "almost impossible."

An important issue in fuzzy logic is inference from qualified propositions for management of uncertainty in expert systems and for the commonsense reasoning. In case of commonsense reasoning, there is a close connection between probability-qualification and usuality-qualification. The role of fuzzy quantifiers is also very important.

Example 3.43 Consider the following disposition:

Swedes are blond. It may be interpreted as most Swedes are blond; or, equivalently, as (Swede is blond) is likely, where "likely" is a fuzzy probability that is numerically equal to the fuzzy quantifier "most,"; or, equivalently, as:

usually (a Swede is blond),

where "usually" qualifies the proposition "a Swede is blond."

Inference from disposition is a main concern of dispositional logic, which is briefly discussed later.

3.5.1 *REPRESENTATION OF MEANING AND INFERENCE*

In fuzzy logic, a proposition p in a natural or synthetic language may be viewed as a collection of elastic constraints, $C_1,...,C_k$, which restrict the values of a collection of variables $X = (X_1,...,X_n)$. The constraints and the variables they constrain are implicit in p. For instance, the representation of the meaning of p is a process by which the implicit constraints and variables in p are made explicit.

In fuzzy logic, this is accomplished by representing p in canonical form:

$$p \xrightarrow{X \text{ is } A}$$

where A is a fuzzy predicate or, equivalently, an n-ary fuzzy relation in $U = U_1 \times U_2 \times ... \times U_n$, where U_i, $i = 1,...,n$, is the domain of X_i.

Representation of p in its canonical form is based on the construction of an explanatory database and a test procedure that tests and aggregates the test scores associated with the elastic constraints $C_1,...,C_k$.

In other words, the canonical form of p implies that the possibility distribution of X is equal to A- that is:

$$\prod_X = A \tag{3.42}$$

which implies that

Poss $\{X = u\} = \mu_A(u), \; u \in U$

where μ_A is the membership function of A and Poss$\{X = u\}$ is the possibility that X may take u as its value. Thus, the meaning of p is represented in the form of Equation (3.42). It signifies that p induces a possibility distribution $\prod_X$ that is equal to A, where A plays the role of an elastic constraint on a variable X that is implicit in p. The possibility distribution of X, $\prod_{X'}$ is the set of possible values of X, so that possibility is a matter of degree. Therefore, a proposition p constrains the possible values of X and defines its possibility distribution. This implies that the meaning of p is defined by identifying the variable that is constrained and characterizing the constraint to which the variable is subjected through its possibility distribution. Equation (3.42) asserts that the possibility that X can take u as its value is numerically equal to the grade of membership, $\mu_A(u)$, of u in A.

Example 3.44 Consider the proposition:

$p \equiv$ John is tall

In this case, X = Height(John), A = TALL, and the canonical form of p reads

Height(John) is TALL

where the fuzzy relation TALL is in upper case letters to underscore that it plays the role of constraint in the canonical form.

From the canonical form, it follows that:

$$\text{POSS} \{\text{Height}(\text{John}) = u\} = \mu_{TALL}(u)$$

where μ_{TALL} is the membership function of TALL and $\mu_{TALL}(u)$ is the grade of membership of u in TALL or, equivalently, the degree to which a numerical height u satisfies the constraint induced by the relation TALL.

When p is a conditional proposition, its canonical form may be expressed as "Y is B if X is A," implying that p induces a conditional possibility distribution of Y given X, written as $\prod_{(Y|X)}$. In fuzzy logic, $\prod_{(Y|X)}$ may be defined in a variety of ways. $\prod_{(Y|X)}$ may be defined in consistent with the definition of implication in Lukasiwe-icz's logic as:

$$\pi_{(Y|X)}(u,v) = 1 \wedge (1 - \mu_A(u) + \mu_B(v)), u \in U, \quad v \in V, \tag{3.43}$$

where

$$\pi_{(Y|X)}(u,v) \equiv \text{Poss}\{X=u, Y=v\}, \text{ and}$$

μ_A and μ_B denote the membership functions of A and B, respectively, and $\wedge$ denotes the operator min.

Consider a quantified proposition of the form

$p \triangleq$ most tall men are not very fat, which can be written as:

$p \triangleq Q \ A's$ are B's

where Q is a fuzzy quantifier and A and B are fuzzy predicates, the constrained variable, X, is the proportion of B's in A's, with Q representing an elastic constraint on X.

Therefore, if U is a finite set $\{u_1, \dots, u_m\}$, the proportion of B's in A's is defined as the relative sigma-count:

$$\sum \text{Count}(B/A) = \frac{\sum_j \mu_A(u_j) \wedge \mu_B(u_j)}{\sum_j \mu_A(u_j)} \qquad (3.44)$$

$j = 1, \dots, m$

where $\mu_A(u_j)$ and $\mu_B(u_j)$ denote the grades of membership of u_j in A and B, respectively. Thus, Equation (3.44) may be written as:

$$\sum \text{Count}(B/A) \text{ is } Q$$

which places in evidence the constrained variable, X, in p and the elastic constraint, Q, to which X is subjected. X is the relative sigma-count of B in A.

The concept of a canonical form provides a framework for formulating the problem of inference in expert systems. Consider a knowledge base (*KB*), which consists of a collection of propositions $\{p_1, \dots, p_N\}$. A constituent proposition $p_i, i = 1, \dots, N$, may be either a fact that may be expressed in a canonical form as "X is A" or a rule that may be expressed in a canonical form as "Y is B_i" if "X is A_i." Both facts and rules may be probability-qualified or, equivalently expressed as quantified propositions.

Example 3.45 A rule of the form "Q A's are B's" may be interpreted as the probability-qualified proposition (X is B if X is A) is λ where λ is a fuzzy probability whose denotation as a fuzzy subset of the unit interval is the same as that of the fuzzy quantifier Q and X is chosen at random in U.

Now, if p_i induces a possibility distribution $\Pi^i_{(X_1, \dots, X_n)}$, where $X_1, \dots, X_n$ are the variables constrained by p_i, then the possibility distribution $\Pi_{(X_1, \dots, X_n)}$, which is induced by the totality of propositions in KB is given by the intersection of the $\Pi^i_{(X_1,...,X_n)}$.

That is:

$$\Pi_{(X_1,...,X_n)} = \Pi^1_{(X_1,...,X_n)} \cap \cdots \cap \Pi^N_{(X_1,...,X_n)}$$

or, equivalently,

$$\pi(x_1,............x_n) = \pi^1(x_1,............x_n) \wedge ... \wedge \pi^N(x_1,.....x_n)$$

$\pi_{(X_1,...,X_n)}$ is the possibility distribution function of $\Pi_{(X_1,...,X_n)}$ The constrained variables $(X_1,...,X_n)$ are the same for all propositions in KB because the set $(X_1,...,X_n)$ may be taken to be the union of the constrained variables for each proposition.

If we want to infer the value of a specified function $f(X_1,...,X_n)$, $f:U \to V$, of the variables constrained by the knowledge base, we cannot deduce the value of $f(X_1,...,X_n)$. But we can obtain its possibility distribution Π_f. By employing the extension principle, it can be shown that the possibility distribution function of f is given by the solution of the nonlinear program:

$$\pi_f(v) = \max_{u_1,...,u_n} \tag{3.45}$$

$$[\pi^1_{(X_1,...,X_n)}(u_1,...,u_n) \wedge ... \wedge \pi^N_{(X_1,...,X_n)}(u_1,...,u_n)]$$

Subject to the constraint

$$v = f(u_1,...,u_n)$$

where $u_j \in U_j, i = 1,...,n, and\ v \in V$.

The reduction to the solution of a nonlinear program constitutes the principal tool for inference in fuzzy logic.

3.5.2   FUZZY SYLLOGISMS

A basic fuzzy syllogism in fuzzy logic that is of considerable relevance to the rules of combination of evidence in expert systems is the intersection/product syllogism—a syllogism that serves as a rule of inference for quantified propositions.

This syllogism may be expressed as the inference rule:

$$Q_1 \text{ A's are B's}$$

$$Q_2 \text{ (A and B)'s are C's} \tag{3.46}$$

$$(Q_1 \otimes Q_2) \text{ A's are (B and C)'s}$$

in which Q_1 and Q_2 are fuzzy quantifiers, A, B, and C are fuzzy predicates, and $Q_1 \otimes Q_2$ is the product of the fuzzy numbers Q_1 and Q_2 in fuzzy arithmetic. (See Figure 6).

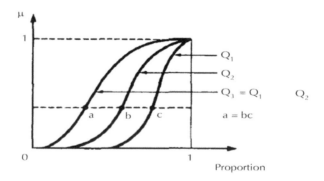

FIGURE 6   Fuzzy Quantifiers in the intersection/product syllogism.

Example 3.46 As a special case of Equation (3.46) we may write:
   Most students are single .
   A little more than a half of single students are male.

(most $\otimes$ a little more than a half) of students are single and male.
Since the intersection of B and C is contained in C, from Equation (3.46) we can write:

$$Q_1 \text{ A's are B's}$$

$$Q_2 \text{ (A and B)'s are C's} \tag{3.47}$$

$$\geq (Q_1 \otimes Q_2) \text{ A's are C's}$$

where the fuzzy number $\geq (Q_1 \otimes Q_2)$ is read as "at least $(Q_1 \otimes Q_2)$" In particular, if the fuzzy quantifiers Q_1 and Q_2 are monotone increasing (for example, when " $Q_1 = Q_2 \equiv$ most"), then

$$\geq (Q_1 \otimes Q_2) = Q_1 \otimes Q_2$$

and Equation (3.47) becomes

$$Q_1 \text{ A's are B's}$$

$$Q_2 \text{ (A and B)'s are C's} \qquad\qquad (3.48)$$

$$\overline{}$$

$$(Q_1 \otimes Q_2) \text{ A's are C's .}$$

Furthermore, if B is a subset of A, then A and B = B, and Equation (3.48) reduces to the chaining rule:

$$Q_1 \text{ A's are B's}$$

$$Q_2 \text{ B's are C's} \qquad\qquad (3.49)$$

$$\overline{}$$

$$(Q_1 \otimes Q_2) \text{ A's are C's .}$$

Example 3.47

Most students are undergraduates.
Most undergraduates are young.

Most^2 students are young.

where "most^2" represents the product of the fuzzy number "most" with itself (See Figure 7).

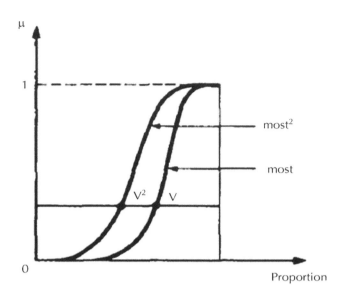

FIGURE 7   Representation of the quantifier most and most².

Remark 3.1 Observe that the chaining rule expressed by Equation (3.49) serves the same purpose as the chaining rules in Mycin, Prospector, and other probability-based expert systems.

Remark 3.2 Equation (3.49) is formulated in terms of fuzzy quantifiers rather than numerical probabilities or certainty factors, and it is a logical consequence of the concept of a relative sigma-count in fuzzy logic.

Remark 3.3 Furthermore, the chaining rule (Equation 3.49) is robust in the sense that if Q_1 and Q_2 are close to unity, so is their product $Q_1 \otimes Q_2$.

More specifically, if Q_1 and Q_2 are expressed as:

$$Q_1 = 1 \ominus \varepsilon_1$$

$$Q_2 = 1 \ominus \varepsilon_2$$

where ε_1 and ε_2 are small fuzzy numbers, then, to a first approximation, Q may be expressed as:

$$Q = 1 \ominus \varepsilon_1 \ominus \varepsilon_2$$

Remark 3.4 The general properties Q_1, Q_2, A, B, and C must have to ensure robustness. As shown above, the containment of B in A and the monotonicity of Q_1 and Q_2 are conditions for robustness in the case of the intersection/product syllogism.

CONSEQUENT CONJUNCTION SYLLOGISM

$$Q_1 \text{ A's are B's}$$

$$Q_2 \text{ A's are C's} \qquad (3.50)$$

$$\text{Q A's are (B and C)'s}$$

where

$$\left(Q_1 \oplus Q_2 \ominus 1\right) \le Q \le Q_1 Q_2$$

$$0 \,\circledcirc\, (Q_1 \oplus Q_2 \ominus 1) \le Q \le Q_1 \circledcirc Q_2$$

in which the operators $\circledwedge$, $\circledvee$, $\oplus$, $\ominus$, and the inequality $\le$ are the extensions of $\wedge$, $\vee$, $+$, $-$, and $\le$, respectively, to fuzzy numbers.

Remark 3.5 The consequent conjunction syllogism plays the same role in fuzzy logic as the rule of combination of evidence for conjunctive hypotheses does in Mycin and Prospector.

Remark 3.6 In Mycin and Prospector, the qualifying probabilities and certainty factors are real numbers, in the consequent conjunction syllogism the fuzzy quantifiers are fuzzy numbers.

Remark 3.7 The result expressed by Equation (3.50) indicates that the conclusion yielded by the application of fuzzy logic to the premises in question is both robust and compositional.

ANTECEDENT CONJUNCTION SYLLOGISM

A more complex problem is stated in terms of quantified premises.

The inference rule in question may be expressed as:

$$Q_1 \text{ A's are C's}$$

$$Q_2 \text{ B's are C's} \qquad (3.51)$$

$$\text{Q (A and B)'s are C's}$$

where the value of Q is to be determined.

Remark 3.8 Antecedent conjunction syllogism corresponds to the conjunction combination of evidence in Mycin and Prospector.

Ramark 3.9 It can be shown that, without any restrictive assumptions on Q_1, Q_2, A, B, and C, there is nothing that can be said about Q, which is equivalent to saying that "Q = none to all."

A basic assumption in Mycin, Prospector, and related systems is that the items of evidence are conditionally independent, given the hypothesis (and its complement). That is:

$$P(E_1, E_2 \mid H) = P(E_1 \mid H) P(E_2 \mid H)$$

where $P(E_1, E_2 \mid H)$ is the joint probability of E_1 and E_2, given the hypothesis H, and $P(E_1 \mid H)$ and $P(E_2 \mid H)$ are the conditional probabilities of E_1 given H and E_2 given H, respectively. Expressed in terms of the relative sigma-counts, this assumption may be written as:

$$\Sigma \text{ Count } (A \cap B / C) = \Sigma \text{ Count } (A/C) \Sigma \text{ Count } (B/C) \qquad (3.52)$$

where $\cap$ denotes the intersection of fuzzy sets.

To determine the value of Q in Equation (3.51), we have to compute the relative sigma-count of C in $A \cap B$. We can verify that, under the assumption (Equation 3.52), the sigma-count in question is given by:

$$\Sigma \text{ Count } (C / A \cap B) = \Sigma \text{ Count } (C/A) \Sigma \text{ Count } (C/B) \, \delta$$

where the factor δ is expressed by:

$$\delta = \frac{\Sigma \text{ Count } (A) \; \Sigma \text{ Count } (B)}{\Sigma \text{ Count } (A \cap B) \; \Sigma \text{ Count } (C)} \qquad (3.53)$$

Equation (3.53) indicates that the assumption expressed by Equation (3.52) does not ensure the compositionality of Q. However, compositionality can be achieved through the use of the concept of a relative ρQ *sigma-count,* which is defined as:

$$\rho Q \Sigma \text{ Count } (B/A) = \frac{\Sigma \; \text{Count } (B/A)}{\Sigma \text{ Count } (\sim B/A)}$$

where $\sim$B denotes the negation of B. The use of ρQsigma-counts in place of sigma-counts is analogous to the use of odds instead of probabilities in Prospector, and it serves the same purpose.

3.5.3 INFERENCE WITH FUZZY PROBABILITIES

Consider a knowledge base $KB = \{p_1, ..., p_N\}$ in which the constituent propositions are true with probability one. We can infer a proposition q which, like the premises, is true with probability one.

Example 3.48 Suppose that each p_i in KB is replaced with a probability-qualified proposition "$p_i \equiv p_i$ is λ_i," in which λ_i is a fuzzy probability. For instance,

$$p_i \equiv X \text{ is small}$$

and

$$p_i \equiv X \text{ is small is very likely.}$$

As a result of the qualification of the p_i, the conclusion, q, is a probability-qualified proposition that may be expressed as:

$$q' = q \text{ is } \lambda$$

in which λ is a fuzzy probability.

The problem is to determine λ as a function of the λ_i, if such a function exists.

Ramark 3.10 A special case of this problem, which is of particular relevance to the management of uncertainty in expert systems, is one in which the fuzzy probabilities λ_i are close to unity.

Ramark 3.11 We say that the inference process is compositional if λ can be expressed as a function of the λ_i, and it is robust if whenever the λ_i are close to unity, so is λ

By reducing the determination of λ to the solution of a nonlinear program, we can show that the inference process is not compositional if the λ_i and λ are numerical probabilities. This result calls into question the validity of the rules of combination of evidence in those expert systems, in which the certainty factor of the conclusion is expressed as a function of the certainty factors of the premises. However, compositionality does hold if the λ_i and λ are assumed to be fuzzy probabilities. For this allows the probability of q to be interval-valued when the λ_i are numerical probabilities, which is consistent with known results in inductive logic.

In general, robustness does not hold without some restrictive assumptions on the premises. For example, the brittleness of the transitivity of implication is an instance of the lack of robustness when no assumptions are made regarding the fuzzy predicates A, B, and C.

On the other hand, if in the inference schema:

    X is A

   ~~Y is B if X is A~~

Y is B

The major premise is replaced by "X is A is probable," where "probable" is a fuzzy probability close to unity, then it can be shown that, under mildly restrictive assumptions on A, the resulting conclusion may be expressed as "Y is B is $\geq$ probable," where "$\geq$ probable" is a fuzzy probability that, as a fuzzy number, is greater than or equal to the fuzzy number "probable." In this case, robustness does hold, for if "probable" is close to unity, so is "$\geq$ probable."

3.5.4 INFERENCE USING METHOD OF INTERPOLATION

An important problem that arises in the operation of any rule-based system is the following. Suppose the user supplies a fact that may be expressed as "X is A," where A is a fuzzy or nonfuzzy predicate. Furthermore, suppose that there is no conditional rule in KB whose antecedent matches A exactly. Then the problem is to choose the rules that should be executed. Also the problem is to combine the results.

An approach to this problem is to use of an interpolation technique which requires computation of the degree of partial match between the user-supplied fact and the rows of decision table. More specifically, suppose that upon translation into their canonical forms, a group of propositions in KB may be expressed as a fuzzy relation of the form given in Table 18.

TABLE 18   Representation of KB by fuzzy relations

R $\quad X_1$	X_2	$\cdot$	X_n	X_{n+1}
R_{11}	R_{12}	$\cdot$	R_{1n}	Z_1
R_{m1}	R_{m2}	$\cdot$	R_{mn}	Z_m

The entries of the table are fuzzy sets. The input variables are X_1, ..., X_n with domains U_1, ..., U_n, and the output variable is X_{n+1}, with domain U_{n+1}.

The problem is:

Given an input n-tuple $(R_1$, ..., $R_n)$, in which R_j j=1, ..., n, is a fuzzy subset of U_j, what is the value of X_{n+1} expressed as a fuzzy subset of U_{n+1}?

A possible approach to the problem is to compute for each pair $(R_{ij}$, $R_j)$ the degree of consistency of the input R_j with the R_{ij} element of R, $i = 1,..,m$, $j = 1, ..., n$. The degree of consistency, Y_{ij}, is defined as:

$$Y_{ij} \triangleq \sup (R_{ij} \cap R_j) = \sup_{u_j} (\mu_{R_{ij}} (u_i) \wedge \mu_{R_j} (u_i))$$

in which $\mu_{R_{ij}}$ and μ_{R_j} are the membership functions of R_{ij} and R_j, respectively; u_i is a generic element of U_i, and the supremum is taken over u_j.

Next, we compute the overall degree of consistency, Y_{ij}, of the input n-tuple (R_1 , ..., R_n) with the ith row of R, i=1, ..., m, by employing $\wedge$(min) as the aggregation operator. Thus,

$$Y_i = Y_{i1} \wedge Y_{i2} \wedge ... \wedge Y_{in}$$

which implies that Y_i may be interpreted as a conservative measure of agreement between the input n-tuple (R_1 , ..., R_n) and the ith-row n-tuple (R_{i1} , ..., R_{in}). Then, employing Y_i as a weighting coefficient, the desired expression for X_{n+1} may be written as a "linear" combination

$$X_{n+1} = Y_i \wedge Z_1 + ... + y_m \wedge Z_m$$

in which + denotes the union, and $Y_i \wedge Z_1$ is a fuzzy set defined by:

$$\mu_{Y_i \wedge Z_i}\left(U_{j+1}\right) = y_i \wedge \mu_{Z_1}\left(U_{i+1}\right), i = 1, ..., m$$

The above approach ceases to be effective, however, when R is a sparse relation in the sense that no row of R has a high degree of consistency with the input n-tuple. For such cases, a more general interpolation technique has to be employed.

3.5.5 BASIC RULES OF INFERENCE

One distinguishing characteristic of fuzzy logic is that premises and conclusions in an inference rule are generally expressed in canonical form. This representation places in evidence the fact that each premise is a constraint on a variable and that the conclusion is an induced constraint computed through a process of constraint propagation – a process that reduces to the solution of a nonlinear program. The following briefly presents – without derivation – some of the basic inference rules in fuzzy logic. Most of these rules can be deduced from the basic inference rule expressed by Equation (3.45).

The rules of inference in fuzzy logic may be classified in a variety of ways. One basic class is categorical rules, that is, rules that do not contain fuzzy quantifiers. A more general class is dispositional rules, rules in which one or more premises may contain, explicitly or implicitly, the fuzzy quantifier "usually."

ENTAILMENT PRINCIPLE

$$X \text{ is } A \qquad\qquad\qquad (3.54)$$

$$A \subset B$$

$$X \text{ is } B$$

where X is a variable taking values in a universe of discourse U, and A and B are fuzzy subsets of U, is a categorical rule.

DISPOSITIONAL ENTAILMENT PRINCIPLE

Usually

$$(X \text{ is } A) \qquad\qquad\qquad (3.55)$$

$$A \subset B$$
_____

usually (X is B)

Remark 3.12 In the limiting case where "usually" becomes "always," Equation (3.55) reduces to Equation (3.54).

In essence, the entailment principle asserts that from the proposition "X is A", we can always infer a less specific proposition "X is B."

Example 3.49 From the proposition "Mary is young," which in its canonical form reads

Age(Mary) is YOUNG

where YOUNG is interpreted as a fuzzy set or, equivalently, as a fuzzy predicate, we can infer "Mary is not old," provided YOUNG is a subset of the complement of OLD. That is:

$$\mu_{YOUNG}(u) \subset 1 - \mu_{OLD}(u), u \in [0, 100]$$

where μ_{YOUNG} and μ_{OLD} are, respectively, the membership functions of YOUNG and OLD, and the universe of discourse is the interval [0, 100].

Remark 3.13 The entailment principle in fuzzy logic may be regarded as a generalization to fuzzy sets of the inheritance principle widely used in knowledge representation systems.

If the proposition "X is A", is interpreted as "X has property A," then conclusion "X is B" may be interpreted as "X has property B," where B is any superset of A. In other words, X inherits property B if B is a superset of A.

Among other categorical rules that play a basic role in fuzzy logic are the following. In all of these rules, X, Y, Z, ... are variables ranging over specified universes of discourse, and A, B, C, ... are fuzzy predicates or equivalently fuzzy relations.

CONJUNCTIVE RULE

X is A
X is B
_____

X is A ∩ B

where A ∩ B is the intersection of A and B represented as:

$$\mu_{A \cap B}(u) = \mu_A(u) \wedge \mu_B(u), u \in U$$

CARTESIAN PRODUCT

X is A

Y is B

(X, Y) is A $\times$ B

where (X, Y) is a binary variable and $A \times B$ is represented as:

$$\mu_{A \times B}(u, v) = \mu_A(u) \wedge \mu_B(v), \quad u \in U, \quad v \in V$$

PROJECTION RULE

(X, Y) is R

X is $_x$R

where $_xR$, the projection of the binary relation R on the domain of X, is represented as:

$$\mu_{X^R}(u) = \sup_v \mu_R(u, v), u \in U, \quad v \in V$$

where $\mu_R(u, v)$ is the membership function of R and the supremum is taken over $v \in V$.

COMPOSITIONAL RULE

X is A

(X, Y) is R

Y is A o R

where A o R, the composition of the unary relation A with the binary relation R, is defined by:

$$\mu_{A \circ R}(v) = \sup_u (\mu_A(u) \wedge \mu_R(u, v)).$$

Remark 3.14 The compositional rule of inference may be viewed as a combination of the conjunctive and projection rules.

GENERALIZED MODUS PONENS

X is A

Y is C if X is B

Y is A o ($\sim$B $\oplus$ C)

where $\sim B$ denotes the negation of B and the bounded sum is defined by:

$$\mu_{\sim B \oplus C}(u, v) = 1 \wedge (1 - \mu_B(u) + \mu_C(v)).$$

Remark 3.15 An important feature of the generalized modus ponens, which is not possessed by the modus ponens in binary logical systems, is that the antecedent "X is B" need not be identical with premise "X is A".

Remark 3.16 It should be noted that the generalized modus ponens is related to the interpolation rule which was described earlier.

Remark 3.17 An additional point that should be noted is that the generalized modus ponens may be regarded as an instance of the compositional rule of inference.

DISPOSITIONAL MODUS PONENS

In many applications involving commonsense reasoning, the premises in the generalized modus ponens are usuality-qualified. In such cases, we may employ a dispositional version of the modus ponens.

It may be expressed as:
- Usually (X is A)
- Usually (Y is B if X is A)
- Usually^2 (Y is B)

where "usually^2" is the square of "usually" (See Figure 8). For simplicity, it is assumed that the premise "X is A" matches the antecedent in the conditional proposition; also, the conditional proposition is interpreted as the statement, *"The value of the fuzzy conditional probability of B given A is the fuzzy number USUALLY."*

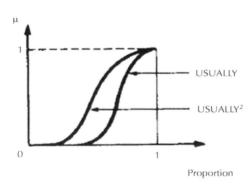

FIGURE 8   Representation of the dispositional quantifier Usually and Usually^2.

EXTENSION PRINCIPLE

The extension principle plays an important role in fuzzy logic by providing a mechanism for computing induced constraints. More specifically, assume that a variable X taking values in a universe of discourse U is constrained by the proposition "X is A." Furthermore, assume that f is a mapping from U to V so that X is mapped into $f(X)$. The question is, what is the constraint on $f(X)$ which is induced by the constraint on X?

The answer provided by the extension principle may be expressed as the inference rule:

$$\frac{X \text{ is } A}{f(X) \text{ is } f(A)}$$

where the membership function of $f(A)$ is defined by:

$$\mu_{f(A)}(v) = \sup_u \mu_A(u) \tag{3.56}$$

subject to the condition

$$v = f(u), \ u \in U, \ v \in V.$$

In particular, if the function f is 1:1, then Equation (3.56) simplifies to:

$$\mu_{f(A)}(v) = \mu_A(v^{-1}), \qquad v \in V$$

where v^{-1} is the inverse of v.

Example 3.50

$$\frac{X \text{ is small}}{X^2 \text{ is small}^2}$$

and

$$\mu_{\text{small}^2}(v) = \mu_{\text{small}}(\sqrt{v}).$$

As in the case of the entailment rule, the dispositional version of the extension principle has the simple form:

$$\frac{\text{usually } (X \text{ is } A)}{\text{usually } (f(X) \text{ is } f(A))}$$

Remark 3.18 The dispositional extension principle plays an important role in inference from commonsense knowledge.

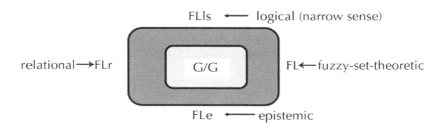

G/G: Graduation/Granulation

FIGURE 9   Principal facets of fuzzy logic (FL). The core of FL is graduation/granulation, G/G.

3.5.6   *GENERAL OBSERVATIONS ABOUT FUZZY LOGIC*

There are many misconceptions about fuzzy logic. Precisely speaking fuzzy logic is not fuzzy. It is a precise logic of imprecision and approximate reasoning. Fuzzy logic may be utilized to mimic the human capabilities to converse, reason, and make rational decisions in an environment of imperfect information. Also it can perform a wide variety of physical and mental tasks, as performed by human being, without any measurements and any computation. One of the principal contributions of fuzzy logic is its high power of precisiation of what is imprecise. This capability of fuzzy logic suggests that it may find important applications in the realms of economics, linguistics, law, and other human-centric fields [310].

In a narrow sense, fuzzy logic is a logical system which is a generalization of multivalued logic. In a wide sense which is in dominant use today, fuzzy logic (FL) is much more than a logical system. The FL has many facets. The principal facets are the logical facet (FLl), the fuzzy-set-theoretic facet (FLs), the epistemic facet (FLe), and the relational facet (FLr) (Figure 9).

The logical facet of FL and FLl is fuzzy logic in its narrow sense. The FLl may be viewed as a generalization of multivalued logic. The agenda of FLl is similar in spirit to the agenda of classical logic.

The fuzzy-set-theoretic facet, FLs, is focused on fuzzy sets, that is, on classes whose boundaries are unsharp. The theory of fuzzy sets is central to fuzzy logic. Historically, the theory of fuzzy sets preceded fuzzy logic in its wide sense.

The epistemic facet of FL, FLe, is concerned with knowledge representation, semantics of natural languages, and information analysis. In FLe, a natural language is viewed as a system for describing perceptions. An important branch of FLe is possibility theory. Another important branch of FLe is the computational theory of perceptions.

The relational facet, FLr, is focused on fuzzy relations and, more generally, on fuzzy dependencies. The concept of a linguistic variable and the associated calculi of fuzzy if-then rules play pivotal roles in almost all applications of fuzzy logic.

The basic concepts of graduation and granulation form the core of FL and are the principal distinguishing features of fuzzy logic. More specifically, in fuzzy logic everything is or is allowed to be graduated, that is, be a matter of degree or, equivalently fuzzy.

Furthermore, in fuzzy logic everything is or is allowed to be granulated, with a granule being a clump of attribute-values drawn together by in distinguishability, similarity, proximity of functionality. Graduated granulation, or equivalently fuzzy granulation, is a unique feature of fuzzy logic. Graduated granulation is inspired by the way in which humans deal with complexity and imprecision.

An instance of granulation is the concept of a linguistic variable – a concept which was introduced in "Outline of a new approach to the analysis of complex systems and decision processes". A simple example of a linguistic variable is shown in Figure 10. Today, the concept of linguistic variable is used in almost all applications of fuzzy logic, especially in the realms of control and consumer products. Granulation may be viewed as a form of information compression of variables and input/output relations.

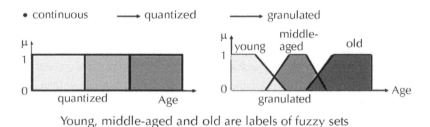

Young, middle-aged and old are labels of fuzzy sets

FIGURE 10   Granulation of Age; young, middle-aged and old are linguistic(granular) values of age.

An important concept which is related to the concept of a linguistic variable is the concept of a granular value. More specifically, consider a variable X, which takes values in U. Let u be a value of X. Informally, if u is known precisely, then u is referred to as a singular (point) value of X. If X is not known precisely, but there is some information which constrains possible values of u, then the constraint on u defines a granular value of X (Figure 11). For example, in what is known about u is that it is contained in an interval [a, b], then [a, b] is a granular value of X. A granular variable is a variable which takes granular values. In this sense, a linguistic variable is a granular variable which carries linguistic labels. It should be noted that a granular value of Age is not restricted to young, middle-aged, or old. For example, "not very young" is an admissible granular value of age. It is important to note that in fuzzy logic, in moving from numerical to linguistic variables, we are moving in a counter traditional direction. This important feature of fuzzy logic is referred to as "the fuzzy logic gambit".

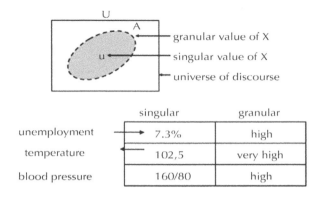

FIGURE 11   Singular and granular values.

The most visible, the best understood and the most widely used contribution of fuzzy logic is the concept of a linguistic variable and the associated machinery of fuzzy if-then rules. But there are other equally important contributions which are much less visible and much less well understood. It is most important to understand these significant contributions which are essentially the landmark of the fuzzy logic in its nontraditional setting.

• **Linguistic variables and fuzzy if-then rules**

The machinery of linguistic variables and fuzzy if-then rules is unique to fuzzy logic. This machinery has played and is continuing to play a pivotal role in the conception and design of control systems and consumer products. However, its applicability is much broader. A key idea which underlies the machinery of linguistic variables and fuzzy if-then rules is centered on the use of information compression. In fuzzy logic, information compression is achieved through the use of fuzzy granulation.

• **FL-generalization**

Fuzzy logic has far greater generality than bivalent logic. This implies that any bivalent-logic-based theory, T, may be generalized and hence upgraded through what is referred to as FL-generalization. The FL-generalization of a bivalent- logic-based theory, T, involves addition to T of concepts and techniques drawn from fuzzy logic. In the limit, FL-generalization of T leads to a fuzzy-logic- based theory, T^+. By construction, T^+ has a much higher level of generality than T, and hence has enhanced capability to deal with imprecision, uncertainty, incompleteness of information, partiality of truth, and partiality of possibility.

• **The concepts of precisiation and cointension**

The concepts of precisiation and cointension play important roles in nontraditional view of fuzzy logic. In nontraditional fuzzy logic, differentiation is made between two concepts of precision: precision of value, v-precision; and precision of meaning, m-precision. Furthermore, differentiation is made between precisiation of meaning which is (a) human-oriented, or mh-precisiation for short; and (b) machine-oriented, or mm-precisiation for short. It is understood that mm-precisiation is mathematically well defined. The object of precisiation, p, and the result of precisiation, p^*, are referred to as precisiend and precisiand, respectively. Informally, cointension is defined as a measure of closeness of the meanings of p and p^*. Precisiation is cointensive if the meaning of p^* is close to the meaning of p. One of the important features of fuzzy logic is its high power of cointensive precisiation. This implies that better models of reality can be achieved through the use of fuzzy logic.

Cointensive precisiation has an important implication for science. In large measure, science is bivalent-logic-based. In consequence, in science, it is traditional to define concepts in a bivalent framework, with no degrees of truth allowed. The problem is that, in reality, many concepts in science are fuzzy, that is, are a matter of degree. For this reason, bivalent-logic-based definitions of scientific concepts are, in many cases, not cointensive. To formulate cointensive definitions of fuzzy concepts, it is necessary to employ fuzzy logic.

- *NL-Computation, computing with words (CW) and precisiated natural language (PNL)*

Much of human knowledge is expressed in natural language. Traditional theories of natural language are based on bivalent logic. The problem is that natural languages are intrinsically imprecise. Imprecision of natural languages is rooted in imprecision of perceptions. A natural language is basically a system for describing perceptions. Perceptions are intrinsically imprecise, reflecting the bounded ability of human sensory organs, and ultimately the brain, to resolve detail and store information. Imprecision of perceptions is passed on to natural languages.

Bivalent logic is intolerant of imprecision, partiality of truth, and partiality of possibility. For this reason, bivalent logic is intrinsically unsuited to serve as a foundation for theories of natural language. As the logic of imprecision and approximate reasoning, fuzzy logic is a much better choice.

The NL-Computation, computing with words (CW) and precisiated natural language (PNL) are closely related formalisms. In conventional modes of computation, the objects of computation are mathematical constructs. By contrast, in NL-Computation the objects of computation are propositions and predicates drawn from a natural language. A key idea which underlies NL-Computation involves representing the meaning of propositions and predicates as generalized constraints. NL-Computation opens the door to a wide-ranging enlargement of the role of natural languages in scientific theories.

- *Computational theory of perceptions*

Human have a remarkable capability to perform a wide variety of physical and mental tasks without any measurements and any computations. In performing such tasks humans employ perceptions. To endow machines with this capability what is needed is a formalism, in which perceptions can play the role of objects of computation. The fuzzy-logic-based computational theory of perceptions serves this purpose. A key idea in this theory is that of computing not with perceptions, but with their descriptions in a natural language. Representing perceptions as propositions drawn from a natural language opens the door to application of NL-Computation to computation with perceptions. Computational theory of perceptions is of direct relevance to achievement of human level machine intelligence.

- *Possibility Theory*

Possibility theory is a branch of fuzzy logic. Possibility theory and probability theory are distinct theories. Possibility theory may be viewed as a formalization of perception of possibility, whereas probability theory is rooted in perception of likelihood. In large measure, possibility theory and probability theory are complementary rather than competitive. Possibility theory is of direct relevance to, knowledge representation, semantics of natural languages, decision analysis, and computation with imprecise probabilities.

- *Computation with imprecise probabilities*

Most real-world probabilities are perceptions of likelihood. As such, real-world probabilities are intrinsically imprecise. Until recently, the issue of imprecise probabilities has been accorded little attention in the literature of probability theory. More recently, the problem of computation with imprecise probabilities has been an object of rapidly growing interest.

Typically, imprecise probabilities occur in an environment of imprecisely defined variables, functions, relations, events, and so on. Existing approaches to computation with imprecise probabilities do not address this reality. To address this reality, what is needed is fuzzy logic and, more particularly, NL-Computation and the computational theory of perceptions.

- *Fuzzy logic as a modeling language*

Science does not deal with reality but with models of reality. In general, reality is fuzzy. For this reason, construction of realistic models of reality calls for the use of fuzzy logic rather than bivalent logic.

Fuzzy logic is logic of imprecision and approximate reasoning. It is natural to employ fuzzy logic as a modeling language when the objects of modeling are not well defined. But what is somewhat paradoxical is that in many of its practical applications fuzzy logic is used as a modeling language for systems which are precisely defined. The explanation is that, in general, precision carries a cost. In those cases in which there is a tolerance for imprecision, reduction in cost may be achieved through imprecisiation, for example, data compression, information compression, and summarization. The result of imprecisiation is an object of modeling which is not precisely defined. A fuzzy modeling language comes into play at this point. This is the key idea which underlies the fuzzy logic gambit. The fuzzy logic gambit is widely used in the design of consumer products, a realm in which cost is an important consideration.

FUZZY LOGIC AS THE BASIS FOR GENERALIZATION OF SCIENTIFIC THEORIES

By construction, fuzzy logic has a much more general conceptual structure than bivalent logic. A key concept in the transition from bivalent logic to fuzzy logic is the generalization of the concept of a set to a fuzzy set. This generalization is the point of departure for what will be referred to as FL-generalization.

More specifically, FL-generalization of any theory, T, involves an addition to T of concepts drawn from fuzzy logic. In the limit, as more and more concepts which are drawn from fuzzy logic are added to T, the foundation of T is shifted from bivalent logic to fuzzy logic. By construction, FL-generalization results in an upgraded theory, T^+, which is at least as rich and in general, significantly richer than T.

As an illustration, consider probability theory (PT) – a theory which is bivalent-logic-based. Among the basic concepts drawn from fuzzy logic which may be added to PT are the following:

- set + fuzzy set,
- event + fuzzy event,
- relation + fuzzy relation,
- probability + fuzzy probility,
- random set + fuzzy random set,
- independence + fuzzy independence,
- stationarity + fuzzy stationarity,
- random variable + fuzzy random variable, and so on.

As a theory, PT^+ is much richer than PT. In particular, it provides a basis for construction of models which are much closer to reality than those that can be constructed through the use of PT. This applies, in particular, to computation with imprecise probabilities.

Some scientific theories have already been FL-generalized to some degree, and many more are likely to be FL-generalized in coming years. Particularly worthy of note are the following FL-generalizations.

- control $\rightarrow$ fuzzy control,
- linear programming $\rightarrow$ fuzzy linear programming,
- probability theory $\rightarrow$ fuzzy probability theory,
- measure theory $\rightarrow$ fuzzy measure theory,
- topology $\rightarrow$ fuzzy topology,
- graph theory $\rightarrow$ fuzzy graph theory,
- cluster analysis $\rightarrow$ fuzzy cluster analysis,
- Prolog $\rightarrow$ fuzzy Prolog, and so on.

The FL generalization is a basis for an important rationale for the use of fuzzy logic. It is conceivable that eventually the foundations of many scientific theories may be shifted from bivalent logic to fuzzy logic.

FUZZY LOGIC AND NATURAL LANGUAGE

Much of human knowledge is described in natural language. Furthermore, natural languages have a position of centrality in human reasoning and communication. For this reasons, as we move further into the age of machine intelligence and automated decision-making, the problem of mechanization of natural language understanding is certain to grow in visibility and importance. Natural languages are pervasively imprecise in the sense that in a natural language almost everything is a matter of degree. Imprecision of natural languages is rooted in imprecision of perceptions. Basically, a natural language is a system for describing perceptions. Perceptions are intrinsically imprecise, reflecting the bounded ability of human sensory organs, and ultimately the brain, to resolve detail and store information. Imprecision of perceptions is passed on to natural languages. This is the principal reason why natural languages are pervasively imprecise. Imprecision of natural languages is as issue of central importance. What is remarkable is that despite its importance, the issue of imprecision has been and continues to be largely ignored in the literatures of linguistics and philosophy of languages. There is an explanation. In large measure, theories of natural language are based on bivalent logic. Bivalent logic is intolerant of imprecision and partial truth. This is why bivalent-logic-based theories of natural language are intrinsically incapable of coming to grips with the issue of imprecision. What is widely unrecognized is that to close the wide gap between the precision of bivalent logic and the imprecision of natural languages what is needed is fuzzy logic, in addition to probability theory. Fuzzy logic can be applied to the development of a better understanding of how to deal with imprecision of natural languages. It should be noted that in fuzzy logic, as in natural languages, everything is or is allowed to be a matter of degree.

FUZZY HARDWARE

Several expert system shells based on fuzzy logic are now commercially available, among them Reveal and Flops. The seminal work of Togai and Watanabe at Bell Telephone Laboratories, which resulted in the development of a fuzzy logic chip, set the stage for using such chips in fuzzy-logic-based expert systems and, more generally, in rule-based systems not requiring a high degree of precision. More recently, the fuzzy computer developed by Yamakawa of Kumamoto University has shown great promise as a general-purpose tool for processing linguistic data at high speed and with remarkable robustness.

Togai and Watanabe's fuzzy inference chip consists of four major components:
- A rule set memory,
- AN inference processor,
- A controller, and
- I/O circuitry.

In a recent implementation, a rule set memory is realized by a random-access memory. In the inference processor, there are 16 data paths; one data path is laid out for each rule. All 16 rules on the chip are executed in parallel. The chip requires 64 clock cycles to produce an output. This translates to an execution speed of approximately 250,000 fuzzy logical inferences per second (FLIPS) at 16 megahertz clock. A fuzzy inference accelerator, which is a coprocessor board for a designated computer, is currently being designed. This board accommodates the new chips.

In the current implementation, the control variables are assumed to range over a finite set having no more than 31 elements. The membership function is quantized at 16 levels, with 15 representing full membership. Once the Togai/Watanabe chip becomes available commercially, it should find many uses in both fuzzy-logic based intelligent controllers and expert systems.

Yamakawa's fuzzy computer, whose hardware was built by OMRON Tateise Electronics Corporation, is capable of performing fuzzy inference at the very high speed of 10 mega FLIPS. Yamakawa's computer employs a parallel architecture. Basically, it has a fuzzy memory, a set of inference engines, a MAX block, and a defuzzifier. The computer is designed to process linguistic inputs, for example, "more or less small" and "very large," which are represented by analog voltages on data buses. A binary RAM, an array of registers and a membership function generator form the computer's fuzzy memory.

The linguistic inputs are fed to inference engines in parallel, with each rule yielding an output. The outputs are aggregated in the MAX block, yielding an overall fuzzy output that appears in the output data bus as a set of distributed analog voltages. In intelligent fuzzy control and other applications requiring nonfuzzy commands, the fuzzy output is fed to a defuzzifier for transformation into crisp output.

Yamakawa's fuzzy computer may be an important step toward a sixth-generation computer capable of processing commonsense knowledge. This capability is a prerequisite to solving many AI problems—for example, handwritten text recognition, speech recognition, machine translation, summarization, and image understanding that do not lend themselves to cost-effective solution within the bounds of conventional technology.

A short list of applications of FL includes: *Controls Applications* – aircraft control (Rockwell Corp.), Sendai subway operation (Hitachi), cruise control (Nissan), automatic transmission (Nissan, Subaru), self-parking model car (Tokyo Tech. Univ.), and space shuttle docking (NASA); *Scheduling and Optimization* – elevator scheduling (Hitachi, Fujitech, Mitsubishi) and stock market analysis (Yamaichi Securities); and *Signal Analysis for Turing and Interpretation* – TV picture adjustment (Sony), handwriting recognition (Sony Palm Top), video camera autofocus (Sanyo/Fisher, Canon), and video image stabilizer (Matshushita/Parasonic).

3.5.7 EXTENDED VERSION OF FUZZY LOGIC

The extended fuzzy logic (FLe) deals with reasoning and formalisms which are quasi-mathematical rather than mathematical. The following is a very brief exposition of some of the basic ideas which underlie FLe [311].

Science generally deals with models of reality. In most of the cases, scientific progress is driven by a quest for better models of reality. In course of building models of reality, a problem that has to be faced is that as the complexity of a system, S, increases, it becomes increasingly difficult to construct a model, M(S), which is both close-fitting and precise. This applies, in particular, to systems in which human judgment, perceptions, and emotions play a prominent role. As the complexity of a system increases further, a point is reached at which construction of a model is impossible. At that juncture extended fuzzy logic comes into picture. But extended fuzzy logic is not the only formalism that comes into play at this point. There are various approximation theories, theories centered on bounded rationality, qualitative reasoning, commonsense reasoning, and theories of argumentation. Extended fuzzy logic differs from these and related theories both in spirit and in substance.

To appreciate the notion of extended fuzzy logic, FLe, we first define fuzzy logic, FL. Fuzzy logic is a precise conceptual system of reasoning, deduction, and computation in which the objects of discourse and analysis are associated with imperfect information. Imperfect information is information which in one or more respects is imprecise, uncertain, incomplete, unreliable, vague, or partially true. In fuzzy logic, the results of reasoning, deduction, and computation are expected to be provably valid (p-valid) within the conceptual structure of fuzzy logic.

Fuzzy logic is precise. In fuzzy logic, precision is achieved through association of fuzzy sets with membership functions and, more generally, association of granules with generalized constraints. Fuzzy logic is called precisiated logic.

At this point, we construct a fuzzy logic, Flu, which, in contrast to FL, is unprecisiated. What this means is that in Flu membership, functions and generalized constraints are not specified, and are a matter of perception rather than measurement. To stress the contrast between FL and Flu, FL may be written as FLp, with p standing for precisiated. In case of Flu, instead of provable validity (p-validity), we have fuzzy validity or f-validity for short. Actually, everyday human reasoning is preponderantly f-valid reasoning. Humans have a remarkable capability to perform a wide variety of physical and mental tasks without any measurements and any computations. In this context, f-valid reasoning is perception-based. In Flu, there are no formal definitions, theorems, or p-valid proofs.

The concept of unprecisiated fuzzy logic provides a basis for the concept of extended fuzzy logic, FLe. More specifically, FLe is the result of adding Flu to FL(FLp),

FLe = FL + Flu,

With Flu playing the role of an extension of, or addendum to, FL.

Expressing FLe as the sum of FL and Flu has important implications. First, to construct a definition of FLe, it is sufficient to delete the word "precise" from the definition of FL. Thus, extended fuzzy logic (FLe) is conceptual system of reasoning, deduction, and computation in which the objects of discourse and analysis are associated with imperfect information. Imperfect information is information which in one or more respects is imprecise, uncertain, incomplete, unreliable, vague, or partially true. In extended fuzzy logic, the result of reasoning, deduction, or computation is not expected to be provably valid. f-valid reasoning is not admissible in FL, but is admissible in FLe when p-valid reasoning is infeasible, and carries an excessively high cost or is unneeded. In many realistic settings, this is the norm rather than exception.

Example 3.51. I hail a taxi and ask the driver to take me to address A. There are two versions: (a) I ask the driver to take me to A the shortest way and (b) I ask the driver to take me to A the fastest way. Based on his/her experience, the driver chooses route (a) for (a) and route (b) for (b).

In version (a), if there is a map of the area, it is possible to construct the shortest way to A. This would be a p-valid solution. Thus, for version (a) there exists a p-valid solution but the driver's choice of route (a) may be viewed as an f-valid solution which in some sense is good enough.

In version (b), it is not possible to construct a cointensive model of the system and hence it is not possible to construct a p-valid solution. The problem is rooted in uncertainties related to traffic conditions, timing of lights, and so on. In fact, if the driver had asked me to define what I mean by "the fastest way," I could not come up with an answer to his/her question. Thus, in version (b) there exists an f-valid solution, but a p-valid solution does not exist.

Basically, extended fuzzy logic, FLe, results from lowering of standards of cointension, and precision in fuzzy logic, FL. In effect, extended fuzzy logic adds to fuzzy logic, a capability to deal imprecisely with imperfect information when precision in infeasible, carries a high cost or is unneeded. This capability is a necessity when repeated attempts at constructing a theory which is both realistic and precise fail to achieve success. Cases in point are the theories of rationality, causality, and decision-making under second order uncertainty, that is, uncertainty about uncertainty. In the following we illustrate this concept by a useful analogy.

Example 3.52 In bivalent logic, the writing/drawing instrument is a ballpoint pen. In fuzzy logic, the writing/drawing instrument is a spray pen; a miniature spray can with an adjustable, precisely specified spray pattern and a white marker for the centroid of the spray pattern, with the marker serving the purpose of precisiation when it is needed. Such a pen is referred to as precisiated. In unprecisiated fuzzy logic, the spray pen has an adjustable spray pattern and a white marker which are not precisiated. In extended fuzzy logic, there are two spray pens that is a precisiated spray pen and an unprecisiated spray pen.

There are three principal rationales for the use of extended fuzzy logic:
- When a p-valid solution is infeasible,
- When a p-valid solution carries an excessively high cost, and
- When there is no need for a p-valid solution, that is, when an f-valid solution is good enough. In much of everyday human reasoning, it is the third rationale that is preponderant.

f-Validity is a fuzzy concept and hence is a matter of degree. When a chain of reasoning leads to a conclusion, we need to consider fuzzy degree of validity, call it the validity index. In most applications involving f-valid reasoning, a high validity index is a desideratum. A high validity index is one of the principal objectives of extended fuzzy logic. It should be noted that in many realistic settings, the question of whether or not a conclusion has a high validity index may be a matter of argumentation.

To construct modes of reasoning which lead to conclusions which are associated with high validity indices, it is expedient to go back to the origin of logical reasoning—Euclidian geometry.

F-GEOMETRY AND F-TRANSFORMATION

In the world of Euclidean geometry (Weg), the drawing instruments are:
- Ruler,
- Compass, and
- Ballpoint pen.

The underlying logic is bivalent (Aristotelian) logic. In the world of f-geometry (Wfg), the drawing instrument is an unprecisiated spray pen, and drawing is done by hand. Figures in Wfg are fuzzy in appearance. We illustrate the basic notion of f-geometry and f-transform using the following examples [311].

Example 3.53 The counterpart of a crisp concept, C, in Weg, is a fuzzy concept, f-C or, more convenient, *C, in Wfg (Figure 12). f-c is referred to as an f-transform of C, with C playing the role of the prototype of f-C. It is helpful to visualize a fuzzy transform of C as the result of execution of the instruction: Draw C by hand with a spray pen. Note that there is no formal definition f-transformation.

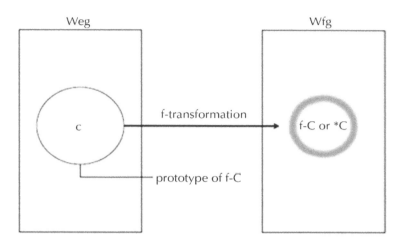

FIGURE 12   f-transformation and f-geometry.

Example 3.54 The f-transform of a point is a f-point, the f-transform of a line is a f-line, the f-transform of a triangle is a f-triangle, f-transform of a square is a f-square, f-transform of a polygon is a f-polygon, the f-transform of a circle is a f-circle, f-transform of a vector is a f-vector, f-transform of a fuzzy vector is a f-fuzzy vector, and the f-transform of parallel is f-parallel (Figure 13).

In f-geometry, the underlying logic is unprecisiated fuzzy logic, Flu. f-Geometry differs both in spirit and in substance fromPoston's fuzzy geometry, coarse geometry, fuzzy geometry of Rosenfeld, fuzzy geometry of Buckley and Eslami, fuzzy geometry of Mayburov, and fuzzy geometry of Tzafestas. The underlying logic in these fuzzy geometries is FL(FLp).

Note that f-transform is one-to-many. f-Transformation may be applied to relations. Thus, in Wfg, we have the concepts of f-parallel, f-similar, f-congruent, and so on. Furthermore, f-transformation may be applied to higher-level concepts, for example, axiom, definition, principle, proof, theorem, truth, and so on. In addition, f-transformation may be applied to concepts drawn from fields other than f-geometry. Examples: f-convex, f-linear, f-stable, and so on. Of particular importance in f-geometry is the concept of f-theorem .

The cointension of f-C is a qualitative measure of the proximity of f-C to its prototype, C. A fuzzy transform, f-C, is cointensive if its cointension is high. Unless stated to the contrary, f-transforms are assumed to be cointensive. The concept of f-transform is distinct from the concept of fuzzy transform (Perfilieva transform) of Perfilieva.

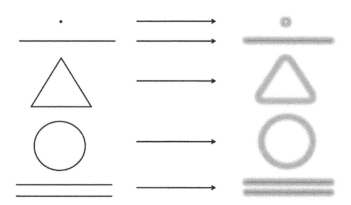

FIGURE 13 Examples of f-transformation.

Remark 3.18 f-geometry may be viewed as the result of application of f-transformation to Euclidean geometry.

A key idea in f-geometry is, if C is p-valid then its f-transform, f-C, is f-valid with a high validity index. For instance, consider the definition of parallelism and triangular similarity in Euclidean geometry.

Definition 3.13 Two lines are parallel if for any transversal that cuts the lines the corresponding angles are congruent.

f-transform of this definition reads:

Definition 3.14 Two f-lines are f-parallel if for any f-transversal that cuts the lines the corresponding f-angles are f-congruent.

Example 3.55 In Euclidean geometry, two triangles are similar if the corresponding angles are congruent. Correspondingly, in f-geometry two f-triangles are f-similar if the corresponding angles are f-congruent.

An f-theorem in f-geometry is an f-transform of a theorem in Euclidean geometry. For instance, an elementary theorem, T, in Euclidean geometry is:

T: the medians of a triangle are concurrent.

A corresponding theorem, f-T, in f-geometry is:

f-T: the f-medians of an f-triangle are f-concurrent.

We state the following result on validation principle.

Proposition 3.1 Let p be a p-valid conclusion drawn from a chain of premises $p_1, \cdots p_n$. Then using the star notation, *p is an f-valid conclusion drawn from $*p_1, \cdots *p_n$, and *p has a high validity index. It is this principle that is employed to derive f-valid conclusions from a collection of f-premises.

Example 3.56 Let us consider two triangles A and B. In Euclidean geometry, if A and B are similar then the corresponding sides are in proportion. The validation principle leads to the following assertion in f-geometry. If A and B are f-similar f-triangles then the corresponding sides are in f-proportion.

In f-geometry, an f-proof may be either empirical or logical. An empirical f-proof involves experimentation. Consistent with the validation principle, a logical f-proof is an f-transform of a proof in Euclidean geometry. Let us consider the following result:

Proposition 3.2 The f-medians of an f-triangle are f-concurrent.

With reference to Figure 14, the logical f-proof of this result follows at once from the property of f-similar triangles.

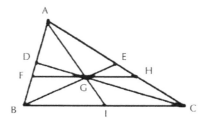

D,E are f-midpoints
DE is f-paralled to BC
FH is f-paralled to BC
AGI is an f-line passing through
f-point G
f-triangles EGH and EBC are f-similar

f-triangles DFG and DBC are f-similar
f-proportionality of corresponding sides of
f-triangles implies that G is f-midpoint of
FH
G is f-midpoint of FH implies that tis
f-midpoint of BC
I is f-midpoint of BC implies that the
f-medians are f-concurrent

FIGURE 14   f-proof of the f-theorem:f-midpoints of an f-triangle are f-concurrent.

Remark 3.19
- The f-theorem and its f-proof are f-transforms of their counterparts in Euclidean geometry.
- Note that the f-theorem and its f-proof could be arrived at without any reference to their counterparts in Euclidean geometry.

Thus there is an intriguing possibility to arrive at systems of f-concepts, f-definitions, f-theorems, f-proofs, f-reasoning, and f-computation in various fields of science and engineering. In the conceptual world of such systems, p-validity has no place.

Remark 3.20
- The concept of f-transformation is not limited to Euclidean geometry.
- f-Transformation may be applied to concepts, definitions, and theorems drawn from various fields.

Consider the definition of a convex set, A, in a linear vector space, U.

Definition 3.15 A is a convex set in U if for any points x and y in A every point in the segment xy is in A.

The f-transform of this definition is the definition of an f-convex set, f-A. Specifically:

Definition 3.16 f-A is an f-convex set in U if for any f-points x and y in f-A every f-point in the f-segment xy is in f-A.

An elementary property of convex sets is:
Property 3.1 If A and B are convex sets, so is their f-intersection $A \cap B$.
An f-transform of property reads:

Property 3.2 If A and B are f-convex sets, so is their f-intersection f-A $\cap$ f-B.
More generally,

Proposition 3.3 If A and B are convex fuzzy sets, so is their intersection.
Applying f-transformation to property, we obtain the result:

Proposition 3.4 If A and B are f-convex fuzzy sets, so is their f-intersection.
A basic problem which arises in computation of f-transforms is the following:
Let g be a function, a functional, or an operator. Using the star notation, let a f-transform, *C, be an argument of g. The problem is that of computing g(*C). Generally, computing g(*C) is not a trivial problem.

A f-valid approximation to g(*C) may be derived through application of a f-principle which is referred to as precisiation/imprecisiation principle or P/I principle, for short.

More specifically, the principle may be expressed as:
g(*C) *= *g(C), where *= should be read as approximately equal.
In words, g(*C) is approximately equal to the f-transform of g(C).

Example 3.57 If g is the operation of differentiation and *C is an f-function, *f, shown in Figure 15, then the f-derivative of this function is an f-function shown in Figure 15.

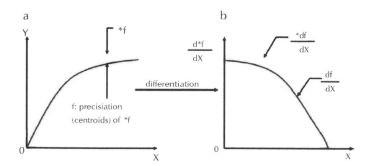

FIGURE 15   f-transform of the derivative of an f-transform.

Example 3.58 If C is a real number and *C is approximately C, then the P/I principle asserts that g(*C) is approximately equal to approximately g(C). More generally, if C is a function from reals to reals, *C is the fuzzy graph of C and g is the operation of differentiation, then the derivative of the fuzzy graph of C is approximately equal to the fuzzy graph of the derivative of C (See Figure 16).

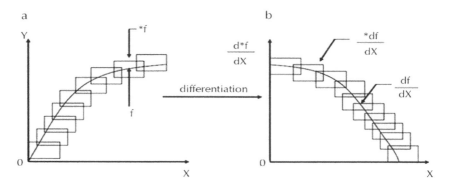

FIGURE 16   f-transform of the derivative of a fuzzy graph.

Remark 3.21

- The P/I principle is widely used in science and engineering.
- It is a common practice to present the results of an analysis, in which the principle is employed without a qualification to the effect that the results are f-valid rather than p-valid and there is no guarantee that the validity index of results is high.

Extended fuzzy logic is perception-based rather than measurement-based. Perceptions are intrinsically imprecise, reflecting the bounded ability of human sensory organs, and ultimately the brain, to resolve detail and store information. The intrinsic imprecision of perceptions underlies the intrinsic imprecision of a major component of extended fuzzy logic, the unprecisiated fuzzy logic. As stated earlier, reasoning in unprecisiated fuzzy logic (f-valid reasoning) is quasi-mathematical rather than mathematical. This is what sets unprecisiated fuzzy logic apart from other logical systems, including precisiated fuzzy logic (FL). The importance of extended fuzzy logic derives from the fact that it adds to fuzzy logic an essential capability to deal with unprecisiated imperfect information. In many realistic settings, decision-relevant information falls into this category. It is important to note that in dealing with many real-world problems as f-valid solution based on a realistic model may be more useful than a p-valid solution based on an unrealistic model.

3.6   ALGEBRIC STRUCTURE IN FUZZY LOGIC

We have experienced the growth and development of fuzzy set and fuzzy logic and have seen the wide spread applications of fuzzy inferences in different areas of science and engineering. Even then, there is a wrong impression among several users of this subject that there is no formal mathematical structure on which fuzzy logic exist. An answer to this problem can be found form the solvability of fuzzy relation equations

$$R \ o \ X = T \text{ and } X \ o \ S = T,$$

introduced by Sanchez, which leads to the theory of *residuated lattices*. The essential content of the work of Goguen, also indicates that the algebra of inexact concepts is based on resituated lattice-like structure. Let us consider this structure in the context of fuzzy logic. In this context, we first introduce some important definitions and properties known in literature.

The fundamental property in fuzzy reasoning is that the Law of the Excluded Middle does not generally hold. Hence we have to look for a logical system, where this law is not valid; thus the residuated lattice structure comes into picture.

We start from classical logic, where the truth value set {0, 1} becomes a residuated lattice L:

$$\langle \{0, 1\}, \leq, \wedge, \vee, *, \rightarrow \rangle,$$

if we equip it in the following way, that is:

$$a \wedge b = a * b = \min\{a, b\}, \tag{3.56a}$$

$$a \vee b = \max\{a, b\}, \tag{3.56b}$$

$$\sim a = 1 - a, \tag{3.56c}$$

$$a \rightarrow b = \sim a \vee b. \tag{3.56d}$$

Therefore. We get:

$$a \rightarrow b = \begin{cases} 1 & \text{if } a \leq b, \\ b & \text{otherwise.} \end{cases} \tag{3.57}$$

Let us substitute, the interval [0, 1] for the set {0, 1} in (3.56). Though such substitution may sound promising but this does not work, because the condition (3.57) and hence the Identity Principle $a \rightarrow a = 1$ among others does not hold good.

Fuzzy logics based on De Morgan algebras faces the similar problems.

In what follows, $\wedge$, $\vee$, $\rightarrow$, and $\sim$ are operations in $\llcorner$, while $\cap$, $\cup$, $\rightarrow$, and $\sim$ are connectives combining formulae. If some of them are interpreted via (3.56), we say that they are classical.

DE MORGAN ALGEBRAS

A De Morgan algebra, also called soft algebra

$$A = \langle A, \wedge, \vee, \sim \rangle$$

is a distributive lattice $\langle A,\wedge,\vee \rangle$ with a unary operation $\sim$ such that the De Morgan laws hold. Fuzzy logical systems based on soft algebras have been studied by Di Nola and Ventre. Preparata and Yeh, Lee and Chang, Negoita and Ralescu, Ishizuka and Kanai, and Kaufmann among others. Ying's logic, too, is De Morgan-type. An example of soft algebras is the unit interval [0, 1], where the operations $\wedge,\vee,\sim$ are defined classically.

In De Morgan algebras, there is no interpretation for implication and hence there is no natural adjoint couple appears. We can define $\rightarrow$ by (3.56d), but doing so implication loses some of its most important roperties and $a \wedge b \leq c$ if $a \leq \sim b \vee c$ does not hold good. Hence, De Morgan algebras need some additional operations to be more enriched.

PSEUDO-BOOLEAN ALGEBRAS

A *pseudo-Boolean algebra* (also called Heyting algebra, Brouwerian algebra, and Gödelian algebra*)* is an algebra:

$$\langle A,\wedge,\vee, \rightarrow, \sim \rangle$$

where $\wedge$ and $\vee$ are the lattice meet and join, respectively $\sim a = a \rightarrow 0$ and $a \wedge b \leq c$ if $a \leq b \rightarrow c$. Therefore, any pseudo-Boolean algebra is a residuated lattice:

$$\langle A, \leq,\wedge,\vee,\wedge, \rightarrow \rangle,$$

where $\leq$ is the lattice order. In the case of $\leq$ being total order we have the condition (3.57) and the connectives $\cap$ and $\cup$ are classical.

Fuzzy and multiple-valued logics in pseudo-Boolean algebras have been studied by Horn, Minari, Tukeuti and Titani, Takano, and Turunen. Raisowa's and Di Zenzo's studies are pseudo-Boolean-like, too, since there the value lattice is Post algebra, that is a pseudo-Boolean algebra equipped with some additional operations. Pseudo-Boolean algebras are present also in Orlowska's and Wierzchon's and Togai's works, since there holds for all models M:

$$\mathrm{val}_M (A \cup B) = \max\{\mathrm{val}_M (A),\mathrm{val}_M (B)\},$$

$$\mathrm{val}_M (A \cap B) = \min\{\mathrm{val}_M (A),\mathrm{val}_M (B)\},$$

$$\mathrm{val}_M (A \rightarrow B) = \begin{cases} 1 & \text{if } \mathrm{val}_M (A) \leq \mathrm{val}_M (B), \\ \mathrm{val}_M (B) & \text{otherwise.} \end{cases}$$

In Nakamura's study only two operations are defined in the unit interval; the adjoint couple of Gödel style. Graham stated that *"toposes implicitly generalize logic in the sense of Intuitionism"*. That means, looking from a category theoretical point of view, fuzzy logic has Heyting algebra structure.

MV-ALGEBRAS

An MV-*algebra*

$$A = \langle A, \otimes, \odot, *, 0, 1 \rangle$$

is an algebra such that $(A, \oplus, 0)$ is an Abelian monoid:

$$x \oplus 1 = 1, x^{**} = x,$$

$$0^* = 1, x \odot y = (x^* \oplus y^*)^*,$$

$$(x^* \oplus y)^* \oplus (y^* \oplus x)^* \oplus x$$

for any $x, y \in A$, originally defined by Chang. Defining

$$x \lor y = (x \odot y^*) \oplus y$$

and

$$x \land y = (x \oplus y^*) \odot y$$

For any $x \ y \in A$ we have that $(A, \leq, \land, \lor)$ is a distributive lattice under the partial ordering $x \leq y$ if $x \land y = x$. In any MV-algebra A there holds $x \leq y = x$ if $x * \oplus y = 1$.

Proposition 3.5 Defining $a \rightarrow b = a * \oplus b$ for $a, b \in A$ obtain a residuated lattice

$$(A, \leq, \land, \lor, \odot \rightarrow)$$.

The Galois correspondence in Proposition 3.5 is established by means of a so-called *Wajsberg algebra* $A = (A, \rightarrow, \sim, 1)$ satisfying the following equations:

$$1 \rightarrow x = x$$

$$(x \to y) \to \big((y \to z) \to (x \to z)\big) = 1$$

$$(x \to y) \to y = (y \to x) \to x,$$

$$(\sim x \to \sim y) \to (y \to x) = 1.$$

In [95] it is shown that any MV-algebra defines a Wajsberg algebra and vice versa.

Chang, Mundici, Belluce, and Belluce, Di Nola, and Sessa have studied fuzzy logic based on multiple-valued algebras, shortly MV-algebras.

ŁUKASIEWICZ ALGEBRAS

The unit interval [0,1] becomes Łukasiewicz-type of residuated lattice if we define binary operations $\wedge$ (min), $\vee$ (max), $\oplus$ and $\to$ where

$$a \oplus b = 0 \vee (a + b - 1),$$

$$a \to b = 1 \wedge (1 - a + b).$$

Similarly, in a finite chain

$$L = \{0 = a_0 < \cdots < a_m = 1\}$$

We set

$$a_k \oplus a_p = a_{\max\{0, k+p-m\}}$$

and

$$a_k \to a_p \, a_{\min\{m, m-k+p\}}$$

for $0 \le k, p \le m$, and obtain a residuated lattice

$$(L, \le, \wedge, \vee, \oplus, \to).$$

Pavelka, Novak, and Gottwald have studied fuzzy logics on Łukasiewicz lattices where L is either the unit interval or a finite chain. In Skala's approach L is the three-valued Łukasiewicz chain. In all these studies the operation $\oplus$ is an interpretation of *bold conjunction*. Pavelka and Novak denote it by &, Gottwald by and Skala by $\odot$ and the interpretation of implication is the operation. In [212] and [202], it is shown that structures isomorphic to Łukasiewicz algebra possess the completeness property. Studies of McNaughton, Woytylak, and Scott in multiple-valued logic imply Łukasiewicz algebra as soon as we add the bold conjunction to them. Features of Łukasiewicz algebra can be found in Dumitrescu's since the values $v(p \cap q)$, $v(p \Rightarrow q)$, for any valuation $v: \{wff\} \rightarrow [0,1]$, define an adjoint couple of Łukasiewicz type.

CONTINUOUS T-NORMS

A continuous T-norm is a continuous function F from [0, 1] x [0, 1] into [0, 1] which is isotone, commutative, associative, and such that $F(1,x) = F(x,1) = x$ for any $x \in$ [0, 1]. The quasi-inverse G of F is the function from [0,1] x [0, 1] into [0, 1] defined by:

$$G(x,y) = \sup\{a \in [0,1] | F(x,a) \leq y\}. \tag{3.58}$$

The min operator, the Łukasiewicz product and the arithmetical product are examples of continuous T-norms.

Thus, we realize that:

$$([0, 1], \leq, \min, \max, F, G),$$

Where F is any continuous T-norm, is a residuated lattice. Continuous T-norms have been used widely in fuzzy framework. Trillas and Valverde and Domingo, Trillas and Valverde have studied implication in fuzzy logic. They define a general implication function I from [0, 1] x [0, 1] into [0, 1] and its three special cases. It is of importance to realize that the only implication function fulfilling the relations

• Identity Principle

$$v(A) \leq v(B) \text{ if } v(I(A,B)) = 1, \tag{3.59}$$

• Principle of Contrapositive Symmetry

$$v(I(A,B)) = v(I(n(B),n(A)), \tag{3.60}$$

where A and B are formulae, v any valuation, and n a so-called strong negation, is that defined by (3.58), the R-impliation. The relations (3.59) and (3.60) belong without any doubt to the most fundamental properties of implication functions.

Trillas and Valverde define an indistinguishability operator E by:

$$E(x,y) \geq \lambda, \qquad \lambda \in [0,1],$$

$$E(x,y) = E(y,x),$$

$$F\big(E(x,y),E(y,z)\big) \le E(x,z),$$

where F is a continuous T-norm.

Now we state the following result.

Proposition 3.6 Let I be an R-implication. Then there exists a continuous T-norm F such that E_1 is an indistinguishability operator.

Proof Let F be the T-norm which is quasi-inverse of I. Trivially:

$$F(I(x,y),I(y,x)) \ge 0.$$

Also

$$F\big(I(x,y),I(y,x)\big) = F\big(I(y,x),I(x,y)\big),$$

Since F is commutative. It also holds that:

$$F(F\big(I(x,y),I(y,x)\big),F\big(I(y,z),I(z,y)\big))$$

$$= F(F\big(I(x,y),I(y,z)\big),F\big(I(x,y),I(y,z)\big))$$

$$\le F(I(x,z),I(z,x)) \text{ (since F is isotone)}$$

In [276], the following problem is stated:

Given an in distinguishability operator E (relatively to an operation *) find out if there exists an implication function I such that:

$$E(x,y) = I(x,y) * I(y,x)'' \qquad (3.61)$$

But no answer to the stated problem is given.

We have:

Proposition 3.7 There exists an R-implication I such that (3.61) holds if $E(x,y) = I(x,y)$ if $x > y$ and $I(y,x)$ otherwise.

Proof Let (3.61) hold and $x \le y$. Since I is an R-implication, we have, by (6), that

$I(x,y) = 1. \text{ So} E(x,y) = I(x,y) * I(y,x) = 1 * I(y,x) = I(y,x).$

Similarly for $x > y$. The converse is trivial.

In [277], Trillas and Valverde define two binary operation $m.t$ called *Modus Ponens generating functions* (MPGf) and *Modus Tollens generating function* (MTGf), respectively, taking values in the units interval, by:

$$m(x, x \rightarrow) \leq y, \qquad \text{(MP1)}$$

$$m\ (1,1) = 1, \qquad \text{(MP2)}$$

$$m(0, y) = 0, \qquad \text{(MP3)}$$

$$\text{If } x \leq x' \text{then } m(x, y) \leq m(x', y), \qquad \text{(MP4)}$$

$$t(n(y), \rightarrow y) \leq n(x), \qquad \text{(MT1)}$$

$$t(1,1) = 1 \qquad \text{(MT2)}$$

$$t(0, y) = 0, \qquad \text{(MT3)}$$

$$\text{If } x \leq x' \text{then } t(x, y) \leq t(x', y). \qquad \text{(MT4)}$$

Proposition 3.8 Let I be an R-implication and m,t the corresponding MTGf. Then we have:

$$m(x, y) \leq z \; iff \; x \leq I(y, z), \qquad \text{(3.62)}$$

$$t(x, y) = n(I(y, n(x))). \qquad \text{(3.63)}$$

Proposition 3.9 Let $(L, \leq, \wedge, \vee, *, \rightarrow)$ be a residuated lattice with **0** and **1**. Then * is MPGf and MTGf.

According to Dubois and Prade, implication function derived via

$$v(P \rightarrow \in [0, 1] | v(P) * v(Q)\}$$

from T-norms * seem to be the best ones if we consider the number of desirable properties they have. Also Weber studies fuzzy connectives based on T-norms.

SOME OTHER APPROACHES

Yager has defined a general class of fuzzy connectives $\cap_p, \cup_p \; (p \geq 1)$, and *, (essentially) as follows:

$$A \cap_p B = 1 - \min\{1, [(1 - A)^p + \left(1 - B)^p]^{\frac{1}{p}}\right\}$$

$$A \cup_p B = \min\{1, [A^p B^p]^{\frac{1}{p}}\},$$

$$A * = 1 - A, \quad A, B \in [0, 1].$$

Yager points out that for any $p \geq 1, A \cap_p$ is a associative, commutative and isotone operation and $\cup_\infty, \cap_\infty$ coincide with max and min operations, respectively. We obtain:

Proposition 3.10 Define $A \to_p B = A^* \cup_p B$, $p \geq 1$. Then, for any $p \geq 1$

$$([0, 1], \leq, \cup_\infty, \cap_\infty, \cap_p, \to_p)$$

Is a residual lattice.

In Mattila's modifier logic, a residuated lattice is present, since there L is $\{0, 1\}$ and the connective $\cap, \cup \to$, and $\sim$ are interpreted classically.

Gaines reports that Heyting implication (the residuum of $\wedge$), Łukasiewicz implication and the residuum of the arithmetical product in the unit interval. The Gaines implication is defined by $x \to y = 1$, if $x \leq y$ and y/x otherwise.

Albert's opinions about the algebra of fuzzy logic is different from those of the majority. He claims *"this algebra is not a lattice"*. In the set M of truth values he defines binary operations $\oplus, \odot$, and a unary operation $*$ and discusses their properties, the associativity and commutativity $\odot$ among others. The isotonicity of $\odot$ follows from the statement.

$$\forall (a \odot b \leq c, a \neq o$$

(o is the zero element of M),
   Implies $b \leq c$).

The operation $\odot$ has a unique inverse operation $\odot^{-1}$ such that $a \odot^{-1} a = e$, the unit element of M, $a \neq o$. A representation of the set M and the operations $\oplus, \odot$, $*$ may be constructed, by Albert, in the interval $[0, 1]$ by means of the usual arithmetical operations as follows:

$$a \oplus b = a + b - ab, a \odot b = ab,$$

$$a * = 1 - a, e = 1, o = 0.$$

Obviously, $\odot^{-1}$ coincides in this case with the usual arithmetical division (/) though the unit interval is not closed with respect to /. We define $x \to y = 1$ if $x \le y$ and y/x otherwise. Then $(\odot), \to)$ becomes an adjoint couple of Gaines' style. Because of the lack of information of the inverse operation of $\odot$ it remains an open question if $\to$ can generally be defined in this way.

In smets and Magrez' paper binary connectives $\to$ $\&_\infty, \&_0$ are defined by means of truth function v taking values in the unit interval.

There are, among others:

$$v(A \to B) = 1 \ iff \ v(A) \le v(B),$$

$$v\big(A \to (B \to C)\big) = v(A \&_\infty, B) \Rightarrow C).$$

After an analysis the authors conclude that "The truth value of $A \Rightarrow B$ is represented by a pseudo- Łukasiewicz functor".

This is to say, by:

$$v(A \to B) = v(A) \to v(B) \tag{3.64}$$

where $\to$ is the Łukasiewicz implication.

Proposition 3.11 The axioms in [266] define a Łukasiewicz-type adjoint couple.

Since valuations in the unit interval for the connectives $\cap, \cup$ and $\sim$ in Lakoff's deiscourse are classical and $v(A \to B) = 1$ if $v(A) \le v(B)$ and otherwise, a residuated lattice structure does not exist. On the other hand Lakoff writes: *"however, it might be interesting to investigate fuzzy propositional logics By doing so we obtain a pseudo-Boolean lattice"*.

THE ADVANTAGES OF RESIDUATED LATTICES

The advantages of discovering/defining adjoint couples in a fuzzy logical system are obvious. In the previous sections, we already used them, but let us have still one more example. Mizumoto studied inference schemas of type:

Ant 1: IF x is A THEN y is B
Ant 2: x is A'

Cons: y is B'.

Without going into details, we mention that truth values are in the unit interval and that the relation between A and A' is for example $A'(x) = A(x)^2$, in this particular case A' is interpreted as 'very A'.

One manner to calculate the value $B'(y)$ from the given ones is via:

$$B'(y) = \sup\{A'(x) \odot (A(x) \to B(y)) | x \in [0,1]\} \qquad (3.65)$$

where $\odot$ is the Łukasiewicz product $\to$ is some implication.

Proposition 3.12 Let $\to$ be the Łukasiewicz implication in (3.65). *Then very* $B(y) \leq B(y)$ *for all y.*

We have studied the structures of truth value sets in different logical systems. The list is not exhaustive but sufficient. We find Heyting, Post, Łukasiewicz, Gaines, MV-algebras, and continuous T-norms, which define a residuated lattice. Studies on implication, category theoretical aspects, some philosophical and other discussions suggest adjoint couples, and residuated structures. The only cases when we do not find this structure seem to be fuzzy logics in soft algebras. On the other hand, soft algebras miss some of the most important properties of implication.

We have studied fuzzy logic from purely mathematical point of view: Fuzzy logic is not yet widely accepted as non-classical mathematical logic. It can obtain this status only if all the concepts are mathematically well-defined and if the semantic-syntactical completeness property holds. We know Boolean algebras play a special role in classical logic. Similarly, given a general algebraic structure (such as residuated lattice or MV-algebra), we have to define the corresponding fuzzy logic.

3.6.1 BASIC CONCEPT OF RESIDUATED LATTICES

In this Section, we briefly review the basic concept and properties of the algebraic structure of the residuated lattices [216–222].

Definition 3.17 A residuated lattice is an algebraic structure $(L, \otimes, \to)$, or simply, L, where:

- $(L, \leq, \wedge, \vee, 0, 1)$ forms a bounded lattice with the smallest element 0 and the

  greatest element 1;

- $(\otimes, \to)$ forms an adjoint coupe on L, that is, for any a,b,c $\in$ L,

  (R1) If $a \leq b$, $c \leq d$, then $a \otimes c \leq b \otimes d$;

  (R2) If $b \leq c$, then $a \to b \leq a \to c$;

  (R3) If $a \leq b$, then $b \to c \leq a \to c$;

  (R4) (adjointness condition) $a \otimes b \leq c \Leftrightarrow a \leq b \to c$.

- $(L, \otimes, 1)$ forms a commutative monoid, that is, for any a, b, c $\in$ L,

  (R5) $(a \otimes b) \otimes c = a \otimes (b \otimes c)$

  (R6) $a \otimes b = b \otimes a$;

  (R7) $1 \otimes a = a$.

Moreover, if L is a chain, then L is called a residuated chain.

We use $\mathcal{R}$ to denote the class of all residuated lattices, and we always suppose that L is a bounded lattice with the smallest element 0 and the greatest element 1, $\otimes$ and $\to$ are two binary operations on L. In addition, we often use the following derived operations:

$$a \leftrightarrow b = (a \to b) \wedge (b \to a); \quad \neg a = a \to 0;$$

$$a^0 = 1, \ a^n = a^{n-1} \otimes a, \quad n \in N, \quad a, b \in L.$$

The following Proposition lists the fundamental properties of residuated lattices.

Proposition 3.13 if $(L, \otimes, \to) \in \mathcal{R}$, then

(R8) $a \leq b \to a \otimes b$;

(R9) $(a \to b) \otimes a \leq b$;

(R10) $f_a : L \to L, \ x \longmapsto x \otimes a$ preserves all joins existing in L;

(R11) $g_a : L \to L, \ x \longmapsto a \to x$ preserves all meets existing in L;

(R12) $h_a : L \to L, \ x \longmapsto a \otimes x$ preserves all joins existing in L;

(R13) $k_a : L \to L, \ x \longmapsto x \to a$ changes all joins existing in L to meets;

(R14) $b \to c \leq (a \to b) \to (a \to c)$;

(R15) $a = 1 \to a$;

(R16) $a \leq b \Longleftrightarrow a \to b = 1$;

(R17) $a \leq b \to c \Longleftrightarrow b \leq a \to c$;

(R18) $a \to b \leq a \otimes c \to b \otimes c$;

(R19) $a \otimes b \to c = a \to (b \to c)$;

(R20) $a \to (b \to c) = b \to (a \to c)$;

(R21) $a \otimes b \leq a \wedge b$;

(R22) $a^n \leq a^m$, $n, m \in N, m \leq n$.

The following Proposition shows that under suitable conditions, the operations $\otimes$ and $\rightarrow$ are not independent.

Proposition 3.14 Suppose that L is a complete lattice.

- If $\otimes$ is a binary operation o L satisfying conditions (R1) and (R10), then there exists a binary operation $\rightarrow$ satisfying conditions (R2), (R3) and (R4). Such operations is unique which is determined by the following formula.

$$a \rightarrow b = \bigvee\{x \in L | x \otimes a \leq b\}, a, b \in L.$$

- If $\rightarrow$ is a binary operation on L satisfying conditions (R2), (R3) and (R11), then there exists a binary operations $\otimes$ satisfying conditions (R1) and (R4), and such operation is unique which is determined by the following formula:

$$a \otimes b = \bigwedge\{x \in L | a \leq b \rightarrow x\}, a, b \in L.$$

We now characterize the residuated lattices with the following Propositions.

Proposition 3.15 $(L, \otimes, \rightarrow) \in \mathcal{R}$ if and only if the following conditions hold, for all $a, b, c \in L$:

- (R4) $a \otimes b \leq c \leftrightarrow a \leq b \rightarrow c$;

- (R7) $1 \otimes a = a$;

- (R20) $a \rightarrow (b \rightarrow c) = b \rightarrow (a \rightarrow c)$

Proposition 3.16 $(L, \otimes, \rightarrow) \in \mathcal{R}$ if and only if the following conditions hold for all $a, b, c \in L$:

- (R8) $(a \rightarrow b) \otimes a \leq b$;

- (R9) $a \leq b \rightarrow a \otimes b$;

- (R7) $1 \otimes a = a$;

- (R20) $a \rightarrow (b \rightarrow c) = b \rightarrow (a \rightarrow c)$;

- (R23) $(a \vee b) \otimes c = (a \otimes c) \vee (b \otimes c)$;

- (R24) $a \rightarrow b \wedge c = (a \rightarrow b) \wedge (a \rightarrow c)$;

Obviously, the inequalities (i-ii) can be translated into equalities. Therefore, $\mathcal{R}$ forms an algebraic variety.

About the independence of the given conditions in the previous two propositions, we have the following results:

Proposition 3.17 The three conditions $R4, R7, R20$ in Proposition 3.15 are mutually independent, that is, every one of them cannot be implied by other two conditions.

Proposition 3.18 Every one of the four conditions (iii)-(iv) in Proposition 3.16 cannot be implied by other five conditions.

Many important fuzzy logic algebras (most of them are given in Section) are residuated lattices. In particular, Heyting algebras are residuated lattices. A bounded lattice $(L, \leq, \wedge, \vee, 0, 1)$ is a Heyting algebra if there exists a binary operation "$\rightarrow$" on L such that for all $a, b, c \in L$ the adjointness condition

$$a \wedge b \leq c \leftrightarrow a \leq b \rightarrow c$$

holds. It is obvious that in a Heyting algebra $L, (\wedge, \rightarrow)$ is an adjoint couple. In addition, according to the related results, the class $\mathcal{R}_H$ formed by all Heyting algebras is also an algebraic variety.

As a kind of important algebraic structures, residuated lattice are all commutative partially ordered semigroups, furthermore, they are all commutative implicative semigroups and commutative residuated semigroups.

3.6.2 NORMAL RESIDUATED LATTICES AND THEIR BASIC PROPERTIES

In this Section, we review the results of normal residuated lattices which form a kind of new algebraic structures for fuzzy logic. This kind of algebraic structures are proposed in [216] to extend the concept of R_0-algebras and BL-algebras, and form a kind of unified algebraic structures for fuzzy logic.

Definition 3.18 If $(L, \otimes, \rightarrow) \in \mathcal{R}$, and satisfies the following condition, (R25)

$$a \rightarrow b \vee c = (a \rightarrow b) \vee (a \rightarrow c).$$

for any $a, b, c \in L$, then If $(L, \otimes, \rightarrow)$ is called a normal residuated lattice.

Moreover, if L is a chain, then L is called a normal residuated chain.

We use the notations $\mathcal{R}_N$ to denote the class of all normal residuated lattices.

We state the properties and characteristics of normal residuated lattices.

The following Proposition shows that normal residuated lattices can be defined in different forms.

Proposition 3.19 In a residuated lattice, the following conditions are equivalent:

(R25) $a \rightarrow b \vee c = (a \rightarrow b) \vee (a \rightarrow c)$;

(R26) $a \wedge b \rightarrow c = (a \rightarrow c) \vee (b \rightarrow c)$;

(R27) $(a \rightarrow b) \vee (b \rightarrow a) = 1$.

The following two Propositions give the main properties of normal residuated lattices.

Proposition 3.20 Let $L \in \mathcal{R}^N$. Then for any $a, b, c \in L$,

(R28) $a \otimes (b \wedge c) = (a \otimes c) \wedge (b \otimes c)$;

(R29) $a \wedge (b \vee c) = (a \wedge b) \vee (b \wedge c)$;

(R30) $a \vee b \to c = (a \to b) \wedge (b \to c)$;

From Proposition 3.20, we see that the normal residuated lattices are bounded distributive lattices.

Proposition 3.21 Let $L \in \mathcal{R}^N$. Then for any $a, b \in L, n \in N$,

(R31) $(a \vee b)^{2^{n-1}} = a^{2^{n-1}} \vee b^{2^{n-1}}$

(R32) $(a \to b)^n \vee (b \to a)^n = 1$.

In view of the following Propositions, we can simplify the definition of normal residuated lattices.

Proposition 3.22 Let $(L, \leq, \wedge, \vee, 0, 1)$ be a bounded distributive lattice, and $\otimes$ and $\to$ be two binary operations on L. Then $(L, \otimes, \to)$ forms a normal residuated lattice if and only if the conditions (R4, R7, and R25) hold.

Proposition 3.23 Let $(L, \leq, \wedge, \vee, 0, 1)$ be a bounded distributive lattice, and $\otimes$ and $\to$ be two binary operations on L. Then $(L, \otimes, \to)$ forms a normal residuated lattice if and only if the conditions (R7, R8,R9, R20, R23, R24, and R25) hold.

We observe the fact that the conditions (R8) and (R9) can be easily changed into equalities. Thus $\mathcal{R}_N$ forms an algebraic variety.

Now we give some important examples of normal residuated lattices.

Example 3.59 Every BL-algebra is a normal residuated lattice. We know that an algebraic structure $(L, \otimes, \to)$ forms a BL-algebra, if it is a residuated lattice satisfying (R27) and the following conditions:

(R33) $a \wedge b = a \otimes (a \to b)$, $a, b \in L$;

Naturally, MV-algebras, G-algebras, and product algebras are all normal residuated lattices because they are all BL-algebras. We use $\mathcal{R}_{BL}, \mathcal{R}_{MV}, \mathcal{R}_G, \mathcal{R}_\Pi$ to denote the algebraic varieties formed by all BL-algebras, all MV-algebras, all G-algebras and all product algebras, respectively.

Obviously, we have $\mathcal{R}_G \subseteq \mathcal{R}_H$.

Example 3.60 Every R_0-algebra is a normal residuated lattice. We know that an algebraic structure $(L, \neg, \vee, \to)$ forms a R_0-algebra if it is a bounded distributive lattice satisfying (R14, R15, R20, R24, R25) and the following conditions:

(R34) (contrapositive symmetry) $\neg a \rightarrow \neg b = b \rightarrow a$;

(R35) $a \rightarrow a = 1$;

(R36) $(a \rightarrow b) \vee (a \rightarrow b) \rightarrow \neg a \vee b) = 1$,

where $\neg: L \rightarrow L$ is an order-reversing involution on L.

In fact, if L is a R_0-algebra, then we can set $a \otimes b = \neg(a \rightarrow \neg b)$. Thus it is not difficult to prove that $(L, \otimes, \rightarrow)$ forms a normal residuated lattice. The algebraic variety of all R_0-algebras is denoted by $\mathcal{R}_0$.

Example 3.61 If $([0, 1], \otimes, \rightarrow)$ is a residuated lattice, then it is also a normal residuated chain.

This is due to the fact that for any adjoint couple $(\otimes, \rightarrow)$ on a residuated chain L. The conditions (R25), (R26), and (R27) are always true.

According to the results given in [216], we know that for any t-norms T which is left-continuous with respect to the first variable (also with respet to the second variable), and the corresponding residuated-typed implication $\rightarrow_T$ determined by T:

$$a \rightarrow_T b = \bigvee \{x \in [0, 1] | T(x, a) \leq b\},$$

the couple $(T, \rightarrow_T)$ forms an adjoint couple on [0, 1]. Thus $([0, 1], T, \rightarrow_T)$ forms a normal residuated chain.

Furthermore, Boolean algebras (we use $\mathcal{B}$ to denote the class of all Boolean algebras), De Morgan algebras and Kleene algebras are all R_0-algebras with $a \rightarrow b = \sim a \vee b$. Thus they are all normal residuated lattices. These facts show that the class $\mathcal{R}^N$ contains many important algebraic structures in nonclassical logic.

We note that lattice implication algebras proposed by Xu are also nirmal residuated lattices because they and MV-algebras are the same algebraic structures in essence. In addition, any regular fuzzy implication algebra $(L, 0, \rightarrow)$ satisfying

$$(a \rightarrow b) \rightarrow b = (b \rightarrow a) \rightarrow a, \quad a, b \in L$$

is also a normal residuated lattice because it is a MV-algebra.

3.6.3 ON HLIHEL'S THEORY

In fuzzy logic algebra, Höhel's theory plays a significant role. In this Section, we briefly introduce this theory, and discuss the relationship between it and the residuated lattice theory.

Definition 3.19 Let $(L, \leq)$ be a bounded lattice with the smallest element 0 and the greatest element 1, $0 \neq 1$, $\otimes$ be a binary operation on L, and $(L, \otimes)$ be a commutative monoid. The triple couple $(L, \leq, \otimes)$ is said to be a residuated, commutative, l-monoid (RCM for short), if there exists another binary operation $\rightarrow$ on L such that the condition (R4) holds for any $a, b, c \in L$.

Definition 3.20 Let $(L, \leq, \otimes)$ be a RCM. If 1 is the unit element w.r.t. the operation $\otimes$, then $(L, \leq, \otimes)$ is called an integral RCM (IRCM for short).

Definition 3.21 Let $(L, \leq, \otimes)$ be a IRCM. If for any $a, b \in L$, there exists $c \in L$ such that $b = a \otimes c$ whenever $a \leq b$, then $(L, \leq, \otimes)$ is called a divisible IRCM (DIRCM for short).

Definition 3.22 An IRCM$(L, \leq, \otimes)$ is called an integral, commutative Girard-monoid (ICGM) if the negation operation $\neg$ is an involution, that is,

$$(R34)\ \sim\sim a = \big((a \rightarrow 0) \rightarrow 0\big) = a,\ a \in L.$$

The classes of all IRCMs, all DIRCMs and all ICGMs are deonted by $\mathcal{H}, \mathcal{H}_D$, *and* $\mathcal{H}_G$, *respectively. Clearly, these classes are all algebraic varieties.*

Proposition 3.24 $\mathcal{R} = \mathcal{H}$.

In fact, if $(L, \leq, \otimes)$ is an IRCM then $(L, \leq, \otimes)$ is a residuated lattice where the binary operation $\rightarrow$ on L is determined by the operation $\otimes$ in the manners of Definition 4.1 and Definition 4.2 Conversely, if $(L, \leq, \otimes)$ is a residuated lattice then obviously, $(L, \leq, \otimes)$ is an IRCM.

We can easily see that Hájek's BL-algebras and Höhel's DIRCMs are the same algebraic structures in essence. Thus we have:

Proposition 3.25 $\mathcal{R}_{BL} = \mathcal{H}_D$.

In addition, normal residuated lattices, and IRCMs satisfying (R27) are the same algebraic structures in essence. Höhel called (R27) "the algebraic strong De Morgan law", and Hájek called it "the prelinearity ". The following conclusions are obvious.

Proposition 3.26 $\mathcal{R}_0 \subseteq \mathcal{H}_G, \mathcal{R}_{MV} \subseteq \mathcal{H}_G$.

3.6.4   *FORMAL DEDUCTIVE SYSTEMS BASED ON RELATED ALGEBRAIC STRUCTURES*

In nonclassical logic, there are many formalized algebraic systems. Many axiomatic systems have been built up, and the logical properties of these systems also have been studied. In this Section, we consider some important formal deductive systems related to residuated-based fuzzy logics.

Höhel proposed the following formal system, which is called the monoidal propositional calculus (SC for short) as a formalization of his IRCM's (that is, residuated lattices).

In the sequel, we let the set $S = \{p_i | i \in N\}$ be the set of all propositional variables, and $F(S)$ the $(\sim\sim, \vee, \wedge, \otimes, \rightarrow)$ –type free algebra generated by S.

Definition 3.23 The formal system SC consists of the following axiom schemes and the inference rule MP (that is modus ponens):

(LA1) $(A \rightarrow B) \rightarrow ((B \rightarrow C) \rightarrow (A \rightarrow C))$;

(LA1) $A \rightarrow (A \vee B)$;

(LA3) $B \rightarrow (A \vee B)$;

(LA4) $(A \rightarrow C) \rightarrow ((B \rightarrow C) \rightarrow (A \vee B \rightarrow C))$;

(LA5) $A \wedge B \rightarrow A$;

(LA6) $A \wedge B \rightarrow B$;

(LA7) $A \otimes B \rightarrow A$;

(LA8) $A \otimes B \rightarrow B \otimes A$;

(LA9) $A \otimes (B \otimes C) \rightarrow (A \otimes B) \otimes C$;

(LA10) $(A \rightarrow B) \rightarrow ((A \rightarrow C) \rightarrow (A \rightarrow B \wedge C))$;

(LA11) $(A \rightarrow (B \rightarrow C)) \rightarrow (A \otimes B \rightarrow C)$;

(LA12) $(A \otimes B \rightarrow C) \rightarrow (A \rightarrow (B \rightarrow C))$;

(LA13) $A \otimes \sim A \rightarrow B$;

(LA14) $(A \rightarrow (A \otimes \sim A)) \rightarrow \sim A$.

Usually, one introduces the provable equivalence relation in a formal system with the following form:

$$A \sim B \text{ if and only if } \vdash A \rightarrow B, \vdash B \rightarrow A.$$

that is, we say that two formulas A, B are provably equivalent in a formal system if both $A \rightarrow B$ and $B \rightarrow A$ are theorem of the system.

The quotient algebra $F(S)/\sim$ of the fomula set $F(S)$ with respect to the relation $\sim$ is called Lindenbaum algebra of the system.

Höhel pointed out that Lindenbaum algebra of SC is an IRCM, that is, a residuated lattice.

We can obtain many important formal fuzzy logical systems by adding some axiom schemes into the system SC.

Adding the idempotent law

$$\text{(LA15)} \; A \rightarrow A \otimes A$$

into SC, we obtain the famous axiom system of intuitionistic propositional calculus (IPC for short), and Lindenbaum algebra of IPC is a Heyting algebra (that is, it belongs to $\mathcal{R}_H$).

Adding the law of double negation

$$\text{(LA16)} \; \sim\sim A \rightarrow A$$

into SC, we can obtain the famous axiom system of Girard's linear logic (LL for short), and Lindenbaum algebra of LL is an ICGM (that is, it belongs to $\mathcal{H}_G$).

If the law of union-preserving

$$\text{(LA17)} \; (A \rightarrow B \vee C) V (A \rightarrow B) \vee (A \rightarrow C)$$

is added into SC, then we can obtain a new formal system $\mathcal{L}^N$, which is recently proposed by the author.

The axiom schemes of the system $\mathcal{L}^N$ are as follows:

$(L^N 1) A \rightarrow (B \rightarrow A)$,

$(L^N 2) (A \rightarrow B) \rightarrow ((B \rightarrow C) \rightarrow (A \rightarrow C))$,

$(L^N 3) A \rightarrow A \vee B$,

$(L^N 4) A \vee B \rightarrow B \vee A$,

$(L^N 5) A \wedge B \rightarrow A$,

$(L^N 6) A \wedge B \rightarrow B \wedge A$,

$(L^N 7) A \otimes B \rightarrow A$,

$(L^N 8) A \otimes B \rightarrow B \otimes A$,

$(L^N 9) (A \otimes B) \otimes C \rightarrow A \otimes (B \otimes C)$,

$(L^N 10) (A \to B \vee C) \to (A \to B)(A \to C),$

$(L^N 11) (A \to B) \to ((A \to C) \to (A \to B \wedge C)),$

$(L^N 12) (A \to C) \to ((B \to C) \to (A \vee B \to C)),$

$(L^N 13) (A \otimes B \to C) \to (A \to (B \to C))$,

$(L^N 14) (A \to (B \to C)) \to (A \otimes B \to C).$

We see that (LA17) indeed is the axiom scheme $(L^N 10)$. In the system $\mathcal{L}^N$ (LA1)–(LA12) are all theorems, and if we use Hájek's method to add a 0-ary connective $\bar{0}$ and an axiom scheme $\bar{0} \to A$, then both (LA13) and (LA14) are theorems of $\mathcal{L}^N$ where $\sim A = A \to \bar{0}$. Moreover, it can be proved that Lindenbaum algebra of $\mathcal{L}^N$ is a normal residuated lattice.

After introducing the suitable logical semantics, we obtain the following interesting results.

Proposition 3.27 Let $A \in F(S)$. Then the following conditions are equivalent:

- $\vdash A$;

- A is a tautology on each R_0-chain L;

- A is a tautology on each $L \in \mathcal{R}_N$.

Proposition 3.28 Adding the law of divisibility

$$(LA18) \ A \wedge B \to A \otimes (A \to B)$$

In to $\mathcal{L}^N$, or adding (LA17) and (LA18) into SC, we can obtain the Hájek's axiom system of basic logic (BL for short), and Lindenbaum algebra of BL is a BL-algebra.

Adding the law of contrapositive symmetry

$$(LA19) \ (\sim A \to \sim B) \to (B \to A)$$

and the following axiom scheme

$$(LA20) \ (A \to B) \vee ((A \to B) \to \sim A \vee B)$$

into $\mathcal{L}^N$, we can obtain Wang's axiom system $\mathcal{L}^*$, and the Lindenbaum algebra of $\mathcal{L}^*$ is a R_0-algebra.

Adding the following axiom scheme:

$$(LA21)\ \big((A \to B) \to B\big) \to \big((B \to A) \to A\big)$$

into $\mathcal{L}^N$, or adding (LA16) into BL, we can obtain the famous Łukasiewicz's axiom system $\mathcal{L}_{Lu}$ is a MV-algebra, or equivalently, a Wajsberg algebra.

Adding (LA15) into BL, or adding (LA18) into IPC, we can obtain Gödel 's axiom system G, and Lindenbaum algebra of G is a G-algebra.

Adding the axiom scheme

$$(LA22)\ \sim\sim\big((A \otimes C \to B \otimes C) \to (A \to B)\big)$$

into BL, we can obtain Hájek's product logic axiom system Π, and Lindenbaum algebra of Π is a product algebra.

We consider all axioms as stated above ((LA1)–(LA22)) to form a formal system. Thus, we obtain a formal system of classical propositional calculus $\mathcal{L}$. Naturally, the Lindenbaum algebra of $\mathcal{L}$ is a Boolean algebra.

We notice here that $\mathcal{L}$ has a simple axiom system:

$$(L1)\ A \to (B \to A);$$

$$(L2)\ \big(A \to (B \to C)\big) \to \big((A \to B) \to (A \to C)\big);$$

$$(L3)\ (\sim A \to \sim B) \to (B \to A).$$

In fact, (L1) is $(L^N 1)$ in $\mathcal{L}^N$, and (L3) is (LA19) in $\mathcal{L}^*$.

3.7   CRITICAL APPRECIATIONS ON FUZZY LOGIC

The grand success of fuzzy logic methods in many real world applications is well established, but the coherence of the foundations of fuzzy logic remains under question. Taken together, these two facts constitute a paradox. A second paradox is that almost all the hundreds or thousands of successful fuzzy logic applications are embedded controllers, while most of the thousands of theoretical papers on fuzzy methods deal with knowledge representation and reasoning. This section attempts to resolve these paradoxes. The aim of this section is to identify which aspects of fuzzy logic make it so popular and which aspects are inessential. The major discussions of this section is based on a mathematical result and on a survey of the literature on the use of fuzzy logic in different areas of science and engineering [75, 76, 77].

A PARADOX IN FUZZY LOGIC

Fuzzy logic is a generalization of standard propositional logic from two truth values *false* and *true* to degrees of truth between 0 and 1.

Let A denotes an assertion. In fuzzy logic, A is assigned a numerical value $t(A)$, called the degree of truth of A, such that $0 \leq t(A) \leq 1$. For a sentence composed from simple assertions and the logical connectives "and" $(\wedge)$, "or" $(\vee)$, and "not" $(\sim)$, degree of truth is defined as follows.

Definition 3.24 Let A and B be arbitrary assertions. Then:

$$t(A \wedge B) = \min\{t(A), t(B)\}$$

$$t(A \vee B) = \max\{t(A), t(B)\}$$

$$t(\sim A) = 1 - t(A)$$

$$t(A) = t(B), \text{ if A and B are logically equivalent.}$$

Depending on how the phrase "logically equivalent" is understood, Definition 3.24 yields different formal systems. A system of fuzzy logic is intended to allow an indefinite variety of numerical truth values. However, for many notions of logical equivalence only two different truth values are possible given the postulates of Definition 3.24.

Theorem 3.1 Given the formal system of Definition 3.24, if $\sim(A \wedge \sim B)$ and $B \vee (\sim A \wedge \sim B)$ are logically equivalent, then for any two assertions A and B, either $t(B) = t(A)$ or $t(B) = 1 - t(A)$.

Proof: Given the assumed equivalence, $t(\sim(A \wedge \sim B)) = t(B \vee (\sim A \wedge \sim B))$, we consider:

$$t(\sim(A \wedge \sim B)) = 1 - \min\{t(A), 1 - t(B)\}$$

$$= 1 + \max\{-t(A), -1 + t(B)\}$$

$$= \max\{1 - t(A), t(B)\}$$

and

$$t(B \vee (\sim A \wedge \sim B)) = \max\{t(B), \min\{1 - t(A), 1 - t(B)\}\}.$$

The numerical expressions above are different if:

$$t(B) < 1 - t(B) < 1 - t(A),$$

that is if $t(B) < 1 - t(B)$ and $t(A) < t(B)$, which happens if $t(A) < t(B) < 0.5$.

So it cannot be true that if $t(A) < t(B) < 0.5$.

Note that the sentences $\sim(A \wedge B)$ and $B \vee (\sim A \wedge \sim B)$ are both re-expressions of the material implication $A \rightarrow B$. One by one, consider the seven other material implication sentences involving A and B, which are:

$$\sim A \rightarrow B$$

$$A \rightarrow \sim B$$

$$\sim A \rightarrow \sim B$$

$$B \rightarrow A$$

$$\sim B \rightarrow A$$

$$B \rightarrow \sim A$$

$$\sim B \rightarrow \sim A.$$

By the same reasoning as before, none of the following can be true:

$$1 - t(A) < t(B) < 0.5$$

$$t(A) < 1 - t(B) < 0.5$$

$$1 - t(A) < 1 - t(B) < 0.5$$

$$t(B) < t(A) < 0.5$$

$$1 - t(B) < t(A) < 0.5$$

$$t(B) < 1 - t(A) < 0.5$$

$$1 - t(B) < 1 - t(A) < 0.5.$$

Let $x = \min \{t(A), 1 - t(A)\}$ and let $y = \min \{t(B), 1 - t(B)\}$. Clearly $x \leq 0.5$ and $y \leq 0.5$. So if $x \neq y$, then one of the eight inequalities derived must be satisfied. Thus $t(B) = t(A)$ or $t(B) = 1 - t(A)$.

Remark 3.22 Theorem 3.1 does not depend on any particular definition of implication in fuzzy logic. Different definitions of fuzzy implication are proposed as different applications of fuzzy logic are investigated; for example by Dubois and Prade.

Proposition 3.29 Let $\mathcal{P}$ be a finite Boolean algebra of propositions and let τ be a truth-assignment function $\mathcal{P} \to [0, 1]$, supposedly truth-functional via continuous connectives. Then for all $p \in \mathcal{P}$, $\tau(p) \in \{0, 1\}$.

The link between Theorem 3.1 and the proposition 3.29 is that $\sim(A \wedge \sim B) \equiv B \vee (\sim A \wedge \sim B)$ is a valid equivalence of Boolean algebra. Theorem 3.1 is stronger in that it only relies on one particular equivalence, while the proposition 3.29 is stronger in that it applies to any connectives that are truth-functional and continuous.

The equivalence used in Theorem 3.1 is rather complicated, but it is plausible intuitively, and it is natural to apply in reasoning about a set of fuzzy rules, since $\sim(A \wedge \sim B)$ and $B \vee (\sim A \wedge \sim B)$ are both re-expressions of the classical implication $A \to B$. It is chosen for this reason, but the same result can also be proved using many other reasonable logical equivalences.

It is necessary to understand what exactly Theorem 3.1 says, and what it does not say. On the one hand, the Theorem 3.1 also applies to any, more general formal system that includes the four postulates listed in Definition 3.24. Any extension of fuzzy logic to accommodate first-order sentences collapses to two truth values if it admits the propositional fuzzy logic of Definition 3.20 as a special case. The Theorem 3.1 also applies to fuzzy set theory given the equation that $\sim(A \cap \sim B) = B \cup (\sim A \cap \sim B)$, because Definition 3.24 can be understood as axiomatizing degrees of membership for fuzzy set intersections, unions, and complements. On the other hand, the Theorem 3.1 does not necessarily apply to versions of fuzzy logic that modify or reject any of the postulates of Definition 3.24. It is however possible to carry through the proof of the Theorem 3.1 in many variant systems of fuzzy logic. In particular, the Theorem 3.1 remains true when negation is modeled by any operator in the Sugeno class, and when disjunction or conjunctions are modeled by operators in the Yager classes.

The last postulate of Definition 3.24 is the most controversial one. In order to preserve a continuum of degrees of truth, we should restrict the notion of logical equivalence. In intuitive descriptions, fuzzy logic is often characterized as arising from the rejection of the law of excluded middle: the assertion $A \vee \sim A$. Unfortunately, rejecting this law is not sufficient to avoid collapse to just two truth values. Intuitionistic logic rejects the law of excluded middle, but the formal system of Definition 3.24 still collapses when logical equivalence means intuitionistic equivalence. Of course, collapse to two truth values is avoided when we admit the equivalences generated by the operator's minimum, maximum, and complement to one. However, these equivalences are just the axiom of de Morgan, which only allow restricted reasoning about collections of fuzzy assertions.

COMMENTS ON THEOREM 3.1 [211]

We analyze two specific reasons that lead Elkan to his conclusions.
- Probably the most polemic point in Elkan's proof is his understanding of the sentence "any assertion A and B". Elkan correctly states that every possible values of t(A) and t(B) must be checked in order to prove theorem 3.1.

Then, he assumes that every point p(t(A), t(B)) must be in some of the regions delimited by the following equivalencies:

$$A \rightarrow B$$
$$\sim A \rightarrow \sim B$$
$$\sim A \rightarrow B$$
$$A \rightarrow \sim B$$
$$B \rightarrow A$$
$$\sim B \rightarrow \sim A$$
$$\sim B \rightarrow A$$
$$B \rightarrow \sim A$$

Given Definition 3.24 (where t(~A) = 1 - t(A)), checking all implications above implies in considering the points in square [1,0] x [1,0] twice. Given the hypothesis *"A and B are any assertions"*, the only assumption regarding t(A) and t(B) is that both points P1(t(A), t(B)) and P2(t(B), t(A)) must hold the theorem (that is, the order is irrelevant). There is no need to check their complements, since there is nothing assumed for these sets.
- During the proof of theorem 3.1, Elkan neglects a region of points when he defines the domain of p(t(A),t(B)) that do not verify the logical equivalence in theorem 3.1. Let us revise this step. By analyzing expression (E1), Elkan concluded that the numerical expressions are different if:

$$t(B) < 1 - t(B) < 1 - t(A)$$

which leads to

$$t(A) < t(B) < 0.5 \text{ (region R1)}$$

This partially true because there are other points that do not hold expression (E1). As we showed before, all points in region R3 (Figure 18(a)) do not hold (E1) and Elkan's region is only half of R3.

The neglected region is given by:

$$0.5 < t(B) < 1 - t(A) \text{ (region R2)}$$

Regions R1 and R2 are showed in Figure 17 and their union in Figure 18(a). The negligence of region R2 did not affect Elkan's proof due to his interpretation of the sentence "any assertions A and B".

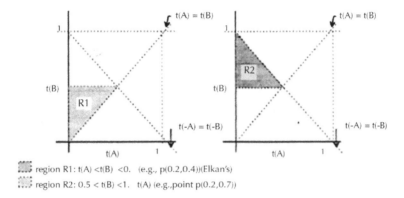

region R1: t(A) <t(B) <0. (e.g., p(0.2,0.4))(Elkan's)
region R2: 0.5 < t(B) <1. t(A) (e.g.,point p(0.2,0.7))

FIGURE 17   Points that do not verify the logical equivalence (E1).

Elkan's paper is conventional and creates some apparent misconceptions among Fuzzy Logic researchers. The author criticizes Fuzzy Logic based upon two different points: first, he introduces a theorem, named "theorem 1", which states that any two logic assertions A and B that meet a given logical equivalence end up in only two combinations of true values, namely the lines t(A) = t(B) or t(A) = t(~B). This means that any multivalent logic that holds the formal system described by definition 1 (see next section) collapses to only two particular relationships. Second, Elkan argues that the success of Fuzzy Logic in industrial applications (fuzzy control) is paradoxical, since it happens despite of this purported drawback.

Most answers presented by well-known Fuzzy Logic researchers do not disagree with the validity of Elkan's theorem. However, the researchers argue that this theorem does not apply to Fuzzy Logic. They argue that, contrary to Fuzzy Logic, theorem 3.1 meets the excluded-middle and contradiction laws, since the definition of logical equivalence assumed in the theorem is too restrict to be kept in Fuzzy Logic. They also examine the supposed reasons for Fuzzy Logic being successful in control applications and show that Elkan's arguments are simply unsupported. For instance; Elkan argues that the industrial applications of fuzzy control are based on a small number of rules which causes its success rather than the fuzzy approach itself. However, the reduced number of rules is not a coincidence but a consequence of fuzzy predicates in the rules.

We decide to investigate theorem 3.1 further. The conclusions we have drawn from this study show that the theorem itself is not correct. There are points p(t(A),t(B)) that do hold the equivalence relation of theorem 3.1 and are not on the lines t(A) = t(B) or t(A) = 1- t(B). We not only disagree with Elkan's opinions, but also with their mathematical basis. Even when the theorem is reformulated, we can conclude that it is only a special case in Fuzzy Logic. In the following we reformulate theorem 3.1 and try to remove the misconception generated by it.

In theorem 3.1, there are two assertions assumed as logically equivalent. According to definition 3.24, if two assertions are logically equivalent they have the same true value.

Therefore:

$$t(\sim(A \wedge -,B)) = t(B \vee (\sim A \wedge \sim B))$$

Considering definition 3.24, we have:

$$1 - t(t(A) \wedge t(\sim B)) = \max\ [t(B), t(\sim A \wedge \sim B)]$$

$$1 - \min[t(A), t(\sim B)] = \max\ (t(B), \min(t(\sim A), t(\sim B)))$$

$$1 - \min[t(A), 1 - t(B)] = \max\ \{t(B), \min[1 - t(A), 1 - t(B)]\}$$

$$(E1)\ \max[1 - t(A), t(B)] = \max\{t(B), \min[1 - t(A), 1 - t(B)]\}$$

The equivalence (1) is true depending upon the relation between the assertions A, B, and their complements. Given a point $p(t(A), t(B))$, the right and left hands of expression (E1) are different iff:

$$t(B) < 1 - t(A) \text{ and } 1 - t(B) < 1 - t(A)$$

which leads us to:

$$t(A) < t(B) < 1 - t(A)$$

The inequalities above define the region R3 of points $p(t(A), t(B))$ that do not hold expression (E1). This region is shown in Figure 18(a).

The hypothesis about assertions A and B in theorem 3.1 is clear: "any two assertions A and B". That means no presumption for them. Region R1 is defined considering points $p(t(A), t(B))$, that is $t(A)$ and $t(B)$ are in a specific order. However, given any two true values (for example, 0.6 and 0.4), we cannot assume a fixed order to verify theorem 3.1 (for example 0.6 can be either $t(A)$ or $t(B)$). In other words, the points that hold expression (E1) must either $p(t(A), t(B))$ or $p(t(B), t(A))$. By switching $t(A)$ by $t(B)$ (and vice-versa) in (E1), we derive the following expression:

$$(E2)\ \max(1 - t(B), t(A)] = \max\ \{t(A), \min[1 - t(B), 1 - t(A)]\}$$

Now, the left and right hands are different iff:

t(B) < t(A) < 1 -t(B), which indicates region R4.

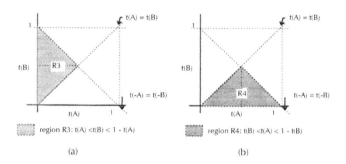

FIGURE 18   Points represented by expression E2.

Figure 18(b) shows region R4. The union between regions R3 and R4 defines all points that do not hold expression (E1) of theorem 3.1. Thus, the complement of this region defines all points that do hold expression (E1).

It is possible to show that the complement of the set (R3 ∪ R4) is given by:

$$\{t(A) \geq 1 - t(B)\} \cup \{t(A) = t(B)\}, \text{ which indicates region R5.}$$

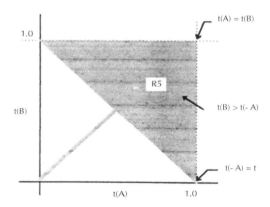

FIGURE 19   Points that violet Elkan's theorem 3.1.

Figure 19 shows region R5. The "arrow" R5 is a consequence of the fact the set $(R3 \cup R4)^c$ includes the fine t(A) = t(B). Contrary to Elkan's proof, there are points p(t(A),t(8)) that do hold the equivalence of theorem 3.1 without meeting the expressions t(A) = t(B) or t(A) = 1- t(B). Table 1 has examples of points that verify (E1) and

(E2) (points in region R5 and bolded in Table 19) and points that hold only one of these equivalencies (points in region R3 or R4).

TABLE 19   Points in R3, R4, and R5 and the respective values of expressions (E1) and (E2)

R_i	t(A)	t(B)	~(A ∧ ~B)	↔	B ∨ (~A ∧ ~B)	~(B ∧ ~A)	↔	A ∨ (~B ∧ ~A)
R1	0.3	0.6	0.7	n	0.6	0.4	y	0.4
R2	0.7	0.1	0.3	y	0.3	0.9	n	0.7
R3	0.8	0.6	0.6	y	0.6	0.8	y	0.8
R3	0.3	0.9	0.9	y	0.9	0.3	y	0.3

The main conclusion is that the thesis of theorem 3.1 is incomplete.

3.7.1   IS THE SUCCESS OF FUZZY LOGIC REALLY PARADOXICAL? [196]

The formal concept of logical equivalence in fuzzy logic, while theoretically sound, seems impractical. The misinterpretation of this concept has led to some pessimistic conclusions. Motivated by practical interpretation of truth values for fuzzy propositions, we take the class (lattice) of all sub-intervals of the unit interval [0, 1] as the truth value space for fuzzy logic, subsuming the traditional class of numerical truth values from [0, 1]. The associated concept of logical equivalence is stronger than the traditional one. Technically, we are dealing with much smaller set of pairs of equivalent formulas, so that we are able to check equivalence algorithmically. The checking is done by showing that our strong equivalence notion coincides with the equivalence in logic programming.

Since fuzzy logic is a formalization of commonsense reasoning, statements that are "equivalent" according to commonsense reasoning must have the same truth values in this logic. This informal argument was used by several researchers in fuzzy logic. The "commonsense equivalence" is not the same as equivalence in 2-valued logic. This difference is mentioned again by Elkan. In this section, we resolve this issue by providing a formal definition of such "equivalence". We also demonstrate that this definition relates exactly the same pairs of formulas as a definition that stems from logic programming. It is a fact that two radically different approaches (fuzzy logic and logic programming) lead to exactly the same notion of equivalence between propositional formulas. Both approaches lead to adequate descriptions of commonsense reasoning (at least as far as equivalence goes).

Elkan describes the difficulties that he has encountered when he tried to describe fuzzy logic formally.

Elkan tried two different formalizations of this "equivalence" based on two most well-known logical formalisms:
- Two-valued propositional logic and
- Intuitionistic logic.

In both cases, he got a contradiction. This contradiction is easy to explain. In both logics (two-valued and intuitionistic), $v_1 \vee (v_2 \& \sim v_2)$ is equivalent to v_1. However, in fuzzy logic, for truth values $t(v_1) = 0.3$ and $t(v_2) = 0.4$, we get $t(\sim v_2) = 1 - t(v_2) = 0.4$ and therefore, $t(v_2 \& \sim v_2) = \min(t(v_2), t(\sim v_2)) = \min(0.6, 0.4) = 0.4 \neq 0.3 = t(v_1)$.

Since both his attempts of formalization (based on reasonable choices of logic) have failed, Elkan concludes that fuzzy logic does not have consistent foundations and that therefore, successes of fuzzy logic are paradoxical.

For the following three reasons we do not agree with such pessimistic conclusion:

- Researchers in mathematical foundations of fuzzy sets and fuzzy control do not use the fact that if F and G are "equivalent" then their truth values coincide $(t(F) = t(G))$ as an independent axiom.
- As far as we know, neither this "postulate" itself, nor any conclusions based on this postulate have ever been used in any real-life fuzzy control applications.
- There exists a consistent formalization of this postulate and this formalization has been proposed by Goguen and Schwartz.

In spite of this confusion, the notion of commonsense equivalence is useful and therefore, worth formalizing. Definitely, this "commonsense equivalence" is not the same as equivalence in 2-valued logic. This difference was noticed by Elkan [75, 76, 77]. The same example works if we identify this "commonsense equivalence" with equivalence in intuitionistic logic.

A consistent formalization of commonsense equivalence has been proposed by Goguen and later by Schwartz. According to Goguen and Schwartz, two propositional formulas F and G with variables v_i are equivalent in fuzzy logic if for all possible assignments of truth values $t(v_i)$ to their variables v_i, the resulting truth values of these two formulas coincide: $t(F) = t(G)$ (actually, instesd of using the interval [0, 1], Goguen uses arbitrary lattices of truth values).

This formalization is not completely satisfactory for the following reasons:

- First, it is not algorithmic. It follows closely the definition of equivalence in two valued logic, in which formulas are equivalent if their truth values coincide for all truth values $t(v_i) \in \{T, F\}$. However, from the computational viewpoint, there is a big difference between these two cases:
  (i) In two-valued logic, each variable v_i has only two possible truth values. Therefore, we can actually enumerate all 2^n combinations of truth values and thus check whether the formulas F and G are equivalent or not.
  (ii) In fuzzy case, each variable v_i has infinitely many possible truth values (the set of truth values coincides with the interval [0, 1]). Therefore, it is impossible to enumerate and test all possible combinations of truth values.
- Second, this definition is very formal. It would be nice to have some extra support for the assumption that this definition reflects commonsense equivalence of two propositional formulas.
- Finally, it is not exactly clear what values of $t(v_i)$ we should use:
  (i) If we use only real numbers from the interval [0, 1], then we neglect the fact that every estimation of the truth values is in itself approximate.

(ii) If we use arbitrary lattices, then we are using mathematical model that may have no relation whatsoever to commonsense reasoning.

The problem of describing of formalization of "commonsense equivalence" that is free from these three drawbacks was, in effect, formulated in the following terms.

It is an open question how to choose a notion of logical equivalence that simultaneously:

(i)   Remains philosophically justifiable,

(ii) Allows useful inferences in practice, and

(iii) Removes the opportunity to prove results similar to Theorem 3.1 (that is, inconsistency).

We address these problems as follows:

(i)   We choose the proper representation of the values as sub-intervals of [0, 1] (this idea also goes back to Goguen and Schwartz).

(ii) We show that the resulting definition of equivalence of propositional formulas is the same as the definition of equivalence stemming from logic programming. The fact that two radically different approaches (fuzzy logic and logic programming) lead to exactly the same notion of equivalence between propositional formulas. It indicates that both approaches lead to adequate descriptions of commonsense reasoning (at least as far as equivalence is concerned).

(iii) This equivalence enables us to design an algorithm that decides whether two propositional formulas F & G are equivalent.

PROPOSITIONAL FORMULAS AND EQUIVALENCE IN 2-VALUED LOGIC

Let us start with reviewing the notion of equivalence in a classical (2-valued) logical setting.

Definition 3.25. Assume that a finite set $V = \{v_1, ..., v_n\}$ is given. Its elements v_i will be called propositional (or Boolean) variables.

A propositional formula with n variables v_i is then defined as follows:

- Every variable v_i is a formula,
- if F is a formula, then $\sim F$ (called not F) is also a formula,
- If F and G are formulas, then the following are formulas:
- F&G (called F and G),
- $F \vee G$ (called F or G),
- Nothing else is a formula.

Formulas that have been used in the construction of a formula F are called its subformulas.

Formulas different from variables are called composite formulas.

Examples 3.62 Let us consider the propositional formulas.

- $v_1 \vee (\sim v_2)$ is a propositional formula that has the following subformulas:

- v_1, v_2, and v_3,

- $\sim v_2$,

- $v_1 \vee (\sim v_3)$.

v_1 and $(v_2 \vee \neg v_1)$ is a propositional formula that has the following subformulas:

- $v_1, v_2,$ and v_3,

- $\sim v_1$.

- $v_2 \vee \sim v_1$.

- $v_1 \& (v_2 \vee \sim v_1)$.

Definition 3.26 By an n—dimensional Boolean vector or a Boolean array t, we mean a function from the set V into the set of truth values {T, F} (where T = 1 stands for "true", and F = 0 stands for "false").

Definition 3.27 Let t be a Boolean vector. Then, for every formula F, we can define its truth value t(F) for this Boolean vector t as follows:

- if $F = v_i$, then $t(F) = t(v_i)$;

- if $F = \sim G$, then $t(F) = \sim tG$;

- if $F = G\&H$, then $t(F) = t(G)\&t(H)$;

- if $F = G \vee H$, then $t(F) = t(G) \vee t(H)$;

(where $\sim, \&,$ and $\vee$ in the right hand sides mean standard operations with Boolean values {T, F}).

Example 3.63 If $t(v_1) = T$ and $t(v_2) = F$, then for $F = v_1 \vee (\sim v_2)$, the truth value $t(F)$ is defined as follows:

- $t(\sim v_2) = \sim F = T$;

- $t(F) = t(v_1 \vee (\sim v_2)) = t(v_1) \vee t(\sim v_2) = T \vee T = T$.

Definition 3.28 We say that formulas F and G are equivalent in 2-valued logic if for every Boolean vector t, t(F) = t(G).

WHAT TRUTH VALUES SHOULD WE CHOOSE?

Usually, the knowledge of an expert contains some statements that this expert is not 100% sure about and these statements from an essential part of the knowledge base. If we want to use this knowledge base, it is important to know the degree of belief that an expert has in each statement, so that, for example, in case of conflicting conclusions, we can choose the conclusion that is supported by the more convincing statements from the knowledge base. So, an adequate computer representation of this knowledge must include not only the representation of the expert's statements themselves, but it must also contain the computer representation of the expert's degrees with which they believe in these statements. Traditionally, these degrees of belief are represented by numbers from the interval [0, 1] (0 corresponds to "false" and 1 to "true").

There are several possible ways to assign a degree of belief to a statement.

Let us just name three of them:

- We can ask an expert to estimate his degree of belief by a number on a scale from, say, 0 to 5. If he marks 3, then we say that his degree of belief is $3/5 = 0.6$.
- We can ask several experts whether they believe in a given statement, and as a degree of belief, take a fraction of those who answered "yes".
- Another way to get $t(S)$ is to ask an expert to compare an alternative "\$100 if S is true else 0" with the lotteries, in which this same amount of money (\$100) is guaranteed with a certain probability p. If there is a probability p for which the above alternative and a lottery are equivalent, then we take p as $t(S)$.

In classical (2-valued) logic, it was sufficient to assign truth values to all basic statements v_i, then we can compute the truth value of any composite statement (that is formed from v_i by applying &, $\lor$, and $\sim$). In case of degrees of belief, it is no longer so. In general, the degree of belief $t(F\&G)$ in a statement $F\&G$ is not uniquely determined by the degrees of belief $t(F)$ and $t(G)$. Let us give an extreme example: assume that we know nothing about a statement F. Then, it is natural to assign both to F and to its negation $\sim F$, the degree of belief 0.5.

Let us now consider two cases:

- If we take G = F, then we have $t(F) = t(G) = 0.5$. Here, $F\&G = F\&F$ means the

  same as F, so $t(F\&G) = 0.5$.

- It we take $G = \sim F$, then $t(F) = t(G) = 0.5$, but $F\&G = F\&\sim F$ is simply false,

  so $t(F\&G) = 0$.

In both cases, $t(F) = t(G) = 0.5$, but the values of $t(F\&G)$ are different.

In view of that, it would be nice to know not only the experts' degrees of belief in elementary statements $v_1, \ldots, v_n$, but also their degrees of beliefs in composite statements. This is not feasible even for pairs $v_i \& v_j$, we need thus to acquire from experts $\approx n^2$ numbers, which for large n is practically impossible. So, in practice, we only know the degrees of belief $t(v_i)$ in the original statements v_i. What should we do if the decision that we are about to make must be based on the degree of belief in $v_i \& v_j$?

A natural approach to this problem is as follows. We must be able, given two numbers $t_1 = t(F)$ and $t_2 = t(G)$, to generate an estimate for $t(F\&G)$. As we have mentioned, there can be different situations with these values t_i that lead to different values of $t(F\&G)$. So, to be on the safe side, it is natural to take the average of these values as the desired estimate for $t(F\&G)$. There have been several experimental papers in which the corresponding averages have been found. It turns out that in most situations, the average for & is best described by either the product $t_1 \cdot t_2$, or by the minimum $\min(t_1, t_2)$. Similarly, the best estimate for $\lor$ is best described either by $t_1 + t_2 - t_1 \cdot t_2$, or by maximum $\max(t_1, t_2)$. All four operations have been originally proposed by L. Zadeh in his pioneer paper on fuzzy set theory.

In other words, if we know the degrees of belief in F and in G, then, as an estimate $t(F\&G)$ for the actual (unknown) degree of belief of $F\&G$, we take either $t(F) \cdot t(F)$, or $\min(t(F), t(F)))$. We consider only the simplest case of min and max. So, we arrive at the following definitions:

Definition 3.29 By an initial fuzzy truth value assignment, we mean a function t from the set V into the set [0, 1].

Definition 3.30 Let t be an initial truth value assignment. Then, for every formula F, we can define its truth value t(F) as follows:

- if $F = v_i$, then $t(F) = t(v_i)$;

- if $F = \sim G$, then $t(F) = t(G)$;

- if $F = G\&H$, then $t(F) = \min(t(G), t(H))$;

- if $F = G \vee H$, then $t(F) = \max(t(G), t(H))$;

Example 3.64. If $t(v_1) = 0.3$ and $t(v_2) = 0.6$, then for $F = v_1 \vee (\sim v_2)$, the truth value $t(F)$ is defined as follows:

- $(\sim v_2) = 1 - 0.6 = 0.4$,

- $t(F) = t(v_1 \vee (\sim v_2)) = t(v_1) \vee t(\sim v_2)) = \max(0.3, 0.4) = 0.4$.

INTERVALS ARE A MORE REALISTIC REPRESENTATION OF DEGREES OF BELIEF THAN REAL NUMBERS

The above definition is based on the assumption that we can describe the degree of belief in a statement by a precise number. However, this is an idealization of the real situation.

Instead of a single value $t(F)$, we get an interval $\mathbf{t}(F) = t^-(F), t^+(F)]$ of possible values of degree of belief.

The fact that we know t(F) means that any number t_1 from this interval can be the degree of belief for F. Similarly, and number t_2 from the interval t(G) can be the degree of belief in G. If we use min for &, then possible values $\min(t_1, t_2)$ form an interval of possible values of degrees of belief for F & G.

To be able to compute this interval, we must thus be able, given two intervals t and s, to compute the interval of possible values of $\min(t, s)$, where $t \in t$ and $s \in s$. For $\vee$ and $\sim$, we must be able to compute similar sets for max and for $1 - t$. Let us describe how to do it.

Definition 3.31 Let f: $R^m \to R$ be an arbitrary function of n real variables, and let $x_1, \ldots x_m$ be m intervals. Then, we denote:

$$f(x_1, \ldots x_m) = \{f(x_1, \ldots x_n) \mid x_1 \in x_1, \ldots x_m \in x_m\}.$$

We will use this definition only for three functions $1 - t$, min, and max that correspond to three logical connectives $\neg$, &, and $\vee$.

Proposition 3.30

- For f(t) = 1-t, we have $1-[t^-, t^+] = [1 - t^+, 1 - t^-]$,

- For f = min, we have min $([t^-, t^+], [s^-, s^+]) = [\min (t^-, s^-) (t^+, s^+)]$.

- For f = max, we have max $([t^-, t^+], [s^-, s^+]) = \max (t^-, s^-) (t^+, s^+)]$.

This Proposition is easy to prove if we take into consideration that all three function $1 - t$, min, and max are monotonic and therefore, we can easily find the values from the corresponding intervals for which this function attains its biggest or its smallest value.

PRACTICAL (INTERVAL) FUZZY LOGIC AND EQUIVALENCE IN PRACTICAL FUZZY LOGIC

Definition 3.32. By an initial practical fuzzy truth value assignment, we mean a function t that assigns to every element v_i from the set of variables V an intervals t $(v_i) \subseteq [0,1]$.

Definition 3.33. Let t be an initial practical truth value assignment. Then, for every formula F, we can define its truth value t(F) as follows:

- If $F = v_i$, then $t(F) = t(v_i)$;

- If $F = {\sim}G$, then $t(F) = 1 - t(G)$;

- If $F = G \& H$, then $t(F) = \min (t(G), t(H))$;

- If $F = G \vee H$, then $t(F) = \max (t(G), t(H))$.

These definitions were originally proposed by Schwartz [24].

Example 3.64. If t $(v_1) = [0.2, 0.4]$, and t $(v_2) = [0.6, 0.7]$, then for $F = v_1 \vee ({\sim}v_2)$, the truth value t(F) is defined as follows:

- t $({\sim}v_2) = 1-[0.6, 0.7] = [1- 0.7, 1-0.6] = [0.3, 0.4]$;

- $t(F) = t\ (v_1 \lor\ (\sim v_2)) = t\ (v_1) \lor t(\sim v_2)) = \max\ ([0.2, 0.4], [0.3, 0.4]) = [\max$

  $(0.2, 0.3), \max\ (0.4, 0.4)] = [0.3, 0.4]$.

Definition 3.34 We say that Formulas F and G are equivalent in practical fuzzy logic if for every initial practical fuzzy truth value assignment t, we have $t(F) = t(G)$.

THE NOTION OF EQUIVALENCE STEMS FROM LOGIC PROGRAMMING

Another approach for representing commonsense reasoning is based on logic programming. But traditional logic programming does not allow all propositional connection (&, $\lor$, and $\sim$) to be used. Recently, an extension of traditional logic programming has been proposed in which all these connectives are well defined.

In application to propositional formulas, this extension is defined as follows:

Definition 3.35 By a literal, we will mean either a variable v_i or its negation $\sim v_i$. Let a set W of literals be given. By induction over F, we can define when a propositional formula F is true or false for W:

- A literal is true for W if it belongs to W, and it is false for W if its negation be-

  longs to W.

- $\sim F$ is true for W if F is false for W, or G is true for W, F $\lor$ G is false for W if

  both F and G are false for W.

- F & G is true for W if both F and G are true for W, F & G is false for W if either

  F if false for W, or G is false for W.

We say that a set W is an answer set for a formula F if the following two conditions are met:
- First, F is true for W and
- Second, F is not true for any proper subset of W.

i. One of the differences between logic programming and 2-valued logic is as follows:
- Logic describes the objective state of the world. Therefore, in logic, for the given Boolean vector t, every formula F is either true or false.
- Logic programming describes our knowledge about the world.

In this interpretation:
a) "F is true for W" means that, if W is what we know, then we know that F is true.
b) Similarly, "F is false for W" means for the knowledge W, F is known to be false.

Since the knowledge need not be complete, for a given set of literals W and a given formula F, in addition to two previous possibilities:
- That F is true for W and

- That F is false for W

We have two more options:
- That F is neither true nor false for W (meaning that if W is all we know, then whether F is true or not is unknown).
- That F is both true and false in W, meaning that the knowledge about F that is contained in W is inconsistent.

For example, if $F = v_1 \vee \sim v_2$, and all is $W = \{v_3\}$ (that is, that v_3 is true), then we have no information about v_1 and v_2 at all, and therefore, it is reasonable to conclude that F is unknown. This is exactly what we will get from Definition 4.1 that the given F is neither true nor false for the given W. For this same F, if we take an inconsistent knowledge $W \{v_1 \sim v_1\}$, then F is both true and false in W.

ii. A formula can have several answer sets.

Example 3.66 Let us consider the formula $F = v_1 \vee \sim (v_2)$. Then, the following two sets of literals are answer sets for this formula: $W_1 = \{v_1\}$ and $W_2 = \{\sim v_2\}$. Let us check the two conditions for W_2:

- For W_2, $\sim v_2$ is true and therefore, $v_1 \vee \sim (v_2)$ is also true for W_2.

- The only proper subset of W_2 is an empty set W. For empty set, none of the formulas v_1 and $\sim v_2$ is true; therefore, $F = v_1 \vee \sim (v_2)$ is also not true.

A set $W_3 = \{v_1, v_2\}$ is not an answer set because although F is true for W_3, but F is also true for a proper subset $W_1 \subset W_3$.

Definition 3.36 We say that propositional formulas F and G are equivalent in logic programming if these two formulas have the same class of answer sets (that is, if every answer set of F is an answer set of G and vice versa).

Now, we are ready to formulate and prove our main result.

Theorem 3.2 Let F and G be any propositional formulas. Then, F is equivalent to G in practical fuzzy logic if and only if F is equivalent to G in logic programming.

Remark 3.23
- So, the desired definition of a logical equivalence that Elkan was looking for can be taken right from logic programming.
- This Theorem was announced in[12] and[19].
- What will happen if instead of the initial interval truth value assignments t, we only consider the numerical truth value assignment (that is, if all intervals t (v_i) contain just one number $t(v_i)$? This situation is described by the following proposition:

Definition 3.37 We say that propositional formulas F and G are equivalent in traditional fuzzy logic if for every initial truth value assignment t, we have t(F)=t(G).

Proposition 3.31

- If the formulas F and G are equivalent in practical fuzzy logic, then they are equivalent in traditional fuzzy logic.
- There exist formulas F and G that are equivalent in traditional fuzzy logic but not equivalent in practical fuzzy logic.

Remark 3.24
- Equivalence classes in practical fuzzy logic are much smaller than in the traditional fuzzy logic case.
- In the next section, we will describe the algorithm that checks when the two given formulas F and G are equivalent in practical fuzzy logic. Suppose now that we are actually interested in whether this they are equivalent in traditional fuzzy logic. To do that, we will apply the algorithm for checking their equivalence in practical logic. Depending on the result of this algorithm, we will have two possibilities:
- If F and G turned out to be equivalent in practical fuzzy logic, then, due to Proposition 2, they are equivalent in traditional fuzzy logic as well.
- If, however, F and G are not equivalent in practical fuzzy logic, then we cannot make any conclusion about whether they are equivalent in traditional fuzzy logic or not.
- This proposition states that the notions of equivalence in traditional and practical fuzzy logics are different. Which of them is closer to commonsense reasoning? To our viewpoint, equivalence in practical fuzzy logic is closer. Indeed, let us consider the following example of formulas F and G that are equivalent in traditional fuzzy logic, but not in the practical one: $F = v_1 \,\&\sim v_1$ and $G = v_1 \,\&\sim v_1 \,\&\sim (v_2 \,\&\sim v_2)$.
- Let us first show that these formulas are equivalent in traditional fuzzy logic. Indeed, in traditional fuzzy logic, we have $t(F) = \min \left(t(v_1), 1 - t(v_1) \right)$, and

$$t(G) = \min \left(t(v_1), 1 - t(v_1) \right), \ 1 - \min(t(v_2), 1 - t(v_2)) = \min(t(F), 1 - \min(t(v_2), 1 - t(v_2))).$$

- Let us consider two cases:

- If $t(v_1) \leq 0.5$, then $1 - t(v_1) \geq 0.5 \geq t(v_1)$, and therefore, $\min \left(t(v_1), 1 - t(v_1) \right) = t(v_1) \leq 0.5$.

- If $t(v_1) \geq 0.5$, then $1 - t(v_1) \leq 0.5 \leq t(v_1)$, and therefore, $\min \left(t(v_1), 1 - t(v_1) \right) = t(v_1) \leq 0.5$.

- In both cases, $t(F) = \min \left(t(v_1), 1 - t(v_1) \right) \leq 0.5$. Similarly, we have $\min \left(t(v_2), 1 - t(v_2) \right) \geq 0.5$, hence, $1 - \min(t(v_2), 1 - t(v_2)) \geq 0.5 \geq t(F)$, and therefore,

- $t(G) = \min(t(F), 1 - \min(t(v_2), 1 - t(v_2))) = t(F)$.

- In interval fuzzy logic, these formulas are not equivalent. For example, if we take $t(v_1) = [0.5, 0.5]$ and $t(v_2) = [0, 1]$, we get $t(F) = [0.5, 0.5]$, but $\min(t(v_2), 1 - t(v_2)) = \min([0, 1], [0, 1]) = [0, 1]$ and therefore, $G = \min([0.5, 0.5], [0, 1]) = [0, 0.5] \neq t(F)$.

- We will now explain why from commonsense point of view these two formulas F and G are not exactly equivalent. To illustrate this point, we will give a commonsense example of these two logical statements. For that, we need an interpretation of the variables v_i. We interpret v_1 as "young", v_2 as "smart". In this interpretation, F would means "young and not young." Informally, any person who is to some extent still young, but at the same time, to some extent not young (that is, who is in the intermediate age category), satisfies the property F. Similarly, a person who is to some extent smart (but not the smartest possible), but who is also to some extent not smart (that is, who is in the intermediate smartness category) satisfies the property $v_2 \&\sim v_2$. In these terms, the property G means that a person is in the intermediate age category, but that he is not in the intermediate smartness category. Now, if a person belongs to both the intermediate age category and to the intermediate intelligence category, then he satisfies the property F but not the property G. So, from the commonsense viewpoint, these properties are indeed not equivalent.

3.7.2 AN ALGORITHM THAT CHECKS EQUIVALENCE IN PRACTICAL FUZZY LOGIC [196]

Definition 3.38 Equivalence of propositional formulas F and G in practical fuzzy logic have been defined as $t(F) = t(G)$ for every initial practical fuzzy truth value assignment 't'.

Definition 3.39 In a 2 valued logic, where equivalence is defined as $t(F) = t(G)$ for every Boolean vector (that is, for every initial 2 valued truth assignment) t.

The above two definitions for equivalence is similar in nature, but for algorithm verification of these two definition needs different approaches.

In 2-valued case, there are finitely many possible Boolean vectors and therefore, we can (potentially) check them all. This gives us the algorithmic way to check whether F is equivalent to G or not.

In practical fuzzy case, there are infinitely many possible initial fuzzy truth value assignments and it is impossible to check them all directly. So, to check whether F and G are equivalent in practical fuzzy logic, we must find some indirect method.

We have shown that two formulas F and G are equivalent in practical fuzzy logic if they are equivalent in logic programming. This result motivates us to check equivalence of practical fuzzy logic in algorithmic form.

The algorithmic approach to check equivalence in logic programming is as follows:

- For each of the formulas F and G, and for every set of literals W, we can use Definition 3.31 to check whether a formula is true for W, neither false for W or neither true nor false for this W.

There are totally $2n$ literals:

- n variables $v_1, \ldots, v_n$, and
- n negations of literals $\sim v_1, \ldots, \sim v_n$.

Therefore, there are 2^{2n} possible sets of literals. We can (in principle) check them all. As a result of this checking, we will have for each of the formulas F and G, the list of all sets of literals W on which this formula is true.

Next, for each of the two formulas F and G, we go through the list of all sets of literals W, for which this formula is true, and eliminate all sets that have proper subsets in the same list. After this elimination, we have for each of the two formulas, the list of all its answer sets.

- If these lists coincide, then these formulas are equivalent. If they differ, then the formulas F and G are not equivalent.

Example 3.67 Let us check whether the formulas $F = v_1 \,\&\sim v_2$ and $G = \sim(\sim v_1 \vee v_2)$ are equivalent. Here, n = 2, so we have to check $2^{2n} = 2^4 = 16$ sets of literals. Let us list them all. First, we will list the sets with no elements; then, the sets with one element, and so on:

- Set with not element: $\emptyset$,
- Sets with one element: $\{v_1\}, \{v_2\}, \{\sim v_1\}, \{\sim v_2\}$,
- Sets with two elements:

$$\{v_1, v_2\}, \{v_1, \sim v_1\}, \{v_1, \sim v_2\}, \{v_2, \sim v_1\}, \{v_2, \sim v_2\}, \{\sim v_1, \sim v_2\}$$,

- Sets with three elements:
$$\{v_1, v_2, \sim v_1\}, \{v_1, v_2, \sim v_2\}, \{v_1, \sim v_1, \sim v_2\}, \text{ and } \{v_2, \sim v_1, \sim v_2\}$$,
- A set with four elements: $\{v_1, v_2, \sim v_1, \sim v_2\}$.

For each set W, in order to check where G is true for W, we must apply Definition 3.31 to all subformulas of G. Let us trace with this procedure for $W = \{v_1, v_2\}$:

- v_1 is true for W because $v_1 \in W$,
- v_2 is also true for W,
- since v_1 is true for W, $\sim v_1$ is false for W,
- since v_2 is true for W, $\sim v_1 \vee v_2$ is true for W, and

- since $\sim v_1 \lor v_2$ is true for W, the formula $G = \sim(\sim v_1 \lor v_2)$ is true for W

After we check all these sets, we will have only one set of variables on which each formula is true: $\{v_1, \sim v_2\}$. So, this very set will be the only answer set for both formulas F and G. So, for F and G, the classes of answer sets coincide therefore, F and G are equivalent.

In the above example, F and G are equivalent in 2-valued logic and they turned out to be equivalent for our case as well. Let us give another example in which formulas are equivalent in 2-valued logic but not in practical fuzzy logic.

Example 3.68 $F = v_1 \lor v_2$, and $G = v_1 \lor v_2 \lor (v_1 \& \sim v_1)$. In this case:
- F is true for the following sets of literals: $\{v_1\}, \{v_2\}, \{v_1, v_2\}, \{v_1, \sim v_2\}, \{\sim v_1, v_2\}$, and $\{v_1, \sim v_1\}$. If we delete the proper supersets from this list, we will be left with three answer sets $\{v_1\}, \{v_2\}$, and $\{v_1, \sim v_1\}$.

The resulting classes of answer sets, so, F and G are not equivalent in logic programming (hence, not equivalent in practical fuzzy logic).

3.7.3   WHEN IS A FORMULA F A CONSEQUENCE OF A FORMULA G?

If formulas F and G are not equivalent, then a natural question to ask is: are these two formulas independent from each other, or one of them is a consequence of another one? In order to answer this question, we must first define what a consequence means. This question is the easiest to answer for 2-valued logic [196]:

Definition 3.40 In 2-valued logic, we say that F is a consequence of G if for every Boolean vector t for which t(G) is true, t(F) is also true.

Remark 3.25 Since we identified 1 with "true" and 0 with "false", we can reformulate this definition as follows.

Definition 3.41 In 2-valued logic, we say that F is a consequence of G is for every Boolean vector t, $t(F) \geq t(G)$.

Remark 3.26
i)   Indeed, if $t(G) = 0$, that is, if G is false in t, then this inequality is always true. If, however, $t(G) = 1$, then this inequality implies that $t(F) = 1$. So, this modified definition is equivalent to the original one.
ii) In traditional fuzzy logic, in addition to the cases when $t(G) = 0$ and $t(G) = 1$, we can have cases when $0 < t(G) < 1$. Intuitively, if we have some reasons to believe in G and F is a consequence of G, then these same reasons can be also viewed as reasons to believe in F. There may be also other reasons to believe in F, that are unrelated to G. Therefore, if F is a consequence of G, this means that in all cases, we have either the same or even more reasons to believe in F than in G. In other words, the degree of belief in F must be always not smaller than the degree of belief in G: $t(F) \geq t(G)$. We can use

this inequality as a definition of the notion of consequence in traditional (non-interval) fuzzy logic:

Definition 3.42 In traditional fuzzy logic, we say that F is a consequence of G if for every initial truth value assignment t, we have $t(F) \geq t(G)$.

Remark 3.27 How to define "consequence" for practical (interval) fuzzy logic? If the degree of belief in G is described by an interval $[t^-(G), t^+(G)]$, this means that the actual degree of belief can take any value form this interval. For each of these degrees of belief, the corresponding degree of belief in F is greater than the degree of belief in G. In other words, every possible degree of belief in F (that is, every number from the interval $t(F)$) must be not smaller than some possible degree of belief in G (that is, some number from the interval $t(F)$). It is natural to make this condition a definition of a consequence in the practical fuzzy case.

We will describe this definition in two steps:
- First, we will describe the corresponding relation between the intervals.
- Second, we will use this relation to describe what a consequence means.

Definition 3.43 We say that an interval a = $[a^-, a^+]$ is not smaller than the interval b = $[b^-, b^+]$ (and denote it by a $\geq$ b) if the following two conditions are satisfied:
- for every value a$\in$a, there exists a b $\in$ b such that a$\geq$b.
- for every b$\in$ b, there exists a a$\in$a such that a$\geq$b.

Proposition 3.32 a$\geq$b if $a^+ \geq b^+$ and $a^- \geq b^-$.

Remark 3.28
- This statement is easy to prove.
- This partial order among intervals coincides with the order imposed by the lattice structure (min, max) on the set of all intervals, and is, therefore, in good accordance with the original ideas.

Definition 3.44 In practical fuzzy logic, we say that F is a consequence of G if for every initial practical fuzzy truth assignment t, we show have $t(F) \geq t(G)$.

Remark 3.29 Similarly to Theorem 3.2, we show that this definition is equivalent to a similar definition from logic programming.

Definition 3.45 In logic programming, we say that F is a consequence of G if F is true for every answer set of G.

Remark 3.30 In Section r, we have already described how to determine all answer sets of a given formula, and how to check whether a given formula F is true for a given set of literals. These two algorithms enable us to check whether F is a consequence of G in logic programming.

Theorem 3.3 Let F and G be any propositional formulas. Then, F is a consequence of G in practical fuzzy logic if and only if F is a consequence of G in logic programming.

Remark 3.31 Because of this theorem, we can apply the above-described method of checking whether F is a consequence of G in logic programming to check whether F is a consequence of G in the sense of practical fuzzy logic.

3.7.4 FUZZY LOGIC IS NOT THE KEY FOR THE FORMALIZATION OF NATURAL LANGUAGE

Fuzzy Logic is not an appropriate tool for a complete formalization of NL. The aspect of vagueness and the relaxations of classical logical truth can only be handled by Fuzzy Logic. In the essay *Vagueness: An Exercise in Logical Analysis* (1937), Max Black first proposed the idea of vague sets and talked about three kinds of imprecision in NL: the generally, the ambiguity, and the vagueness. The generality is the power of a word to refer to a lot of things which can be very different each other. The ambiguity is the possibility of a linguistic expression to have many different meanings. The vagueness is the absence of precise confines in the reference of a lot of adjective and common names of human language, for example, "table", "house", "tall", "rich", "strong", "young", and so on. More precisely, vagueness is an approximate relation between a common name or a quantitative adjective and the objects of the world which can be referred by this name or predicated of this adjective. By the term "quantitative adjective" we mean an adjective which refers to qualities which have variable intensities, that is qualities which can be predicated of the subject more or less. Fuzzy Logic can completely handle the linguistic vagueness.

The successes of Fuzzy Logic in the field of engineering and the birth of fuzzy sets (vague set as proposed by Black) theory from the study of linguistic vagueness may initiate the idea that Fuzzy Logic can give solution to the problems that the bivalent logic leaves unsolved in artificial intelligence (AI). Kosko proposes the idea that an artificial system may be a good imitation of a natural system, like a brain, if the artificial system is able to learn, to get experience and to change itself without the intervention of a human programmer. This idea may be correct, but we do not believe that it is enough to put Fuzzy Logic into a dynamic system to solve the problems of AI. Kosko also hypothesizes that the employment of Fuzzy Logic is the key to give the common sense to a system. We think that this is not correct. The common sense is the result of many experiences, intuitions, and so many other complex processes of our faculty that it is not enough to substitute bivalent logic with Fuzzy Logic to obtain a system which can behave on the basis of common sense.

The success on Fuzzy Logic in many fields of science and engineering may create the illusion that Fuzzy Logic is an appropriate tool for the formalization of NL. The vagueness is only one of the many aspects of NL that classical logic cannot treat.

A calculus may reproduce a good part of the richness of NL only having:
1)   A sufficient meta-linguistic power,
2)   The ability to interpret the metaphors, and
3)   The devices to calculate all the variables of the pragmatic context of the enunciation.

The first problem is solvable with a very complicated syntax and the large employment of the set theory. With regard to the second problem, there are a lot of theories on the treatment of metaphor, but none of them seems to be adequate to reach the objective of a "formal" interpretation. The third problem is very far from a solution. The pragmatics studies of physical, cultural, and situational context of linguistic expressions show only that the pragmatics is fundamental for semantics: the Wittgenstein's theory of linguistic games (1953) is the best evidence of this fact. With regard to pragmatics, it is impossible that an artificial cognitive system could process sentences semantically, if the system is not capable of perception and emotional action (cf. Marconi, 1997). The problem of vagueness is important in semantics, but we think that the solutions of the problems 1), 2), and 3) are more important and more structural to reach a good automatic treatment of NL. A good automatic treatment of NL does not necessarily require a rigorous logical formalization of NL. With regard to the formalization of NL, we believe that formalized languages are always founded on NL and their semantic richness is always a parasitical part of the semantic richness of NL.

Thus the objectives of the research in NLP (Natural Language Processing) are:

I)   The automatic production of artificial sentences which human speakers can easily understand and

II) A sufficiently correct interpretation of sentences of NL.

In a static system, which is not able to program itself, I) and II) are realized on the basis of a formalized language, NL', which is semantically rich enough to be similar to NL, but the semantic richness of NL' is however founded on NL. In a dynamic system, the conceivable imitations of natural phenomena like "the extensibility of the meaning of the words", "the change of meaning of words along time", and other kinds of "rule changing creativity" or of "metaphorical attitude", on the basis of the auto-programming activity of the system are very important aspects. Also in dynamic systems, like the hypothetical neural nets, the substitution of bivalent logic with Fuzzy Logic is a good improvement, but it is not the key of the solution of all problems. The concept of dynamic system, understood as a system which learns and changes on the basis of experience is very important, but we are still very far form a concrete realization of a system like this and the treatability of semantic vagueness through Fuzzy Logic is only a little solution of this task. Hence it is a very high ambitious thinking that Fuzzy Logic is the key of formalization of NL.

3.7.5   THE POSITION OF FUZZY LOGIC (FL) IN THE CONTEXT OF THE MANY-VALUED LOGICS [174]

Fuzzy logic is a polyvalent logic which is based upon another many-valued calculus. A mathematical relationship between Fuzzy Logic and many-valued logics can be stated as a fuzzy logic calculus is a logic, in which the truth-values are fuzzy subsets of the set of truth-values of a non-fuzzy many-valued logic. A simple many-valued logic has a fix number of truth values (3, 4, …, n), while a Fuzzy Logic has a free number of truth values. It is the user's choice to select the number of truth values he wants to consider. The user finds the truth-values of the fuzzy system inside the evaluation set of the many-valued calculus, which is the basis of the fuzzy system. This freedom in the choice, of how many truth-values are to employ, makes Fuzzy Logic a very popular technique to treat the complex phenomena.

The basis of FL is the system L_{N1} of Łukasiewicz. L_{N1} is a many-valued logic in which the set of truth values contains all the real numbers of the interval [0, 1]. The FL admits, as truth values, "linguistic" truth values which belong to a set T of infinite cardinality: T={True={Very True, Not very True, Moe or less True, Not True, ...}, False={Very False, Not very False, More or less False, not False, ...}, ...}. Each linguistic truth-value of FL is a fuzzy subset of the set T of the infinite numeric truth values of L_{N1}. The employment of linguistic truth values permits to formulate vague answers to vague questions. Let us consider an example to illustrate a fuzzy truth. Consider the question "Is John YOUNG?". An answer to the question is, "It is Very True that John is YOUNG". As we see in this example, FL works with vague sentences, that are with sentences which contain vague or fuzzy predicates. As in the case of truth values, the fuzzy predicates are fuzzy subsets of the universe of discussion X. The universe of discussion is a classical (non fuzzy) set which contains for example, ages, temperatures, velocities, and all kind of adjectival quantities which can have a numerical translation. In the case of our example the universe of discussion is the "age". The set A ("age") contains finite numeric values [0, 120]. Inside the classical set A it is possible to define the linguistic variables (YOUNG, OLD, ...) as fuzzy subsets. A = { YOUNG = {Very YOUNG, Not very YOUNG, More or less YOUNG, Not YOUNG, ...}, OLD = {Very OLD, Not very OLD, More or less OLD, Not OLD, ...}, ...}. Given that inside the set A = {0, 120}, a subset of values which can be considered internal to the vague concept of "young" for example {0, 35}, the employment of modifiers (Very ..., Not very ..., More or less ..., and so on) makes fuzzy the subset YOUNG. The membership function of the elements of A establish how much each element belongs to the fuzzy subset YOUNG. The membership function $\mu_{YOUNG}\ (a_n) = [x]$ of the element a_n establishes that the age a_n belongs to the fuzzy set YOUNG at the degree x, which is a real number of the interval [0, 1]. The interval [0, 1] is called "Evaluation set". Let's consider some examples. The membership degree of the age "20" to the fuzzy set YOUNG is 0.80. In symbols this is written as $\mu_{YOUNG}\ (20) = [0.80]$. The membership degree of the age "30" to the fuzzy set YOUNG is 0.50. In symbols this is $\mu_{YOUNG}\ (30) = [0.50]$. If we write the membership degree of each age of the fuzzy set YOUNG, we obtain a bend which gives an idea of the fuzzy membership of the elements to a fuzzy set. The Zadeh's modifiers of FL are arithmetical operators on the value of the membership function of the primary term. In this way it is possible to obtain secondary terms. If the primary term is "YOUNG", the secondary terms are "Very YOUNG ", "Not very YOUNG ", "More or less YOUNG", "Not YOUNG", and so on. For the application of the modifiers it is necessary to give an average value to the fuzzy set YOUNG. Let's suppose that the membership value of the average element of YOUNG is μ_{YOUNG}. The modifier "Not" defines the value "Not YOUNG" in this way:

$$\mu_{Not\ YOUNG} = 1 - \mu_{YOUNG}\ .$$

The modifier "Very" defines the value "Very YOUNG" in this way:

$$\mu_{\text{Very YOUNG}} = (\mu_{\text{YOUNG}})^2.$$

The modifier "More or less" defines the value "More or less YOUNG" in this way:

$$\mu_{\text{More or less YOUNG}} = (\mu_{\text{YOUNG}})^{1/2}.$$

The Zadeh's modifiers give a concrete idea of what is a fuzzy set, because they are the linguistic translation of the degree of membership of the elements. Their mathematical definition is necessary for their employment in the calculus.

In a calculus, it is possible to introduce a lot of different universes discourse: "age", "strength", "temperature", "tallness", and so on. A fuzzy system can treat vague sentences like "Maria is rich enough" or "The fever of Bill is very high", or more complicated sentences like "It is not very true that a high fever is dangerous for life". In this way it is possible to build a logical system, which can be employed to translate the vague sentences of natural language in a formal calculus, and it is possible to make formal demonstrations about a scientific phenomenon. It is clear that the fuzziness of the sentence can be transferred from the predicate to the truth value. The sentence "John is Not very YOUNG" is synonym of the sentence "It is not very true that John is YOUNG". Now it is clear how is possible to have, in a logical system, "linguistic" truth-values as fuzzy sets. These truth-values must be the subsets of a classical set: the set of truth-values of a simple many valued logic.

It is possible to obtain a great advantage employing Fuzzy Logic in the clinical diagnosis of a concrete clinical case, in those cases the linguistic variables are the so called "hedges", that is sets of values which are in correspondence to the numerical values of the universe of discourse. In the example of the "age", the set A = {0, 120} can be split into five subsets: A = {VERY YOUNG, YOUNG, ADULT, OLD, VERY OLD}. The 120 values of A are distributed in these five sets. VERY YOUNG= {0,18}, YOUNG = {19,35}, ADULT={36, 55}, OLD={56,75}, and VERY OLD = {76,120}. These five sets are fuzzy sets because we consider that each value belongs to a subset of a more or less, following a fuzzy membership function. We mean that, for example, the element "70" has a higher degree of membership than the element "60" to the set OLD, or that the element "2" has higher degrees of membership than the element "10" to the set VERY YOUNG with respect to Zadeh's FL, this is another way to create a correspondence between linguistic variables and fuzzy values. The unchanged matter is that, even if we work with vague predicates, this vagueness has however a precise reference to scalar values. Moreover, when the phenomenon we want to treat has no a scalar shape, we must give to this phenomenon a scalar shape following its intensity, to put this datum in a fuzzy inference. In clinical diagnosis when we put the "pain" or the "liver enlargement" in fuzzy inferences, we have to give to these factors a scalar shape, employing percent values. Thus we create a correspondence between "linguistic" and "numeric" intensities: a pain with value "20%" is "Light", a pain with value "50%" is "Mild"; a liver enlargement with value "15%" is "Little", and a liver enlargement with value "85%" is "Very big". Thus we obtain intensity values for the diseases found in the patient, for example we conclude "the patient suffers from a 'moderate-severe' Congestive Heart Failure (80%) and from a 'moderate' Congestive Hepatopathy (50%)". The great precision and richness of this new kind of diagnosis is the advantage of the use of Fuzzy Logic in clinical diagnosis. Anyway, it is important to notice here that the correspondence between linguistic and numerical values is what permits the processes of fuzzification and defuzzification. The fuzzification is the transformation of a numerical value in a linguistic value, the defuzzification is the reverse. It is clear that Zadeh's FL system does not need diagrams of correspondence or fuzzification- defuzzification process, because the linguistic variables (for predicates and for truth-values) represent fuzzy sets through the modifiers. However, also in FL system (as in all fuzzy systems), we find a precise correspondence between numerical and linguistic values. This happens because fuzzy sets can be theorized only as subsets of a classical set X and the possibility to use linguistic vague predicates is given by the reference to a great number, or an infinite number of values into the classical set X. Thus, the "formal" vagueness of Fuzzy Logic is only the result of a great numerical precision.

An "indicator function" or a "characteristic function" is a function defined on a set X that indicates the membership of an element x to a subset A of X. The indicator function is a function $\mu_A : X \rightarrow \{0, 1\}$. It is defined as $\mu_A(x) = 1$ if $x \in A$ and $\mu_A(x) = 0$ if $x \notin A$. In the classical set theory, the characteristic function of the elements of the subset A is assessed in binary terms according to a crisp condition: an element either belongs (1) or does not belong (0) to the subset. By contrast, fuzzy set theory permits a gradual membership of the elements of X (universe of discourse) to the subset B of X. Thus, with a generalization of the indicator function of classical sets, we obtain the membership function of a fuzzy set:

$$\mu_A : X \rightarrow [0, 1]$$

The membership function indicates the degree of membership of an element x to the fuzzy subset B, its value is from 0 to 1. Let's consider the braces as containing the elements 0 and 1, while the square parentheses as containing the finite/infinite interval from 0 to 1. The generalization of the indicator function corresponds to an extension of the valuation set of B: the elements of the valuation set of a classical subset A of X are 0 and 1, those of the valuation set of a fuzzy subset B of X are all the real numbers in the interval between 0 and 1. For an element x, the value $\mu_B(x)$ is called "membership degree of x to the fuzzy set B", which is a subset of X.

The universe X is never a fuzzy set, so we can write:

$$\forall x \in X, \mu_X(x) = 1$$

As the fuzzy set theory needs the classical set theory as its basis, in the same way, the fundament of the logic, also of polyvalent logic, is however the bivalence.

In conclusion, it seems that the dispute between bivalent and polyvalent logic proposed by Kosko is not a real opposition. The notion of vagueness, may insist polyvalence, but the Aristotelean bivalence is however fundamental in our knowledge. A lot of circumstances in our life require the bivalence. Often our decisions are choices between two alternatives and the alternative true/false is one of the most fundamental rules of our language (Wittgenstein, 1953). As Quine (1960) underlines, the learning of a foreign language has at its basis the "yes" and the "no", as answers to sentences. Kosko, instead, affirms that the advent of Fuzzy Logic is a real revolution in science and in philosophy, also from a metaphysical point of view. Kosko prefers the principle of "A $\wedge$ non A" to the principle "A $\vee$ non A". He believes that the world can be understood only if we forget the principle of non-contradiction, because always the objects of the world have in the same time opposite determinations. On the other hand, Zadeh does not think that Fuzzy Logic is so in contrast with classical logic. Zadeh and Bellman writes (1977: 109): *"Although fuzzy logic represents a significant departure from the conventional approaches to the formulization of human reasoning, it constitutes – so far at least – an extension rather than a total abandonment of the currently held views on meaning, truth and inference"*. Fuzzy logic is just an extension of standard Boolean logic: if we keep the fuzzy values at their extremes of 1 (completely true) and 0 (completely false), the laws of classical logic are valid.

3.7.6   QUANTUM MECHANICS AND MANY-VALUED LOGIC

The theorists of quantum mechanics treated the complexity of quantum interaction employing many-valued logics. The passage from classical particles to waves corresponds to the passage from two-valued logic to many-valued logics. It is very interesting, to recall the birth of quantum physics, that the employment of probabilistic logic marks this birth and that many-valued systems, and fuzzy logic are connected to quantum paradigm.

At the beginning of twentieth century, undulatory mechanics theorizes that the behavior of the smallest constituent of matter can be described through waves of frequency (v) and length (λ). In the hypothesis of undulatory mechanics, variables of corpuscular kind are connected to variables of undulatory kind.

The photon, the quantum of light, is connected to the electromagnetic wave with energy E and quantity of motion p, which are given by the equations E = hv and p = h/ λ. The fundamental hypothesis of undulatory mechanics is that each particle is connected to wave described by these equations. The law of propagation of these waves of "matter" was found by Schrödinger, who in analogy with classical mechanics formulated the right wave equation. The energy of a classic particle is a function of position and of velocity, thus the probability to find a particle of mass m in the position x at the instant t was expressed by the wave function $\varphi(x, t)$ which satisfies the Schrödinger's equation:

$$ih\frac{\partial \varphi}{\partial t} = -\frac{h^2}{2m}\frac{\partial^2 \varphi}{\partial x^2} + V(x)\varphi$$

where the field of forces around the particle derives from the potential $V(x)$ and h is a variant of the Plank's constant h, $h = h/2\pi$. This hypothesis mark the birth of quantum mechanics. Undulatory mechanics permits to calculate the energetic levels of atoms and the spectral terms. In this way, the old theory of quanta based on classical principles, unable to interpret the spectrum of black body, the photoelectric effect, and the atomic spectra was surpassed. Born gave to the wave function the following probabilistic interpretation, which was refused by Schrödinger. In a one-particle-system, with a wave function $\varphi(r, t)$ the probability to find a particle in the volume dv, centered around the point r_1, is:

$$\varphi^*(r_1, t)\, \varphi(r_1, t)\, dv$$

where φ^* is the conjugated complex of φ. In the same time Heisenberg theorized the mechanics of matrices, in which a dynamic variable is represented by a matrix Q. The equation of motion of mechanics of matrices is:

$$ih\frac{dQ}{dt} = Qh - HQ$$

Where H is the matrix obtained from the classic Hamiltonian function, through the substitution of classic dynamic variables with the correspondent Heisenberg's matrices. The second member QH-HQ is the commutator, and it is commonly written [QH]. Quantum mechanics derives from the acknowledgement of the equivalence between the undulatory mechanics and the mechanics of matrices. In quantum mechanics, the status of a physical system is represented by a vector of Hilbert's space. Dynamic variables are represented by linear operators in the Hilbert's space. The evolution of a physical system can be described in two ways. In the first way, proposed by Schrödinger, the operators are fixed, while the vector of status evolves in time following the equation:

$$ih\frac{\partial}{\partial t}\varphi = H\varphi$$

Where φ represents the vector of the status and H is the operator of energy. In the second way, proposed by Heisenberg, the vector of status is fixed while the operators evolve in time following the equation

$$ihQ' = [Q, H]$$

Where Q' is the derivate respect to time of the operator Q. Over these two ways, it is possible to give an intermediate representation of the evolution of a physical system in which both the vector of status and the operators evolve in time. It is a postulate of quantum mechanics that the operators of position and of impulse of a particle satisfy the relation of commutation.

$$[Q, P] = ith$$

Thus the position and the impulse cannot be measured simultaneously with arbitrary precision. This is the principle of indetermination enounced by Heisenberg. The measure of a dynamic variable Q gives a determined and exact result q only when the vector ψ, the vector of the status of the system, satisfies the equation Q $\psi = q\psi$. In this case ψ is an autostatus of Q, which corresponds to the auto-value q. If the system is not in an auto-status of the dynamic variable measured, it is impossible to predict the result of the measure, it is only possible to assign the probability to obtain a determinate value q. For this statistic character of quantum mechanics some physicists, like Einstein, believed that this theory is not complete. Kosko (1993: 67) writes that the operator ψ represents the matter's wave in an infinitesimally little volume dV, Born interpreted the square of the absolute value of the wave, $|\psi|^2$, as a measure of probability. Thus the infinitesimal quantity $|\psi|^2 \, dV$ measures the probability that a particle of matter is in the infinitesimally little region dV. This entails that all the infinitesimal particles are casual point. On the other hand, the fuzzy thinking considers $|\psi|^2 \, dV$ as the measure of how much the particle is in the region dV. According to this point of view, the particles are to some extent in all the regions of the space, hence the particles are deterministic clouds. Telling that the quantum particles, in fuzzy thinking, are "deterministic" clouds, Kosko means that it is precisely determinable the measure of the quantity of matter in the volume dV, as we see, fuzzy thinking is always connected to the precision. However, the adjective "deterministic" is too much employed to describe the old scientific paradigm, thus we prefer to say that, in this anti-probabilistic interpretation, quantum particles are fuzzy clouds.

In quantum physics, which study the subatomic particles, we find the unforeseeability and the uncertainty that, at the level of macroscopic chemistry and of macroscopic physics, is substituted by foreseeability and bivalence. In the classical physics of Galileo and Newton the phenomena were reduced to the properties of material and rigid bodies. From 1925, quantum mechanics showed that, at subatomic level, material bodies dissolve in undulatory schemas of probability. Subatomic particles are not understood as rigid but very little entities, they are instead relationships or interconnections between processes which can be only theoretically distinguished. The schemas of probability (or fuzziness) are not probabilities of material objects (electrons, quarks, neutrins, and so on.), but probabilities of interconnections between events. Capra (1996: 41) writes that *"when we move our attention from macroscopic objects to the atoms and to subatomic particles, nature does not show isolated bricks, but it appears as a complex weft of relations between parts of an unified everything"*. The father of the idea of vague (fuzzy) sets, M. Black, was an expertise of quantum mechanics. And the studies of Łukasiewicz on many-valued logic, from 1920, were soon connected with the development of quantum physics. In 1936 Birkhoff and von Neumann wrote a famous essay on the logic of quantum mechanics. The fact that the Schrödinger's wave function ψ was interpreted in a probabilistic way and the fact that the father of the idea of vague/fuzzy sets was an expertise of quantum mechanics are very important for two reasons, they show us that:

i) A many-valued logic system is much more adequate to quantum physics than classical logic and that

ii) A scientific theory becomes much clearer if we find an adequate logic system to explain the phenomena. Mathematic has been especially in the last four centuries, the language of science, if logics is another useful point of view to understand natural phenomena, then Fuzzy Logic is a very good instrument to build explanations, even it is not the solution of so many problems as Kosko believes.

3.7.7 PROBABILISTIC AND FUZZY LOGIC IN DISTINCT SIDES OF KNOWLEDGE

We think that the fuzzy interpretation, proposed by Kosko, of the wave-function $|\psi|^2$ in Scröndinger's equation is very interesting. Indeed it seems to me that Scröndinger's equation regards the quantity and the quantum distribution of matter and not the probability to find the particle in the region dV. However, in other fields of science it is not useful to try to reduce probabilistic logic to Fuzzy Logic or to treat the problems of probability with Fuzzy Logic. It is also wrong to reduce Fuzzy Logic to probabilistic logic. These two kinds of calculus have different fields of employment, different aims, and give different information about phenomena. Evidence is that probabilistic diagnosis and fuzzy diagnosis give different kinds of information about the health of the patient. In particular: probabilistic diagnosis drives in the choice of the possible diseases, which could cause the symptoms, while fuzzy diagnosis gives the exact quantification of the strength of diseases. They are both useful in the study and in the cure of pathology but they do different tasks (cf. Licata, 2007). It is usual in literature to distinguish probabilistic logic form fuzzy logic, telling that the first is a way to formalize the "uncertainty" while the second is a method to treat "vagueness". In technical sense, uncertainty is the incompleteness of information, while vagueness is the absence of precise confines in the reference of quantitative adjectives, common names, and so on to objects of world. Nevertheless, some researchers employed Fuzzy Logic to treat uncertainty (in the sense of incompleteness of information) and many theorists of probability think that probabilistic logic is a good way to treat vagueness. In general, it is clear that vagueness and uncertainty (in technical sense) can be theorized as two distinct areas of knowledge, studied by distinct methods. Given that uncertainty is understood as incompleteness of information, while vagueness regards an indefinite relationship between words and objects, it is possible to say that uncertainty and probabilistic logic fall in the area of "subjective knowledge", while vagueness and Fuzzy Logic fall in the area of "objective knowledge".

3.8 GENERATING LOGIC FOR FUZZY SET

The idea of fuzzy set is developed to appreciate the notion of vagueness in a manner which is completely different from the way classical mathematics does. Formally, each fuzzy set A is a fuzzy subset of a given universe of discourse U, characterized by its membership function $\mu_A: U \to [0, 1]$. The value $\mu_A(x)$ is the membership degree of x with respect to the fuzzy set A.

Zadeh introduces fuzzy sets in his seminal paper but he essentially does not relate it to non-classical logics. However, there is a minor exception in the meaning of the membership degrees. He mentions with respect to two thresholds $0 < \beta < \alpha < 1$, one may interpret the case $\mu_A(x) \geq \alpha$ as saying that x belongs to the fuzzy set A, the other may interpret $\mu_A(x) \leq \beta$ as saying that x does not belong to the fuzzy set A, and leaving the case $\beta < \mu_A(x) < \alpha$ is left as an indeterminate status for the membership of x in A.

Nevertheless, the overwhelming majority of fuzzy set papers that follow Zadeh 1965 and the other early Zadeh papers on fuzzy sets treat fuzzy sets in the standard mathematical context, that is with an implicit reference to a naively understood classical logic as argumentation structure.

Even Max Black 1937 and Carl Hemple at the time of discussing vague notions refer only to classical logic. They discuss the problem of some incompatibilities of the naively correct use of vague notions and principles of classical logic, for example, concerning the treatment of negation-like statements.

Zadeh not only proposes to define union $A \cup B$ and intersection $A \cap B$ of fuzzy sets A and B by the well known formulas:

$$\mu_{A \cup B}(x) = \max\{\mu_A(x), \mu_B(x)\}, \qquad (3.66)$$

$$\mu_{A \cap B}(x) = \min\{\mu_A(x), \mu_B(x)\}, \qquad (3.67)$$

but also introduces in [298] other operations for fuzzy sets, called an algebraic product AB and an algebraic sum $A + B$ defined via the equations:

$$\mu_{AB}(x) = \mu_A(x) \cdot \mu_B(x), \qquad (3.68)$$

$$\mu_{A+B}(x) = \min\{\mu_A(x) + \mu_B(x), 1\}. \qquad (3.69)$$

The core point here is that it is mathematically more or less obvious that these two additional operations are particular cases of further generalized intersection and union operations for fuzzy sets besides the "standard" versions [111–114].

3.8.1 EARLY APPROACH OF KLAUA INVOLVING NON-CLASSICAL LOGIC

As early as 1965, independent Zadeh's approach, the German mathematician Dieter Klaua presents two versions for a cumulative hierarchy of many-valued sets. In both cases he considers as membership degrees the real unit interval $W_\infty = [0,1]$ or a finite, m-element set $W_\infty = \{\frac{k}{m-1} | 0 \leq k < m\}$ of equidistant points of [0, 1]. He considers these membership degrees as the truth degrees of the corresponding Łukasiewicz systems L_∞ or L_m, respectively. Additionally, he starts these hierarchies with a given set U of urelements.

The first one of these hierarchies, presents in [134, 135] in 1965, offers an interesting simultaneous definition of a graded membership and a graded equlity predicate, but does not work well and is almost immediately abandoned. The main reason for this failure is that the class of objects that is intended to act as many-valued sets is not well chosen.

The second one of these hierarchies, presents in 1966 by Klaua, has as its objects A functions into the truth degree set $\mathcal{W}$, the values $A(x)$ being the membership degrees of the object x in the generalized set A.

The first level of this second hierarchy is formed just of all $\mathcal{W}$-valued fuzzy subsets of the set U. Thus, the set of elements in the second Klaua approach plays the role of the universe of discourse in the Zadeh approach. And each first-level many-valued set of this hierarchy is nothing but a particular fuzzy subset of U.

So it is reasonable to identify the many-valued sets of Klaua with the fuzzy sets of Zadeh.

Therefore the 1966 approach by Klaua offers immediately the Łukasiewicz systems of many-valued logic as the suitable logics to develop fuzzy set theory within their realm.

The majority of results are presented using the language of these Łukasiewicz systems by Klaua. Some examples are:

$$\vDash A \subseteq B \,\&\, B \subseteq C \to_L A \subseteq C,$$

$$\vDash a\varepsilon B \,\&\, B \subseteq C \to_L a\varepsilon C,$$

$$\vDash A \equiv B \,\&\, B \subseteq C \to_L A \subseteq C.$$

Here $\to_L$ si the Łukasiewicz implication, & the strong (or: arithmetical) conjunction with truth degree function $(u, v) \mapsto \max\{0, u + v - 1\}$, ε the graded membership predicate, and $\vDash \varphi$ means that the formula φ of the language of Łukasiewicz logic is logically valid, that is assumes always truth degree 1.

A graded inclusion relation $\subseteq$ is defined (for fuzzy sets of the same level in the hierarchy) as:

$$A \subseteq B =_{\text{def}} \forall x(x\varepsilon A \to_L x\varepsilon B), \tag{3.70}$$

and a graded equality $\equiv$ for fuzzy sets is defined as:

$$A \equiv B =_{\text{def}} A \subseteq B \wedge B \subseteq A. \tag{3.71}$$

This direction of development continues in the early 1970s by Gottwald. The topic is the formulation of (crisp) properties of fuzzy relations to consider graded properties of fuzzy relations, follow only in the 1991 by Gottwald. The topic of [115] is the formulation of generalized versions of the standard ZF axioms valid in a modified version of Klaua's second hierarchy of fuzzy sets.

3.8.2 RELATION BETWEEN NON-CLASSICAL LOGIC AND ZADEH'S APPROACH TO FUZZY LOGIC

Starting from Zadeh's approach to fuzzy logic Goguen introduces a close relationship between fuzzy logic and non-classical logic. In [107, 108] Goguen considers membership degrees as generalized truth values, that is as truth degrees. He establishes a "solution" of the sorites paradox, that is the heap paradox, using the ordinary product * in [0, 1] as a generalized conjunction operation. Based upon these ideas and finding some analogies with the intuitionistic logic, he proposes completely distributive lattice ordered monoids (closg) as suitable structures for the membership degrees of fuzzy sets. This structure is enriched with a (right) residuation operation $\rightarrow$ characterized by the well known adjointness condition:

$$a * b \leq c \leftrightarrow b \leq a \rightarrow c, \tag{3.72}$$

and with the "implies falsum" negation. He introduces the notion of tautology, with the neutral element of the monoid as the only designated truth degree. He defines a graded notion of inclusion which is same as equation (3.70) and which is equipped with the residual implication $\rightarrow$ instead of the implication $\rightarrow_L$ of the Łukasiewicz systems. But he does not mention any results for this graded implication.

Robin Giles also points out a strong relationship between fuzzy sets and many-valued logic. He proposes a general treatment of reasoning with vague predicates by means of a formal system based upon a convenient dialogue interpretation. This dialogue interpretation deals with subjective belief and the foundations of physics.

The main idea is stated as follows:

"a sentence represent a belief by expressing it tangibly in the form of a bet". In this setting then a "sentence ψ is considered to follow from sentences $\varphi_1, ..., \varphi_n$ just when he who accepts the bets $\varphi_1, ..., \varphi_n$ can at the same time bet ψ without fear of loss".

Thus we obtain a (formal) language, which is closely related to Łukasiewicz's infinite-valued logic L_∞. In fact the two systems coincide if we assign to a sentence φ the truth value $1 - \langle \varphi \rangle$, with $\langle \varphi \rangle$ for the risk value of asserting φ. He further adds, *"that, with this dialogue Łukasiewicz logic is exactly appropriate for the formulation of the 'fuzzy set theory' first described by L. A. Zadeh; indeed, it is not too much to claim that L_∞ is related to fuzzy set theory exactly as classical logic is related to ordinary set theory".*

Thus it is clear from the very beginning that from the mathematical point of view the set-algebraic operations for fuzzy sets can be reduced, in a many-valued setting, to generalized connectives in the same way as standard set-algebraic operations for classical sets can be reduced to connectives of classical logic.

Now the question is, if we consider the definitions (3.68) and (3.69), then what structural consequence would have for generalized intersections and unions. On the other hand, the "reverse" question is which structural conditions, besides (3.66) and (3.67), it can eliminate such generalizations. An answer to this "reverse" question is given by Bellman and Giertz 1973 and Gaines 1976. Some natural "boundary conditions" together with the inclusion maximality of the standard intersection with respect to each other generalized intersection, with the inclusion minimality of the standard union with respect to each other generalized union with commutativity and associativity and with the mutual distributivity of the generalized union and intersection force a restriction to the "standard" case (3.66) and (3.67).

The set of all above mentioned structural restrictions seems to be very restrictive. Hence it does not look very convincing. Therefore the restriction to the "standard" operations (3.66) and (3.67) is not appealing to the majority of the mathematically oriented people of the fuzzy community.

To find out the suitable choices of such "fuzzy" connectives which might be used to define unions and intersections for fuzzy sets different from (3.66) and (3.67) people look at the types of restrictive conditions discussed by Bellman and Giertz in 1973 as functional equations or functional inequalities, to reduce this set of functional conditions, to look also at other conditions, and to discuss the solutions of suitable sets of such functional conditions. In [278] Alsina et al., a focus is given on pairs of generalized conjunctions and disjunctions. Other attempts with emphasis on generalized implication operations are given in [275].

3.8.3 BASIC INFINITE VALUED LOGICS

If we look for infinite valued logics of the kind which is needed as the underlying logic for a theory of fuzzy sets, we find three main systems.

These are:

- The Łukasiewicz logic L,
- The Gödel logic G, and
- The product logic II.

These logics look rather different, regarding their propositional parts. For the first order extensions, however, there is a unique strategy, we add a universal and an existential quantifier such that quantified formulas get, respectively, as their thruth degrees the infimum and the supremum of all the particular cases in the range of the quantifiers.

GÖDEL LOGIC

The simplest one of these logics is the Gödel logic G which has a conjuction $\wedge$ and a disjunction $\vee$ defined by the minimum and the maximum, respectively, of the truth degrees of the constituents:

$$u \wedge v = \min\{u, v\}, \qquad u \vee v = \max\{u, v\},. \qquad (3.73)$$

We denote here and later on the connectives and the corresponding truth degree functions by the same symbol.

The Gödel Logic has also a negation ~ and an implication $\rightarrow_G$ defined by the truth degree functions:

$$\sim u = \begin{cases} 1, if\ u = 0; \\ 0, if\ u > 0. \end{cases} \text{and } u \rightarrow_G v = \begin{cases} 1, if\ u \leq v; \\ v, if\ u > v. \end{cases} \quad (3.74)$$

ŁUKASIEWICZ LOGIC

The Łukasiewicz logic L is originally designed with only two primitive connectives, an implication $\rightarrow_L$ and a negation ~ characterized by the truth degree functions:

$$\sim u = 1 - u, \qquad u \rightarrow_L v = \min\{1, 1 - u + v\}. \quad (3.75)$$

It is possible to define further connectives from these primitive ones. With

$$\varphi \,\&\, \varphi =_{df} \sim(\varphi \rightarrow_L \sim\varphi), \qquad \varphi \veebar \psi =_{df} \sim\varphi \rightarrow_L \psi \quad (3.76)$$

we get a (strong) conjunction and a (strong) disjunction with the truth degree functions:

$$u \,\&\, v = \max\{u + v - 1, 0\}, \qquad u \veebar v = \min\{u + v, 1\}. \quad (3.77)$$

which are called the Łukasiewicz (arthmetical) conjunction and the Łukasiewicz (arthmetical) disjunction. Note that these connectives are linked together via a De Morgan law using the standard negation of the system.

$$\sim(u \,\&\, v) = \sim u \veebar \sim v \quad (3.78)$$

From the additional definitions:

$$\varphi \wedge \psi =_{df} \varphi \,\&\, (\varphi -_L \psi) \qquad \varphi \vee \psi =_{df} (\varphi \rightarrow_L \psi) \rightarrow_L \psi \quad (3.79)$$

we get another (weak) conjunction ∧ with truth degree function min, and a further (weak) disjunction ∨ with max as truth degree function, that is we have the conjunction and the disjunction of the Gödel logic.

PRODUCT LOGIC

The product logic Π has a fundamental conjunction $\odot$ with the oridinary product of reals as its truth degree function, as well as an implication $\sim_\pi$ with truth degree function.

$$u \rightarrow_\Pi v = \begin{cases} 1, \text{if } u \leq v \\ \frac{u}{v}, \text{if } u < v \end{cases} \qquad (3.80)$$

It has a truth degree constant $\overline{0}$ to denote the truth degree zero. In this conext, a negation and a further conjunction are defined as:

$$\sim \varphi =_{df} \varphi \rightarrow_\Pi \overline{0}, \qquad \varphi \wedge \psi =_{df} \varphi \odot (\varphi \rightarrow_\Pi \psi). \qquad (3.81)$$

Routine calculation show that both connectives coincide with the corresponding ones of the Gödel logic. The disjunction $\vee$ of the Gödel logic is also available, via the definition.

$$\varphi \wedge \psi =_{df} \varphi \& (\varphi \sim_L \psi) \qquad \varphi \vee \psi =_{df} \varphi \& (\varphi \rightarrow_L \psi) \rightarrow_L \psi. \qquad (3.82)$$

3.8.4   STANDARD AND ALGEBRAIC SEMANTICS

These fundamental infinite valued logics have their standard semantics as explained: the real unit interval [0,1] as truth degree set, and the connectives (and quantifiers) as mentioned.

As known from classical logic, we can introduce for each formula φ the notion of its validity in a model, which in these logics means that φ has the truth degree 1 with respect to this model. By a model we mean either – in the propositional case – an evaluation of the propositional variables by truth degrees, or in the first-order case, a suitable interpretation of all the non-logical constants together with an assignment of the variables.

Based upon this, we define logical validity of a formula φ in each model, and the entailment relation holds between a set Σ of forumulas and a formula φ if each model Σ is also a model of φ. Thus, all the three systems G, L, II have the truth degree one as their only designated truth degree. All three basic infinite valaued logics have algebraic semantics determined by suitable classes $\mathcal{K}$ of truth degree structures. This is similar to the case of classical logic where logically valid formulas in classical logic are just those formulas which are valid in all Boolean algebras.

These strucutres have the same signature as the language $\mathcal{L}$ of the corresponding logic. This means that these structures provide for each connective of the language $\mathcal{L}$, an operation of the same arity and they have suprema and infima for all those subsets which may appear as value sets of formulas. Hence, they have to be (partially) ordered, or at least preordered.

For each formula φ of the language $\mathcal{L}$ of the corresponding logic, for each such structure A, and for each evaluation e which maps the set of propositional variables of

$\mathcal{L}$ into the carrier of A, we have to define a value $e(\varphi)$ and finally we have to define what it means that such a formula φ is *valied in* A. Then a formula φ is logically valid with respect to the class $\mathcal{K}$ if φ is valid in all structures from $\mathcal{K}$.

The standard way to arrive at such classes of structures is to start from the Lindenbaum algebra of the corresponding logic, that is its algebra of formulas modulo the congruence relation of logical equvalence. For this Lindenbaum algebra, we have to determine a class of similar algebraic structures which forms a variety.

For the Gödel logic such a class of structures is the class of all Heyting algebras, that is of all relatively pseudo-complemented lattices, which satisfy the prelinearlity condition.

$$(u \rightarrowtail \vartheta) \sqcup (\vartheta \rightarrowtail u) = 1. \tag{3.83}$$

where $\sqcup$ is the lattice join and $\rightarrowtail$ the relative pseudo-complement.

For the Łukasiewicz logic, the corresponding class of structures is the class of all MV-algebras. For the product logic the class of structure is the class of lattice ordered semigroups which is called product algebras. All these structures viz. Heyting algebras, MV-algebras, and product algebras are abelian lattice ordered semigroups with an additional "residuation" operation.

3.8.5 INVOKING T-NORMS

In early 1980s, the mathematical fuzzy community considers t-norms as suitable candidates for connectives upon which generalized intersection operations for fuzzy sets should be based. These t-norms, shorthand for "triangular norms", become important in discussions of the triangle inequality within probabilistic metric spaces. They are binary operations in the real unit interval, which make this interval into an ordered abelian monoid with 1 as unit element of the monoid.

In the present context the basic examples of t-norms are the Łukasiewicz t-norm T_L, the Gödel t-norm T_G, and the product t-norm T_P defined by the equations:

$$T_L(u, v) = \max\{u + v - 1, 0\},$$

$$T_G(u, v) = \min\{u, v\}, \text{ and}$$

$$T_P(u, v) = u \cdot v.$$

The general understanding in the context of fuzzy connectives is that t-norms form a suitable class of generalized conjunction operators.

From logic point of view, the class of left-continuous t-norms is of particular interest. The left-continuity for a t-norm $T: [0, 1]^2 \rightarrow [0, 1]$ means that for each $a \in [0, 1]$ the unary function $T_a(x) = T(a, x)$ is left-continuous. The main idea of left-continuous t-norms is the fact that just for left-continuous t-norms $*$ a suitable implication function, usually called R-implication, is uniquely determined via the adjointness condition (3.72). Suitability of an implication function means that it allows for a corresponding sound detachment, or modus ponens rule: if one infers a formula ψ from formulas $\varphi \rightarrow \psi$ and φ then the logical validity.

$$\vDash \varphi \& (\varphi \rightarrow \psi) \psi \tag{3.84}$$

yields the inequality $[\![\varphi]\!][\![\varphi \rightarrow \psi]\!] \leq [\![\psi]\!]$ for the truth degrees.

A propositional language with connectives $\wedge$, $\vee$ for the truth degree functions min, max, and with connectives $\&$, $\rightarrow$ for a left-continuous t-norm T and its residuation operation offers a suitable framework for fuzzy set theory as long as the complementation of fuzzy sets remains out of scope. With this limitation, that is disregarding complementation, this framework offers a suitable extension of Zadeh's standard set-algebraic operations. Additionally, this framework, with the "implies falsum" construction, yields a natural way to define a negation, that is to introduce a t-norm related complementation operation for fuzzy sets, via the definition $-T \; \varphi =_{\text{def}} \varphi \rightarrow \bar{0}$ using a truth degree constant $\bar{0}$ for the truth degree 0. This particular complementation operation does not always become the standard complementation of Zadeh's approach.

The t-norm based construction gives the infinite-valued Łukasiewicz system L_∞ provided we consider the t-norm T_L, and the right negation for Zadeh's complementation. This construction gives the infinite-valued Gödel system G_∞ if we start with the t-norm T_G, and it gives the product logic if we start with the t-norm T_Π The "implies falsum" negations of the latter two systems coincide, but are different from the negation operation of the Łukasiewicz system L_∞. So these two cases do not offer Zadeh's complementation. But this can be achieved if we add the Łukasiewicz negation to these systems.

It is essentially a routine job to generate this type of t-norm based logic to some suitable extent. Also the development of fuzzy set theory on this basis does not offer problems, including essential parts of fuzzy set algebra, some fuzzy relation theory up to a fuzzified version of the Szpilrajn order extension theorem and some solvability considerations for systems of fuzzy relation equations.

There is another way to develop t-norm based logics for fuzzy set theory. It avoids the introduction of the R-implications via the residuation operation and so it does not depend on the restriction of left-continuous t-norms. Instead it uses additionally negation functions, that is unary functions $N : [0,1] \rightarrow [0,1]$ which are at least order reversing and satisfy $N(0) = 1$ as well as $N(1) = 0$. The strategy to introduce an implication function $I_{T,N}$ in this setting is to define

$$I_{T,N}(u, v) = N\Big(T\big(u, N(v)\big)\Big). \tag{3.85}$$

The implication connectives defined in this way usually are called S-implications.

But the fact that S-implications do not necessarily satisfy (3.84) means that the corresponding rule of detachment is not always correct. And this seems to be the main reason that this type of approach is not popular among logicians interested in fuzzy set matters.

3.8.6 LOGICS WITH T-NORM BASED CONNECTIVES

The basic infinite valued logics as stated earlier in section 3.8.3 look quite different if we consider the form in which they are initially presented. However, there is a common generalization which allow us to present all these three logics in a uniform way. In this uniform presentation one of the conjunction connectives becomes a core role: $\wedge$ in the system G, & in the system L, and $\odot$ in the system II.

This uniform generalization covers a much larger class of infinite valued logics over [0,1]: the core conjunction connective, which is denoted &- has a truth degree function $\otimes$, which should be an associative, commutative, and isotonic operation which has 1 as neutral element, that is should satisfy for arbitrary $x, y, z, \in [0,1]$:

$$(T1)\ x \otimes (y \otimes z) = (x \otimes y) \otimes z,$$

$$(T_2)\ x \otimes y = y \otimes x,$$
$$(T_3)\ x \otimes y = y \otimes x \text{ then } x \otimes z \le y \otimes z,$$
$$(T_4)\ x \otimes 1 = x.$$

Such binary operations known as t-norms are used in the context of probablistic metric spaces. At the same time they are considered as natural candidates for truth degree functions of conjunction connectives. From such a t-norm, we are able to derive all the other truth degree functions for further connectives.

The minimum operation $u \wedge v$ from (3.37), the Łukasiewicz arithmetic conjunction $u \& v$ from (3.77) and the ordinary product are the best known examples of t-norms.

In algebraic terms, such a t-norm $\otimes$ makes the real units interval into an ordered monoid, that is into an abelian semigroup with unit element. And this ordered monoid is even integral, that is its unit element is at the same time the universal upper bound of the ordering.

Additionally this monoid has because of:

$$0 \otimes x \le 0 \otimes 1 = 0 \tag{3.86}$$

the number 0 as an annihilator.

From a t-norm $\otimes$ we find a truth degree function $\rightarrowtail$ for an implication connective via the adjointness condition:

$$x \otimes z \le y \longleftrightarrow z \le (x \rightarrowtail y). \tag{3.87}$$

To guarantee that this ajointness condition (3.87), determines the operation $\rightarrowtail$ uniquely, we suppose that the t-norm $\otimes$ is a leftcontinuous function in both arguments. Indeed, the adjointness condition (3.87) is equivalent to the condition that $\otimes$ is left continuous in both arguments.

Instead of this adjointness condition (3.87), we can equivalently either give the direct definition:

$$x \rightarrowtail y = sup\{z | x \otimes z \le y\} \tag{3.88}$$

of the residuation operation $\rightarrowtail$, or we can force the t-norm $\otimes$ to have the sup-preservation property

$$\sup_{i \to \infty} (x_i \otimes y) = \left(\sup_{i \to \infty} x_i \right) \otimes y \tag{3.89}$$

for each $y \in [0, 1]$ and each non-decreasing sequence $(x_i)_{i \to \infty}$ from the real unit interval.

In this framework, we additionally introduce a further unary operation:

$$-x =_{df} x \to 0, \tag{3.90}$$

and considers this as the truth degree function of a negation connective.

Finally, we like to have weak conjunction and disjunction connectives $\wedge, \vee$ available. These connectives are added to the vocabulary. However, it suffices to add only the min conjunction $\wedge$, because then for each left continuous t-norm $\otimes$ and its residuated implication $\rightarrowtail$ we have, completely similar situation (3.82) in the product logic:

$$u \vee v = ((u \rightarrowtail \vartheta) \rightarrowtail \vartheta) \wedge ((\vartheta \rightarrowtail u) \rightarrowtail u). \tag{3.91}$$

All these consideratios lead in a natural way to algebraic structures which, starting from the unit interval, consider a left continuous t-norm $\otimes$ together with its residuation operation $\rightarrowtail$, with the minimum-operation $\wedge$, and the maximum operation $\vee$ as basic operations of such an algebraic structure, and with the particular truth degrees 0,1 as fixed objects (that is as nullary operations) of the structure.

Such an algebraic structure:

$$\langle [0,1], \wedge \vee \otimes, \rightarrowtail, 0.1 \rangle \tag{3.92}$$

is coined as a t-norm algebra.

3.8.7   RESIDUATED IMPLICATIONS VERSUS S-IMPLICATIONS

With the basic properties of classical logic in mind, particularly because of the logical equivalence of the formulas:

$$\varphi \rightarrow \psi \text{ and } \sim \varphi \vee \Psi \text{ and } \sim \varphi \wedge \sim \Psi \qquad (3.93)$$

In classical logic, the introduction of the implication concective directly as residuation via (3.88) or via the adjointness condition (3.87) seems to be quite sophisticated, and perhaps unnecessarily complicated.

If we consider an arrow-free approach similar to (3.93) for the present case, we should consider a definition of an implication connective either with a generalized disjunction or with a generalized conjunction and have to add a generalized negation.

In this case the implication, defined according to one of the equivalences in (3.93), is often coined "S-implication".

But this approach does not really become simpler as the former one because we need to fix either an additional negation, or we have to fix a negation together with a disjunction.

The main disadvantage of such a modification is that we loose a quite natural strong soundness property for the rule of detachment in the former t-norm based approach.

From the adjointness condition (3.87) we always have:

$$u \otimes (u \rightarrowtail \vartheta) \leq \vartheta \qquad (3.94)$$

because of

$$u \otimes (u \rightarrowtail \vartheta) \leq \vartheta \text{ if } (u \rightarrowtail \vartheta) \otimes u \leq \vartheta \text{ if } u \rightarrowtail v \leq u \rightarrowtail v.$$

Therefore we have in the t-norm based approach with implication defined as residuation, a natural lower bound for the truth degree of a formula ψ which is derived from $\varphi \rightarrow \psi$ and φ via the rule of detachment: the truth degree of the formula $\varphi \& (\varphi \rightarrow \psi)$.

A similar property is lacking in general for the approach via S-implications. In this case, say starting from a t-norm $\otimes$ and a negation $\sim$, the corresponding property (3.94) becomes:

$$u \otimes \sim (u \otimes \sim v) \leq v. \qquad (3.95)$$

But this fails already in the case that, independent of the choice of the t-norm $\otimes$, the negation $\sim$ is the Gödel negation $\sim$ of (3.74), that is the common negation of the systems G and II. For this negation and any $v > 0$ one has $\sim v = 0$, hence $u \otimes \sim v =$

0, which means $\sim (u\otimes \sim v)=1$ and $u\otimes \sim (u\otimes \sim v)= u$. Now we may choose $u > v$ to see that (3.95) fails.

3.8.8 CONTINUOUS T-NORMS

Among the large class of all t-norms the continuous ones are the best understood. A t-norm is continuous if it is continuous as a real function of two variables or equivalently, if it is continuous in each argument [111–114].

All continuous t-norms are ordinal sums of the Łukasiewicz arthmetic t-norm u & v from (3.77), the ordinary product t- norm, and the minimum operation $u \wedge v$. The definition of an ordinal sum of t-norms is the following one.

Definition 3.46 Suppose that $\left([a_i,b_i]\right)_{i\in I}$ is a countable family of non-overlapping proper subintervals of the unit interval [0,1], let $(t_i)_{i\in I}$ be a family of t-norms, and let $(\varphi_i)_{i\in I}$ be a family of mappings such that each φ_i is an order isomorphism from $[a_i,b_i]$ onto [0,1]. Then the (generalized) ordinal sum of the combined family $\left(([a_i,b_i],t_i,\varphi_i)\right)_{i\in I}$ is the binary function $T:[0,1]^2 \rightarrow [0,1]$ characterized by:

$$T(u,v)= \begin{cases} \varphi_k^{-1}\left(t_k\left(\varphi_k(u),\varphi_k(v)\right)\right), & if\ u,\ v\in [a_k b_k] \\ \min\ \{u,\ v\} & otherwise \end{cases} \qquad (3.96)$$

We depict the construction of an ordinal sum in Figure 20 .

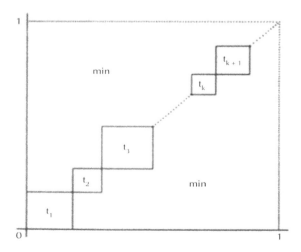

FIGURE 20   The basic construction of an ordinal sum.

An order isomorphic copy of the minimum t-norm is again the minimum operation. Thus the whole construction of ordinal sums of t-norms allows to assume that the summands are formed from t-norms different from the minimum t-norm.

Note that all endpoints a_i, b_i of the interval family $([a_i, b_i])_{i \in I}$ give idempotents of the resulting ordinal sum t-norm T:

$$T(a_i a_i) = a_i, \qquad T(b_i b_i) = b_i \quad \text{for all } i \in I$$

Conversely, if we know all the idempotents of a given continuous t-norm t, that is all $u \in [0,1]$ with $t(u,u) = u$, then we are able to give a representaiton of t as an ordinal sum.

Now we state the following result:

Theorem 3.4 Each continuous t-norm t is the (genralized) ordinal sum of (isomorphic) copies of the Łukasiewicz t-norm, the product t-norm, and the minimum t-norm.

There should be a natural way to get an algebraic semantics for these considerations. The class of all t-norm algebras with a continuous t-norm should eihter form such an algebraic semantics, or should be a constitutive part of a variety of algebraic sturctures which form such an algebraic semantics. However, there is an inadequacy in the description of this algebraic semantics. On the one hand the notion of t-norm algebra is a purely algebraic notion, the notion of continuity of a t-norm on the other hand is an analytical one. Fortunately, there is a possibility of an algebraic characterization for the continuity of t-norms as stated below.

Definition 3.47 A t-norm algebra $\langle [0,1], \wedge, \vee, \otimes, \rightarrowtail, 0, 1 \rangle$ is divisible if one has for all $a, b \in L$:

$$a \wedge b = a \otimes (a \rightarrowtail b). \tag{3.97}$$

Proposition 3.33 A t-norm algebra $\langle [0,1], \wedge, \vee, \otimes, \rightarrowtail, 0, 1 \rangle$ is divisible if the t-norm $\otimes$ is continuous.

3.8.9   THE LOGIC OF CONTINUOUS T-NORMS

The class of t-norm algebras (with a continuous t-norm or not) is not a variety. It is not closed under direct products becuase each t-norm algebra is linearly ordered, but the direct products of linearly ordered structures are not linearly orderd, in general. Hence we may expect that it would be helpful for the development of a logic of continuous t-norms to extend the class of all divisible t-norm algebras in a moderate way to get a variety.

The main point we consider instead of the divisible t-norm algebras, which are linearly ordered integral monoids as mentioned previously, now latice ordered integral monoids which are divisible, which have an additional residuation operation connected with the semigroup operation via an adjointness condition like (3.87) and which satisfy a prelinearity condition like (3.83). These structures are called BL-algebras.

Definition 3.48 A BL-algebra is an algebraic structure

$$L = \langle L, V, \wedge, *, \rightarrowtail, 0.1 \rangle \tag{3.98}$$

With four binary operations and two constants such that:

$(L, \vee, \wedge, 0, 1)$ is a bounded lattice 4, that is has 0 and 1 as the universal lower and upper bounds w.r.t. the lattice order $\leq$,

$(L *, 1)$ is an abelian monoid, that is a commutative semigroup with unit 1 such tha the multiplication $*$ is associative, commutative and satisfies $1 * x$ for all $x \in L$,

The binary operations $*$ and $\rightarrow$ form an adjoint pair, that is satisfy for all $x, y, z \in L$ the adjointness condition

$$z \leq (x \rightarrow y) \quad iff \quad x * z \leq y, \tag{3.99}$$

and moreover, for all $x, y \in L$ one has satisfied the pre-linearity condition

$$(x \rightarrow y) \vee (y \rightarrow x) = 1 \tag{3.100}$$

as well as the divisibility condition

$$x * (x \rightarrow y) = x \wedge y. \tag{3.101}$$

The axiomatization of Hajek for the basic t-norm logic BL, that is for the class of all well-formed formulas which are valid in all BL- algebras, is given in a language $\mathcal{L}_T$, which has as basic vocabulary the connective $\rightarrow$, $\&$, and the truth degree constant $\overline{0}$, taken in each BL-algebra $\langle L, \cap, U, *, \rightarrowtail, 0, 1 \rangle$ as the operations $\rightarrowtail, *,$ and the element 0.

Then this t-norm based logic has as axiom system $\mathrm{Ax_{BL}}$ the following schemata:

$\mathrm{Ax_{BL}} 1 \qquad (\varphi \rightarrow \psi) \rightarrow ((\psi \rightarrow \chi) \rightarrow (\varphi \rightarrow \chi)),$

$\mathrm{Ax_{BL}} 2 \qquad \varphi \& \psi \rightarrow \varphi,$

$\mathrm{Ax_{BL}} 3 \qquad \varphi \& \psi \rightarrow \psi \& \varphi,$

$$\text{Ax}_{\text{BL}}\,4 \qquad (\varphi \to (\psi \to \chi)) \to (\varphi \& \psi \to \chi),$$

$$\text{Ax}_{\text{BL}}\,5 \qquad (\varphi \& \psi \to \chi) \to (\varphi \to (\psi \to \chi)),$$

$$\text{Ax}_{\text{BL}}\,6 \qquad \varphi \& (\varphi \to \psi) \to \psi \& (\psi \to \varphi),$$

$$\text{Ax}_{\text{BL}}\,7 \qquad ((\varphi \to \psi) \to \chi) \to (((\psi \to \varphi) \to \chi) \to \chi),$$

$$\text{Ax}_{\text{BL}}\,8 \qquad \overline{0} \to \varphi,$$

and has as its (only) inference rule the rule of detachment, or: modus ponens (with respect to the implication connective $\to$).

The logical calculus which is constituted by this axiom system and its inference rule, and which has the standard notion of derivation, shall be denoted by K_{BL} or just by BL.

Starting from the primitive connectives $\to, \&$, and the truth degree constant $\overline{0}$, the language $\mathcal{L}_T$ of BL is extended by definitions of additional connectives $\wedge, \vee, \neg$:

$$\varphi \wedge \psi =_{df} \varphi \& (\varphi \to \psi) \qquad\qquad (3.102)$$

$$\varphi \vee \psi =_{df} ((\varphi \to \psi) \to \psi) \wedge ((\psi \to \varphi) \to \varphi) \qquad\qquad (3.103)$$

$$\neg \varphi =_{df} \varphi \to \overline{0}, \qquad\qquad (3.104)$$

where φ, ψ are formulas of the language of that system.

Calculations (in BL-algebras) show that the additional connectives $\wedge, \vee$ just have the lattice operations, $\cap, \cup$ as their truth degree functions.

We can check that this logical calculus K_{BL}, usually called the axiomate system BL, is sound, that is derives only such formulas which are valid in all BL-algebras.

Corollary 3.1 The Lindenbaum algebra of the axiomatic system BL is a BL-algebra.

Theorem 3.5 [111] (General Completenss) A formula φ of the language $\mathcal{L}_T$ is derivable within the axiomatic system BL if φ is valid in all BL-algebras.

Corollary 3.2 (General Completeness; Version 2) A formula φ of $\mathcal{L}_T$ is derivable within the axiomatic system BL if φ is valid in all BL-chains.

But even more is provable and leads back to the starting point of the whole approach: the logical calculus K_{BL} characterizes just those formulas which hold true with respect to all divisible t-norm algebras.

Theorem 3.6 [111] (Standard Completeness) The class of all formula which are provable in the system BL coincides with the class of all formulas which are logically valid in all t-norm algebras with a continuous t-norm.

Another generalization of Theorem 3.5 deserves to be mentioned. Let us *call schematic extension* of BL. Let us denote such an extension by $\text{BL}(C)$. And call $\text{BL}(C)$ - algebra each BL-algebra A which makes A- valid all formulas of C.

We state even more general completeness result.

Theorem 3.7 [111] (Extended General Completeness) For each finite set C of axiom schemata and any formula φ of $\mathcal{L}_T$ there are equivalent:

φ is derivable within BL(C);

φ is valid in all BL(C)-algebras;

φ is valid in all BL(C) – chains.

The algebraic machinery allows even deeper insights. After some particular result, the study of such sub varieties of the variety of all BL-algebras which are generated by single t-norm algebras $\langle [0,1], \wedge, \vee, \otimes, \mapsto, 0, 1 \rangle$ with a continuous t-norm $\otimes$ led to (finite) axiomatizations of those t-norm based logics which have a standard semantics determined just by this continuous t-norm algebra.

3.8.10   THE LOGIC OF LEFT CONTINUOUS T-NORMS [111]

We can arrive at the logic of left continuous t-norms if we start from the logic of continuous t-norms and delete the continuity condition, that is the divisibility condition (3.97).

The algebraic approach needs only a small modification in Definition 3.44 of BL-algebras by deleting the divisibility condition (3.10.1). The resulting algebraic structures are called MTL-algebras. They again form a variety.

Following this idea, we modify the previous axiom system in a suitable way. We have to delete the expression (3.10.2) of the connective $\wedge$, because this expression (together with suitable axioms) essentially codes the divisibility condition. The expression (3.10.3) of the connective $\vee$ remains unchanged.

Thus we consider a new system MTL of mathematical fuzzy logic, characterized semantically by the class of all MTL-algebras.

It is connected with the axiom system:

$(\text{Ax}_{\text{MTL}}\ 1)$ $(\varphi \to \psi) \to ((\psi \to \chi) \to (\varphi \to \chi)),$

$(\text{Ax}_{\text{MTL}}\ 2)$ $\varphi\ \&\ \psi \to \varphi,$

$(\text{Ax}_{\text{MTL}}\ 3)$ $\varphi\ \&\ \psi \to \psi\ \&\ \varphi,$

$(\text{Ax}_{\text{MTL}}\ 4)$ $(\varphi \to (\psi \to \chi)) \to (\varphi\ \&\ \psi \to \chi),$

$(\text{Ax}_{\text{MTL}}\ 5)$ $(\varphi\ \&\ \psi \to \chi) \to (\varphi \to (\psi \to \chi)),$

$(\text{Ax}_{\text{MTL}}\ 6)$ $\varphi \wedge \psi \to \varphi,$

$(\text{Ax}_{\text{MTL}}\ 7)$ $\varphi \wedge \psi \to \psi \wedge \varphi,$

$(\text{Ax}_{\text{MTL}}\ 8)$ $\varphi\ \&\ (\varphi \to \psi) \to \varphi \wedge \psi,$

$(\text{Ax}_{\text{MTL}}\ 9)$ $\overline{0} \to \varphi,$

$(\text{Ax}_{\text{MTL}}\ 10)$ $((\varphi \to \psi) \to \chi) \to (((\psi \to \varphi) \to \chi) \to \chi),$

together with the rule of detachment (with respect to the implication connective $\to$) as (the only) inference rule.

We can verify that this logical calculus K_{MTL} is sound, that is derives only such formulas which are valid in all MTL-algebras.

Corollary 3.3 The Lindenbaum algebra of the logical calculus K_{MTL} is an MTL-algebra.

Proofs of this result and also of the following completeness theorem are given in [111].

Theorem 3.8 [111] (*General Completeness*) A formula φ of the language $\mathcal{L}_T$ is derivable within the logical calculus K_{MTL} if φ is valid in all MTL-algebras.

Again the proof method yields hat each MTL-algebra is (isomorphic to) a subdirect product of linearly ordered MTL-algebras, that is of MTL-chains.

Corollary 3.4 [111] (General Completeness, Version 2) A formula φ of $\mathcal{L}_T$ is derivable within the axiomatic system MTL if φ is valid in all MTL-chains.

And again, similar as for the BL-case, even more is provable: the logical calculus K_{MTL} characterizes just these formulas which hold true with respect to all t-norm based logics, which are determined by a left continuous t-norm.

Theorem 3.9 [111] (Standard Completeness) The class of all formulas which are provable in the logical calculus K_{MTL} coincides with the class of all formulas which are logically valid in all-t-norm algebras with a left continuous t-norm.

This result again means, as the similar one for the logic of continuous t-norms, that the variety of all MTS-algebras is the smallest variety which contains all t-norm algebras with a left continuous t-norm.

Because of the fact that the BL-algebras are the divisible MTL-algebras, we get another adequate axiomatization of the basic t-norm logic BL if one extends the axiom system K_{MTL} with additional axiom schema.

$$\varphi \wedge \psi \to \varphi \& (\varphi \to \psi). \qquad (3.105)$$

To prove that this implication is sufficient, is to show that the inequality $x * (x \to y) \le x \cap y$, which corresponds to the converse implication, holds true in each MTL-algebra. Similar remarks apply to further extensions of MTL we are going to mention.

Also for MTL an extended completeness theorem similar to Theorem 3.7 remains true.

Theorem 3.10 [111] (Extended General Completeness) For each finite set C of axiom schemata and formula φ of $\mathcal{L}_T$ the following are equivalent:

φ is derivable within the logical calculus $K_{MTL} + C$,

φ is valid in all MTL(C) – algebras, and

φ is valid in all MTL(C) – chains.

SOME GENERALIZATIONS

The standard approach toward t-norm based logics, as explained earlier, has been modified in various ways. The main ideas are the extension or the modification of the expressive power of these logical systems.

An addition to the standard vocabulary of the languages of t-norm based systems is as follows:

a unary propositional operator Δ which has for t-norm algebras the semantics

$$\Delta(x) = 1 \text{ for } x = 1, \ \Delta(x) = 0 \text{ for } x \ne 1. \qquad (3.106)$$

This unary connective can be added to the systems BL and MTL via the additional axioms:

$(\Delta 1)$ $\Delta\varphi \vee \neg\Delta\varphi,$

$(\Delta 2)$ $\Delta(\varphi \vee \varphi) \to (\Delta\varphi \vee \Delta\psi),$

$(\Delta 3)$ $\Delta\varphi \to \varphi,$

$(\Delta 4)$ $\Delta\varphi \to \Delta\ \varphi,$ and

$(\Delta 5)$ $\Delta(\varphi \to \psi) \to (\Delta\varphi \to \Delta\varphi).$

This addition leaves all the essential theoretical results, like correctness and completeness theorems, valid with respect to suitably expanded algebraic structures.

Hajek gives a common generalization of all these generalized fuzzy logics, thus giving up divisibility, the falsity constant, and commutativity. The corresponding algebras are called *fleas* (or flea algebras), are the logic is the flea logic FIL. There are examples of fleas on (0,1] not satisfying divisibility, nor commutativity, and having no least element.

LOGIC WITH PAVELKA STYLE EXTENSIONS

Fuzzy logic should be a (mathematical) tool for approximative reasoning which deals with graded inferences.

The systems of t- norm based logics discussed up to now have been designed to formalize the logical background for fuzzy sets and they allow themselves for degrees of truth of their formulas. But they all have crisp notions of consequence, that is of entailment and of provability.

Now the question is whether it is possible to generalize these considerations so that we start from fuzzy sets of formulas and that we get from them as consequence hulls again fuzzy sets of formulas. This problem is first treated by Pavelka. We discuss in the present section this kind of approach, because it uses graded relations of entailment and of provability.

It should be mentioned that there is also another more algebraically oriented approach toward consequence operations for the classical case, originating from Tarski. This approach treats consequence operations as closure operations. And this type of approach has been generalized to closure operations in classes of fuzzy set of formulas by Gerla.

The Pavelka-style approach deals with fuzzy sets $\Sigma^\sim$ of formulas, that is besides formulas φ also their membership degrees $\Sigma^\sim(\varphi)$ in $\Sigma^\sim$. And these membership degrees are just the truth degrees. We may assume that these degrees again form a residuated lattice $L = \langle L. \cap, \cup, *, \rightarrow, 0, 1 \rangle$. Thus we generalize the standard notion of fuzzy set (with membership degrees from the real unit interval). Therefore the appropriate language has the same logical connectives as in the previous considerations.

The Pavelka-style approach is an easy matter as long as the entailment relationship is considered. An evaluation e is a *model* of a fuzzy set $\Sigma^\sim$ of formulas if

$$\Sigma^\sim(\varphi) \le e(\varphi) \tag{3.107}$$

holds for each formula φ. This immediately yields as definition of the entailment relation that the semantic consequence hull of $\Sigma^\sim$ should be characterized by the membership degrees:

$$C^{sem}(\Sigma^\sim)(\psi) = \wedge\{e(\psi) \mid e \bmod el \text{ of } \Sigma^\sim\} \tag{3.108}$$

for each formula ψ.

For a syntactic characterization of this entailment relation, it is necessary to have some calculus K which treats formulas of the language together with truth degrees. So the language of this calculus has to extend the language of the basic logical system by having also symbols for the truth degrees. Depending upon the truth degree structure, this may mean that the language of this calculus becomes an uncountable one.

We indicate these symbols by over lined letters like $\bar{a}, \bar{c}$. We realize the common treatment of formulas and truth degrees by considering evaluated formulas, that is ordered pairs $(\bar{a}, \varphi)$ consisting of a truth degree symbol and a formula. This transforms each fuzzy set $\Sigma^\sim$ of formulas into a (crisp) set of evaluated formulas again denoted by $\Sigma^\sim$.

So K has to allow to derive evaluated formulas out of sets of evaluated formulas, of course using suitable axioms and rules of inference. These axioms are usually only formulas φ which, however, are used in the derivations as the corresponding evaluated formulas $(\bar{1}, \varphi)$. Derivations in K out of some set $\Sigma^\sim$ of evaluated formulas are finite sequences of evaluated formulas which either are axioms, or elements of (the support of) $\Sigma^\sim$, or result from former evaluated formulas by application of one of the inference rules.

Each K – derivation of an evaluated formula $(\bar{a}, \varphi)$ counts as a derivation φ to the degree $a \in L$. The provability degree of φ from $\Sigma^\sim$ in K is the supremum over all these degrees. This now yields that the syntactic consequence hull of $\Sigma^\sim$ should be the fuzzy set C_K^{syn} of formulas characterized by the membership function:

$$C_K^{syn}(\Sigma^\sim)(\psi) = v\{a \in L \mid K \text{ derives } (\bar{a}, \psi) \text{ out of } \Sigma^\sim\} \qquad (3.109)$$

for each formula ψ.

Despite the fact that K is a standard calculus, this is an infinitary notion of provability.

For the infinite-valued Łukasiewicz logic L this machinery works particularly well because it needs in an essential way the continuity of the residuation operation. In this case, we can form a calculus K_L which gives an adequate axiomatization for the graded notion of entailment in the sense that one has suitable soundness and completeness results.

This calculus K_L has as axioms any axiom system of the infinite-valued Łukasiewicz logic L which provides together with the rule of detachment an adequate axiomatization of L, but K_L replaces this standard rule of detachment by the generalized form:

$$\frac{(\bar{a}, \varphi) \qquad (\bar{c}, \varphi \to \psi)}{(\overline{a * c}, \psi)} \qquad (3.110)$$

for evaluated formulas.

The soundness result for this calculus K_L yields the fact that the K_L provability of an evaluated formula $(\bar{a}, \varphi)$ says that $a \le e(\varphi)$ holds for every valuation e, that is that the formula $\bar{a} \to \varphi$ is valid – however as a formula of an *extended* propositional language which has all the truth degrees constants among its vocabulary. Of course, now the evaluation e have also to satisfy $e\overline{a} = a$ for each $a \in [0,1]$.

And the soundness and completeness results for K_L say that a strong completeness theorem hold true giving:

$$C^{sem}\left(\Sigma^{\sim}\right)(\psi) = C_{K_L}^{syn}\left(\Sigma^{\sim}\right)(\psi) \qquad (3.111)$$

for each formula ψ and each fuzzy set $\Sigma^{\sim}$ of formulas.

If one takes the previously mentioned turn and extends the standard language of propositional L by truth degree constants for all degrees $\overline{a} \to \varphi$, then a slight modification K_L^+ of the former calculus K_L again provides an adequate axiomatization, we add the bookkeeping axioms.

$$\left(\overline{a} \,\&\, \overline{c}\right) \equiv \overline{a * c}\,,$$

$$\left(\overline{a} \to \overline{c}\right) \equiv \overline{a \rightsquigarrow_L c}\,,$$

And if one is interested to have evaluated formulas together with the extension of the language by truth degree constants, one has also to add the degree introduction rule:

$$\frac{\left(\overline{a}, \varphi\right)}{\overline{a} \to \varphi}\,.$$

However, even a stronger result is available with refers only to a notion of derivability over a countable language. The completeness result (3.111), for K_L^+ instead of K_L becomes already provable if one adds truth degree constants only for all the rationals in [0,1]. And this extension of L is even only a conservative one, that is K_L^+ proves only such constant-free formulas of the language with rational constants, which are already provable in the standard infinite-valued Łukasiewicz logic L.

LOGIC WITH GERLA'S APPROACH

For completeness we mention also a much more abstract approach toward fuzzy logics with graded notions of entailment as the previously explained one for the t-norm based fuzzy logics as stated earlier.

The background for this generalization is that (already) in systems of classical logic the syntactic as well as the semantic consequence relations, that is the provability as well as the entailment relations, are closure operators within the set of formulas. This is a fundamental observation made by Tarski already in 1930. The same holds true for the Pavelka style extensions and the operators C^{sem} and C^{sen} introduced in (3.108) and (3.109), respectively.

The context of L- fuzzy sets, with $L = \langle L \le \rangle$ an arbitrary complete lattice. A closure operator *in* **L** is a mapping $J: L \to L$ satisfying for arbitrary $x, y \in L$ the well-known conditions:

$$x \le J(x),$$ (increasingness)

$$x \le y \Rightarrow J(x) \le J(y),$$ (isotonicity)

$$J(J(x)) = J(x).$$ (idempotency)

And a closure system in L is a subclass $C \subseteq L$, which is closed under arbitrary lattice meets.

For fuzzy logic such closure operators and closure systems are considered in the lattice $\mathcal{F}_L \mathbb{F}$ of all fuzzy subsets of the $\mathbb{F}$ of formulas of some suitable formalized language.

An abstract fuzzy deduction system now is an ordered pair $D = (\mathcal{F}_L (\mathbb{F}), D)$ determined by a closure operator D in the lattice $\mathcal{F}_L \mathbb{F}$. And the fuzzy theories T of such an abstract fuzzy deduction system, also called D- theories, are the fixed points of D:T = D(T), that is the deductively closed fuzzy sets of formulas.

A rather abstract setting is also chosen for the semantics of such an abstract fuzzy deduction system:

An abstract fuzzy semantics $\mathcal{M}$ is nothing but a class of elements of the lattice $\mathcal{F}_L \mathbb{F}$, that is a class of fuzzy sets of formulas. These fuzzy sets of formulas are called models. The only restriction is that the universal set over $\mathbb{F}$, that is the fuzzy subset of $\mathbb{F}$, which has always membership degree one, is not allowed as a model. The background idea here is that, for each standard interpretation (in the sense of many-valued logic, including an evaluation of the individual variables) for the formula $\mathbb{F}$, a model M is determined as the fuzzy set which has for each formula $\varphi \in \mathbb{F}$ the truth degree of φ in A as membership degree.

Accordingly the satisfaction relation $\vDash_{\mathcal{M}}$ coincides with inclusion for models M $\in \mathcal{M}$ and fuzzy sets Σ of formulas one has:

$$M \vDash_{\mathcal{M}} \Sigma \Longleftrightarrow \Sigma \subseteq M. \tag{3.112}$$

In this setting, one has a semantic and a syntactic consequence operator, both being closure operators, that is one has for each fuzzy set Σ of formulas from $\mathbb{F}$ a semantic as well as a syntactic consequence hull, given by:

$$C^{sem}(\Sigma) = \bigcap\{M \in M | M \vDash_{\mathcal{M}} \Sigma\}, \qquad C^{syn}(\Sigma) = D(\Sigma). \tag{3.113}$$

Similar to the classical case one ha $C^{sem}(M) = M$ for each model $M \in M$, that is each such model provides a C^{sem} theory.

However, a general completeness theorem is not available.

3.9   FUZZIFYING NON-CLASSICAL LOGICS

The major application of logic in computer science is AI. Non-monotonic reasoning is a challenging problem of AI.

Now the question is how the basic ideas of non-monotonic inference can be generalized from the crisp case to the fuzzy case, that is to the case in which either the knowledge comes for example. with degrees of vagueness, or of confidence, of in which for example the defaults are accepted only to some degrees.

A first idea on the circumscription approach in a straightforward way from classical logic to the infinite-valued Łukasiewicz logic L_∞, and gives some basic properties of the non-monotonic inference operator defined via minimal models.

It is possible to define for abstract fuzzy semantics $\mathcal{M}$ the model class of a fuzzy set Σ of formulas as:

$$\mathrm{mod}_{\mathcal{M}}(\Sigma) = \{M \in \mathcal{M} | M \vDash_{\mathcal{M}} \Sigma\}, \tag{3.114}$$

and to define the theory of a class $\mathbb{K} \subseteq \mathcal{M}$ of models as:

$$\mathrm{th}(\mathbb{K}) = \cup\{u \in \mathcal{F}_L(\mathbb{F}) | M \vDash_u \text{ for all } M \in \mathbb{K}\}, \tag{3.115}$$

which means that we have:

$$\mathrm{th}(\mathbb{K}) = \cup\{u \in \mathcal{F}_L(\mathbb{F}) | \subseteq \cap\mathbb{K}\} = \cap\mathbb{K}.$$

We can prove that for each fuzzy set $\Sigma \in \mathcal{F}_L(\mathbb{F})$ of formulas we get:

$$C^{\text{sem}}(\Sigma) = \mathrm{th}(\mathrm{mod}_{\mathcal{M}}(\Sigma)),$$

that is $\mathrm{th}(\mathrm{mod}_{\mathcal{M}}(\Sigma))$ is a C^{sem}-theory.

Therefore, it is possible to adapt within this abstract setting the model theoretic method of non-monotonic inference which connects with each set Σ of formulas as its non-monotonic inference hull $C_\sim(\Sigma)$ the theory of a subclass $\Phi(\mathrm{mod}(\Sigma))$ of the class $\mathrm{mod}(\Sigma)$ of all models of Σ:

$$C_\sim(\Sigma) = \mathrm{th}\big(\Phi(\mathrm{mod}(\Sigma))\big),$$

For example, the subclass of all normal or of all minimal models. Thus we can prove quite similar theoretical results as in the crisp case.

Another tool from non-monotonic reasoning has a natural generalization to a fuzzy setting: *Poole systems*. A crisp Poole system P is determined by a pair (D, C) of sets of sentences understood as the relevant defaults and constraints. For each set Σ of formulas and a suitably chosen closure operator C it defines a class $\mathbb{E}_P$ of extensions by

$E_P(\Sigma) = \{C(\Sigma \cup D_m) | D_m \subseteq D$ maximal with respect to consistency of $\Sigma \cup C \cup D_m\}$, and an inference operator C_P by:

$$C_P(\Sigma) = \bigcap E_P(\Sigma).$$

All these definitions allow a natural extension to the case of fuzzy sets of defaults and constraints.

Fuzzy belief revision is another important application area.

A fuzzy belief base B is just a fuzzy set of formulas $B \in \mathcal{F}_L(\mathbb{F})$. The revision information (φ/a), understood as the fuzzy singleton of φ with membership degree a, tells that a "new" formula φ should be integrated with degree a.

As in the AGM framework for the crisp case this may happen in the following steps:

- From the family $B \perp (\varphi/a)$ of all maximal $X \in \mathcal{F}_L(B)$ consistent with (φ/a),
- Select a subset $\gamma(B \perp (\varphi/a)) \subseteq B \perp (\varphi/a)$ and form its meet, and
- Add the revision information to get the revised belief base.
  $B * (\varphi/a) = \cap \gamma(B \perp (\varphi/a)) \cup (\varphi/a).$

The adaptation of this procedure to the case of the revision of fuzzy theories is not as straightforward as in the crisp case, but can also be handled sufficiently well with some extra case regarding the moment for taking (deductive) closures.

Another combination of the ideas from fuzzy set theory and non-classical logic, which is known as philosophical logic, has been offered by the work of Fitting. In these works graded modalities appear in the context of applications to multi-agent systems.

Description logic is another area where integration of fuzzy sets and vague notions is considered.

The potential field of applications is much wider. Let us look at deontic notions like that one that something is "forbidden", or "allowed", or "obligatory" (for someone or everybody), and also at epistemic notions like that somebody "knows" something, or "beliefs" it or is "convinced of" it. All these notions have, at least in everyday discourse and in commonsense reasoning, an intrinsic fuzzy component. And these effects we need to represent in suitable formalized systems of fuzzified non-classical logics. This appears to be a challenging topic for AI fields like knowledge representation and even knowledge engineering.

3.10 BRIDGING THE GAP BETWEEN FUZZY LOGIC AND QUANTUM LOGIC

The development of the mathematical fuzzy logics leads to a series of interesting systems of such logics. The prototypical ones of them have an adequate (standard) semantics provided by a logical matrix over the real unit interval, like Łukasiewicz infinite valued logic L_{∞} or infinite valued logic G_{∞}.

But all of them have algebraic semantics provided by suitable algebraic structures. This development started with the introduction of the MV-algebras in a completeness proof for L_{∞} the by Chang in 1958, continued much later with the product algebras which provide an algebraic semantics fort product logic Π and culminated in the introduction of BL-algebras by Hájek to get a semantics for the logic BL of all continuous t-norms.

Birkhoff/von Neumann developed a particular logic, the quantum logic which deals with quantum theoretical propositions. This logic has also an algebraic semantics, provided by the class of all orthomodular lattices.

Such an orthomodular lattice reflects the essential algebraic properties of the system of closed subspaces of a Hilbert space. It is an ortholattice, that is a bounded lattice with a universal upper bound 1 and a universal lower bound 0 which has an orthocomplementation$^{\perp}$, which is order reversing and involutive, and satisfies $a \vee a^{\perp} = 0$ as well as the orthomodularity condition:

$$x \leq y \Rightarrow y = x \vee (x^{\perp} \wedge$$

For generalization of the MV-algebras and the orthomodular lattices either we have to consider QMV-algebras and more general the S-algebras, or we have to consider effect algebras and the D-posets.

The S-algebras are abelian monoids $(M, \oplus, 0)$ with an idempotent orthocomolement $*$ and an annihilator 1, such that $x \oplus x^* = 1$ and $0^* = 1$ hold true.

They become MV-algebras if we add the condition:

$$(x^* \oplus y)^* \oplus y = (x \oplus y^*)^* \oplus x,$$

and become the (more general) QMV-algebras if we add the condition:

$$x \oplus ((x^* \cap y) \cap (z \cap x^*)) = (x \oplus y) \cap (x \oplus z).$$

with the operation $\cap$ defined via $x \odot y =_{def} (x^* \oplus y^*)^*$ by $x \cap y =_{def} (x \oplus y^*) \odot y$.

For each QMV-algebra the class of all $\oplus$-idempotent elements, that is those ones which satisfy $x \oplus x = x$, forms an orthomodular lattice.

The standard example of a QMV-algebra is the class of all self-adjoint operators A with $0 \leq A \leq I$, called effects, which has the null operator 0 and the identity operator I together with the operations

$$E \oplus F = \begin{cases} E + F, & \text{if } E + F \text{ is self-adjoint} \\ I, & \text{otherwise} \end{cases}$$

and $E^* = I - E$.

The effect algebras are partial abelian semigroups $(M, \oplus \quad , 0, 1)$ with two distinguished elements such that $\forall x \exists! \, y(x \oplus y = 1)$ holds, and such that $x \oplus 1$ is defined if $x = 0$.

Standard examples of effect algebras are:

(i)   The real unit interval together with the ordinary sum and

(ii) The set of all effects with respect to some Hillbert space together with operator addition.

We can also consider the D-ordirings structures. These are bounded ordering $\leq$ together with some partial operation $\ominus$ such that $y \ominus x$ is defined if $x \leq y$, and such that for $x \leq y \leq z$ there holds $y \ominus x \leq y$ and $z \ominus y \leq z \ominus x$ as well as $y \ominus (y \ominus x) = x$ and $(z \ominus x) \ominus (z \ominus y) = y \ominus x$.

The class of all D-lattices, that is of all D-orderings which are lattice orderings, and the classes of all effect algebras are categorically equivalent.

A D-lattice is an MV-algebra if it satisfies:

$$x \ominus (x \wedge y) = (x \vee y) \ominus y.$$

The bounded BCK-algebras form a kind of further common generalization. A BCK-algebra is an ordered set $(M, \leq, *, 0)$ with universal lower –bound 0 and an operation $*$, such that $x \leq y$ holds true if $x * y = 0$, and such that $(x * y) * (x * z) \leq (z * y)$ and $x * (x * y) \leq y$ are satisfied. The bounded BCK-algebras additionally have a universal upper bound.

Theorem 3.11 Let $\mathcal{A} = (A, \leq, *, 0, 1)$ be a bounded BCK-algebra. Adding the partial operation

$$x \div y = \begin{cases} x * y, & \text{if } y \leq x, \\ \text{undefined}, & \text{otherwise.} \end{cases}$$

and the total operations

$$x \oslash y = x \div (y \sqcap x), x^* = 1 \div x,$$

$$x \oplus y = (x^* \oslash y)^*, x \odot y = x \oslash y^*,$$

Yields:

- $(A, \leq, \div, 0, 1)$ is a D-ordering.

- $(A, \leq, *, 0, 1)$ is a bounded, commutative BCK-algebra.

- $(A, \oplus, *, 0, 1)$ is an MV-algebra.

The comparison of these types of algebraic structures shows that the algebraic discussions in the realm of fuzzy logic and in the realm of quantum theory on the other hand offer structures which have the MV-algebras as common specifications. These MV-algebras are important for infinite valued logics and quantum logic. Furthermore these algebraic structures of different origin have the BCK-algebras as a common generalization. And these BCK-algebras are also generalizations of the BL-algebras.

From a logicians point of view this leads to the problem which ones of these different classes of algebraic structures are suitable to provide algebraic semantics for interesting logics and how we may find adequate calculi to axiomatize these logics. Additionally these classes of structures offer a whole family of algebraic structures which, in some sense, "interpolate" between the structures we have introduced for fuzzy logics and those ones introduced for the logic of quantum theory. Now the problem is to select a similar family of logics which "interpolate" between the mathematical fuzzy logics and the quantum logic and thus bring quantum logic(s) in closer relationship to the class of well understood and well accepted logics. Such an interpolating family of logics would offer a bridge into the realm of partial logics.

3.11 FUTURISTIC AMBITIONS OF FUZZY LOGIC

Fuzzy logic is a special kind of multivalued logic addressing the vagueness phenomenon and developing tools for its modeling via truth degrees taken from an ordered scale. Basically fuzzy logic is a precise logic of imprecision and approximate reasoning.

Fuzzy logic is an attempt to formalize/mechanize two remarkable human capabilities, viz.

(i)   The capability to converse, reason and make rational decisions in an environment of imprecision, uncertainty, incompleteness of information, conflicting information, partiality of truth and partiality of possibility – in short, in an environment of imperfect information and

(ii) The capability to perform a wide variety of physical and mental tasks based on manipulation of perception instead of any measurements or any computations.

The principal contribution of fuzzy logic which is widely unrecognized is its high power of precisiation of what is imprecise. Hence, under such circumstances we list some properties which are not exhaustive and which a fuzzy logic (FL) system should possess [202–206].

- The FL should be well established sound and complete formal system so that its applications are well justified.
- The FL should be an open system. It must be possible to extend it by new connectives and by generalized quantifiers. Moreover, some specific phenomena of natural language semantics should also be expressible, such as non-commutativity of conjunction and disjunction.
- The FL should have a specific agenda, special technique and concepts. Amomg them we can rank evaluating linguistic expressions, linguistic variable, fuzzy IF-THEN rules, fuzzy quantification, defuzzification, fuzzy equality, and so on.

- The FL should enable to develop special inference schemes including sophisticated inference schemes of human reasoning (For example, compositional rule of inference, reasoning based natural language expressions, non-monotonic reasoning, abduction, commonsense reasoning, and so on).
- The FL must have features to be compatible with classical bivalued logic and multivalued logic so that a workable environment to handle combination of logics can be created.

3.11.1 ALGEBRAIC STRUCTURES OF FUZZY LOGIC

The fundamental problem that determines any kind of logic (including fuzzy, general many-valued and other ones) is the structure of truth values. In fuzzy logic, it is generally accepted that it should basically be a residuated lattice:

$$\mathcal{L} = \langle L, \vee, \wedge, \otimes, \rightarrow, 0, 1 \rangle \tag{3.116}$$

where $\vee$ and $\wedge$ are lattice operations, 0, 1 are the smallest and the greatest elements $\langle L, \otimes, 1 \rangle$ is a commutative monoid and the operations $\otimes$ (product) and $\rightarrow$ (residuum) fulfil the adjunction condition

$$a \otimes b \leq c \text{ if } a \leq b \rightarrow c \tag{3.117}$$

for all $a, b, c \in L$. The residuated lattice is complete if its lattice reduct is complete.
Two specific operations closely related to logic are negation

$$\sim a = a \rightarrow 0$$

and biresiduation

$$a \leftrightarrow b = (a \rightarrow b) \wedge (b \rightarrow a)$$

where $a, b \in L$. Alternatively, we can define biresiduation in a weaker form by $a \leftrightarrow b = (a \rightarrow b) \otimes (b \rightarrow a)$.

We can further extend (3.116) by further specific operations and claiming more properties. The residuated lattice (3.116) is MTL-algebra if it is prelinear, that is:

$$(a \rightarrow b) \vee (b \rightarrow a) = 1, \ a, b \in L. \tag{3.118}$$

Remark 3.32 This property is essential for the proof of completeness of fuzzy logics.

We can prove that every MTL-algebra is isomorphic to a sub direct product of linearly ordered MTL-algebras.

The *IMTL-algebra* is MTL-algebra in which double negation

$$\sim\sim a = a \quad a \in L$$

holds true.

The MTL-algebra is a *BL-algebra* if it is divisible, that is:

$$a \otimes (a \to b) = a \wedge b, a, b \in L \tag{3.119}$$

holds true.

A Π-algebra is a BL-algebra fulfilling

$$\sim\sim a \leq (a \to a \otimes b) \to b \otimes \sim\sim b, \qquad a, b \in L.$$

The MV-algebra introduced by C. C. Chang, is a nontrivial generalization of a Boolean algebra.

$$\mathcal{L} = \langle L, \oplus, \otimes, \neg, 0, 1 \rangle \tag{3.120}$$

satisfying the following axioms:

- $(a \oplus b) \oplus c = a \oplus (b \oplus c),$
- $a \oplus b = b \oplus a,$
- $a \oplus 0 = a,$
- $\sim\sim a = a,$
- $a \oplus = 1,$
- $\sim 0 = 1,$
- $a \otimes b = \sim(\sim a \oplus \sim b),$
- $\sim(\sim a \oplus b) \oplus b = \sim(\sim b \oplus a) \oplus a$

for all $a, b, c \in L$. If we put:

$$a \vee b = (a \otimes \sim b) \oplus b, \text{ and}$$
$$a \wedge b = (a \oplus \sim b) \otimes b, a, b \in$$

then $\langle L,\vee,\wedge,0,1\rangle$ is a bounded distributive lattice. The operation $a \to b = \sim a \oplus b$ is adjoint with $\otimes$ and so, it is a residuation.

Remark 3.33 MV-algebra is a residuated lattice.

Remark 3.34 MV-algebra is a BL-algebra fulfilling the law of double negation. ŁΠ-algebra is the algebra

$$\mathcal{L} = \langle L,\vee,\wedge\ \oplus,\odot,\ \overset{L}{\to},\overset{n}{\to}\ 0,1\rangle \tag{3.121}$$

Where

- $\langle L,\vee,\wedge,\otimes,\overset{L}{\to},0,1\rangle$ is MV-algebra,

- $\langle L,\vee,\wedge,\odot,\overset{n}{\to},0,1\rangle$ is Π-algebra,

- $a\odot(b\ominus c) = (a\odot b)\ominus(a\odot c)$ holds for all $a,b,c \in L$ where $a \ominus b = a\otimes \underset{\sim}{L}b$ and $\underset{\sim}{L}a = a \overset{L}{\to} 0$.

We further define $\underset{\sim}{\pi}a = a \overset{\pi}{\to} 0$ and $\Delta a = \underset{\sim}{\pi}\underset{\sim}{L}a$.

Baaz delta operation is a unary operation on L, fulfilling the following properties:

$$\Delta a \vee \sim \Delta a = 1, \Delta(a \vee b) \le \Delta a \vee \Delta b,$$

$$\Delta a \le a, \Delta a \le \Delta\Delta a,$$

$$\Delta(a \to b) \le \Delta a \to \Delta b, \Delta 1 = 1.$$

Example 3.69 The simplest example of residuated lattice is a Boolean algebra, of course, including the two-valued one for classical logic $\langle\{0,1\},\vee,\wedge,\sim,0,1\rangle$, where $\otimes$ $=\wedge$ and $a \to b = \sim a \vee b$.

Otherwise, examples of the above introduced algebras should have the support $L = [0,1]$ so that the residuated lattice is complete and has the general form:

$$\mathcal{L} = \langle[0,1],\vee,\wedge\ \oplus,\to,0,1\rangle \tag{3.122}$$

where $\otimes$ is a left-continuous t-norm. The obtained algebra is MTL-algebra.

Example 3.70 IMTL-algebra is (3.122) where:

$$a\otimes b = \begin{cases} a\wedge b, & \text{if } a+b > 1, \\ 0 & \text{otherwise,} \end{cases} \quad \text{(nilpotent minimum)}$$

$$a \to b = \begin{cases} 1, & \text{if } a \le b, \\ \neg a \vee b & \text{otherwise,} \end{cases} \text{(residuum)}$$

$\sim a \ = \ 1 - a,$ (negation)

$a \leftrightarrow b \ = \ (\sim a \wedge \sim b) \vee (a \wedge b).$ (biresiduation)

Example 3.71 BL-algebra is any residuated lattice (3.122) where $\otimes$ is a continuous t-norm. For the case when $\otimes$ is product or minimum, we get:

$$\sim a \ = \ a \rightarrow 0 \ = \ \begin{cases} 1 & \text{if } a = 0, \\ 0 & \text{otherwise,} \end{cases}$$

$$\sim \sim a \ = \ \begin{cases} 0 & \text{if } a = 0, \\ 1 & \text{otherwise.} \end{cases}$$

Example 3.72 Łukasiewicz MV-algebra is a residuated lattice (3.120) where

$$a \otimes b \ = \ 0 \vee (a + b - 1), \qquad \text{(Łukasiewicz conjunction)}$$

$$a \oplus b \ = \ 1 \wedge (a + b), \quad \text{(Łukasiewicz disjunction)}$$

$$\sim a \ = \ 1 - a. \text{ (negation)}$$

We can put $a \rightarrow b = 1 \wedge (1 - a + b)$ to obtain the residuation that is called Łukasiewicz implication. The biresiduation is defined by $a \leftrightarrow b \ = \ 1 - |a - b|$.

Example 3.73 $Ł\prod$-algebra is:

$$\mathcal{L} = \langle L, \vee, \wedge, \otimes, \overset{L}{\rightarrow}, \overset{n}{\rightarrow} 0, 1 \rangle$$

where

$$a \overset{L}{\rightarrow} b \ = \ 1 \wedge (1 - a + b), a \otimes b \ = \ 0 \vee (a + b - 1),$$

$$a \overset{\pi}{\rightarrow} b = \begin{cases} 1 & a \leq b, \\ \frac{b}{a} & \text{otherwise,} \end{cases} \overset{L}{\sim} a = 1 - a,$$

$$\overset{\pi}{\sim} a \ = \ \begin{cases} 1 & a = 0, \\ 0 & \text{otherwise,} \end{cases} a \ominus b = 0 \vee (a - b).$$

The Baaz delta operation is

$$\Delta(a) \ = \ \begin{cases} 1 & \text{if } a = 1, \\ 0 & \text{otherwise.} \end{cases}$$

3.11.2   CLASSIFICATION OF FUZZY LOGICS

As stated above, fuzzy logic is a special many-valued logic for dealing with the vagueness phenomenon via degrees. Any formal logic has two basic constituents: syntax and semantics. Then, fuzzy logics can be classified into two kinds [202–206]:

FUZZY LOGIC IN NARROW SENSE (FLN)

Mathematical fuzzy logic (MFL) is established as a sound and complete formal system to provide tools for the development of a working mathematical model of vagueness phenomenon and to offer well justified applications of it. The mathematization of vagueness is based on the introduction of degrees of truth, which form a special algebra.

The journey of MFL starts with the seminal paper on fuzzy logic written by Goguen, which appears shortly after the seminal paper on fuzzy set theory written by Zadeh. Goguen proposes to split the operation representing conjunction into two operations (minimum and multiplication) and considers the residuated lattice as a convenient structure of truth values. Thus a convenient basis for the semantics of fuzzy logics is established. But the approach of Goguen is not sufficiently formal. More mathematically sophisticated approach on fuzzy logic is written by Pavelka. Since then, significant developments are achieved in FLn. The Pavelks's work has been continued by Novák. Subsequent development of MFL is given in the monograph written by Hájek. The significant development of logic results in generating corresponding algebra by Höhel and Mundici. Esteva, Godo, Gottwald, DiNola. Montagns, Cignoli, Gerla, Turunen, Cintula, Noguera, and others have significant contributions on development of MFL [203, 204].

We can distinguish two directions in FLn:
- Fuzzy logic with traditional syntax and
- Fuzzy logic with evaluated syntax.

FUZZY LOGICS WITH TRADITIONAL SYNTAX

This class of logics has been significantly developed by Hájek. Formulas in these logics are dealt with classically, that is, the language of fuzzy logic differs from that of classical logic in particular by having more connectives. On the other hand, the concepts of inference rule, theory, proof, and many other ones remain classical. The language ℓ of fuzzy logics contains disjunction $\vee$, conjunction $\wedge$, implication $\rightarrow$, a specific new connective of strong conjunction &, and a logical (truth) constant $\perp$ for falsity. Of course, depending on the chosen logic, some of the connectives can be defined in terms of the others. The connectives of negation ~ and equivalence $\leftrightarrow$ are derived.

The semantics is many valued based on a corresponding algebra, as discussed above. For convenience, we speak about a ℓ – algebra, where each connective from ℓ is interpreted by the corresponding algebraic operation (namely, $\vee$ is interpreted by $\vee$, $\wedge$ by $\wedge$, & by $\otimes$, $\Rightarrow$ by $\rightarrow$, and accordingly for all other possible connectives).

The most prominent fuzzy logic is MTL, whose algebraic semantic is formed by MTL-algebras. Its axioms are as follows:

(A1) $(A \vee B) \rightarrow ((B \rightarrow C) \rightarrow (A \rightarrow C))$

(A2) $(A \vee B) \rightarrow A$

(A3) $(A \vee B) \rightarrow (B \wedge A)$

(A4) $(A \& (A \rightarrow B)) \rightarrow (A \wedge B)$

(A5a) $(A \rightarrow (B \rightarrow C)) \rightarrow ((A \& B) \rightarrow C)$

(A5b) $((A \& B) \rightarrow C) \rightarrow (A \rightarrow (B \rightarrow C))$

(A6) $(A \rightarrow B) \rightarrow C) \rightarrow (((B \rightarrow A) \rightarrow C) \rightarrow C)$

(A7) $\bot \rightarrow A$

This logic is the basis for the core fuzzy logics.

The latter are expansions of MTL-logic satisfying the following additional properties:

- For any formulas A, B , C in the language of MTL, $A \leftrightarrow B \vdash C(A) \leftrightarrow C(B)$.
- For every theory T and formulas A, B, the following holds (Local Deduction Theorem):

$$T \cup \{A\} \vdash B \text{ if } T \vdash A^n \rightarrow B$$

For some n, where A^n is a short for A&...&A(n-times).

Prominent examples of core fuzzy logics include IMTL, BL, product, and Łukasiewicz, amog others.

All the core fuzzy logics enjoy the following form of completeness.

Theorem 3.12 For every formula A and theory T, the following are equivalent:

- $T \vdash A$.

- A is true in degree 1 in every linearly ordered ℓ -algebra that is a model of T.

- A is true in degree 1 in every ℓ –algebra that is a model of T.

This theorem gave rise to the idea that a given logic deserves to be called "fuzzy", if it is complete with respect to linearly ordered ℓ – algebras. Even more, it raises the question whether it is possible to confine our attention only to the standard algebras.

The answer is partly positive. We call a logic *standard* complete if it is complete with respect to standard chains. It is hyperreal chain complete if it is complete with respect to a class of chains whose lattice reduct is an ultrapower of [0, 1]. At the same time, if the theory T in Theorem 3.12 is arbitrary, then we speak about strong completeness. If it is only allowed to be finite, then we speak about finite strong completeness. If $T = \emptyset$, then it is complete.

Strong standard completeness implies finite strong standard as well as standard completeness. It also implies strong hyperreal-chain as well as finite strong hyperreal-chain and hyperreal-chain completeness.

The following results of Table 20 hold for some of the core fuzzy logics.

TABLE 20 Results of core fuzzy logic

Logic	Standard complete	Finite strong st. complete	Strong st. complete
MTL, IMTL, SMTL, Gödel, WNM, NM	Yes	Yes	Yes
BL, SBL, Łukasiewicz, product, Π_{MTL}	Yes	Yes	Yes

At present, there are many core fuzzy logics, both in propositional and in predicate versions.

The FLn has been studied in detail, especially from the algebraic and metamathematical points of view. We can hardly estimate how far this work may reach. It seems that FLn offers a deeply justified technique enabling us to model various manifestations of the phenomenon of vagueness and to develop other applications. However, there are not yet many results on the applied side.

FUZZY LOGIC WITH EVALUATED SYNTAX $(Ev_\pounds)$

This logic is specific by introducing formulas that are also evaluated on the syntactic level. The basic concept is that of an evaluated formula a/A, where A is a formula and $a \in L$ is its syntactic evaluation. This has a nice interpretation since it allows us to consider axioms that need not be fully satisfactory, so their initial truth values can be lower than 1. Moreover, it enables us to derive statements about intermediate truth values.

A propositional version of this logic is established by Pavelka and extended to a predicate version by Novák. As usual, $Ev_\pounds$ is a mathematical logic with clearly distinguished syntax and semantics. The syntax, however, is generalized, and in addition to evaluated formulas, it also has precise definitions of evaluated proof, fuzzy theory, evaluated provability, model, etc. Its semantics is determined by a finite Łukasiewicz algebra, or, in the case of $L = [0, 1]$, the standard Łukasiewicz algebra. It has been proved that completeness of the syntax with respect to semantics requires the corresponding algebra to satisfy the following four equations:

$$\bigvee_{i \in I}(a \to b_i) = a \to \bigvee_{i \in I} b_i \; , \bigwedge_{i \in I}(a \to b_i) = a \to \bigwedge_{i \in I}(b_i) \; ,$$

$$(3.123)$$

$$V_{i \in I}(a \to b_i) = \Lambda_{i \in I} \; a_i \to b \; , \Lambda_{i \in I}(a \to b_i) = V_{i \in I} \, a_i \to b.$$

$$(3.124)$$

These equations are equivalent in [0, 1] to the continuity of $\to$, which is satisfied only by the Łukasiewicz implication and its isomorphs.

The resulting logic is quite strong and has a lot of interesting properties. As mentioned, its syntax is evaluated, which means that evaluated formulas are manipulated using special inference rules. A formal fuzzy theory T is determined by a triple $T = \langle LA_X, SA_X, R \rangle$, where $LA_X \subset F_j$ is a fuzzy set of logical axioms, $SA_X \subset F_j$ is a fuzzy set of special axioms and R is a set of inference rules.

The evaluated formal proof of A in T is sequence of evaluated formulas where each (evaluated) formula is an axiom (in a certain degree) or has been derived using an inference rule. The evaluation of the last formula in the proof is a value of the proof.

This gives rise to the notion of provability degree:

$$a = V\{Val(w)|w \text{ is a proof of A in T}\}. \qquad (3.125)$$

Then we say that a formula A is a theorem in degree a in T and write $T \vdash_a A$. Note that (3.125) naturally generalizes the classical definition of provability where finding one proof is sufficient, while here, the provability is obtained as a supremum of values of still "better and better" proofs.

The completeness of $Ev_Ł$ takes the form of a generalization of the Gödel-Henkin completeness theorem:

$$T \vdash_a A \text{ if } T \vDash_a A, a \in L, \qquad (3.126)$$

for all formulas A and all fuzzy theories T, where a in $T \vDash_a A$ is the infimum of the truth values of A in all models of T.

It is a special property of this logic that its language, in addition to the connectives introduced above, also contains logical (truth) constants as names for the truth values. In its original version, all the values from L were considered, which in the case of L = [0, 1] makes the language uncountable.

The system of $(Ev_Ł)$ is open to extension by new connectives, which makes it a fairly rich logical system. However, in the case of L = [0, 1], all the connectives must be continuous. On the other hand, the fact that it is the only logic of this kind (up to isomorphism) leaves many researchers unsatisfied with it. This has led to attempts at partial approaches to $Ev_Ł$ via the introduction of logical constants a for rational truth values in the language of the corresponding logic, which enables us to take into account evaluated formulas, these are identified with formulas $a \to A$ which is possible because in any model $\mathcal{M}, \mathcal{M}(a \to A) = 1$ is equivalent with $\mathcal{M}(A) \geq a$. Completeness (in the classical sense) for a wide class of such logics has been proved. However, the generalized completeness (3.126) does not hold.

FUZZY LOGIC IN BROADER SENSE

The paradigm of fuzzy logic in the broader sense (FLb) is proposed by Novák as a program to extend FLn as follows:

To develop a formal theory of natural human reasoning, this is characterized by the use of natural language. Thus, the theory should encompass mathematical models of special expressions of natural language, take into account their vagueness and develop specific reasoning schemes. This paradigm overlaps with two other paradigms proposed in the literature, namely common sense reasoning and precisiated natural language (PNL).

The idea of common sense reasoning has been proposed by McCarthy as a part of the program of logic-based artificial intelligence. Its paradigm is to develop formal common sense theories and systems using mathematical logics that exhibit common-sense behavior. The reason is that commonsense reasoning is a central part of human behavior, and no real intelligence is possible without it. The main drawback of the up-to-date formalizations of commonsense reasoning, in our opinion, is that neglects the vagueness present in the meaning of natural language expression.

The concept of a precisiated natural language (PNL) has been proposed by Zadeh. Its idea is to develop a *"reasonable working formalization of the semantics of natural language without pretensions to capture it in detail and fineness"*. The goal is to provide an acceptable and applicable technical solution. It should also be noted that the term perception is not considered here as a psychological term but rather as a result of intrinsically imprecise human measurement. The concept of PNL is based on two main premises:

i)   Much of the world's knowledge is perception based,
ii)   Perception based information is intrinsically fuzzy.

The PNL methodology requires presence of World Knowledge Database and Multiagent, Modular Deduction Database. The former contains all the necessary information, including perception based propositions describing the knowledge acquired by direct human experience, which can be used in the deduction process. The latter contains various rules of deduction. Until recently, however, no exact formalization of PNL had been developed, so it should be considered mainly as a reasonable methodology.

The concept of FLb is a sort of fusion between the two paradigms that takes the best of each. It has been slowly developed over the years, and at present, FLb consists of the following theories:

- Formal theory of evaluative linguistic expressions,
- Formal theory of fuzzy IF-THEN rules and approximate reasoning (derivation of a conlusions),
- Formal theory of intermediate and generalized quantifiers, and
- Model for commonsense (human) reasoning.

The first attempt to develop these theories was based on $Ev_\bot$. The essential constituent of FLb, however, is a model of natural language semantics. Many logicians and linguists have argued that the first order logic is not sufficient for this task. Although the first-order $Ev_\bot$ has greater explicative power than classical first-order logic, the formalization of the above two items is not fully satisfactory. A more suitable formal system has been chosen as the basis for further development of FLb, namely the fuzzy type theory.

THEORY OF EVALUATIVE LINGUISTIC EXPRESSIONS

Recall that evaluative linguistic expressions are special expressions of natural language with which people evaluate phenomena around them.

They include them the following classes of linguistic expressions:

- *Basic* trichotomous evaluative expressions (small, medium, big; weak, medium strong, strong; silly, normal, intelligent, and so on).
- *Fuzzy numbers (25,* roughly 100, and so on).
- *Simple evaluative expressions* (very short, more or less medium, roughly big, about 25, and so on).
- *Compound evaluative expressions* (roughly small or medium, small but not very (small), and so on).
- *Negative evaluative expressions* (not small, not very big, and so on).

An indispensable role in the formation of these expressions is played by hedges, which are formed on a surface level by a special subclass of adverbs. We distinguish narrowing hedges(very, extremely, significantly, and so on), widening hedges (more or less, roughly, very roughly, and so on) and specifying hedges (approximately, about, rather, precisely, and so on).

When joining evaluative expressions with nouns, we obtain evaluative linguistic predications (temperature is low, very intelligent man, more or less weak force, medium tension, extremely long bridge, short distance and pleasant walk, roughly small or medium speed, and so on). In FLb, we usually simply evaluative predications to:

$$X \quad \text{is} \quad A.$$

where X is a variable whose values are the values of some measurable feature of the noun, while the noun itself is omitted from consideration. The A is an evaluative expression.

Since evaluative expressions are omnipresent in natural language, they occur in the description of any process, decision situation, procedure, characterization of objects, and so on. Therefore, the mathematical model of their meaning initiated in the seminal works by Zadeh can be ranked among the most important contributions of fuzzy logic.

The formalization of the semantics of evaluative expressions is based on the standard assumptions of the theory of semantics developed in linguistics and logic. Namely, the fundamental concepts are context (=possible world), intension, and extension. In FLb, a formal theory T^{Ev} is developed as a special theory of Łukasiewicz fuzzy type theory (Ł-FTT) formalizing certain general characteristics of the semantics of evaluative expressions.

The intension of an evaluative expression (or prediction) A is obtained as interpretation of a formula $\lambda w \lambda x (Aw)x$ of Ł-FTT in a special model $\mathcal{M}$: Let U (we usually put $U = R$).

- Recall that by a context (a possible world) we mean, in general, a state of the world at a given point in time and space. It is very difficult to formalize such a definition. However, it is argued that extensions of evaluative expressions are classes of elements taken from scale representing.

The context is a nonempty, linearly ordered and bounded, in which three distinguished limit points can be determined: a left bound v_L, a right bound v_R, and a central point v_S. Hence, each context is identified with an ordered triple:

$$w = (v_L, v_S, v_R),$$

where $v_L, v_S, v_R \in U$.

Example 3.74 A straightforward example is the prediction " $\mathcal{A}$ town", for example "small town", "very big town", and so on. Then, the corresponding context for the Czech Republic can be (3000, 50 000, 1 000 000), while for the USA it can be (30 000, 200 000, 10 000 000).

We introduce a set W of contexts. Each $w \in W$ gives rise to an interval $w = [v_L, v_R] \subset U$.

- The *i*ntension Int (A) of an evaluative expression A is a property that attains various truth values in various contexts but is invariant with respect to them. Therefore, it is modeled as a function Int $(A): W \rightarrow F(U)$ where $F(U)$ is a set of all fuzzy sets over U.
- The extension $\text{Ext}_w (A)$ of an evaluative expression A in the context $w \in W$ is a fuzzy set of elements

$$\text{Ext}_w (A) = \text{Int}(w)A \subseteq w.$$

In example 3.73, the truth value of a "small town having 30 000 inhabitants" could be, for example, 0.7 in the Czech Republic and 1 in the USA.

FUZZY/LINGUISTIC IF-THEN RULES AND APPROXIMATE REASONING

The theory of fuzzy IF-THEN rules is the most important and popular area of fuzzy logic, which has a wide variety of applications. However, there is still no general agreement about what we are discussing.

Let us recall the general form of a fuzzy IF-THEN rule:

$$\text{IF X is } \mathcal{A} \text{ THEN } Y \text{ is } B. \tag{3.127}$$

where X is A, Y is B are evaluative predications. A typical example is:

IF the temperature is small, THEN the amount of gas is very big.

Such a rule has a surface form of a conditional linguistic clause. A (finite) set of rules (3.127) is called a linguistic description.

The rules (3.127) (and the linguistic descriptions) apparently characterize some kind of relation between values of X and Y. There are two basic approaches to how the rules can be construed: relation and logical/linguistic.

Relation Approach: The relation approach assumes some chosen formal system of predicate fuzzy logic. Then, certain first-order formulas $A(x), B(x)$ are assigned to the evaluative predications "X is A", "Y is B", respectively, and are interpreted in a suitable formal model. Although the surface form of the rules (3.127) is linguistic, they are treated in this way. The whole linguistic description is construed as a fuzzy relation resulting from the interpretation of one of two normal forms; disjunctive, and conjunctive. This approach has been well-elaborated inside BL-fuzzy logic and also inside $(Ev_\natural)$. This method of interpretation of fuzzy IF-THEN rules is very convenient when we need a nice tool for the approximation of functions but is less convenient as a model of human reasoning. Therefore, it does not fit paradigm of FLb.

Logical/linguistic Approach: The logical/linguistic approach follows the paradigm of FLb, namely, the rules (3.127) are taken as genuine conditional clauses of natural language and the linguistic description is taken as a text characterizing some situation, strategy of behavior, control of some process, etc. The goal of constructed FLb model is to mimic the way how people understand natural language. Then, a formal theory of FTT (fuzzy type theory) is considered (it must include a formal theory T^{Ev} of evaluative expressions) so that the intension of each rule (3.127) can be constructed:

$$\text{Int}\,(\mathcal{R}) := \lambda w \lambda w'. \lambda x \lambda y.\, Ev^A wx \Rightarrow Ev^C w'y, \tag{3.128}$$

where w, w' are contexts of the antecedent and consequent of (3.127), respectively, Ev^A is the intension of the predication in the antecedent and Ev^C the intension of the predication in the consequent. The linguistic description is interpreted as a set of intensions (3.128). When considering a suitable model, we obtain a formal interpretation of (3.128) as a function that assigns to each pair of contexts $w, w' \in W$ a fuzzy relation among objects. It is important to realize that in this case, we introduce a consistent model of the context and provide a general rule for the construction of the extension in every context.

A further widely discussed problem concerns approximate reasoning (that is, the derivation of a conclusion): given a linguistic description consisting of n rules of the form (3.127), let us learn that "X is A_0" where A_0 differs slightly from all the $A_1, \dots, A_n$. How should we construct a conclusion Y is B_0, that is what should be B_0?

A detailed logical analysis of the relation-based approximate reasoning inside the predicate fuzzy logic with traditional syntax has been provided and inside the predicate ($Ev_\natural$). When taking a specific model of such logic, we derive a conclusion as a certain composition of fuzzy relations. This interpretation, however, does not lie in the realm of FLb because natural language is neglected. The main outcome of this approach is the well founded and nicely working approximation of functions that are specified imprecisely (we speak of the fuzzy approximation of functions).

The most elaborated approximate reasoning method in logical/linguistic interpretation is the so-called perception based logical deduction. The main idea is to consider the linguistic description as a specific text, which has a topic (what we are speaking about) and focus. Each rule is understood as local but vague information about the relation between X and Y. The given prediction "X is A_0''" is taken as a perception of some specific value of X. On this basis, the most proper rule from the linguistic description is applied (fires), and the best value of Y with respect to this rule is taken as a result. Hence, despite the vagueness of the rules forming the linguistic description, the procedure can distinguish among them.

GENERALIZED (FUZZY) QUANTIFIERS

Generalized quantifiers occur quite often in natural language. Recall that these are words such as Most, a lot of , many, a few, a great deal of , a large part o , and so on. A general theory of generalized quantifiers was initiated by Mostowski and further elaborated by Lindström, Westerståhl, Keenan, Barwise, and Cooper. Generalized quantifiers were introduced into fuzzy logic by Zadeh and further elaborated by Hájek, Glöckner, Holčaped and Dvořák and others.

A class of particular interest for FLb consists of the so-called intermediate quantifiers, for example, "many, a lot of, most, almost all", and so on. Clearly, they are quantifiers which lay between the classical quantifiers "for all" and "exists". Hence, the main idea of how their semantics can be captured is the following: Intermediate quantifiers refer to elements taken from a class that is "smaller" than the original universe in a specific way. Namely, they are classical quantifiers "for all" or "exists" taken over a class of elements that is determined using an appropriate evaluative expression. Classical logic has no substantiation for why and how the range of quantification should be made smaller.

In fuzzy logic, we can apply the theory of evaluative linguistic expressions as follows:

Let $Ev \in Form_{(o\alpha)(\alpha o)}$ be an evaluative predication. Then we define:

$$\left(Q_{Ev}^{\forall} x\alpha\right)(B_{o\alpha} A_{o\alpha}) = \left(\exists z_{o\alpha}\right)((\vartriangle\left(z_{o\alpha} \subseteq B_{o\alpha}\right) \& \left(\forall x_{\alpha}\right)\left(z_{o\alpha} x_{\alpha} \to A_{o\alpha} x_{\alpha}\right)) \wedge Ev((\mu B_{o\alpha}) z_{o\alpha})),$$

$$(3.129)$$

$$\left(Q_{Ev}^{\exists} x\alpha\right)(B_{o\alpha}, A_{o\alpha}) = \left(\exists z_{o\alpha}\right)((\vartriangle\left(z_{o\alpha} \subseteq B_{o\alpha}\right) \& \left(\exists x_{\alpha}\right)\left(z_{o\alpha} x_{\alpha} \wedge A_{o\alpha} x_{\alpha}\right)) \wedge Ev((\mu B_{o\alpha}) z_{o\alpha})).$$

$$(3.130)$$

The interpretation of formula (3.129) is as follows: there is a fuzzy set $z_{o\alpha}$ of objects having the property $B_{o\alpha}$, the size of which (determined by a measure μ) is characterized by the evaluative expression Ev, and all these objects also have the property $A_{o\alpha}$. The interpretation of (3.130) is similar. The property is here, for simplicity, represented by a fuzzy set. However, it is also possible to introduce possible worlds.

Note that the theory also includes classical quantifiers. Special natural language quantifiers can be specified, e.g.for example, by the following formulas:

$$Most = Q_{Very\ big}^{\forall} \qquad Many = Q_{Big}^{\forall}$$

$$Several = Q_{Small}^{\forall} \qquad Some = Q_{Small}^{\exists}.$$

Altogether total of 105 generalized syllogisms are informally introduced (including the basic Aristotelian syllogisms). All of them are also valid in this theory, for example:

ATK:	AKK:
All M are Y	All M are Y
Most X are M	Many X are M
-------------------	-------------------
Many X are Y	Many X are Y .

A Model of Commonsense (Human) Reasoning

The principal goal of FLb specified in the beginning of this section is to develop a model of natural human (common sense) reasoning. In this section, we briefly demonstrate a possible way to approach this goal.

A typical example of human reasoning is the reasoning of detectives. Therefore, we have chosen a simple story based on one episode form the famous TV series about Lt. Columbo. Let us emphasize that the method outlined below can be taken as a more general methodology that has a variety of specific applications.

Example 3.75.

The Story:

Mr. John Smith has been shot dead in his house. He was found by his fried, Mr. Robert Brown. Lt. Columbo suspects Mr. Brown to be the murderer.

Mr. Brown's Testimony:

I have started from my home at about 6:30, arrive at John's house at about 7, finds John dead and go immediately to the phone booth to call police. They come immediately.

Evidence of Lt. Columbo:

Mr. Smith has a high quality suit and a broken wristwatch stopped at 5:45. There is no evidence of a hard blow to his body. Lt. Columbo touches the engine of Mr. Brown's car and finds it to be more or less cold.

Lt. Columbo concludes that Mr. Brown is lying because of the following:

- Mr. Brown's car engine is more of less cold, so he must have been waiting long (more than about 30 min). Thereore, he cannot arrive and call the police (who come immediately),
- A high quality wristwatch does not break after not too hard blow. A man having high quality dress and a luxurious house is supposed to also have a high quality wristwatch. The wristwatch of John Smith is of low quality, so it does not belong to him. It does not display the time of Mr. Smith's death.

The reasoning of Lt. Columbo inside FLb can be modeled as a combination of logical rules, world knowledge and evidence with the help of non-monotonic reasoning. This procedure is realize syntactically in Ł-FTT (fuzzy type theory).

The world knowledge includes common sense knowledge of the context and further knowledge, which can be characterized using linguistic descriptions:

Context:

- Drive duration to heat the engine (minutes): $w_D = \langle 0,5,30 \rangle$.
- Temperature of engine (degrees Celsius): $w_T = \langle 0,45,100 \rangle$.
- Abstract degrees: quality, state, strike strength: $\langle 0,0.5,1 \rangle$.

Logical rules. These are logical theorems of Ł-FTT (fuzzy type theory) and theorems given by some considered theory, for example

IF X is Sm_v THEN X is ~Bi,

IF X is Bi_v THEN X is ~Sm.

Common sense knowledge from physics:

IF drive duration is Bi THEN engine temperature is Bi,

IF drive duration is Sm THEN engine temperature is ML Sm,

Common sense knowledge of customs of people:

IF quality of x's suit is Bi AND quality of x's house is VeBi

THEN wealth of x is Bi,

Some other kinds of common sense knowledge, for example, properties of products, etc.and so on.

Finally, we construct a specific model M determined by the evidence, which includes the context (for example, the wealth or quality of Mr. Smith's house) and perceptions, for example:

Touching Mr. Brown's car engine does not burn the hand, i.e.that is, its temperature is more or less low.

The quality of Mr. Smith's house is very high.

On the basis of a formal analysis which includes the use of perception-based logical deduction, Lt. Columbo concludes that the two special constructed theories are contradictory. Since his perceptions and the evidence cannot be doubted, Mr. Brown is lying, so he has an opportunity to kill Mr. Smith. It is important to emphasize that the contradictory theories have been constructed as nodes of a graph representing the structure of non-monotonic reasoning.

Other applications of FLb

There are several other successful applications of FLb, which we very briefly mention in this section to demonstrate the power of FLb. Let us emphasize that we confine only to specific applications in which the formal theory of FLb (and , consequently, of FLn) Is applied.

- Applications of the theory of evaluative expressions. Because evaluative linguistic expressions are very often used in human reasoning, they have a great potential for practical applications. One of such applications described is a geological problem of identifying rock sequences on the basis of expert geologists' knowledge. The problem is normally solved at the table by a geologist on the basis of his/her expert knowledge, which contains evaluative expressions such as "too thin", "too thick", "sufficiently thick", etc.and so on. The algorithm developed using FLb works with at least 81% success in comparison with the geologist's results.

- Linguistic control of technological processes. This is the most successful area of applications. The main tool is the perception-based logical deduction that employs linguistic descriptions of the control strategy. The ability to imitate human way of reasoning makes this method of control attractive. The main idea is to make the computer act like a "human partner" who understands and follows the linguistic description of the control strategy. Unlike classical fuzzy control where the control strategy described in natural language serves only as a rough guide to how a relational interpretation of linguistic description can be constructed, in linguistic control the control strategy in formed directly using the conditional linguistic clauses (3.127).

Example 3.76 Consider the old classical problem of how to avoid an obstacle on the basis of the following strategy: if the obstacle is very near then avoidavoiding it to the left (turn the steering wheel to the left), and if it is near then avoid it to the right. Otherwise do nothing. The corresponding linguistic description is given in Table 21.

TABLE 21   Linguistic description of control.

	Distance → turn of steering wheel	
1.	VeSm	-Bi
2.	Sm	+Bi
3.	Me	Ze
4.	Bi	Ze

(Sm, Bi, Me means "small, big, medium", respectively, Ze means "zero" and Ve means "very"). If we construct a fuzzy relation using triangular fuzzy sets, then the approximate reasoning using the composition of fuzzy relations leads to colliding with the obstacle. The FLb solution (using perception based logical deduction (PbLD) rule) successfully avoids it.

We have developed a general methodology for successful linguistic control and tested it on many practical examples. We can also learn linguistic descriptions on the basis of monitoring the run of successful control. Moreover, when specifying a suitable context, the linguistic description provides control of various kinds of processes if their control strategies are similar. A nice practical example is described, where the control of 5 aluminum-melting furnaces is developed using the same linguistic description for each furnace.

- ***Decision making:*** The decision situation can be effectively described by a set of linguistic Descriptions, which consist of rules, such as:

IF prices is rather small AND size of garden is very big, THEN the house is very good.

This method has the following advantages:

- The decision situation is well understandable to people.
- It is easy to include non-quantifiable information.
- The degree of importance is naturally included in the linguistic characterization of the decision situation, so there is no need to assign weights.

For example, in time series analysis and forecasting where the proper linguistic description is learned from the previous development and then using the PbLD method, the future development of the time series is forecasted.

3.11.3 POSSIBLE FUTURE DIRECTIONS OF MATHEMATICAL FUZZY LOGIC (MFL)

Let us now summarize how the current situation in mathematical fuzzy logic can be regarded. There is a deeply developed fuzzy logic in narrow sense, in which meta-mathematics of many formal (residuated lattice-based) logical systems has been studied in detail, including their interrelations. Therefore, the structure of FLn is already quite well known. It is still not fully clear which logic is the most convenient to solve problems related to models of vagueness and their applications. Therefore, we think that it is already time to turn our attention to the proclaimed goals of fuzzy logics so that its power can be fully recognized. As can be seen from the presentation above, some steps in this direction have already been accomplished.

We think that there are good reasons to continue the development of models of vagueness using the tools of FLn. We also propose to continue the development of FLb so that the intricate principles of human (that isi.e., common sense) reasoning can be more properly captured. The resulting logic would have many important applications (some of them were outlined above) in artificial intelligence, robotics, and in many other areas of human activities. We see also great potential in the development of fuzzy mathematics in the frame of MFL.

Vagueness is one facet of a wider phenomenon of indeterminacy, another facet of which is uncertainty. The latter is usually mathematically modeled using probability theory (but also using possibility or belief theory). Thus, a promising direction is also to consider uncertainty in the sense that has been nicely established by Flaminio and Montagna and to develop the corresponding models.

Below is a short list of some of the possible future tasks in the study of MFL and its applications:

- Develop or improve mathematical models of the phenomenon of vagueness with the goal of capturing the ways in which the latter manifests itself in various situations (without pretensions to capture its substance in all details).
- Extend the repertoire of evaluative linguistic expressions for which a reasonable working mathematical model can be elaborated.
- Extend the theory of generalized quantifiers using the formalism of FLn (some steps have already been accomplished. Introduce models of a wider class of specific natural language quantifiers.
- Fund a reasonable class of "intended modes" for theory of intermediate and generalized quantifiers.
- Study various forms of commonsense (human) reasoning and search for a reasonable formalization of them. As a subgoal, extent the list of intermediate quantifiers and the list of generalized syllogisms .
- Develop a reasonable formalization of FLb on the basis of which the above mentioned constituents of the PNL methodology (namely the World Knowledge

Database and Multiagent, Modular Deduction Database) can be formed. Furthermore, extent the results obtained in the AI theory of common sense reasoning.

- Extend the technique by joining fuzzy logic with probability theory so as to be able to include also uncertainty inside FLb and thus to develop a concise theory of the phenomenon of indeterminacy.
- Study the ways in which other formal systems of FLn (besides the fuzzy type theory) can be used for the solution of problems raised in FLb and develop them accordingly.
- Develop other aspects of fuzzy mathematics. Try to find problems specific to fuzzy mathematics, which are either unsolvable or meaningless in classical mathematics.

In general, we propose to shift the interest in MFL from its outer structure (metamathematics of fuzzy logics) to the inner structure of some reasonably chosen systems. One of the problems we face quite often is also the great complexity of formal means when they are applied. The question is raised as to whether or not it is possible to simplify the formalization without losing the expressive power. We thus face a wide variety of interesting problems, both inside mathematical fuzzy logic and in its applications, thatapplications, which are interesting to solve in the future.

As the real world is a mixed environment which is neither exclusively fuzzy and nor exclusively nonfuzzy and where changeover from fuzzy environment to nonfuzzy environment and vice versa is gradual (not abrupt), we need a well equippedwell-equipped mathematical fuzzy logical system which is perfectly compatible with its nonfuzzy counterpart for peaceful coexistence of both the logical systems (fuzzy and nonfuzzy) to describe the universe in a more enriched fashion to reveal the mystery of nature. For instance, we want to capture the legacy of Buddha and Aristotle in one mathematical frame, i.e.that is $(A \wedge \sim A)$ and $(A \vee \sim A)$ where the conjunction "and" is from the natural language and not the conjunction $\wedge$ of a formalized language, because only the natural language has the power to maintain the conjunction between two principles which express different metaphysical systems.

From car parking to moonlanding, from physical science to social science, from social science to biological science, from medical science to management science; these vast range of complex dynamics cannot be appropriately described and manipulated by fuzzy logic alone; rather we need a combination of logics (combination between fuzzy logic and nonfuzzy logic, where nonfuzzy logic includes classical twovaluedtwo valued concept, classical multivalued concept, probabilistic logic etc., and so on) to perform the task.

In real world, in almost every field of science and engineering we need perfect and precise measurement to represent and manipulate a system; whereas in real life there are many challenging situations which are essentially highly chaotic in nature. Physical measurement of any parameter for any real time application is not possible and which are nicely represented and manipulated by perception derived from experience and/or intuition of individual (expert). Hence, it is not only measurement but also perception both are equally important and both have significantly meaningful position/status in our knowledgebase which makes us rational on the surface of the earth.

Therefore, it is not important whether we compute with number or compute with words, whether we go by measurement or go by perception,; but it is most important how to combine the above stated advanced features in an intelligent way so that they can mutually share each other's benefit in a compatible manner to face the challenge of the real world.

KEYWORDS

- **Łukasiewicz Logic**
- **Modus ponens**
- **Abductive reasoning**
- **Syllogism**
- **Modus tollens**

CHAPTER 4

FUZZY IMPLICATIONS AND FUZZY IF-THEN MODELS

4.1 INTRODUCTION

Material implication is a conditional proposition normally represented as $(x \rightarrow y)$, where x is the antecedent, y is the consequent. A conditional proposition is a complex proposition consisting of the two sub-propositions x and y connected with the material implication connective "→". The natural language interpretation of material implication is "if x is TRUE, then y is TRUE", or simply as "x implies y". But the natural language interpretation of material implication does not say anything about the case, when x is FALSE. The material implication is defined both in case x is TRUE and x is FALSE. The natural language interpretation thus only covers half the definition of material implication and this gap in interpretation is the source of the confusion around material implication.

4.2 SYNTAX AND SEMANTICS OF MATERIAL IMPLICATION

Let p = "x is in A" and q = "y is in B" are crisp propositions, where A and B are crisp sets. Therefore we get the implication as, $p \rightarrow q$, which is interpreted as $\sim (p \wedge \sim q)$. "p entails q" means that it can never happen that p is true and q is not true.

Thus we get:

$$p \rightarrow q = \sim p \vee q. \tag{4.1}$$

The full interpretation of the material implication $p \rightarrow q$ is that the degree of truth of $p \rightarrow q$ quantifies to what extent q is at least as true as p, that is:

$p \rightarrow q$ is true $\Leftrightarrow \tau(p) \leq \tau(q)$, where τ is the degree of truth that is:

$$p \rightarrow q = \begin{cases} 1 & if \ \tau(p) \leq \tau(q) \\ 0 & otherwise. \end{cases} \tag{4.2}$$

The truth table of material implication is given in Table 1

TABLE 1   Truth table of material implication

p	q	~p	p $\longrightarrow$ q
1	1	0	1
0	1	1	1
0	0	1	1
1	0	0	0

Example 4.1 Let p = "x is taller than 6ft" and let q = "x is taller than 5ft". It is easy to see that p → q is true, because it can never happen that x is taller than 6ft and x is not taller than 5ft.

This property of material implication can be interpreted as:

$$\text{If } X \subseteq Y \text{ then } X \rightarrow Y. \tag{4.3}$$

An alternative interpretation of the implication operator is:

$$X \rightarrow Y = \sup\{Z | X \cap Z \subseteq Y\}. \tag{4.4}$$

4.2.1   FUZZY IMPLICATIONS

Consider the proposition, "if air flow is high then temperature is low".

The membership function of the fuzzy set A, air flow, is shown in the Figure 1,

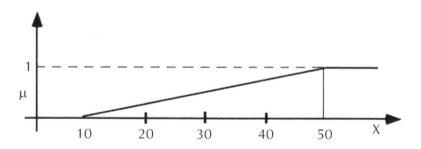

FIGURE 1   Membership function (μ) for "air flow is high".

The membership function of the fuzzy set A, air flow, is shown in the Figure 1 is interpreted as:

- 10 is in the fuzzy set high air flow with grade of membership 0,
- 20 is in the fuzzy set high air flow with grade of membership 0.25,
- 40 is in the fuzzy set high air flow with grade of membership 0.75, and
- x is in the fuzzy set high air flow with grade of membership 1, for all x $\geq$ 50.

Therefore,

$$A(x) = \begin{cases} 1 & \text{if } x \geq 50 \\ 1 - \frac{50-x}{40} & \text{if } 10 \leq x \leq 50 \\ 0 & \text{otherwise.} \end{cases} \quad (4.5)$$

The membership function of the fuzzy set B, small volume, is interpreted as (See Figure 2)
- 5 is in the fuzzy set low temperature with grade of membership 0,
- 4 is in the fuzzy set low temperature with grade of membership 0.25,
- 2 is in the fuzzy set low temperature with grade of membership 0.75, and
- x is in the fuzzy set low temperature with grade of membership 1, for all $x \leq 1$.

Therefore,

$$B(y) = \begin{cases} 1 & \text{if } y \leq 1 \\ 1 - \frac{y-1}{4} & \text{if } 1 \leq y \leq 5 \\ 0 & \text{otherwise.} \end{cases} \quad (4.6)$$

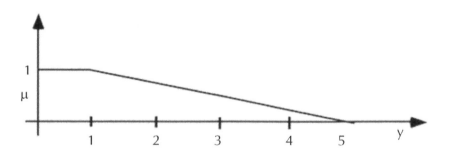

FIGURE 2   Membership function for "temperature is low".

If p is a proposition of the form:

$$x \text{ is } A$$

where A is a fuzzy set, for example, high air flow and q is a proposition of the form:

$$y \text{ is } B$$

for example, low temperature then we define the fuzzy implication $A \rightarrow B$ as a fuzzy relation.

It is clear that $(A \rightarrow B)(x, y)$ should be defined point wise and likewise, that is, $(A \rightarrow B)(x, y)$ depends only on $A(x)$ and $B(y)$.

That is,

$$(A \to B)(x, y) = I(A(x), B(y)) = A(x) \to B(y),$$

where I is an implication operator.

In our interpretation $A(x)$ is considered as the truth value of the proposition
"x is high air flow",

and $B(y)$ is considered as the truth value of the proposition:
"y is low temperature".

That is,

x is high air flow $\to$ y is low temperature $\equiv A(x) \to B(y)$.

Remember the full interpretation of the material implication:

$$p \to q = \begin{cases} 1 & if \ \tau(p) \le \tau(q) \\ 0 & otherwise. \end{cases}$$

One possible extension of material implication to implications with intermediate
truth values can be:

$$A(x) \to B(y) = \begin{cases} 1 & if \ A(x) \le B(y) \\ 0 & otherwise. \end{cases} \tag{4.7}$$

"4 is high air flow" $\to$ "1 is low temperature" $= A(4) \to B(1) = 0.75 \to 1 = 1$.

However, it is easy to see that this fuzzy implication operator sometimes is not appropriate for real-life applications. Namely, let $A(x) = 0.8$ and $B(y) = 0.8$.

Then we have:

$$A(x) \to B(y) = 0.8 \to 0.8 = 1.$$

Suppose there is a small error of measurement in $B(v)$, and instead of 0.8 we have
0.7999. Then:

$$A(x) \to B(y) = 0.8 \to 0.7999 = 0$$

This example shows that small changes in the input can cause a big deviation in
the output, that is our system is very sensitive to rounding errors of digital computation
and small errors of measurement.

A smoother extension of material implication operator can be derived from the
equation:

$$X \to Y = \sup\{ Z \mid X \cap Z \subseteq Y \}. \tag{4.8}$$

That is,

$$A(x) \to B(y) = \sup \{z \mid \min \{ A(x), z \} \le B(y) \}$$

So:

$$A(x) \to B(y) = \begin{cases} 1 & \text{if } A(x) \leq B(y) \\ B(y) & \text{otherwise.} \end{cases} \tag{4.9}$$

This operator is called Gödel implication. Other possibility is to extend the original definition:

$$p \to q = {\sim} p \lor q$$

using the definition of negation and union:

$$A(x) \to B(y) = \max \{ 1 - A(x), B(y) \}. \tag{4.10}$$

This operator is called Kleene-Dienes implication.

In many practical applications we use Mamdani's implication operator to model causal relationship between fuzzy variables.

This operator simply takes the minimum of truth values of fuzzy predicates:

$$A(x) \to B(y) = \min \{A(x), B(y)\}.$$

It is easy to see this is not a correct extension of material implications, because $0 \to 0$ yields zero. However, in knowledge-based systems we are usually not interested in rules, where the antecedent part is false.

We can categorize the fuzzy implication operators into following three classes:

• **S-implications**: defined by:

$$x \to y = S(n(x).y)$$

where S is a t-conorm and n is a negation on [0, 1]. These implications arise from the Boolean formalism $p \to q = {\sim} p \lor q$. Typical examples of S-implications are the Łukasiewicz and Kleene-Dienes implications.

• **R- implications**: obtained by residuation of continuous t-norm T, that is,:

$$x \to y = \sup\{z \in [0, 1] | T(s, z) \leq y\}.$$

These implications arise from the Intutionistic Logic Formalism. Typical examples of R-implications are the Gödel and Gaines implications.

• **t-norm implications**: if T is a t-norm then:

$$x \to y = T(x, y).$$

Although these implications do not verify the properties of material implication they are used as model of implication in many applications of fuzzy logic. Typical example of t-norm implication is the Mamdani ($x \to y = \min\{x, y\}$) implication.

The most often used fuzzy implication operators are listed in Table 2.

TABLE 2   Laws of fuzzy implication

Larsen	$x \to y = xy$
Łukasiewicz	$x \to y = \min \{ 1, 1 - x + y \}$
Mamdani	$x \to y = \min \{ x, y \}$
Standard Strict	$x \to y = \begin{cases} 1 & \text{if } x \leq y \\ 0 & \text{otherwise} \end{cases}$
Gödel	$x \to y = \begin{cases} 1 & \text{if } x \leq y \\ y & \text{otherwise} \end{cases}$
Gaines	$x \to y = \begin{cases} 1 & \text{if } x \leq y \\ y/x & \text{otherwise} \end{cases}$
Kleene-Dienes	$x \to y = \max \{ 1 - x, y \}$
Kleene-Dienes – Łuk.	$x \to y = 1 - x + xy$

4.3   FUZZY MODIFIERS (HEDGES)

Fuzzy sets provide a basis for a systematic way for the manipulation of vague and imprecise concepts. For instance, the statement "old" is a vague concept, which we express as our perceptual representation of an individual's age. Such perceptual representation is not unique and its degree of imprecision depends on the environment (universe) to which we are exposed. We can employ fuzzy sets to represent such linguistic statement to represent and quantify our perception.

A linguistic hedge or modifier is an operation that modifies the meaning of a term or a fuzzy set. For example, if hot is a fuzzy set, then very hot, more or less hot, and extremely hot are examples of hedges that are applied to that fuzzy set. Hedges can be viewed as operators that act upon a fuzzy set's membership function to modify it. Hedges play the same role in fuzzy production rules that adjectives and adverbs play in English sentences. There are hedges that intensify the characteristics of a fuzzy set (very, extremely), that dilute the membership curve (somewhat, rather, and quite), that form the complement (not), and that approximate a scalar to a fuzzy set (about, close to, and approximately). The mechanics underlying the hedge operation is generally heuristic in nature. For example, $\mu_A^{1.3}(x)$ is used frequently to implement the hedge slightly. Zadeh's original definition of the hedge very intensifies the fuzzy region by squaring the membership function at each point in the set $\mu_A^2(x)$. On the other hand, the hedge somewhat dilutes the fuzzy region by taking the square root of the membership function at each point along the set $\mu_A^{0.5}(x)$.

A generalization of the concentrator hedge is:

$$M_{con(A)}(x) = \mu_A^n(x) \tag{4.11}$$

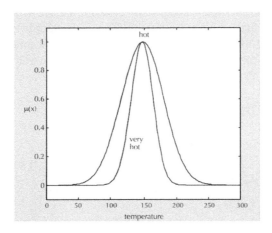

FIGURE 3   Representation of concentrator hedge.

where n $\geq$ 1. This hedge simply replaces the exponent of the intensification function with a real positive number greater than unity. Figure 3 shows the hedge that uses the general concentrator form with n = 3. The complement of very is a hedge group represented by somewhat, rather, and quite. These hedges basically dilute the force of a fuzzy set membership function. A generalization of the dilator hedge simply replaces the exponent of the intensification function with a real positive number less than unity, expressed as a fraction (1/n).

The generalized dilator edge is defined as:

$$M_{dil(A)}(x) = \mu_A^{1/n}(x) \tag{4.12}$$

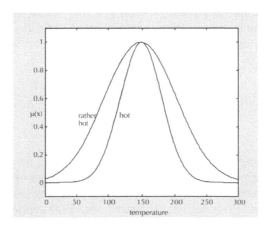

FIGURE 4   Representation of dilator hedge.

where n ≥ 1. Generalized dilator hedges are shown in Figure 4. The contrast hedges change the nature of fuzzy regions by making the region either less fuzzy (intensification) or more fuzzy (diffusion). Hedges such as positively, absolutely, and definitely are contrast hedges, changing a fuzzy set by raising the truth values above (0.5) and decreasing all the truth values below (0.5), thus reducing the overall fuzziness of the region (Figure 5).

These hedges are represented by:

$$\mu_{inf}(A) = \begin{cases} 2(\mu_A^2(A)) & \text{if } \mu_A(A) \geq 0.5 \\ 1 - 2(\mu_A''(A)) & \text{otherwise} \end{cases}. \tag{4.13}$$

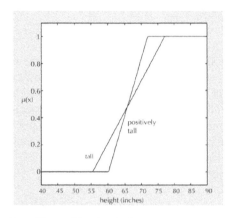

FIGURE 5   Representation of intensification hedge.

Similarly, a hedge such as generally changes the fuzzy surface by reducing all truth values above (0.5) and increasing all truth values below (0.5), as shown in Figure 6.

These hedges are represented by:

$$\mu_{def}(A) = \begin{cases} \dfrac{1}{2}(\mu_A^{1/2}(A)) & \text{if } \mu_A(A) \geq 0.5 \\ 1 - \dfrac{1}{2}(\mu_A^{1/2}(A)) & \text{otherwise} \end{cases} \tag{4.14}$$

Since hedge is linguistic in nature, multiple hedges can be applied to a singly fuzzy region. The approximation hedges are an important class of transformers. They not only broaden or restrict existing bell-shaped fuzzy regions, but also convert scalar values into bell-shaped fuzzy regions. The most often used approximate hedge is the about hedge, which creates a space that is proportional to the height and width of the generated fuzzy space [97].

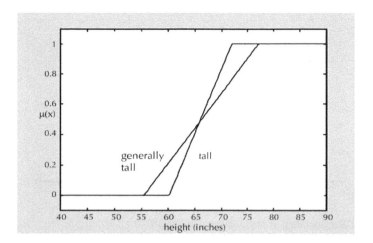

FIGURE 6 Representation of Diffusion hedge.

Definition 4.1 Let A be a fuzzy set in X. Then the fuzzy sets "very A" and "more or less A" can be defined by (very A) (x) = $A(x)^2$, (more or less A) (x) = $\sqrt{A(x)}$.

Example 4.2 The Figure 7 and 8 represent the modifiers "very" and "more or less" to represent the vague concept "old", which can be formally represented by a fuzzy set.

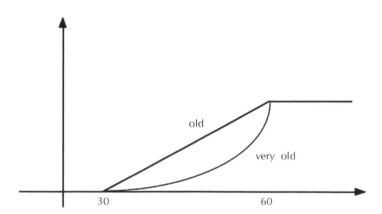

FIGURE 7 Representation of modifier "very".

A linguistic variables can be regarded either as a variable, whose value is a fuzzy number or as a variable, whose values are defined in linguistic terms.

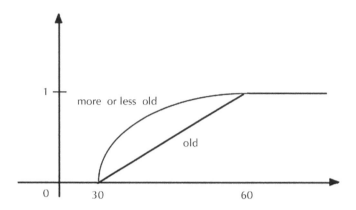

FIGURE 8   Representation of modifier "more or less".

Definition 4.2 A linguistic variable is defined by a quintuple:

$$(x, T(x), X, G, M),$$

Where:
- x is the name of variable,
- T(x) is the term set of x, that is, the set of names of linguistic values of x with each value being a fuzzy number defined on X,
- G is a syntactic rule for generating the names of values of x, and
- M is a semantic rule for associating with each value its meaning.

Example 4.3 Let us consider "speed" as a linguistic variable. The term set T of "speed" is represented as:

T = {slow, moderate, fast, very slow, more or less fast, ... }

where each term in T (speed) is represented by a fuzzy set in a universe of discourse X = [0, 100].

Let, "speed below 30 mph" be represented as slow, "speed around 60 mph" be represented as moderate and "speed above 80 mph" be represented as fast.

These terms are represented by fuzzy sets whose membership functions are (See Figure 9):

$$Slow(x) = \begin{cases} 1 & \text{if } x \le 30 \\ 1 - \frac{x-40}{15} & \text{if } 40 \le x \le 60 \\ 0 & \text{otherwise;} \end{cases}$$

$$moderate(x) = \begin{cases} 1 - \frac{|x-55|}{30} & \text{if } 60 \le x \le 80 \\ 0 & \text{otherwise;} \end{cases}$$

$$\text{fast(x)} = \begin{cases} 1 & \text{if } x \le 80 \\ 1 - \frac{(70-x)}{15} & \text{if } 60 \le x \le 80 \\ 0 & \text{otherwise.} \end{cases}$$

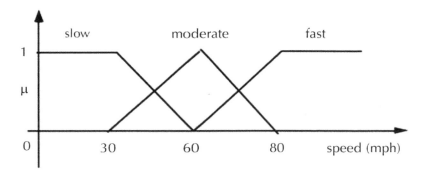

FIGURE 9 Values of linguistic variable speed.

In many practical applications we normalize the domain of inputs and use the following type of fuzzy partition (See Figure 10).

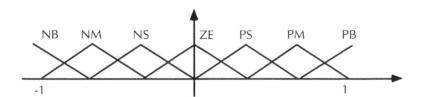

FIGURE 10 A possible fuzzy partition of [-1, 1].

Here we use the abbreviations:
- NB Negative Big, [NM] Negative Medium,
- NS Negative Small, [ZE] Zero,
- PS Positive small, [PM] Positive Medium, and
- PB Positive Big.

4.4 LINGUISTIC TRUTH VALUE

Let, Truth = {Absolutely false, Very false, False, Fairly true, True, Very true, and Absolutely true}.

We may define the membership function of linguistic terms of truth as:

$$\text{True(x)} = x$$

for each $x \in [0,1]$.

$$\text{False}(x) = 1 - x$$

for each $x \in [0,1]$.

$$\text{Absolutely false}(x) = \begin{cases} 1 & if & x = 0 \\ 0 & otherwise. \end{cases}$$

$$\text{Absolutely true}(x) = \begin{cases} 1 & x = 1 \\ 0 & otherwise. \end{cases}$$

The linguistic truth pattern is depicted in Figure 11.

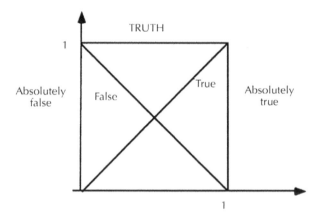

FIGURE 11   Linguistic truth status.

The word "Fairly" is interpreted as "more or less" (See Figure 12).

$$\text{Fairly true}(x) = \sqrt{x}$$

for each $x \in [0,1]$ and

$$\text{Very true }(x) = x^2$$

for each $x \in [0,1]$.

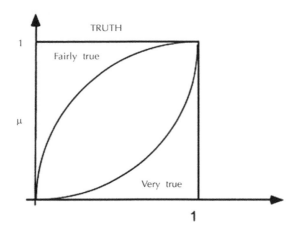

FIGURE 12   Truth pattern "fairly true and very true".

The word "Fairly" is interpreted as "more or less" (See Figure 13). Therefore,

$$\text{Fairly false}(x) = \sqrt{1-x}$$

for each $x \in [0,1]$, and

$$\text{Very false }(x) = (1-x)^2$$

for each $x \in [0,1]$.

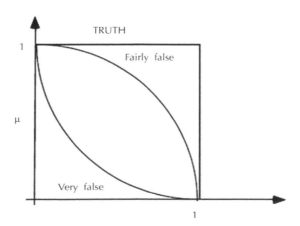

FIGURE 13   Truth pattern of Fairly false and very false.

Suppose we have the fuzzy statement "x is A". Let τ be a term of linguistic variable Truth.

Then the statement "x is A is τ" is interpreted as "x is τ o A", where:

$$(\tau \text{ o A}) (x) = \tau (A (x))$$

for each $x \in [0,1]$.

For example, let τ = "true", Then:

"x is A is true"

is defined by:

"x is τ o A" = "x is A"

because,

$$(\tau \text{ o A}) (x) = \tau (A (x)) = A(x)$$

for each $x \in [0,1]$.

That is why *"everything we write is considered to be true"* (See Figure 14).

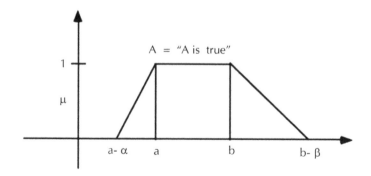

FIGURE 14   A is true.

Let τ = "absolutely true". Then the statement *"x is A is Absolutely true"* is defined by *"x is τ o A"* (See Figure 15),

Where,

$$(\tau \text{ o A}) (x) = \begin{cases} 1 & if \ A(x) = 1 \\ 0 & otherwise. \end{cases}$$

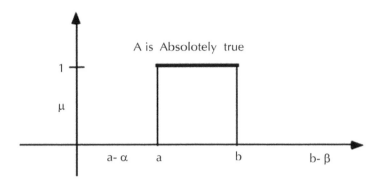

FIGURE 15   A is absolutely true.

Let τ = "absolutely false". Then the statement "*x is A is Absolutely false*" is defined by "*x is τ o A*" (See Figure 16),
Where,

$$(\tau \text{ o A}) (x) = \begin{cases} 1 & \text{if } A(x) = 0 \\ 0 & \text{otherwise.} \end{cases}$$

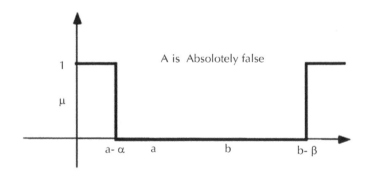

FIGURE 16   A is absolutely false.

Let τ = "Fairly true". Then the statement "*x is A is Fsirly true*" is defined by "*x is τ o A*" (See Figure 17),
Where,

$$(\tau \text{ o A}) (x) = \sqrt{A(x)} \, .$$

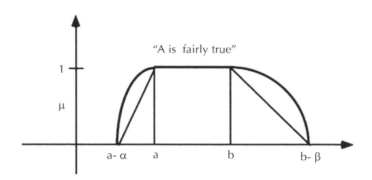

FIGURE 17   A is fairly true.

Let τ = "Very true". Then the statement "*x is A is Fairly true*" is defined by "*x is τ o A*" (See Figure 18),
   Where,

$$(\tau \text{ o A}) (x) = \left(A(x)\right)^{2}.$$

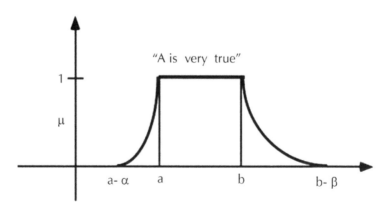

FIGURE 18   A is very true.

4.5   GROUP DECISION MAKING BASED ON LINGUISTIC DECISION PROCESS

A group decision making process can be formulated based on the following components:
   • A group is formed by two or more individuals.
   • Each member of the group has his or her own perception, attitude, motivation, and personality.
   • The group as a whole recognizes a common problem to be solved, and

- The group as a whole tries to reach a collective decision to solve the problem, which is recognized as stated above.

In this section we present a linguistic decision process in group decision making. Assuming a set of linguistic preferences, representing the preferences of the individuals, we develop a linguistic decision process [134, 135].

The use of preference relations is usual in group decision making. As human judgments including preferences are often vague, the concept of fuzzy set plays an important role in group decision making process. Several researchers have provided interesting results on group decision making or social choice theory with the help of fuzzy sets.

Let there be a finite set of alternatives $X = \{x_1, \ldots\ldots x_n\}$ as well as a finite set of individuals $N = \{1, \ldots\ldots, m\}$. Each individual $k \in N$ provides his/her preference (fuzzy concept) relation on X, that is, $P_k \subset X \times X$, and $\mu_{P_k}(x_i, x_j)$ denotes the degree of preference of alternative x_i over x_j, $\mu_{P_k}(x_i, x_j) \in [0,1]$.

As an individual may have vague information about the degree of preference between the alternative x_i and x_j and cannot estimate the degree of preference with an exact numerical value, linguistic assessments instead of numerical values, are applied by means of linguistic terms. A scale of certainty expressions (linguistically assessed) is presented to the individual, who could then use it to describe his/her degree of certainty in a preference. In Figure 19 we depict the linguistic decision process.

We consider a linguistic ordered weighted averaging (LOWA) operator based on two concepts: the ordered weighted averaging operator, and the convex combination of linguistic labels. The fuzzy majority concept, represented by a fuzzy linguistic quantifier and the LOWA operator, is used to obtain a collective linguistic preference. Finally, the non-dominated alternative concept is used for defining a linguistic non-dominance degree, which allows us to obtain the solution alternative(s) in the process of choice.

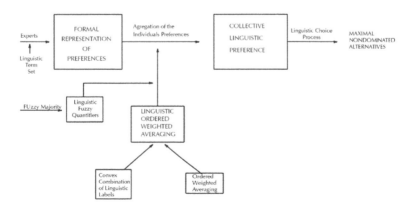

FIGURE 19   Schematic representation of Linguistic decision process.

4.6   LINGUISTIC ASSESSMENTS AND COMBINATION OF LINGUISTIC VALUES

The linguistic approach as proposed by Zadeh assesses the variables in the problem by means of linguistic terms instead of numerical values. This approach is appropriate since it allows a representation of the experts knowledge in a more direct and appropriate form though the experts cannot express the preferences with precision.

To make the finest level of distinction among different quantifications of uncertainty we consider term set to describe granularity of uncertainty. People studied the use of term sets with odd cardinality, representing the middle term by a probability of "approximately 0.5", with the remaining terms placed symmetrically around it.

The semantic of the elements of the term set is given by fuzzy numbers defined in the [0,1] interval, described by membership functions. As the linguistic assessments are estimates given by the experts or decision-makers, we consider the linear trapezoidal membership function to represent the vagueness of those linguistic assessments. The Figure 20 shows the hierarchical structure of linguistic values or labels.

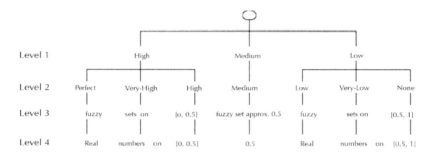

FIGURE 20   Representation of different hierarchy of labels.

First we have to determine the type of label set to be used. Let $S = \{l_i\}$, $i \in H = \{0, \ldots, T\}$ be a finite and totally ordered term set on [0.1]. A label l_i represents a possible value for a linguistic real variable, that is, a vague property or constraint on [0,1]. The representation is achieved by the 4-tuple $(a_i, b_i, \alpha_i, \beta_i)$. The first two parameters indicate the interval in which the membership value is 1.0 and the third and fourth parameters indicate the left and right width of the distribution. We consider a term set with odd cardinality, where the middle label represents an uncertainty of "approximately 0.5", and the remaining terms are placed symmetrically around it. We require the following properties for the term set;

The set is ordered: $l_i \geq l_j$ if $i \geq j$.
The negation operator is defined as: $Neg(l_i) = l_j$ such that $j = T - i$.
$\quad$ $Max(l_i, l_j) = l_i$ if $l_i \geq l_j$.
$\quad$ $Min(l_i, l_j) = l_i$ if $l_i \geq l_j$.

Example 4.4 Consider the term set of level 2:

$S = \{l_6 = P, l_5 = V H, l_4 = H, l_3 = M, l_2 = L, l_1 = V L, l_0 = N\}$, where
$P = $ Perfect, V H = Very_High, H = High, M = Medium, L = Low, VL = Very_Low,
N = None.

The term set verifies each of the above properties.

The Figure 21 shows a possible domain of the term set.

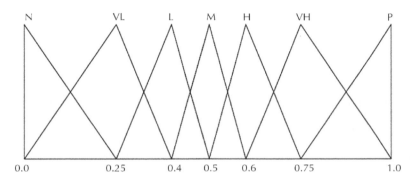

FIGURE 21   Representation of Domain at level 2

The representation values are:
P = (1,1,0,0)   V H = (.75,.75,.15,.25)   H = (.6,.6,.1,.15)
M = (.5,.5,.1,.1)   L = (.4,.4,.15,.1)   V L = (.25,.25,.25,.15)
N = (.0,.0,.0,.25).

Aggregation of uncertainty information is a recurrent need in the decision process. Hence, the combinations of linguistic values are needed.

We consider an aggregation operator (LOWA) of linguistic labels by direct computation on labels, based on the ordered weighted averaging (OWA) operator, and the convex combination of linguistic labels.

A mapping F:

$$I^n \rightarrow I(\text{where } I = [0, 1])$$

is called an OWA operator of dimension n if it is associated with a weighting vector $W = [w_1, \ldots\ldots, w_n]$, such that: i) $w_i \in [0, 1]$, ii) $\sum_i w_i = 1$, and $F(a_1 \ldots\ldots, a_n) = w_1 . B_1 + w_2 . b_2 + \ldots\ldots + w_n . b_n$, where b_i is the i-th largest element in the collection $a_1, \ldots\ldots, a_n$. If we denote B as the vector consisting of the arguments of F in descending order:,

$$F(a_1, \ldots\ldots, a_n) = W . B^T$$

provides an aggregation type operator that always lies between the "and" and the "or" aggregation (See Chapter 2).

Yager (1992b) extended the OWA operator to linguistic elements. Here, we extend it to linguistic arguments using the convex combination of linguistic labels. In fact, let

M be a collection of linguistic labels, $l_k \in M, k = 1, ..., m$, and assume without loss of generality $l_m \leq l_{m-1} \leq ..... \leq l_1$. For any set of coefficients $\{\lambda \in [0, 1], k = 1, 2, ..., m, \sum \lambda_k = 1\}$, the convex combination of these m generalized labels is the label given by:

$$C\{\lambda_k, l_k, k = 1, ..., m\} = \lambda_1 \, l_1 \oplus (1 - \lambda_1) \odot C\{\beta_h, l_h, h = 2, ...m\}$$

With,

$$\beta_h = \lambda_h / \sum_2^n \lambda_k ; h = 2, ..., m$$

The aggregation of labels is defined by addition, the difference of generalized labels, and the product by a positive real number over a generalized label space S, based on S, that is, the Cartesian product $S = SxZ^+$, with the basic label set $S = \{(l_i, 1, i \in H\}$. In our context all the operations are made over the basic set S. Briefly, the result of the expression $\lambda \odot l_j \oplus (1 - \lambda) \odot l_i, j \geq i$, is l_k where $k = \min\{T, i + round(\lambda. (j - i))\}$.

Example 4.5 Consider the term set of level 2 (See Table 3);

TABLE 3   Term set of level 2

		$1 - \lambda = 0.6$			
		VL	VH	P	VL
	P	M	VH	P	M
$\lambda = 0.4$	N	VL	M	H	VL
	L	VL	M	H	VL
	M	L	H	VH	L

where,

$$k_{11} = \min\{6, 1 + round(0.4*(6-1))\} = 3 \Rightarrow l_{k_{11}} = M$$
$$k_{21} = \min\{6, 0 + round(0.6 * (1 - 0))\} = 1 \Rightarrow l_{k_{21}} = VL$$

Therefore the linguistic ordered weighted aggregation (LOWA) operator is defined as:

$$F(a_1, ..., a_m) = W . B^T = C\{w_k, b_k, k = 1, ..., m\}$$

$$= w_1 \odot b_1 \oplus (1 - w_1) \odot C\{\beta_h, b_h, h = 2, ..., m\}$$

where $\beta_h = w_h / \sum_2^m w_k, h = 2,....,m, and B$ is the associated ordered label vector.

Each element $b_i \in B$ is the i-th largest label in the collection $a_1, ..., a_m$.

Basically, there are two approaches to obtain the values of w_i;

- The first approach is to use a learning mechanism. In this approach, sample data are used along with arguments and associated aggregated values, and then weights are fitted to the sample date.
- The second approach is to give some semantics or meaning to the weights. Then, based upon these semantics we can directly provide the values for the weights.

In the following section, we consider a semantic for the weights based on fuzzy linguistic quantifiers, and obtain a collective linguistic preference relation.

4.7 LINGUISTIC PREFERENCE RELATIONS AND LINGUISTIC CHOICE PROCESS

Let there be a set of n alternatives $X = \{x_1,......,x_n\}$ and a set of individuals N = $\{1,........,m\}$. Each individual K $\in$ N provides a preference relation linguistically assessed into the term set S,

$$\varphi P_k : X \times X \to solution \subseteq X.$$

On the basis of the individual preference relations, a solution is derived. Alternatively an indirect approach is:

$$\{P_1....., P_m\} \to P \to solution \subseteq X$$

which provides the solution on the basis of a collective preference relation, P, which is a preference relation of the group of individuals as a whole.

Here we consider the indirect derivation.

Hence we have to consider the following two issues:

- Derivation of a collective linguistic preference P from $\{P_1,......, P_m\}$, and
- Generation of the linguistic choice process to obtain the soution from P.

4.7.1 LINGUISTIC PREFERENCE RELATION

We need to aggregate the linguistic preference relations to obtain $l_{ij} \in S$ from

$\{l_{ij}^1,...........,l_{ij}^m\}$ for all i, j. Using a fuzzy majority specified by a fuzzy linguistic quantifier, we deal with this problem. Fuzzy linguistic quantifiers provide tools to deal with fuzzy majority. It can be used to define a weight vector necessary for using LOWA operator.

We use the LOWA operator to obtain the collective preference relation P as:

$$P = F(P_1,......,P_m)$$

with $I^{n} = E\left(I^{n}_{1}, \ldots, I^{n}_{w}\right)$ and the weight vector, W, representing the fuzzy majority over the individuals.

The fuzzy linguistic quantifiers were introduced by Zadeh (1983). Linguistic quantifiers are represented by terms such as most, at least half, all, as many as possible. A quantifier Q assumed to be a fuzzy set in [0,1]. Zadeh distinguished between two types of quantifiers; absolute, and proportional or relative. Absolute quantifiers are used to represent amount that are absolute in nature. These quantifiers are closely related to the number of elements. Zadeh suggested that these absolute quantifier values can be represented as fuzzy subsets of the non-negative reals R^{+}. In particular, he suggested that an absolute quantifier can be represented by a fuzzy subset Q, where for any $r \in R^{+}$, Q(r) indicated the degree to which the value r satisfies the concept represented by Q. Relative quantifiers represent proportion type statements. Thus, if Q is a relative quantifier, then Q can be represented as a fuzzy subset of [0,1] such that for each $r \in [0,1]$, Q(r) indicates the degree to which r portion of objects satisfies the concept devoted by Q.

Here, we consider relative quantifiers as stated below.

Definition 4.3 A relative quantifier, $Q: [0,1] \rightarrow [0,1]$, satisfies:

$$Q(0) = 0,$$

$$\exists r \in [0,1] \text{ such that } Q(r) = 1.$$

It is non-decreasing if it has the following property:

$$\forall a, b \in [0,1] \text{ if } a > b \text{ then } Q(a) \geq Q(b)$$

The membership function of a relative quantifier can be represented as:

$$Q(r) = \begin{cases} 0 & \text{if } r < a \\ \dfrac{r-a}{b-a} & \text{if } b \leq r \leq a \\ 1 & \text{if } r > b \end{cases}$$

with $a, b, r \in [0,1]$.

Example 4.6 Relative quantifiers are shown in Figure 22, where the parameters, (a,b) are (0.3, 0.8), (0, 0.5), and (0.5, 1), respectively.

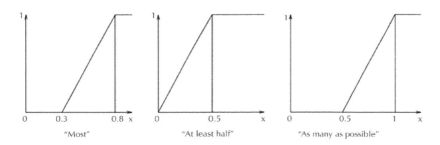

FIGURE 22   Representation of Relative quantifiers.

Yager (1988) computes the weights w_i of the aggregation from the function Q describing the quantifier. In the case of a relative quantifier.

$$W_i = Q(i/m) - Q((i-1)/m), \; i=1, \, ..., m, \; with \; Q(0) = 0.$$

4.7.2 LINGUISTIC CHOICE PROCESS

Numerous solutions derived from a collective fuzzy preference are available in the literature, including a consensus winner a competitive-like pooling, and a fuzzy α-majority uncovered fuzzy set based on the concept of fuzzy tournaments [134, 135].

We propose a process to derive a solution on the basis of the collective preference relation, a process based on the concept of non-dominated alternatives.

Let P^s be a linguistic strict preference relation $\mu p^s(x_i, x_j) = l_j^l$ such that;

$$l_{ij}^s = None \; if \; l_{ij} < l_{ji},$$

or $\qquad l_{ij}^s = l_k \in S \; if \; l_{ji} \geq l_{ji} \; with \; l_{ji} = l_i, l_{ji} = l_t, \; and \; l = t + k.$

The linguistic non-dominance degree of x_i is sated as follows;

Definition 4.4 $\mu ND(x_i) = Min \, x_j \in X[Neg(\mu P^s(x_j, x_i))]$

where the value $\mu ND(x_i)$ is to be interpreted as the linguistic degree to which the alternative x_i is not dominated by any of the elements in X.

A set of maximal non-dominated alternatives, $X^{ND} \subset X$, is stated as:

Definition 4.5 $X^{ND} = \{x \in X / \mu^{ND}(x) = Max_{y \in x}[\mu_{ND}(y)]\}.$

The knowledge of the experts, X^{ND} is selected as the set of preferred alternatives in the linguistic choice process.

Example 4.7 We consider the above seven term set as stated in Figure 21 and a situation with four individuals whose linguistic preferences are:

$$P_1 = \begin{bmatrix} - & VL & VH & VL \\ VH & - & H & H \\ VL & L & - & VL \\ VH & L & VH & - \end{bmatrix} P_2 = \begin{bmatrix} - & L & H & VL \\ H & - & VH & L \\ L & VL & - & VL \\ VH & H & VH & - \end{bmatrix}$$

$$P_3 = \begin{bmatrix} - & M & VH & N \\ M & - & VH & L \\ VL & VL & - & VL \\ P & H & VH & - \end{bmatrix} P_4 = \begin{bmatrix} - & L & VH & VL \\ H & - & L & VL \\ VL & H & - & VL \\ VH & VL & VH & - \end{bmatrix}.$$

We apply the choice process with different fuzzy quantifiers:
- Based on the linguistic quantifier "As many as possible" with the pair (0.5, 1.0), and the corresponding LOWA operator, with W = [0,0,0.5,0.5], we obtain the collective linguistic preference as:

$$P = \begin{bmatrix} - & VL & H & N \\ M & - & M & VL \\ VL & VL & - & VL \\ VH & M & VH & - \end{bmatrix}.$$

The linguistic strict preference relation is:

$$P^s = \begin{bmatrix} - & L & VH & VL \\ H & - & VH & M \\ VL & M & - & VL \\ VH & H & VH & - \end{bmatrix}$$

and the linguistic non-dominance degree is:

$$\mu ND(x_1, x_2, x_3, x_4) = [V\ L, H, L, P].$$

The set of maximal non-dominated alternatives, X^{ND} is;

$$X^{ND} = \{x_4\}.$$

Therefore, x_4 is the maximal non-dominated alternative and the solution to the linguistic decision process.
- Based on the linguistic quantifier "At least half" with the pair (0.0, 0.5), and the corresponding LOWA operator, with W = [0.5, 0.5, 0.0, 0.0], we obtain the collective linguistic preference as:

$$P = \begin{bmatrix} - & VL & H & N \\ M & - & M & VL \\ VL & VL & - & VL \\ VH & M & VH & - \end{bmatrix}.$$

The linguistic strict preference relation is:

$$P = \begin{bmatrix} - & VL & VH & VL \\ VH & - & H & H \\ VL & L & - & VL \\ VH & L & VH & - \end{bmatrix}$$

$$P^s = \begin{bmatrix} - & N & H & N \\ L & - & L & N \\ N & N & - & N \\ H & VL & H & - \end{bmatrix}$$

and the linguistic non-dominance degree is:

$$\mu ND(x_1, x_2, x_3, x_4) = [L, VH, L, P].$$

The set of maximal non-dominated alternatives, X^{ND}, is:

$$X^{ND} = \{x_4\}.$$

Therefore, x_4 is the maximal non-dominated alternative and the solution to the linguistic decision process.

We have presented a representation of commonsense knowledge by means of linguistic labels and developed a linguistic decision process in group decision making for this representation. The linguistic decision process has been defined as an indirect approach based on the concepts of fuzzy majority and non-dominated alternatives, where fuzzy linguistic quantifiers have been used as tools to deal with fuzzy majority. This model seems to be very consistent to the social choice in an imprecise environment. Note that in group decision making, the linguistic approach is a tool, which provides a framework with more human-consistency than usual ones, and therefore helps the development of decision processes.

4.8 FUZZY SYSTEMS AS FUNCTION APPROXIMATORS

A fuzzy system can be used to approximate a function. Kosko [170] described a class of additive fuzzy systems. An additive fuzzy system approximates a function by covering its graph with fuzzy patches. The approximation improves as the fuzzy patches grow in number. Additive fuzzy systems have a feed-forward architecture that resembles the feed-forward multilayer neural systems used to approximate functions. Additive fuzzy systems are different from conventional fuzzy inference systems. Additive fuzzy systems add the then parts of fired if-then rules, whereas conventional fuzzy inference systems combine the then part with pairwise maxima. The fuzzy mapping function for the adaptive fuzzy system F: X → Y that approximates a function f: x → Y is shown in figures 23 and 24. Fuzzy patches approximate the function. The approximation improves with the number of patches. However, the computational cost also increases with the number of patches. A schematic diagram for an additive fuzzy system is presented in Figure 25. A Cartesian product space for the system is shown in Figure 26. Rules for the additive system are of the form "If X is A, then Y is B." Additive fuzzy systems fire all rules in parallel and average the scaled then part sets. The class of additive fuzzy systems represents a large number of additive systems. The most commonly used model for an additive fuzzy system is the standard additive model (SAM), which defines a function given by Kosko [169], *viz.*,

$$y = F(x) = \frac{\int y b(y) dy}{\int b(y) dy}$$

$$= \frac{\sum_{j=1}^{m} w_j v_j a_j(x) c_{yj}}{\sum_{j=1}^{m} w_j v_j a_j(x)} \qquad (4.15)$$

where V_j is the volume of the jth then-part set Bj and wj is the weight of the jth rule (often, $w_j = 1$). The term c_y is the centroid of the jth output set. Fit value $a_j(x)$ scales the then-part set B_j and m is the number of rules. The complexity of a SAM system depends on the complexity of the if-part fuzzy sets A_j and the dimensionality of the problem. Simple sets such as trapezoids and bell curves lead to efficient approximation.

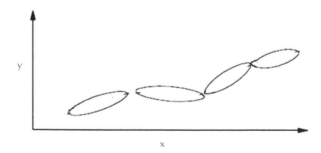

FIGURE 23   Function approximation with four fuzzy patches.

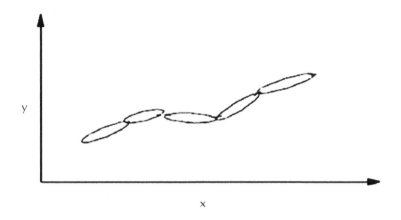

FIGURE 24 Function approximation with five fuzzy patches.

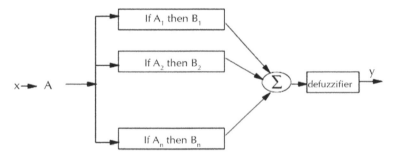

FIGURE 25 Additive fuzzy interference system.

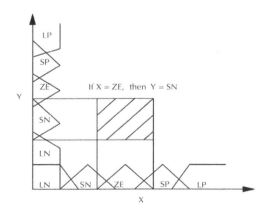

FIGURE 26 Fuzzy rule as a state patch.

4.9   EXTRACTING FUZZY RULES FROM SAMPLE DATA POINTS

Usually to design a fuzzy inference system (FIS), we need a rule base that contains fuzzy rules. These rules are obtained from expert knowledge. However, on many occasions, we may not know rules, but we may have sample data points or training samples in the input/output spaces. In situations like this, it is possible to generate fuzzy rules that define the mapping surface. The generated rules then can be used to design an FIS that performs the desired mapping. In 1991 Wang and Mendel suggested a systematic method for extracting fuzzy rules from sample data points. The method consists of five steps. They have also shown that the mapping surface can approximate any real continuous function on a compact set to a desired degree of accuracy. In this method, it is possible to combine information of two kinds: numeric and linguistic.

Consider a function $y = f(x_1, x_2)$. We can design FIS with two inputs and one output to approximate the function, using the following algorithm;

ALGORITHM

Step 1. Divide the input/output space into fuzzy regions: Divide each domain interval into $2N + 1$ regions. Let the regions be denoted as S_N(small N), ..., S_1(small 1), CE(central), B_1(big 1), ..., B_N(big N). The number of regions can be different for each variable. Assign each region a fuzzy membership function. Fuzzy membership functions for x_1, x_2, and y are shown in Figure 27. a–c.

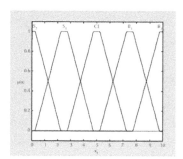

FIGURE 27 (a)   Fuzzy membership function.

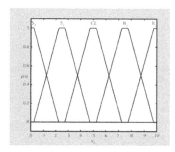

FIGURE 27 *(continued)*

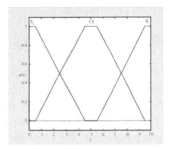

FIGURE 27 (b)   Fuzzy membership function.

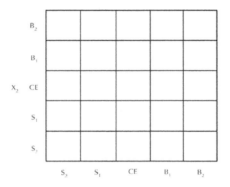

FIGURE 27 (C)   Fuzzy membership function.

Step 2. Generate fuzzy rules from given data points: First determine the degree of the given data point x_1 (i), x_2 (i), and y(i) for each membership function, and assign the point to the region with the maximum degree of membership. Then obtain a rule from the given data point.

The rule may look like the following:

$$R_i: \text{if } x_i \text{ is } B_i \text{ and } x_2 \text{ is CE, then } y \text{ is } B_1.$$

Step 3. Assign a degree to each rule: There are many data points, each generating a rule. Therefore, some rules may conflict. The degree of a rule can be defined as follows:

For rule R_i *viz.*, if x_1 is A and x_2 is B, then y is C, the degree of the rule is defined as:

$$D(R_i) = \mu_A(x_1)\, \mu_B(x_2)\mu_c(y) \qquad (4.16)$$

where $\mu_A(x_1)$, $\mu_B(x_2)$, and $\mu_c(y)$ represent membership values in fuzzy sets A, B, and C, respectively. In practice, we may have a priori information about data points. We therefore assign a degree to each data point that represents expert belief in the rule.

The degree of the rule then can be written as:

$$D(R_j) = \mu_A(x_1)\, \mu_B(x_2)\, \mu_c(y)\, \mu_i \, .$$ (4.17)

Step 4. Create a combined Fuzzy Associative Memory (FAM) Bank: Cells in the FAM bank are to be filled with fuzzy rules, by assignment. If there is more than one rule in any cell, then the rule with the maximum degree is used. If there is a rule with an OR operator, it fills all the cells in that row or column. (Shown in Figure 27(d))

Step 5. Determine a mapping based on the combined FAM bank: We used the following defuzzification to determine output y for given inputs $(x_1 m\, x_2)$.

The output membership region o_1 is given by:

$$\mu_{i0} = \mu_1\,(x_1)\,\mu_{2i}(x_2)$$ (4.18)

The centroid defuzzification method can be used to obtain the crisp output y.

Example 4.8 We view the above algorithm as a block. Input to the block consists of examples and expert rules, and the output of the block is a mapping from input to output space. Wang and Mendel used the five-step process for a chaotic time-series prediction problem. A chaotic time series, which is sufficiently complicated that it appears to be "random" can be:

Generated from a deterministic nonlinear system. The time series Wang and Mendel used is generated from the differential equation.

$$\frac{dx(t)}{dt} = \frac{0.2x(t-\tau)}{1+x^{10}(t-\tau)} - 0.1x(t),$$ (4.19)

where t>17. Those two researchers generated and plotted the time series with 1,000 points, using the first 700 points to train the system and the last 300 points to test the system. They approximated the time series using both a FIS and a neural network and compare the results. They show that the approximation could be greatly improved by dividing the domain into finer intervals. An FIS can approximate any arbitrary continuous function to any desired degree of accuracy. The ability to approximate an arbitrary function is an important property that can be used in many applications. Given discrete data points, we can generate a function passing through those points.

4.10   FUZZY BASIS FUNCTIONS

From the previous section, we know that a FIS is a nonlinear system that maps a crisp input vector X to a scalar y. The mapping can be represented as y = f(x). Discussions in the previous sections offer a geometric interpretation of a FIS. In 1995 Kim and Mendel provided the mathematical formula that defines the mapping function for a FIS. Their expansion for the FIS mapping function is:

$$y = f(x) = \frac{\sum\limits_{l=1}^{M} y'_1 \prod\limits_{i=1}^{p} \mu'_i(x_i)}{\sum\limits_{i=1}^{M} \prod\limits_{i=1}^{p} \mu'_i(x_i)} \tag{4.20}$$

where M denotes the number of rules, y'_i represents the center of gravity of the output fuzzy set that is associated with the rule R_i, p is the dimension of vector X, and $\mu'_i(x_i)$ represents input membership functions. This expansion is valid only when we choose singleton fuzzification functions, product inference, maximum-product composition, and height defuzzification.

Equation 4.20 can be rewritten as:

$$y = f(x) = \sum\limits_{i=1}^{M} y' \varphi_i(x) \tag{4.21}$$

where the $\phi_i(x)$ are called fuzzy basis functions (FBFs) and are given by:

$$\phi_i(x) = \frac{\prod\limits_{i=1}^{p} \mu_i(x_i)}{\sum\limits_{i=1}^{m} \prod\limits_{i=1}^{p} \mu'_i(x_i)} \tag{4.22}$$

The Equation 4.22 is valid for singleton fuzzification. The representation in Equation 4.20 is referred to as the fuzzy basis function expansion. Relationships between the fuzzy function and other basis functions (such as trigonometric functions) were studied extensively by Kim and Mendel. It can be seen that the FBF expansion is essentially a sum over M rules, each of which generates an FBF. The rules in the FBF expansion can be obtained from numeric data as well as from expert' knowledge. It is therefore convenient to decompose f(x) as:

$$Y = f(x) = f_N(x) + f_L(x) \tag{4.23}$$

The Equation 4.23 can be rewritten as:

$$y = f(x) = \sum\limits_{i=1}^{M_n} y \, Ni\phi_{Ni}(x) + \sum\limits_{k=1}^{M_1} y' \phi_{LK}(x) \tag{4.24}$$

where $M = M_N + M_L$ and M_N FBFs are associated with numeric data, and M_L FBFs are associated with linguistic information. These FBFs are given by:

$$\phi_N\left(x\right) = \frac{\displaystyle\prod_{s=1}^{p}\mu_s{}'(x_s)}{\displaystyle\sum_{j=1}^{M_N}\prod_{s=1}^{p}\mu_{s'}(x_s)} \qquad (4.25)$$

$$\phi_{L_k}\left(x\right) = \frac{\prod_{s=1}^{p}\mu_s{}'(x_s)}{\sum_{j=1}^{M_L}\prod_{s=1}^{p}\overline{\omega}_s(x_s)} \qquad (4.26)$$

It can be seen from Equations 4.25 and 4.26 that each FBF is normalized by information that is associated with both numeric and linguistic information.

Because the decomposition of an FBF depends on M, where $M = M_N + M_L$, a mapping function associated with an FIS can be expressed as a summation over FBFs. Unlike other classical basis functions (for example, trigonometric functions), which are inherently orthogonal, FBFs are not orthogonal. They are, however, important and unique, because of the fact that they are the only basis functions that can include numeric, as well as linguistic, information.

4.11   EXTRACTING FUZZY RULES FROM CLUSTERING OF TRAINING SAMPLES

Extracting fuzzy rules from training samples establishes a relationship among the data to be modeled by "if-then" rules. The rule extraction method is based on estimating clusters in the data. Each cluster obtained corresponds to a fuzzy rule that relates a region in the input space to an output region. After the number of rules and initial rule parameters are obtained by cluster estimation, the rule parameters are optimized by gradient descent method.

For function approximation, where the output data correspond to a continuous-valued variable, the extracted rules express continuous-valued relationships (for example, "if input is small then output is big"). For pattern classification, where the output data correspond to class assignments, the extracted rules have discrete-valued consequents (for example, "if input is small then output is class 1"). In both cases, fuzzy rules provide a powerful framework for capturing the behavior of the input/output data. The concept of function approximation has already been discussed in section 4.8. The problem of extracting fuzzy rules from data for function approximation has been studied in section 4.9 and 4.10. Several methods for extracting fuzzy rules for function approximation have used clustering to determine the number of rules and initial rule parameters. Each cluster essentially identifies a region in the data space that contains a sufficient mass of data to support the existence of a fuzzy input/output relationship. Because a rule is generated only where there is a cluster of data, the resultant rules are scattered in the input space rather than placed according to grid-like partitions in the input space. This fundamental feature of clustering-based rule extraction methods helps avoid combinatorial explosion of rules with increasing dimension of the input space. Also, because the clustering step provides good initial rule parameter values, the subsequent rule parameter optimization process usually converges quickly to a good solution.

A clustering method called subtractive clustering is considered for the approach. Subtractive clustering is a fast and robust method for estimating the number and location of cluster centers present in a collection of data points. Initial fuzzy rules with rough estimates of membership functions are obtained from the cluster centers. The membership functions and other rule parameters are then optimized with respect to some output error criterion. This approach can be applied to extract rules for both function approximation and pattern classification, with some small differences in the detailed methods for these two types of applications.

In the following sections, we describe the rule extraction methods in detail. We also illustrate their use in a function approximation example and in a pattern classification example [47].

4.11.1 CLUSTER ESTIMATION

Yager and Filev proposed a simple and effective algorithm, called the mountain method, for estimating the number and initial location of cluster centers. Their method is based on gridding the data space and computing a potential value for each grid point based on its distances to the actual data points. A grid point with many data points nearby has a high potential value. The grid point with the highest potential value is chosen as the first cluster center. The key concept is that once the first cluster center is chosen, the potential of all grid points is reduced according to their distance from the cluster center. Grid points near the first cluster center have reduced potential. The next cluster center is then placed at the grid point with the highest remaining potential value. This procedure of acquiring new cluster center and reducing the potential of surrounding grid points repeats until the potential of all grid points falls below a threshold. Although this method is simple and effective, the computation grows exponentially with the dimension of the problem. For example, a clustering problem with 4 variables and having a resolution of 10 grid lines for each dimension results in 10^4 grid points evaluation.

Chiu proposed an extension of Yager and Filev's mountain method, called subtractive clustering, in which each data point, not a grid point, is considered as a potential cluster center. Using this method, the number of effective "grid points" to be evaluated is simply equal to the number of data points, independent of the dimension of the problem. Another advantage of this method is that it eliminates the need to specify a grid resolution, in which trade-offs between accuracy and computation complexity are considered. The subtractive clustering method extends the mountain method's criterion for accepting and rejecting cluster centers.

SUBTRACTIVE CLUSTERING

Consider a collection of n data points $\{x_1, x_2, ..., x_n\}$ in an M dimensional space. The data points are normalized in each dimension so that they are bounded by a unit hypercube. We consider each data point as a potential cluster center and define a measure of the potential of data point x_j as:

$$P_i = \sum_{j=1}^{n} e^{-\alpha \|x_i - x_j\|^2}$$

(4.27)

where,

$$\alpha = 4/r_a^2,$$

(4.28)

$\|\cdot\|$ denotes the Euclidean distance, and r_a is a positive constant. Thus, the measure of the potential for a data point is a function of its distances to all other data points. A data point with many neighboring data points have a high potential value. The constant r_a is effectively the radius defining a neighborhood. Data points outside this radius have little influence on the potential.

After the potential of every data point has been computed, we select the data point with the highest potential as the first cluster center. Let x_1^* be the location of the first cluster center and P_1^* be its potential value. We then revise the potential of each data point x_i by the formula:

$$P_i \Leftarrow P_i - P_1^* e^{-\beta \|x_i - x_1^*\|^2}$$

(4.29)

where $\beta = 4/r_b^2$ and r_b is a positive constant.

Thus, we subtract an amount of potential from each data point as a function of its distance from the first cluster center. The data points near the first cluster center have reduced potential, and are unlikely to be selected as the next cluster center. The constant r_b is effectively the radius defining the neighborhood, which has measurable reductions in potential. To avoid obtaining closely spaced cluster centers, we set r_b to be somewhat greater than r_a. A good choice is $r_b = 1.25\, r_a$.

When the potential of all data points has been revised according to Equation 4.29, we select the data point with the highest remaining potential as the second cluster center. We .further reduce the potential of each data point according to their distance to the second cluster center. In general, after the k'th cluster center has been obtained, the potential of each data point is revised by the formula:

$$P_i \Leftarrow P_i - P_k^* e^{-\beta \|x_i - x_k^*\|^2}$$

where x_k^* is the location of the k'th cluster center and P_k^* is its potential value.

The process of acquiring new cluster center and revising potentials we repeat the process until the remaining potential of all data points are below some fraction of the potential of the first cluster center. We use $P_k^* < 0.15\, P_1^*$ as the stopping criterion.

4.11.2 OBTAINING THE INITIAL FUZZY MODEL

Each cluster center is a prototypical data point that characterizes input/output behavior of the system to be modeled. Hence, each cluster center is used as the basis of a rule that describes the system behavior.

Consider a set of c cluster centers $\{x_1^*, x_2^*, \dots x_c^*\}$ in an M dimensional space. Let the first N dimensions correspond to input variables and the last M–N dimensions correspond to output variables. We decompose each vector x_i^* into two component vectors y_i^* and z_i^*, where y_i^* is the location of the cluster center in input space and z_i^* is the location of the cluster center in output space.

That is:

$$x_i^* = \begin{bmatrix} y_i^* \\ z_i^* \end{bmatrix}$$

where,

$$y_i^* \in R^N \text{ and } z_i^* \in R^{M-N}.$$

We consider each cluster center x_i^* as a fuzzy rule that describes the system behavior. Intuitively, cluster center x_i^* represents the rule "if input is near y_i^* then output is near z_i^*."

Given an input vector y, the degree to which rule i is fulfilled is defined as:

$$\mu_i = e^{-\alpha \|y - y_i^*\|^2}$$

where α is the constant defined by Equation 4.28. We compute the output vector z via.,

$$z = \frac{\sum_{i=1}^{c} \mu_i z_i^*}{\sum_{i=1}^{c} \mu_i}.$$

We can view this computational model in terms of a fuzzy inference system employing traditional fuzzy in-then rules.

Each rule has the following form:

$$\text{If } Y_1 \text{ is } A_{i1} \text{ \& } Y_2 \text{ is } A_{i2} \text{ \& } \dots \text{ then } Z_1 \text{ is } B_{i1} \text{ \& } Z_2 \text{ is } B_{i2} \dots$$

where Y_j is the j'th input variable and Z_j is the j'th output variable, A_{ij} is an exponential membership function in the I'th rule associated with the j'th input and B_{ij} is a singleton in the i'th rule associated with the j'th output.

For the i'th rule, which is represented by cluster center x_i^*, A_{ij} and B_{ij} are given by:

$$A_{ij}(Y_j) = \exp\left\{-\frac{1}{2}\left(\frac{Y_j - y_{ij}^*}{\sigma_{ij}}\right)^2\right\} \tag{4.30}$$

$$B_{ij} = z_{ij}^* \tag{4.31}$$

where y_{ij}^* is the j'th element of y_i^*, z_{ij}^* is the j'th element of z_i^*, and $\sigma_{ij}^2 = 1/(2\alpha)$. The computational scheme is equivalent to an inference method that uses multiplication as the AND operator, weights the output of each rule by the rule's firing strength, and computes the output value as a weighted average of each rule's output.

Remark 4.1 Although the number of rules (or clusters) is automatically determined by this method, we should note that the user specified parameter r_a (that is, the cluster radius) strongly affects the number of rules/clusters that are generated. A large r_a results in fewer rules/clusters and hence a coarser model, while a small r_a can produce excessive numbers of rules/clusters and hence a model that does not generalize well. Therefore, r_a can be regarded as an approximate specification of the desired resolution of the model, which can be adjusted based on the resultant complexity and generalization ability of the model. Fortunately, the input variable selection method is not sensitive to the resolution of the initial model, as long as the initial model does not excessively over-fit the training data.

4.11.3 OPTIMIZING THE FUZZY MODEL

There are several approaches as stated below to optimize the rules obtained from the cluster estimation method.

- One approach is to apply a gradient descent method to optimize the parameters y_{ij}^*, z_{ij}^*, and σ_{ij} in Equations 4.30 and 4.31 to minimize the root mean square (RMS) output error with respect to the training data. Backpropagation formulas to perform this optimization have been derived by Wang and Mendel in 1992. This is the approach adopted by Yager and Filev in 1994 to optimize the rules obtained from the mountain clustering method.

- Another approach is to consider the consequent parameter z_{ij}^* be a linear function of the input variables, instead of a single constant.
  That is, we let:

$$z_{ij}^* = G_{ij}\, y + h_{ij}$$

where G_{ij} is an N-element vector of coefficients and h_{ij} is a scalar constant. The if-then rules then become the Takagi-Sugeno type. As shown by Takagi and Sugeno in 1985, given a set of rules with fixed premise membership functions, optimizing G_{ij} and h_{ij} in all consequent equations to minimize the RMS output error is a simple linear least-squares estimation problem. Chiu [47] adopted this approach to optimize the rules obtained from the subtractive clustering method, optimizing only the coefficients in the consequent equations allows a significant degree of model optimization to be performed without adding much computational complexity. This approach produces models that are compared favorably with those obtained from more computationally intensive methods.

- A third approach involves using the Takagi-Sugeno rule format, but it combines optimizing the premise membership functions by gradient descent with optimizing the consequent equations by linear least squares estimation. This is the ANFIS (Adaptive Network-Based Fuzzy Inference System) methodology developed by Jang [142]. When the ANFIS approach is used to optimize the same rules, the resultant model is generally more accurate than that obtained from either of the two preceding approaches.

4.11.4   SELECTING INPUT VARIABLES

After an initial fuzzy model that incorporates all possible input variables has been generated by using the subtractive clustering method in conjunction with one of the aforementioned rule optimization methods, we can ascertain the importance of each input variable from this initial model. The fuzzy rule framework provides an easy mechanism to test the importance of each input variable without having to generate new models. The basic idea is to simply remove all antecedent clauses associated with a particular input variable from the rules and then evaluate the performance of the model.

For example, suppose that initial model has three inputs, with rules of the from:

$$\text{If } Y_1 \text{ is } A_i 1 \text{ and } Y_2 \text{ is } A_i 2 \ \& \ Y_3 \text{ is } A_i 3 \text{ then } Z_1 \text{ is } B_i 1.$$

We can test the importance of the Y_2 variable in the model by temporarily removing the antecedent clauses that involve Y_2.

Thus we truncate rules to the form:

$$\text{If } Y_1 \text{ is } A_i 1 \ \& \ Y_3 \text{ is } A_i 3 \text{ then } Z_1 \text{ is } B_i 1.$$

If the resultant model performance dose not degrade with respect to some performance measure (for example, by testing the model with respect to an independent set of checking data), then we can eliminate Y_2 from the list of possibly important variables. In practice, we need not actually remove antecedent clauses from the rules, but simply let the associated clauses (for example, "Y_2 is $A_i 2$") be assigned a truth value of 1.o to achieve the effect.

ALGORITHM (INPUT VARIABLE SELECTION)

Step 1. Evaluate the performance of the initial model with all candidate input variables in the model.

Step 2. For each remaining input variable, evaluate the performance of the initial model with this variable temporarily removed.

Step 3. Permanently remove the variable associated with the best model performance obtained in step 2. Record the resultant reduced variable set and associated model performance.

Step 4. If there are still variables remaining in the model, go back to step 2 to eliminate another variable. Otherwise go to step 5.

Step 5. Choose the best variable set from among the sets recorded in step 3.

This is essentially a backward selection procedure that starts with all possible variables and reduces the number of variable by one at each stage. For example, starting with 4 input variables, this procedure first selectively removes one variable to arrive at the best 3 variable set, from among the 3 remaining variables, it then selectively removes one more variable to arrive at the best 2 variable set, and so on, among these "best" variable sets, the set that provides the best overall performance is chosen at the end, after we have reached a model with no input variable. Figure 28 shows the variable selection process for a four – input model. Because testing the different combination of variables requires only truncating the rules in an initial full model and not generating any new models, the variable selection process is highly efficient.

While a backward selection process typically stops when the model's performance becomes unacceptable at some stage, we find it more useful to carry the process to the end until the performance of a model with no input variable is evaluated. It is important to let the human designer examine the model performance as a function of the number of variables removed and determine how to trade off accuracy for simplicity. The role of human judgment in the variable selection method is illustrated below.

There are four conditions under which removing an input variable from the model does not degrade model performance:

- The output doses not vary with respect to the given input.
- The output variation with respect to the given input is due to noise.
- The given input is redundant such that the output variation can be predicted equally well by using other inputs.
- The model is a highly over-fitted model.

The first three conditions occur when an input variable is not important. The last condition occurs when the model is so over-fitted to noise that removing an important input variable can nonetheless improve the model's performance. Hence, we must be careful to avoid a highly complex initial model that over-fits the training data. The initial model does not have to be a highly accurate model because variable selection is based on comparing relative performances of the model as each variable is removed. In view of the problems associated with over-fitting the training data, it is generally preferable to use a coarse initial model for the purpose of variable selection.

After the input variables have been selected, we then reapply the clustering-based model extraction method to the training data to obtain the final model. This time we use only the selected input variables in the training data. It is important to note that the truncated rules evaluated during variable selection are merely the mathematical mechanism for collapsing the initial full model's output surface to a lower dimension input space, and that these truncated rules usually bear no resemblance to the final rules that would be extracted using the same subset of input variables. The final model extracted using only the selected variables have significantly fewer rules. We do not re-optimize the truncated rules, when comparing models during variable selection, since it is problematic that optimization will help a truncated-rule model to more accurately reflect the performance of the corresponding final model. In particular, if optimized, a truncated-rule model would tend to over-fit the training data due to the excessive number of tunable rules.

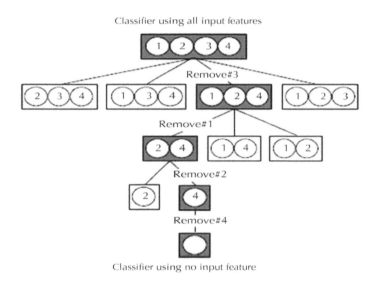

FIGURE 28   Variable selection process.

The Figure 28 represents the variable selection process for a four-input initial model. The different subsets of variables considered at each stage are shown, the shaded subsets are the ones that provided the best performance at each stage. After the variable removal process is carried to the end, we select from among the shaded subsets the subset that provides the best performance/complexity trade-off.

4.11.5   MODEL SELECTION CRITERIA

The variable selection procedure can be used with various performance criteria for model selection.

The simplest performance criterion is the model's RMS output error with respect to an independent set of checking data. That is, we first divide the available data into two groups: A and B, we then generate the initial model by using the data in group A and call this model "model A".

The checking error criterion is then defined as:

$$J_C = [\sum_{i=1}^{nB}(z_i^B - z_i^{BA})^2/nB]^{1/2} \tag{4.32}$$

where z_i^B is the i'th output data in group B; z_i^{BA} is the corresponding predicted output for group B obtained from model A; and nB is the number of data points in group B. We repeatedly evaluate this criterion as each input variable is removed from model A and choose the variable subset that produced the smallest J_C at each stage. Although the checking error criterion favors model structures with high prediction accuracy, a drawback of this criterion is that the results are sensitive to the choice of training data and checking data.

Other possible performance criteria include the unbiased criterion and regularity criterion. These criteria are based on dividing the data into two groups and generating two separate models, one from group A and one from group B.

• The unbiased criterion is defined as:

$$J_U = \left[\sum_{i=1}^{nA}(z_i^{AB} - z_i^{AA})^2 + \sum_{i=1}^{nB}(z_i^{BA} - z_i^{BB})^2\right]^{1/2} \tag{4.33}$$

The unbiased criterion is designed to make the chosen model insensitive to the data on which it was built. This criterion seeks to minimize only the difference between the output of the two separate models, without regard to the model's prediction accuracy, hence this criterion often does not result in selecting variables with the best prediction ability.

• The regularity criterion is defined as:

$$J_{R1} = \left[\sum_{i=1}^{nA}(z_i^A - z_i^{AB})^2/n_A + \sum_{i=1}^{nB}(z_i^B - z_i^{BA})^2/n_B\right]/2 \tag{4.34}$$

The regularity criterion is simply the mean square of the checking error criteria for the two separate models (there are other definitions of regularity criterion that involves only one model). This criterion provides a good compromise between prediction accuracy and insensitivity to the choice of data. We prefer to use the square root of this criterion so that it becomes an RMS type of error, which gives the human designer a better feel for the error magnitude.

Hence, we define the regularity criterion J_{R2} as:

$$J_{R2} = \sqrt{J_{R1}} \tag{4.35}$$

We may use either the unbiased criterion or the regularity criterion for variable selection. But our procedure generates only two initial models instead of two models for each combination of variables to be tested.

The variable selection method can be applied to both conventional fuzzy models, where the rule consequent is a singleton or membership function and Takagi-Sugeno models, where the rule consequent is a linear equation in the input variables. However, application to conventional fuzzy models is straightforward, while application to Takagi-Sugeno models requires recomputation of some coefficients in the consequent equations as each variable is removed from the rules. For computational efficiency, and because the variable selection mechanism is not sensitive to the absolute accuracy of the initial model, we always choose the initial model to be a conventional fuzzy model (with singleton consequents) optimized by gradient descent. After the input variables have been selected from the initial model, we typically generate the final model as a Takagi-Sugeno model optimized by the ANFIS technique. This approach, which consists of generating a conventional fuzzy model from high dimension data for the variable selection phase and then generating a Takagi-Sugeno model from the reduced dimension data in the final phase, generally provides the best result in terms of both model accuracy and computation time.

4.11.6 APPLICATION OF THE RULE EXTRACTION METHOD

To illustrate the rule extraction methods, we now apply them to a function approximation problem and to a pattern classification problem [47].

AUTOMOBILE TRIP PREDICTION

We consider a function approximation problem in which we wish to predict the number of automobile trips generated from an area based on the area's demographics. The data used for rule extraction consists of demographic and trip data for 100 traffic analysis zones is New Castle Country, Delaware.

The original data set contains five input variables:
- Population,
- Number of dwelling units,
- Number of car ownerships,
- Median household income, and
- Total employment.

For simplicity of demonstration we consider only two input variables:
- Car ownership,
- Employment.

A discussion on how to select the most important input variables is discussed in section 4.11.4.

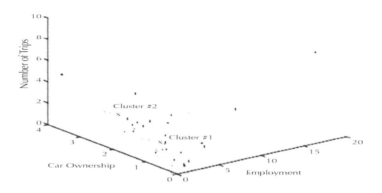

FIGURE 29   Clustering of training data set.

Out of 100 data points, we randomly select 75 points as training data for generating the rules and 25 points as checking data for validating the rules. Using cluster radius $r_a = 0.5$, two cluster centers are found in the training data. Recall that the cluster radius is expressed relative to the normalized data space, hence $r_a = 0.5$ corresponds to half the width of the data space. The training data and the cluster centers are shown in Figure 29, where the cluster centers are marked by Xs. The two cluster centers are translated into two rules of the Takagi-Sugeno type, with initial premise membership functions obtained from the cluster center positions using Equation 4.32. The ANFIS approach is then applied to optimize the model. That is, the rules' premise membership functions are optimized by gradient descent, while the consequent equations are optimized by linear least squares estimation. The optimization process stops when the improvement in RMS error after a pass through the data becomes less than 0.1% of the previous RMS error. The resultant rules are shown in Figure 30. A comparison of the actual output versus the output predicted by the fuzzy model is shown in Figure 31. The fuzzy model has an RMS output error of 0.582 with respect to the training data and an error or 0.586 with respect to the checking data, indicating the model generalizes well.

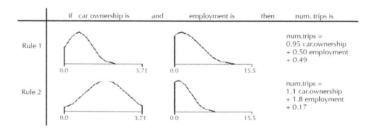

FIGURE 30   Representation of the rules extracted from the training data set of trip prediction model.

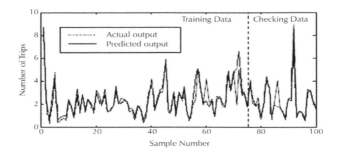

FIGURE 31   Comparison of actual output with predicted output.

IRIS CLASSIFICATION

We now consider Fisher's iris flower data. The iris data consists of a set of 150 data samples that maps 4 input feature values (sepal length, sepal width, petal length, and petal width) into one of 3 species of iris flower. There are 50 samples for each species. We use 120 samples as training data (40 samples of each species) and 30 samples as checking data (10 samples of each species). To simplify the illustration, we consider only two input variables: petal width and petal length.

The training data are normalized and then separated into 3 groups according to their species. Using a cluster radius of 0.5, one cluster is found in each group of data, resulting in one rule for classifying each species. The rules' membership functions are allowed to be two-sided Gaussians and are optimized by gradient descent.

The optimization process stops when the improvement in the error measure after a pass through the data becomes less than 0.1% of the previous error measure (the error measure is defined as the average of the individual error measure). The resultant rules are shown in Figure 32. The fuzzy classifier misclassifies 3 samples out of 120 samples in the training data and classified all samples correctly in the checking data.

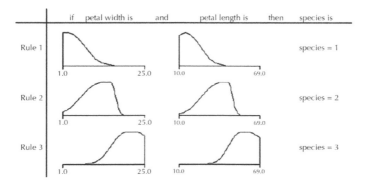

FIGURE 32   Representations of rules extracted from training data for the Iris classification problem.

4.12   REPRESENTATION OF FUZZY IF-THEN RULES BY PETRI NET

In this section we discuss about visualization of modeling and decisional processes described by fuzzy IF-THEN rules represented by Petri Nets [160].

Classical Petri Nets are defined as a structure N=(S, T, F), where S means set of places, T is set of transitions and F is $F \subseteq (S \times T) \cup (T \times S)$, where $(\forall t \in T)(\exists p, q \in S)(p, t), (t, q) \in F$. Graphical representation is set up by following symbols:

- Places – rings,
- Transitions – rectangle, and
- Relations – pointers between transitions and places or places and transitions.

During process simulation by Petri Nets we have to illustrate the status. In classical Petri Nets there is token placed if the expression is true (1) or false (0). Let's now try to create such a Petri Net, which works with vague values ("a lot, "big", ...). We use tools of fuzzy logic for work with such values especially fuzzy IF THEN rules.

Token is the bearer of fuzzy sets in our case, edges are evaluated by language expression from IF THEN rule. Creation of that relation is depend on the chosen inferential method.

Example 4.9 We illustrate the correspondence between IF THEN rules and Petri Nets:

Let's introduce simple model of weather behavior in dependency on various factors. We set up temperature of the air, pressure and cloudy weather at the entry statuses of Petri Nets. According to these values we finally receive forecast of nice weather, rain and storm.

We create a model according to our expert knowledge, which consists of following observations:

- If temperature is high, weather is highly cloudy and pressure is low then storm occurs.
- If temperature is high, weather is not too cloudy and pressure is high then, weather is nice.
- If temperature is medium, and weather is highly cloudy then rain occurs.

We model dependencies by Petri Nets according to the rules as visible on figures (Figures 33–35).

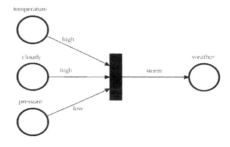

FIGURE 33   Rule 1.

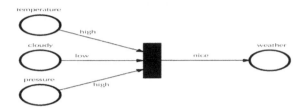

FIGURE 34   Rule 2.

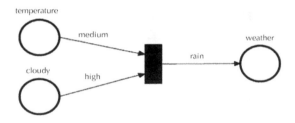

FIGURE 35   Rule 3.

We can simply join all the rules into Petri Net as shown in Figure 36. Such a connection is quite synoptic. But if we like to find out the level of membership of all items of the final fuzzy set we have to repeatedly proceed all possible transitions Petri Nets and find out maximum of levels individual items of output.

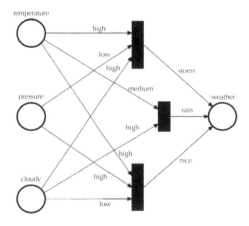

FIGURE 36   Simple connection of rules.

We can resolve this problem by modification of Petri Nets into final version as it is shown on the Figure 37. The last transition provides conjunction of output fuzzy sets from individual IF-THEN rules. After the transition of tokens through the Petri Net, place marked by symbol of weather contain the final fuzzy set is achieved. According to the level of membership we can conclude the status of the weather.

We see the main usage of our approach in facilitating the layout of fuzzy IF-THEN rules and making them more synoptic. These rules can be linked to each other. Finally we can draw the conclusion.

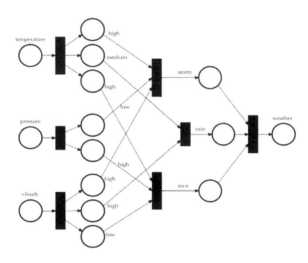

FIGURE 37   Last version of the model.

4.13   TRANSFORMATIONS AMONG VARIOUS RULE BASED FUZZY MODELS [161,162, 167]

Classical expert systems operate with symbols and discrete knowledge that refers to the actual knowledge base. The space complexity of such an expert system is enormous. The size of the rule base is proportional to the number of elements in the input state space. Fuzzy rules contain knowledge that states something exactly for a certain domain of the input space (in the case of the non-fuzzy expert systems this domain might be a single point), while for the fuzzy neighborhood of this exact domain(core), vague knowledge is given (that has a decreasing degree of truth when going farther from the core) for a certain neighborhood of these domains. Figure 38 illustrates this concept.

It depicts a part of fuzzy model consisting of rules of type:

$$\text{If } x \text{ is } A_i \text{ then } y \text{ is } B_i$$

($X = \{x\}$ is the input, $Y = \{y\}$ is the output space, usually $X = \prod_{i=1}^{k} X_i$) In the figure, the domains of exact knowledge (cores, $\mu = 1$), and fuzzy knowledge ($0 < \mu < 1$) are indicated by the appropriate membership values, in the latter parts of X. Conclusions can be obtained by interpolating the fuzzy pieces of knowledge covering that area partially. This type of model is the most fundamental one, used in many application oriented problem.

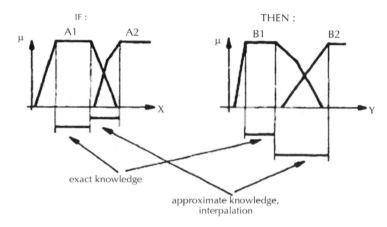

FIGURE 38   Interpolativity of Z type fuzzy if...then...rules.

Having such a model (Z-model), and an observation on the input (that might be crisp or fuzzy, like "x is A' "), a conclusion can be calculated by applying some version of the Compositional Rule of Inference (See Chapter 3):

$$B' = A' \, 0 \, R$$

where o denotes some relational composition (for example, the max-min one), and R is the fuzzy relation representing the set of rules in the model.

Technically, the composition is usually calculated by:

$$B' = \bigcup_{i=1}^{r} \min\{height(A', A_i) \; B_i\}$$

or by:

$$B' = \bigcup_{i=1}^{r} height(A', A_i) \times B_i$$

(where x denotes the algebraic product and U stands for max). Almost all industrial applications of fuzzy control use this technique, as it was used first by Mamdani in his famous steam engine control, this reasoning method is often referred to as "Mamdani-controller". (A similar model was later proposed by Larsen with a different t-norm for weighting the consequents, this latter can also be considered as a version of the Mamdani-model).

Rules of type:

If x is A_i then y is B_i

are not the only possibilities to accumulate knowledge on a system. Consider that for simpler systems, often the analytical model is known in the form of an equation (See Section 1.2 of chapter 1 of volume 2 of this book).

$$Y = f(x).$$

If the system is more complex, in certain areas of the space X a similar analytical (may be, approximative) model might exist. Then, it is obvious to approximate the system by determining the local tendencies of behavior, by identifying simpler segments through analytical rules, whose validity is true on a fuzzy domain. The core is the domain where the analytical expression is considered to be exactly true. This type of model was proposed by Takagi and Sugeno so that linear consequents are represented as (See Chapter 1 of volume 2 of this book),

$$\text{If x is } A_i \text{ then } y = a_i x + b_i.$$

It is quite obvious to extend this model to:

$$\text{If x is } A_i \text{ then } y = f_i(x)$$

for virtually arbitrary functions $f_i(x)$. As a matter of fact, this model is reasonable only, if $f_i(x)$ is quite simply computable; this is why its main importance lies with linear consequents.

In the TS-model [or its extended version, with arbitrary $f_i(x))$] the interpolative property of rules with fuzzy antecedents is clearly used. As the domains A_i form a fuzzy cover of X in the same way as in the Z-model.

$$\bigcup_{i=1}^{r} A_{\alpha i} = X$$

$$(4.36)$$

(r denotes the number of rules in the base), in the transition areas where no exact knowledge is available, the conclusion is calculated by the interpolation of the neighboring consequents.

Generally, rule bases, where Equation 4.36 holds, are called dense. In a dense rule base, there is no such $x \in X$ for which $\mu_a(x) \geq \alpha > 0$ is not satisfied for some reasonably high membership degree α, and at least one i. Usually, $1 > \mu_{A_i}(x) > 0$ holds for several (at least two)different is. This means that none of the affected rules is true in the Boolean sense, although they are true to some extent, for the given observation point x. The conclusion obtained by applying all the rules that have any positive degree of truth, weighting their importance by their degrees, and calculating the average, is clearly a kind of interpolation.

This might be true for the TS-model, as well. If the consequents contain linear functions, for all x-s that lie in the "grey Zones" where more than one antecedents are partially true, the connection between y and x is the weighted average of two or more linear connections, that is, a nonlinear function in reality. The great advantage of this approach is that by using only linear consequents, nonlinear functions can be approximated by the interpolative ability of fuzzy rule-based models. Figure 39 depicts a possible application of the TS-model (with only two rules being indicated), where a nonlinear section of the real f(x) is approximated by two "fuzzy linear segments,"(that is, two linear segments whose validity is less than 1).

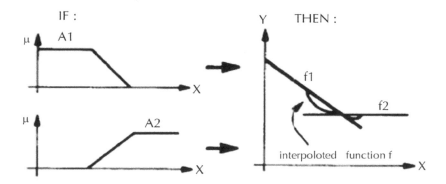

FIGURE 39   Using the TS-model for function interpolation.

The common point in the two different models (*viz.* Z-model and TS model) is that both give an approximation of the system's behavior by "partitioning" the input state space into "exactly known" domains (the cores of A_i may be approximately true, in reality) and approximately known domains (the areas where all antecedents have $0 < \mu(x) < 1$).

This is a fuzzy cover, if the union of the supports covers the full universe:

$$\bigcup_{i=1}^{r} Supp(A_i) = X$$

even for some reasonable high $\alpha > 0$:

$$\bigcup_{i=1}^{r} A_{i\alpha} = X$$

while the union of the cores is always a proper subset of X:

$$\bigcup_{i=1}^{r} Core(A_i) \subset X.$$

The models and corresponding control algorithms are overviewed and discussed in full detail in chapter 1 and 3 of volume 2 of this book.

Having overviewed the two main fuzzy model classes, the question is quite obvious. Do these two model types fit for two different classes of systems? Is there an intersection of the two, or are they equivalent in some sense?

It is obvious that the Sugeno-model is a special case of both these models, for example, there is a class of systems that corresponds to both the Zadeh-Mamdani-Larsen and the Takagi-Sugeno style rules. However, in a way, all these models can be considered as equivalent, concerning the class of systems that correspond, which will be shown in the next section.

4.13.1   INTERPOLATION OF RULES

Despite the inherent interpolativity of fuzzy rules, no conclusion can be drawn by the Compositional Rule of Inference or similar methods, if an observation on X hits into one of the gaps, as A' 0 R = Ø always holds if:

$$A' \cap \bigcup_{i=1}^{r} A_i = \theta.$$

Instead, some method of inference should be applied that allows the approximation of B' in arbitrary case, independent of whether the actual observation overlaps with any of the antecedents in the rule base.

Suppose that all terms in the rules are convex and normal, are referred as CNF set. It is an extension of the definition of fuzzy numbers for arbitrary universes.

It is necessary to assume that the input and output state spaces have partial ordering, furthermore, a metric. Then, partial ordering between two comparable CNF sets and a kind of fuzzy distance can be introduced.

With these assumptions, the problem of approximating the conclusion when the observation hits a gap, can be reduced to a family of function approximation ("curve fitting") problems.

The simplest solution is to apply linear interpolation of the two flanking rules, where the formulas for calculating the membership function of B' on level α are the following:

$$\inf\{B_\alpha'\}=\frac{\dfrac{1}{d_{\alpha L}(A_{1\alpha},A_\alpha')}\inf\{B_{1\alpha}\}+\dfrac{1}{d_{\alpha L}(A_{2\alpha},A_\alpha')}\inf\{B_{2\alpha}\}}{\dfrac{1}{d_{\alpha L}(A_{1\alpha},A_\alpha')}+\dfrac{1}{d_{\alpha L}(A_{2\alpha},A_\alpha')}}$$

and   (4.37)

$$\sup\{B_\alpha'\}=\frac{\dfrac{1}{d_{\alpha l}(A_{1\alpha},A_\alpha')}\sup\{B_{1\alpha}\}+\dfrac{1}{d_{\alpha l}(A_{2\alpha},A_\alpha')}\sup\{B_{2\alpha}\}}{\dfrac{1}{d_{\alpha l}(A_{1\alpha},A_\alpha')}+\dfrac{1}{d_{\alpha l}(A_{2\alpha},A_\alpha')}}.$$

It should be mentioned that executing the rule interpolation algorithm on a rule base with CNF sets and a CNF (eventually, crisp) observation does not necessarily lead to a CNF conclusion. Analysis of various necessary and sufficient conditions already exists.

4.13.2 RULE REDUCTION AND MODEL CONSTRUCTION BY INTERPOLATION

While rule interpolation in the stricter sense is useful in obtaining conclusions when the observation is not overlapping with the antecedents, obviously, its importance is much greater. By fitting the α-level curves, a new "continuous" model is generated. It is easy to recognize the relationship of the interpolative model with the TS-model that also uses continuous functions both in and between the cores of the antecedents, however, the interpolative model is more general, as it preserves fuzziness also in the consequent space [167].

The interpolative technique of model construction can be utilized for the reduction of dense models, where some of the rules might contain redundant information that can be deducted from the other rules. The main idea is that from the starting Z-type model $M = \{R_i; I = 1, \ldots\ldots, r\}$, an interpolative model is generated, $M_i = \{R_i, F_j; i = 1, \ldots\ldots, r; j = 1, \ldots\ldots, f, f < r\}$, from where, by elimination of some redundant rules,

a compressed Z-type model is generated: $M^I = \{R_{ik}: i_k \in I \subset \{1, \ldots\ldots, r\}, |I| < r\}$.

Once the "resolution" of the qualitative (Z-type) model is determined, it must be investigated whether the information in the original rule base is still preserved despite the omission of certain rules.

Example 4.10 We consider a problem where an 11-rule linguistic model is compressed to a three-rule model under polynomial (quadratic) interpolation (in reality, there exist several, equally good compressions).

The original model is the following:

    $R = \{$If x is NVB then y is NB

    If x is NB then y is NS

    If x is NM then y is ZO

If x is NS then y is PS
If x is NZ then y is PM
If x is ZO then y is PM
If x is PZ then y is PM
If x is PS then y is PM
If x is PM then y is PS
If x is PB then y is ZO
If x is PVB then y is NS}.

The linguistic terms NVB, NB, ... PVB are defined in the universe X = [0,10], and y = [0,6], respectively, by equidistant", and identical triangular membership functions of width 2. The resolution for every α-level, and every neighborhood in X is n = 1.

Applying quadratic interpolation, the model reduces to
R' = { If x is NM then y is ZO
If x is ZO then y is PM
If x is PM then y is PS; $y = ax^2 + bx + c$}.

All the omitted rules can be reconstructed by applying:

$$y = -\frac{1}{6}x^2 + \frac{11}{6}x$$

for α = 1, (for both the inf and the sup, because of the triangularity), and

$$y = -\frac{1}{6}x^2 + \frac{3}{2}x + \frac{5}{6}$$

for α = 0,L (the inf), finally:

$$y = -\frac{1}{6}x^2 + \frac{13}{6}x - 1$$

for α = 0,U (the sup), namely, all eliminated rules are approximated within the error bound n/2 = 0.5. In this example, the three parabolas can be obtained from each other by a simple translation, however, if the terms are not identically shaped, the resulting functions are also different. It is interesting to note that the choice of remaining rules is very critical, and there is no monotonicity in the omission of rules, for example, having three rule bases:

$$R'' \subset R' \subset R.$$

may be R'' is a compression of R, while R' is not. Because of this, no computationally effective serial search algorithms for the best reduction can be constructed (at least for polynomial interpolation).

Example 4.11 The original rule base is:
R = { If x is NVB then y is NM
     If x is NB then y is NM
     If x is NM then y is NM
     If x is NS then y is NS
     If x is NZ then y is NS
     If x is ZO then y is NS
     If x is PZ then y is NS
     If x is PS then y is NS
     If x is PM then y is ZO
     If x is PB then y is ZO
     If x is PVB then y is ZO}.
This can be written in the more compressed linguistic form:
     R = { If x is NVB or NB or NM then y is NM
     If x is NS or NZ or ZO or PZ or PS then y is NS
     If x is PM or PB or PVB then y is ZO}.
Using quadratic interpolation this knowledge base turns out to be linear, and re-
duces to two rules;
     R' = { If x is NVB then y is NM
     If x is PVB then y is ZO; $y = ax + b$}.
     R is reconstructable from the three level functions:

$$Y_{1L/U}\, y = \frac{1}{5}x + 1$$

$$Y_{0L} = \frac{1}{5}x + \frac{1}{5}$$

and

$$Y_{0U} = \frac{1}{5}x + \frac{9}{5}.$$

Let us consider an observation be A'(2,3,3,4) (that is, the "trapezoidal," in reality
triangular, membership function characterized by the given four break-points), which
is identical with NS. So the conclusion should be $y = $ NS by:

$$R_4 = \text{If } x \text{ is NS then } y \text{ is NS}.$$

Substituting the characteristic points of A', the following is obtained for B':

$$b_{0L} = Y_{0L}(2) = 0.6$$
$$b_{1L/U} = y_{1L/U}(3) = 1.6$$
$$b_{0U} = y_{0U}(4) = 2.6$$

The obtained conclusion B'(0.6, 1.6, 1.6, 2.6) is "rounded up" to the closest exist-ing linguistic term in Y. As NM = (0,1,1,2) and NS = (1,2,2,3), the solution is B' = NS, in accordance with the expectations.

4.13.3   A GENERAL FUZZY MODEL AND THE CNS SETS

Let us consider the two fuzzy models as stated above. Both models can be considered as approximations (in simplified ways) to describe the behavior of the eventually very complex system. The Z-model is a kind of discrete one, listing typical cases for the behavior of the system S, an extension of the non-fuzzy symbolic AI model, while the TS-model is a fuzzy approximation of a hypothetical non-fuzzy analytical model, where the latter might be an approximation itself, if the system S is inherently fuzzy itself [167].

Let us propose the method of the exact description of S.

Definition 4.6 $C(X)$ is the CNF (convex and normal fuzzy) power set of X:

$$C(x) = \{A = \{X, \mu_A(x)\} : height(A) = 1;$$
$$\mu_A(\lambda x_1 + (1-\lambda)x_2) \geq \min\{\mu_A(x_1), \mu_A(x_2)\}$$
$$\lambda \in (0,1)\} \cup \{\theta\}$$

C(X) is the set of all convex and normal fuzzy sets of the universe X (including the empty set θ, as a special element). When constructing a general fuzzy model, it is reasonable to restrict both inputs and outputs to elements of the respective CNF sets of X and Y.

Definition 4.7 The general fuzzy model of a system S is described by the CNF mapping:

$$F_S: C(X) \rightarrow C(Y). \tag{4.38}$$

F_S is a functional, mapping membership functions to membership functions. A direct graphic representation of F_S is impossible even in the simplest case of one-dimensional (1-D) X and Y. One of the possibilities of depicting F_S is to fix the input width for every α, so that $w(\alpha_1) \leq w(\alpha_2)$ if $\alpha_2 \leq \alpha_1$ is satisfied. Then the locus of all A_α

x $F_{w\alpha}(A_\alpha)$ (where A is a general CNF set of X for which $|A_\alpha| = w_\alpha$) is a connected relation in X x Y that can be illustrated as a "band" $F_{w\alpha}$. For various w, there are various $F_{w\alpha}$ nested into each other:

$$F_{w1\alpha} \subset F_{w2\alpha} \textit{iff } w_1 < w_2. \tag{4.39}$$

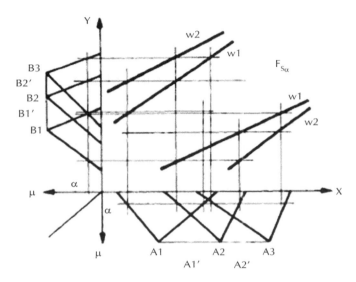

FIGURE 40 α-cuts of a fuzzy model (with triangular CNF-sets as examples: $F_S(A1) = B1$, $F_S(A2) = B2$, $F_S(A3) = B3$, $F_S(A1') = B1'$, and $F_S(A2') = B2'$.

The Figure 40 illustrates some α-cuts of a possible F_S, with two different values of w. In the figure, examples for input-output pairs with two different widths are shown, A_1, A_2, and A_3, with their respective images, represent the width w_1, while $A_1^!$ and $A_2^!$ the two sets obtained by the convex hull of the previous ones, united pair wise, and their images illustrate the width w_2. The two cuts are nested indeed. This figure also suggests an idea of representing F_S by its α-cuts in the space X x Y x w, where w is the universe of possible width $[0, |X|]$. Even though theoretically arbitrary α-cuts satisfying Equation 4.39 could be assumed for some F_S, it is shown later that it is reasonable to assume several properties of the mapping, in accordance with the behavior of rule-based models and common sense.

Usually, F_S is rather complicated, and so, calculations directly with F_S are not possible, because of the immense computational complexity, that is, practical intractability. Instead, several levels of approximation is proposed that provide a somewhat easier manageable model.

As mentioned above, it is necessary to state a few properties of reasonable fuzzy models. In order to do that, let us first discuss operations among CNF sets. Considering that F_s refers to only CNF sets, it is necessary to discuss first the algebra of CNF sets. Considering that none of the usual set operations are closed under the three basic set theoretic (or logical) operations (complement, t-norm/intersection, and S-norm/union), it is necessary to introduce some new operations that actually have very different properties than in the usual fuzzy algebra. In order to find some properties, let us discuss the semantics of If.... Then rules containing CNF sets.

The unary operation of complementation is impossible in the usual sense among CNF sets, as $\overline{A}$ is often non-convex, if A is convex itself. So, instead of $\overline{A}$ in the usual sense, the following definition is proposed:

Definition 4.8 The CNF complement $\dfrac{\wedge}{A}$ of the CNF set A is the convex hull of $\overline{A}$.

There are various interesting cases for $\dfrac{\wedge}{A}$, as stated in the following:

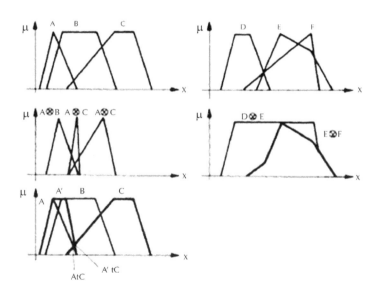

FIGURE 41   Examples for CNF intersection and union.

Remark 4.2

$$\frac{\wedge}{A} = \text{ if and only if all } \alpha\text{-cuts of A are half hyper-planes of X,}$$

$$\frac{\wedge}{A} = \Phi \text{ if A = X.}$$

$$\frac{\wedge}{A} = X \text{ if supp}(A) \text{ bounded.}$$

Example 4.12 An obvious example for a CNF set is the cylindrical extension of an S-shaped membership function, that is, where for one of the components X_i of X

$$\mu A(x) = \mu A(x_i) \begin{cases} = 0, \text{ if } x_1 \le x_{i1} \\ \in (0,1) \text{ and } \mu A(x_{i3}) < \mu_A(x_{i4}) \\ \text{ if } x_{i3} < x_{i4} \text{ for } x_{i1} < x_i < x_{i2} \\ = 1 \text{ if } x_1 \ge x_{i2} \end{cases}.$$

Similarly, its symmetric pair, or any rotation of it behaves in the same way.

Remark 4.3 The intersection of two CNF sets AtB is always convex, and it normal if and only if:

Core$(A) \cap core(B) \neq \phi.$
The CNF intersection can be defined:

Definition 4.9 The CNF intersection $A \otimes B$ is:

$$A \otimes B = \begin{cases} \lambda(AtB), \lambda = \dfrac{1}{Height(AtB)}, & \text{if } AtB \neq \varphi \\ \varphi & \text{if } AtB = \varphi \end{cases} \tag{4.40}$$

Obviously, $A \otimes B$ is always normal, except in the case of the empty set, which is, however, element of C(X). From Remark 4.3,

$$A \otimes B = AtB$$

if and only if Core$(A) \cap$ Core$(B) \neq \phi$, AB $= \phi$. Some examples for $\otimes$ can be found in Figure 41.

It must be noted that the CNF intersection is not a t-norm. Any t-norm must satisfy four axioms: the boundary conditions, commutativity, associativity, and monotonicity. The next statement explains the relation of CNF intersection to these axioms.

Remark 4.4 The CNF intersection satisfies the boundary axiom and it is always commutative, but it is not always associative and monotone.

Definition 4.10 CNF union is defined by:

$$A \oplus B = \text{Conv}(AsB)$$

where Conf(AsB) denotes the convex hull of the ordinary union.

Some examples are shown in Figure 41.

If the CNF are in a 1-D universe, more can be said about $A \oplus B$.

Remark 4.5 If the sets A and B are 1-D, $A \otimes B = AsB$ if:

$$\text{Core}(A) \cap \text{Core}(B) \neq \phi.$$

Let us examine the four axiomatic properties of the CNF union.

Remark 4.6 The CNF union is always commutative, associative and monotone, but it does not always satisfy the boundary axioms.

Let us return to the fuzzy models. If we suppose that all the primary linguistic terms used in the vague description of approximate values or domains of the state variables (like "very large", and so on) are convex, and also can be considered normal (there is at least one such a value to which they refer with crisp truth), it is worthwhile analyzing the semantics of the combination of rules, and of combined rules themselves.

Suppose that the following two rules are in the model (for simplicity, let us adopt the universes and linguistic resolutions used in the examples in Section 4.13.2):

If x is NVB then y is NM

If x is NB then y is NM $\in$ R .

These two can be formulated by a single, combined rule:

If x is NVB or NB then y is NM.

The interesting point is what is the semantics of "NVB or NB"? Both linguistic expressions ("negatively very big," and "negatively big") are represented by CNF terms, in our example, by symmetrical triangular sets (the former being truncated at x = 0, so they are NVB(0,0,0,1) and NB(0,1,1,2), their characteristic points indicated). Is "NVB or NB" the union of these two, for example, by applying max? If so, the truth of the statement:

If x is 0.5 then y is NM

would be only $\mu_{AsB}(0.5) = 0.5$ (by application of the Mamdani-method for reasoning with A' = 0.5), however, it seems to be rather reasonable to assume (especially as there is no contradicting evidence), that everywhere between NVB and NB the same consequent (conclusion) NM is valid with the same degrees of truth (which is identical with the principle of interpolation). Because of that, the semantics of "NVB or NB" is $A \oplus B$ rather than AsB. These considerations open a new way for simplifying rules [165, 167].

Example 4.13 We consider merging of rules with identical consequents.

According to this, the model:

R = {If x is NVB then y is NM

If x is NB then y is NM

If x is NM then y is NM

If x is NS then y is NS
If x is NZ then y is NS
If x is ZO then y is NS
If x is PZ then y is NS
If x is PS then y is NS
If x is PM then y is ZO
If x is PB then y is ZO
If x is PVB then y is ZO},

can be compressed into:

$\breve{R} = \{$*if* x *is NVB or NB or NM then* y *is NM*

    if x *is NS or NZ or ZO or PZ or PS then* y *is NS*

    if x *is PM or PB or PVB then* y *is ZO*} ,

where all the combined terms are CNF sets themselves (See Figure 42).

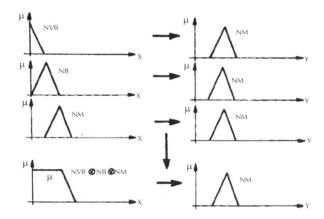

FIGURE 42   Compression of three rules with identical consequents into a single one by using CNF union.

Definition 4.11 The rule base $\breve{R}$ obtained from the rule base R by merging two or more rules with identical consequents. Applying CNF union in the antecedent part is a compression of R.

Example 4.14 Let us combine two rules with different consequents:.

If x is NM then y is NM

If x is NS then y is NS $\in$ R

are two "neighboring" rules (in the sense that there is no antecedent term between NM and NS) of the same model. These two rules can be merged. However, merging rules with different consequents means loss of information.

Similarly to the previous example, the linguistic form is:,

$$R_{3,4} = \text{If } x \text{ is NM or NS then } y \text{ is NM or NS}$$

Apparently, this rule also allows the possibilities:

$$\text{If } x \text{ is NM then } y \text{ is NS}$$

And:

$$\text{If } x \text{ is NS then } y \text{ is NM,}$$

both of which are excluded from the original model. The semantics of $R_{3,4}$ is expressible the CNF union:

$$R3,4 = \text{If } x \text{ is NM} \oplus \text{NS then } y \text{ is NM} \oplus \text{NS.}$$

An illustration of such a rule merge is shown in Figure 43. In the bottom part of the figure, it can be seen that the support of the new merged rule contains areas that have not been included in either original rule. Merging rules in this way might compress the rule base to an arbitrarily small size (to a minimal single rule), in the case of R (or $\breve{R}$) the merge of all the rules would be:

$$\breve{R} = \{ \text{ If } x \text{ is } X \text{ then } y \text{ is NM} \oplus \text{NS} \oplus \text{ZO}\},$$

an almost completely meaningless rule. Indeed, from the model of R it seems that the universe assumed for Y is mistaken, as no consequent goes above 4 (in $Y = [0,6]$), and a similar model could be very well given in the universe $Y' = [1,3]$, with renaming the linguistic terms NM $\rightarrow$ N (negative), NS $\rightarrow$ ZO (approximately zero) , and ZO $\rightarrow$ P (positive), NS $\rightarrow$ ZO (approximately zero), and ZO $\rightarrow$ P (positive). In this new environment, and generally, in every well-chosen universe, the ultimate compression of every dense rule base is:

$$\ddot{R} = \{\text{If } x \text{ is } X \text{ then } y \text{ is } Y\}$$

an absolutely meaningless rule. Merging rules with different consequents always results in loss of information because the new model becomes rougher; however, it might be still motivated by the gain in the decrease of complexity. The new rule base obtained by uniting rules in this way "covers" the original rule base in a geometrical sense (but is not identical with it), so we have the next definition.

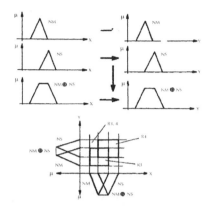

FIGURE 43 Merging two neighboring rules with different consequents.

Definition 4.12 Rule base $\overset{\cdot\cdot}{R}$ obtained from R by merging rules with different antecedents and consequents, applying CNF union in both the antecedent and consequent parts is called a cover of R.

A connection of compression and cover is the following:

Remark 4.7 The minimal cover $\overset{\leftrightarrow}{\tilde{R}}$ of the minimal compression $\tilde{R}$ of rule base R is identical with the minimal cover $\overset{\leftrightarrow}{R}$ of R. Here "minimal" means that all possible rules are united.

The proof is rather straightforward from the definitions. From the two types of rule merging by the CNF union, an important and rather general property of F_s can be deduced.

Property 4.1

$$F_s(A \oplus B) = F_s(A) \oplus F(B).$$

As a matter of fact, F_s not satisfying Property 4.1 can be easily constructed.

In the following similar properties for the CNF intersection is discussed. Let us transform the model in question by uniting the neighboring rules pair by pair in the model of the example discussed above.

Example 4.15
      R' = { If x is NVB $\oplus$ NB then y is NM
      If x is NB $\oplus$ NB then y is NM

      If x is NM $\oplus$ NS then y is NM $\otimes$ NS
      If x is NS $\oplus$ NZ then y is NS
      If x is NZ $\oplus$ ZO then y is NS
      If x is ZO $\oplus$ PZ then y is NS
      If x is PZ $\oplus$ PS then y is NS

If x is PS $\oplus$ PM then y is NS $\otimes$ ZO
If x is PM $\oplus$ PB then y is ZO
If x is PB $\oplus$ PVB then y is ZO}

$$= \left\{ R_1^{'}, \ldots\ldots\ldots, R_{10}^{'} \right\}.$$

R` is a cover of R (although for from being minimal), but its size is not smaller than the size of the original rule base, so it has little motivation to replace R by it. Nevertheless, the use of this model is helpful in identifying some properties of the CNF intersection. Let us take the CNF intersection of the antecedents of the first two rules (having identical consequents):

$$(\text{NVB} \oplus \text{NB}) \oplus (\text{NB} \oplus \text{NM}) = \text{NM}$$

so we get:

$$R_2 = \text{If } x \text{ is NB then } y \text{ is NM}$$

in accordance with the primary model of the system. By generalizing this example, the cover can be replaced by:

$$\widehat{R}^{'} = \{ \text{ If } x \text{ is NVB} \oplus \text{NB then } y \text{ is NM}$$

If x is NB then y is NM
If x is NM $\oplus$ NS then y is NM $\oplus$ NS
If x is NZ then y is NS
If x is ZO then y is NS
If x is PZ then y is NS
If x is PS $\oplus$ PM then y is NS $\oplus$ ZO
If x is PB then y is ZO
If x is PB $\oplus$ PVB then y is ZO}

where all the neighboring rules with identical consequents have been intersected. As a matter of fact, the procedure can be continued as long as the antecedents have non-empty intersections, so, for example,

If x is NZ $\otimes$ ZO then y is NS

can also be obtained (where NZ $\otimes$ ZO is single triangular CNF set not expressible by the set of primary linguistic terms in the example). While intersecting rules with non-overlapping antecedents would result in completely meaningless rules, for example from:

If x is NZ then y is NS

And:

$$\text{If } x \text{ is PZ then } y \text{ is NS,}$$

the nonsense rule:

$$\text{If } x \text{ is } \theta \text{ then } y \text{ is NS}$$

can be obtained, which is a rule that is formally true but valid for no input. The following definition summarizes the idea of applying CNF intersection for obtaining new rules.

Definition 4.13 The rule base $\widehat{R}$ obtained from rule base R by combining two or more rules with identical consequents, applying CNF intersection in the antecedent part is an extension of R.

Now let us combine rules with different antecedents and different consequents in R'. Taking the two combined rules:

$$R_1' = \text{If } x \text{ is NB} \oplus \text{NM then } y \text{ is NM}$$

$$R_2' = \text{If } x \text{ is NM} \oplus \text{NS then } y \text{ is NM} \oplus \text{NS}$$
the CNF intersection of the two can be calculated:

$$R_1' \otimes R_2' = \textbf{If } x \textbf{ is NM then } y \textbf{ is NM.}$$
This is nothing else but R_3 of the original rule base, and so, fully in accordance with the starting model. By generalizing the observation on combining arbitrary rules by CNF intersection, the following second general property for F_s can be deduced:

Property 4.2 $F_s(A \otimes B) = F_s(A) \otimes F(B).$

Obviously, like Property 4.1, it is possible to construct F_s not satisfying Property 4.2. But it is reasonable to assume that all consistent rule models satisfy both of them. So, the following definition can be accepted:

Definition 4.14 F_s is consistent if it satisfies Properties 1 and 2.

By applying CNF intersection on all rules with semantic overlapping in R', the following is obtained:

$$\widehat{R} = \{\text{If } x \text{ is NVB} \oplus \text{NB then } y \text{ is NM}$$
If x is NB then y is NM
If x is NM then y is NM
If x is NS then y is NS
If x is NZ then y is NS
If x is ZO then y is NS
If x is PZ then y is NS
If x is PS then y is NS
If x is PM then y is ZO
If x is PB then y is ZO
If x is PB $\oplus$ PVB then y is ZO$\}$

$$= \{ R_1', R_2, R_3, \ldots\ldots, R_0, R_1' \}$$

an 11-rule base, almost identical with the starting model R (the first and last rules are impossible to be reconstructed in this case). In general, the following definition can be adopted:

Definition 4.15 Rule base $\vec{R}$ obtained from R by combining rules with different antecedents and consequents, applying CNF intersection in both the antecedent and consequent parts is called a refinement of R.

The maximal refinement of a rule base is reached when no antecedents overlap any more. In the case of refining R', furthermore, such rules are obtained, for example,

If x is NB $\otimes$ NM then y is NM

If x is NM $\otimes$ NS then y is NM $\otimes$ NS

and in the next step,

If x is NB $\otimes$ NM $\otimes$ NS then y is NM

that is,

If x is ϕ then y is NM.

By intersecting all rules with each other, the ultimate refinement is obtained that is entirely meaningless.

If x is θ then y is θ.

The Figure 44 depicts an example for refining a three rules base. Because of the properties of the two CNF operations, in addition to the two properties of consistent models, the following three basic equalities should always hold for arbitrary F_s:

E1. $F_s(A \otimes B) = F_s(B \otimes A)$.

E2. $F_s(A \oplus B) = F_s(B \oplus A)$.

E3. $F_s((A \oplus B) \oplus C) = F_s(A \oplus (B \oplus C))$.

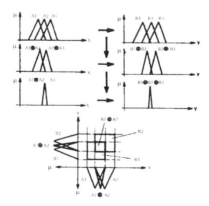

FIGURE 44   The combination of two neighboring rules with different consequents by CNF intersection.

Let us return now to the question, "How can a general fuzzy model be represented and interpreted?" Let us consider an arbitrary (Z- or TS-type) practical fuzzy model. There are usually a series of rules that can be ordered according to their antecedents $A_1 < A_2 < ..... < A_r$. An exception is formed by the inconsistent rule bases where, for example, $A_i = A_{i+1}$, or more generally, $A_i \subset A_{i+1}$ might occur (with different, or contradicting, consequents). If the antecedents form an ordered series, taking any $\alpha \in [0,1]$, the following hold:

$$\min\{A_{i\alpha}\} < \min\{A_{i+1\alpha}\} \quad \max\{A_{i\alpha}\} < \max\{A_{i+1\alpha}\}.$$

If the model is Z-type, and, in addition, all α-cuts have monotone borders, for given α, it is possible to construct two continuous functions $F_{\alpha L}, F_{\alpha U}: X \rightarrow Y$ so that for every i:

$$\min\{B_{i\alpha}\} = F_{\alpha L}\left(\min\{A_{i\alpha}\}\right)$$

And:

(4.41)

$$\max\{B_{i\alpha}\} = F_{\alpha L}\left(\max\{A_{i\alpha}\}\right)$$

for example, by taking the most obvious piecewise linear function fitting all r points. (If any of the minima or maxima of the cuts are identical, as in the case of some inconsistent rule bases, the two functions might not exist, as more than one value in Y is attached to the same value in X,) As a matter of fact, there are an infinite number of pairs of functions satisfying these conditions. If a reasonably dense resolution $\{0, \alpha_2, ..., \alpha_{n-1}, 1\}$ of $[0,1]$ is taken, and all $F_{\alpha i,L}, F_{\alpha i,U}$ are given, a rather easily interpretable approximative representation of the system model F is given.

For this representation, the following holds:

$$[F_{\alpha 1L}(x), F_{\alpha 1U}(x)] \subset [F_{\alpha 2L}(x), F_{\alpha 2U}(x)] \text{ if } \alpha_1 > \alpha_2$$

(where $[f_1, f_2=]$ denotes the area between f_1 and f_2), because of the properties of cuts If $F_{\alpha,L}$ and $F_{\alpha,U}$ are known, it should be possible to determine the conclusion for any observation by simply applying these two mappings for every cut of the observation. Depending on whether the two families of functions are known exactly, or only approximately, the conclusions calculated in this way will be exactly, or

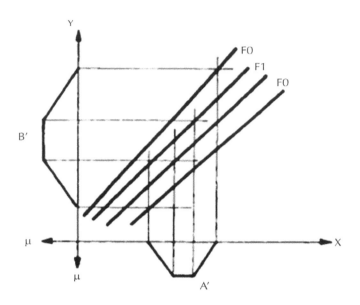

FIGURE 45   Calculation of the conclusion by α-cuts.

approximately, identical with the real conclusion for the given observation. Figure 45 depicts an example for the calculation of the conclusion when the resolution is only {0,1}. This is exactly the method used in rule interpolation, where the α-cuts of the fuzzy mapping are obtained from the respective points of the rules.

It is interesting to check how the α-cuts representation behaves in respect to the CNF operations. Figure 46 presents two antecedent/consequent (or observation/conclusion) pairs, and furthermore, their CNF unions. From this figure, it can be easily understood why monotonicity of the cut borderlines is necessary. If it is not so, the formula for the determination of B_i had to be changed to:

$$B_i = proj_Y \left(F_\alpha \cap (A_i \times Y) \right) \tag{4.42}$$

Note that Equation 4.41 is a special case of Equation 4.42. The Figure 47 shows the problem with non-monotone cuts for a single α. In this general case, the approximation between two rules can be done in the same way as in the monotone case. Restricting the possible approximation functions to such that are monotone between two neighboring points, or to polynomial functions, and so on might reduce the theoretically infinite number of possible approximation, whose reduced number depends on the additional conditions assumed, and might result into even a single solution (for example the minimal degree Lagrange polynomial).

Let us discuss now the representation of the CNF intersection. It is obvious that if $A_1 \cap A_2$ and $B_1 \cap B_2$ are subnormal, the α-cuts of $A_1 \otimes A_2$ and $B_1 \otimes B_2$ depend in a much more complicated way on the cuts of the arguments themselves than in the case of union. By knowing only the 0- and 1-cuts, it is impossible to reconstruct the core of the CNF intersection, (that is, from a known rule base no refinement can be constructed by using only the support and core, theoretically, not even by knowing a finite number of cuts).

A very special case is when all terms in the rules are crisp sets. For crisp sets, the CNF intersection is identical with the ordinary intersection, so refinements can be reconstructed by knowing the supports only (which are in this case identical with the cores).

The Figure 48 presents such an example.

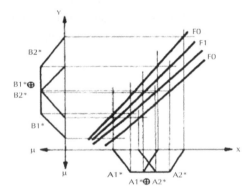

FIGURE 46 False conclusion obtained with CNF union (consistent mode) by using the single α-cut method.

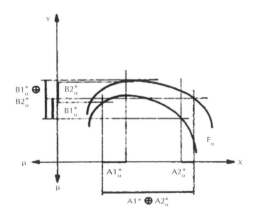

FIGURE 47 Consistency of F (cover) with non-monotonic cuts.

4.13.4 APPROXIMATIVE FUZZY MODEL

The general fuzzy mapping is too complex to be used in practical applications where the major advantage of applying fuzzy models is usually the lower computations complexity. Both fuzzy models discussed in Section 4.13.2 are such approximations. However, the information contained in these models is different, and seemingly not compatible. Also, their structure is different from that of the general model, as they both operate with a particular fuzzy cover (or "partial cover") of the input universe, rather than with the fuzzy power set. In the following, a general approximative model is considered that includes both Z and TS.

The common point in the two models is that they both consist of a set of rules, partitioning the behavior of the system into smaller areas of the input universe, where this behavior can be described by some simple method – considerably simpler than the overall behavior. This feature is kept in the general approximative model, as well. In the consequent part, first the most general approach is adopted [164, 167].

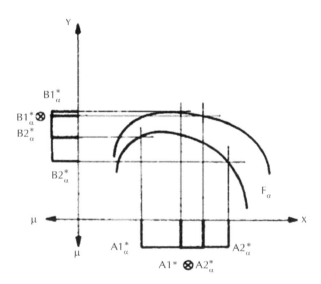

FIGURE 48   Consistency of F (CNF refinement) with crisp terms.

Definition 4.16 The general approximative fuzzy model of a system S is a rule set with CNF mappings in the consequent:

$$R = \left\{ \text{If x is } A_i \text{ then } C_Y = F_{S_i}\left(C_x\right), \qquad i = 1, \ldots\ldots, r \right\} \qquad (4.43)$$

Where C_X and C_Y are general CNF variables (elements of the CNF power sets of X and Y).

This model is seemingly even more complicated than the non-approximative one, formally it is a generalization of F_S, which is a special case, when $r = 1$, and that single rule is:

$$\text{If x is X then } C_Y = F_S(C_X) \tag{4.44}$$

Such an approximative model has importance when the consequents are easily computable (for example, when F_{Si} denotes some simpler fuzzy mappings, such as extended linear mappings, that is, where all level functions are linear:

$$F_{i\alpha} = \left[a_{i\alpha}L_x + b_{i\alpha L}, a_{i\alpha}U_x + b_{i\alpha}U \right]$$

For any constant width input sequence. If, in addition, the piecewise linearity of the membership functions described by these cuts can be assumed, a very simply tractable rule system is obtained.

If the shape of all terms is restricted to trapezoidal, it is efficient to use only the $\alpha = 0, 1$ cuts (supports and cores), and so, every consequent can be given in the form:

$$\text{Supp}(F_i) = \left[a_{i0Lx} + b_{i0L}, a_{i0Ux} + b_{i0U} \right]$$
$$\text{Core}(F_i) = \left[a_{i1Lx} + b_{i1L}, a_{i1Ux} + b_{i1U} \right]$$

In general, if it is possible to calculate easily with $F_{i\alpha}$ (including piecewise linear, polynomial, or simple rational functions), Equation 4.43 can be considered as a practically implementable approximate model of S, more accurate than the two models treated earlier. Furthermore, it is an advantageous property that, because of the property of preserving (or at least, approximately preserving) piecewise linearity between the characteristic points (breakpoints) of the input and output terms, this approach still offers a computationally effective way to deal with fuzzy systems if only trapezoidal membership functions C_X are taken into consideration. C_Y is also(approximately) trapezoidal. This is certainly true if piecewise linear level functions are taken. In general, it might be a promising new means of doing approximate reasoning in fuzzy rule-based models.

Remark 4.8 The two mentioned models (Z- and TS-models) as well as the general non-approximative fuzzy model and the non-fuzzy model, fit into Equation 4.43 as special cases:

i)   If $F_{i\alpha}(x) = B_{i\alpha}$ for every i, that is,the local approximation "functions" are constant CNF sets, the Z model is obtained,

If $Fi\alpha(x) = fi(x)$ for every $\alpha \ \square \ (0,1)$, that is, the fuzzy functional are ordinary (crisp) functions, the TS-model is generated. (In this case, necessarily $f_{\alpha L}(x) = f_{\alpha U}(x) = f(x)$ for every $\alpha \in [0,1]$),

The general model itself is a special case of the approximative model Equation 4.43, as it was shown by Equation 4.44, and

The non-fuzzy analytical model $y = f(x)$ is the special case when $A_i = X$, or

$$R_{TS} = \{\text{If x is } A_1 \text{ then } y = f_1(x)$$

$\text{Supp}(A_i) = X$, and for every input $\text{If x is } A_2 \text{ then } y = f_2(x)\}$., while the model

does not restrict the behavior of $B' = F(A')$ when $A' \neq y \epsilon Y$

The Z approach considers the functions constant "values" for the core domains of the antecedent sets, although these values are fuzzy sets, while the TS approach is crisp in Y, but allows the change of the substitution value even within the core of a given A_i. Depending on the real behavior of S, both models might be good enough approximations (but usually not both for the same system), however, with more complex systems, a type (4) approach might be unavoidable. The importance of the fuzzy functional model F is usually only theoretical, as using this model directly in the general case would mean continuum infinite steps in obtaining B'. An exception is when all level functions of F are explicit, as it is in the compressed model approximating the 11-rule model in the example of Section 4.13.2. If the parabolic level functions are accepted as exact (or good enough) descriptions of the system, the substitution of an arbitrary piecewise linear CNF observation into this function can be done very fast.

4.13.5 TRANSFORMATION OF VARIOUS MODELS

After having discussed the general fuzzy model including both "classical" models, it seems to be quite obvious that the transformation of Z- and TS-models into each other is possible *via,* the general model under certain circumstances. It must be seen clearly, however, that both the Z- and TS-models are approximative ones as compared to the general F, or even the approximative ones as compared to the general F, or even the approximative one given buy Equation 4.43, and so, by the transformations, some more loss of exactness of the knowledge might occur.

Let us consider the problem of $Z \rightarrow TS$ transformation first.

Suppose that two rules are given (as a part of Z-model of S):

$$R_Z \{\text{If x is } A_i \text{ then } y \text{ is } B_i$$

$$\text{If x is } A_2 \text{ then } y \text{ is } B_2 \}$$

with the triangular rules and the characteristic values (bottom points, and peak point) a_{1L0}, $a_{1L/U1}$, a_{1U0} and b_{1L0}, $b_{1L/U1}$, and b_{1U0} for the first rule, a_{2L0}, $a_{2L/U1}$, a_{2U0} and b_{2L0}, $b_{2L/U1}$, and b_{2U0} for the second rule. Applying linear interpolation between the two rules, the three level functions F_{L0}, $F_{L/U1}$, and F_{U0} can be determined (See Figure 49). The fuzzy fraction obtained by interpolating F_{L0}, $F_{L/U1}$, and F_{U0} for $\alpha \in (0, 1)$ can be defuzzified, for example, by center of gravity method, and so f is obtained.

This is the consequent of the single TS rule:

$$R_{TS} = \text{If x is A then } y = f(x)$$

the partial model corresponding to R_Z. A can be obtained by the CNF union of A_1 and A_2: $A = A_1 \oplus A_2$ is a single trapezoidal domain described by the four characteristic values $a_{L0} = a_{2L0}$, $a_{L1} = a_{2L/U1}$, $a_{U1} = a_{2L/U1}$, and $a_{U0} = a_{1U0}$ because $A_2 < A_1$.

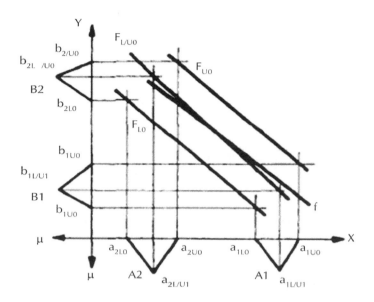

FIGURE 49   Transformation form Z-() to *TS*-model.

The opposite transformation, that is, TS → Z, is also possible, however, as the antecedents in the TS-model are crisp functions, the obtained Z model is a classical discrete one. Let the original model be:

$$R_{TS} = \{\text{If } x \text{ is } A_1 \text{then } y = f_1(x)$$
$$\text{If } x \text{ is } A_2 \text{ then } y = f_2(x)\}.$$

Then, several characteristic points of $f_i(x)$ is determined, depending on the type of these functions, the antecedent terms, and the method of interpolation applied. If, for example, $f_i(x)$ are linear, it might be sufficient to choose a few points in Gray (A_1, A_2), and piecewise linear or polynomial interpolation might reconstruct the original knowledge with an acceptable accuracy. If the functions themselves are nonlinear, several more points are necessary, eventually also in Core(A_1) and Core(A_2). A simple example is shown in Figure 50.

As a matter of fact, if model Equation 4.43 is adopted as a primary model, it is possible to transform it into a real fuzzy Z-model. The technique is similar to the one applied in 2, however, for the characteristic levels (at least for 0 and 1) separate transformations are necessary, from where the antecedents and consequents can be reconstructed by piecewise linear interpolation.

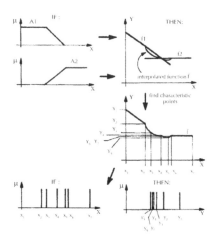

FIGURE 50   Transformation of TS-model to sdiscrete Z-() model (Sugeno-controllers). The original consequent functions are linear.

In this section both Mamdani-type and T-S type have been overviewed. In both model types, the input universe is covered densely by the union of antecedents. There is an essentially different case, when the rule base is sparse, then from Mamdani-style rules it is necessary to construct interpolation functions; (however, in general, for all α-cuts in the unit interval, as an interval valued function, that is, pair of function). This solution has a strong resemblance with the generalized TS model, except that here really fuzzy functions are generalized, while the TS-model operates with crisp functions. Such crisp functions, however, is interpreted as unfuzzified functions. These considerations lead to the proposition of a general fuzzy model that contains all previous ones as its special cases (Mamdani, TS, and interpolative models).

4.14   LOSLESS RULE REDUCTION TECHNIQUES FOR FUZZY SYSTEM

Following the wide spread usage of Fuzzy Systems, Rule Reduction has emerged as one of the most important areas of research in different application domain. It is well known that an increase in the number of input variables and/or the number of membership functions in the input domains quickly lead to combinatorial explosion in the number of rules.

But very little work has been done on rule reduction techniques that preserve the inference, that is, the outputs of the original and the reduced rule bases are identical. This section proposes a novel [6] rule reduction technique for a restricted class of Fuzzy Systems that preserves the inference.

4.14.1 DIFFERENT STAGES OF A FUZZY INFERENCE SYSTEM

A Fuzzy inference system consist of the following stages:

- **Fuzzification:** Given crisp input "a" is fuzzified to get a fuzzy set $\tilde{X}$ on the corresponding input space, that is, $a \rightarrow \tilde{X}$.
- **Matching:** The input fuzzy sets ($\tilde{X}_1$, $\tilde{X}_2$, ..., $\tilde{X}_3$) are matched against their corresponding if-part sets of their input spaces in each of the rule antecedents in the Fuzzy System, that is,

$$a_i^j = S(a_i^j, \tilde{X}) \qquad (4.45)$$

- Combining: In a multi-antecedent fuzzy system, the various matching degrees a_i^j of the n input fuzzy sets to the antecedent of a fuzzy if-then rule is combined to:

$$\mu_j = T(a_j^i,...., a_n^j) \qquad (4.46)$$

- Rule Firing: The combined value μ_j fires the rule consequent or the output fuzzy set Y_j. In many models of fuzzy systems, this Y_j is taken as its centroid y_j, that is,

$$f_j = f(\mu_j, y_j) \qquad (4.47)$$

- Aggregation of Inference: The fired output fuzzy sets (or crisp sets) $f_j, j = 1, 2,$ ..., m; are aggregated to obtain the final output fuzzy set:

$$y = g(f_1, f_2, ... f_m) \qquad (4.48)$$

4.14.2 DIFFERENT EXISTING MODELS OF FUZZY INFERENCE SYSTEM

Let us consider the following system of m fuzzy if-then rules:

R_i If X_1 is A_1^1 and .... X_n is A_n^1 Then Y is B_1

R_j : If X_1 is A_1^j and .... X_n is A_n^j Then Y is B_j

R_m : If X_1 is A_1^m and .... X_n is A_n^m Then Y is B_m

where $A_i^j \in F(X_i)$ for i = 1, 2, ..., n are the input fuzzy sets over the n input domains $X_1, X_2, \ldots\ldots, X_n$, and $B_j \in F(Y)$ for j = 1, 2, ..., m are the output fuzzy sets over the single output domain Y.

The following are the three most widely used models of fuzzy systems.

- Takagi – Sugeno Fuzzy System

$$F(x) = \frac{\sum^m_{j=1} \mu_j b_j}{\sum^m_{i=1} \mu_j} \qquad (4.49)$$

where we use singleton fuzzification. For the input $X = (x_1, x_2, (fix_n)$, the matching values are given by $a_i^j = A_i^j \wedge \tilde{X}_i$ or $A_i^j \cdot \tilde{X}_i = A_i^j (x_i)$. The combined value of the multi-antecedent if-part is given by $\mu_j = a_1^j \cdot a_2^j \cdots a_n^j = A_1^j(x_1) \cdot A_2^j(x_2) \cdots A_n^j(x_n)$, and b_j is the centroid of the output fuzzy sets B_j, j=1, 2, ..., m.

- **Mamdani Fuzzy System:** The output fuzzy set B given by μ_b is as follows:

$$\mu_b(w) = \vee^m_{j=1} f_j = \vee^m_{j=1} \wedge^n_{i=1} (a_i^j \wedge \mu_{b_j}(w)) \qquad (4.50)$$

where $a_i^j = A_i^j \wedge \tilde{X}_i$, $\mu_j = \wedge^n_{i=1} a_i^j$, $f_j = \mu_j \wedge \mu_{b_j}(w)$ and $\mu_{b_j}(w)$ is the output fuzzy set B_j of the jth rule.

- **Kosko's Standard Additive Model (SAM):** The output is given by:

$$F(x) = \frac{\sum^m_{j=1} w_j a_j(x) v_j c_j}{\sum^m_{j=1} w_j a_j(x) v_j} \qquad (4.51)$$

where $a_j(x) = a_1^j(x_1) \cdot \ldots \ldots e a_n^j(x_n)$, v_j and c_j are the volume and centroid of the output fuzzy set B_j of the j'th fuzzy if-then rule and w_j are the rule weights. Letting $\mu_j = w_j \cdot a_j(x) \cdot v_j$ we get the Takagi – Sugeno fuzzy system.

4.14.3   A GENERAL FRAMEWORK FOR FUZZY SYSTEMS

From the above two sub-sections, it appears that the different stages can be mapped to different functions capturing the actions performed at every stage. To this end, we do not consider 'fuzzification' stage since a crisp input to the fuzzy system can be thought of as a singleton – fuzzified input fuzzy set.

Then the different stages and the corresponding mappings capturing their actions can be given by:

- **Matching:** $a_i^j : S(A_i^j, \tilde{X}_i) : F(X_i) \times F(X_i) \rightarrow [0, 1]$

- **Combining:** $\mu_j : \mu(a_1^j, \text{in } a_n^j) : [0,1]^n \rightarrow [0,1]$

- **Firing:** $f_j : f(\mu_1, \ \mu_m)$

- **Aggregation:** $g = g(f_1, \ g f_m).$

The corresponding functions for $s, \mu, f,$ and g for the different models of fuzzy inference systems are tabulated in Table 4.

TABLE 4   S,μ,f, and g for the different models of fuzzy inference systems

Name / Type	S	μ	f	g	Fuzzification
Takagi-Sugeno	$\wedge$	Product	Product	Weighted Average	Singleton
Mamdani-Type I	$\wedge$	$\wedge$	Product/ Minimum	V	Any
Mamdani-Type II	V	V	Product/ Minimum	$\wedge$	Any
Kosdo's SAM	$\wedge$	Product	Product	Weighted Average	Singleton

4.14.4   RULE REDUCTION FOR A RESTRICTED CLASS OF FUZZY SYSTEMS

Inference in multi input single output (MISO) – Fuzzy Inference Systems under g, f, μ, and S.

A general Multi Input Single Output (MISO) – fuzzy inference system is given as follows [6]:

$$R_i : \text{If } X_1 \text{ is } A_1^1 \text{ and } \ldots\ldots\ldots\ldots X_n \text{ is } A_n^1 \text{ Then Y is } B_1$$

$$R_j : \text{If } X_1 \text{ is } A_1^j \text{ and } \ldots\ldots\ldots\ldots X_n \text{ is } A_n^j \text{ Then Y is } B_j$$

$$R_m : \text{If } X_1 \text{ is } A_1^m \text{ and } \ldots\ldots\ldots\ldots X_n \text{ is } A_n^m \text{ Then Y is } B_m$$

where $A_1^j \in F(X_i)$ for i=1, 2, ..., n and $B_j \in F(Y)$ for j = 1, 2, ..., m. Then the general inference in the absence of any input is given by:

$$g\{f[\mu(A_1^1, A_2^1, [rA_n^1), B_1], f[\mu(A_1^2, A_2^2, f[A_n^2), B_2], \ldots f[\mu(A_1^m, A_2^m, f[A_n^m, B_m]\}$$

$$(4.52)$$

where μ is any antecedent combiner, f is any function representing the rule firing and g is the aggregation.

RULES WITH THE SAME CONSEQUENTS

In many cases, the number of fuzzy sets (membership functions) defined on the single output domain, say r, is typically much less than the number of rules m, that is, $r \ll m$. To eliminate this redundancy, we propose a new type of rule reduction, where the rules with the same consequents but different antecedents are merged into a single rule. Then we have only as many rules as there are output membership functions, in fact only those that are part of the original fuzzy inference system.

The issue involved here is that despite the merging of the above rules, there should be no loss of inference, that is, the output that would have been obtained for a given input to the original model should be the same as that of the reduced model for the same input.

This necessitates the functions g, f, μ, and S to possess some properties. These are discussed as follows:

THE RESTRICTIONS ON g, f, μ

Let us consider a MISO – fuzzy inference system. Without loss of generality, let us take a 2-input 1-output fuzzy system, where X_1 and X_2 are the input domains and Y the output domain. Again, without loss of generality, let us consider the fuzzy system with the following rules:

$$R_1: \quad A_1, B_1,$$

$$R_2: \quad A_2, B_2, \quad (4.53)$$

$$R_3: \quad A_3, B_3,$$

Then the inference under g, f, and μ in the absence of any input to the fuzzy inference system is given by:

$$g\{f[\ \mu(A_1,\ B_1),\ C],\ f[\mu(A_2,\ B_2),\ C],\ f[\mu(A_3,\ B_3),\ D]\}. \quad (4.54)$$

Since we need to merge the rules R_1 and R_2 having the same consequents, we do the following:

From Equation 4.54 we have,

$$g\{f[\mu(A_1,B_1),o_g\mu(A_2,B_2),C],f[\mu(A_3,B_3),D]\}$$

$$(4.55)$$

$$=g\{f[\mu(A_1\ o_\mu\ A_2,B_1o_\mu B_2),C],f[\mu(A_3,B_3),D]\}$$

$$(4.56)$$

COMBINING "COMBINED' VALUES

From Equation 4.54 we obtain Equation 4.55 by composing the antecedents $\mu(A_1,B_1)$ and $\mu(A_2,B_2)$ of the rules R_1 and R_2 having the same consequents. This introduces a new operator

$$o_g : I\times I \to I \text{ such that } g\left[\ f(A,\ C),\ f(B,\ C)\right] = f(A\ o_g\ B,\ C). \quad (4.57)$$

Thus the function g should possess a corresponding operator o_g such that Equation 4.57 is satisfied. Also g should be associative.

COMBINING FUZZY SETS ON THE SAME DOMAIN

From Equation 4.55 we obtain Equation 4.56 by combining fuzzy sets that are defined on the same input domain, that is, $A_1, A_2 \in F(X_1)$ and $B_1, B_2 \in F(X_2)$. To this end, we introduce another operator:

$$o_\mu: I\times I \to \text{ such that } \mu(A_1,\ B_1)\ o_g\ \mu(A_2,\ B_2) = \mu(A_1\ o_\mu A_2,\ B_1\ o_\mu B_2) \quad (4.58)$$

In the absence of any input to the fuzzy system, the restrictions applied so far are: g is associative.

- $g\left[f(A,\ C),\ f(B,\ C)\right] = f(A\ o_g\ B,\ C).$

- $\mu(A_1,\ B_1)\ o_g\ \mu(A_2,\ B_2) = \mu(A_1\ o_\mu\ A_2,\ B_1\ o_\mu\ B_2)$

The above technique is applied when g and μ obey the given equations apossess functions o_g and o_μ.

THE REDUCED RULE BASE AND INFERENCE IN THE PRESENCE OF INPUTS

In the above discussion, the function S has not figured. This is because one of the parameters for S is the current input. Let us consider the inference in the above MISO – fuzzy system in the presence of input, say $\tilde{X} = (A, B)$ where $A \in F(X_1)$, $B \in F(X_2)$. The MISO inference can be stated as:

$$g\{f[\mu(S(A_1,A),S(B_1,B)),C],f[\mu(S(A_2,A),S(B_2,B)),C],f[\mu(S(A_3,A),S(B_3,B)),D]\}$$
(4.59)

$$= g\{f[\mu(S(A_1,A),S(B_1,B))\ o_g\mu(S(A_2,A),S(B_2,B)),C],f[\mu(S(A_3,A),S(B_3,B)),D]\}$$ (4.60)

$$= g\{f[\mu(S(A_1,A)\ o_\mu S(A_2,A)\ (S(B_1,B)o_\mu S(B_2,B)\},C],f[\mu(S(A_3,A),S(B_3,B)),D]\}$$
(4.61)

$$= g\{f[\mu(S(A_1\ o_s A_2,A),\ S(B_1 o_s B_2,B\},C),\ f[\mu(S(A_3,A),S(B_3,B)),D]\}$$
(4.62)

In the presence of an input $\tilde{X} = (\tilde{A}_1, \ldots\ldots\ldots, \tilde{A}_n)$, the matching fit values $a_i^j = S(A_i^j, \tilde{A}_i)$ are calculated and thus the function S features in Equation 4.59, which is otherwise another form of Equation 4.54.

We obtain Equation 4.60 from Equation 4.59 by using Equation 4.57 and Equation 4.61 from Equation 4.60 by applying Equation 4.58. Since in the reduced rule base A_1 and A_2 are not separately accessible, we go a step further and combine the fuzzy sets on the antecedents on the same domain. To enable us to perform this, we introduce a new operator $o_g : F(X) \times F(X) \rightarrow I$ i.e. such that $S(A_1, A)\ o_\mu$

$$S(A_2, A) = S(A_1 o_s A_2, A)$$
(4.63)

A careful inspection on Equation 4.56 and Equation 4.62 reveals that for the inference to hold even after the rule reduction, we need:

$$o_s \equiv o_\mu$$
(4.64)

and thus S and μ are related. Thus the only properties g, f, μ, and S should posses are:
- g is associative.
- g [f(A, C), f(B, C)] = f(A o_g B, C).

- $\mu(A_1, B_1) \circ_g \mu(A_2, B_2) = \mu(A_1 \circ_\mu A_2, B_1 \circ_\mu B_2).$

- $S(A_1, A) \circ_\mu S(A_2, A) = S(A_1 \circ_g A_2, A),$

since $\circ_s \equiv \circ_\mu$

The above equations are the well-established Aggregation Equations.

Example 4.16 Mamdani-type models with Residuated Implications.

For simplicity of demonstration we consider, without any loss of generality, the 2-input 1-output fuzzy system with 3 rules as stated above:

$$A_1, B_1 \to C,$$

$$A_2, B_2 \to C,$$

$$A_3, B_3 \to D.$$

A Residuated Implication $I : [0.1] \times [0,1] \to [0,1]$ is obtained as the residuation of a binary operator, in our case a t-norm, $t : [0.1] \times [0,1] \to [0,1]$ such that:

$$a \ tb \le c \Leftrightarrow a \le bIc, \forall a, b, c \in [0,1].$$

The pair (t,I) is called the adjoin couple.

Some of the well-known R-implications and their corresponding t-norms are given in Table 5.

TABLE 5 Some of the well-known R-implications and their corresponding t-norms

Name	t(a, b)	I(a, b)
Łukasiawicz	max(0, a+b-1)	Min(1, 1-a+b)
Mamdani	min (a, b)	$a \to b = \begin{cases} 1, & \text{if } a) \\ b, & \text{otherwise} \end{cases}$
Larsen	a . b	$a \to b = \begin{cases} 1, & \text{if } ase \\ b/a, & \text{otherwise} \end{cases}$

Since $L = ([0, 1], \wedge, \vee, t, \to)$ forms a Linearly Ordered Residuated Lattice, we have the following properties of L:

$$\overset{\vee}{_i}(a_i \to c) = (\overset{\wedge}{_i} a_i) \to c \qquad (4.65)$$

$$\overset{\wedge}{_i}(a_i \to c) = (\overset{\vee}{_i} a_i) \to c \qquad (4.66)$$

MAMDANI MODEL – TYPE I

From Table 4, we know that for the Mamdani model of type 1, we have g = V, $\mu = \wedge$ and S = $\wedge$. Taking f an R – implication, denoted f = →, we have from 4.52, in the absence of any external input to the fuzzy system in 4.53,

$$\left[\left(A_1 \wedge B_1\right) \to C\right] \vee \left[\left(A_2 \wedge B_2\right) \to C\right] \vee \left[\left(A_3 \wedge B_3\right) \to D\right]$$
$$= \left\{\left[\left(A_1 \wedge A_2\right) \wedge \left(B_1 \wedge B_2\right)\right] \to C\right\} \vee \left[\left(\left(A_3 \wedge B_3\right) \to D\right)\right] \qquad (4.67)$$

from 4.65 and grouping $A_i{}'s$ and $B_i's$. Also (4.67) is:

$$= \left[\left(A_1^* \wedge B_1^*\right) \to C\right] \vee \left[\left(\left(A_3 \wedge B_3\right) \to D\right)\right]. \qquad (4.68)$$

Thus with $O_g = \wedge$ and $O_\mu = \wedge$ we have the fuzzy system in 4.53 with 3 rules reduced to a fuzzy system with 2 rules 4.68 without any loss of inference. Thus we have g = V, $\mu = \wedge$, S = $\wedge$, f = →, $O_g = \wedge$, and $O_\mu = \wedge$.

In the presence of an input, say $\tilde{X} = (A, B)$, we have:

$$\left[\left(S(A_1, A) \wedge S(B_1, B)\right) \to C\right] \vee \left[\left(S(A_2, A) \wedge S(B_2, B)\right) \to C\right] \vee \left[\left(S(A_3, A) \wedge S(B_3, B)\right) \to D\right].$$
$$(4.69)$$

Since in the above model, S=$\wedge$, we have, by substituting for S in 4.69

$$\left[\left(\left(A_1 \wedge A\right) \wedge \left(B_1 \wedge B\right)\right) \to C\right] \vee \left[\left(\left(A_2 \wedge A\right) \wedge S(B_2 \wedge B)\right) \to C\right] \vee \left[\left(\left(A_3 \wedge A\right) \wedge \left(B_3 \wedge B\right)\right) \to D\right].$$
$$(4.70)$$

From (4.70) by applying (4.57), (4.58) and (4.63) coupled with the fact that $O_g \equiv O_\mu = \wedge$ we obtain:

$$\left[\left(S\left(A_{1} \wedge A_{2}, A\right) \wedge S\left(B_{1} \wedge B_{2}, B\right)\right) \rightarrow C\right] \vee \left[\left(S\left(\left(A_{3} \wedge A\right) \wedge S\left(B_{3} \wedge B\right)\right) \rightarrow D\right]\right. \quad \langle \text{since } S = \wedge \rangle$$

$$=\left[\left(S\left(A_{1}^{*}, A\right) \wedge S\left(B_{1}^{*}, B\right)\right) \rightarrow C\right] \vee \left[\left(S\left(\left(A_{3} \wedge A\right) \wedge S\left(B_{3} \wedge B\right)\right) \rightarrow D\right]\right..$$

MAMDANI MODEL – TYPE II

In the above Mamdani Model, by replacing $g = \wedge$, $\mu \vee$, $S = \vee$ and retaining f to be an R implication, it can similarly be shown using 4.66 that rule reduction of the proposed type is possible with $o_g = \vee$ and $o_s \equiv o_\mu = \vee$.

Detail discussion of rule simplification based on similarity measure is given in the following section [246].

4.15 SIMPLIFICATION OF FUZZY RULE BASE USING SIMILARITY MEASURE

Fuzzy rule-based models obtained from numerical data (See Section 4.9), may contain redundancy in the form of similar fuzzy sets, which make the models unnecessarily complex and less transparent in nature. Using a measure of similarity, we propose a rule base simplification method that reduces the number of fuzzy sets in the model. Similar fuzzy sets are merged to create a common fuzzy set to replace them in the rule base. If the redundancy in the model is high, merging similar fuzzy sets might result in equal rules that also can be merged, thereby reducing the number of rules as well. The simplified rule base is computationally efficient and linguistically tractable.

4.15.1 FUZZY MODELING

Fuzzy modeling is either based on data or based on knowledge acquisition. In the latter case, the model is based on human expert knowledge. This knowledge is captured by IF-THEN rules with fuzzy predicates that establish a qualitative description of the system.

Knowledge acquisition is not a trivial task because either experts are not available or their knowledge is not always consistent, systematic and complete. Whereas, automated modeling using systems measurements gives a more versatile approach in the sense that it is independent of domain experts. It facilitates adaptation and self-tuning based on information becoming available during operation. Moreover, data and knowledge can be easily combined when building fuzzy models.

Different types of fuzzy models exist. The Mamdani model, which uses linguistic rules with a fuzzy premise part and a fuzzy consequent part. Another structure is the Takagi-Sugeno (TS) model. In Example 4.17, we use TS approach as it is well suited for automatic approaches to fuzzy modeling.

TS FUZZY MODEL

The TS fuzzy model uses rules that differ from the Mamdani type in that their consequents are mathematical functions instead of fuzzy sets. The TS model is based on the idea describing the system with a set of local input-output relations that have the following structure:

$$R_i: w_i \text{ (IF } x_1 \text{ is } A_{i1} \text{ and } x_2 \text{ is } A_{i2} \text{ and } \ldots \text{ and } x_n \text{ is } A_{in} \text{ THEN } y_i = f_i(.)) \tag{4.71}$$

where R_i is the ith rule base $x_1, \ldots, x_n$ are the premise variables, y_i is the rule output, $A_{i1}, \ldots, A_{in}$ are fuzzy sets defined for the respective premise variables, and $w_i = 1, \forall_i$, but it can be adjusted during model reduction. Usually, $f_i(.)$ is a linear function of the premise variables.

$$f_i(x_i, x_2)x_n) = p_{i0} + p_{i1} x_1 + p_{i2} x_2 + \ldots + p_{in} x_n. \tag{4.72}$$

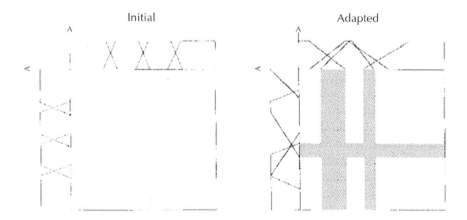

FIGURE 51   Fuzzy partition of two premise variables.

The overall output of the model (the inferred value $\bar{y}$) is calculated by taking the weighted average of the rule consequences:

$$\overline{y} = \frac{\sum_{i=1}^{N} w_i \beta y_i}{\sum_{i=1}^{N} w_i \beta_i} \tag{4.73}$$

where N is the number of rules, β_i is the degree of activation of the ith rule's premise, and y_i is the contribution of that rule.

Given the inputs $x_1, x_2, ... x_n$, the degree of activation is calculated as:

$$\beta = \prod_{j=1}^{n} \mu_{ij}(x_j), i = 1,2,........N \tag{4.74}$$

where $\mu_{ij}(x_j)$ is the membership function of the fuzzy set A_{ij} for input variable x_j in the premise of the ith rule. Because of the linear structure of the rule consequents, well-known parameter estimation techniques such as least squares can be used to estimate the consequent parameters.

AUTOMATED MODELING

Two common approaches for obtaining fuzzy models from systems measurements are parameter adaptation and fuzzy clustering. In the first case, we tune an initial partition of the premise space, while in the second case a partition suitable for a given number of rules is sought automatically. Both techniques can be combined too.

- *Parameter Adaptation:* In this approach the initial partition of the input space is represented by a number of equidistant symmetrical fuzzy sets defined for all the premise variables of the system. This partition creates a uniform grid in the premise space. The parameters of the membership function are adapted using learning algorithms such as backpropagation. During adaptation, the fuzzy sets can drift closer to each other and may end up in overlapping positions. The resulting rule base may contain redundancy in terms of similar fuzzy sets, as illustrated in Figure 51. A drawback with this approach is that the number of rules increased exponentially with the number of inputs, and that an initially transparent model may become unreadable after adaptation.

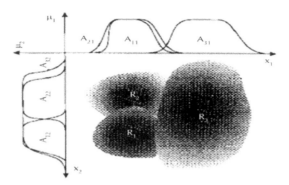

FIGURE 52   Schematic diagram of three fuzzy clusters in a two dimensional premise space.

- **Fuzzy Clustering:** Fuzzy clustering approach (See Section 4.11) is unsupervised algorithm that partition data points into a given number of clusters with fuzzy boundaries. Each cluster represents a fuzzy relation, and corresponds to a rule in the rule base. The fuzzy sets in the premise part of the rules are usually identified by projecting the clusters onto the corresponding axis of the data space. This projection usually results in similar fuzzy sets, as illustrated in Figure 52. In Mamdani models, the fuzzy consequents of the rules are determined by projection too. In TS models, the consequent parameters are derived from the cluster covariance matrix or estimated using a parameters estimation technique. Different approaches to clustering can be found, such as clustering in the output space or clustering in the product pace of input and output variables. Two well known fuzzy clustering algorithms are the fuzzy c-means and the Gustafson–Kessel (GK) algorithm. The latter is especially suitable for the identification of TS fuzzy models and has been successfully applied to modeling of dynamic systems. It can be used to identify a systems mode by clustering data from system (input-output) measurements. However, before applying clustering, the number of clusters must be specified explicitly. Correct specification of the number of clusters is important. A large number results in an unnecessarily complicated rule base, while a small number may result in a poor model. Methods for finding the optimal number of clusters (rules) are already suggested.
- **Redundancy:** Fuzzy models obtained from data, may contain redundant information in the form of similarity between fuzzy sets.

Three unwanted effects that can be recognized are:
i)   Similarity between fuzzy sets in the model,
ii) Similarity of a fuzzy set A to the universal set

$$U : \mu_u (x) = 1, \forall x \in X;$$

iii) Similarity of a fuzzy set A to singleton set.

Similar fuzzy sets represent compatible concepts in the rule base. A model with many similar fuzzy sets becomes redundant, unnecessarily complex and computationally heavy. Linguistic interpretation of such a model is difficult to assign qualitatively meaningful labels to highly similar fuzzy sets. Some of the fuzzy sets extracted from data may be similar to the universal set U (for example, A_{32} in Figure 52). Such fuzzy sets are irrelevant. The opposite effect is similarity to a singleton set. During adaptation, membership functions may get narrow, resulting in fuzzy sets almost like singletons (spikes). If a rule has one or more such fuzzy sets in its premise, it will practically never fire, and thus the rule does not contribute to the output of the model. However, it should be noted that such rules may represent exceptions from the overall model behavior.

4.15.2 SIMILARITY

The notion of similarity is interpreted in different ways depending on the context. We define similarity between fuzzy sets as the degree to which the fuzzy sets are equal. Consider the fuzzy sets A and B in Figure 53(a). They have exactly the same shape, but represent clearly distinct concepts, for example, a low and a high value of x, respectively. They have zero degree of equality and are considered dissimilar. On the other hand, the two fuzzy sets C and D in Figure 53(b), even though they differ in shape, can be said to have a high degree of equality. They represent compatible concepts and are considered similar. For further discussion on similarity measure interested readers should go through [246] and chapter 2 of volume 2 of this book.

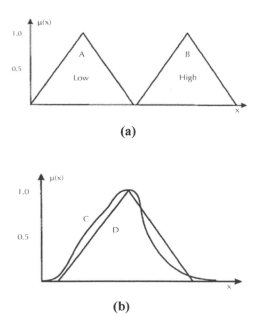

FIGURE 53 (a)Distinct fuzzy sets with no degree of equality and (b) overlapping fuzzy sets with a high degree of equality.

SIMILARITY AS DEGREE OF EQUALITY

Fuzzy sets are considered similar if they are defined by overlapping membership functions that assign approximately the same values of membership to the elements in their universe of discourse. Their similarity is the degree to which they can be considered as equal. The classical definition of equality is crisp. Let μ_a and μ_b be the membership functions of fuzzy sets A and B, respectively. Then A and B are equal, if $\mu_a(x) = \mu_b(x), \forall x \in X$. If we apply this concept of equality to the fuzzy sets in Figure 53 we get $A \neq B$ and $C \neq D$ since their membership functions are different. However, C and D can be said to have a high degree of equality and hence they are similar. A similarity measure captures a gradual transition between equality and non-equality:

$$s = S(A, B) = \deg ree(A = B), s \in [0,1] \qquad (4.75)$$

where S is a similarity measure. The similarity measure is a function assigning a similarity value s to the pair of fuzzy sets (A, B) that indicates the degree to which A and B are equal or how similar they are.

SIMPLIFICATION OF RULE BASE USING SIMILARITY MEASURE

A similarity measure for fuzzy sets detects highly similar fuzzy sets representing more or less compatible concepts in a fuzzy rule base. Such fuzzy sets should be assigned a high similarity value, whereas more distinct sets should be assigned a lower similarity value. For a correct comparison of similarity values, the similarity measure should not be influenced by the scaling of the domain on which the fuzzy sets are defined. This avoids the need for normalization of the domains.

Let A and B be (two) fuzzy subsets of X with membership functions $\mu_A(x)$ and $\mu_B(x)$, respectively. A similarity measure is considered as a candidate for an automated rule base simplification scheme if it satisfies the following four criteria:

- Non-overlapping fuzzy sets should be considered totally nonequal, s = 0

$$S(A, B) = 0 \Leftrightarrow \mu_A(x)\mu_B(x) = 0, \forall x \in X. \qquad (4.76)$$

Remark 4.9 Criterion 1 assures that dissimilar (non-overlapping) fuzzy sets are excluded from the set of similar fuzzy sets. Various degrees of dissimilarity between distinct fuzzy sets are related to the distance between them, and can be quantified by a distance measure.

- Overlapping fuzzy sets should have a similarity value $s > 0$

$$S(A, B) > 0 \Leftrightarrow \exists x \in X, \mu_A(x)\mu_B(x) \neq 0 \qquad (4.77)$$

Remark 4.10 Criterion 2 states that overlapping fuzzy sets should be assigned a nonzero degree of similarity and should not be regarded as totally nonequal.

- Only equal fuzzy sets should have a similarity value s = 1

$$S(A,B) = 1 \Leftrightarrow \mu_A(x) = \mu_B(x), \qquad \forall x \in X. \tag{4.78}$$

Remark 4.11 Criterion 3 assures that equality is a special case of similarity, in the same way that crisp sets can be considered as a special case of fuzzy sets.
- Similarity between two fuzzy sets should not be influenced by scaling or shifting the domain on which they are defined:

$$S(A',B') = S(A,B), \quad \mu_{A'}(l+kx) = \mu_A(x),$$
$$\mu_{B'}(l+kx) = \mu_B(x) \quad k,l \in R, \quad k > 0. \tag{4.79}$$

Remark 4.12 Criterion 4 is required for a fair comparison of similarities in the rule base as a similarity measure that satisfies this criterion is not influenced by the numerical values of the domain variables.

Different similarity measures have been proposed for fuzzy sets (See Chapter 2 of volume 2 of this book).

In general, they can be divided into two main groups:
- Geometric similarity measures;
- Set-theoretic similarity measures.

The theoretical analysis of similarity has been dominated by geometric models. These models represent fuzzy sets as points in a metric space and the similarity between the sets is regarded as an inverse of their distance in this metric space.

If the distance between A and B is D(A, B), the similarity of A and B can be written as:

$$s = S(A,B) = \frac{1}{1 + D(A+B)}, s \in (0,1] \tag{4.80}$$

Examples of geometric similarity measures are the generalizations of the Hausdorff distance to fuzzy sets. Another example is similarity transformed from the well-known Minkowski class of distance functions:

$$D_r(A,B) = \left(\sum_{j=1}^m |\mu_A(x_j) - \mu_B(x_j)|^r \right)^{1/r}, r \geq 1 \tag{4.81}$$

assuming that the fuzzy sets A and B are defined on a discrete universe of discourse $X = \{x_j | j = 1, 2, ..., m\}$. For continuous universes, the sum is replaced by integration.

It has been argued that geometric similarity measures are best suited for measuring similarity (or dissimilarity) among distinct fuzzy sets, while the set-theoretic measures are the most suitable for capturing similarity among overlapping fuzzy sets. The geometric similarity measures represent similarity as proximity of fuzzy sets, and not as a measure of equality. The interpretation of similarity as "approximate equality" can better be represented by a set-theoretic similarity measures. Such measures are based on set-theoretic operations like union and intersection. They also have the advantage above geometrical measures that they are not influenced by scaling and ordering of the domain.

A set-theoretic measure often encountered in the literature is the so-called consistency-index, which is the maximum membership degree of the intersection of two fuzzy sets:

$$S_c(A, B) = \sup_{x \in X} \mu_{A \cap B} = \max_{x \in X} [\mu_A(x) \wedge \mu_B(x)] \qquad (4.82)$$

where $\wedge$ is the minimum operator. Some authors use this measure for rule base reduction purposes. However, this measure does not fulfill criterion 3 as it focuses attention on only one value of the variable x, rather than performing some sort of averaging or integration.

We consider the following similarity measure, based on the set-theoretic operations of intersection and union, to determine the similarity between fuzzy sets:

$$S(A, B) = \frac{|A \cap B|}{|A \cup B|} \qquad (4.83)$$

where $| \cdot |$ denotes the cardinality of a set, and the $\cap$ and $\cup$ operators represent the intersection and union respectively. Rewriting this expression in terms of the membership functions gives:

$$S(A, B) = \frac{\sum_{j=1}^{m} [\mu_A(x_j) \wedge \mu_B(x_j)]}{\sum_{j=1}^{m} \mu_A(X_j) \vee \mu_B(x_j)} \qquad (4.84)$$

in a discrete universe $X = \{x_j | j = 1, 2, ..., m\}$. $\wedge$ and $\vee$ are the minimum and maximum operators, respectively. In computer implementation, continuous domains need to be discretized. This similarity measure complies with the four criteria above, and reflects the idea of a gradual transition from equal to completely nonequal fuzzy sets (with $S(A, B) = 0$).

An example of the behavior of this similarity measure for fuzzy sets with a varying degree of overlap is shown in Figure 54.

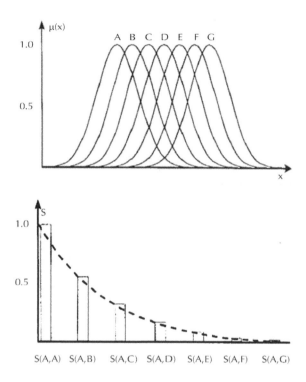

FIGURE 54 Fuzzy sets A,B,...,G and the similarity computed for S(A,A), S(A,B),...S(A,G).

4.15.3 SIMPLIFICATION OF RULE BASE

Automated approaches to fuzzy modeling often introduces redundancy in terms of several similar fuzzy sets that describe almost the same region in the domain of some model variable. The similarity measure Equation 4.83 can be used to quantify the similarity between fuzzy sets in the rule base. Two or more such similar fuzzy sets can be merged to create a new fuzzy set representative of the merged sets. By substituting this new fuzzy set for the ones merged in the rule base, the number of fuzzy sets needed to constitute the model decreases. In this way rule base simplification is achieved. This simplification may result in equal rules. In the rule base, only one of the equal rules is needed, and the others can be deleted. In this way rule base reduction is achieved. Hence, in our approach, there is a difference between rule base simplification and rule base reduction. The former is the primary objective, and the latter may follow indirectly if the redundancy is high. Figure 55 illustrates the idea of merging similar fuzzy sets, which results in both rule base simplification and reduction. This idea is exploited in this section for developing the rule base simplification and reduction algorithm that is described at the subsequent stage [246].

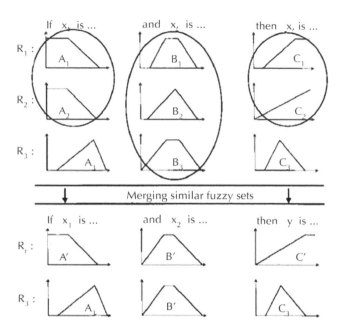

FIGURE 55 Example of a Mamdani-type model. Similar fuzzy sets are merged. Rules R_1 and R_2 become equal and can be represented by one rule R.

REMOVING FUZZY SETS

The rule base may contain irrelevant fuzzy sets. If a fuzzy set in the premise of a rule has a membership function $\mu(x) \approx 1, \forall x \in X$, it is similar to the universal set U and can be removed. The similarity of a fuzzy set A to the universal set is quantified by $S(A, U)$. An example of a fuzzy set quite similar to the universal set is illustrated in Figure 52. Here A_{32} can be removed, and only A_{31} is necessary in the premise of rule R_3 to distinguish the associated region in the premise product space.

A rule whose premise only consists of fuzzy sets very similar to the universal set can be removed. Its contribution is then only biasing the result, and the same output can be achieved by adjusting the consequents of the other rules. The opposite may also occur. During adaptation, the support of one or more fuzzy sets may become so narrow that they become almost like spikes (singletons). Singleton fuzzy sets have extremely low similarity to the universal set (that is, $S(A, U) \approx 0$). In some cases, rules with such fuzzy sets in their premise can be removed from the rule base, but in general care must be taken as the rules may represent exceptions. Interaction from the user is typically needed in such cases. Since our aim is to develop an automated simplification method, we do not consider removing singletons from the rule base.

MERGING FUZZY SETS

In general, when two fuzzy sets A and B are considered to be very similar, there are three possibilities for simplifying the rule base:
- Replace A by B,
- Replace B by A, and
- Replace both A and B by a new fuzzy set C.

Two important aspects of the simplified model are its accuracy and coverage of the premise space. Let the model's accuracy be measured by some function J (for example, sum of squared errors). The effect of replacing A and B by C should be as small as possible with respect to J. Thus, finding the fuzzy set C best suited to replace A and B evaluates the function J. In general, if the model is more sensitive to changes in A than to changes in B, A should replace B, or the common fuzzy set C should resemble A more than B. In particular applications, additional aspects like model granularity (number of linguistic terms per variable), interpretability or physical relevance may be important.

For the discussion about merging fuzzy sets, we define a fuzzy set A using a parametric membership function:

$$\mu_A(x: a_1, a_2, a_3, a_4) a_1 < a_2, a_3, a_4$$

$$\mu_A(x: a_1, a_2, a_3, a_4) = \begin{cases} 0 & x \leq a_1, \quad \text{or } x \geq a_4 \\ 1 & a_2 \leq x \leq a_3 \\ \alpha & \alpha \in (0,1), \quad \text{otherwise} . \end{cases} \quad (4.85)$$

To merge the fuzzy sets we consider the support of $A \cup B$ as the support of the new fuzzy set C. This guarantees preservation of the coverage of the whole premise space, when C replaces A and B in the premise of the rule base. The kernel of C is given by aggregating the parameters describing the kernels of A and B. Thus merging A and B, defined by $\mu_A(x; a_1, a_2, a_3, a_4)$ and $\mu_B(x; b_1, b_2, b_3, b_4)$, respectively, Equation 4.85 gives a fuzzy set C defined by $\mu_C(x; c_1, c_2, c_3, c_4)$ where:

$$c_1 = \min(a_1, b_1) \quad (4.86)$$

$$c_2 = \lambda_2 a_2 + (1 - \lambda_2) b_2 \quad (4.87)$$

$$c_3 = \lambda_3 a_3 + (1 - \lambda_3) b_3 \quad (4.88)$$

$$c_4 = \max(a_4, b_4). \quad (4.89)$$

The parameters λ_2, $\lambda_3 \in [0, 1]$ determines which of the fuzzy sets A or B has the most influence on the kernel of C. In the rest of the article we use $\lambda_2 = \lambda_3 = 0.5$.

This averaging of the kernels gives a tradeoff between contributions of the rules, in which the fuzzy sets occur.

The Figure 56 illustrates this method for merging two fuzzy sets A and B to create C.

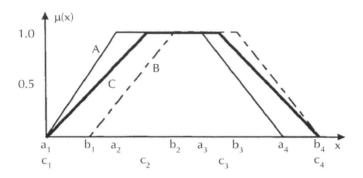

FIGURE 56   Creating fuzzy set C to replace A and B in the rule base.

MERGING RULES

In Mamdani fuzzy model, if k rules become equal as a result of rule base simplifica-tion, k-1 of them can be removed, resulting in rule base reduction, as shown in Figure 55. If only the premises of the rules become equal, and the consequents do not, this can indicate a contradiction in the rule base that might need further attention. In the rest of this article we concentrate on TS models since they are well suited for (semi) automated generation of rules from data.

In TS models, the consequents of the rules are not fuzzy, and the similarity is considered only in the premise part of the rules. When the premise parts of k rules get equal, we remove k-1 of these rules. However, the consequent parameters of the rule remaining in the rule base, called R_r , must be reestimated. This can be done by weighting R_r with $k(w_r = k)$ and averaging the consequents of all the k rules with equal premise parts. Thus, the k rules with equal premise parts, $R_1, R_2, ..., R_k$, are represented by a single rule R_r with weight $w_r = k$ and consequent parameters:

$$P_r = \frac{1}{k}\sum_{i=1}^{k} P_i \qquad (4.90)$$

where P_i is a vector of the consequent parameters $p_{io}, p_{i1}, ..., p_{in}$ in the ith of the rules with equal premise parts. The model output must now be calculated accord-ing to:

$$\widehat{y} = \frac{\sum_{i=1, i \neq r}^{N-(k-1)} w_i \beta_i y_i + w_r \beta_r y_r}{\sum_{i=1, i \neq r}^{N-(k-1)} w_i \beta_i + w_r \beta_r} \tag{4.91}$$

Another approach is to re-estimate the consequent parameters in the reduced rule base using training data. This requires more computation, but usually gives a numerically more accurate result than weighting and averaging. Independently of the method used, we refer to this as merging rules.

RULE BASE SIMPLIFICATION ALGORITHM

This section describes an algorithm that is developed for rule base simplification is TS models. The same concept can be used also for Mamdani models. Simplification is achieved by removing fuzzy sets similar to the universal set and by merging similar fuzzy sets. Based on the result, rule base reduction is obtained by merging rules with equal premise parts. The approach uses the similarity measure Equation 4.83 for determining the similarity between the fuzzy sets in the rule base, and requires two thresholds γ for removing fuzzy sets similar to the universal set and λ for merging fuzzy sets that are similar to one another.

The algorithm starts by iteratively merging similar fuzzy sets. In each iteration, the similarity between all pairs of fuzzy sets for each variable is considered, and the pair of fuzzy sets having the highest similarity $s > \lambda$ is merged to create a new fuzzy set. Then the rule base is updated by substituting this new fuzzy set for the fuzzy sets merged to create it. The algorithm then again evaluates the similarities in the updated rule base. This continues until there are no more fuzzy sets for which $s \geq \lambda$. Therefore, the fuzzy sets that have similarity $s > \gamma$ to the universal set U are removed. Finally, the rule base is checked for rules with equal premise parts. Such rules are merged as discussed earlier.

The Figure 57 depicts a flowchart of the algorithm that is stated below [246];

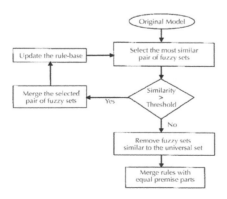

FIGURE 57   The simplification algorithm.

ALGORITHM

Given a fuzzy rule base $R = \{R_i\}_{i=1}^N$, where R_i is given by Equation 4.71, select thresholds $\gamma, \lambda \in (0, 1)$.

Repeat:

Step 1: Select two most similar fuzzy sets in

R. Calculate $s_i k_j = S(A_{ij}, A_{kj})$, $j = 1, \ldots, n$, $i = 1, \ldots, N$, $k = 1, \ldots, N$. Select A_{lq}

and A_{mq}, $s_{lmq} = \max_{i \neq k}\{s_i k_j\}$.

Step 2: Merge similar fuzzy sets and update **R.** If $s_{lmq} \geq \lambda$ merge A_{lq} and A_{mq} to create a new fuzzy set A. Set $A_{lq} = A$ and $A_{mq} = A$.

Until: no more fuzzy sets have similarity $s_i k_j \geq \lambda$, $i \neq k$.

Step 3: Remove fuzzy sets similar to the universal set. For each fuzzy set A_{ij} calculate $S(A_{ij}, U)$, $\mu_U(x_j) = 1$, $\forall x_j$. If $S(A_{ij}, U) \geq \gamma$ remove A_{ij} from the premise of R_i

Step 4: Merge rules with equal premise part.

The threshold γ for removing the fuzzy sets that are similar to the universal set should generally be higher than the threshold λ for merging. In our applications, $\gamma = 0.8$ gives good results. The choice of a suitable threshold λ depends on the application. The lower the threshold λ, the less fuzzy sets are used in the resulting model. In general, one can expect the numerical accuracy of the model to decrease as λ decreases. However, this need not always be the case. If the model is highly redundant or over determined, the numerical accuracy may improve as a result of simplification.

By using different thresholds, different versions of the model can be obtained. For instance, for explaining the working of a system (operator training, expert evaluation), a comprehensible linguistic description is important. In such cases, it is reasonable to trade some numeric accuracy for extra transparency and readability. This implies the use of a lower threshold λ than when aiming at applications for prediction or simulation.

The algorithm only merges one pair of fuzzy sets (A_{lq}, A_{mq}) per iteration. Merging in different premise variables is independent of each other, making it possible to merge more fuzzy sets in one variable than in another. It might happen that the fuzzy sets to be merged were created themselves by merging in a previous iteration. For the fuzzy sets in the original rule base to have an equal influence on the final result, we make use of the fact that if a fuzzy set D is created by merging, it has multiple occurrences in the rule base. For instance, if D is created by merging (A, B), and later D is merged with C, two occurrences of D and one of C are merged to create E. Using the parametric description in Equation 4.86, the parameters of the membership function $\mu_s(x; e_1, e_2, e_3, e_4)$ become: $e_1 = \min(c_1, d_1)$, $e_2 = (c_2 + c_2 + d_2)/3$, $e_3 = (c_3 + c_3 + d_3)/3$, and $e_4 = \max(c_4, d_4)$. This corresponds to merging the three original membership functions A, B, and C.

After rule base simplification, rules with equal premise parts are merged. In the following, we re-estimate the consequent parameters of the resulting rule base using the same training data from which the original rule base is identified.

Example 4.17 We consider fuzzy modeling of enzymatic soil removal [246]. Enzymes are agents that break down soil chemically. The rate of the soil removal is affected by such factors as alkalinity of the solution and temperature. The fuzzy model should predict the percentage soil that is removed by the enzymes, given the elapsed time for the reaction, the temperature of the solution and the alkalinity. It is assumed that the enzyme concentration is large enough, so that it has no influence on the rate of the reaction.

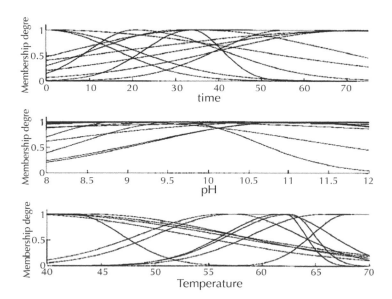

FIGURE 58   The membership functions of the original model.

- ***Original Model:*** The process is identified from measurements of the time responses under particular temperature and alkalinity conditions. Based on these measurements, a TS fuzzy model has been identified by fuzzy clustering in the product space of the three input variables time (t), alkalinity (pH), and temperature (T) and one output variable, the remaining soil (y). The rule base obtained from clustering with $K = 11$ can be written:

$$R_i : \text{IF t is } A_{i1} \text{ and pH is } A_{i2} \text{ and T is } A_{i3}$$

$$\text{THEN } y_i, \quad i = 1, 2, \ldots, 11. \tag{4.92}$$

The output (consequent) of each rule is a linear combination of the process variables:

$$y_i = p_{i_0} + p_{i1} \cdot t + p_{i2} \cdot pH + p_{i3} \cdot T \tag{4.93}$$

where the parameters p_{i0}, p_{i1}, re p_{i3} have been estimated with least mean square (LMS). The model obtained from clustering consists of 11 rules and has the total of 33 fuzzy sets [15]. The fuzzy sets in the premise of this original model are shown in Figure 58.

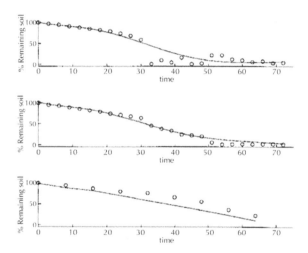

FIGURE 59 The original model's response to the evaluation data for three different experimental conditions.

TABLE 6 Results that are obtained using different values for λ and γ = 0.8

Threshold λ	Number of fuzzy sets per variable				rules	MSE
	Time	pH	Temp	total		
Original model	11	5	11	33	11	0.0108
0.90	10	2	9	21	11	0.0106
0.80	8	2	6	16	11	0.0108
0.70	4	2	6	12	10	0.0119
0.60	2	2	5	9	9	0.0116
0.40	2	1	3	6	7	0.0120

- *Model Validation:* The original model is validated using a validation data set. The original model's response to this data is shown in Figure 59. The original model's response to the evaluation data has been found satisfactory, the mean square error (MSE) is 0.0108. However, the model contains a lot of overlapping fuzzy sets, Figure 58 shows that there is a high redundancy in terms of similarity among the fuzzy sets in the model. Assigning meaningful labels to all these fuzzy sets for linguistic description and expert evaluation is almost impossible.
- *Results:* The proposed rule base simplification algorithm is applied several times with different values of the threshold λ for merging. The threshold γ for removing fuzzy sets similar to the universal set is held constant at 0.8. Both rule base simplification and reduction occurs, and different versions of the rule base are obtained, varying in both the number of fuzzy sets (granularity) and the number of rules. The MSE is calculated for the different models from their response to the evaluation data, and the obtained results are reported in Table 6. The table shows that the original model can be both simplified and reduced quite substantially without sacrificing the accuracy too much. Also we see that lowering the threshold does not always decrease the numerical accuracy. From this, we conclude that the original model is highly redundant and over-determined.

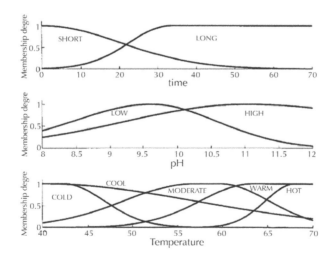

FIGURE 60   Membership function obtained with λ=0.6 and ⬚=0.8.

In Figure 60, the fuzzy sets of the model obtained by using $\lambda = 0.6$ are plotted. For this case, obtaining a qualitative model by assigning linguistic labels to the fuzzy sets is much easier than for the original model. As shown in the figure, the variable time is partitioned into two regions, "short" and "long;" the variable alkalinity (pH) is partitioned into "low" and "high", and for the variable temperature one obtains the five regions "cold", "moderate", "warm", and "hot."

The response of this model to the evaluation data is shown in Figure 61. There is little difference from the response of the original model (compare with Figure 59). See Table 6 for the MSE values.

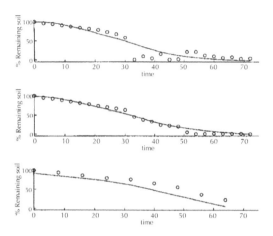

FIGURE 61   Response of model obtained with λ=0.6 and γ=0.8.

From Table 6, we see that for a threshold $\lambda \leq 0.6$ all the fuzzy sets defined for the premise variable alkalinity are merged. If we decrease the threshold γ, the process variable alkalinity will be removed from the premise of the rule base. However, it will still remain in the rule consequents, having a linear influence on the process. Expert knowledge confirms that alkalinity is the least influential premise parameter for this process, and that the temperature is the most important quantity that influences the enzyme activity in this application. This is reflected in the higher granularity in the partitioning of this variable.

4.16   QUALITATIVE MODELING BASED ON FUZZY LOGIC [270]

This section discusses a general approach to qualitative modeling based on fuzzy logic. The method of qualitative modeling is related to fuzzy modeling and linguistic modeling. It is based on to use a fuzzy clustering method (fuzzy c-means method) to identify the structure of a fuzzy model. To illustrate the proposed method, a model of a dynamical process and a model of a human operator's control action are discussed. Qualitative modeling is not so popular in general but this concept is indirectly implied by fuzzy modeling or linguistic modeling. Here we deal with a qualitative model as a system model based on linguistic descriptions just as we use them in sociology or psychology. Though the terminology of "linguistic modeling" may be straightforward and more appropriate, we use "qualitative modeling" partly because we like to discuss certain problems in comparison with the "qualitative reasoning" approach considered in artificial intelligence (AI) and also because "qualitative modeling" has been one of the most important issues since the very beginning of fuzzy theory.

First we give an overview of fuzzy modeling in fuzzy theory and qualitative reasoning in AI, then we state the problems concerning qualitative modeling based on fuzzy logic from a systems theory point of view.

We propose a method of qualitative modeling in a general framework known as the black box approach in systems theory. Thus, we build a qualitative model of a system without a priori knowledge about a system provided that we are given numerical input-output data.

4.16.1 FUZZY MODELING

The concept of fuzzy modeling has a history of more than four decades. In fact we can find the seminal ideas of fuzzy modeling in the early works of Zadeh. There are many interpretations of fuzzy modeling. For instance, we can consider a fuzzy set as a fuzzy model of a human concept. In this section we illustrate the term fuzzy modeling as an approach to form a system model using a description language based on fuzzy logic with fuzzy predicates. In a broader sense we can interpret the fuzzy modeling as a qualitative modeling scheme by which we qualitatively describe system behavior using a natural language. The fuzzy modeling in a narrow sense is a system description with fuzzy quantities. Fuzzy quantities are expressed in terms of fuzzy numbers or fuzzy sets associated with linguistic labels, where a fuzzy set usually does not have a tight relation with a linguistic label.

Qualitative model is essentially a generalized fuzzy model consisting of linguistic explanations about system behavior. Linguistic terms in linguistic explanations are found such that they linguistically approximate the fuzzy sets in and underlying fuzzy model. If a relation of state variables in a system is to be expressed linguistically in a qualitative model, we can use a method of linguistic approximation to accomplish this aim.

Fuzzy sets and/or fuzzy logic were suggested by Zadeh with qualitative modeling in mind.

In 1968, Zadeh suggested an idea of fuzzy algorithm, which is nothing but qualitative descriptions of a human action, or decision making. The most remarkable contribution related to qualitative modeling is his works of 1973 on linguistic analysis, where he states "the principle of incompatibility," according to which "*as the complexity of a system increases, our ability to make precise and yet significant statements about its behavior diminishes until a threshold is reached beyond, which precision and significance (or relevance) become almost mutually exclusive characteristics. It is in this sense that precise quantitative analyses of the behavior of humanistic systems are not likely to have much relevance to the real world societal, political, economic, and other types of problems, which involve humans either as individuals or in groups.*"

Based on the above considerations Zadeh suggested linguistic analysis in place of quantitative analysis. If we look at his idea of linguistic analysis from the viewpoint of modeling, it is seen to be precisely qualitative modeling. As the main characteristics of this approach, he suggests "*1) use of so-called linguistic variables in place of or in addition to numerical variables, 2) characterization of simple relations between variables by conditional fuzzy statements, and 3) characterization of complex relations by fuzzy algorithms.*"

It is well-known that, motivated by these ideas of "fuzzy algorithm" and "linguistic analysis," Mamdani first applied fuzzy logic to control. Fuzzy control can be viewed in a certain sense as the result of the qualitative modeling of a human operator working at plant control.

The main problem of fuzzy control is to design a fuzzy controller, where we usually take an expert-system-like approach. That is, we derive fuzzy control rules from a human operator's experience and/or engineer's knowledge, which are mostly based on their qualitative knowledge of an objective system.

The design procedure is thus something like the following:
- We build linguistic control rules,
- We adjust the parameters of fuzzy sets by which the linguistic terms in the control rules are quantitatively interpreted.

For example, let us look at the linguistic rules for controlling a cement kiln, as shown in Table 7. From these, we can easily derive fuzzy control rules. In this sense, we may say that a set of fuzzy control rules is a linguistic model of human control actions, which is not based on a mathematical description of human control actions, but is directly based on a human way of thinking about plant operation.

TABLE 7   Operator's manual of cement klin control

Case	Condition	Action to be taken
1	BZ low	When BZ is drastically low:
	OX low	reduce klin speed
	BE low	reduce fuel
		When Bz is slightly low;
		Increase I. D. speed
		decrease fuel rate
2	BZ low	reduce klin speed
	OX low	reduce fuel rate
	BE O.K.	reduce I.D. fan speed
3	BZ low	reduce klin speed
	OX low	reduce fuel rate
	BE high	reduce I.D. fan speed

BE = back end temperature, BZ = burning zone temperature, OX = percentage of oxygen gas in klin exit Gas, Total of 27 rules.

Apart from fuzzy control, we have many studies on fuzzy modeling. Those are divided in two groups. The studies of the first group deal with fuzzy modeling of a system itself or a fuzzy modeling for simulation. Some of those are considered as examples of qualitative modeling. The studies of the second group deal with fuzzy modeling of a plant for control. Just as with the modern control theory, we can design a fuzzy controller based on a fuzzy model of a plant if a fuzzy model can be identified. Fuzzy modeling in the latter sense is not necessarily viewed as qualitative modeling unless the derivation of a qualitative model from the identified fuzzy model is discussed. It is, of course, quite interesting to derive qualitative control rules based on the qualitative model of a plant.

For example, assume that we have a dynamical plant model such as:

- If u_n is positive and y_{n-1} is positive, then y_n is positive big,

- If u_n is negative and y_{n-1} is positive, then y_n is positive small,

- If u_n is positive and y_{n-1} is negative, then y_n is negative small, and

- If u_n is negative and y_{n-1} is negative, then y_n is negative big.

Then given a reference input $r = 0$, we can derive the following control rules based on the above model:

- If y_{n-1} is positive and y_n is negative, then u_n is negative big,

- If y_{n-1} is positive and y_n is negative, then u_n is positive,

- If y_{n-1} is negative and y_n is positive, then u_n is negative, and

- If y_{n-1} is negative and y_n is negative big, then u_n is positive big.

Here the error e_n is equal to $-y_n$ since the reference input (the set point) is zero.

In the fuzzy modeling, the most important problem is the identification method of a system. The identification for the fuzzy modeling has two aspects as usual structure identification and parameter identification. This problem is discussed in subsection "identification in fuzzy modeling".

QUALITATIVE REASONING

Outside the research area of fuzzy logic, the concept of qualitative reasoning has been suggested in AI. Earlier studies of qualitative reasoning were found on mechanical systems in 1975 [8], and also on naïve physics in 1979 [9].

We can identify as typical studies of qualitative reasoning the following:
- Qualitative physics or naïve physics,
- Qualitative process theory, and
- Qualitative simulation.

Here we call these ideas qualitative reasoning.

There are small distinctions and big similarities between fuzzy modeling and qualitative reasoning. One distinction is that fuzzy modeling starts from the fact that a precise mathematical model of a complex system cannot be obtained, whereas qualitative reasoning starts from the fact that, although a complete model may be available, it cannot provide insight into the system, a description based on deep knowledge is needed. On the other hand, similarities are found in the confidence of the advantage of qualitative expressions, in the goals, and in some parts of description languages for modeling. The common idea of qualitative system theory should be emphasized.

From the existing references we understand qualitative reasoning and fuzzy modeling, we may conclude:

1) Motivations are different,
2) Goals look similar,
3) Tools are much more powerful in fuzzy modeling, and
4) Methods of approach to modeling are different and those in fuzzy modeling are more varied and applicable.

In any case, however, we see similarities between qualitative reasoning and fuzzy modeling rather than differences.

QUALITATIVE MODELING

What we imply here by a qualitative model is a linguistic model. A linguistic model is a model that is described or expressed using linguistic terms in the framework of fuzzy logic instead of mathematical equations with numerical values or conventional logical formula with logical symbols.

For example, as we shall see later, a linguistic model of a two inputs-single output system is something like the following [270]:

i.   If x_1 is more than medium and x_2 is more than medium, then y is small, $\partial y/\partial x_1$ is sort of negative, and $\partial y/\partial x_2$ is sort of negative.

ii. If x_1 is small and x_2 is more or less small or medium small, then y is big, $\partial y/\partial x_1$ is very negative, and $\partial y/\partial x_2$ is very negative.

We can regard most of fuzzy models and fuzzy control rules as qualitative models.

We distinguish, a qualitative model from a fuzzy model. The terminology "a fuzzy model" is used in a narrow sense. A qualitative model is considered a fuzzy model with something more, that is, with the more linguistic expressions.

For example, a fuzzy model of the type:

• If x is approximately 3, then y is approximately 5,
• If x increases by approximately 5, then y decreases by approximately 4.

It should not be called a qualitative model. We can call the above model a fuzzy number model to distinguish it from a qualitative model.

Further, in an ordinary fuzzy model that is used in fuzzy control such as:

• If x is positive small, then y is negative small,
• If x is positive medium, then y is positive small.

The terms "positive small," "negative small," and so on, are the labels conventionally attached to fuzzy sets, where the fuzzy sets play an important role, not the labels.

We go beyond this stage by utilizing of the concept of "linguistic approximation." That is, given a conventional fuzzy model with fuzzy sets, we improve its qualitative nature by using linguistic approximation techniques in fuzzy logic. In other words, we deal with a model, in which we focus our attention on how to linguistically or qualitatively explain a system behavior as we shall see in what follows.

Now let us discuss available sources, that is information or data, for qualitative modeling. We find the following classification of the sources:

- Conventional mathematical models,
- Observation based on knowledge and/or experience,
- Numerical data,
- Image data, and
- Linguistic data.

In qualitative reasoning as we have seen, a model is built based on 1) and 2). A conventional mathematical model is usually identified based on 2) and 3). A fuzzy model is also based on 2) and 3), as in the case of a mathematical model. Sources 4), and 5) are also useful to build a qualitative model. A qualitative model based on 4), image data, can be interpreted as image understanding, that is a linguistic explanation of an image. As for the examples concerned with 5), we can consider translation of one language into another or making a summary of a story.

In this section we deal with qualitative modeling based partly on 2), and mainly on 3), as usual, a black box approach. The reason for this is that system identification is a key issue in the black box approach and all the basic matters in model building appear in the context of system identification.

TABLE 8   Classification of identification

Structure Identification I	a: Input candidates
	b: Input variables
Structure Identification II	a: Number of rules
	b: Partition of input space
Parameter Identification	

Let us first consider the problems in modeling. Modeling is classified from the viewpoint of a description language. However, there are some common problems to be solved in modeling independently of both the description language and the data type. Thus we refer to the systems theory. The most complicated problems arise, when we take a black box approach to modeling. In the black box approach, we have to build a dynamical model using only input-output data. This stage of modeling is usually referred as identification. It is worth noting that the concept of system identification and its formal definition were introduced by Zadeh in the early 1960's. We may suppose that Zadeh suggested the idea of fuzzy sets since he found difficulties in the identification of a complex system based on differential equations with numerical parameters.

According to Zadeh's definition [17], given a class of models, system identification involves finding a model, which may be regarded as equivalent to the objective system with respect to input-output data.

IDENTIFICATION IN FUZZY MODELING

Now let us look at the problems in the identification of a fuzzy model. The identification is divided into two kinds: structure identifications and parameter identification.

Structure identification can be divided into two types, called, type I and type II, where each type is also divided into two subtypes (See Table 8).

By summing up the above-mentioned tasks to be done for modeling, we could say that the ratio of importance of the structure identification of type I to that of II and the parameter identification would be, moderately speaking, 100:10:1. In any event, if we know the input candidates to a system, our problem is almost solved. After this, we can certainly find an algorithm of the identification depending on a description language. Unfortunately, we do not have a systematic approach to structure identification of type Ia: it is a problem of induction. Structure identification of type Ib is a combinatorial problem. Type IIa is similar to the identification of the model order in ordinary identification. Type IIb is also a combinatorial problem, which appears only in the case of if-then rules. The parameter identification is merely an optimization problem with an objective function.

In this section we deal with structure identification. We consider a multi-input and single output system [270].

4.16.2   FUZZY MODEL

We consider a fuzzy model for a multi-input and single-output system:

$$R^i : \text{if } x_1 \text{ is } A_1^i \text{ and } x_2 \text{ is } A_2^i \text{ ... and } x_n \text{ is } A_n^i \text{ then y is } B^i,$$

where R^i is the ith rule $(1 \leq i \leq m)$, $x_j (1 \leq j \leq n)$ are input variables, y is the output, and A_j^i and B^i are fuzzy variables.

We can simply rewrite the above form as:

$$R^i : \text{if x is } A^i \text{ then y is } B^i \tag{4.94}$$

Where

$$x = (x_1, ..., x_n) \text{ and A=}(A_1, ..., A_n).$$

For simplicity, the membership function of A_j^i is denoted $A_j^i(\bullet)$. In this section we regard the fuzzy variables A and B as those taking as values fuzzy numbers, which are not necessarily associated with linguistic labels. Our method of qualitative modeling consists of two steps. In the first step we deal with a fuzzy model in terms of fuzzy numbers. In the second step we give linguistic interpretations to this fuzzy model. That is, we deal with a fuzzy model with linguistic terms, which we call a qualitative model. Occasionally, we let B^i take singletons, that is real numbers, instead of fuzzy numbers. As far as fuzzy control is concerned, it is well known that we can use fuzzy rules with singletons in the consequents without losing the performance of the control. However, in order to derive a qualitative model from the fuzzy model in Equation 4.94, it is better to use fuzzy numbers in the consequents.

As for reasoning, we modify partly the ordinary method as seen in the following steps 2) and 3):

Given the inputs x_1^0, x_2^0, ..., and x_n^0, calculate the degree of match, w^i, in the premises for the ith rule, ($1 \leq i \leq m$) as:

$$w^i = A_1^i(x_1^0) \times A_2^i(x_2^0) \times ... \times A_n^i(x_n^0) \qquad (4.95)$$

Then defuzzify B^i in the consequents by taking the center of gravity:

$$b^i = \int B^i(y)y\,dy / \int B^i(y)\,dy \qquad (4.96)$$

Calculate the inferred value:

$$\hat{y} = \sum_{i=1}^{m} w^i b^i / \sum_{i=1}^{m} w^i, \qquad (4.97)$$

where m is the number of rules.

As we find in the process of reasoning, the rule R^i translate to the form:

$$R^i : \text{if x is } A^i \text{ then y is } b^i. \qquad (4.98)$$

We call a fuzzy model in the form Equation 4.94 a position type model.

Next we consider position-gradient type model. It is often the case that we cannot build a fuzzy model over the whole input space because we lack data. In this case we need to take an extrapolation for estimating the output using local fuzzy rules. Note that in conventional fuzzy reasoning we take an interpolation using some number of rules.

A position-gradient model is of the following form:

$$R^i : \text{if x is } A^i \text{ then y is } B^i \text{ and } \partial y/\partial x \text{ is } C^i, \qquad (4.99)$$

where $\partial y/\partial x = (\partial y/\partial x_1, ..., \partial y/\partial x_n)$. $C^i = (C_1^i, ..., C_n^i)$, and $\partial y/\partial x_j$ is the partial derivative of y with respect to x_j.

Using the rules shown in Equation 4.99, we can infer the output for a given input for which no rule of the position type is available, if $w^i = 0$ in all the rules for the inputs, $\hat{y}$ cannot be inferred in the position type model.

The reasoning algorithm of the position-gradient rules is the following:

Defuzzify B^i and C^i, and let those values be b^i and c^i, respectively, where $c^i = (c_1^i, ..., c_n^i)$. We can rewrite Equation 4.98 as:

$$R^i : \text{if x is } A^i \text{ then y is } b^i \text{ and } \partial y/\partial x \text{ is } c^i . \qquad (4.100)$$

Calculate the distance d^i between the input and the core region of the ith rule as shown in Figure 62. As we see, the core region, in a two-dimensional case, of the ith rule:

" if x_1 is A_1^i and x_2 is A_2^i ... then y is B^i," is the crisp region determined by the fuzzy sets A_1^i and A_2^i, where membership grades A_1^i and A_2^i are 1.

Calculate the inferred output, $\hat{y}$,

$$\hat{y} = \sum_{i=1}^{m}\left\{ w(d^i) * \left(b^i + \sum_{j=1}^{n}(d_j^i \times c_j^i) \right) \right\} / \sum_{i=1}^{m} w(d^i), (4.101)$$

where n is the number of inputs, m the number of rules, d_j^i the component of d^i on the x_j coordinate axis, and $w(d^i) = \exp(- d^i)$ is the weight of the ith rule depending on the distance d^i.

As is seen in Equation 4.101 the term $b^i + \sum_{j=1}^{n}(d_j^i \times c_j^i)$ is the extrapolated value of the output using the value of its partial derivatives $\partial y / \partial x_j$.

We shall see below that the membership functions in this study are almost always of a trapezoidal type as shown in Figure 62.

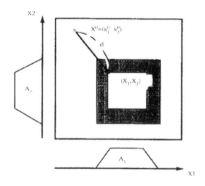

FIGURE 62   Distance from the input X to the rule.

STRUCTURE IDENTIFICATION

Let us now discuss the method of structure identification. As stated earlier we have to deal with structures of type Ib: to find a set of input variables among the possible candidates, and with structures of type II: to find the number of rules and a fuzzy partition of the input space (See Table 8). We shall use an ordinary method for Ib but propose a new method based on fuzzy clustering for II. In general, it seems that we can neither separate the identification of type Ib from that of type II nor separate the structure identification from the parameter identification; these are mutually related. However, we can separate these by using our method. This is a great advantage of the method discussed in this section.

In principle, the algorithm for the identification is of the iterative type. We present the algorithm through numerical examples.

Example 4.18 Let us consider the following nonlinear statistic system with two points, x_1 and x_2, and a single output, y:

$$y = (1 + x_1^{-2} + x_1^{-1.5})^2, \quad 1 \le x_1, x_2 \le 5. \tag{4.102}$$

We show a three-dimensional input-output graph of this system in Figure 63. From this system equation, 50 input-output data are obtained (Table 9). The data of x_3 and x_4 are put as dummy inputs to check the appropriateness of the identification method [270].

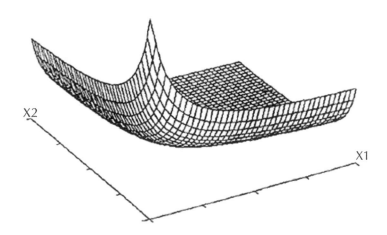

FIGURE 63 Input output relation of nonlinear system.

- *Structure Identification of Type 1:* In the proposed algorithm, the identification of type Ib is done between the identification of type II and the parameter identification. Let us, however, first consider the identification Ib.

We have four candidates, x_1–x_4, for the inputs to the system and have to find among them the actual inputs affecting the output, y. This is a combinatorial problem. For instance we can count 15 cases in this example: four cases if the system has only one input, six cases if it has two inputs, and so on. In general, let X be a set of possible input candidates $x_1, x_2, ..., x_n$, then the total number of cases is the number of subsets except an empty subset of X, that is, $2^n - 1$. Here we take a heuristic method to select some inputs from among the candidates, we increase the number of inputs one by one, watching a criterion.

TABLE 9   Input-output data of nonlinear system

Group A						Group B				
No	$x1$	$x2$	$x3$	$x4$	Y	No	$x1$	$x2$	$x3$	$x4$	y
1	1.40	1.80	3.00	3.80	3.70	26	2.00	2.06	2.25	2.37	2.52
2	4.28	4.96	3.02	4.39	1.31	27	2.71	4.13	4.38	3.21	1.58
3	1.18	4.29	1.60	3.80	3.35	28	1.78	1.11	3.13	1.80	4.71
4	1.96	1.90	1.71	1.59	2.70	29	3.61	2.27	2.27	3.61	1.87
5	1.85	1.43	4.15	3.30	3.52	30	2.24	3.74	4.25	3.26	1.79
6	3.66	1.60	3.44	3.33	2.46	31	1.81	3.18	3.31	2.07	2.20
7	3.64	2.14	1.64	2.64	1.95	32	4.85	4.66	4.11	3.74	1.30
8	4.51	1.52	4.53	2.54	2.51	33	3.41	3.88	1.27	2.21	1.48
9	3.77	1.45	2.50	1.86	2.70	34	1.38	2.55	2.07	4.42	3.14
10	4.84	4.32	2.75	1.70	1.33	35	2.46	2.12	1.11	4.44	2.22
11	1.05	2.55	3.03	2.02	4.63	36	2.66	4.42	1.71	1.23	1.56
12	4.51	1.37	3.97	1.70	2.80	37	4.44	4.71	1.53	2.08	1.32
13	1.84	4.43	4.20	1.38	1.97	38	3.11	1.06	2.91	2.80	4.08
14	1.67	2.81	2.23	4.51	2.47	39	4.47	3.66	1.23	3.62	1.42
15	2.03	1.88	1.41	1.10	2.66	40	1.35	1.76	3.00	3.82	3.91
16	3.62	1.95	4.93	1.58	2.08	41	1.24	1.41	1.92	2.25	5.05
17	1.67	2.23	3.93	1.06	2.75	42	2.81	1.35	4.96	4.04	1.97
18	3.38	3.70	4.65	1.28	1.51	43	1.92	4.25	3.24	3.89	1.92
19	2.83	1.77	2.61	4.50	2.40	44	4.61	2.68	4.89	1.03	1.63
20	1.48	4.44	1.33	3.25	2.44	45	3.04	4.97	2.77	2.63	1.44
21	3.37	2.13	2.42	3.95	1.99	46	4.82	3.80	4.73	2.69	1.39
22	2.84	1.24	4.42	1.21	3.42	47	2.58	1.97	4.16	2.95	2.29
23	1.19	1.53	2.54	3.22	4.99	48	4.14	4.76	2.63	3.88	1.33
24	4.10	1.71	2.54	1.76	2.27	49	4.35	3.90	2.55	1.65	1.40
25	1.65	1.38	4.57	4.03	3.94	50	2.22	1.35	2.75	1.01	3.39

First we divide the data into two group, A and B, as in Table 9. As a criterion to this purpose, we use the so-called regularity criterion (RC) in group method of data handling (GMDH), which is defined as follows:

$$RC = \left[\sum_{i=1}^{k_A}(y_i^A - y_i^{AB})^2/k_A + \sum_{i=1}^{k_B}(y_i^B - y_i^{BA})^2/k_B\right]/2, \quad (4.103)$$

TABLE 10   Structure identification Ib of nonliner system

	Input Variables	RC	
Step 1	$x1$	**0.630**	0
	$x2$	0.863	
	$x3$	0.830	
	$x4$	0.937	
Step 2	$x1 - x2$	**0.424**	0 0
	$x1 - x3$	0.571	
	$x1 - x4$	0.583	
Step 3	$x1 - x2 - x3$	0.483	x
	$x1 - x2 - x4$	0.493	x

Where,

K_A and K_B : the number of data of the groups A and B,

y_i^A and y_i^B: the output data of the groups A dn B,

y^{AB} : the model output for the group A input estimated by the model identi-fied using the Group B data, and

y^{BA}: the model output for the group B input estimated by the model identi-fied using the Group A data.

As we can guess from the form of *RC*, we build two models for two data groups at each stage of the identification. Note that we have to make the structure identification of type II and the parameter identification in order to calculate *RC*.

Now we show the outline of a heuristic algorithm for lb. First, we begin with a fuzzy model with one input. We make four models, one model for one particular input. After the identification of the structure II and parameter identification, which will be described later, we calculate RC of each model and select one model to minimize RC from among the one-input models. Next we fix the one input selected above and add another input to our fuzzy model from among the remaining three candidates. Our fuzzy model has two inputs at this stage. We select the second input as we do at the first step, according to the value of RC.

We continue the above process until the value of RC increased. The result is shown in Table 10. As shown, x_1 is selected at the first step, x_2 at the second step. At the third step, however, both the values of RC for the third inputs, x_3 and x_4 are bigger than the minimal RC at the second step. So the search is terminated at this stage. As a result we have evaluated nine of the 15 cases and succeeded in finding the true inputs, x_1 and x_2.

2)Structure Identification of Type II: Usually in the design of a fuzzy controller we first pay attention to rule premises and find an optimal partition based on a certain criterion. Here we propose a different method, that is, we first pay attention to the consequents of the rules and then find a partition concerning the premises. Also in our method, we do not take an ordinary fuzzy partition of the input space, as is shown in Figure 64, for if we take this kind of partition, the number of rules increases exponentially with the number of inputs. For this reason, we introduce the fuzzy c-means method, abbreviated FCM, for the structure identification of type IIb. Using FCM, we make fuzzy clustering of the output data, we use all the data. As a result, every output y is associated with the grade of membership belonging to a fuzzy cluster B. Notice that we now have the following data associated with the grade of the membership of y^i in B^j $(1 \leq j \leq c)$:

$$(x^i, y^i): B^1 (y^i) B^2 (y^i), ..., B^c (y^i). \tag{4.104}$$

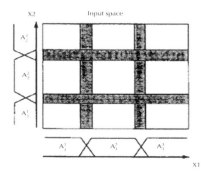

FIGURE 64   Ordinary fuzzy partition of input space.

We can induce a fuzzy cluster A in the input space as in shown in Figure 65. By making the projection of the cluster A onto the axes of the coordinated x_1 and x_2, we obtain the fuzzy sets A_1 and A_2 as shown in Figure 66. Thus, we have, at this stage, the following relation:

$$A_1\left(x_1^i\right) = A_2\left(x_2^i\right) = \left(y^i\right), \qquad (4.105)$$

where B is the output cluster.

This cluster generates a fuzzy rule if x_1 is A_1 and x_2 is A_2, then y is B.

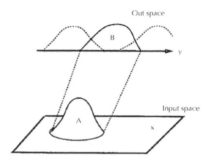

FIGURE 65   Fuzzy cluster in the input space.

Remark 4.13 Although the output cluster B is convex, the input cluster A corresponding to B might not be convex for instance we might obtain A_1, as is shown in Figure 67(a). In this case we approximate the input cluster in Figure 67(a) with a convex fuzzy set as in Figure 67(b). Finally, we approximate this convex fuzzy set and B as well, with a fuzzy set of trapezoidal type as shown in Figure 67(c), which is used in the fuzzy model.

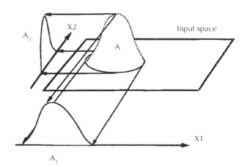

FIGURE 66   Projection of a fuzzy cluster.

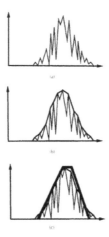

FIGURE 67 Construction of a membership function: (a) input cluster, (b)approximated convex fuzzy set, and (c) approximated trapezoid fuzzy set.

Remark 4.14 We might have more than two fuzzy clusters, A^1 and A^2 in the input space, which corresponds to the same fuzzy cluster B in the output space. In this case we carefully form two convex fuzzy clusters as illustrated in Figure 68. We obtain the following two rules with the same consequent:

$$R^1 : \text{if } x_1 \text{ is } A_1^1 \ x_2 \text{ is } A_2^1 \text{ then y is B}$$

$$R^2 : \text{if } x_1 \text{ is } A_1^2 \ x_2 \text{ is } A_2^2 \text{ then y is B.}$$

Here, a fuzzy partition of the input space is obtained as a direct result of fuzzy clustering, we do not have to consider the structure identification of type IIb.

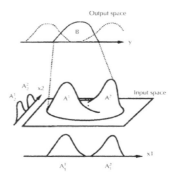

FIGURE 68 Two fuzzy clusters induced from one output cluster.

Let us discuss a method to determine the number of rules, which is related to the number of fuzzy clusters in fuzzy clustering. Note that, because of Remark 4.14 the number of fuzzy rules is not exactly the same as that of fuzzy clusters in the output space, as we have just discussed above.

The determination of the number of clusters is the most important issue in clustering. There are many studies on this issue. Here we use the following criterion [20] for this purpose:

$$S(c) = \sum_{k=1}^{n} \sum_{i=1}^{c} (\mu_i k)^m \left(\| x_k - v_i \|^2 - \| v_i - \bar{x} \|^2 \right), \quad (4.106)$$

Where,

    n——number of data to be clustered,

    c——number of clusters, $c \geq um$

    x_k—— k th data, usually vector,

    $\bar{x}$ ——average of data: $x_1 . x_2 ...., x_n$,

    v_i——vector expressing the center of ith cluster,

    $\|.\|$ ——norm,

    $\mu_i k$——grade of kth data belonging to ith cluster, and

    m——adjustable weight (usually m = $1.5 \sim 3$).

The number of clusters, c, is determined so that $S(c)$ reaches a minimum as c increases: it is supposed to be a local minumum as usual. As in seen in Equation 4.106, the first term of the right-hand side is the variance of the data in a cluster and the second term is that of the clusters themselves. Therefore the optimal clustering is considered to minimize the variance in each cluster and to maximize the variance between the clusters. Figure 69 shows the change of $S(c)$ in fuzzy modeling of the system Equation 4.102. In this case, the optimal number of fuzzy clusters is found to be 6. From this, the number of rules is identified by taking account of the case, where a fuzzy cluster in the input space is divided into two fuzzy clusters.

As it is easily seen, in the process of fuzzy clustering, we refer neither to the input nor to parameters in premises. Therefore we can separate the identification of type II from that of Ib and the parameter identification. Further as we find in the above discussion, a fuzzy partition of the input space IIb as well as the parameters A^i in the premises and B^i in the consequents are obtained as by –products of IIa. We use these A^i and B^i to calculate RC in the identifucation of type Ib.

S
-20
-30
-40
-50
-21.58
-32.47
-39.77
-40.86
-42.70
-41.69
2
3
4
5
6
7
c

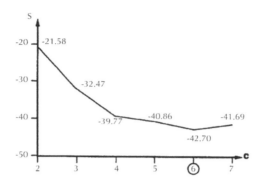

FIGURE 69 Behavior of S(c) in nonlinear system model.

After identifying the structure of type Ib (input variables), we combine the two groups of the data and induce fuzzy clusters in the input space from the output clusters to find the parameters A. We use those parameters obtained in the process of fuzzy clustering as an initial guess in the parameter identification. Figure 70 shows the fuzzy model of Equation 4.102. Below we shall use the mean square error of output as a performance index of a fuzzy model:

$$PI = \sum_{i=1}^{m} (y^i - \hat{y}^i)^2 / m \tag{4.107}$$

where m is the number of data, y^i is the ith actual output, and $\hat{y}^i$ is the ith model output. In this example, we have $PI = 0.318$.

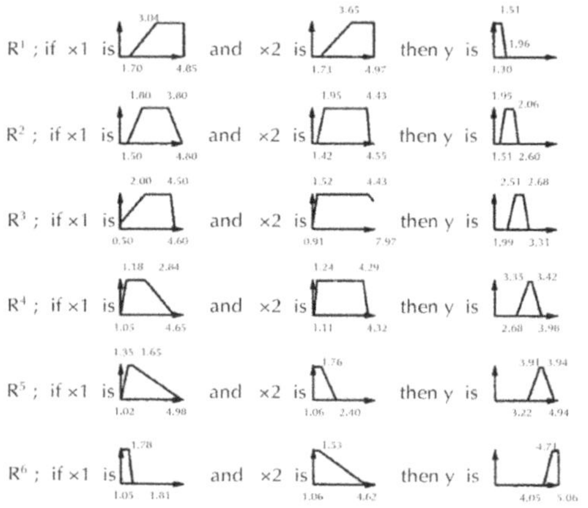

R1 ; if x1 is and x2 is then y is
R2 ; if x1 is and x2 is then y is
R3 ; if x1 is and x2 is then y is
R4 ; if x1 is and x2 is then y is
R5 ; if x1 is and x2 is then y is
R6 ; if x1 is and x2 is then y is

FIGURE 70 Model of the nonlinear system.

3) Identification of a Position-Gradient Model: Finally let us discuss the identification of a position-gradient type model of the form Equation 4.99, the determination of the term "$\partial y/\partial x_j$ is C_j. "Since the partial derivative $\partial y/\partial x_i$ is not given as data, we have to estimae it from the given input-output data.

We assume an equation around the input-output data $\left(x_1^0,\ldots\ldots,x_n^0,y^0\right)$:

$$y = y^0 + \partial y/\partial x_1(x_1 - x_1^0) + _{\ldots} + \partial y/\partial x_n(x_n - x_n^0).(4.108)$$

We estimate the coefficients $\partial y/\partial x_j$ in Equation 4.108 by using the method of weighted least squares using the other input-output data. As weights, we use:

$$w^k = \exp\left(-\left|x_1^0 - x_1^k\right| - 2\sum_{j=2}^n\left|x_j^0 - x_j^k\right|\right), \qquad (4.109)$$

where $x_j^k(1ej \leq n)$ is the kth data. Then we can obtain a fuzzy set C_j^i in the form of Equation 4.99 from the output cluster B^i just as we do to obtain the fuzzy sets A_j^i. Summing up the above method of identification, we arrive at the algorithm given in Figure 71 [270].

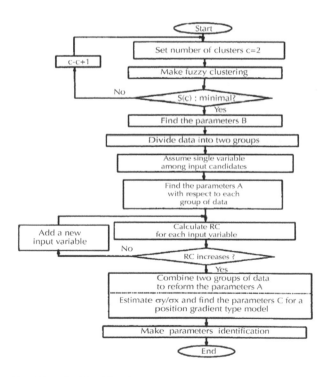

FIGURE 71   Algorithm for identification.

We should notice that the parameter identification can be done separately from the structure identification since the parameters obtained as by-products in fuzzy clustering, are available to calculate RC in the process of the structure identification Ib. In ordinary algorithms of identification, the parameter identification must be performed in the process of the structure identification, which makes an algorithm complicated. We can also omit the identification IIb of the partition of the input space.

PARAMETER IDENTIFICATION

At the stage of parameter identification we determine the values of parameters in a system model. In the case of a fuzzy model, the parameters are those concerned with membership functions. We approximate a convex fuzzy set with a trapezoidal fuzzy set. A trapezoidal fuzzy set has four parameters, as shown in Figure 72, where $p1 \leq p2 \leq p3 \leq p4$. We have already found the parameters by making the projection of the clusters onto the axes of coordinates. We can derive a qualitative model from a fuzzy model with these parameters. However, it is better to improve the parameters in order to use a fuzzy model for simulation. So we adjust the parameters as we do in the ordinary parameter identification.

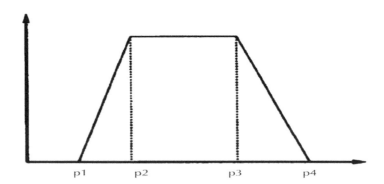

FIGURE 72   Trapezoidal fuzzy set.

In the method, we can find the approximate values of the parameters, which can be used as an initial guess in the parameter identification.

ALGORITHM (IDENTIFICATION PROCESS)

Step 1: Set the value f of adjustment.

Step 2: Assume that the kth parameter of the jth fuzzy set is p_j^k.

Step 3: Calculate $p_j^k + f$ and $p_j^k - f$. If $k = 2, 3, 4,$ and $p_j^k - f$ is smaller than p_j^{k-1}, then $\hat{p}_j^k = p_j^{k-1}$;, else $\hat{p}_j^k = p_j^k - f$. Also if $k = 1, 2, 3$ and $p_j^k + f$

is bigger than p_j^{k+1}, then $\hat{\hat{p}}_j^k = p_j^{k+1}$, else $\hat{\hat{p}}_j^k = p_j^k + f$. f is a constraint for ad-

justing parameters, as shown in Figure 73.

Step 4: Choose the parameters, which shows the best performance *PI* in Equation

4.107 among $\{\hat{p}_j^k, p_j^k, \hat{\hat{p}}_j^k\}$ and replace p_j^k with it.
  Step 5: Go to step 2, while unadjusted parameters exist.
  Step 6: Repeat step 2 until we are satisfied with the result.
  We use 5% of the width of the universe of discourse as the value of f and we repeat
20 times steps 1 to 6. Note that we do not adjust the parameters in the consequents of
the rules [270].

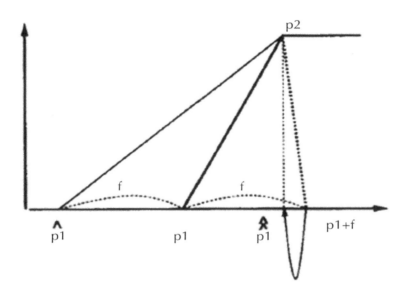

FIGURE 73   Constraint for adjusting parameter.

4.16.3   QUALITATIVE MODEL

LINGUISTIC APPROXIMATION

In this section we derive a qualitative model from a fuzzy model. To achieve this target
we use a method of linguistic approximation of fuzzy sets. We can state our problem
as follows:
  Given a proposition with fuzzy predicates find a word or a phrase out of a given
set of words to linguistically approximate it, with hedges and connectives. After this

procedure, we can obtain a qualitative model with linguistic rules from the identified fuzzy model.

We use the following two indices to measure the matching degree of two fuzzy sets:

- Degree of similarity:

$$S(N,L) = \| N \cap L \| / \| N \cup L \|, \qquad (4.110)$$

where $\| \cdot \|$ is the cardinality of the fuzzy set, and N and L are fuzzy sets.

- Degree of inclusion:

$$(N,L) = \| N \cap L \| / \| L \|. \qquad (4.111)$$

In the above setting, N is a fuzzy set considered as a fuzzy number and L is a fuzzy set associated with a linguistic label.

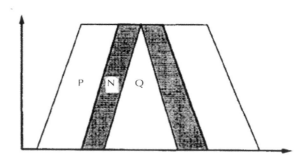

FIGURE 74   Fuzzy set N and linguistic approximations P and Q.

In order to choose the closest L to a given N, we may refer only $S(N,L)$. In some cases, however, it is better to refer also $I(N,L)$. In Figure 74, for two fuzzy sets P and Q, we have:

$$S(N,P) = S(N,Q)$$

$$I(N,P) < I(N,Q).$$

As Q is included in N, we can say that Q approximates more appropriately N than P. We suggest leaving the exact use of these to the user's preference.

We consider linguistic approximation on three levels.

- **Level 1:** Approximation with linguistic terms.

- **Level 2:** Approximation with linguistic terms and hedges.
- **Level 3:** Approximation with linguistic terms, hedges and connectives.

We use the following hedges: very, more or less, slightly, sort of, not, more than, and less than, as shown in Figure 75. We apply certain constraints in the use of hedges. For instance we may say "very big," or "more than middle," but we do not say "more than big."

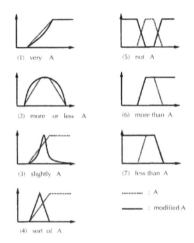

FIGURE 75   Linguistic hedges.

As an example, let us approximate two fuzzy numbers, A and B, concerning the strength of wind in Figure 76(a) with the linguistic terms in Figure 76(b). The top and bottom parts of Table 11 show the linguistic approximations of A and B according to three levels, where the values of two indices are shown.

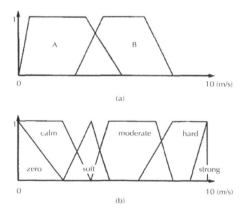

FIGURE 76   Fuzzy numbers and words for linguistic approximation: (a) fuzzy numbers and (b) wind scale.

It is often the case that we are asked to explain phenomena "more precisely" or "more simply." We have a limitation in responding to this sort of request if we merely try to refine or simplify the linguistic approximation. We can manage this problem by increasing or decreasing the number of linguistic rules.

Two features contribute to this flexibility: hedges and connectives.

TABLE 11   Results of linguistic approximation

Level	Linguistic Expression	S	I
1	calm	0.62	0.96
2	less than soft	0.87	0.97
3	more or less calm or more or Less soft	0.94	0.94

(A)

Level	Linguistic Expression	S	I
1	moderate	0.76	0.92
2	more or less moderate	0.81	0.83
3	not strong but more or less Moderate	0.86	0.98

(B)

As we adopt a fuzzy clustering method for the identification of IIa that is, the number of rules, we can simply control the number of linguistic rules by adjusting the number of fuzzy clusters. This is also a great advantage of the proposed method.

For further illustration of the method we consider three examples. The first example involves qualitative modeling of a nonlinear system. The second example is concerned with qualitative modeling of human operation at process control. In the third example we make a qualitative model to explain the trend in the time series data of the price of a stock [270].

In order to understand the examples in connection with the preceding discussions, let us list the key points:

- Fuzzy model of position type,
- Fuzzy model of position-gradient type,
- Qualitative model,
- Structure of type Ib: Input variables,
- Control of the number of linguistic rules,
- Structure of type IIa: number of rules, and
- Parameter identification.

We attach symbols (a) – (e) to each example.

Example 4.19 *Nonlinear Systems (a, b, c, d)*

This example deals with the explanation of the proposed method of identification. Let us call a static and nonlinear two input-single output system of the type shown in Equation 4.102.

$$y = (1 + x_1^{-2} + x_2^{-1.5})^2, 1 \le x_1, x_2 \le 5.$$

This system shows the non linear characteristic illustrated in Figure 63 and we use the data in Table 9. The process of the identification of type IIa has been shown in Table 10 and we have found the true inputs x_1 and x_2. The optimal number of rules has been found to be 6. In this example, the number of rules is found to be equal to the number of clusters. After the parameter identification, we obtain a fuzzy model as in Figure 77, where the performance index of the model is $PI = 0.079$. Before the parameter identification, we have obtained the fuzzy model with unadjusted parameters as we see in Figure 70, where $PI = 0.318$. We can certainly improve the model by adjusting its parameters [270].

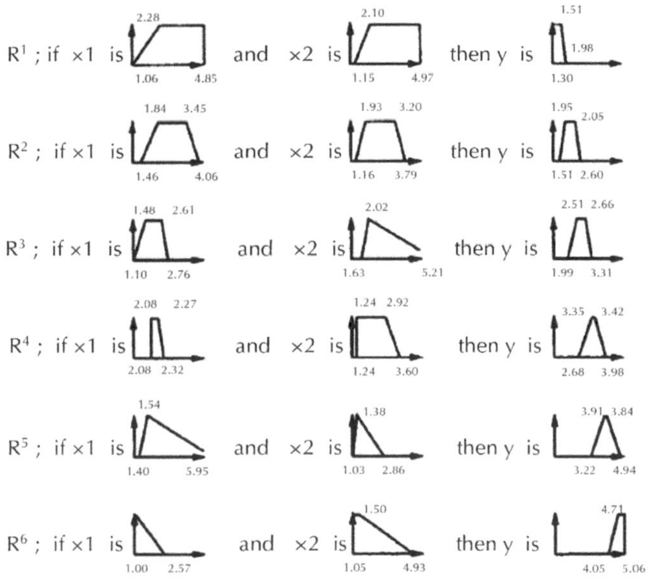

FIGURE 77   Model of nonlinear system after parameter identification.

In this example, we also obtain a fuzzy model of position-gradient type as illustrated in Table 12. In the case of the latter model, the performance is greatly improved. We have $PI = 0.010$. Finally we show a qualitative model of the position-gradient type.

- If x_1 is more than MEDIUM and x_2 is more than MEDIUM, then y is SMALL, $\partial y/\partial x_1$ is sort of NEGATIVE, and $\partial y/\partial x_2$ is sort of NEGATIVE.

- If x_1 is not SMALL but less than MEDIUM BIG and x_2 is not SMALL but less than MEDIUM BIG, then y is MEDIUM SMALL, $\partial y/\partial x_1$ is sort of NEGA-TIVE, and $\partial y/\partial x_2$ is sort of NEGATIVE.

- If x_1 is not SMALL but less than MEDIUM BIG and x_2 is more or less ME-DIUM BIG, then y is more or less MEDIUM SMALL and MEDIUM, $\partial y/\partial x_1$ is sort of NEGATIVE, and $\partial y/\partial x_2$ is sort of NEGATIVE.

- If x_1 is less than MEDIUM and x_2 is less than MEDIUM BIG, then y is ME-DIUM and more or less MEDIUM BIG, $\partial y/\partial x_1$ is sort of NEGATIVE, and $\partial y/\partial x_2$ is sort of NEGATIVE.

- If x_1 is more or less MEDIUM SMALL or MEDIUM and x_2 is more or less SMALL, then y is MEDIUM BIG, $\partial y/\partial x_1$ is sort of NEGATIVE, and $\partial y/\partial x_2$ NEGATIVE.

- If x_1 is SMALL and x_2 is more or less SMALL or MEDIUM SMALL, then y is BIG, $\partial y/\partial x_1$ is very NEGATIVE, and $\partial y/\partial x_2$ very NEGATIVE.

TABLE 12 Position-gradient model of nonlinear system

Rule	Premise	y	$\partial y/\partial x_1$	$\partial y/\partial x_2$
1		1.42	-0.71	-0.79
2		2.02	-0.58	-0.57
3	the same	2.58	-0.43	-0.43
4	as Fig. 77	3.39	-0.50	-0.56
5		3.94	-0.59	-1.04
6		4.90	-1.20	-1.35

*Consequents are singletons.

Example 4.20 *Human Operation at a Chemical Plant (a, c, d, e)*
We deal with a model of an operator's control of a chemical plant. The plant is for producing a polymer by the polymerization of some monomers. Since the start-up of the plant is very complicated, a man has to make the manual operation at the plant [270].

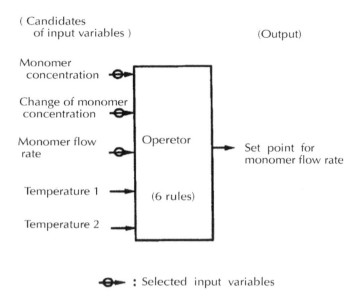

(Candidates
of input variables)   (Output)

Monomer
concentration

Change of monomer
concentration

Monomer flow   Operetor
rate   Set point for
monomer flow rate

Temperature 1   (6 rules)

Temperature 2

 ⊖➤ : Selected input variables

FIGURE 78   Structure of plant operation.

The structure of the human operation is shown in Figure 78. There are five input candidates, which a human operator might refer to for his control, and one output, that is, his control.

These are the following:

  $u\ 1$: Monomer concentration,
  $u\ 2$: Change of monomer concentration,
  $u\ 3$: Monomer flow rate,
  $u\ 4,\ U\ 5$: local temperatures inside the plant, and
  y: Set point for monomer flow rate.

where and operator determines the set point for the monomer flow rate and the actual value of the monomer flow rate to be put into the plant is controlled by a PID controller. We obtain 70 data points of the above six variables from the actual plant operation as shown in Appendix I. First we find six clusters by fuzzy clustering, we obtain six rules in this case. Figure 79 shows the change of $S(c)$ in the process of IIa. The identification process of type Ib is as shown in Table 13. As a result, we conclude that the operator must refer to the three information $u1$ (monomer concentration), $u2$ (change of $u1$) and $u3$ (monomer flow rate) to decide his control action.

We show the obtain fuzzy model in Figure 80. Figure 81 shows the excellent performance of the fuzzy model.

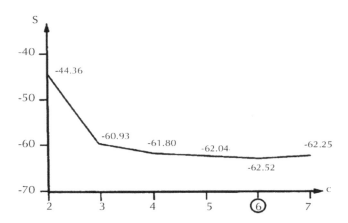

FIGURE 79   Behavior of S(c) in plant operation model.

TABLE 13   Structure identification Ib of chemical plant operation

	Input Variables	RC	
	$u1$	602715	
	$u2$	6077539	
Step 1			
	$u3$	**60756**	O
	$u4$	6663660	
	$u5$	5570199	
	$u3 - u1$	46178	
Step 2			
	$u3 - u2$	**41418**	OO
	$u3 - u4$	64124	×
	$u3 - u5$	60277	
	$u3 - u2 - u1$	**38950**	OOO
Step 3			
	$u3 - u2 - u5$	41846	×

From the fuzzy model, we can derive the following qualitative model.

- If $u1$ is more or less BIG, and $u2$ is not INCREASED, and $u3$ is SMALL, then y is SMALL or MEDIUM SAMLL.
- If $u1$ is more or less MEDIUM, and $u2$ DECREASED, and $u3$ is SMALL or MEDIUM SMALL, then y is MEDIUM SMALL.
- If $u1$ is MEDIUM, and $u2$ shows NO CHANGE, and $u3$ is MEDIUM SMALL or MEDIUM, then y is MEDIUM.
- If $u1$ is more or less MEDIUM, and $u2$ is ANY VALUE, and $u3$ is MEDIUM, then y is MEDIUM or MEDIUM BIG.
- If $u1$ is more or less SMALL, and $u2$ is very INCREASED, and $u3$ is MEDIUM BIG, then y is BIG.
- If $u1$ is more or less SMALL, and $u2$ is sort of INCREASED, and $u3$ is BIG, then y is very BIG.

We have shown this qualitative model to some operators and obtained their agreements with the model. It is worth noticing that we can make a fuzzy controller using the obtain fuzzy model to automate the operator's control.

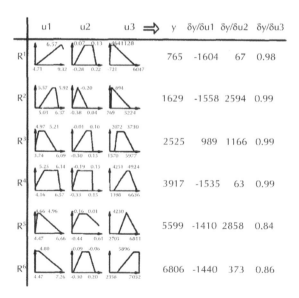

FIGURE 80 Fuzzy model of plant operation (position-gradient type).

In general it is difficult to evaluate this sort of a qualitative model since a model error in an ordinary sense is not available. One method is taken here is to ask an expert about the performance of a model.

If we are asked to explain the operator's action in a simple form, we can present a qualitative model, for instance, with three linguistic rules by adjusting the number of clusters.

Those are the following:.

- M1) If $u1$ is MEDIUM SMALL, and $u2$ is less than NO CHANGE and $u3$ is sort of SMALL, then y is sort of SMALL or more or less MEDIUM SMALL.
- M2) If $u1$ is more or less MEDIUM, and $u2$ is ANY, and $u3$ is more less MEDIUM, then y is more or less MEDIUM.
- M3) If $u1$ is sort of SMALL or more or less MEDIUM SMALL, and $u2$ is more or Less NO CHANGE, and $u3$ is more than MEDIUM BIG, then y is more then MEDIUM BIG.

By comparing those M1-M3 with the above 1–6, we can find that M1 is a summary of 1, 2, and 3, M2 is that of 3 and 4, and M3 is that of 4, 5, and 6. That is, the original six rules are fuzzily summarized in three rough rules.

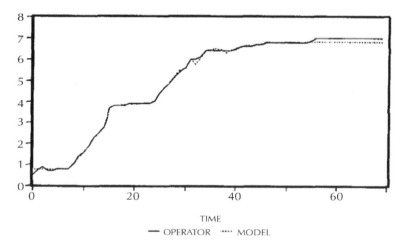

TIME

— OPERATOR ···· MODEL

FIGURE 81   Output of plant operation model.

Example 4.21 *Trend of Stock Prices (a, c)*

Finally we deal with the trend data of stock prices. We use the daily data of two different stocks: 100 data points of the first stock, A, and 150 data points of the second stock, B. The data of stock A are shown in Appendix II. Both data consists of ten inputs and one output [270]. These are:

$x1$: Past change of moving average (1) over a middle period,

$x2$: Present change of moving average (1) over a middle period,

$x3$: Past separation ratio (1) with respect to moving average over a middle

peirod,

$x4$: Present separation ratio (1) with respect to moving average over a middle

period,

$x5$: Present change of moving average (2) over a short period,

$x6$: Past change of price (1), for instance, change on one day before,

$x7$: Present change of price (1),

$x8$: Past separation ratio (2) with respect to moving average over a short

period,

$x9$: Present change of moving average (3) over a long period,

$x10$: Present sepatation ratio (3) with respect to moving average over a short

period, and

y: Prediction of stock price.

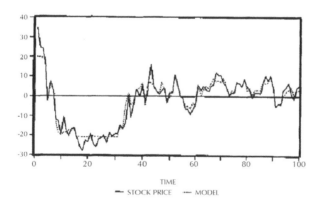

TIME

— STOCK PRICE   ···· MODEL

FIGURE 82   Output of stock price model A.

Here the separation ratio is a value concerning the difference between a moving average of a stock price and price of a stock. Making fuzzy clustering, we obtain five rules in both cases. Here we omit fuzzy models. The Figure 82 and 83 show a comparison of the price with the actual price, we can see the good performance of the models. The qualitative models of the trend data of the two stock prices are shown in Tables 14 and 15. This sort of study is quite interesting. It implies that we induce "qualitative laws," by observing data, to which economic phenomena are subject.

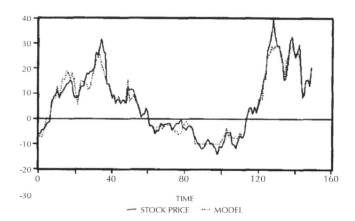

FIGURE 83   Output of stock price model B.

We have discussed an approach to qualitative modeling based on fuzzy logic. A qualitative model is derived from a fuzzy model using the linguistic approximation method. We have proposed the use of a fuzzy clustering for the structure identification of a fuzzy model. The proposed method has been examined in several case studies. What we have to do further in qualitative modeling is to improve the linguistic approximation method.

TABLE 14   Qualitative model of trend of stock price A

Rule	Change of Moving Average 1		Separation Ratio 1		ChangeOf Moving Average2	Change of Price 1		Separation Ratio2	ChangeOf Moving Average3	Separation Ratio 3	Prediction
	Past	Now	Past	Now	Now	Past	Now	Past	Now	Now	
1	more or less rise	level or rise	sort of plus	less than zero	level	level	rise	more or less zero	level	more less zero	rise
2		level or decline		minus	more or less level		level	more or less zero	level	more or less zero	sort of rise
3		level or decline	more or zero	sort of minus	more or less level	level or rise	sort of decline	more orless zero	more or less level	more or less zero	level
4	more or less rise	level	plus	more or less zero	more or less level	sort of rise	level	more or less zero	more or less level	more or less zero	sort of decline
5	level or rise	Rise	more than zero	plus	sort of rise	sort of rise	level	sort of plus	level or rise	more than zero	decline

TABLE 15 Qualitative model of trend of stock price B

Rule	Change of Moving Average 1		Separation Ratio 1		Change Of Moving Average 2	Change of Price I		Separation Ratio 2	Change Of Moving Average 3	Separation Ratio 3	Prediction
	Past	Now	Past	Now	Now	Past	Now	Past	Now	Now	
1	sort of rise	level or decline	less than zero	sort of minus	level	sort of decline	more or less level	sort of minus	sort of decline	more less zero	rise
2	level or rise	level or decline	less than zero	more or less zero	level or rise	sort of decline			sort of rise	more than zero	sort of rise
3	level or rise	level	more or less zero	more or less zero		level or rise	level or rise		sort of rise		level
4		more or less rise	more or less zero	Slightly plus	more or less level	sort of rise	level or rise	more or less zero	level or decline	less than zero	sort of decline
5	more or less rise	more or less rise	plus	more than zero	level	sort of decline	level	sort of minus		more or less zero	decline

APPENDIX I

Data of Human Operation At a Chemical Plant

u1	u2	u3	u4	u5	y
6.80	-0.05	401.00	-0.20	-0.10	500.00
6.59	-0.21	464.00	-0.10	0.10	700.00
6.59	0.00	703.00	-0.10	0.10	900.00
6.50	-0.90	797.00	0.10	0.10	700.00
6.48	-0.20	717.00	-0.10	0.10	700.00
6.54	0.60	706.00	-0.20	0.10	800.00
6.45	-0.90	784.00	0.00	0.10	800.00
6.45	0.00	794.00	-0.20	0.10	800.00
6.20	-0.25	792.00	0.00	0.00	1000.00
6.02	-0.18	1211.00	0.00	0.10	1400.00
5.80	-0.22	1557.00	-0.20	0.00	1600.00
5.51	-0.29	1782.00	-0.10	0.00	1900.00
5.43	-0.08	2206.00	-0.10	0.10	2300.00
5.44	0.01	2404.00	-0.10	-0.10	2500.00
5.51	0.07	2685.00	0.10	0.00	2800.00

APPENDIX I   *(Continued)*

5.62	0.11	3562.00	-0.40	0.10	3700.00
5.77	0.15	3629.00	-0.10	0.00	3800.00
5.94	0.17	3701.00	-0.20	0.10	3800.00
5.97	0.03	3775.00	-0.10	0.00	3800.00
6.02	0.05	3829.00	-0.10	-0.10	3900.00
5.99	-0.03	3896.00	0.20	-0.10	3900.00
5.82	-0.17	3920.00	0.20	-0.10	3900.00
5.79	-0.03	3895.00	0.20	-0.10	3900.00
5.65	-0.14	3887.00	-0.10	0.00	3900.00
5.48	-0.17	3930.00	0.20	0.00	4000.00
5.24	-0.24	4048.00	0.10	0.00	4400.00
5.04	-0.20	4448.00	0.00	0.00	4700.00
4.81	-0.23	4462.00	0.00	0.10	4900.00
4.62	-0.19	5078.00	-0.30	0.30	5200.00
4.61	-0.01	5284.00	-0.10	0.20	5400.00
4.54	-0.07	5225.00	-0.30	0.10	5600.00
4.71	0.17	5391.00	-0.10	0.00	6000.00
4.72	0.01	5668.00	0.00	-0.10	6000.00
4.58	-0.14	5844.00	-0.20	0.10	6100.00

u1	u2	u3	u4	u5	y
4.55	-0.03	6068.00	-0.20	0.00	6400.00
4.59	0.04	6250.00	-0.20	-0.10	6400.00
4.65	0.06	6358.00	-0.10	-0.10	6400.00
4.70	0.05	6368.00	-0.10	0.00	6400.00
4.81	0.11	6379.00	-0.30	0.00	6400.00
4.84	0.03	6412.00	-0.10	-0.10	6400.00
4.83	-0.01	6416.00	0.10	-0.10	6500.00
4.76	-0.07	6514.00	0.00	0.00	6600.00
4.77	0.01	6587.00	-0.10	0.10	6600.00
4.77	0.00	6569.00	0.00	-0.10	6600.00

APPENDIX I   *(Continued)*

4.77	0.00	6559.00	0.00	0.00	6700.00
4.73	-0.04	6672.00	0.00	0.00	6700.00
4.73	0.00	6844.00	-0.10	0.00	6800.00
4.74	0.01	6775.00	-0.20	0.00	6800.00
4.77	0.03	6779.00	0.00	-0.10	6800.00
4.71	-0.06	6783.00	0.00	0.00	6800.00
4.66	-0.05	6816.00	0.00	0.00	6800.00
4.70	0.04	6812.00	0.00	0.00	6800.00
4.63	-0.07	6849.00	0.00	0.00	6800.00
4.61	-0.02	6803.00	0.00	0.00	6800.00
4.57	-0.04	6832.00	0.00	0.10	6800.00
4.56	-0.01	6832.00	-0.10	0.10	6900.00
4.54	-0.02	6862.00	-0.10	-0.10	7000.00
4.51	-0.03	6958.00	0.10	-0.10	7000.00
4.47	-0.04	6998.00	0.00	0.10	7000.00
4.47	0.00	6986.00	-0.10	0.10	7000.00
4.48	0.01	6975.00	0.00	0.00	7000.00
4.48	0.00	6973.00	0.00	0.00	7000.00
4.50	0.02	7006.00	0.00	0.10	7000.00
4.50	0.00	7027.00	0.00	0.00	7000.00
4.48	-0.02	7032.00	0.00	0.00	7000.00
4.54	0.06	6995.00	0.00	0.00	7000.00
4.57	0.03	6986.00	0.10	-0.10	7000.00
4.56	-0.01	7009.00	-0.10	0.10	7000.00
4.56	0.00	7022.00	0.00	0.00	7000.00
4.57	0.01	6998.00	-0.10	0.00	7000.00

APPENDIX II

Daily Data of Stock A

x1	x2	x3	x4	x5	x6	x7	x8	x9	x10	y
0.239	0.227	8.307	2.820	-0.498	0.870	-3.281	-2.562	-2.523	-3.355	34.512

APPENDIX II *(Continued)*

0.279	0.246	16.771	5.222	-0.250	.588	1.696	-4.568	0.848	-0.502	24.390
0.319	0.272	21.253	5.819	-0.418	0.841	-0.834	-3.255	4.352	0.756	24.187
0.346	0.270	19.867	4.654	-0.420	-0.834	-0.841	-0.502	2.588	0.338	17.662
0.351	0.303	19.447	7.848	0.084	3.364	-2.545	0.756	3.364	3.626	-2.441
0.269	0.268	14.320	5.809	0.253	-1.627	0.870	0.338	0.834	1.682	7.444
0.250	0.267	11.157	5.527	0.084	0.0	2.588	3.626	1.682	1.597	2.481
0.256	0.336	12.787	11.263	0.756	5.790	0.841	1.682	4.068	6.672	-11.728
0.296	0.379	12.453	14.309	1.168	3.127	-0.834	1.597	9.098	8.739	-12.889
0.326	0.400	12.088	16.444	1.649	2.274	3.364	6.672	11.580	9.408	-20.015
0.354	0.350	13.587	14.317	1.379	-1.483	-1.627	8.739	3.909	6.320	-10.534
0.395	0.315	15.971	14.815	1.200	0.752	0.0	9.408	1.516	5.850	-17.924
0.388	0.295	19.383	12.767	0.949	-1.494	5.790	6.320	-2.224	3.289	-20.470
0.433	0.294	22.512	16.698	1.410	3.791	3.127	5.850	3.010	5.714	16.801
0.466	0.350	28.465	19.689	1.390	2.922	2.274	3.289	5.228	7.311	-16.324
0.466	0.340	26.015	21.823	1.752	2.129	-1.483	5.714	9.098	7.710	-20.848
0.391	0.404	19.058	26.391	2.171	4.170	0.752	7.311	9.496	9.817	-26.017
0.346	0.478	13.125	30.825	2.051	4.003	-1.494	7.710	1.0646	11.917	-27.582
0.348	0.401	11.815	29.467	1.651	-0.641	3.791	9.817	7.644	9.393	-22.595
0.357	0.427	10.504	28.084	1.342	-0.646	2.922	11.917	2.668	7.247	-23.392
0.357	0.361	11.021	20.990	0.906	-5.198	2.129	9.393	-6.414	0.760	-19.191
0.314	0.378	10.674	22.186	0.967	1.371	4.170	7.247	-4.519	1.163	-24.341
0.292	0.413	13.067	25.798	1.436	3.381	4.003	0.760	-0.650	3.102	-26.161
0.297	0.457	11.830	26.044	1.146	0.654	-0.641	1,163	5.483	2.600	-22.092
0.266	0.455	9.733	28.734	1.133	2.599	-0.646	3.102	6.761	4.087	-21.533
0.255	0.408	5.862	25.776	0.725	-1.900	-5.198	2.600	1.308	1.374	-20.013
0.264	0.415	7.374	28.491	0.589	2.582	1.371	4.087	3.249	3.383	-23.9`4
0.249	0.404	6.214	25.557	0.0	-1.888	3.381	1.374	-1.267	1.431	-18.602
0.243	0.394	5.066	24.262	0.0	-0.641	0.654	3.383	0.0	0.781	-20.658
0.223	0.410	2.165	24.554	0.130	-0.646	2.599	1.431	-1.888	1.299	-19.243
0.227	0.364	2.820	24.102	0.650	0.0	-1.900	0.781	0.0	0.646	-19.243
0.246	0.318	5.222	17.360	0.0	-5.131	2.582	1.299	-4.519	-4.519	-14.875
0.272	0.238	5.819	17.873	-0.258	0.676	-1.888	0.646	-4.490	-3.625	-16.790

APPENDIX II *(Continued)*

0.270	0.176	4.654	10.554	-0.906	-6.044	-0.641	-4.519	-10.263	-8.622	-13.581
0.303	-0.026	7.848	-5.226	-2.482	-14.296	0.646	-3.625	-18.932	-19.692	0.0
0.268	0.070	5.809	2.607	-1.674	8.340	0.0	-8.622	-12.760	-11.512	-10.778
0.267	0.053	5.527	-2.184	-2,384	-4.619	-5.131	-19.692	-11.437	-13.538	-4.033
0.336	-0.035	11.263	-10.837	-3.001	-8.878	0.676	-11.512	-5.838	-18.777	3.543
0.379	-0.044	14.309	-9.218	-2.878	-1.771	-6.044	-13.538	-11.547	-14.889	0.0
0.400	-0.097	16.444	-14.666	-3.556	-6.092	-14.296	-18.777	-12.914	-17.127	5.561
0.350	0.0	14.317	-5.967	-2.842	10.195	8.340	-14.889	5.314	-6.008	-3.364
0.315	-0.070	14.815	-13.023	-3.004	-7.569	-4.619	-17.127	-4.352	-10.432	5.459
0.295	-.0.114	12.767	-16.885	-3.586	-4.550	-8.878	-6.008	-2.780	-11.327	-16.206
0.294	-0.026	16.698	-9.731	-2.198	8.580	1.771	-10.432	-4.205	-q1.556	5.268
0.350	0.026	19.689	-6.515	-0.173	3.512	-6.092	-11.327	7.279	2.078	2.544
0.340	0.053	21.823	-9.802	-1.385	-3.393	10.195	-1.556	8.580	0.0	0.878
0.404	0.035	26.391	-12.209	-1.141	-2.634	-7.569	2.078	-2.634	-1.510	2.705
0.478	0.018	30.825	-10.641	0.0	1.803	-4.550	0.0	-4.241	0.266	4.429
0.401	0.105	29.467	-5.201	0.444	6.200	8.580	-1.510	5.268	6.012	-3.336

x1	x2	x3	x4	x5	x6	x7	x8	x9	x10	y
0.427	0.123	28.084	-6.897	0.884	-1.668	3.512	0.266	6.312	3.330	1.696
0.361	0.088	20.990	-6.978	-0.088	0.0	-3.393	6.012	4.429	3.421	1.696
0.378	0.061	22.186	-11.766	0.175	-5.089	-2.634	3.330	-6.672	-2.014	10.724
0.413	0.017	25.798	-10.993	0.700	0.089	1.803	3.421	-4.241	-1.826	6.200
0.457	0.061	26.044	-5.533	0.522	6.200	6.200	-2.014	1.696	3.720	0.0
0.455	0.105	28.734	-2.484	0.519	3.336	-1.668	-1.826	10.724	6.626	-0.807
0.408	0.149	25.776	-2.628	0.861	0.0	0.0	3.720	9.743	5.717	-6.457
0.415	0.113	28.491	-5.094	0.853	-2.421	-5.089	6.626	0.834	2.284	-6.617
0.404	0.174	25.557	-0.557	1.184	4.963	0.894	5.717	2.421	6.104	-9.456
0.394	0.148	24.262	-3.834	0.251	-3.152	6.200	2.284	-0.807	2.502	-6.509
0.410	0.174	24.554	-1.658	0.667	2.441	3.336	6.104	4.136	4.308	-3.971
0.364	0.130	24.102	-1.786	0.663	0.0	0.0	2.502	-0.788	3.621	5.560
0.318	0.052	17.360	-1.837	1.152	0.0	-2.421	4.308	2.441	2.441	3.177
0.238	-0.009	17.873	-3.388	0.896	-1.589	4.963	3.621	-1.589	-0.081	4.843
0.176	-0.026	10.554	-5.702	0.081	-2.421	-3.152	2.441	-3.971	-2.579	3.308
-0.026	-0.035	-5.226	-6.450	-0.322	-0.827	2.441	-0.081	-4.766	-3.072	2.502

APPENDIX II   *(Continued)*

0.070	-0.026	2.607	-9.547	-0.647	-3.336	0.0	-2.579	-6.457	-5.696	5.177
0.053	0.026	-2.184	-7.230	-0.163	2.588	0.0	-3.072	-1.654	-3.097	5.887
-0.035	-0.009	-10.837	-8.783	-0.815	-1.682	-1.589	-5.696	-2.502	-3.944	11.976
-0.044	-0.026	-9.218	-10.320	-0.657	-1.711	-2.421	-3.097	-0.863	-4.963	10.444
-0.097	-0.035	-14.666	-11.070	-0.993	-0.870	-0.827	-3.944	-4.205	-4.845	10.536
0.0	-0.043	-5.967	-10.250	-0.919	0.878	-3.336	-4.963	-1.711	-3.120	6.962
-0.070	-0.061	-13.023	-9.414	-0.843	0.870	2.588	-4.845	0.870	-1.446	5.177
-0.114	-0.043	-16.885	-4.683	-0.170	5.177	-1.682	-3.120	7.024	3.833	0.820
0.026	-0.096	-9.731	-6.157	-0.085	-1.641	-1.711	-1.446	4.352	2.217	1.668
0.026	-0.148	-6.585	-5.234	0.085	0.834	-0.870	3.833	4.314	2.981	1.654
0.053	-0.183	-9.802	-9.772	-0.085	-4.963	0.878	2.217	-5.742	-2.046	6.962
0.035	-0.131	-12.209	-10.440	-0.426	-0.870	0.870	2.981	-5.004	-2.483	7.024
0.018	-0.044	-10.641	-7.255	0.086	3.512	5.177	-2.046	-2.481	0.855	5.089
0.105	-0.052	-5.201	-8.780	0.0825	-1.696	-1.641	-2.483	0.870	-0.940	8.628
0.123	-0.009	-6.897	-5.624	0.513	3.451	0.834	0.855	5.268	1.956	5.004
0.088	-0.017	-6.978	-5.607	0.426	0.0	-4.963	-0.940	1.696	1.524	2.502
0.061	-0.017	-11.766	-2.475	0.677	3.336	-0.870	1.956	6.902	4.205	-0.807
0.017	-0.044	-10.993	-5.582	-0.168	-3.228	3.512	1.524	0.0	1.011	1.668
0.061	-0.035	-5.533	-5.549	0.0	0.0	-1.696	4.205	0.0	1.011	1.668
0.105	0.009	-2.484	-3.194	0.168	2.502	3.451	1.011	-0.807	3.364	1.627
0.149	-0.017	-2.628	-8.692	0.084	-5.696	0.0	1.011	-3.336	-2.605	6.040
0.113	-0.016	-5.094	-11.001	-0.084	-2.588	3.336	3.364	-5.838	-5.046	10.629
0.174	-0.035	-0.557	-9.393	-0.252	1.771	-3.228	-2.605	-6.509	-3.120	7.833
0.148	-0.026	-3.834	-9.369	-0.084	0.0	0.0	-5.046	-0.863	-3.038	10.444
0.174	0.053	-1.658	-4.686	0.084	5.222	2.502	-3.120	7.086	1.939	4.963
0.130	0.149	-1.786	4.618	1.096	9.926	-4.696	-3.038	15.666	10.842	-5.267
0.052	0.096	-1.837	2.158	0.500	-2.257	-2.558	1.939	13.055	7.801	-3.849
-0.009	0.087	-3.388	2.069	0.830	0.0	1.7711	0.842	7.444	6.914	-3.849
-0.026	0.52	-5.702	-1.911	0.412	-3.849	0.0	7.801	-6.020	2.377	3.203
-0.035	0.0	-6.450	-3.482	0.0	-1.601	5.222	6.914	-5.389	0.738	4.882
-0.026	0.009	-9.547	-4.275	0.492	-0.814	9.926	2.377	-6.159	-0.571	6.563
0.026	0.44	-7.230	-1.177	1.060	3.281	-2.257	0.738	0.801	1.614	0.794

-0.009	0.026	-8.783	2.720	1.291	3.971	0.0	-0.571	6.509	4.303	-1.528
-0.026	-0.044	-10.320	-0.375	0.956	-3.056	-3.849	1.614	4.102	0.158	4.728
-0.035	-0.079	-11.070	-1.082	0.395	-0.786	-1.601	4.303	0.0	-1.022	4.766

KEYWORDS

- **Fuzzy modifiers**
- **Interpolation**
- **Linguistic approach**
- **Petri Net**
- **Takagi-Sugeno model**

CHAPTER 5

ROUGH SET

5.1 INTRODUCTION

The notion of a set is very fundamental in mathematics. It also plays an important role in natural language. We often speak about sets (collections) of various objects of interest, for example, collection of books, paintings, people, and so on. Thus a set is a collection of things, which are somehow related to each other but the nature of this relationship is not specified.

According to Cantor a set is a collection of any objects, which according to some law can be considered as a whole. All mathematical objects, for example, relations, functions, numbers, and so on, are some kind of sets. In fact set theory is needed in mathematics to provide rigor.

Bertrand Russell discovered that the intuitive notion of a set has given by Cantor leads to antinomies (contradictions). One of the best known antinomies called the power set antinomy goes as follows: consider (infinite) set X of all sets. Thus X is the greatest set. Let Y denote the set of all subsets of X. Obviously, Y is greater than X, because the number of subsets of a set is always greater the number of its elements. For example, if X = {1, 2, 3} then Y = {∅,{1}, {2}, {3}, {1, 2}, {1, 3}, {2, 3}, and {1, 2, 3}}, where ∅ denotes the empty set. Hence X is not the greatest set as assumed and we arrived at contradiction.

Thus the basic concept of mathematics, the concept of a set, is contradictory. That means that a set cannot be a collection of arbitrary elements as is stipulated by Cantor.

To overcome such contradiction several improvements of set theory have been proposed.

For example
- Axiomatic set theory (Zermelo and Fraenkel, 1904),
- Theory of types (Whitehead and Russel, 1910), and
- Theory of classes (V. Neumann, 1920).

All these improvements consist of restrictions. The restrictions are expressed by properly chosen axioms, which say how the set can be build. They are called, in contrast to Cantors' intuitive set theory, axiomatic set theories. Instead of improvements of

Cantor's set theory by its axiomatization, some mathematicians proposed alternative approach to classical set theory by creating completely new idea of a set, which is free from antinomies.

Some of them are listed below:

- Mereology (Lesniewski, 1915),
- Alternative set theory (Vopenka, 1970), and
- "Penumbral" set theory (Apostoli and Kanada, 1999).

No doubt the most interesting proposal is given by Stanislaw Lesniewski, who proposes (instead of membership relation between elements and sets, employed in classical set theory), the relation of "being a part". In this set theory, called mereology, this relation is a fundamental one.

None of the three mentioned above "new" set theories are accepted by mathematicians, however, Lesniewski's mereology attracts attention of philosophers and (recent past) computer scientists, (for example, Lech Polkowski and Andrzej Skowron).

In classical set theory, a set is uniquely determined by its elements. In other words, it means that every element must be uniquely classified as belonging to the set or not. That is to say the notion of a set is a crisp (precise) one. For example, the set of odd numbers is crisp because every number is either odd or even. In mathematics we have to use crisp notions, otherwise precise reasoning would be impossible. However, philosophers for many years are interested also in vague notions. For example, in contrast to odd numbers, the notion of a beautiful painting is vague, because we are unable to classify uniquely all paintings into two classes: beautiful and not beautiful. Some paintings cannot be decided whether they are beautiful or not and thus they remain in the doubtful area. Thus beauty is not a precise but a vague concept. Almost all concepts we are using in natural language are vague. Therefore common sense reasoning based on natural language must be based on vague concepts and not on classical logic. That is why vagueness is so important to philosophers and also to computer scientists.

Vagueness is usually associated with the boundary region of any concept (that is, existence of objects, which cannot be uniquely classified to the set or its complement), which is first visualized in 1893 by the father of modern logic Gottlob Frege.

According to Frege, *"The concept must have a sharp boundary. To the concept without a sharp boundary there would correspond an area that has no sharp boundary-line all around."*

Mathematics must use crisp, not vague concepts, otherwise it would be impossible to reason precisely. Thus we can say, vagueness is, not allowed in mathematics, but interesting for philosophy and necessary for computer science.

Rough set theory is an alternative approach to handle imperfect knowledge. The problem of imperfect knowledge has been considered for a long time by philosophers, logicians, and mathematicians. Recently it becomes a crucial issue for computer scientists, particularly in the area of commonsense reasoning as enunciated by the researchers of Artificial Intelligence.

There are many existing approaches to this problem:

- Based on the concept of crisp set and non-monotonic logic,
- Based on probabilistic approach, and
- Based on fuzzy set and fuzzy logic.

Rough set and rough logic proposed by Z. Pawlak presents another approach to this problem. The theory has attracted attention of many researchers and practitioners all over the world, who contribute essentially to its development and applications.

Rough set philosophy is based on the concept that with every object of the universe of discourse some information (data and knowledge) is associated. For instance, if objects ate patients suffering from a certain disease, symptoms of the disease form information about patients. Objects characterized by the same information are indiscernible (similar) in view of the available information about them. Thus, the indiscernibility relation is generated, which is the essence of rough set theory. Any set of all indiscernible (similar) objects is called an elementary set, which forms a basic granule (atom) of knowledge about the universe. Any union of some elementary sets is referred to as a crisp (precise) set, otherwise the set is rough (vague). Each rough set has boundary-line cases, that is, objects, which cannot be with certainty classified, by employing the available knowledge, as members of the set or its complement. Obviously, rough sets, in contrast to precise sets, cannot be characterized in terms of information about their elements. With any rough set a pair of precise sets, called the lower and the upper approximation of the rough set, is associated. The lower approximation consists of all objects, which surely belong to the set and the upper approximation contains all objects, which possibly belong to the set. The difference between the upper and lower approximation constitutes the boundary region of the rough set. Approximations are fundamental concepts of rough set theory [213, 214, 215].

Rough set based data analysis starts from a data table called a decision table. The columns of the decision table are labeled by attributes and rows are labeled by objects of interest. The entries of the table are attribute values. Attributes of the decision table are divided into two disjoint groups called condition and decision attributes respectively. Each row of a decision table induces a decision rule, which specifies decision (action, results, outcome, and so on) if some conditions are satisfied. If a decision rule uniquely determines decision in terms of condition – the decision rule is certain. Otherwise the decision rule is uncertain. Decision rules are closely connected with approximations. Roughly speaking, certain decision rules describe lower approximation of decisions in theorems of conditions, whereas uncertain decision rules refer to the boundary region of decisions.

With every decision rule two conditional probabilities, called the certainty and the coverage coefficient, are associated. The certainty coefficient expresses the conditional probability that an object belongs to the decision classified by decision rule, given it satisfies conditions of the rule. The coverage coefficient gives the conditional probability of reasons for a given decision. It turns out that the certainty and coverage coefficients satisfy Bayes theorem that gives a new look into the interpretation of Bayes theorem and offers a new method to draw conclusions from data.

Rough set theory has an overlap with many theories dealing with imperfect knowledge, for example, evidence theory, fuzzy sets, Bayesian inference, and others. The rough set theory can be regarded as an independent discipline, in its own rights. It is basically a complementary (not competing) discipline of other existing theories of uncertainty and vagueness.

Rough sets have been proposed for a very wide variety of applications. In particular, the rough set approach seems to be important for Artificial Intelligence and cognitive sciences, especially in machine learning, knowledge discovery, data mining, expert systems, approximate reasoning, and pattern recognition.

The main advantages of the rough set approach are as follows:

- It does not need any preliminary or additional information about data – like probability in statistics, grade of membership in the fuzzy set theory.
- It provides efficient methods, algorithms and tools for finding hidden patterns in data.
- It allows to reduce original data, that is to find minimal sets of data with the same knowledge as in the original data.
- It allows to evaluate the significance of data.
- It allows to generate in automatic way the sets of decision rules from data.
- It is easy to understand.
- It offers straightforward interpretation of obtained results.
- It is suited for concurrent (parallel/distributed) processing.

5.2   GATEWAY TO ROUGH SET CONCEPT

Let us consider a very simple example [120] on churn modeling problem in telecommunications. In Table 1, six facts concerning six client segments are presented. Each row in the table determine a decision rule. For instance, row 2 determines the following decision rule, "if the number of incoming calls is high and the number of outgoing calls is high and the number of outgoing calls to the mobile operator is low then these is no churn."

Churn model in telecommunication industry predicts customers, who are going to leave the current operator. The main problem that has to be solved by marketing departments of wireless operators is to find the way of convincing current clients that they should continue to use the services.

TABLE 1   Client segments

Segment	In	Out	Change	Churn	N
1	medium	medium	low	no	200
2	high	high	low	no	100
3	low	low	low	no	300
4	low	low	high	yes	150
5	medium	medium	low	yes	220
6	medium	low	low	yes	30

Key

In ≡ Incoming calls,

Out ≡ Outgoing calls within the same operator,

Change ≡ Outgoing calls to other mobile operator,

Churn ≡ The decision attribute describing the consequence, and

N ≡ The number of similar cases.

Precisely speaking we explain churn in terms of client's profile, that is, to describe market segments {4, 5, 6} (or {1, 2, 3}) in terms of conditional attributes In, Out and Change. The problem cannot be solved uniquely because the data set is inconsistent, that is, segments 1 and 5 have the same profile but different consequences.

Let us observe that:

Segments 2 and 3 (4 and 6) can be classified as sets of clients, who certainly do not churn (churn),

Segments 1, 2, 3, and 5 (1, 4, 5, and 6) can be classified as sets of clients, who possibly do not churn (churn), and

Segments 1 and 5 are undecidable sets of clients.

This leads us to the following notions:

- The set {2, 3} ({4, 6}) is the lower approximation of the set {1, 2, 3} ({4, 5, 6}),
- The set {1, 2, 3, 5} ({1, 4, 5, 6}) is the upper approximation of the set {1, 2, 3} ({4, 5, 6}), and
- The set {1, 5} is the boundary region of the set {1, 2, 3} ({4, 5, 6}).

Any decision table induces a set of "if … then" decision rules. Any set of mutually, exclusive, and exhaustive decision rules, that covers all facts in an information system and preserves the indiscernibility relation included by the information system is called a decision algorithm of information system, say, S.

An example of decision algorithm in the decision Table 1 is given below:

TABLE 2   Decision algorithm

		Certainty factor
1.	If (In, high) then (Churn, no)	1.00
2.	If (In, low) and (Change, low) then (Churn, no)	1.00
3.	If (In, med) and (Out, med.) then (Churn, no)	0.48
4.	If (Change, high) then (Churn, yes)	1.00
5.	If (In, med) and (Out, low) then (Churn, yes)	1.00
6.	If (In, med) and (Out, med) then (Churn, yes)	0.52

Finding a minimal decision algorithm associated with a given decision table is rather complex. Many methods have been proposed to solve this problem, but we do not consider this problem here.

If we are interested in explanation of decisions in terms of conditions, we need as inverse decision algorithm, which is obtained by replacing mutually conditions and decisions in every decision rule in the decision algorithm.

For example:

The following inverse decision algorithm as given in Table 3 can be understood as explanation of churn (no churn) in terms of client profile:

TABLE 3. Inverse decision algorithm

		Certainty factor
1.	If (Churn, no) then (In, high) and (Out, med)	0.33
2.	If (Churn, no) then (In, high)	0.17
3.	If (Churn, no) then (In, low) and (Change, low)	0.50
4.	If (Churn, yes) then (Change, yes)	0.38
5.	If (Churn, yes) then (In, med) and (Out, med)	0.55
6.	If (Churn, yes) then (In, med) and (Out, low)	0.07

Observe that certainty factor for inverse decision rules are coverage factors for the original decision rules.

The above properties of decision tables (algorithms) give a simple method of drawing conclusions from the data and giving explanation of obtained results.

From the decision algorithm and the certainty factors we can draw the following conclusions:
- No churn is implied with certainty by:
- High number of incoming calls
- Low number of incoming calls and low number of outgoing calls to other mobile operator.
- Churn is implied with certainty by:
- High number of outgoing calls to other mobile operator
- Medium number of incoming calls and low number of outgoing calls.
- Clients with medium number of incoming calls and low number of outgoing calls within the same operator are undecided (no churn, certainty factor = 0.48, churn, certainty factor = 0.52).

From the inverse decision algorithm and the coverage factors we get the following explanations:
- The most probable reason for no churn is low general activity of a client,
- The most probable reason for churn is medium number of incoming calls and medium number of outgoing calls within the same operator.

5.3   APPROXIMATION SPACES AND SET APPROXIMATION

Rough set theory is alternative tool for vagueness. Similarly to fuzzy set theory it is not an alternative to classical set theory but it is embedded in it. Rough set theory can be viewed as a specific implementation of Frege's idea of vagueness, that is, imprecision in this approach is expressed by a boundary region of a set, and not by a partial membership, like in fuzzy set theory.

Rough set theory proposes a new mathematical approach to imperfect knowledge, that is to vagueness (or imprecision). In this approach, vagueness is expressed by a boundary region of a set. Rough set concept can be defined by means of topological operations, interior, and closure called approximations.

We describe the basic concept of rough set as follows:

- Let a finite set of objects U and a binary relation $R \subseteq U \times U$ be given. The sets U, R are called the universe and an indiscernibility relation1, respectively. The discernibility relation represents our lack of knowledge about elements of U. For simplicity, we assume that R is an equivalence relation on U. A pair (U, R) is called an approximation space, where U is the universe and R is an equivalence relation on U.

- Let X be a subset of U, that is $X \subseteq U$. Our goal is to characterize the set X with respect to R.

In order to do it, we need additional notion and basic concepts of rough set theory, which are presented below.

BY R(x) we denote the equivalence class of R determined by element x. The indiscernibility relation R describes – in a sense – our lack of knowledge about the universe U. Equivalence classes of the relation R, called granules, represent an elementary portion of knowledge we are able to perceive due to R. Using only the indiscernibility relation, in general, we are not able to observe individual objects from U but only the accessible granules of knowledge described by this relation.

The set of all objects, which can be with certainty classified as members of X with respect to R is called the R-lower approximate of a set X with respect to R, and denoted by $R_*(X)$, that is.

$$R_*(X) = \{ x : R(x) \subseteq X \}.$$

The set of all objects, which can be only classified as possible members of X with respect to R is called the R-upper approximation of a set X with respect to R and denoted by $R^*(X)$, that is

$$R^*(X) = \{x : R(x) \cap X \neq \emptyset\}.$$

The set of all objects, which can be decisively classified neither as members of X nor as members of $-X$ with respect to R is placed in the boundary region of the set X with respect to R and is represented as $RN_R(X)$,

$$RN_R(X) = R^*(X) - R_*(X).$$

The set of objects, which can be certainly classified as do not belonging to X is placed in the outside region of the set X with respect of R and is represented by U - R*(X).

---

1   R-indiscernibility relation in the context of an information system S is represented as INDS(R).

Example 5.1 Let us consider the medical data set as given in Table 4.

TABLE 4   Medical data

Object	Attributes	
U	$c_1\, c_2$	d
x_1	0 L	0
x_2	0 H	0
x_3	0 H	0
x_4	1 L	0
x_5	1 L	1
x_6	1 H	1
x_7	1 H	1
x_8	2 L	0
x_9	2 L	1
x_{10}	2 H	1

Equivalence Classes (granules)
  $\{x_1\}$
  $\{x_2, x_3\}$
  $\{x_4, x_5\}$
  $\{x_6, x_7\}$
  $\{x_8, x_9\}$
  $\{x_{10}\}$

In the information system (Table 4) S, the universe U consists of ten objects U = $\{x_1, x_2, \ldots\ldots, x_{10}\}$ each representing one patient. Each object (patient) is described by the set of three attributes Q = $\{c1\ c2\ d\}$ with discrete values (numerical and symbolic) representing results of the medical tests and diagnoses. The set of all discrete (numerical) values of the attribute c1 is V_{c_1} = $\{0, 1, 2\}$. The second attribute c2 takes two discrete non-numerical values V_{c_2} = $\{L, H\}$ (L = low and H = high). The third attribute d with two discrete (binary) values Vd = $\{0, 1\}$ represents Doctor's decision about a certain disease based on test results. d = 0 indicates that a patient does not have a disease and d = 1 indicates that a patient does have disease. From Table 4 we observe that objects can be divided into six disjoint groups according to equal values of attributes c1 and c2.

Let us consider a subset X of objects from U, namely objects representing sick patients (a concept sick, d = 1):

$$X = \{x_5, x_6, x_7, x_9, x_{10}\}.$$

According to the definition, the lower approximation of the set X based on the attributes $\{c_1, c_2\}$ is:

$$R_*(X) = \{x_6, x_7\} \cup \{x_{10}\}$$

$$= \{x_6, x_7, x_{10}\}.$$

Similarly, the upper approximation of the set X based on the attributes $\{c_1, c_2\}$ is;

$$R^*(X) = \{x_4, x_5\} \cup \{x_6, x_7\} \cup \{x_8, x_9\} \cup \{x_{10}\}$$

$$= \{x_4, x_5, x_6, x_7, x_8, x_9, x_{10}\}.$$

The boundary region of X is;

$$RN_R(X) = R^*(X) - R_*(X)$$

$$= \{x_4, x_5, x_8, x_9\}.$$

Now we are ready to formulate the definition of the rough set notion. These are:

- A set X is called crisp (exact) with respect to R, if and only if the boundary region of X is empty.
- A set X is called rough (inexact) with respect to R, if and only if the boundary region of X is nonempty.

The definitions of set approximations presented above can be expressed in terms of granules of knowledge in the following way. The lower approximation of a set is union of all granules, which are entirely included in the set, the upper approximation is union of all granules, which have non-empty intersection with the set, the boundary region of a set is the difference between the upper and the lower approximation of the set.

The Figure 1 represents the graphical illustration of the set approximations defined above.

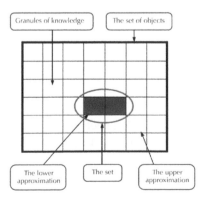

FIGURE 1   Graphical representation of rough set approximation.

It is interesting to compare definitions of classical sets, fuzzy sets, and rough sets. Classical set is a primitive notion and is defined intuitively or axiomatically. Fuzzy sets are defined by employing the fuzzy membership function, which involves advanced mathematical structures, numbers, and functions. Rough sets are defined by approximations. Thus this definition also requires advanced mathematical concepts.

We state the following properties of approximations:

- $R_*(X) \subseteq X \subseteq R^*(X)$
- $R_*(\emptyset) = R^*(\emptyset) = \emptyset; R_*(U) = R^*(U) = U$
- $R^*(X \cup Y) = R^*(X) \cup R^*(Y)$
- $R_*(X \cap Y) = R_*(X) \cap R_*(Y)$
- $R_*(X \cup Y) \supseteq R_*(X) \cup R_*(Y)$
- $R^*(X \cap Y) \subseteq R^*(X) \cap R^*(Y)$
- $X \subseteq Y \rightarrow R_*(X) \subseteq R_*(Y) \& R^*(X) \subseteq R^*(Y)$
- $R_*(-X) = -R_*(X)$
- $R^*(-X) = -R_*(X)$
- $R_* R_*(X) = R^* R_*(X) = R_*(X)$
- $R^* R^*(X) = R_* R^*(X) = R^*(X)$

It is easily seen that the lower and the upper approximations of a set are, respectively the interior and closure of the set in the topology generated by the indiscernibility relation.

In rough set theory, set X is either definable or undefinable. A set $X \subseteq U$ is definable in R, denoted by R-definable, if $R_*(X) = R^*(X)$, otherwise X is not definable, denoted by R-undefinable.

We can define the following four basic classes of rough sets that is, four categories of vagueness:

Definition 5.1 A set X is roughly R-definable, if $R_*(X) \neq \emptyset$ and $R^*(X) \neq U$.

Remark 5.1 A set X is roughly R-definable, means that with respect to R we are able to decide for some elements of U that they belong to X and for some elements of U that they belong to –X.

Definition 5.2 A set X is internally R-undefinable, if $R_* = \emptyset$ and $R^*(X) \neq U$.

Remark 5.2 A set X is internally R-undefinable, means with respect to R we are able to decide for some elements of U that they belong to –X, but we are unable to decide for any element of U whether it belongs to X.

Definition 5.3 A set X is externally R-undefinable, if $R_*(X) \neq \emptyset$ and $R^*(X) = U$.

Remark 5.3 A set X is externally R-undefinable means that with respect to R we are able to decide for some elements of U that they belong to X, but we are unable to decide for any element of U whether it belongs to X.

Definition 5.4 A set X is totally R-undefinable, if $R_*(X) = \emptyset$ and $R^*(X) = U$.

Remark 5.4 A set X is totally R-undefinable, means that with respect to R we are able to decide for any element of U whether it belongs to X or –X.

A rough set X can be characterized by the following coefficient:

$$\alpha_R(X) = \frac{|R_*(X)|}{|R^*(X)|}$$

which represents the accuracy of approximation, and where |X| denotes the cardinality of $X \neq \emptyset$.

Obviously, $0 \le \alpha_R(X) \le 1$. If $\alpha_R(X) = 1$ then X is crisp with respect to R (X is precise with respect to R), and otherwise, if $\alpha_R(X) < 1$, X is rough with respect to R (X is vague with respect to R).

Example 5.2 Let S =< U, Q, V, f>, where U = $\{x_1, \ldots\ldots, x_{11}\}$ and $R \subseteq Q$ with the following equivalence classes:

$$E_1 = \{x_1, x_2\},$$
$$E_2 = \{x_3, x_4\},$$
$$E_3 = \{x_5, x_6, x_7\},$$
$$E_4 = \{x_8, x_9\},$$
$$E_5 = \{x_{10}, x_{11}\}.$$

The sets:

$$X_1 = \{x_3, x_4, x_8, x_9\},$$
$$Y_1 = \{x_5, x_6, x_7\},$$
$$Z_1 = \{x_5, x_6, x_7, x_{10}, x_{11}\}.$$

are examples of R-definable sets. The sets:

$$X_2 = \{x_1, x_5, x_6, x_7, x_8, x_9, x_{11}\},$$

$$Y_2 = \{x_3, x_5, x_{10}, x_{11}\},$$

$$Z_2 = \{x_1, x_2, x_5, x_7\}$$

are examples of roughly R-definable sets as shown by their approximations:

$$R_*(X_2) = E_3 \cup E_4 = \{x_5, x_6, x_7, x_8, x_9\},$$

$$R^*(X_2) = E_1 \cup E_3 \cup E_4 \cup E_5 = \{x_1, x_2, x_5, x_6, x_7, x_8, x_9, x_{10}, x_{11}\},$$

$$R_*(Y_2) = E_5 = \{x_{10}, x_{11}\},$$

$$R^*(Y_2) = E_2 \cup E_3 \cup E_5 = \{x_3, x_4, x_5, x_6, x_7, x_{10}, x_{11}\},$$

$$R_*(Z_2) = E_1 = \{x_1, x_2\},$$

$$R^*(Z_2) = E_1 \cup E_3 = \{x_1, x_2, x_5, x_6, x_7\}.$$

The sets:

$$X_3 = \{x_1, x_2, x_3, x_5, x_8, x_{10}\},$$

$$Y_3 = \{x_1, x_3, x_4, x_6, x_7, x_9, x_{10}\},$$

$$Z_3 = \{x_2, x_4, x_6, x_8, x_9, x_{11}\}.$$

are examples of externally R-undefinable sets as shown by their approximations:

$$R_*(X_3) = E_1 = \{x_1, x_2\},$$

$$R^*(X_3) = U,$$

$$R_*(Y_{3)} = E_2 = \{x_3, x_4\},$$

$$R^*(Y_3) = U,$$

$$R_*(Z_3) = E_4 = \{x_8, x_9\},$$

$$R^*(Z_3) = U.$$

The sets:

$$X_4 = \{x_1, x_3, x_8\},$$

$$Y_4 = \{x_2, x_4, x_6, x_8\},$$

$$Z_4 = \{x_3, x_5, x_8\}.$$

are examples of internally R-undefinable sets as shown by their approximations:

$$R_*(X_4) = \emptyset,$$

$$R^*(X_4) = E_1 \cup E_2 \cup E_4 = \{x_1, x_2, x_3, x_4, x_8, x_9\},$$

$$R_*(Y_4) = \emptyset,$$

$$R^*(Y_4) = E_1 \cup E_2 \cup E_3 \cup E_4 = \{x_1, x_2, x_3, x_4, x_5, x_6, x_7, x_8, x_9\},$$

$$R_*(Z_4) = \emptyset,$$

$$R^*(Z_4) = E_2 \cup E_3 \cup E_4 = \{x_3, x_4, x_5, x_6, x_7, x_8, x_9\}.$$

The sets:,

$$X_5 = \{x_1, x_3, x_5, x_8, x_{10}\},$$

$$Y_5 = \{x_2, x_4, x_6, x_9, x_{11}\},$$

$$Z_5 = \{x_1, x_4, x_7, x_8, x_{11}\}.$$

are examples of totally A-undefinable sets.

Example 5.3 Consider the information system of Table 5.

The set $Y_1 = \{x_2, x_4, x_8\}$ is roughly R-definable, since:

$$R_*(Y_1) = X_2 = \{x_4, x_8\},$$

$$R^*(Y_1) = X_2 \cup X_3 = \{x_2, x_4, x_6, x_8\}.$$

The set $Y_2 = \{x_1, x_2, x_5\}$ is internally R-undefinable, since:

$$R_*(Y_2) = \emptyset,$$

$$R^*(Y_2) = X_1 \cup X_3 = \{x_1, x_2, x_3, x_5, x_6, x_7, x_9\}.$$

The set $Y_3 = \{x_1, x_2, x_4, x_6\}$ is externally R-undefinable, since:

$$R_*(Y_3) = X_3 = \{x_2, x_6\},$$
$$R^*(Y_3) = X_1 \cup X_2 \cup X_3 = U.$$

The set $Y_4 = \{x_1, x_2, x_4\}$ is totally R-undefinable, since:

$$R_*(Y_4) = \emptyset.$$
$$R^*(Y_2) = X_1 \cup X_2 \cup X_3 = U.$$

TABLE 5   Data set numerical

Object	Attributes			
U	p	q	r	s
x_1	0	1	1	0
x_2	2	1	0	1
x_3	0	0	0	1
x_4	1	0	2	0
x_5	0	1	1	0
x_6	2	1	0	1
x_7	0	1	1	0
x_8	1	0	2	1
x_9	0	0	0	1

5.4   ROUGH MEMBERSHIP FUNCTION

Rough sets can be also defined by rough membership function proposed in [215].

In classical set theory, either an element belongs to a set or not. The corresponding membership function is the characteristic function for the set, that is the function take values 1 and 0, respectively. In the case of rough sets, the notion of membership is different. The rough membership function quantifies the degree of relative overlap between the set X and the equivalence class R(x) to which belongs.

It is defined as follows:

$$\mu_X^R : U \rightarrow < 0,1 >$$

Where

$$\mu_X^R(x) = \frac{|X \cap R(x)|}{|R(x)|}$$

And |X| denotes the cardinality of X.

The rough membership function expresses conditional probability that x belongs to X given R and can be interpreted as a degree that x belongs to X in view of information about x expressed by R.

The meaning of rough membership function can be depicted as shown in Figure 2.

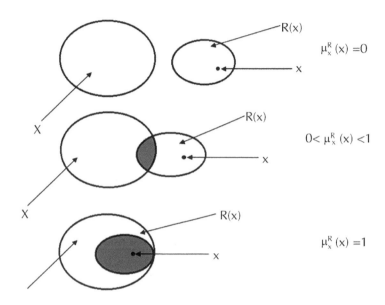

FIGURE 2   Representation of rough set membership function.

The rough membership function can be used to define approximations and the boundary region of a set, as shown below:

$R_*(X) = \{\, x \in U: \mu_X^R(x) = 1 \,\}$,

$R^*(X) = \{\, x \in U: \mu_X^R(x) > 0 \,\}$,

$RN_R(X) = \{\, x \in U: 0 < \mu_X^R(x) < 1 \,\}$.

Example 5.4 With respect to Example 5.1 and $X = \{x_5, x_6, x_7, x_9, x_{10}\}$ the accuracy of approximation:

$$\alpha R(X) = \frac{|R_*(X)|}{|R^*(X)|}$$

$$= \frac{|\{x_6, \; x_7, \; x_{10}\}|}{|\{x_4, \; x_5, \; x_6, \; x_7, \; x_8, \; x_9, \; x_{10}\}|}$$

$$= \frac{3}{7} = 0.428.$$

Further, the membership function of the element x_6 of $R^*(X) = \{x_6, x_7, x_{10}\}$ is:

$$\mu_X^R(x_6) = \frac{|X \cap R(X)|}{|R(X)|}$$

$$= \frac{|\{x_5, x_6, x_7, x_8, x_9, x_{10}\} \cap \{x_6, x_7\}|}{|\{x_6, x_7\}|}$$

$$= \frac{2}{2} = 1.$$

Similarly, the membership function of the element, x_4 of $R^*(X) = \{x_4, x_5, x_6, x_7, x_8, x_9, x_{10}\}$ is,

$$\mu_X^R(x_4) = \frac{|\{x_5, x_6, x_7, x_8, x_9, x_{10}\} \circ \{x_4, x_5\}|}{|\{x_4, x_5\}|}$$

$$= \frac{|\{x_5\}|}{|\{x_4, x_5\}|}$$

$$= \frac{1}{2} = .5.$$

Note that membership function x_5 and x_4 are same because of the fact that they belong to same equivalence class. As $R^*(X) \subseteq X \subseteq R^*(X)$, the membership function of the element x_6, x_7 and x_{10} are always 1.

The membership function of x_8 of R N_R $(X) = \{x_4, x_5, x_8, x_9\}$ is:

$$\mu_X^R(x_8) = \frac{|\{x_5, x_6, x_7, x_9, x_{10}\} \circ \{x_8, x_9\}|}{|\{x_8, x_9\}|}$$

$$= \frac{|\{x_9\}|}{|\{x_8, x_9\}|}$$

$$= \frac{1}{2} = 0.5$$

It can be shown that the rough membership function has the following properties:

$$\mu_X^R(x) = 1 \text{ iff } x \in R_*(X)$$

$$\mu_X^R(x) = 0 \text{ iff } x \in U - R^*(X)$$

$$0 < \mu_X^R (x) < 1 \text{ iff } x \in RN_R (X)$$

$$\mu_{U-X}^R (x) = 1 - \mu_X^R (x) \text{ for any } x \in U$$

$$\mu_{X \cup Y}^R (x) \geq \max (\mu_X^R (x), \mu_Y^R (x)) \text{ for any } x \in U$$

$$\mu_{X \cap Y}^R (x) \leq \min (\mu_X^R (x), \mu_Y^R (x)) \text{ for any } x \in U.$$

From the above properties it follows that the rough membership differs essentially form the fuzzy membership. Properties P5 and P6 show that the membership for union and intersection of sets, in general, cannot be computed – as in the case of fuzzy sets – from their constituents membership. Besides, the rough membership function, in contrast to fuzzy membership function, has a probabilistic flavor. The rough membership function can alternatively be interpreted as a frequency based estimate of Pr(x ∈ X | u), the conditional probability that object x belongs to set X, given knowledge u of the information signature of x with respect to attribute R.

The formulae for the lower and upper set approximations can be generalized to some arbitrary level of precision $\pi \in \left(\frac{1}{2}, 1\right)$ by means of the rough membership function in the following way:

$$R_*^\pi (X) = \{x \in U : \mu_X^R (x) \geq \pi\}$$

$$R_\pi^* (X) = \{x \in U : \mu_X^R (x) > 1 : \pi\}$$

Note that the lower and upper approximations as originally formulated are obtained as a special case with $\pi = 1.0$.

Approximations of concepts are constructed on the basis of background knowledge. Obviously, concepts are also related to unseen so far objects. Hence it is very useful to define parameterized approximations with parameters tuned in the searching process for approximations of concepts. This idea is crucial for construction of concept approximations using rough set methods. For more information about the parameterized approximation spaces the reader is referred to [215].

Rough sets can thus approximately describe sets of patients, events, outcomes, and so on that may be otherwise difficult to circumscribe.

5.5   INFORMATION SYSTEMS

A data set is represented as a table, where each row represents a case, an event, a patient, or simply an object. Every column represents an attribute (a variable, an observation, a property, and so on) that can be measured for each object, the attribute may be also supplied by a human expert of the user. Such table is called an information system. Formally, an information system is a pair S = (U, A), where U is a non-empty finite set of objects called the universe and A is a non-empty finite set of attributes such that a: U $\rightarrow$ V_a for every a ∈ A. The set V_a is called the value set of a.

Example 5.5 Let us consider a very simple information system in Table 6. The set of objects U consists of seven objects: x_1, x_2, x_3, x_4, x_5, x_6, x_7, and the set of attributes includes two attributes: Age and LEMS (Lower Extremity Motor Score).

TABLE 6   Simple information system

U	Age	LEMS
x_1	15-30	50
x_2	15-30	0
x_3	35-45	1-20
x_4	35-45	1-20
x_5	50-60	25-50
x_6	15-30	25-50
x_7	50-60	25-50

One can easily notice that objects x_3 and x_4 as well as x_5, and x_7 have exactly the same values of attributes. The objects are (pairwise) indiscernible using the available attributes.

In many applications there is an outcome of classification that is known. This a posteriori knowledge, which is expressed by one distinguished attribute called decision attribute, the process is known as supervised learning. Information systems of this kind are called decision systems. A decision systems (a decision table) is any information system of the form S = (U, A ({d}), where d ∉ A is the decision attribute. The elements of A are called conditional attributes or simply conditions. The decision attribute may take several values though binary outcomes are rather frequent.

Example 5.6 Consider a decision system presented in Table 7. The table includes the same seven objects as in Example 5.5 and one decision attribute (Walk) with two values: Yes, No.

TABLE 7   Decision table

U	Age	LEMS	Walk
x_1	15-30	50	Yes

TABLE 7   *(continued)*

x_2	15-30	0	No
x_3	35-45	1-20	No
x_4	35-45	1-20	Yes
x_5	50-60	25-50	No
x_6	15-30	25-50	Yes
x_7	50-60	25-50	No

We notice that objects x_3 and x_4 as well as x_5 and x_7 still have exactly the same values of conditions, but the first pair has different value of the decision attribute while the second pair has the same value.

5.6   INDISCERNIBILITY RELATION

A decision system expresses all the knowledge about the model. This table may be unnecessarily large in part because it is redundant in at least two ways. The same or indiscernible objects may be represented several times, or some of the attributes may be superfluous. We shall look into these issues now.

Let S = (U, A) be an information system, and R $\subseteq$ A. A binary relation IND_S (R) defined in the following way:

$$IND_S (R) = \{(x, x') \in U^2 \mid a \in R\, a\,(x) = a(x')\}$$

is called the R-indiscernibility relation. It is easy to see that IND_S (R) is equivalence relation. If (x, x') $\in$ IND_S (R), then objects x and x' are indiscernible from each other by attributes from R. The equivalence classes of the R-indiscernibility relation are denoted $[x]_R$. The subscript S in the indiscernibility relation is usually omitted if it is clear which information system is meant.

The rough membership function has the following properties:

If IND_S(R) = {(x, x): x $\in$ U}, then $\mu_x^R (x)$ is the characteristic function of X.

If x IND_S(R)y, then $\mu_x^R (x) = \mu_y^R (y)$ provided IND_S(R).

Some extensions of standard rough sets do not require from a relation to be transitive. Such a relation is called tolerance relation or similarity.

Example 5.7 In order to illustrate how a decision system from Table 7 defines an indiscernibility relation, we consider the following three non-empty subsets of the conditional attributes: {Age}, {LEMS}, and {Age, LEMS}.

If we take into consideration the set {LEMS} then objects x_3 and x_4 belong to the same equivalence class, they are indiscernible. From the same reason x_5, x_6, and x_7 belong to another indiscernibility class. The relation IND defines three partitions of the universe.

IND ({Age}) = {{x_1, x_2, x_6}, {x_3, x_4}, {x_5, x_7}}

IND ({LEMS}) = {{x_1}, {x_2}, {x_3, x_4}, {x_5, x_6, x_7}}

IND ({Age, LEMS}) = {{x_1}, {x_2}, {x_3, x_4}, {x_5, x_7}, {x_6}}

5.7 SOME FURTHER ILLUSTRATION ON SET APPROXIMATION

Let S = (U, A) be an information system and let R $\subseteq$ A and X $\subseteq$ U. Now, we can approximate a set X using only the information contained in the set of attributes R by constructing the *R-lower* and *R-upper approximations of X*, denoted R_*X and R^*X respectively, where $R_*X = \{x | [x]_R \subseteq X\}$ and $R^*X = \{x | [x]_R \cap X \neq X\emptyset\}$.

Analogously as in a general case, the objects in R_*X can be certainly classified as members of X on the basis of knowledge in R, while the objects in R^*X can be only classified as possible members of X on the basis of knowledge in R. The set RN_R (X) = R^*X - R_*X is called the *R-boundary region of X,* and thus consists of those objects that we cannot decisively classify into X on the basis of knowledge in R. The set U - R^*X is called the *R – outside region of X* and consists of those objects, which can be certainly classified as do not belonging to X (on the basis of knowledge in R). A set is said to be *rough* (respectively *crisp*) if the boundary region is non-empty (respectively empty).

Example 5.6 Let X = {x: *Walk* (x) = *Yes*}, as given by Table 7. In fact, the set X consists of three objects: x_1, x_4, x_6 . Now, we want to describe this set in terms of the set of conditional attributes A = {*Age, LEMS*}. Using the above definitions, we obtain the following approximations: the A-lower approximation $A_*X = \{x_1, x_6\}$, the A-upper approximation $A^*X = \{x_1, x_3, x_4, x_6\}$, the A-boundary region RN_S (X) = {x_3, x_4}, and the A-outside region U - $A^*X = \{x_2, x_5, x_7\}$. It is easy to see that the set X together with the equivalence classes contained in the corresponding approximations are shown in Figure 3.

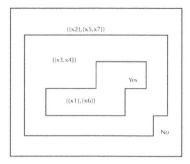

FIGURE 3   Representation of equivalent classes.

It is easily seen that the lower and the upper approximations of a set, are respectively, the interior and the closure of this set in the topology generated by the indiscernibility relation.

Example 5.9 Let us consider a decision system shown in Table 8 in order to explain the above definitions.

TABLE 8   Decision system

Patient	Headache	Muscle-pain	Temperature	Flu
P1	No	yes	high	yes
P2	Yes	no	high	yes
P3	Yes	Yes	very high	yes
P4	No	yes	normal	no
P5	Yes	no	high	no
P6	No	yes	very high	yes

Let X = {x: Flu(x) = Yes} = {p1, p2, p3, p6} and the set of attributes R = {*Headache, Muscle-pain, Temperature*}. The set X is roughly R-definable, because $R_*(X)$ = {p1, p3, p6} $\neq \emptyset$ and $R^*(X)$ = {p1, p2, p3, p5, p6} $\neq$ U. For this case we get the accuracy of approximation $\alpha_R(X)$ = 3/5. It means that the set X can be characterized partially employing symptoms (attributes) *Headache, Muscle-pain* and *Temperature*. Taking only one symptom R = {*Headache*} we get $R_*(X) = \emptyset$ and $R^*(X)$ = U, which means that the set X is totally undefinable in terms of attribute *Headache*, that is, this attribute is not characteristic for the set X whatsoever. However, taking single attribute R = {*Temperature*} we get $R_*(X)$ = {p3, p6} and $R^*(X)$ = {p1, p2, p3, p5, p6}. Thus the set X is again roughly definable, but in this case we obtain $\alpha_R(X)$ = 2/5, which means that the single symptom *Temperature* is less characteristic for the set X, than the whole set of symptoms, and patient p1 cannot be now classified as having flu in this case.

5.8   DEPENDENCY OF ATTRIBUTES

An important issue in data is discovering dependencies between attributes. Intuitively, a set of attributes D depends totally on a set of attributes C, denoted C $\Rightarrow$ D, if all values of attributes from D are uniquely determined by values of attributes from C. In other words, D depends totally on C, if there exists a functional dependency between values of D and C.

Formally, a functional dependency can be defined in the following way. Let D and C be subsets of A.

We say that D depends on C in a degree k ($0 \leq k \leq 1$), denoted C $\Rightarrow$ D_k
If:

$$K = \gamma(C,D) = \frac{|POS_C(D)|}{|U|}$$

where $POS_C(D) = \bigcup_{X \in U/D} C_*(X)$ called a positive region of the partition U/D with respect to C, is the set of all elements of U that can be uniquely classified to blocks of the partition U/D, by means of C.

Obviously:

$$\gamma(C,D) = \sum_{X \in U/D} \frac{|C_*(x)|}{|U|}.$$

If k = 1 we say that D depends totally on C, and if k $<$ 1, we say that D depends partially (in a degree k) on C.

The coefficient k expresses the ratio of all elements of the universe, which can be properly classified to blocks of the partition U/D, employing attributes C and is called the degree of the dependency.

Example 5.10 Let us consider again a decision system shown in Table 8. For example, for dependency {Headache, Muscle-pain, Temperature} $\Rightarrow$ {Flu} we get k = 4/6 = 2/3, because four out of six patients can be uniquely classified as having flu or not, employing attributes Headache, Muscle-pain and Temperature.

If we were interested in how exactly patients can be diagnosed using only the attribute Temperature, that is – in the degree of the dependence {Temperature} $\Rightarrow$ {Flu}, we would get k = 3/6 = 1/2, since in this case only three patients p3, p4, and p6 out of six can be uniquely classified as having flu. In contrast to the previous case patient p4 cannot be classified now as having flu or not. Hence the single attribute Temperature offers worse classification than the whole set of attributes Headache, Muscle-pain and Temperature. it is interesting to observe that neither Headache nor Muscle-pain can be used to recognize flu, because for both dependencies {Headache} $\Rightarrow$ {Flu} and {Muscle-pain} $\Rightarrow$ {Flu} we have k = 0.

It can be easily seen that if D depends totally on C then IND(C) $\subseteq$ IND(D). This means that the partition generated by C is finer than the partition generated by D. Let us notice that the concept of dependency discussed above corresponds to that considered in relational databases.

Summing up: D is totally (partially) dependent on C, if employing C all (possibly some) elements of the universe U may be uniquely classified to blocks of the partition U/D.

Example 5.11 Consider the information given in Table 9.

TABLE 9 Information Table CAR

Object	Condition attributes (C)			Decision attributes (D)
u	Engine	Size	Color	d
x_1	Propane	Compact	Black	Good
x_2	Diesel	Medium	Gold	Bad
x_3	Diesel	Full	White	Bad
x_4	Diesel	Medium	Red	Bad
x_5	Gasoline	Compact	Black	Good
x_6	Gasoline	Medium	Silver	Good
x_7	Gasoline	Full	White	Bad
x_8	Gasoline	Compact	Silver	Bad

Let us select two subsets of attributes A = {Engine, Size} and B = {Engine}. The partition $\overline{A}$ (classification U/IND(A)) corresponding to equivalence relation IND(Engine), imposed by attributes set A, is $\overline{A} = \{Y_1 = \{x_1\}, Y_2 = \{x_2, x_4\}, Y_3 = \{x_3\}, Y_4 = \{x_5, x_8\}, Y_5 = \{x_6\}, Y_6 = \{x_7\}\}$.

The partition $\overline{B}$ (classification U/IND(B)) corresponding to the equivalence relation IND(Engine), imposed by attributes set B, is $\overline{B} = \{X_1 = \{x_1\}, X_2 = \{x_2, x_3, x_4\}, X_3 = \{x_5, x_6, x_7, x_8\}\}$.

The A-positive region of B is:

$$POS_A(B) = \bigcup_{X \in \overline{B}} A_* X = A_* X_1 + A_* X_2 + A_* X_3 = \{x_1\} + \{x_2, x_3, x_4\} + \{x_5, x_6, x_7, x_8\}.$$

Hence, $K = \gamma(A, B) = \dfrac{POS_A(B)}{|U|} = \dfrac{8}{8} = 1$, which indicates that B is totally dependent on A, that is A → B.

Let us select two other subsets of attributes A = {Engine, Size} and B = {Color}. The partition $\overline{A}$ is now, $\overline{A} = \{Y_1 = \{x_1\}, Y_2 = \{x_2, x_4\}, Y_3 = \{x_3\}, Y_4 = \{x_5, x_8\}, Y_5 = \{x_6\}, Y_6 = \{x_7\}\}$.

The partition $\overline{B}$ (classification U/IND(B)) corresponding to the equivalence relation IND(Engine), imposed by attributes set B = {Color}, is $\overline{B} = \{X_1 = \{x_1, x_5\}, X_2 = \{x_2\}, X_3 = \{x_3 x_7\}, X_4 = \{x_4\}, X_5 = \{x_6, x_8\}\}$. The A-positive region of B is,

$$POS_A(B) = \bigcup_{X \in \overline{B}} A_* X = A_* X_1 + A_* X_2 + A_* X_3 + A_* X_4 + A_* X_5$$

$$= \{x_1\} + \{ \quad \} + \{ x_3, x_7 \} + \{ \quad \} + \{x_6\}.$$

Hence, $K = \gamma(A, B) = \dfrac{4}{8} = 0.5$, which indicates that B is dependence of A in degree 0.5, that is $A \rightarrow B$.

5.9 APPROXIMATION AND ACCURACY OF CLASSIFICATION

The concept of set approximation can be extended to approximation of a classification related to the family Υ of objects subsets {X1, X2, ..., Xn} from U. Let S=<U,Q,V,f> be an information system and let R⊆Q, and let Υ={X1, X2,............, Xn} for every Xi⊆U(1<=i<=n) be a classification(a partition, a familyof subsets) of U. The family of sets Υ={X1, X2, ..., Xn} is a classification in U in S, if Xi∩Xj= Ø for every i,j<=n, i≠j and $\bigcup_{i=1}^{n} X_i = U$. Xi are called classes of Υ. For R⊆Q the R-lower and R-uper approximation of a classification Υ on S, denoted by $R_* \Upsilon$ and $R^* \Upsilon$ respectively are defined as follows:

$$R_* \Upsilon = \{R_* X1, R_* X2, ..., R_* Xn\}$$

$$\overline{A}\Upsilon = \{R^* X1, R^* X2, ..., R^* Xn\}$$

The set $R_* \Upsilon$ is called R-positive region of classification Υ and BNR(Υ)= $R^*\Upsilon$-R_* Υ is called R-boundary of classification Υ. The R-positive region of classification Υ with respect to R is defined as:

$$POS_R(\Upsilon) = \bigcup_{x_i \in \Upsilon} R_* X_i$$

and:

$$BN_R(\Upsilon) = \bigcup_{x_i \in \Upsilon} BN_R(X_i)$$

is called R-doubtful region of a classification Υ in S.

Since $U = \bigcup_{x_i \in \Upsilon} R_* X_i$, thus there is no R-negative region of a classification Υ in S. The classification Υ is called R-definable iff every class Xi $\in \Upsilon$ is R-definable, otherwise the classification Y is called non-definable. And the classification Y is called roughly R-definable iff $\exists\ Xi \in Y$, $R^*Xi=\emptyset$.

The accuracy of approximation of classification of Y by the set of attributes R (or shortly accuracy of classification) is defined as follows:

$$\alpha_R(Y)=\frac{\sum_{i=1}^{n} card\,(R_*X_i)}{\sum_{i=1}^{n} card(R^*X_i)}$$

The quality of approximation of classification Y by R (or shortly quality of classification) is defined as follows:

$$\rho_R(Y)=\frac{\sum_{i=1}^{n} card(R_*X_i)}{card(U)}$$

which represents the ratio of all R-correctly classified objects to all objects in the system S.

The idea of accuracy of classification allows us to define how close one can approximate a partition (classification) B^* generated by the set of attributes $B \subseteq Q$ by another partition R^* generated by the set of attributes $R \subseteq Q$. The accuracy of approximation of classification B^* by R^* can be defined as:

$$\rho_R(B^*) = \frac{card\,POS_R(B^*)}{card(U)}$$

Where

$$POS_R(B^*) = \bigcup_{X_i \in B^*} R_*X_i$$

is called a positive region of B^* with respect to R. Of course the following inequality hold $0 \le \rho_R(B^*) \le 1$ for every R, $B \subseteq Q$.

Example 5.12 Suppose we are given the information system from Table 5. Let R = {p, q, r, s} (R = Q) and the classification is defined as $Y = \{Y_1, Y_2, Y_3\}$, where:

$Y_1 = \{x_1, x_2, x_3\}$

$Y_2 = \{x_4, x_5, x_6, x_7\}$

$Y_3 = \{x_8, x_9\}$

We recall that R-elementary sets are: $Z_1 = \{x_1, x_5, x_7\}$, $Z_2 = \{x_2, x_6\}$, $Z_3 = \{x_3, x_9\}$, $Z_4 = \{x_4\}$, and $Z_5 = \{x_8\}$.

The information system with this classification is shown in Table 10.

TABLE 10   An information system with classification

Y	U	p	q	r	s

TABLE 10   *(continued)*

Y_1	x_1	0	1	1	0
	x_2	2	1	0	1
	x_3	0	0	0	1
Y_2	x_4	1	0	2	0
	x_5	0	1	1	0
	x_6	2	1	0	1
Y_3	x_7	0	1	1	0
	x_8	1	0	2	1
	x_9	0	0	0	1

Then, the classification accuracy $\alpha_A(Y)$ and classification quality $\rho_A(Y)$ are computed as follows:

$$R_*Y = \{R_*Y_1,\ R_*Y_2,\ R_*Y_3\} = \{\{\}, Z_4, Z_5\} = \{\{\}, \{x_4\}, \{x_8\}\}$$

$$R^*Y = \{R^*Y_1, R^*Y_2, R^*Y_3\} = \{\{Z_1,\ Z_2,\ Z_3\}, \{Z_1,\ Z_2,\ Z_4\}, \{Z_3,\ Z_5,\}\} =$$
$$\{\{x_1, x_2, x_3, x_5, x_6, x_7, x_9\}, \{x_1, x_2, x_4, x_5, x_6, x_7,\}, \{x_3, x_8, x_9\}\}$$

$$\alpha_R(Y) = \frac{0+1+1}{7+6+3} = 0.125$$

$$\rho_R(Y) = \frac{0+1+1}{9} = 0.222.$$

5.10   REDUCTION OF ATTRIBUTES

In the Section 5.4 we investigated one of the natural aspects of reducing data which concerns identifying equivalence classes, that is objects that are indiscernible based on the available attributes. In order to make some savings only one element of the equivalence class is needed to present the entire class. The other aspect in data reduction is to keep only those attributes that preserve the indiscrenibility relation and consequently, set approximation. The rejected attributes are redundant since their removal cannot worse the classification.

In order to express the above idea more precisely we need some auxiliary notions. Let $S = (U, A)$ be an information system, $R \subseteq A$, and let $A \in R$.

We say that a is dispensable in R if $IND_S (R) = IND_S (R - \{a\})$, otherwise a is indispensable in R.

A set R is called independent if all its attributes are indispensable.

Any subset R' of R is called a reduct of R if R' is independent and $IND_S (R') = IND_S (R)$.

Hence, a reduct is a set of attributes that preserves partition. It means that a reduct is the minimal subset of attributes that enables the same classification of elements of the universe as the whole set of attributes. In other words, attributes that do not belong to a reduct are superfluous with regard to classification of elements of the universe.

There is usually several such subsets of attributes and those, which are minimal are called reducts. Computing equivalence classes is straightforward. Finding a minimal reduct (that is reduct with a minimal number of attributes) among all reducts is NP-hard. It is easy to that the number of reducts of an information systems with m attributes may be equal to:

$$\binom{m}{[m/2]}.$$

This means that computing reducts is not a trivial task. This fact is one of the bottlenecks of the rough set methodology. Fortunately, there exist good heuristics based on genetic algorithms that compute sufficiently many reducts in often acceptable time, unless the number of attributes is very high.

The reducts have several important properties. In what follows we present two of them. First, we define a notion of a core of attributes.

Let B be a subset A. The core of B is the set of all indispensable attributes of R.

The following is an important property, connecting the notion of the core and reducts:

$$\text{Core } (R) = \bigcap \text{ Red } (R),$$

where Red (R) is the set of all reducts of R.

Because the core is the intersection of all reducts, it is included in every reduct, that is, each element of the core belongs to some reduct. Thus, in a sense, the core is the most important subset of attributes, for none of its elements can be removed without affecting the classification power of attributes.

To further simplification of an information table we can eliminate some values of attribute from the table in such a way that we are still able to discern objects in the table as the original one. To this end we can apply similar procedure as to eliminate superfluous attributes, which is defined next.

We say that the value of attribute $a \in R$, is dispensable for x, if $[x]_R = [x]_{R-\{a\}}$, otherwise the value of attribute a is indispensable for x.

If for every attribute $a \in R$ the value of a is indispensable for x, then R is called orthogonal for x.

A subset $R' \subseteq R$ is a value reduct of R for x, if R' is orthogonal for x and $[x]_R = [x]_{R'}$.

The set of all indispensable values of attributes in R for x is called the value core of R for x, and is denoted CORE* (R).

Also in this case have:

CORE* (R) == $\cap$ Red* (R),

where Red* (R) is the family of all reducts of R for x.

Suppose we are given a dependency $C \Rightarrow D$. It may happen that the set D depends not on the whole set C but on its subset C' and therefore we might be interested to find this subset. In order to solve this problem we need the notion of a relative reduct, which is defined and discussed next.

Let $C, D \subseteq A$. Obviously, if $C' \subseteq C$ is a D-reduct of C, then C' is a minimal subset of C such that $\gamma\ (C, D) = \gamma\ (C', D)$.

We say that attribute $a \in C$ is D-dispensable in C, if $POS_C(D) = POS_{(C-\{a\})}(D)$, otherwise the attribute a is D-indispensable in C.

If all attributes $a \in C$ are C-indispensable in C, then C is called D-independent.

A subset $C' \subseteq C$ is a D-reduct of C, iff C' is D-independent and $POS_C(D) = POS_{C'}(D)$.

The set of all D-indispensable attributes in C is called D-core of C and is denoted by $CORE_D(C)$. In this case we have also the property:

$$CORE_D(C) = \cap\ RED_D(C),$$

where RED_D (C) is the family of all D-reducts of C. If D = C we get the previous definitions.

Example 5.13 In Table 7, there are two relative reducts with respect to Flu, {Headache, Temperature} and {Muscle-pain, Temperature} of the set of condition attributes {Headache, Muscle-pain, and Temperature}. That means that either the attribute Headache or Muscle-pain can be eliminated from the table and consequently instead of Table 7 we can use either Table 11 or Table 12.

TABLE 11   Reduced order decision table with headache and temperature

Patient	Headache	Temperature	Flu
p1	no	high	yes
P2	yes	high	yes
P3	yes	very high	yes

TABLE 11   *(continued)*

P4	no	normal	no
P5	yes	high	no
P6	no	very high	yes

TABLE 12   Reduced order decision table with muscle pain and temperature

Patient	Muscle-pain	Temperature	Flu
p1	Yes	high	yes
P2	no	high	yes
P3	yes	very high	yes
P4	Yes	normal	no
P5	No	high	no
P6	yes	very high	yes

For Table 7 the relative core of with respect to the set {Headache, Muscle-pain, and Temperature} is the Temperature. This confirms our previous considerations showing that Temperature is the only symptom that enables, at least, partial diagnosis of patients.

We also need a concept of a value reduct and value core. Suppose we are given a dependency $C \implies D$, where C is relative D-reduct of C. For further investigation of the dependency we might be interested to know exactly how values of attributes from D depend on values of attributes from C. To this end we need a procedure eliminating values of attributes form C, which does not influence on values of attributes from D.

We say that value of attribute $a \in C$, is D-dispensable for $x \in U$, if $[x]_C \subseteq [x]_D$ implies $[x]_{C-\{a\}} \subseteq [x]_D$; , otherwise the value of attribute a is D-indispensable for x.

If for every attribute $a \in C$ value of a is D-indispensable for x, then C will be called D-independent (orthogonal) for x.

A subset $C' \subseteq C$ is a D-reduct of C, for x (a value reduct), if C' is D-independent for x and $[x]_C \subseteq [x]_D$ implies $[x]_{C'} \subseteq [x]_D$.

The set of all D-indispensable for x values of attributes in C is called D-core of C for x (the value core), and is denoted $CORE_D^x(C)$ (C).

We have also the following property:

$$CORE_D^x(C) = \cap \, Red_D^x(C),$$

where $Red_D^x(C)$ is the family of all D-reducts of C for x.

Using the concept of a value reduct, Table 11 and Table 12 can be simplified as follows:

TABLE 13   Further reduction of Table 11

Patient	Headache	Temperature	Flu
p1	no	high	yes
P2	yes	high	yes
P3	--	very high	yes
P4	--	normal	no
P5	yes	high	no
P6	--	very high	yes

TABLE 14   Further reduction of Table 12

Patient	Muscle-pain	Temperature	Flu
p1	Yes	high	yes
P2	no	high	yes
P3	--	very high	yes
P4	--	normal	no
P5	no	high	no
P6	--	very high	yes

We can present the obtained results in a form of a decision algorithm. For Table 13 we get:
- If (Headache, no) and (Temperature, high) then (Flu, yes),
- If (Headache, yes) and (Temperature, high) then (Flu, yes),
- If (Temperature, very high) then (Flu, yes),
- If (Temperature, normal) then (Flu, no),
- If (Headache, yes) and (Temperature, high) then (Flu, no), and
- If (Temperature, very high) then (Flu, yes).

and for Table 14 we have:
- If (Muscle-pain, yes) and (Temperature, high) then (Flu, yes),
- If (Muscle-pain, no) and (Temperature, high) then (Flu, yes),
- If (Temperature, very high) then (Flu, yes),
- If (Temperature, normal) then (Flu, no),
- If (Muscle pain, no) and (Temperature, high) then (Flu, no), and
- If (Temperature, very high) then (Flu, yes).

The following important property:

$B' \implies B - B'$, where B' is a reduct of B,

connects reducts and dependency.

Besides, we have:

If $B \implies C$, then $B \implies C'$, for every $C' \subseteq C$, in particular:

If B $\Rightarrow$ C, then B $\Rightarrow$ {a}, for every a $\in$ C.

Moreover, we have:

If B' is a reduct of B, the neither {a} $\Rightarrow$ {b} nor {b} $\Rightarrow$ {a} holds, for every a, b $\in$ B'

that is, all attributes in a reduct are pair wise independent.

5.11 DISCERNIBILITY MATRICES AND FUNCTIONS

In order to compute reducts and the core easily we can use discernibility matrix, which is defined below.

Let S = (U, A) be an information system with n objects.

The discernibility matrix S is a symmetric n x n matrix with entries c_{ij} as given below:

$$c_{ij} = \{ a \in A \mid a\,(x_1) \neq a(\,x_j)\} \text{ for } i, j = 1, ..., n.$$

Each entry thus consists of the set of attributes upon, which object x_i and x_j differ. Since discernibility matrix is symmetric and $c_{ij} = \emptyset$ (the empty set) for i = 1, ..., n. Thus, this matrix can be represented using only elements in its lower triangular part, that is for $1 \leq j \leq i \leq n$.

With every discernibility matrix we can uniquely associate a discernibility function defined below:

A discernibility function f_s for an information system S is a Boolean function of m Boolean variables a_1^*, ..., a_m^* (corresponding to the attribute a_1, ..., a_m) defined as follows:

$$f_s(a_1^*, ..., a_m^*) = \forall \{ \exists c_{ij}^* \mid 1.j \leq i \leq n, c_{ij} \leq \phi\}$$

where $c_{ij}^* = \{ a^* \mid a \in c_{ij}\}$. The set of all prime implicants of f_s determines the set of all reducts of A.

Example 5.14 Using the above definitions for the information system S from Example 5.7 (Table 7), we obtain the following discernibility matrix presented in Table 15 and discernibility function presented below.

TABLE 15 Descernibility matrix

	P1	P2	P3	P4	P5	P6
P1						
P2	H, M					
P3	H, T	M, T				
P4	T, F	H, M, T, F	H, T, F			
P5	H, M, F	F	M, T, F	H, M, T		
P6	T	H, M, T	H	T, F	H, M, T, F	

In this table H, M, T, and F denote Headache, Muscle-pain, Temperature and Flu, respectively. The descernibility function for this table is:

$$f_S \ (H, M, T, F) = (H \lor M) \ (H \lor T)(T \lor F) \ (H \lor M \ \lor F) \ T$$

$$\Rightarrow (M \lor T) \ (H \lor M \ \lor T \ \lor F) \ F \ (H \lor M \ \lor T)$$

$$\Rightarrow (H \lor T \ \lor F) \ (M \lor T \ \lor F)H$$

$$\Rightarrow (H \lor M \ \lor T \ ) \ (T \ \lor F)$$

$$\Rightarrow (H \lor M \ \lor T \ \lor F)$$

where $\lor$ denotes the disjunction and the conjunction is omitted in the formula.

Let us also notice that each row in the above discernibility function corresponds to one column in the discernibility matrix. This matrix is symmetrical with the empty diagonal. Each parenthesized tuple is a conjunction in the Boolean expression, and where the one-letter Boolean variables correspond to the attribute names in an obvious way. After simplification, the discernibility function using laws of Boolean algebra we obtain the following expression HTF, which says that there is only one reduct {H, T, F} in the data table and it is the core.

Relative reducts and core can be computed also using the discernibility matrix as follows;

$$c_{ij} = \{ a \in C : a(x_i) \ \neq \ a(x_j) \ \text{and} \ w(x_i, x_j)\},$$

where $w(x_i, x_j \equiv x_i \in POS_C \ (D) \ \text{and} \ x_j \notin POS_C \ (D) \ \text{or}$

$$x_i \notin POS_C \ (D) \ \text{and} \ x_j \in POS_C \ (D) \ \text{or}$$

$$x_i, x_j \in POS_C \ (D) \ \text{and} \ (x_j , x_j)\notin \text{IND} \ (D)$$

For I, j = 1, 2, ..., n.

If the partition defined by D is definable by C then the condition $w \ (x_i, x_j)$ in the above definition can be reduced to $(x_i, x_j)) \notin \text{IND} \ (D)$.

Thus, entry c_{ij} is the set of all attributes, which discern objects x_i and x_j that do not belong to the same equivalence class of the relation IND (D).

If we instead construct a Boolean function by restricting the conjunction to only run over column k in the discernibility matrix (instead of over all columns), we obtain the so-called k-relative discernibility function. The set of all prime implicants of this function determines the set of all k-relative reducts of A. These reducts reveal the minimum amount of information needed to discern $x_k \in U$ (or, more precisely, [x_k] $\subseteq U$) from all other objects.

Example 5.15 Considering the information system S from Example 5.7 as a decision system, we can illustrate the above considerations by computing relative reducts for the set of attributes {Headache, Muscle-pain, Temperature} with respect to Flu. The corresponding discernibility matrix is shown in Table 16.

TABLE 16   Discernibility matrix using relative reducts

	P1	P2	P3	P4	P5	P6
P1						
P2						
P3						
P4	T	H, M, T				
P5	H, M		M, T			
P6				T	H, M, T	

The descernibility function for this table is:

$$T(H \lor M)(H \lor M \lor T)(M \lor T).$$

After simplication the discernibility function, we obtain the following expression THVTM, Which represents two reducts TH and TM in the data table and T is the core.

5.12   SIGNIFICANCE OF ATTRIBUTES AND APPROXIMATE REDUCTS

As it follows from considerations concerning reduction of attributes, they (attributes) cannot be equally important, and some of them (attributes) can be eliminated from an information table without losing information contained in the table. The idea of attribute reduction can be generalized by introducing a concept of significance of attributes, which enables us evaluation of attributes not only by two-valued scale, dispensable – indispensable, but by assigning to an attribute a real number from the closed interval [0, 1], expressing how important is an attribute in an information table.

Significance of an attribute can be evaluated by measuring effect of removing the attribute from an information table on classification defined by the table. Let us first start our consideration with decision tables.

Let C and D be sets of condition and decision attributes respectively and let a be a condition attribute, that is, $a \in C$. As shown previously the number $\gamma(C, D)$ expresses a degree of consistency of the decision table or the degree of dependency between attributes C and D, of accuracy of approximation of U/D by C. We can ask how the coefficient $\gamma(C, D)$ changes when removing the attribute a, that is, what is the difference between $\gamma(C, D)$ and $\gamma(C-\{a\}, D)$.

We can normalize the difference and define the significance of the attribute a as:

$$\sigma_{(C,D)}(a) = \frac{(\gamma(C,D) - \gamma(C - \{a\}, D))}{\gamma(C,D)} = 1 - \frac{\gamma(C - \{a\}, D)}{\gamma(C,D)},$$

and denoted simple by $\sigma(a)$, when C and D are understood.

Obviously, $0 \leq \sigma(a) \leq 1$. The more important is the attribute a the greater is the number $\sigma(a)$. For example for condition attributes in Table 7 we have the following results:

$$\sigma(Headache) = 0,$$

$$\sigma(Muscle - pain) = 0,$$

$$\sigma(Temperature) = 0.75.$$

Because the significance of the attribute Temperature or Muscle-pain is zero, removing either of the attributes from condition attributes does not effect the set of consistent decision rules, whatsoever. Hence the attribute Temperature is the most significant one in the table. That means that by removing the attribute Temperature, 75% (three out of four) of consistent decision rules disappear from the table, thus lack of the attribute essentially effects the "decisive power" of the decision table.

For a reduct of condition attributes, for example {Headache and Temperature}, we get:

$$\sigma(Headache) = 0.25,$$

$$\sigma(Temperature) = 1.00.$$

In this case, removing the attribute Headache from the reduct, that is, using only the attribute Temperature, 25% (one out of four) of consistent decision rules are lost, and dropping the attribute Temperature, that is, using only the attribute Headache 100% (all) consistent decision rules are lost. That means that in this case making decisions is impossible at all, whereas by employing only the attribute Temperature some decision can be made.

Thus the coefficient $\sigma(a)$ can be understood as an error, which occurs when attribute a is dropped. The significance coefficient can be extended to set of attributes as follows:

$$\sigma_{(C,D)}(B) = \frac{(\gamma(C,D) - \gamma(C - B, D))}{\gamma(C,D)} = 1 - \frac{\gamma(C - B, D)}{\gamma(C,D)}$$

denoted by $\varepsilon(B)$, if C and D are understood, where B is a subset of C.

If B is a reduct of C, then $\varepsilon(B) = 1$, that is, removing any reduct from a set of decision rules unables to make sure decisions, whatsoever.

Any subset B of C will be called an approximate reduct of C, and the number:

$$\varepsilon_{(C,D)}(B) = \frac{(\gamma(C,D) - \gamma(B,D))}{\gamma(C,D)} = 1 - \frac{\gamma(B,D))}{\gamma(C,D)}$$

denoted simple as ε (B), is called an error of reduct approximation. It expresses how exactly the set of attributes B approximates the set of condition attributes C. Obviously, ε (B)= $1 - \sigma(B)$ and ε (B) = $1 - \varepsilon(C - B)$. For any subset B of C we have $\varepsilon(B) \leq \varepsilon(C)$. If B is a reduct of C, then ε (B)=0.

For example, either of attributes Headache and Temperature can be considered as approximate reducts of {Headache, Temperature}, and:

$$\varepsilon(Headache) = 1,$$

$$\varepsilon(Temperature) = 0.25.$$

But for the whole set of condition attributes {Headache, Muscle-pain, and Temperature} we have also the following approximate reduct:

$$\varepsilon(Headache, \ Muscle - pain) = 0.75.$$

The concept of an approximate reduct is a generalization of the concept of a reduct considered previously. The minimal subset B of condition attributes C, such that $\gamma(C,D) = \gamma(B,D)$, or $\varepsilon_{(C,D)}(B) = 0$ is a reduct in the previous sense. The idea of an approximate reduct can be useful in cases, when a smaller number of condition attributes is preferred over accuracy of classification.

5.13 DECISION RULE SYNTHESIS

We have realized that the reducts (of all the various types) can be used to synthesize minimal decision rules. Once the reducts have been computed, the rules are easily constructed by overlaying the reducts over the originating decision table and reading off the values.

Example 5.16 Given the reduct {Headache, Temperature} in Table 11, the rule read off the first object is "if Headache is no and Temperature is high then Flu is yes."

We shall make these notions precise.

Let S = (U, A $\cup$ {d} be a decision system and let V = U {V_a: a $\in$ A} $\cup$ V_d. Atomic formulae over:

B $\subseteq$ A $\cup$ {d} and V are expressions of the form a = v, they are called descriptors over B and V, where a $\in$ B and v $\in$ V_a. The set F(B, V) of formulae over B and V is the least set containing all atomic formulae over B and V and closed with respect to the prepositional connectives $\wedge$ (conjunction), $\vee$ (disjunction), and $\neg$ (negation).

Let ϕ $\in$ F(B, V). $\| \phi_A \|$ denotes the meaning of φ in the decision table A, which is the set of all objects in U with the property φ.

These sets are defined as follows:

1. If φ is of the form $a = v$ then $\| \varphi_a \| = \{x \in U \mid a(x) = v\}$

2. $\| \varphi \wedge \varphi'_A \| = \| \varphi_A \| \cap \| \varphi'_A \|$; $\| \varphi \vee \varphi'_A \| = \| \varphi_A \| \cup \| \varphi'_A \|$; $\| \sim \varphi_A \| = U - \| \varphi_A \|$

The set F(B, V) is called the set of conditional formulae of A and is denoted C(B, V).

A decision rule for A is any expression of the form $\varphi \Rightarrow d = v$, where $\varphi \in C(B, V)$, $v \in V_d$ and $\| \varphi_A \| \neq 0$. Formulae φ and $d = v$ are referred to as the predecessor and the successor of decision rule $\varphi \Rightarrow d = v$.

Decision rule $\varphi \Rightarrow d = v$ is true in A if, and only if, $\| \varphi_A \| \subseteq \| d = v_A \|$;, $\| \varphi_A \|$ is the set of objects matching the decision rule, $\| \varphi_A \| \cap \| d = v_A \|$ is the set of objects supporting the rule.

Example 5.17 Looking again at Table 14, some of the rules are:
(Headache = no) $\wedge$ (Temperature = high) $\Rightarrow$ (Flu = yes),
(Headache = yes) $\wedge$ (Temperature = high) $\Rightarrow$ (Flu = yes).
The first rule is true in Table 14, while the second one is not true in that table.

Several numerical factors can be associated with a synthesized rule. For example, the support of a decision rule is the number of objects that match the predecessor of the rule. Various frequency-related numerical quantities may be computed from such counts like the accuracy coefficient equal to:

$$\frac{\| \varphi_A \| \cap \| d = v_A \|}{\| \varphi_A \|}.$$

For a systematic overview of rule synthesis see for example [213].

5.13.1 DECISION TABLES AND DECISION RULES

If we distinguish in an information system two disjoint classes of attributes, called condition and decision attributes, respectively, then the system is called a decision table and will be denoted by S = (U, C, D), where C and D are disjoint sets of condition and decision attributes, respectively.

Let s = (U, C, D) be a decision table. Every $x \in U$ determines a sequence $c_1(x)$, ..., $c_n(x)$, $d_1(x)$, ..., $d_m(x)$, where $\{c_1, ..., c_n\} = C$ and $\{d_1, ..., d_m\} = D$.

The sequence is called a decision rule induced by x (in S) and is denoted by $c_1(x)$, ..., $c_n(x) \rightarrow d_1(x)$, ..., $d_m(x)$ or in short $C \rightarrow_x D$.

The number $\text{supp}_x (C, D) = |A(x)| = |C(x) \cap D(x)|$ is called a support of the decision rule $C \rightarrow_x D$

And the number:

$$\sigma_x (C, D) = \frac{\text{supp}_x (C, D)}{|U|}$$

is referred to as the strength of the decision rule C $\rightarrow_x$ D, where |X| denotes to cardinality of X.

With every decision rule C $\rightarrow_x$ D we associate the certainty factor of the decision rule, denoted:

$$cer_x (C, D) = \frac{|C(x) \cap D(x)|}{|C(x)|} = \frac{supp_x (C,D)}{|C(x)|} = \frac{\sigma_x (C,D)}{\pi(C(x))},$$

where $\pi(C(x)) = \frac{|C(x)|}{|U|}$.

The certainty factor may be interpreted as a conditional probability that y belongs to D(x) given y belongs to C(x), symbolically π_x (D|C).

If cer_x (C, D) = 1, then C $\rightarrow_x$ D will be called a certain decision rule, if $0 < cer_x$ (C, D) < 1 then decision rule will be referred to as an uncertain decision rule.

Besides, we also use a coverage factor of the decision rule, denoted cov_x (C, D) and defined as:

$$cov_x (C, D) = \frac{|C(x) \cap D(x)|}{|D(x)|} = \frac{supp_x (C,D)}{|D(x)|} = \frac{\sigma_x (C,D)}{\pi(D(x))},$$

where $\pi(C(x)) = \frac{|D(x)|}{|U|}$.

Similarly,

$$cov_x (C, D) = \pi_x (C|D).$$

If C $\rightarrow_x$ D is a decision rule then D $\rightarrow_x$ C is called an inverse decision rule. The inverse decision rules can be used to give explanations (reasons) for a decision.

For Table 1 of section 5.2, we have the certainty and coverage factors are as shown in Table 17.

TABLE 17   Parameters of the decision rules

Decision rule	Strength	Certainty	Coverage
1	0.20	0.48	0.33
2	0.10	1.00	0.17
3	0.30	1.00	0.50
4	0.15	1.00	0.38
5	0.22	0.52	0.55
6	0.03	1.00	0.07

Let us observe that if C $\rightarrow_x$ D is a decision rule then:

$$\bigcup_{y \in D(x)} \{ C(y) : C(y) \subseteq D(x) \}$$

is the lower approximation of the decision class D(x), by condition classes C(y), whereas the set:

$$\bigcup_{y \in D(x)} \{ C(y) : C(y) \cap D(x) \neq \emptyset \}$$

is the upper approximation of the decision class by condition classes C(y).

Approximations and decision rules are two different methods to express properties of data. Approximations suit better to express topological properties of data, whereas decision rules describe in a simple way hidden patterns in data.

5.13.2 PROBABILISTIC PROPERTIES OF DECISION TABLES

Decision tables (and decision algorithms) have important probabilistic properties, which are discussed next.

Let $C \rightarrow_x D$ be a decision rule and let $\Gamma = C(x)$ and $\Delta = D(x)$.
Then the following properties are valid:

$$\sum_{y \in \Gamma} cer_y (C, D) = 1, \tag{5.1}$$

$$\sum_{y \in \Delta} cov_y (C, D) = 1, \tag{5.2}$$

$$\pi (D(x)) = \sum_{y \in \Gamma} cer_y (C, D). \; \pi (C(y)) =$$

$$= \sum_{y \in \Gamma} \sigma_y (C, D), \tag{5.3}$$

$$\pi (C(x)) = \sum_{y \in \Delta} cov_y (C, D). \; \pi (D(y))$$

$$= \sum_{y \in \Delta} \sigma_y (C, D), \tag{5.4}$$

$$cer_x (C, D) = \frac{cov_x (C, D). \; \pi (D(x))}{\sum_{y \in \Delta} cov_y (C, D). \; \pi (D(y))} = \frac{\sigma_x (C, D)}{\pi (C(x))}, \tag{5.5}$$

$$cov_x\left(C,D\right) = \frac{cer_x\left(C,D\right).\ \pi\left(C(x)\right)}{\sum_{y\ \in\ \Gamma}cer_y\left(C,D\right).\ \pi\left(C(y)\right)} = \frac{\sigma_x\left(C,D\right)}{\pi\left(D(x)\right)}. \tag{5.6}$$

That is, any decision table satisfies Equations (5.1)–(5.6). Observe that formulae (5.3) and (5.4) refer to the well-known total probability theorem, whereas (5.5) and (5.6) refer to Bayes' theorem.

Thus, in order to compute the certainty and coverage factors of decision rules according to formula (5.5) and (5.6), it is enough to know the strength (support) of all decision rules only. The strength of decision rules can be computed from data or can be a subjective assessment (See Section 5.2).

5.14   CASE STUDY: DIAGNOSIS OF DENGUE BASED ON ROUGH SET CONCEPT

In this section, we attempt to diagnose the disease dengue based on rough set concept. Table 18 shows the patients data set and respective symptoms. The data are of the discreet type. The elimination of redundant data and the development of a set of rules that can aid the doctor in the elaboration of the diagnosis are based on rough set concept.

5.14.1   INFORMATION SYSTEM CONSISTS OF THE DATA GIVEN IN TABLE 18

TABLE 18   Patients with respective symptoms

Patient	Condition Attributes			Decision Attribute
	blotched_red_skin	muscular_pain_ articulations	Temperature	Dengue
P1	No	No	Normal	No
P2	No	No	High	No
P3	No	No	Very High	Yes
P4	No	Yes	High	Yes
P5	No	Yes	Very High	Yes
P6	Yes	Yes	High	Yes
P7	Yes	Yes	Very High	Yes
P8	No	No	High	No
P9	Yes	No	Very High	Yes
P10	Yes	No	High	No
P11	Yes	No	Very High	No
P12	No	Yes	Normal	No

TABLE 18   *(continued)*

P13	No	Yes	High	Yes
P14	No	Yes	Normal	No
P15	Yes	Yes	Normal	No
P16	Yes	No	Normal	No
P17	Yes	No	High	No
P18	Yes	Yes	Very High	Yes
P19	Yes	No	Normal	No
P20	No	Yes	Normal	No

The set B = {P1, P2, P3, P4, P5, P6, P7, P8, P9, P10, P11, P12, P13, P14, P15, P16, P17, P18, P19, and P20} represents the objects, the set C = {blotched_red_skin, muscular_pain_articulations, and Temperature} represents the conditional attribute and the set D = {dengue} represents the decision attribute.

Table 19 shows the relation between the nominal values and considered attributes.

TABLE 19   Nominal Values of Attributes

	Attributes	Nominal Values
Conditional	blotched_red_skin,	Yes, No
Attributes	muscular_pain_articulations,	Yes, No
	Temperature	Normal, High, Very High
Decision Attributes	Dengue	Yes, No

5.14.2   INDISCERNIBILITY RELATION

Indiscernibility relation is the relation between two objects or more, where all the values are identical in relation to a subset of considered attributes. From Table 18 it can be observed that the attributes that are directly related to patients symptoms are represented by the set C = {blotched_red_skin, muscular_pain_articulations, and temperature}. The indiscernibility relation is given to IND(C).

When Table 14 is broken down, it can be seen that indiscernibility relation is given in relationship to conditional attributes:

The blotched_red_skin attribute generates two indiscernibility sets (See Table 20): IND({blotched_red_skin}) = {{P1, P3, P4, P5, P8, P12, P13, P14, P20},{P6, P7, P9, P10, P11, P15, P16, P17, P18, P19}}.

TABLE 20 Table 18 is organized in relation to blotched_red_skin attribute

Patient	Condition Attributes			Decision Attribute
	blotched_red_skin	muscular_pain_articulations	Temperature	Dengue
P1	No	No	Normal	No
P12	No	Yes	Normal	No
P13	No	Yes	High	Yes
P14	No	Yes	Normal	No
P2	No	Yes	High	No
P20	No	Yes	Normal	No
P3	No	No	Very High	Yes
P4	No	Yes	High	Yes
P5	No	Yes	Very High	Yes
P8	No	No	High	No
P10	Yes	No	High	No
P11	Yes	No	Very High	No
P15	Yes	Yes	Normal	No
P16	Yes	No	Normal	No
P17	Yes	No	High	No
P18	Yes	Yes	Very High	Yes
P19	Yes	No	Normal	No
P6	Yes	Yes	High	Yes
P7	Yes	Yes	Very High	Yes
P9	Yes	No	Very High	Yes

The muscular_pain_articulations attribute generates two indiscernibility sets (See Table 21):

IND({muscular_pain_articulations}) = {{P1, P2, P3, P8, P9, P10, P11, P16, P17, P19}, {P4, P5, P6, P7, P12, P13, P14, P15, P18, P20}}.

TABLE 21　Table 18 is organized in relation to muscular_pain_articulations attribute

Patient	Condition Attributes			Decision Attribute
	blotched_red_skin	muscular_pain_articulations	Temperature	Dengue
P1	No	No	Normal	No
P2	No	No	High	No
P3	No	No	Very High	Yes
P8	No	No	High	No
P9	Yes	No	Very High	Yes
P10	Yes	No	High	No
P11	Yes	No	Very High	No
P16	Yes	No	Normal	No
P17	Yes	No	High	No
P19	Yes	No	Normal	No
P4	No	Yes	High	Yes
P5	No	Yes	Very High	Yes
P6	Yes	Yes	High	Yes
P7	Yes	Yes	Very High	Yes
P12	No	Yes	Normal	No
P13	No	Yes	High	Yes
P14	No	Yes	Normal	No
P15	Yes	Yes	Normal	No
P18	Yes	Yes	Very High	Yes
P20	No	Yes	Normal	No

The temperature attribute generates three indiscernibility sets (See Table 22):
IND({temperature})={{P2, P4, P6, P8, P10, P13, P17}, {P3, P5, P7, P9, P11, P18}, {P1, P12, P14, P15, P16, P19, P20}}.

Table 20, 21, and 22 are organized in relation to conditional attributes and Table 23 is organized in relation to decision attribute.

TABLE 22　Table 18 is organized in relation to temperature attribute

Patient	Condition Attributes			Decision Attribute
	blotched_red_skin	muscular_pain_articulations	Temperature	Dengue

TABLE 22 *(continued)*

P13	No	Yes	High	Yes
P2	No	Yes	High	No
P4	No	Yes	High	Yes
P8	No	No	High	No
P10	Yes	No	High	No
P17	Yes	No	High	No
P6	Yes	Yes	High	Yes
P1	No	No	Normal	No
P12	No	Yes	Normal	No
P14	No	Yes	Normal	No
P20	No	Yes	Normal	No
P15	Yes	Yes	Normal	No
P16	Yes	No	Normal	No
P19	Yes	No	Normal	No
P3	No	No	Very High	Yes
P5	No	Yes	Very High	Yes
P11	Yes	No	Very High	No
P18	Yes	Yes	Very High	Yes
P7	Yes	Yes	Very High	Yes
P9	Yes	No	Very High	Yes

5.14.3 APPROXIMATION

Using is Rough Set Theory the approximations concepts are applied in the Table 18:

TABLE 23 Table 18 is organized in relation to decision attribute

Patient	Condition Attributes			Decision Attribute
	blotched_red_skin	muscular_pain_articulations	Temperature	Dengue
P1	No	No	Normal	No
P2	No	No	High	No
P8	No	No	High	No
P10	Yes	No	High	No
P11	Yes	No	Very High	No
P12	No	Yes	Normal	No

TABLE 23   *(continued)*

P14	No	Yes	Normal	No
P15	Yes	Yes	Normal	No
P16	Yes	No	Normal	No
P17	Yes	No	High	No
P19	Yes	No	Normal	No
P20	No	Yes	Normal	No
P3	No	No	Very High	Yes
P4	No	Yes	High	Yes
P5	No	Yes	Very High	Yes
P6	Yes	Yes	High	Yes
P7	Yes	Yes	Very High	Yes
P9	Yes	No	Very High	Yes
P13	No	Yes	High	Yes
P18	Yes	Yes	Very High	Yes

Lower Approximation set (B_*):
- Lower Approximation set (B_*) of the patients that definitely have dengue is identified as:
  $B_* = \{P3, P4, P5, P6, P7, P13, \text{and } P18\}$,
- Lower Approximation set (B_*) of patients that certainly do not have is identified as:
  $B_* = \{P1, P2, P8, P10, P12, P14, P15, P16, P17, P19, \text{and } P20\}$,

Upper Approximation set B^*
- Upper Approximation set (B^*) of the patients that possibly have dengue are identified as:
  $B_* = \{P3, P4, P5, P6, P7, P9, P13, \text{and } P18\}$,
- Upper Approximation set (B^*) of the patients that possibly have not dengue are identified as:
  $B_* = \{P1, P2, P8, P10, P11, P12, P14, P15, P16, P17, P19, \text{and } P20\}$,
- Boundary Region (BR)

  Boundary Region (BR) of the patients that do not have dengue are identified as:

  $BR = \{P1, P2, P8, P10, P11, P12, P14, P15, P16, P17, P19, \text{and } P20\} - \{P1, P2, P8, P10, P12, P14, P15, P16, P17, P19, \text{and } P20\} = \{P11\}$

- Boundary Region (BR) the set of the patients that do have dengue are identified as:

  $BR = \{P3, P4, P5, P6, P7, P9, P13, \text{and } P18\} - \{P3, P4, P5, P6, P7, P9, P13, \text{and } P18\} = \{P9\}$.

Observation: In Boundary Region (BR), the set constituted by elements P9 and P11, cannot be classified, since they possess the same characteristics in conditional attributes but with different conclusions in the decision attribute.

5.14.4 QUALITY OF APPROXIMATIONS

The two coefficients of quality of approximation are:

IMPRECISION COEFFICIENT

- For the patients with possibility that they are having dengue $\alpha B(X) = 7/8$,

- For the patients with possibility that they are not having dengue $\alpha B(X) = 8/12$.

QUALITY COEFFICIENT OF UPPER AND LOWER APPROXIMATION:

- $\alpha B(B^*(X)) = 8/20$, for the patients that have the possibility of dengue,

- $\alpha B(B^*(X)) = 11/20$, for the patients that do not have the possibility of dengue,

- $\alpha B(B. (X)) = 7/20$, for the patients that have dengue, and

- $\alpha B(B. (X)) = 8/20$, for the patients that do not have dengue.

OBSERVATIONS

Patient with dengue: $\alpha B(B. (X)) = 7/20$, that is, 35% of patients certainly having dengue.

Patient without dengue: $\alpha B(B^*(X)) = 11/20$, that is, approximately 55% of patients certainly do not have dengue.

10% of patients (P9 and P11) cannot be classified neither with dengue nor without dengue, since the characteristics of all conditional attributes are the same, with different decision attribute and generate an inconclusive diagnosis for dengue.

5.14.5 DATA REDUCTION IN INFORMATION SYSTEM

The process of reduction of information is presented below.

Verification inconclusive data:

Step 1 – Analysis of data contained in Table 18 shows that information contained is inconclusive that means, the values of conditional attributes are same and the value of decision attribute is different.

Remark 5.5 The symptoms of patient P9 and patient P11 are both inconclusive, since they possess equal values of conditions attributes together with a value of decision attribute that is different. Therefore, the data of patient P9 and patient P11 are excluded from Table 18.

Verification of equivalent information:

Step 2 – Analysis of data contained in Table 18 shows that it possesses equivalent information.

P2	No	No	High	No

P8	No	No	High	No

P4	No	Yes	High	Yes
P13	No	Yes	High	Yes

P7	Yes	Yes	Very High	Yes
P18	Yes	Yes	Very High	Yes

P10	Yes	No	High	No
P17	Yes	No	High	No

P12	No	Yes	Normal	No
P14	No	Yes	Normal	No
P20	No	Yes	Normal	No

P16	Yes	No	Normal	No
P19	Yes	No	Normal	No

Remark 5.6 The Table 18 has reduced data presented in a revised version in Table 20 shown below:

TABLE 24   Reduct of Information of Table 18

Patient	Condition Attributes			Decision Attribute
	blotched_red_skin	muscular_pain_articulations	Temperature	Dengue
P1	No	No	Normal	No
P2	No	No	High	No
P3	No	No	Very High	Yes
P4	No	Yes	High	Yes
P5	No	Yes	Very High	Yes
P6	Yes	Yes	High	Yes
P7	Yes	Yes	Very High	Yes
P8	No	No	High	No

TABLE 24 *(continued)*

P10	Yes	No	High	No
P12	No	Yes	Normal	No
P15	Yes	Yes	Normal	No
P16	Yes	No	Normal	No
P19	Yes	No	Normal	No

Step 3 – Analysis of each condition attributes with the attributes set (See Table 25, 26, and 27).

TABEL 25   Analysis of Attribute blotc hed_red_skin in Table 24

Patient	Condition Attributes	Decision Attribute
	blotched_red_skin	Dengue
P1	No	No
P2	No	No
P3	No	Yes
P4	No	Yes
P5	No	Yes
P6	Yes	Yes
P7	Yes	Yes
P8	No	No
P10	Yes	No
P12	No	No
P15	Yes	No
P16	Yes	No
P19	Yes	No

TABLE 26   Analysis of Attriubute muscular pain articulations in Table 24

Patient	Condition Attributes	Decision Attribute
	muscular_pain_articulations	Dengue
P1	No	No
P2	No	No
P3	No	Yes
P4	Yes	Yes

TABLE 26   *(continued)*

P5	Yes	Yes
P6	Yes	Yes
P7	Yes	Yes
P8	No	No
P10	No	No
P12	Yes	No
P15	Yes	No
P16	No	No
P19	No	No

TABLE 27   Analysis of Attribute Temperature in Table 24

Patient	Condition Attributes	Decision Attribute
	Temperature	Dengue
P1	Normal	No
P2	High	No
P3	Very High	Yes
P4	High	Yes
P5	Very High	Yes
P6	High	Yes
P7	Very High	Yes
P8	High	No
P10	High	No
P12	Normal	No
P15	Normal	No
P16	Normal	No
P19	Normal	No

Remark 5.7 in this analysis, no data can be excluded.

Given analysis of condition attributes in Table 24, it can be observed that the same data exists in proceeding tables.

Analysis of attributes blotched_red_skin and muscular_pain_articulations in Table 24 is given in Table 28.

TABLE 28   Analysis of Attributes blotched_red_skin and muscular_pain_articulations in Table 24

| Patient | Condition Attributes | | Decision Attribute |
	blotched_red_skin	muscular_pain_articulations	Dengue
P1	No	No	No
P2	No	No	No
P3	No	No	Yes
P4	No	Yes	Yes
P5	No	Yes	Yes
P12	No	Yes	No
P6	Yes	Yes	Yes
P7	Yes	Yes	Yes
P8	No	No	No
P16	Yes	No	No
P19	Yes	No	No
P10	Yes	No	No
P15	Yes	Yes	No

Result of analysis is given in Table 29.

TABLE 29   Result of Analysis blotched_red_skin and muscular_pain_articulations in Table 24

| Patient | Condition Attributes | | Decision Attribute |
	blotched_red_skin	muscular_pain_articulations	Dengue
P1	No	No	No
P3	No	No	Yes
P4	No	Yes	Yes
P6	Yes	Yes	Yes
P10	Yes	No	No
P15	Yes	Yes	No

Analysis of Attributes attributes blotched_red_skin and Temperatue in Table 24 is given in Table 30.

TABLE 30   Analysis of Attributes blotched_red_skin and temperature in Table 24

Patient	Condition Attributes		Decision Attribute
	blotched_red_skin	Temperature	Dengue
P1	No	Normal	No
P12	No	Normal	No
P2	No	High	No
P8	No	High	No
P3	No	Very High	Yes
P5	No	Very High	Yes
P7	Yes	Very High	Yes
P4	No	High	Yes
P6	Yes	High	Yes
P10	Yes	High	No
P15	Yes	Normal	No
P16	Yes	Normal	No
P19	yes	Normal	No

Result of Analysis is given in Table 31.

Table 31. Result of it Analysis blotched_red_skin and temperature in Table 13

Patient	Condition Attributes		Decision Attribute
	blotched_red_skin	Temperature	Dengue
P1	No	Normal	No
P2	No	High	No
P3	No	Very High	Yes
P4	No	High	Yes
P6	Yes	High	Yes
P10	Yes	High	No
P15	Yes	Normal	No

Analysis of attributes muscular_pain_articulations and temperature given in Table 24 is given in Table 32.

Table 32 Analysis of Attributes muscular_pain_articulations and temperature in Table 24

Patient	Condition Attributes		Decision Attribute
	muscular_pain_articulations	Temperature	Dengue
P1	No	Normal	No
P16	No	Normal	No
P19	No	Normal	No
P2	No	High	No
P8	No	High	No
P10	No	High	No
P3	No	Very High	Yes
P4	Yes	High	Yes
P6	Yes	High	Yes
P5	Yes	Very High	Yes
P7	Yes	Very High	Yes
P12	Yes	Normal	No
P15	Yes	Normal	No

Result of analysis is given in Table 33.

TABLE 33 Result of it analysis of Attributes muscular_pain_articulations and temperature in Table 24

Patient	Condition Attributes		Decision Attribute
	muscular_pain_articulations	Temperature	Dengue
P1	No	Normal	No
P2	No	High	No
P3	No	Very High	Yes
P4	Yes	High	Yes
P5	Yes	Very High	Yes
P20	Yes	Normal	No

Step 4 – Verification of equivalent (intersection) data in the Tables 29, 31, and 33 provide reduct information in relation to Table 24.

TABLE 34   Table with result of information reduct of Table 24

Patient	Condition Attributes			Decision Attribute
	blotched_red_skin	muscular_pain_articulations	Temperature	Dengue
P1	No	No	Normal	No
P3	No	No	Very High	Yes
P4	No	Yes	High	Yes

5.14.6   DECISION RULES

With the information reduct shown above, it can generate the necessary decision rules for aid to the diagnosis of dengue. The rules are presented below:

Rule-1
- R1: If patient
- Blotched_red_skin = No and
- Muscular_pain_articulations = No and
- Temperature = Normal
- Then dengue = No.

Rule-2
- R2: If patient
- Blotched_red_skin = No and
- Muscular_pain_articulations = No and
- Temperature = Very High
- Then dengue = Yes.

Rule-3
- R3: If patient
- Blotched_red_skin = No and
- Muscular_pain_articulations = Yes and
- Temperature = High
- Then dengue = Yes.

5.15   ROUGH SETS, BAYES' RULE, AND MULTIVALUED LOGIC

Inference rules, like modus ponens, play an essential role in logical reasoning and are fundamental in deduction logic, whereas decision rules are basic tools of reasoning in many branches of AI, particularly in data mining, machine learning decision support, and others.

Both inference rules and decision rules are implication, but there are essential differences between these two concepts described by premises and by conclusions of implication. Inference rules are used to draw true conclusions from true premises, whereas decision rules are prescription of decision (actions) that must be made when some condition are satisfied. Therefore some probabilistic, fuzzy or rough measures must be associated with decision rules, to measure the closeness of concepts in contrast to inference rules, where truth values are propagated from premises to conclusions. The rough set approach bridges somehow both concepts – inference and decision rules.

With every implication two conditional probabilities are associated, called credibility and coverage factors respectively. The credibility factor may be considered as partial truth value of the implication and was first introduced by Łukasiewicz in 1913 – whereas the covering factor, introduced recently by Tsumoto, shows how strongly a decision rule covers decision of the decision rule.

It can be shown that the relationship between these two factors is disclosed by the Bayes' Theorem. However, the meaning of Bayes' Theorem in this case differs from that postulated in statistical inference. In statistical data analysis based on Bayes' Theorem, we assume that prior probability about some parameters without knowledge about the data is given. The posterior probability is computed next, which tells us, what can be said about prior probability in view of the data. In the rough set approach the meaning of Bayes' Theorem is different. It reveals some relationships in the database, without referring to prior and posterior probabilities and it can be used to reason about data in terms of approximate (rough) implications. Thus, the proposed approach can be seen as a new model for Bayes' Theorem.

Thus, the rough set approach combines together both logical and probabilistic aspects of implications. This idea is due to Lukasiewicz, who first pointed out the relationship between implications and Bayes' Theorem. In this section, the above ideas are formulated precisely and discussed from the rough set perspective.

5.15.1 MULTIVALUED LOGICS AS PROBABILITY LOGICS – A ŁUKASIEWICZ'S APPROACH

In this section we briefly discuss the ideas of Łukasiewicz's approach to multivalued logics as probability logics.

Łukasiewicz associates with every indefinite proposition of one variable x, $\Phi(x)$ a true value $\pi(\Phi(x))$, which is the ratio of the number of all values of x, which satisfy $\Phi(x)$, to the number of all possible values of x. For example, the true value of the proposition "x is greater than 3" for $x = 1, 2, ..., 5$ is 2/5.

It turns out that assuming the following three axioms:

A1) Φ is false if and only if $\pi(\Phi) = 0$,

A2) Φ is true if and only if $\pi(\Phi) = 1$,

A3) If $\pi(\Phi \to \Psi) = 1$ then $\pi(\Phi) + \pi(\sim \Phi \wedge \Psi) = \pi(\Psi)$;

we can show that:

A4) If $\pi(\Phi \equiv \Psi) = 1$ then $\pi(\Phi) = \pi(\Psi)$;

A5) $\pi(\Phi) + \pi(\sim \Phi) = 1$;

A6) $\pi(\Phi \vee \Psi) = \pi(\Phi) + \pi(\Psi) - \pi(\Phi \wedge \Psi)$;

A7) $\pi(\Phi \wedge \Psi) = -$ iff $\pi(\Phi \vee \Psi) = \pi(\Phi) + \pi(\Psi)$.

Obviously, the above properties have probabilistic flavor. With every implication $\Phi \to \Psi$ one can associate conditional probability $\pi(\Psi|\Phi) = \frac{\pi(\Phi \wedge \Psi)}{\pi(\Phi)}$. In what follows the above ideas are used to define the Rough Modus Ponens. Let us mention that in applications we are often interested in properties more specific than (A1) – (A7)s related to properties of π defined by data tables.

5.15.2 INFORMATION SYSTEM AND DECISION TABLE

An information system is a data table, whose columns are labeled by attributes, rows are labeled by objects of interest and entries of the table are attribute values.

Formally by an information system we understand a pair S = (U, A), where U and A are finite nonempty sets called the universe and the set of attributes, respectively. With every attribute a ∈ A we associate a set V_a, of its values, called the domain of a. Any subset R of A determines a binary relation I(R) on U, which is called an indiscernibility relation and is defined as follows:

(x, y) ∈ I(R) if and only if $a(x) = a(y)$ for every a ∈ A, where $a(x)$ denotes the value of attribute a for element x. Obviously, I(R) is an equivalence relation. The family of all equivalence classes of I(R), that is, partition determined by R, will be denoted by U/ I(R), or simple U/R, an equivalence class of I(R). that is, block of the partition U/R, containing x will be denoted by R(X).

If (x, y) belongs to I(R) we say that x and y are B-indiscernible or indiscernible with respect to R. Equivalence classes of the relation I(R) (or blocks of the partition U/R) are referred to as R-elementary sets or R-granules.

If we distinguish in an information system two classes of attributes, called condition and decision attributes, respectively, then the system will be called a decision table.

Example 5.18 Table 35 is an information system.

TABLE 35   An example of a decision table

Car	F	P	S	M
1	med.	med.	med.	poor
2	high	med.	large	poor
3	med.	low	large	poor
4	low	med.	med.	good
5	high	low	small	poor
6	med.	low	large	good

The table contains data about six cars, where F, P, S, and M is the decision attribute. Each row of the decision table determines a decision obeyed, when specified conditions are satisfied.

For example, let $C = \{F, P, S\}$ be the set of all condition attributes. Then for the set $X = \{1, 2, 3, 5, \text{and } 6\}$ and $BN_C(X) = \{3, 6\}$.

Certainty and coverage factors for decision rules associated with Table 31 are given in Table 36.

TABLE 32   Certainty and coverage factor

Car	F	P	S	M	Cert.	Cov.
1	med.	med.	med.	poor	1	1/4
2	high	med.	large	poor	1	1/4
3	med.	low	large	poor	1/2	1/4
4	low	med.	med.	good	1	1/2
5	high	low	small	poor	1	1/4
6	med.	low	large	good	1/2	1/2

5.15.3   DECISION RULES AND APPROXIMATIONS

Let $\{\Phi_i \to \Psi\}_n$ be a set of decision rules such that: all conditions Φ_i are pairwise mutally exclusive, that is, $||\Phi_i \wedge \Phi_j||_S = \varnothing$, for any $1 \le i, j \le n, i \ne j$, and $\sum_{i=1}^{n} \pi_S(\Phi_i|\Psi) = 1$.   (5.7)

Let C and D be condition and decision attributes, respectively, and let $\{\Phi_i \to \Psi\}_n$ be a set of decision rules satisfying (5.7).

Then the following relationships are valid:

$$C_*\left(||\Psi||_S\right) = ||V_{\pi(\Psi|\Phi_i)=1}\,\Phi_i||_S,$$

$$C^*\left(||\Psi||_S\right) = ||V_{0<\pi(\Psi|\Phi_i)\le 1}\,\Phi_i||_S,$$

$$B N_C\left(||\Psi||_S\right) = ||V_{0<\pi(\Psi|\Phi_i)<1}\,\Phi_i||_S = V_{i=1}^{n}||\Phi_i||_S,$$

The above properties enable us to introduce the following definitions:

Definition 5.5 If $||\Phi||_S = C_*(||\Psi||_S)$, then formula Φ is called the C-lower approximation of the formula Ψ and is denoted by $C_*(\Psi)$,

Definition 5.6 If $||\Phi||_S = C^*(||\Psi||_S)$, then formula Φ is called the C-upper approximation of the formula Φ and is denoted by $C^*(\Psi)$,

Definition 5.7 If $||\Phi||_S = BN_C(||\Psi||_S)$, then Φ is called the C-boundary of the formula Ψ and is denoted by $BN_C(\Psi)$.

Example 5.19 The C-lower approximation of (M, poor) is the formula:

$$C_*(M, poor) = ((F, med.) \wedge (P, med.) \wedge (S, med.))$$

$$((F, high) \wedge (P, med.) \wedge (S, large)) \vee$$

$$((F, high) \wedge (P, low) \wedge (S, small)).$$

$$C^*(M, poor) = ((F, med.) \wedge (P, med.) \wedge (S, med.))$$

$$((F, high) \wedge (P, med.) \wedge (S, large)) \vee$$

$$((F, med.) \wedge (P, low) \wedge (S, large)) \vee$$

$$((F, high) \wedge (P, low) \wedge (S, small)).$$

The C-boundary of $(M, poor)$ is the formula:

$$BN_C(M, poor) = ((F, med.) \wedge (P, low) \vee (S, large)).$$

After simplification we get the following approximations:

$$C_*(M, poor) = ((F, med.) \wedge (P, med.) \vee (P, high)),$$
$$C^*(M, poor) = (F, med.) \vee (F, high).$$

The concepts of the lower and upper approximation of a decision allow us to define the following decision rules:

$$C_*(\Psi) \to \Psi,$$

$$C^*(\Psi) \to \Psi,$$

$$BN_C(\Psi) \to \Psi.$$

For instance, from the approximations given in the example above, we get the following decision rules:

$$((F, med.) \wedge (P, med.) \vee (P, high)) \to (M, poor),$$

$$(F, med.) \vee (F, high) \to (M, poor),$$

$$((F, med.) \wedge (P, low) \vee (S, large)) \to (M, poor).$$

From these definitions it follows that any decision Ψ can be uniquely described by the following two decision rules:

$$C_*(\Psi) \to \Psi ,$$
$$BN_c(\Psi) \to \Psi .$$

From the above calculations we can get two decision rules:

$$((F, med.) \wedge (P, med.) \vee (F, high)) \to (M, poor),$$
$$((F, med.) \wedge (P, low) \wedge (S, large)) \to (M, poor),$$

Which are associated with the lower approximation and the boundary region of the decision $(M, poor)$, respectively and describe decision $\to (M, poor)$.

Obviously, we can get similar decision rules for the decision $\to (M, poor)$, which are as follows:

$$(F, low) \to (M, good),$$
$$((F, med.) \wedge (P, low) \wedge (S, large)) \to (M, good).$$

This coincides with the idea given by Ziarko to represent decision tables by means of three decision rules corresponding to positive region the boundary region and the negative region of a decision.

5.15.4 DECISION RULES AND BAYES' RULES

If Let $\{\Phi_i \to \Psi\}_n$ is a set of decision rules satisfying condition (5.7), then the well known formula for total probability holds:

$$\pi_S(\Psi) = \sum_{i=1}^{n} \pi_S(\Psi|\Phi_i) \cdot \pi_S(\Phi_i). \tag{5.8}$$

Moreover for any decision rule $\Phi \to \Psi$ the following Bayes' formula is valid:

$$\pi_S(\Phi_j|\Psi) = \frac{\pi_S(\Psi|\Phi_j) \cdot \pi_S(\Phi_j)}{\sum_{i=1}^{n} \pi_S(\Psi|\Phi_i) \cdot \pi_S(\Phi_i)}. \tag{5.9}$$

That is, any decision table or any set of implications satisfying condition (5.7) satisfies the Bayes' formula, without referring to prior and posterior probabilities – fundamental in Baysian data analysis philosophy. Bayes' formula in our case says that: if an implication $\Phi \to \Psi$ is true to the degree $\pi_S(\Psi|\Phi)$ then the implication $\Psi \to \Phi$ is true to the degree $\pi_S(\Phi|\Psi)$.

This idea can be seen as a generalization of a modus tollens inference rule, which says that is the implication $\Phi \to \Psi$ is true so is the implication $\sim\Psi \to \sim\Phi$.

Example 5.20 For the set of decision rules:

$$((F, med.) \wedge (P, med.) \vee (F, high)) \to (M, poor),$$

$$((F, med.) \wedge (P, low) \wedge (S, large)) \rightarrow (M, poor)$$

$$(F, low) \rightarrow (M, good),$$

$$((F, med.) \wedge (P, low) \wedge (S, large)) \rightarrow (M, good).$$

We get the values of certainty and coverage factors shown in Table 37.

TABLE 37   Initial decision rules

Rule	Decision	Certainty	Coverage
certain	poor	1	3/4
boundary	poor	1/2	1/4
certain	good	1	1/2
boundary	good	1/2	1/2

The above set of decision rules can be "reversed" as:

$$(M, poor) \rightarrow ((F, med.) \wedge (P, med.) \vee (F, high)),$$

$$(M, poor) \rightarrow ((F, med.) \wedge (P, low) \wedge (S, large)),$$

$$(M, good) \rightarrow (F, low),$$

$$(M, good) \rightarrow ((F, med.) \wedge (P, low) \wedge (S, large)).$$

Due to Bayes' formula the certainty and coverage factors for inverted decision rules are mutually exchanged as shown in Table 38 below:

TABLE 38   Reversed decision rules

Rule	Decision	Certainty	Coverage
certain	poor	3/4	1
boundary	poor	1/4	1/2
certain	good	1/2	1
boundary	good	1/2	1/2

This property can be used to reason about data in the way similar to that allowed by modus tollens inference rule in classical logic.

It is shown that any decision table satisfies Bayes' rule. This enables to apply Bayes' rule of inference without referring to prior and posterior probabilities, inherently associated with "classical" Bayesian inference philosophy. From data tables one can extract decision rules – implications labeled by certainty factors expressing their degree of truth. The factors can be computed from data. Moreover, one can compute from data the coverage degrees expressing the truth degrees of "reverse" implications. This can be treated as generalization of modus tollens inference rule.

5.16 ROUGH SETS AND DATA MINING

Rough set theory has proved to be useful in Data Mining and Knowledge Discovery. It constitutes a sound basis for data mining applications. The theory offers mathematical tools to discover hidden patterns in data. It identifies partial or total dependencies (that is cause-effect relations) in data bases, eliminates redundant data, gives approach to null values, missing data, dynamic data, and others. The methods of data mining in very large data bases using rough sets have been developed.

There are some important steps in the synthesis of approximations of concepts related to the construction of:
- Relevant primitive concepts from which approximations of more complex concepts will be constructed,
- (Closeness) similarity measures between concepts, and
- Operations for construction of more complex concepts from primitive ones.

These problems can be solved by combining the classical rough set approach and recent extensions of rough set theory. Methods for solving problems arising in the realization of these steps are crucial for knowledge discovery and data mining (KDD) [228] as well.

New methods for extracting patterns from data, decomposition of decision tables as well as a new methodology for data mining in distributed and multi-agent systems [271] have been developed.

Here, we consider an example showing some relationships between association rules and approximate reducts.

In some applications, instead of reducts we prefer to use their approximations called α-reducts, where $\alpha \in [0, 1]$ is a real parameter.

The set of attributes $B \subset A$ is called α-reduct if:

$$B \text{ is } \alpha\text{-reduct in } \mathcal{A} \text{ if } \frac{|\{c_{ij} : B \cap c_{ij} \neq \emptyset\}|}{|\{c_{ij} : c_{ij} \neq \emptyset\}|} \geq \alpha$$

One can show that for a given α, the problems of searching for shortest α-reducts and for all α-reducts are also NP-hard.

Given an information table $\mathcal{A} = (U, A)$. By descriptors we mean terms of the form $(a = v)$, where $a \in A$ is an attribute and $a \in V_a$ is a value in the domain. The notion of descriptor can be generalized by using terms of form $(a \in S)$, where $S \subseteq V_a$ is a set of values. By template we mean the conjunction of descriptors, that is $T = D_1 \wedge D_2 \wedge \ldots \wedge D_m$, where $D_1 \backslash, \ldots D_m$ are either simple or generalized descriptors. We denote by length (T) the number of descriptors being in T. An object $u \in U$ is satisfying the template $T = (a_{i_1} = v_1) \wedge \ldots \wedge (a_{i_m} = v_m)$ if and only if $\forall_j a_{ij}(u) = v_j$. Hence the template T describes the set of objects having the common property: "the values of attributes a_{j_1} , ..., a_{j_m} on these objects are equal to $v_1, ..., v_m$, respectively". The support of T is defined by support $(T) = |\{u \in U: u$ satisfies $T\}|$. The long templates with large support are preferred in many Data Mining tasks.

Regarding on a concrete optimization function, problems of finding optimal large templates are k known as being NP- hard with respect to the number of attributes involved into descriptors, or open problems. Nevertheless, the large templates can be found quite efficiently by Apriori and Apriori Tid algorithms. A number of other methods for large template generation has been proposed.

Association rules and their generations can be defined in many ways. Here, according to the presented notation, association rules can be defined as implications of the form $(P \Rightarrow Q)$, where P and Q are different simple templates, that is formulas of the form:

$$(a_{i_1} = v_{i_1}) \wedge ... \wedge (a_{i_k} = v_{i_k}) \Rightarrow (a_{j_1} = v_{j_1}) \wedge ... \wedge (a_{j_l} = v_{j_l}) (5.10)$$

These implication can be called generalized association rules, because association rules are originally defined by formulas $P \Rightarrow Q$, where P and Q are the sets of items (that is goods or articles in stock market) for example $\{A, B\} \Rightarrow \{C, D, E\}$. One can see that this form can be obtained from Equation 5.10 by replacing values on descriptors by 1 that is $(A = 1) \wedge (B = 1) \Rightarrow (C = 1) \wedge (D = 1) \wedge (E = 1)$.

Usually, for a given information table $\mathcal{A}$, the quality of the association rule $\mathcal{R} \Rightarrow$ $P \Rightarrow Q$ can be evaluated by two measures called support and confidence with respect to $\mathcal{A}$. The support of the rule $\mathcal{R}$ is defined by the number of objects from $\mathcal{A}$ satisfying the condition $(P \wedge Q)$ that is support $(\mathcal{R})$ = support $(P \wedge Q)$. The second measure – confidence of $\mathcal{R}$ - is the ratio between the support of $(P \wedge Q)$ and the support of P that is confidence $(\mathcal{R}) = \frac{\text{support } (P \wedge Q)}{\text{support } (P)}$. The following problem has been investigated by many authors. For a given information table $\mathcal{A}$, an integer s, and a real number c $\in [0, 1]$, find as many as possible association rules $\mathcal{R} = (P \Rightarrow Q)$ such that support $(\mathcal{R}) \geq$ s and confidence$(\mathcal{R}) \geq$ c.

All existing association rule generation methods consists of two main steps:

Generate as many as possible templates $T = D_1 \wedge D_2 \wedge ... \wedge D_k$ such that support$(T) \geq$ s and support$(T \wedge D) <$ s for any descriptor D (that is maximal templates among those, which are supported by more than s objects).

For any template T, search for a partition $T = P \wedge Q$ such that support$(P) <$ $\frac{\text{support}(T)}{c}$ and P is the smallest template satisfying this condition.

We can show that the second step can be solved using rough set methods and Boolean reasoning approach.

Let us assume that the template $T = D_1 \wedge D_2 \wedge ... \wedge D_m$, which is supported by at least s objects, has been found. For a given confidence threshold $c \in (0, 1)$ the decomposition $T = P \wedge Q$ is called c-irreducible if confidence $(P \Rightarrow Q) \geq c$ and for any decomposition $T = P' \wedge Q'$ such that P' is a sub-template of P, confidence (P' $\Rightarrow$ Q') < c.

One can prove that for any $c \in [0, 1]$. The problem of searching for the shortest association rule from the template T for a given table S with the confidence limited by c (Optimal c-Association Rules Problem) is NP-hard.

For solving the presented problem, we show that the problem of searching for optimal association rules from the given template is equivalent to the problem of searching for local α-reducts for a decision table, which is a well known problem in Rough set theory.

We construct the new decision table $\mathcal{A}|_T = (U, \mathcal{A}|_T \cup d)$ from the original information table $\mathcal{A}$ and the template T as follows:

- $A|_T = \{a_{D_1}, a_{D_2}, ..., a_{D_m}\}$ is a set of attributes corresponding to the descriptors of T such that $a_{D_i}(u) = \begin{cases} 1 & \text{if the object u satisfies } D_i, \\ 0 & \text{otherwise.} \end{cases}$

- The decision attribute d determines if the object satisfies template T that is d(u)
  $= \begin{cases} 1 & \text{if the object u satisfies } T, \\ 0 & \text{otherwise.} \end{cases}$

The following facts describe the relationship between the association rules problem and the reduct searching problem.

For a given information table $\mathcal{A} = (U, A)$, the template T, the set of descriptors P.

The implication:

$$\left(\bigwedge_{D_i \in P} D_i \Rightarrow \bigwedge_{D_j \notin P} D_j \right) \text{ is:}$$

- 100% - irreducible association rule from T if and only if P is reduct in $A|_T$.

- c- irreducible association rule from T if and only if P is α-reduct in $A|_T$, where

$\alpha = 1 \Leftrightarrow \left(\frac{1}{c} \Leftrightarrow 1 \right) \left(\frac{n}{s} \Leftrightarrow 1 \right)$, n is the total number of objects from U and s

= support (T).

Searching for minimal α-reducts is another well known problem in rough set theory. One can show, that the problem of searching for the all α-reducts as well as the problem of searching for shortest α-reducts is NP-hard. Great effort has been done to solve those problems.

Example 5.21 In the following, we illustrate the main idea of our method. Let us consider the information table $\mathcal{A}$ with 18 objects and 9 attributes (Table 39). Assume that the template $T = (a_1 = 0) \wedge (a_3 = 2) \wedge (a_4 = 1) \wedge (a_6 = 0) \wedge (a_8 = 1)$ has been extracted from the information table $\mathcal{A}$. One can see that support $(T) = 10$ and length$(T) = 5$. The new constructed decision table $\mathcal{A}|_T$ is presented in Table 40. The discernibility function for $\mathcal{A}|_T$ can be described as follows:

$$f(D_1, D_2, D_3, D_4, D_5) = (D_2 \vee D_4 \vee D_5) \wedge (D_1 \vee D_3 \vee D_4) \wedge$$

$$(D_2 \vee D_3 \vee D_4)$$

$$\wedge (D_1 \vee D_2 \vee D_3 \vee D_4) \wedge (D_1 \vee D_3 \vee D_5)$$

$$\wedge (D_2 \vee D_3 \vee D_5) \wedge (D_3 \vee D_4 \vee D_5) \wedge (D_1 \vee D_5)$$

After its simplification we obtain six reducts:

$$f(D_1, D_2, D_3, D_4, D_5) = (D_3 \wedge D_5) \vee (D_4 \wedge D_5) \vee (D_1 \wedge D_2 \wedge D_3) \vee (D_1 \wedge$$

$D_2 \wedge D_4) \vee (D_1 \wedge D_2 \wedge D_5) \vee (D_1 \wedge D_3 \wedge D_4)$ for the decision table $\mathcal{A}|_T$. Thus, we

have found from T six association rules with (100%)-confidence. For c = 90%, we

would like to find α-reducts for the decision table $\mathcal{A}|_T$, where $\alpha = 1 \iff \dfrac{\frac{1}{c} - 1}{\frac{n}{s} - 1} = 0.86$.

Hence we would like to search for a set of descriptors that covers at least $[(n \iff s)\,(\alpha)] = [8.0.86] = 7$ elements of discernibility matrix $\mathcal{M}(\mathcal{A}|_T)$. One can see that the fol-

lowing sets of descriptions:
$\{D_1, D_2\}$, $\{D_1, D_3\}$, $\{D_1, D_4\}$, $\{D_1, D_5\}$, $\{D_1, D_3\}$, $\{D_3, D_3\}$, $\{D_2, D_5\}$, and $\{D_3, D_4\}$ have nonempty intersection with exactly 7 members of the discernibility matrix $(\mathcal{M}(\mathcal{A}|_T)$. In Table 40 we present all association rules achieved from those sets.

TABLE 38 Information table $\mathcal{A}$

$\mathcal{A}$	a_1	a_2	a_3	a_4	a_5	a_6	a_7	a_8	a_9
u_1	0	1	1	1	80	2	2	2	3
u_2	0	1	2	1	81	0	aa	1	aa

TABLE 38 *(continued)*

u_3	0	2	2	1	82	0	aa	1	aa
u_4	0	1	2	1	80	0	aa	1	aa
u_5	1	1	2	2	81	1	aa	1	aa
u_6	0	2	1	2	81	1	aa	1	aa
u_7	1	2	1	2	83	1	aa	1	aa
u_8	0	2	2	1	81	0	aa	1	aa
u_9	0	1	2	1	82	0	aa	1	aa
u_{10}	0	3	2	1	84	0	aa	1	aa
u_{11}	0	1	3	1	80	0	aa	2	aa
u_{12}	0	2	2	2	82	0	aa	2	aa
u_{13}	0	2	2	1	81	0	aa	1	aa
u_{14}	0	3	2	2	81	2	aa	2	aa
u_{15}	0	4	2	1	82	0	aa	1	aa
u_{16}	0	3	2	1	83	0	aa	1	aa
u_{17}	0	1	2	1	84	0	aa	1	aa
u_{18}	1	2	2	1	82	0	aa	2	aa

TABLE 39 An example of information table $\mathcal{A}$ and template T supported by 1o objects and the new decision table $\mathcal{A}|_T$ constructed from $\mathcal{A}$ and template T

$\mathcal{A}|_T$	D_1	D_2	D_3	D_4	D_5	d
	$a_1=0$	$a_3=2$	$a_4=1$	$a_6=0$	$a_8=1$	
u_1	1	0	1	0	0	
u_2	1	1	1	1	1	1
u_3	1	1	1	1	1	1
u_4	1	1	1	1	1	1
u_5	0	1	0	0	1	
u_6	1	0	0	0	1	
u_7	1	0	0	0	1	
u_8	1	1	1	1	1	1
u_9	1	1	1	1	1	1
u_{10}	1	1	1	1	1	1
u_{11}	1	0	1	1	0	
u_{12}	1	0	0	1	0	
u_{13}	1	1	1	1	1	1
u_{14}	1	1	0	0	0	
u_{15}	1	1	1	1	1	1
u_{16}	1	1	1	1	1	1
u_{17}	1	1	1	1	1	1
u_{18}	0	1	1	1	0	

TABLE 40   The simplified version of discernibility matrix $\mathcal{M}\ (\mathcal{A}|_T)$ and association rules

$\mathcal{M}\ (\mathcal{A}|_T)$	u_8
	$u_2, u_3, u_4 \qquad u_9$
	$u_{10}, u_{13}, u_{15}, u_{16}$
	u_{17}

u_1	$D_2 \vee D_4 \vee D_5$
u_5	$D_1 \vee D_3 \vee D_4$
u_6	$D_2 \vee D_3 \vee D_4$
u_7	$D_1 \vee D_2 \vee D_3 \vee D_4$
u_{11}	$D_1 \vee D_3 \vee D_5$
u_{12}	$D_2 \vee D_3 \vee D_5$
u_{14}	$D_3 \vee D_4 \vee D_5$
u_{18}	$D_1 \vee D_5$

$$D_3 \wedge D_5 \Rightarrow D_1 \wedge D_2 \wedge D_4$$

$$D_1 \wedge$$
$$D_4 \wedge D_5 \Rightarrow \qquad D_2 \wedge D_3$$
$$= 100\% \Rightarrow D_1 \wedge D_2 D_3 \Rightarrow D_4 \wedge D_5$$
$$D_1 \wedge D_2 D_4 \Rightarrow D_3 \wedge D_5$$
$$D_1 \wedge D_2 D_5 \Rightarrow D_3 \wedge D_5$$
$$D_1 \wedge D_3 D_4 \Rightarrow D_2 \wedge D_5$$

$$= 90\% \Rightarrow \quad D_1 \wedge D_2 \Rightarrow D_3 \wedge D_4 \wedge D_5$$

$$D_1 \wedge D_3 \Rightarrow D_3 \wedge D_4 \wedge D_5$$

$$D_1 \wedge D_4 \Rightarrow D_2 \wedge D_3 \wedge D_5$$

$$D_1 \wedge D_5 \Rightarrow D_2 \wedge D_3 \wedge D_4$$

$$D_2 \wedge D_3 \Rightarrow D_1 \wedge D_4 \wedge D_5$$

$$D_2 \wedge D_5 \Rightarrow D_1 \wedge D_3 \wedge D_4$$

$$D_3 \wedge D_4 \Rightarrow D_1 \wedge D_2 \wedge D_5$$

The classical rough set approach is based on crisp sets. A generalization of rough set approach for handling different types of uncertainty has been proposed for example, in [271, 272]. Further investigations of techniques transforming crisp concepts (features) into fuzzy ones will certainly show more interesting results.

One of the main problems in soft computing is to find methods allowing measuring the closeness of concept extensions. Rough set methods can also be used to measure the closeness of (fuzzy) concepts.

In classical rough set approach sets are represented by definable sets, that is unions of indiscernibility classes. Extensions of this approach have been proposed by several researchers. Instead of taking equivalence relations as the indiscernibility relations the tolerance relation (or even more arbitrary binary relation) is considered. This leads to a richer family of definable sets but it is harder (from computational complexity point of view) to construct concept approximations of high quality. Searching problems for optimal tolerance relations are NP-complete or NP-hard. However, it has been possible to develop efficient heuristics searching for relevant tolerance relation(s) that allow extracting interesting patterns in data. The reported results are promising. A successful realization of this approach is possible because in the rough set approach relevant tolerance relations determining patterns can be extracted from the background knowledge represented in the form of data tables. The extracted patterns can be further fuzzyfied and applied in construction of concept approximation.

Rough set approach combined with rough mereology can be treated as an inference engine for computing with words and granular computing. For example, the construction of satisfactory target fuzzy concept approximations from approximations of the input (primitive) fuzzy concepts can be realized in the following stages:

- First the fuzzy primitive (input) and the target (output concept are represented by relevant   families of cuts,
- Next by using rough set methods the appropriate approximations of cuts are constructed in terms of available (conditions) measurable features (attributes) related to concepts,
- The approximations of input cuts obtained in stage 2 are used to construct schemes defining to a satisfactory degree the approximations of output cuts from approximated input cuts (and other sources of background knowledge), and
- The constructed family of schemes represents satisfactory approximation of the target concept by the input concepts, (in this step more compact descriptions of the constructed family of schemes can be created, if needed).

Progress in this direction seems to be crucial for further developments in soft computing and KDD.

KEYWORDS

- **Artificial intelligence**
- **Bayes theorem**
- **Decision tables**
- **Expert systems**
- **Pattern recognition**

REFERENCES

1. Adams, E. W. and Levine, H. F. On the Uncertainties Transmitted from Premises to Conclusions in Deductive Inferences, Synthese, 30, 429–460 (1975).
2. Akhmetov, D. F. and Dote, Y. General parameter approach for signalprocessing, J. Appl. Fast Signal Process., 1(1), 5–30 (1997).
3. Albert, P. The algebra of fuzzy logic. Fuzzy Sets Syst., 1, 203–230 (1978).
4. Alchourron, C., Gardenfors, P., and Makinson, D. On the logic of theory change: partial meet contraction and revision functions. J. Symbolic Logic, 50, 510–530 (1985).
5. Aliev, R. A., Fazlollahi, B., Aliev, R. R., and Guirimov, B. G. Fuzzy time series prediction method based on fuzzy recurrent neural network. Lecture Notes in Computer Science (LNCS), 860–869 (2006).
6. Balasubramaniam, J. and Jagan Mohan Rao, C. A Lossless Rule Reduction Technique for a Class of Fuzzy System. Nikos E. Mastorakis (Ed.), Recent Advances in Simulation, Computational Methods and Soft Computing, Proc. of 2002 WSEAS Intl. Conf. on Fuzzy Sets and Fuzzy Systems (3rd WSEAS Conference), Interlaken, Switzerland, WSEAS Press, pp. 228–233 (February 12–14, 2002).
7. Balasubramaniam, Jayaram, and Jagan Mohan Rao, C. On the distributivity of implication operators over T and S norms. IEEE Trans. Fuzzy Syst., 12(2), 194–98 (2004).
8. Baldwin, J. F. A new approach to approximate reasoning using fuzzy logic. Fuzzy Sets Syst., 2, 309–325 (1979).
9. Baldwin, J. F. and Pilsworth, B. W. Axiomatic approach to implication for approximate reasoning with fuzzy logic, Fuzzy Sets Syst., 3 193–219 (1980).
10. Baldwin, J. F. and Zhou, S. Q. A New Approach to Approximate Reasoning Using a Fuzzy Logic. Fuzzy Sets and Systems, 2, 302–325 (1979).
11. Barai, S. V. and Reich, Y. Ensemble modelling or selecting the best model: Many could be better than one. Artificial Intelligence for Engineering Design, Analysis and Manufacturing, 13 377–386 (1999).
12. Baranyi, P. and Yam, Y. Fuzzy rule base reduction in fuzzy IF-THEN rules. D. Ruan and E. E. Kerre (Eds.), Computational Intelligence: Theory and Applications, pp. 135–160 (2000).
13. Baranyi, P., Yam, Y., Tikk, D., and Patton, R. J. Trade-off between approximation accuracy and complexity: HOSVD based complexity reduction. Period. Polytech. Ser. Trans. Eng., 29(1–2), 3–26 (2001).
14. Baranyi, P., Yam, Y., Tikk, D., and Patton, R. J. Trade-off between approximation accuracy and complexity: TS controller design via HOSVD based complexity minimization. J. Casil-las, O. Cordon, F. Herrera, and L. Magdalena (Eds.), Studies in fuzziness and soft computing, Interpretability Issues in Fuzzy Modeling, 128, Springer-Verlag, pp. 249–277 (2003).
15. Bardossy, A., and Duckstein, L. Fuzzy Rule-based Modelling with Application to Geophysical. Biological and Engineering Systems, CRC Press (1995).
16. Bargiela, A. and Pedrycz, W. Granular Computing. Kluwer Academic Publishers (2002).

17. Běhounek, L. and Cintula, P. From fuzzy logic to fuzzy mathematics: a methodological manifesto. Fuzzy Sets and Systems, 157(5), 642–646 (2006).
18. Běhounek, L. and Cintula, P. Fuzzy logics as the logics of chains. Fuzzy Sets and Systems, 157, 604–610 (2006).
19. Bellman, R. and Giertz, M. On the analytic formalism of the theory of fuzzy sets. Inf. Sci., 5, 149–156 (1973).
20. Bellman, R. E. and Zadeh, L. A. Decision-making in a fuzzy environment. Management Sci-ence, 17, B141–B164 (1970).
21. Bellman, R. E. and Zadeh, L. A. Local and Fuzzy Logics. G. Epstein (Ed.), Modern Uses of Multiple-Valued Logic, Reidel, Dordrecht, pp. 103–165 (1977).
22. Belluce, L. P., Di Nola, A., and Sessa, S. Triangular norms, MV-algebras and bold fuzzy set theory. Math. Japonica, 36(3), 481–487 (1991).
23. Belluce, L. P. Semisimple algebras on infinite valued logic and bold fuzzy set theory. Func. Anal., 38(6), 1356–1379 (1986).
24. Bě'lohlávek, R. and Novák, V. Learning rule base of the linguistic expert systems. Soft Com-putting, 7, 79–88 (2002).
25. Belohlavek, R. and Vychodil, V. Attribute implications in a fuzzy setting. B. Ganter and L. Kwuida (Eds.), ICFCA 2006, Lecture Notes in Artificial Intelligence, vol. 3874, Springer-Verlag, Heidelberg, pp. 45–60 (2006).
26. Birkhoff, G. and von Neumann, J. The logic of quantum mechanics. Ann. Math., 37, 823–834 (1936).
27. Birkhoff, G. Lattice Theory, third edition, AMS Coll. PubL, Providence, New York (1967).
28. Blok, W. J. and Pigozzi, D. Algebraizable logics. Memoirs Amer. Math. Soc., 77, 396 (1989).
29. Blyth, T. S. and Janowitz, M. F. Residuated Theory. Pergamon Press. London (1972).
30. Bodjanova, S. Complement of fuzzy k-partitions. Fuzzy Sets Syst., 62, 175–184 (1994).
31. Bonissone, P. P. Soft Computing and meta heuristics: using knowledge and reasoning to control search and vice-versa. in Proc. Of the SPIE, Vol 5200, Application and science of neural network, Fuzzy Systems and evolutionary computation, V. San Diego, California, pp 133–144 (August, 2003).
32. Bonissone, P. P. Soft Computing: The convergence of emerging reasoning technologies, Soft Computing, 1(1), 6–18 (1997).
33. Bonissone, P. P, Chen, T. T., Goebel, K., and Khedkar, P. S. Hybrid soft computing Sys-tems: Industrial and commercial applications. Proceedings of IEEE, 87(9), 1641–1667 (1999).
34. Brzozowski, J. A. De Morgan bisemilattices. In Proc. 30th IEEE Int. Symp. Multiple-Valued Logic, Portland, OR, pp. 173–178 (May 23–25, 2000.)
35. Buckley, J. Fuzzy complex analysis I: Differentiation. Fuzzy Sets Syst., 41, 269–284 (1991).
36. Buckley, J. Fuzzy complex analysis II: integration. Fuzzy Sets Syst., 49, 171–179 (1992).
37. Buckley, J. Solving fuzzy equations: a new solution concept. Fuzzy Sets Syst., 39, 291–301 (1991).
38. Bui, T. X. A Group Decision Support System for Cooperative Multiple criteria Group Decision making. Springer- Verlag, berlin (1987).
39. Bustince, H., Burillo, P., and Soria, F. Automorphisms, negation, and implication opera-tors. Fuzzy Sets Syst., 134, 209–229 (2003).
40. Bustince, H., Kacprzyk, J., and Mohedano, V. Intuitionistic fuzzy generators: application to intuitionistic fuzzy complementation. Fuzzy Sets Syst., 114, 485–504 (2000).

41. Cao, T. H., Creasy, P. N., and Wuwongse, V. Fuzzy types and their lattices. in Proc. 1997 Int. Conf Fuzzy Systems, Barcelona, Spain, pp. 805–812 (July 1–5, 1997).

42. Carlsson, C. and Fuller, R. Possibility and necessity in weighted aggregation. R. R. Yager and J. Kacprzyk (Eds.), The ordered weighted averaging operators: Theory, Methodology, and Applications, Kluwer Academic Publishers, Boston, 18–28, (1997), [ISBN 0-7923-9934-X].

43. Chan, M. W. and Shurn, K. P. Hornornorphisrns of implicative semigroups. Semigroup Fo-rum, 46, 7–15 (1993).

44. Chang, C. C. A new proof of the completeness of the Lukasiewicz axioms. Trans. Amer. Math. Soc., 93, 74–80 (1959).

45. Chang, C. C. Algebraic analysis of many valued logics. Trans. Amer. Math. Soc., 88, 467–490 (1958).

46. Chang, C. C. Algebraic analysis of many valued logics. Transactions American Mathematical Society, 88, 476–490 (1958).

47. Chiu, S. L. Extracting Fuzzy Rules from Data for Function Approximation and Pattern Classification. Chapter 9 in Fuzzy Information Engineering: A Guided Tour of Applications, D. Dubois, H. Prade, and R. Yager (Eds.), John Wiley & Sons (1997).

48. Cintula, P., Hájek, P., and Horčík, R. Formal systems of fuzzy logic and their fragments. Annals of Pure and Applied Logic, 150, 40–65 (2007).

49. Cintula, P. and Hájek, P. Triangular norm based predicate fuzzy logics. Fuzzy Sets and Systems, 161(3) 311–346 (2010).

50. Cordero, P., Enciso, M., Mora, A., and de Guzman, I. A complete logic for fuzzy functional dependencies over domains with similarity relations, In proc. of INANN 09 (2009).

51. Cvetkovic, D. and Parmee, I. Agent-based support within an interactive evolutionary design system. Artificial Intelligence for Engineering Design, Analysis, and Manufacturing, 16, 331–342 (2002).

52. Dalla Chiara, M. L. Quantum logic. D. Gabbay/F. Guenthner (Eds.), Handbook of Philosoph. Logic, , Reidel, Dordrecht, 3, 427–469 (1986).

53. Daniel, R. and Torrens, J. Distributive strong implications from uninorms. In: Proceedings of the AGOP-2005, pp. 103–108 (2005).

54. Daniel, R. and Torrens, J. Distributivity and conditional distributivity of a uninorm and a continuous r-conorm. IEEE Trans. Fuzzy Syst., 180–190 (2006).

55. Daniel, R. and Torrens, J. Distributivity of residual implications over conjunctive and disjunctive uninorms. Fuzzy Sets Syst., 158, 23–37 (2007).

56. Daniel, R. and Torrens, J. Distributivity of strong implications over conjunctive and disjunctive uninorms, Kybernetika, 42, 319–336 (2006).

57. Daňková, M. Representation of logic formulas by normal forms. Kybernetika, 38, 711–728 (2002).

58. Davis, E. and Morgenstern, L. Introduction: progress in formal commonsense reasoning. Artificial Intelligence. 153, 1–12 (2004).

59. De Baets, B. and Fodor, J. Residual operators of uninorms. Soft Comput., 3, 89–100 (1999).

60. Delgado, M. verdegay, J. L, and Vila, M. A. On Aggregation Operations of Linguistic Labels. International Journal of Intelligent Systems, 8, 351–370 (1993b).

61. Delgado, M., Verdegay, J. L, and Vila, M. A Linguistic decision Making Models International journal of intelligent systems. 7, 479–492 (1993a).

62. Di Nola, A. and Ventre, A. G. S. On fuzzy implication in De Morgan Algebra. Fuzzy Sets and Systems, 33, 155–164 (1989).

63. Dilworth, R. P. and Ward, N. Residuated lattices. Trans. Amer. Math. Soc., 45, 335–354 (1939). 600 Soft Computing and Its Applications.

64. Domingo, X., Trilias, E., and Valverde, L. Pushing Łukasiewicz-Tarski implication a little father. In: Proc. 11th IEEE Int. Symp., On Multiple-valued Logic, Oklahoma City 232–243 (1981).

65. Dote, Y and Osaka, S.J. Industrial applications of soft computing: A review. Proceedings of the IEEE, 89(9), 1243–1265 (2001).

66. Dubois, D. and Prade, H. Fuzzy Sets and Systems: Theory and Applications. Academic Press, New York (1980).

67. Dumitrescu, D. A note on fuzzy logic. University of Cluj-Napoca, Preprint No. 9 (1988).

68. Dutta, P., Boruah, H., and Ali, T. Fuzzy arithmetic with and without using α-cut method : A comparative study. International Journal of Latest Trends in Computing, 2(1),99–107 (2011).

69. Dvořák, A. and Novák, V. Formal theories and linguistic descriptions. Fuzzy Sets and Systems ,143, 169–188 (2004).

70. Dvořák, A. and Novák, V. Fuzzy logic deduction with crisp observations. Soft Computing, 8, 256–263 (2004).

71. Dvořák, A. and Novák, V. Towards automatic modeling of economic texts. Mathware & Soft Computing, 14(3), 217–231 (2007).

72. Dvurecenskij, A. and Pulmannova, S. New Trends in Quantum Structures. Mathematics and Its Applications, 516, Kluwer, Dordrecht (2000).

73. Dvurecenskij, A. and Chovanec, F. Fuzzy Quantum spaces and compatibility. International journal of theoretical physics, 27, 1069–1075 (1988).

74. Edmonds, E. A. Lattice fuzzy logics. Int. J. Man-Machine Stud., 13, 455 465 (1980).

75. Elkan, C. Paradoxes of Fuzzy Logic. Revisited International journal of approximate reasoning, 26(2), 157 159 (2001)

76. Elkan, C. The paradoxical success of fuzzy logic. IEEE Expert, 6(6), 3–8 (August, 1994). With fifteen responses on pp. 9–46 and a reply by the author on pp. 47–49.

77. Elkan, C., The paradoxical success of fuzzy logic in Proc. 11th Nat. Conf. Artificial Intelligence, Washington, DC 698 703 (July 11–15, 1993).

78. El-Zekey, M., Representable good EQ-algebras. Soft Computing, 14, 1011 1023 (2009).

79. El-Zekey, M., Novdk, V., and Mesiar, R. On good EQ-algebras. Fuzzy Sets and Systems, 178(1), 1–23 (September 1, 2011).

80. Esteva, F., Godo, L., and Garcfa-Cerdana, A. On the hierarchy of t-norm based residuated fuzzy logics. M. Fitting and E. Orlowska (Eds.) Beyond Two: Theory and Applications of Multiple-Valued Logic Series, Springer, Berlin, 235 270 (2003).

81. Esteva, F., Godo, L., and Noguera, C. On expansions of WNM t-norm based logics with truth-constants. Fuzzy Sets and Systems, 161, 347 368 (2010).

82. Esteva, F., Godo, L., and Montagna, F., The Ł Π and Ł Π½ logics: two complete fuzzy systems joining Lukasiewicz and product logics. Archive of Mathematical Logic, 40, 39 67 (2001).

83. Esteva, F. and Godo, L. Towards the generalization of Mundici's gamma functor to IMTL algebras: the linearly ordered case. Algebraic and Proof-theoretic Aspects of Non-classical Logics, 127 137 (2006).

84. Esteva, F. On a representation theorem of De Morgan algebras by fuzzy sets, Stochastica, 5(2), 109 115 (1981).

85. Esteva, F. Some representable de Morgan algebras. J. Math. Anal Appl. 100(2), 463 469 (1984).

86. Esteva, F. and Godo, L. Monoidal t-norm based logic: towards a logic for left-continuous t-norms, Fuzzy Sets and Systemsm, 124, 271–288 (2001). References 601.
87. Fan, J. and Xie, Weixin. Some notes on similarity measures and proximity measure. Fuzzy Sets and Systems, 101, 403 312 (1999).
88. Feynmann, R. P. Quantum Mechanical Computers. Foundations of Physics, 16, 507 531 (1986).
89. Filev, D. and Yager, R. R. On the issue of obtaining OWA operator weights. Fuzzy Sets and Systems, 94, 157 169 (1998).
90. Fitting, M. C. Many-valued modal logics: I—II. Fundamenta Informaticae, 15, 235 254 (1991); 17, 55 73 (1992).
91. Fitting, M. C. Tableaus for many-valued modal logic, Studia Logica, 55, 63 87 (1995).
92. Flaminio, T. and Montagna, F. MV-algebras with internal states and probabilistic fuzzy logics. International Journal of Approximate Reasoning, 50, 138 152 (2009).
93. Fodor J. and Roubens, M. Fuzzy Preference Modeling and Multicriteria Decision Support, Kluwer, Dordrecht (1994).
94. Fodor, J. C. Contrapositive symmetry of fuzzy implications, Fuzzy Sets and Systems, 69, 141 156 (1995).
95. Font, J. M., Rodriquez, A. J., and Torres, A. Wajsberg algebras, Stochastica, 8(1), 5 31 (1984).
96. Fuller, R. and Majlender, P. An analytic approach for obtaining maximal entropy OWA operator weights. Fuzzy Sets and Systems, 124, 53 57 (2001).
97. Robert, F. Neural Fuzzy Systems, Abo Akademi University (1995).1995ISBN/ASIN: 951-650-624-0.
98. Robert, F. and Majlender, P. On obtaining minimal variability OWA operator weights, Turku centre for Computer Science, TUCS Technical Report No 429 (November, 2001).
99. Gaines, B. R. Fuzzy reasoning and the logics of uncertainty in Proc. 6th Int. Symp. Multiple-Valued Logic, Logan, Utah, 179 188 (May 25–28, 1976).
100. Galatos, N., Jipsen, P., Kowalski T., and Ono, H. Residuated lattices: An Algebraic Glimpse at Substructural Logics, Elsevier, Amsterdam (2007).
101. Gallant, S. I., Neural Network Learning and Expert Systems, The MIT Press (1993).
102. Garcia, P. and Esteva, F. Representation of symmetric algebras and its subvarieties. In: The Eighteenth International Symposium on Multiple-Valued Logic, Palma de Mallorca, Spain (1988).
103. Georgescu, G.and Popescu, A. Concept lattices and similarity in noncommutative fuzzy logic. Fundamenta Informaticae, 53, 23 54 (2002).
104. Gericke, H., Lattice Theory. New York: Frederick Ungar (1966).
105. Gerla, G. An extension principle for fuzzy logics Math. Logic Quart., 40, 357–380 (1994).
106. Gerla, G. Closure operators, fuzzy logic and constraints. D. Dubois, H. Prade, and E. P. Klement (Eds.), Fuzzy Sets, Logics and Reasoning About Knowledge, Applied Logic Series, Kluwer Academic Publishers, Dordrecht, 15, 101–120 (1999).
107. Goguen, J. A. The logic of inexact concepts, Synthese, 19 325 373 (1968/69).
108. Goldberg, D. E. The Design of Innovation, Kluwer Academic Publishers, Massachusetts, (2002).
109. Gottwald, S. Fuzzy Sets and Fuzzy Logic: The Foundations of Application—from a Mathematical Point of View, Vieweg, Braunschweig/Wiesbaden and Teknea, Toulouse, (1993).
110. Gottwald, S. and Hajek. P. T-norm based mathematical fuzzy logics. Logical, Algebraic, Analytic, and Probabilistic Aspects of Triangular Norms. E. P. Klement and R. Mesiar, (Eds.), Elsevier, Dordrecht, 275 299 (2005).

111. Gottwald, S. Mathematical fuzzy logic as a tool for the treatment of vague information, Inf. Sci. 172(1 2) 41 71 (2005). 602 Soft Computing and Its Applications.
112. Gottwald, S. A Treatise on Many-valued Logics. Research Studies Press, Baldock (2001).
113. Gottwald, S. Fuzzy prepositional logics. Fuzzy Sets and Systems, 3, 181–192 (1980).
114. Gottwald, S. Mathematical fuzzy logics. Bulletin of Symbolic Logic, 14(2), 210–239 (2008).
115. Gottwald, S. A cumulative system of fuzzy sets. A. Zarach (Ed.), Set Theory Hierarchy Theory, Mem. Tribute A. Mostowski, Bierutowice 1975, Lect. Notes Math., Springer, Berlin, 537, 109–119 (1976).
116. Gottwald, S. Fuzzy set theory. Some aspects of the early development. Aspects of Vagueness (H. J. Skala, S. Termini, and E. Trillas (Eds.), Theory and Decision Libr., Reidel, Dordrecht, 39, 13–29(1984).
117. Gottwald, S. Universes of fuzzy sets and axiomatizations of fuzzy set theory. Part I: Model-based and axiomatic approaches. Studia Logica, 82(2), 211–244 (March 2006).
118. Gottwald, S. Universes of fuzzy sets and axiomatizations of fuzzy set theory. Part II: Category theoretic approaches. Studia Logica, 84(1), 23–50 (September, 2006).
119. Graham, I. Fuzzy sets and topazes–Towards higher order fuzzy logic. Fuzzy Sets and Systems, 23, 19–32 (1987).
120. Grant, J. Churn modeling by rough set approach, manuscript (2001)
121. Haack, S. Deviant Logic Fuzzy Logic - Beyond the Formalism. The University of Chicago Press, Chicago (1974).
122. Hajek, P. Fuzzy logic and arithmetical hierarchy. Fuzzy Sets Sxst., 73, 359–363 (1995).
123. Hájek, P., Godo, L., and Esteva, F. A complete many-valued logic with product conjunction. Arch. Math. Logic, 35, 191–208 (1996).
124. Hájek, P. Meta mathematics of Fuzzy Logic. Kluwer Academic Publishers, Dordrecht (1998).
125. Hájek, P. and Cintula, P. On theories and models in fuzzy predicate logics. Journal of Symbolic Logic, 71(3), 863–880 (2006).
126. Hájek, P. and Paris, J. A dialogue on fuzzy logic. Soft Computing, 1(1), 3–5 (1997).
127. Hájek, P. Ten questions and one problem on fuzzy logic. Annals of Pure and Applied Logic 96, 157–165 (1999).
128. Hájek, P. and Novak, V. The sorties paradox and fuzzy logic. International Journal of General Systems, 32, 373–383 (2003).
129. Hájek, P. What is mathematical fuzzy logic. Fuzzy Sets and Systems, 157, 597–603 (2006).
130. Hájek, P. Why fuzzy logic? A Companion to Philosophical Logic, Blackwell Publishers, Massachusetts, 22, 595–605 (2002).
131. Hájek, P. and Hanikova, Z. A development of set theory in fuzzy logic. M. Fitting and E. Orlowska (Eds.), Beyond Two: Theory and Applications of Multiple-Valued Logic, Physica-Verlag, Heidelberg, pp. 273–285 (2003).
132. Henkin, L. A theory of prepositional types. Fundamenta Mathematica, 52, 323–344 (1963).
133. Henkin, L. Completeness in the theory of types. Journal of Symbolic Logic, 15, 81–91 (1950).
134. Herrera, F. and Verdegay, J. L. Linguistic assessments in group decision. In proc. of First European Congress on Fuzzy and Intelligent Technologies, Aachen (1993).
135. Herrera, F., herrera-Viedma, E., and verdegay, J. L. A linguistic Descision process in Group Decision making. Technical Report, ETS Ingenieria Informatica (February, 1994).
136. Higashi, M. and Klir, G. J. On measures of fuzziness and fuzzy complements. Int. J. Gen. Syst., 8, 169–180 (1982) References 603.

137. Hirota, K. and Pedrycz, W. Fuzzy computing for data mining. Proc. IEEE, 87, 1575–1600 (September, 1999).
138. Höhle, U. Classification of subsheaves over GL-Algebras. Logic Colloquium '98, Natick, Massachusetts, pp. 238–261 (2000).
139. Höhle, U. Commutative residuated l-monoids. U. Hohle and E. P. Klement (Eds.), Non-Classical Logics and Their Applications to Fuzzy Subsets: A Handbook of the Mathematical Foundations of Fuzzy Set Theory, Kluwer Academic Publishers, Dordrecht, pp. 53–106 (1995).
140. Höhle, U. M-valued sets and sheaves over integral commutative CL-monoids. Appl. of Category Theory to Fuzzy Subsets, Dordrecht, pp. 33–72 (1992).
141. Höhle, U. Presheaves over GL-monoids. Non-Classical Logics and Their Appl. to Fuzzy Subsets, Dordrecht, pp. 127–157 (1995).
142. Jang, J. S. R. and Sun, C. T. Functional equivalence between radial basis function networks and fuzzy inference systems. IEEE Transactions on Neural Networks, 4(1), 156–159 (January, 1993).
143. Julian, P. and Rubio-Manzano, C. A similarity based wam for bousi-prolog. In proc. of IWANN'09 (2009).
144. Julian, P., Moreno, G. and Penabad, J. On the declarative semantics of multi-adjoint logic programs. In proc. of IWANN'09 (2009).
145. Kacprzyk, J., Fedrizzi, M., and Nurmi, H. Group decision making with fuzzy majorities represented by linguistic quantifiers. J. L. Verdegay and M. Delgado (Eds.), Approximate reasoning tools for artificial Intelligence, Verlag TUV Rheinland, Cologne (1990).
146. Kacprzyk, J., Fedrizzi, M., and Nurmi, H. Fuzzy logic with linguistic Quantifiers in Group Decision Making. R. R. Yager and L. A. Zadeh (Eds), An Introduction to Fuzzy Logic Applications in Intelligent Systems, Kluwer Academic, Boston (1992).
147. Karnik, N. N., Mendel, J. M., and Liang, Q. Type-2 fuzzy logic systems. IEEE Transaction on Fuzzy systems, 7, 643–658 (1999).
148. Kaufman, A. and Gupta, M. M. Introduction to Fuzzy Arithmetic. Van Nostrand Reinhold, New York (1985).
149. Kaufmann, A. Theory of expertons and fuzzy logic. Fuzzy Sets and Systems, 28, 295–304 (1988).
150. Keefe, R. Theories of Vagueness. Cambridge University Press, Cambridge (2000).
151. Keenan E. and Westerståhl, D. Quantifiers in formal and natural languages. J. van Benthem and A. ter Meulen (Eds.), Handbook of Logic and Language, Elsevier, Amsterdam, pp. 837–893 (1997).
152. Kerre, E. and De Cock, M. Linguistic modifiers: An overview. J. Martinez (Ed.), Fuzzy Logic and Soft Computing, Kluwer Academic, Boston, pp. 69–86 (1999).
153. Kikuchi, H. and Takagi, N. De Morgan bisemilattice of fuzzy truth value. In Proc. 32nd IEEE Int. Symp. Multiple-Valued Logic, Boston, Massachusetts, pp. 180–184 (May 15–18, 2002).
154. Klaua, D. Über einen Ansatz zur mehrwertigen Mengenlehre. Monatsber. Deutsch. Akad. Wiss. Berlin, 7, 859–867 (1965).
155. Klaua, D. Uber einen zweiten Ansatz zur mehrwertigen Mengenlehre. Monatsber. Deutsch. Akad. Wiss. Berlin, 8, 161–177 (1966).
156. Klement, E. P., Mesiar, R., and Pap, E. Triangular Norms, Kluwer, Dordrecht (2000).
157. Klement, E. P. and Navara, M. A survey on different triangular norm-based fuzzy logics. Fuzzy Sets and Systems, 101, 241–251 (1999).
158. Klir, G. J. and Yuan, B. Fuzzy Sets and Fuzzy Logic: Theory and Applications. Upper Saddle River, Prentice-Hall, New Jersey, (1995).
604 Soft Computing and Its Applications

159. Klir, G. J. Uncertainty and Information: Foundations of Generalized Information Theory. Wiley-Interscience, Hoboken, New Jersey (2006).

160. Knybel, J. and Pavliska, V. Reprentation of Fuzzy IF-THEN rules by Petri Nets. Research report No. 84, University of Ostrava (2005).

161. Koczy, L. T. and Hirota, K. Interpolation and size reduction in fuzzy rule bases. TR 93–94/401, LIFE Chair of Fuzzy Theory, Tokyo Inst.,Technology, Yokohama, Japan (1993).

162. Koczy, L. T. and Hirota, K. Ordering, distance, and closeness of fuzzy sets. Fuzzy Sets Syst., 59, 281–293 (1993).

163. Koczy, L. T. and Kovics, S. On the preservation of convexity and piecewise linearity in linear fuzzy rule interpolation. TR 9.1–94/402, LIFE Chair of Fuzzy Theory, Tokyo Inst. Technology, Yokohama, Japan (1993).

164. Koczy, L. T. Algorithmic aspects of fuzzy control. International Journal of Approximate Reasoning, 12(3–4), 159–219 (April–May, 1995).

165. Koczy, L. T. and Zorat, A. Optimal fuzzy rule bases– the cat and mouse problem. FUZZ-IEEE'96, pp. 1865–1870 (1996).

166. Kóczy, L. T. Fuzzy graphs in the evaluation and optimization of networks. Fuzzy Sets and Systems, 46(3), 307–319 (1992).

167. Koczy, L. T. Fuzzy if-then rule models and their transformation into one another. IEEE Trans. Syst. Man Cyber. Part A, 26(5), 621–637 (1996).

168. Kodandapani, K. L. and Setlur, R. V. Reed-Muller canonical forms in multivalued logic. IEEE Trans. Comput., C-24(6), 628 636 (June, 1975).

169. Kosko, B, Fuzzy systems as universal approximators. IEEE Trans. Computers. 1994;an early version appears in Proc. 1st IEEE Int. Conf. on Fuzzy Systems, pp. 1153–1162 (March, 1992).

170. Kosko, B. Fuzzy Engineering. Prentice Hall, Upper Saddle River, New Jersey (1997).

171. Kosko, B. and Dickerson, J. A. Function approximation with additive fuzzy systems. Theoretical Aspects of fuzzy control, pp. 313–347, ISBN:0-471-02079-6.

172. Kwang, H. Lee. First course on Fuzzy theory and Application, Springer ,New York (2005).

173. Lehmke, S. and Thiele, H. On fuzzy circumscription. EUSFLAT '96. Proc. Fourth Europ. Congr. Intell. Techniques and Soft Computing, Aachen, 1, 641–645 (1996).

174. Licata, G. Fuzzy Logic, Knowledge and Natural Language. Fuzzy Inference System: Theory and Applications, Dr. Mohammad Fazle Azeem (Ed.), In Tech, Available from: http://www.intechopen.com/books/fuzzy-inference-system-theory-and-applications/fuzzy-logic-knowledge-andnatural-language, (2012) ISBN: 978-953-51-0525-1.

175. Liu, L. Z. and Wang, G. J. Fuzzy implication algebras arid MV-algebra. Fuzzy Systems and Mathematics, 12(1), 20–25 (1998).

176. Lopez-Molina, E. barrenechea, H., Bustine, P., Couto, B., Dacts, D., and Fernander, J. Edge detection based on gravitional forces. In Proc. of IWANN'09 (2009).

177. Lowen, R. On fuzzy complements. Inf. Sci., 14, 107–113 (1978).

178. Maczynski, M. J. Functional properties of quantum logics. International Journal of Theoretical physics, 11, 149–155 (1974).

179. Magdalena, L. What is soft computing? Revisiting Possible Answers. International Journal of computational Intelligence systems, 3(2), 148–159 (2010).

180. Mamdani, E. H. and Assilian, S. An experiment in linguistic synthesis with a fuzzy logic controller. International Journal of Man Machine Studies, 7, 1–13 (1975).

181. Martin, J., Mayor, G., and Torrens, J. On locally internal monotonic operators. Fuzzy Sets Syst., 137 27–42 (2003). References 605

182. Mencattini, A., Salmeri, M., and Lojacono, R. Type-2 fuzzy sets for modelling uncertainty in measurement. AMUEN 2006-International Workshop on Advanced Methods for Uncertainty Estimation in Measurement, Sardagna, Trento, Italy, pp. 20–21 (2006).

183. Mendel, J.Type-2 Fuzzy sets Made simple. IEEE Transaction on Fuzzy Systems. 10(2), 117–126 (2002).

184. Mendel, J. Uncertain Rule-Based Fuzzy Logic Systems - Introduction and New Directions, Prentice Hall, Upper Saddle River, NJ (2001).

185. Mich, L., Gaio, L., and fedrizzi, M. On Fuzzy Logic-Based Consensus in group Decision. In Proc. of Fifth IFSA World congress, Seoul (1993).

186. Minari, P. Completeness theorems for some intermediate predicate calculi. Studia Logica, 42(4) 431–441 (1980).

187. Mizraji, E. Vector logics: the matrix-vector representation of logical calculus. Fuzzy Sets Syst., 50, 179–185 (1992).

188. Mizraji, E. The operators of vector logic. Math. Logic Quart, 42(1), 27–40 (1996).

189. Montagna, F. An algebraic approach to propositional fuzzy logic. J. Logic, Lang. Inf., 9, 91–124 (2000).

190. Mundici, D. Interpretation of AF C*-algebras in Łukasiewicz sentential calculus. J. Func. Anal., 65(1) 15–63 (1986).

191. Mundici, D. Mapping Abelian l-groups with strong unit one-one into MV-algebras. J. Algebra, 98 76–81 (1986).

192. Mundici, D. Ulanrs game, Lukasiewicz logic and AF c*-algebras. Fundamenta Informaticae, 18 151–161 (1993).

193. Nakamura, A. A note on truth-value functions in the infinitely-many-valued logics. Zeitsch. f. Math. Logik, 9 141–144 (1963).

194. Negoita, C.V. and Ralescu, D. A. Applications of Sets to System Analysis, Birkhaiiser, Basel-I (1975).

195. Nguyen, H. T., Kandel, A., and Kreinovich, V. Complex fuzzy sets: toward new foundations. In Proc. 2000 IEEE Int. Conf. Fuzzy Systems, San Antonio, TX, pp. 1045–1048 (May 7–10, 2000).

196. Nguyen, H. T., Kosheleva, O. M., and Kreinovich, V. Is the success of fuzzy logic really paradoxical?: Toward the actual logic behind expert systems. Int. J. Intell. Syst., 11, 295–326 (1996).

197. Nguyen, H. T. A note on the extension principle for fuzzy sets. J. Math Anal. and Appl, 64, 359–380 (1978)

198. Nguyen, H. T. Some mathematical tools for linguistic probabilities. Fuzzy Sets and systems, 2, 53–65(1979).

199. Nguyen, H. T, Olga, M., Kosheleva, and Kreinovich, V. Is the success of Fuzzy Logic Really paradoxical? Or: towards the actual logic behind expert systems. International Journal of Intelligent Systems, 11(5), 295–326 (May 1996).

200. Nguyen, H. T and Kreinovich, V. On logical Equivalence in Fuzzy Logic. Sixth International Fuzzy Systems Association World Congress, San Paulo, Brazil, (July 22–28, 1995).

201. Nguyen, H. T. lecture Notes on fuzzy logic, LIFE, Tokyo Institute of technology (1993).

202. Novak, V. First-order fuzzy logic. Studia Logica, 46(1), 87–109 (1987).

203. Novák, V., Fuzzy logic theory of evaluating expressions and comparative quantifiers, in: Proceedings of the 11th International Conference on IPMU, Paris, Editions EDK, Us Cordeliers, Paris, 2, pp. 1572–1579 (July, 2006).

204. Novák, V. Fuzzy Sets and Their Applications. Soft Computing and its Applications, Adam Hilger, Bristol, (1989).

205. Novák, V. Towards formalized integrated theory of fuzzy logic. Z. Bien, K. Min (Eds.), Fuzzy Logic and Its Applications to Engineering, Information Sciences, and Intelligent Systems, Kluwer, Dordrecht, pp. 353–363 (1995).

206. Novak, V. Which logic is the real fuzzy logic? Fuzzy Sets and Systems, 157, 635–641 (2006).

207. Nurmi, H. and Kacprzyk, J. On fuzzy tournaments and their solution concept in group decision making. European Journal of Operational Research, 51, 223–232 (1991).

208. O'Hagan, M. Aggregating template or rule antecedents in real-time expert systems with fuzzy set logic, Proc. 22nd Annual IEEE Asilomar Conf. Signals, Systems, Computers, Pacific Grove, California, 81–689 (1988).

209. G. M. P O'Hare and N. R. Jennings (Eds.). Foundations of Distributed Artificial Intelli-gence, New York: Wiley (1996).

210. Orlovski, S. A. Decision making with fuzzy preference relation. Fuzzy Sets and Systems, 1, 155–167 (1978)

211. Pacheco, R., Alejandro, Martins, Abraham, Kandel. On the power of fuzzy logic. International Journal of Intelligent Systems, 11(10), 779–789, (October, 1996).

212. Pavelka, J. On fuzzy logic (I, II, III), Z. Math. Logik Grundl Math., 25, 45–52; 119–134; 447–464 (1979).

213. Pawlak, Z. Decision rules, Bayes' rule and rough sets, in New Direction in Rough Sets. N. Zhong, A. Skowron, and S. Ohsuga, (Eds), Data Mining, and Granular-Soft Computing, Springer, pp. 1–9 (1999).

214. Pawlak, Z. New look Bayes' theorem - the rough set outlook, in Proc. Int. RSTGC-2001, Bull. Int. Rough Set Soc., Matsue Shimane, Japan, 5(1/2), 1–8 (May, 2001).

215. Pawlak, Z., Rough Sets: Theoretical Aspects of Reasoning about Data. Boston, London, Dordrecht, Kluwer, (1991).

216. Pei, Daowu. Fuzzy Logic Algebras on Residuated Lattices, Southeast Asian Bulletin of Mathematics, 28, 519–531(2004).

217. Pei, D. W. A unified normal residuated based logic system and its completeness, to appear in this journal, Southeast Asian Bulletin of Mathematics, 28(6), 1089–1098 (2004)

218. Pei, D. W. The operation Ä and deductive theorem of the formal system £*. Fuzzy Systems and Mathematics, 15(1), 21–26 (2001).

219. Pei, D. W. The studies on fuzzy logic and fuzzy reasoning based on the formal system £*. Ph.D. Thesis, Sichuan Univ., Chengdu, (2000).

220. Pei, D. W. and Wang, G. J. A kind of new algebraic systems for fuzzy logic. J. Southwest Jiaotong University, 35(5), 564–568 (2000).

221. Pei, D. W. and Wang, G. J. The completeness and applications of the formal system £*. Science in China (Series F), 45, 40–50 (2002).

222. Pei, D. W. and Wang, S. M. The completeness of the formal systems £*(n), Applied Mathematics J. of Chinese Universities, 16, 253–262 (2001).

223. Perfilieva, I. Normal forms in BL-algebra of functions and their contribution to universal approximation. Fuzzy Sets and Systems, 143 111–127 (2004).

224. Peters, S.and Westerståhl, D. Quantifiers in Language and Logic, Clarendon Press, Oxford, (2006).

225. Peterson, P. Intermediate Quantifiers. Logic, Linguistics, and Aristotelian Semantics, Ashgate, Aldershot (2000).

226. Peterson, G. I. Rough classification of pneumonia patients using a clinical database, W. Ziarko (Eds.), Rough Sets, Fuzzy Sets and Knowledge Discovery. Proceedings of the International Workshop on Rough Sets and Knowledge Discovery (RSKD'93), Banff, Alberta, Canada, October 12–15, Springer-Verlag, Berlin, 412–419 (1993).

227. Polkowski, L. and A. Skowron (Eds.). Rough Sets and Current Trends in Computing. Lecture Notes in Artificial Intelligence, 1424, Springer (1998).

228. L. Polkowski and A. Skowron (Eds.). Rough Sets in Knowledge Discovery. (1–2), Springer, (1998).

229. Polkowski, L., Tsumoto, S., and T. Y. Lin (Eds.). Rough Set Methods and Applications - New Developments in Knowledge Discovery in Information Systems, Springer (2000).

230. Pradera, A., Trillas, E., and Moraga, C. Clarifying Elkan's theoretical results European Society for Fuzzy Logic and Technology - EUSFLAT, pp. 604–608 (2003).

231. Preparata, F. P. and Yeh, R. T. Continuously valued logic. J. Compute and System Sci. 6 397–418 (1972).

232. Priest, G. An Introduction to Non-Classical Logics. Cambridge Univ. Press, Cambridge, UK (2001).

233. Pykacz J. Lukasiewicz operations in fuzzy set and many-valued representations of quantum logics. Found. Phys., 30(9), 503–1524 (2000).

234. Pykacz, J. Fuzzy Set Ideas in Quantum Logics. International Journal of Theoretical physics, 31(9), (1992).

235. Rahardja, S and Falkowski, B. J. A new algorithm to compute quaternary Reed-Muller expansions. in Proc. 30th IEEE Int. Symp. Multiple-Valued Logic, Portland, Oregon, pp. 153–158 (May 23–25, 2000).

236. Ramot, D., Friedman, M., Langholz, G., and A. Kandel. Complex fuzzy logic IEEE Trans. Fuzzy Syst., 11(4), 450–461, (Aug, 2003).

237. Ray, K. S. and Mandrita, Mondal. Similarity-based fuzzy reasoning by DNA Computing. International Journal of Bio-Inspired computation, 3(2), 112–122 (2011).

238. Ray, K. S. and Chatterjee, Piyali. Approximate Reasoning on a DNA-chip. International Journal of Intelligent Computing and Cybernetics, 3(3), 514–553.

239. Ray, S. The difference, symmetric difference, and sigma-rings of fuzzy sets. Fuzzy Sets Syst., 50, 315–329, (1992).

240. Reghis, M. and Roventa, E. Classical and Fuzzy Concepts in Mathematical Logic and Applications, CRC-Press (1998).

241. Richter, E. Nonmonotonic inference operators for fuzzy logic. S. Benferhat, E. Giunchiglia, (Eds.), In: Proc. 9th Internat. Workshop on Nonmonotonic Reasoning, NMR'2002, Toulouse, France, Toulouse, 321–329 (2002).

242. Saridakis, K. M. and Dentsoras, A. J. Soft Computing in Engineering design- A review, Ad-vance Engineering Informatics, 22, 202–221 (2008).

243. Sato, S. Arai, Y., and K. Hirota. Pattern recognition using fuzzy inference with lacked input data. In Proc. IEEE Int. Conf. Fuzzy Systems, San Antonio, Texas, pp. 100–104 (2000).

244. Scott, M. J. Formalizing negotiation in engineering design, PhD thesis, California Institute of Technology, Pasadena, California (1999).

245. Seki, H., Ishii, Hiroaki, and Mizumoto, Masaharu. On the Property of Single input Rule Modules Connected type fuzzy Reasoning Method. FUZZ-IEEE 2007, IEEE International Fuzzy Systems Conference (2007).

246. Setnes, M., Babuska, Robert, Kaymak, Uzay, and Hans R van Nauta Lemke. Similarity Measures in Fuzzy Rule Base Simplifications. IEEE Transactions on System Man and Cybernetics-Part B: Cybernetics, 28(3) (June, 1998).

247. Shenoi, S. Rough sets in fuzzy databases. P. P. Wang (Ed.), Soft Computing and its Applications, Second Annual Joint Conference on Information Sciences Proceedings, Wrightsville Beach, North Carolina, USA, 608, 263–264 (September 28–October 1, 1995).

248. Simpson, T. W., Peplinski, J. D. Koch, P. N, and Allen, J. N. Metamodels for computer-based engineering design: Survey and recommendations, Engineering with computers, 17 129–150 (2001).

249. Skala, H. J. On many-valued logics, fuzzy sets, fuzzy logics and their applications. Fuzzy Sets and Systems, 1, 129–149 (1978).

250. Skolem, T. Bemerkungen zum Komprehensionsaxiom. Zeitschr. math. Logik Grundl. Math., 3, 1–17 (1957).

251. Skowron, A. and Crzymala-Busse, J. W. From rough set theory to evidence theory. K. H Yaeger, M. Fedrizzi, and J. Karprzyk (Eds.). Advances in the Dempster Shafer Theory of Evidence, John Wiley & Sons, Inc., New York, Chichester, Brisbane, Toronto, Singapore, 193–236 (1991).

252. Skowron, A. and Rauszer, C. The discertiibiiity matrices and functions in information systems. R. Slowinski (ed.), Intelligent Decision Support. Handbook of Applications and Advances of the Rough Set Theory, Kluwer Academic Publishers, Dordrecht, 311–362 (1992).

253. Skowron, A. Extracting laws from decision tables, Computational Intelligence, 11/2, 371–388 (1995).

254. Skowron, A. Synthesis of adaptive decision systems from experimantal data. A. Aamadt and J. Komorowski (eds.), Proc. of the Fifth Scandinavian Conference on Artificial Intelligence SCAl-95, IOS Press, Amsterdam, 220–238 (1995).

255. Skowron, A. and Stepaniuk, J. Decision rules based on discernibility matrices and decision. T. Y. Lin (Ed.), The Third International Workshop on Rough Sets and Soft Computing Proceedings (RSSC'94), San Jose State University, San Jose, California, USA, 602–609 (November 10–12, 1994).

256. Slowiński, R. and Stefanowski J. Rough classification with valued closeness relation. E. Diday, Y. Lechevallier, M. Schrader, P. Bertrand, and B. Burtschy (Eds.), New Approaches in Classification and Data Analysis, Springer-Verlag, Berlin, 482–489 (1994).

257. Slowiński, K. Rough classification of HSV patients. R. Slowiriski (Ed.), Intelligent Decision Support: Handbook of Applications and Advances of the Rough Set Theory, Kluwer Academic Publishers, Dordrecht, 77–93 (1992).

258. Slowiński, K. and Sharif, E. S. Rough sets approach to analysis of data of diatnostic peritoneal lavage applied for multiple injuries patients. W. Ziarko (Ed.), Rough Sets, Fuzzy Sets and Knowledge Discovery: Proceedings of the International Workshop on Rough Sets and Knowledge Discovery (RSKD'93), Banff, Alberta, Canada, Springer-Verlag, Berlin, 420–425 (October 12–15, 1993).

259. Slowiński, K., Slowiński, R., and Stefanowski, J. Rough sets approach to analysis of data from peritoneal lavage in acute pancreatitis. Medical Infonnatics, 13/3, 143–159 (1988).

260. Slowiński, K., Stefanowski, J., Antczak, A, and Kwias, Z. Rough sets approach to the verification of indications for treatment of urinary stones by extracorporeal shock wave lithotripsy (ESWL). T. Y. Lin and A. M. Wildberger (Eds.), The Third International Workshop on Rough Sets and Soft Computing Proceedings (RSSCJ94), San Jose State University, San Jose, California, USA, 93–96 (November 10–12, 1995).

261. Slowiński, R. Rough Set Approach to Decision Analysis, AI Expert, 10, 18–25 (1995).

262. Slowiński, R. Rough set learning of preferential attitude in multi-criteria decision making. J. Komorowski and Z. W. Ras (Eds.), Methodologies for Intelligent Systems. Lecture Notes in Artificial Intelligence, Springer-Verlag, Berlin, 689, 642–651 (1993).

263. R. Slowiński. (Eds.). Intelligent Decision Support Handbook of Applications and Advances of the Rough Set Theory, Kluwer Academic Publishers, Dordrecht.References, 609 (1992).

264. Slowiński, R. and Stefanowski, J. RoughDAS and RoughClass' software implementations of the rough sets approach. R. Slowiński (Ed.), Intelligent Decision Support: Handbook of Applications and Advances of the Rough Set Theory, Kluwer Academic Publishers, Dordrecht, 445–456 (1992).

265. Slowiński, R. and Zopounidis, C. Applications of the rough set approach to evaluation of bankruptcy risk, Working Paper 93–08, Decision Support System Laboratory, Technical University of Crete, Chania (June, 1993).

266. Smets, P. and Magres, P. Implication in fuzzy logic. Internat. J. Approximate Reasoning, 1 327–347 (1987).

267. Smets, P. and Magres, P. The measure of the degree of truth and of the grade of membership. Fuzzy Sets and Systems, 25, 67–72 (1988).

268. Soto, A. R. de and Trillas, E. On antonym and negate in fuzzy logic. Int. J. Intell. Syst., 14, 295–303 (1999).

269. Straccia, U. Reasoning within fuzzy description logics. J. Artif. Intell. Res., 14, 137–166, (2001).

270. Sugeno, M. and Takahiro Yasukawa. A Fuzzy-Logic-based Approach to Qualitative Modeling. IEEE Transactions on Fuzzy Systems, 1(1) (February, 1993).

271. Szladow, A. Datalogic/R: Mining the knowledge in databases, PC AI, 7/1, 40–41 (1993).

272. Szladow, A. and Ziarkom, W. Rough sets: Working with imperfect data, AI Expert, 7, 36–41 (1993).

273. Takagi, H. R&D in intelligent technologies: Fusion of NN, FL, GA, chaos, and human, in Half-Day Tutorial/Workshop, IEEE Int. Conf. Systems, Man, and Cybernetics, Orlando, Florida (1997).

274. Takagi, N., Kikuchi, H., and K. Nakashima. Multi-interval truth-value logic, in Proc. 10th IEEE Int. Conf. Fuzzy Systems, Melbourne, Australia, pp. 1119–1122 (December 2–5, 2001)

275. Torra, V, A review of the construction of hierarchical fuzzy systems, International journal of intelligent systems, 17, 531–543 (2002).

276. Trillas, E. and Valverde, L. On implication and indistinguishability in the setting of fuzzy logic. R. R. Yager and J. Kacprzyk (Eds.), Management Decision Support Systems using Fuzzy Set and Possibility Theory, Verlag TÜV Rheinland, Köln (1984).

277. Trillas, E. and. Valverde, L. On Mode and Implication in Approximate Reasoning. M. M. Gupta, A. Kandel, W. Beudler, and J. B. Kiszka (Eds.), Approximate Reasoning in Expert Systems, Elsevier Science Publ., Amsterdam, (1985).

278. Trillas, E. and Alsina, C. On the law $[\{p \wedge q\} \Rightarrow r] = [\{p \Rightarrow r\} \vee \{q \Rightarrow r\}]$ in fuzzy logic. IEEE Trans. Fuzzy Syst., 10(1) 84–88 (2002).

279. Trillas, E.and Alsina, C. Comments to "Paradoxes of fuzzy logic, revisited. Int. Journal of Approximate Reasoning, 26, 157–159 (2001).

280. Trillas, E. and Alsina, C. Elkan's theoretical argument, reconsidered. Int. Journal of Approximate Reasoning, 26, 145–152 (2001).

281. Trillas, Enric. On the use of words and fuzzy sets. Information Sciences, 176(11), 1463–1487 (2006).

282. Tsumoto, S. and Tanaka, H. PRIMEROSE: Probabilistic rule induction method based on rough set theory. V. V. Ziarko (Ed.), Rough. Set*, Fuzzy Sets and Knowledge Discovery. Proceedings of the International Workshop on Rough Sets and Knowledge Discovery (RSKD'93), Banf F, Alberta, Canada, Springer-Verlag, Berlin, 274–281 (October 12–15, 1993).

283. Turksen, I. B. Fuzzy normal forms. Fuzzy Sets Syst., 69, 319–346, (1995).610 Soft Computing and Its Applications

284. Turksen, I. B. The first and second order lattices in fuzzy logic. In Proc. 1995 IEEE Int. Conf Systems, Man, and Cybernetics, Vancouver. IK. Canada, pp. 3642–3646 (October 22–25, 1995).

285. Turunen, E. Algebraic structures in fuzzy logic. Fuzzy Sets Sysi., 52, 181–188 (1992).

286. Walker, C. L and Elbert, A. Walker. Automorphisms of the algebra of fuzzy, Truth values. International Journal of uncertainity, Fuzziness and knowledge-based systems, 14(6), 711–732 (2006).

287. Weber, S. A general concept of fuzzy connectives, negations and implications based on t-norms and t-conorms. Fuzzy Sets and Systems, 11, 115–134 (1983).

288. Wu, W. M. Fuzzy implication algebras. Fuzzy Systems and Mathematics, 4(1), 56–64 (1990).

289. Wu, D. A brief tutorial on internal type -2 fuzzy sets and systems, personal communication. https://sites.google.com/site/drwu09/publications/completepubs.

290. Xu, Y. et al. L-vaiued propositional logic Lvpi. Inform.Sci. 114, 205–235 (1999).

291. Yager, R. and A. Rybalov. Uninorm aggregation operators. Fuzzy Sets Syst., 80, 111–120 (1996).

292. Yager, R. On some new classes of implication operators and their role in Approximate Reasoning. Inform. Sci., 167, 193–216 (2004).

293. Yager, R. R. Families of OWA operators, Fuzzy Sets and Systems, 59, 125–148 (1993).

294. Yager, R. R. On ordered weighted averaging aggregation operators in multicriteria decisionmaking. IEEE Trans. Systems, Man and Cybernet., 18, 183–190 (1988).

295. Yager, R. R. Applications and extensions of OWA operator. Int. J. of Man Machine Studies, 37, 103–132 (1992b).

296. Ying, M. and Bouchon-Meunier, B. Quantifiers, modifiers and qualifiers in fuzzy logic. Journal of Applied Non-Classical Logics, 7, 335–342 (1997).

297. Zadeh, L. A. Fuzzy logic, neural networks and soft computing, in Proc. IEEE Int. workshop Neuro Fuzzy control, Muroran, Japan, P1 (1993).

298. Zadeh, L. A. Fuzzy sets, Information and Control, 8, 338–353 (1965).

299. Zadeh, L. A. Generalized theory of uncertainty (GTU)-principal concepts and ideas, Computational Statistics & Data Analysis, 51, 15–46 (2006).

300. Zadeh, L. A. On the analysis of large scale systems. H. Gottinger (Ed.), Systems Approaches and Environment Problems, Vandenhoeck and Ruprecht, Gottingen, pp. 23–37 (1974).

301. Zadeh, L. A. Outline of a computational approach to meaning and knowledge representation based on the concept of a generalized assignment statement. M. Thoma and A. Wyner (Eds.), Proceedings of the International Seminar on Artificial Intelligence and Man Machine Systems, Springer-Verlag, Heidelberg, pp. 198–211 (1986).

302. Zadeh, L. A. Outline of a computational theory of perceptions based on computing with words. N. K. Sinha, M. M. Gupta, and Lot A. Zadeh (Eds.), Soft Computing & Intelligent Systems: Theory and Applications, Academic Press, London, pp. 3–22 (2000).

303. Zadeh, L. A. Outline of a new approach to the analysis of complex systems and decision processes. IEEE Trans. Syst. Man Cyber., 3, 28–44 (1973).

304. Zadeh, L. A. Possibility theory and soft data analysis. L. Cobb and R. M. Thrall (Eds.), Mathematical Frontiers of the Social and Policy Sciences, Westview Press, CO, Boulder, pp. 69–129 (1981).

305. Zadeh, L. A. Precisiated natural language (PNL). AI Magazine, 25(3), 74–91 (2004).

306. Zadeh, L. A. Precisiation of meaning via translation into PRUF. L. Vaina, J. Hintikka (Eds.), Cognitive Constraints on Communication, Reidel, Dordrecht, pp. 373–402 (1984).

307. Zadeh, L. A. PRUF-a meaning representation language for natural languages. International Journal of Man-Machine Studies, 10, pp. 395–460 (1978).

308. Zadeh, L .A. Quantitative fuzzy semantics, Information Sciences, 3, 159–176 (1971).

309. Zadeh, L. A. Test-score semantics as a basis for a computational approach to the representation of meaning, in: Proceedings of the 10th Annual Conference of the Association for Literary and Linguistic Computing (1983).

310. Zadeh L. A. Is There any Need for Fuzzy Logic? Information Sciences, 178, 2751–2779 (2008).

311. Zadeh, L. A. Towards Extended Fuzzy Logic – A First Step. Fuzzy Sets and Systems, 160, pp. 3175-3181 (2009).

312. Zadeh, L. A. The concept of a linguistic variable and its application to approximate reasoning. Part I. Information Sciences, 8, 199–249 (1975).

313. Zadeh, L. A. The concept of a linguistic variable and its application to approximate reasoning. Part II, Information Sciences, 8, 301–357 (1975)

314. Zadeh, L. A. Toward a generalized theory of uncertainty (GTU) - an outline. Information Sciences, 172, 1–40 (2005).

315. Zadeh, L. A. Toward a perception-based theory of probabilistic reasoning with imprecise probabilities. Journal of Statistical Planning and Inference, 105, 233-264 (2002).

316. Zechman, E. M. and Ranjithan, S. R. An evolutionary algorithm to generate alternatives (EAGA) for engineering optimization problems. Engineering Optimization, 36(5) 539–553 (2004).

317. Zha, X. F. Soft computing framework for intelligent human–machine system design, simulation and optimization. Soft Computing, 7184–198 (2003).

318. Zhong, N., Skowron, A., and S. Ohsuga (Eds.). New Direction in Rough Sets, Data Mining, and Granular-Soft Computing, Springer (1999).

319. Ziarko, V. V. Variable Precision Rough Set Model. Journal of Computer and System Sciences, 40, 39–59 (1993).

320. Ziarko, V. V. Golan, R., and Edwards, D. An application of DATALOCIC/R knowledge discovery tool to identify strong predictive rules in stock market data in: Proc. AAAI Workshop on Knowledge Discovery in Databases, Washington, DC, 89–101 (1993).

321. Ziarko, W. Data analysis and case-based expert system development tool Rough, in: Pivc. Case-Based Reasoning Workshop, Morgan Kaufmann, Los Altos, California, 356–361 (1989).

322. Ziarko, W. The discovery, analysis and representation of data dependencies in databases. G. Piatetsky-Shapiro and W. J. Frawley (Eds.), Knowledge Discovery in Databases, AAAI Press/MIT Press, 177–195 (1991).

323. Ziarko, W. Acquisition of control algorithms from operation data. R. Slowiriski (Ed.), Intelligent Decision Support: Handbook of Applications and Advances of the Rough Set Theory, Kluwer Academic Publishers, Dordrecht, 61–75 (1992).

INDEX

Milton Keynes UK
Ingram Content Group UK Ltd.
UKHW030901141024
449569UK00025B/1284